Peter Norton's Visual Basic for Windows
Third Edition
Covering Release 3.0

Peter Norton's Visual Basic for Windows
Third Edition
Covering Release 3.0

Steven Holzner and
The Peter Norton Computing Group

////Brady

New York   London   Toronto   Sydney   Tokyo   Singapore

**Copyright © 1993 by Steven Holzner and
The Peter Norton Computing Group**

Brady Publishing
A Division of Prentice Hall Computer Publishing
15 Columbus Circle
New York, NY 10023

ISBN: 1-56686-093-8

Library of Congress Catalog No.: 93-8216

Printing Code: The rightmost double-digit number is the year of the book's printing; the rightmost single-digit number is the number of the book's printing. For example, 93-1 shows that the first printing of the book occurred in 1993.

96 95 94 93   4 3

Manufactured in the United States of America

Limits of Liability and Disclaimer of Warranty

Trademarks

Credits

Publisher
Michael Violano

Acquisitions Director
Jono Hardjowirogo

Managing Editor
Kelly D. Dobbs

Acquisitions Editor
Michael Sprague

Production Editor
Bettina A. Versaci

Copy Editors
Gail S. Burlakoff
Becky Whitney

Editorial Assistant
Lisa Rose

Book Designer
Michele Laseau

Cover Designer
Hub Graphics

Indexers
Jeanne Clark, Craig A. Small

Production Team
Diana Bigham, Katy Bodenmiller, Scott Cook, Tim Cox,
Terri Edwards, Mark Enochs, Linda Koopman, Wendy Ott,
Tom Loveman, Beth Rago, Joe Ramon, Carrie Roth,
Greg Simsic, Marcella Thompson, Suzanne Tulley

Note for Professional Edition Users

The screens shown in this book were captured from the Standard Edition. Therefore, the Standard Edition's toolbar usually is visible and will not match the toolbar you see on-screen.

Contents at a Glance

INTRODUCTION ....**XV**

Chapter 1:   The First Windows 1
Chapter 2:   Buttons, Text Boxes, and an Alarm Clock Program 37
Chapter 3:   Menus 85
Chapter 4:   Dialog Boxes and a Database Program.......................137
Chapter 5:   What About Files? 191
Chapter 6:   Graphics 233
Chapter 7:   The Mouse and a Mouse-driven Paint Program.........297
Chapter 8:   Advanced Data Handling, Sorting, and a
                Spreadsheet Program 357
Chapter 9:   Error Handling and Debugging...................................409
Chapter 10:   Connecting to Other Windows Applications
                (DDE and OLE) 455
Chapter 11:   Advanced Control and Form Handling 505
Chapter 12:   Linking to C and to Windows Directly 539
Chapter 13:   Using the Professional Edition's Custom Controls ...583
Chapter 14:   Creating Custom Controls 635

Appendix A: Creating Customized Windows Help 687
Appendix B: Windows Program Design..701
Appendix C: Converting Visual Basic for Windows to DOS
                and Back: A Few Problems 709
Appendix D: About the Disk 715
Appendix E: More About the Diskette 723

DISK CONTENTS **739**

INDEX **741**

CONTENTS

INTRODUCTION XV

CHAPTER 1. THE FIRST WINDOWS 1
About Windows 2
    A Brief Windows History 3
    The Parts of a Window 4
    Preserving the Feel of Windows 5
About Windows Programming 6
    Windows Events 7
About Visual Basic Programming 9
Your First Window 10
The Form 11
Properties 12
Controls 14
    The Toolbox 14
Command Buttons 20
Using the Code Window 22
Visual Basic Projects 28
    Visual Basic Forms 29
Visual Basic Modules 29
    Using Visual Basic Projects 30
Saving Your Work on Disk 31
    Saving Your Project 32
Adding More Power to Your Text Box 33
Summary 35

CHAPTER 2. BUTTONS, TEXT BOXES, AND AN ALARM
CLOCK PROGRAM 37
A Calculator Example 39
    Labels 42
Variables in Visual Basic 43
    Type Conventions for Variables 44
    Scope of Variables in Visual Basic 46
Storing the Calculator's Data 48
Formatting Text 53
    Displaying Date and Time 55
A Notepad Example—Complete with
  Cut and Paste 55

Using Selected Text in Text Boxes 58
   How To Cut Selected Text 60
Using Access Keys 65
An Alarm Clock Example 67
Interpreting Individual Keystrokes 68
   Displaying the Time 71
   Visual Basic Timers 71
Using Option (Radio) Buttons 75
Arrays of Controls 76
Selecting Fonts 79
Summary 81

CHAPTER 3. MENUS **85**
A Menu-Driven Tic-Tac-Toe Game 88
Adding A Menu to the Tic-Tac-Toe Game 90
Beginning the Editor Example..99
Selecting Fonts from Menus 109
Marking Menu Items with Check Marks 114
Adding Access Keys to Menus...118
Adding Shortcut Keys to Menus 119
Giving the Editor Application an Icon 122
Changing Menu Items at Run Time 124
Adding and Deleting Menu Items 127
Summary 135

CHAPTER 4. DIALOG BOXES AND A DATABASE PROGRAM...........**137**
No Windows Needed 139
Displaying a Message Box with MsgBox( ) 140
An InputBox$() Application—a Windows Shell ....ﯨ...144
Creating Applications with Multiple Windows 147
The First Form 148
Creating Custom Dialog Boxes...150
Adding a Control Panel to Your Applications........................154
Using Scroll Bars 156
Setting Colors in Visual Basic 162
Creating List Boxes 167
Creating Your Own Data Types 178
Creating Combo Boxes 183
Multiple Document Interface (MDI) Programs 187
Summary 189

CHAPTER 5. WHAT ABOUT FILES? 191

Saving Data in a File 193
Opening Files in Visual Basic....................................... 195
   The Types of Visual Basic Files 196
Writing to Files in Visual Basic 200
Using the Visual Basic File Controls 202
   Drive List Boxes 204
   Directory List Boxes 205
   File List Boxes 207
Reading from Files in Visual Basic 210
Using Random Files in Visual Basic 221
Writing Random-Access Files 222
Reading Random Access Files 225
   Using the Seek Statement 230
Summary 230

CHAPTER 6. GRAPHICS 233

Drawing with Visual Basic 235
   Drawing Points 235
   Selecting Colors 239
   Drawing Lines 244
   Drawing Rectangles 252
   Filling Figures with Patterns 255
   Drawing Circles 257
Loading Pictures... 259
Displaying Text in Visual Basic 262
Determining the Length of the
  String on the Screen 267
Creating Your Own Animation 277
Creating Customized Icons in Visual Basic 281
Using a Printer from Visual Basic 286
Changing Coordinate Systems 287
Summary 293

CHAPTER 7. THE MOUSE AND A MOUSE-DRIVEN PAINT PROGRAM 297

MouseDown Events 299
MouseMove Events 303
MouseUp Events 306
Drawing Lines 306
Drawing Boxes 316

Drawing Circles 318
    Drawing Text 322
Saving Your Paint Image on Disk 326
Reading the Image Back from Disk 328
Changing the Drawing Color 331
Printing the Paint Program's Graphics 339
Using the Windows Clipboard 341
Graphics Scaling 352
Summary 354

CHAPTER 8. ADVANCED DATA HANDLING, SORTING, AND STORING A SPREADSHEET PROGRAM 357

Variables 359
Arrays 361
Data Structures 366
Linked Lists 367
Circular Buffers 371
Binary Trees 372
Shell Sorts 379
Quicksorts 389
Searching Your Data 395
A Spreadsheet Example 401
Summary 407

CHAPTER 9. ERROR HANDLING AND DEBUGGING 409

How to Test Programs 412
Handling Run-time Errors 413
The On Error GoTo Statement 413
The Err and Erl Functions 415
The Error$ Function 420
Creating Customized Error Handlers 421
The Resume Statement 423
    Resume Next and Resume Line # 426
Debugging 433
Debugging an Investment Calculator 445
Summary 453

CHAPTER 10. CONNECTING TO OTHER WINDOWS APPLICATIONS (DDE AND OLE) 455

What Is DDE? 457
How DDE Works 458

Design-time Client Links 459
    DDE's LinkMode..461
    DDE's LinkTopic..462
    DDE's LinkItem 463
    DDE's LinkTimeout 463
Design-time Source Links 464
Run-time Client Links 465
    Changing the LinkItem at Run-time...............................468
    Manual Run-time Client Links 469
Run-time Source Links 472
Maintaining a Picture Box Link..477
Sending Data Back to a DDE Source 480
Sending Commands through DDE...483
Handling DDE Errors 484
The LinkOpen and LinkClose Events 488
Pasting Links in Code 489
Customized Source Applications 492
How to Use Object Linking and Embedding (OLE) 496
    Object Linking and Embedding Version 1 (OLE1) 497
    Object Linking and Embedding Version 2 (OLE2) 499
Summary 502

CHAPTER 11. ADVANCED CONTROL AND FORM HANDLING..........505
A Desktop Organizer Example 508
Passing Controls to Procedures Ourselves 520
Passing Forms As Arguments to Procedures 523
Creating An Array of Forms 529
Determining Which Control is Active 530
Affecting Tab Order 532
Summary 536

CHAPTER 12. LINKING TO C AND TO WINDOWS DIRECTLY 539
Linking to Windows System Calls 542
A Screen-Capture Program 542
    Declaring External Code 543
    Starting the Screen-Capture Program 546
    Accessing the Screen Directly in Windows 550
Connecting Visual Basic to C 568
    The Visual Basic Part of the Code 576
Summary 579

CHAPTER 13. USING THE PROFESSIONAL EDITION'S CUSTOM CONTROLS 583

Updating Your Notepad with Key Status Controls 585
Updating the Notepad's Buttons
   to 3-D Appearance 590
Updating Your Animation Example
   with Animated Buttons 593
Improving Your Plotter with Custom
   Control Graphs 598
     Other Types of Graphs 602
     Using ThisPoint To Set Graph Data 603
     Setting Your Own X Coordinates.....................604
     Pie Charts 605
Updating Your C Interface with Windows Gauges 608
Updating Your Notepad with Prewritten
   Dialog Boxes 611
     A Font Selection Dialog Box 612
     A File Open Dialog Box 618
     A Save File Dialog Box 622
     A Color Selection Dialog Box 623
     A Print Dialog Box 624
Pen Computing 630
Summary 631

CHAPTER 14. CREATING CUSTOM CONTROLS 635

The Box Custom Control...................................637
Initializing and Registering a Control 639
     Registering a Property................................640
     Registering an Event 647
Designing the Control's Toolbox Bitmap 658
Your Box Control Procedure...............................660
Using Your New Custom Control 682
And That's It 684
Summary 684

APPENDIX A. CREATING CUSTOMIZED WINDOWS HELP 687

Creating the Help Text: Editor.Rtf...........................688
Creating the Project File: Editor.Hpj 696
Creating the Help File: Editor.Hlp 697
Connecting Editor.Hlp to the Editor Program 698

APPENDIX B. WINDOWS PROGRAM DESIGN 701
Windows Programming Philosophy 702
Mouse Actions 703
Keyboard Actions 704
The Edit Menu 707
The File Menu 707
The Help Menu 708

APPENDIX C. CONVERTING VISUAL BASIC FOR WINDOWS TO DOS AND BACK: A FEW PROBLEMS 709
Translating Visual Basic Projects with Trnslate.Exe 712
Rewriting for Compatibility 713

APPENDIX D. ABOUT THE DISK 715

APPENDIX E. MORE ABOUT THE DISKETTE 723
CSMeter   \CRESCENT\ 723
VBToolsKan 728
TKCHART   \TOOLSKAN\CHART\CHART.EXE 729
Ribbon/Icon Bar
  \TOOLSKAN\RIBBON\RIBBON.EXE 731
Status Bar   \TOOLSKAN\STATBAR\STATBAR.EXE 732
Table   \TOOLSKAN\TABLE\TABLE.EXE 734
TKTBOX   \TOOLSKAN\TOOLBOX\TOOLBOX.EXE 736

DISK CONTENTS 739

INDEX 741

Introduction

Why Visual Basic?

Visual Basic is, without question, one of the best programming tools ever created for the PC. It is the stuff of programmers' dreams, especially Windows programmers. If you have done any Windows programming in C, then you know what it can be like—difficult and time-consuming, and the programs can be hard to debug. Just getting started with the Microsoft Windows Software Development Kit (SDK) takes hours of reading and absorbing. Writing the actual code usually takes many more hours, including time for experimentation and fixing problems. Graphical User Interfaces—GUIs—may definitely be the wave of the future, but they can make life very tough for the programmer.

Even the most elementary Windows application, which might do nothing more than pop an "About" window on the screen, telling you who created it, can take about five pages of C code and four separate files (although it is getting better now with C++). The enormous complexity of writing an actual, useful application often slows development time down to a snail's pace. To make matters worse, Windows programming tools were (until now) far from complete. The Windows Software Development Kit can sometimes be as much a hindrance as a help.

Visual Basic changes this picture entirely. Finally, it adds the programming tools that have been lacking for so long in Windows. Working with Visual Basic for the first time, experienced Windows programmers can hardly believe their eyes. The ideas are simple. If you want a window of a certain size, you simply draw it that size. If you want a text box at a particular point in your window, simply select the correct tool and draw the text box there. Visual Basic does what programs excel at—handling the details for you. That is useful because, at last, the aid of the computer is being enlisted in the Windows programming process. You can draw just about anything—listboxes, buttons, combo boxes—anywhere you need it. When you are finished, you write a few (often a very few) lines of Basic code to make things work,

XV

and Visual Basic creates the working .Exe file for you. From the Windows programmer's point of view, this package is nothing short of astonishing.

Our Approach

This is a book for would-be Windows programmers, so you are going to spend a lot of time seeing Visual Basic at work. In other words, you are going to see what the software is capable of. To do that, you will have to see plenty of examples, which is always the best way to learn about software. These examples start in Chapter 1, where you put a window on the screen and work with it. As the book progresses, you will see many other examples: an alarm clock, a text editor, a database program, a paint program, calculators, and many others.

In addition, as the name Visual Basic implies, you will spend some time looking at windows on the screen and learning about what makes them tick. This book is unlike other programming books you might have read in that much of what it covers has to do with using Visual Basic to design your software—visually—instead of working through long programs. If you are unfamiliar with Windows programming, you will also find that the code you develop is different from what you might expect. In particular, Windows programs are *event driven*, which means that your code will be divided into many small sections to handle specific events, rather than the linear, continuous programs you might be used to. This can take some getting used to, but after a while, thinking in terms of Windows events like mouse clicks or key presses comes naturally. You will see more about this in Chapter 1.

In a nutshell, then, the book's approach is the programmer's approach: task- and example-oriented, without a great deal of unneccessary theory. In this book, Visual Basic will be put to work for you.

What Is In This Book?

Visual Basic is a tremendous toolbox of programming resources, and this book is going to explore them. You will work our way up, from the most basic examples to the most polished. In the beginning of the book, you will get the essentials down, and then you will be able to progress beyond them. You will follow the natural course of Windows programming development. You will start with a blank window, embellish it a little with color and graphics, and then start to add buttons and text boxes—what Visual Basic calls *controls.* When you become comfortable with the idea of controls, you will add dialog boxes, messages boxes, and then menus themselves. As you work your way through the book, you will get into the kinds of topics that real Windows applications deal with, like the clipboard, bitmaps and icons, and error handling. One chapter deals with debugging; another, with dynamic data exchange, which enables you to communicate with other Windows applications like Microsoft Excel or Word for Windows.

Then you will press on to the realm of the expert: you will see how to add to Visual Basic from outside (often with the help of code written in C). If you want to stick to pure Visual Basic (not C) and see everything Visual Basic can do, this book is for you. But if you want to go on as an advanced programmer and reach the professional level by making full use of the Visual Basic Professional Edition and augmenting Visual Basic with the help of C, the Microsoft Windows Software Development Kit (SDK), and the Visual Basic Control Development Kit (CDK), then this book is also for you. All this makes for quite an ambitious plan: learning how to design and put to work useful Windows applications with a minimum of trouble. But that is what Visual Basic does best.

As previously mentioned, your orientation will be about seeing your programs work and getting functioning results. To do that, however, you must understand what you are doing. Therefore, you will have to take the time to understand all the concepts involved in Visual Basic; concepts like forms, methods, projects, and modules. And you will see that Visual Basic is object oriented (although not in the true C++ sense), which means that you will have to take the time to understand those objects before you can work with them.

For that reason, part of the first chapter will get you started by exploring the concepts you will need. You will begin with fundamental Windows concepts, like windows and buttons, and then you will work through some Windows programming concepts. Finally, you will get an introduction to the essential Visual Basic programming concepts as well. Because this first chapter lays the foundation for the rest of the book, make sure that you get all the basic ideas down before continuing.

From then on, the book is as task-oriented as possible. Many of the chapters are purposely designed to cover one specific type of Visual Basic "control"—buttons, listboxes, combo boxes, dialog boxes, or menus, for example. In this way, you will build your expertise by building your windows—piece by piece—steadily adding more and more power to your Windows applications. This will enable you to handle in a systematic, gradual way any complexities that might arise.

After you build and design your applications to add power to the programming part of your applications—rather than to the I/O part, which is handled by menus and buttons—you will investigate how to work with files and how to pass data in and out of the Windows clipboard. Then you will continue with other, more advanced concepts, such as developing and using custom controls and linking to the C language, on your way to becoming a Visual Basic wizard.

So What Is New In Version 3.0?

This book covers Version 3.0 of Visual Basic. This version is similar to Version 2.0; programmers used to Version 1.0 will see a number of differences as they move along. If you are familiar with version 1.0, the differences you will see in this book include the following:

▼ The properties bar is gone—now it is the properties window.

▼ No more CtlNames or FormNames—they are all just Names now.

▼ New Grid and OLE custom controls now come in each edition.

▼ There is no default global module.

▼ The Immediate window has changed into the Debug window.

▼ True and False are now predefined.

▼ The Multiple Document Interface (MDI) is now supported.

▼ Arrays can be as big as available memory.

▼ A new toolbar makes frequently used actions easy to perform.

▼ You can select groups of controls with the mouse.

▼ Graphics controls (Shape, Line, Image) have been added.

▼ Debugging is more powerful.

▼ Global variables can be declared in any module.

▼ The hWnd property has been added to all controls.

▼ A new keyword (Me) enables you to refer to the current form.

▼ New fonts have been added.

▼ The file format of .Mak, .Frm, and .Bas files have changed.

▼ .Mak files are now stored in English.

You will see all of these items, and more, as we cover Visual Basic 3.0.

What You Will Need

To read this book profitably, you will need to have some knowledge of Basic, but not much; the programming here is generally not very advanced, and new Basic constructions are introduced as needed. Even so, you should be familiar enough with Basic (such as BASICA, QuickBasic, or QBasic) to be able to write your own simple programs in it. If you find yourself lost in the first chapter, you should probably become familiar with Basic before continuing. The best Basic to review is Microsoft QuickBasic or QBasic; for straight programming, Visual Basic is very close to these packages.

In addition, you will need Windows, Version 3.0 or later, because Visual Basic requires it. There is nothing special here, just the normal Win.Exe program. Please note that you should be a Windows *user* before becoming a Windows *programmer*. That is, if you do not know how to use Windows and are not used to the customary feel of Windows applications, you should take some time to learn before working on programs. Windows users expect their applications to conform pretty closely to Windows' conventions, and the best way to know what is expected is to be a Windows user yourself (see Appendix B on Windows Program Design).

Note also that you will need a mouse for the work you will do in this book. Although Windows applications are supposed to run with either the mouse or the keyboard, it is very difficult to do real work without a mouse—it is almost certainly impossible to program in Visual Basic without one. That is, casual Windows users may be able to get along without a mouse, but for the more serious Visual Basic programmer, the mouse is an essential tool.

If you want to follow the examples that allow you to link to other Windows applications, you will need Microsoft Excel or Word for Windows as well (although you do not need either package to use what you learn in Visual Basic). You will also create a dynamic link library to interface Visual Basic to C, and creating dynamic link libraries can be done only by specialized software—for example, Microsoft QuickC for Windows, or Microsoft C 6.0/7.0 and the Windows SDK.

We also intend to create our own customized Visual Basic controls later in the book. To do that, you will use Microsoft C 6.0/7.0 (you will see how to use both packages here) and the Windows 3.1 Software Development Kit (although you could use Microsoft QuickC for Windows), together with the Visual Basic Custom Control Kit (CDK)— and the CDK is now bundled in the Visual Basic Professional Edition. In addition, you will take the time to explore the custom Visual Basic controls that come with the Professional Edition of Visual Basic; to follow along, you will need that package. Finally, of course, you will need Visual Basic itself; here we will use version 3.0.

That's it. It is time to begin. Your first task will be to review Visual Basic and create some simple programs. Then you will be off on a comprehensive behind-the-scenes tour of this exceptional—and powerful—programming package.

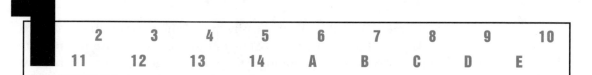
The First Windows

T his chapter is your introduction to Visual Basic. In it, you will see how to put together your first functioning Windows program. You will also see the following:

▼ The parts of a window

▼ How to program in Windows

▼ All about event-oriented programming

▼ Creating a window

▼ Adding text boxes to windows

▼ Adding buttons to windows

▼ Creating a Visual Basic project

▼ Running a Visual Basic program

▼ Saving work on disk

Here you will develop your first program, which responds to a button click and places a welcoming message into a Windows text box. Also, you will find a discussion of some fundamentals about Windows and Visual Basic programming and programming design, which will be useful when you start creating your own programs.

1

Welcome to Visual Basic. It is easily one of the most exciting software packages in the PC marketplace and one of the components of a revolution in Windows programming. This powerful package is one of the new generation of programming tools that are beginning to open up Windows programming as never before. No longer does it take a great deal of patience, experience, and expensive software to produce valuable Windows applications—under Visual Basic (and programs like it), developing Windows programs is easier than ever. In this chapter, you will put together your first Visual Basic programs, which will run under Windows 3+. You will see that it is easier than you might expect, because Visual Basic handles most of the details for you.

You can think of Visual Basic as an immense box of tools and resources, waiting for you to use it. To use these tools and resources, however, you have to understand them. In other words, you have to know what is available—and all about the environment in which it is available—before you can take advantage of what Visual Basic has to offer.

Accordingly, you will begin your tour of Visual Basic by examining the environment in which you will work—Windows itself. Next, you will see how Visual Basic works in this environment and what tools it offers you to manipulate that environment. Then, when you are ready, you will put Visual Basic to work and get some results. Now to begin...by examining the host operating environment, Windows.

About Windows

Many people believe that Graphical User Interfaces (GUIs) are the wave of the future in microcomputing, and they could be right. Certainly Windows 3.0 was one of the quickest selling software packages in history (500,000 copies in its first six weeks; 3,000,000 in its first nine months). In all significant ways, Windows is a full operating environment by itself (soon to become a full operating system with the introduction of Windows NT).

Windows is very different from DOS in many ways. One of the most fundamental differences is that Windows is a Graphical User Interface, which introduces many new concepts. One of the primary ideas here is that most of the available options are presented to the user at once, in the form of objects on the screen, much like tools ready to be used. The utility of this simple approach is surprising—rather than remembering complex techniques and keywords, a user can simply select the correct tool for the task at hand and begin work. In this way, graphical interfaces fufill much of the promise of computers as endlessly adaptable tools. In the next section you will take a look at some of the background of this operating environment.

A Brief Windows History

Microsoft started working on Windows in 1983, only two years after the PC had appeared, but the original version (Windows 1.01) did not actually ship until 1985. This version was supposed to run on the standard machine of that time: an IBM PC with two 360K disk drives, 256K, and an 8088. The display was automatically tiled; that is, the windows were arranged to cover the whole screen, and it looked less than impressive.

The next major version, Windows 2, came out two years later. For the first time, windows could overlap on the screen. However, Windows 2 could only run in 80x86 real mode, which meant that it was limited to a total of one megabyte of memory. For a while, Windows even split into Windows 286 and Windows 386 to take advantage of the capabilities of the (then new) 80386 chip. Progress had been made, but it was clear that much more was still needed.

In May of 1990, Microsoft introduced Windows 3.0. The look and feel of Windows 3.0 was a great improvement over its ancestors, and it featured proportional fonts, which made displays look more refined. Version 3.0 also had better support for DOS programs, and many users started to use Windows as the primary operating system for the PC.

The MS-DOS Executive of earlier versions was replaced by a trinity of windows that manage Windows: the *Program Manager*, the *Task List*, and the *File Manager*. From a programming point of view, one of the most important features of Windows 3.0 was that it could support extended memory—up to 16 megabytes of RAM. And in its 386-enhanced mode, Windows 3.0 used the built-in virtual memory (storing sections of memory temporarily on disk) capabilities of the 80386 to give programmers access to up to four times the amount of actual installed memory. In a machine that has 16 megabytes, then, Windows could actually provide 64 megabytes. Now Windows 3.1 has been introduced with proportional fonts, common dialog boxes, and other improvements. With Windows 3+, then, Windows has arrived at last.

The Parts of a Window

A typical Windows 3+ window appears in figure 1.1. You should be familiar with its parts before starting to program Windows applications. In fact, if you are not a Windows user, you should spend time with Windows before continuing. As you will see, it is important to know what the user expects from a Windows application before you write one.

Before starting to program, then, you should spend a little time reviewing Windows terminology; this will help you later in the book. At the upper left of the window in figure 1.1 is a system menu box, which, when selected, displays a menu that typically allows the user to move the window, close it, or minimize it. At the top center is the title or caption bar (Visual Basic refers to the text as the window's caption, not its title), and this provides an easy way of labelling an application.

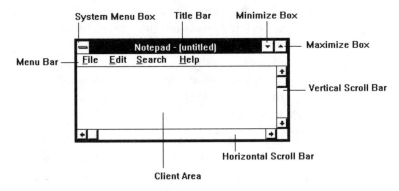

Figure 1.1. A Windows 3+ window.

Next to the title bar are the minimize and maximize boxes, which allow the user to reduce the window to an icon (called an application's *iconic* state), or expand it fully, usually to the whole screen. Under the title bar is usually a menu bar offering the currently available menu options for the application. Almost every stand-alone application will have a menu bar with at least one menu item in it: the File menu. This is the menu that usually offers the Exit item at the bottom (see figure 1.2).

> **How users quit windows programs.**
> The Exit item is the usual way for users to leave an application, so if your application supports file handling, you should include the Exit item at the bottom of the File menu.

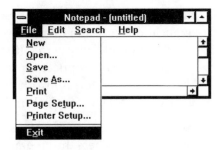

Figure 1.2. A Windows 3+ window with menu.

Under the menu bar is the *client area*; in fact, the client area makes up the whole of a window under the menu bar except for the borders and scroll bars (it is the area that the window is designed to display). This is the drawing area, the area you will work with directly in Visual Basic; that is, this is the part of the window on which you will place buttons, list boxes, text boxes, and the other parts of your programs.

Next to the client area is a vertical scroll bar, a common part of a window that displays text. If there is too much text to fit in the window at once, scroll bars let you look at some subsection of the whole, moving around in the document. (By the way, the small square that moves up and down and which you use to manipulate your position in the scroll bar is called a *thumb*.)

At the bottom of the window is a horizontal scroll bar that scrolls the text in the client area horizontally. Everything in the window but the client area is called the nonclient area; even the border is part of the nonclient area. Visual Basic is responsible for maintaining the nonclient area of the window, and you are responsible for the client area.

Preserving the Feel of Windows

As mentioned, before you begin programming in Visual Basic you should be very familiar with the way the user expects Windows programs to work and feel. In particular, you should be at home with the language of mouse clicks and double-clicks, and anticipating what the user might expect from your application.

For example, the fact that the File menu usually has an Exit item, and that item—if present—is always last, is part of the Windows interface you will be programming in. Before producing applications yourself, you should be familiar with many other aspects of the way users expect Windows applications to work; in other words, there are many Windows conventions you should adhere to. Although these conventions are discussed as you reach the appropriate topics, as well as in Appendix B of this book, there is no substitute for working with existing Windows applications to get the correct feel for the Windows interface.

After a while, these conventions become quite automatic; for instance, in file list boxes (where the program is showing you which files are available to be opened), one click of the mouse should highlight a filename (called *selecting*), and two clicks should open the file (called *choosing*). On the other hand, it is also supposed to be possible to use Windows without a mouse at all—just with the keyboard—so you must provide keyboard support at the same time (in this case, the user would use the tab key to move to the correct box, the arrow keys to highlight a filename, and the Enter key to choose it).

> **You should use the mouse for program design.**
> For the purposes of program design, this book assumes that you have a mouse to go along with Visual Basic. Although it is possible to use Windows *applications* without a mouse, Windows *programmers* (or even experienced Windows users) are severely hampered without one, and their productivity is seriously hampered.

There are other conventions that Windows users expect; if there is some object that can be moved around the screen, users expect to be able to drag it with the mouse. They expect shortcut keys in menus, System menus that let them close a window, and windows that can be moved, resized, or minimized. As mentioned earlier, the best way to know what will be expected of your program is to work with existing Windows applications. For more information on this topic, please refer to Appendix B, which covers Windows program design.

About Windows Programming

Now you will take a look at how one programs applications for Windows and what makes it different from programming under DOS. To start, DOS programs are written sequentially; that is, one event follows the other. In a DOS program, control goes down the list of statements, more or less in the order that the programmer designed. For example, this is the way an introductory program from a Basic book might appear as follows:

```
WHILE INKEY$ = "": WEND
PRINT "Hello from Basic."
```

In the first line, you are simply waiting until the user presses a key. When the key is pressed, control goes sequentially to the next line, and the message "Hello from Basic." appears on the screen. If there were more statements, control would continue on with them, looping and progressing in the way the programmer designed it to work. Windows, however, is different.

Windows Events

An application under Windows typically presents on the screen all possible options (in the form of visual objects) for the user to select. In this way, it represents an entirely new kind of programming—*event*-driven and object-oriented programming. That is to say, the programmer is no longer completely responsible for the flow of the program—the user is. The user selects among all the options presented, and it is up to the program to respond correctly. For example, there may be three buttons on a window, as shown in figure 1.3. Clearly, you cannot just write your program assuming that the user is going to push them in some sequence. Rather, you have to write separate code for each button.

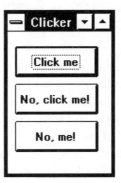

Figure 1.3. A clicker window.

That is the case in general, and it will have significant consequences for you in this book. Instead of monolithic programs you can read from beginning to end, your code will necessarily be divided into smaller sections, one such section for one kind of event. For example, you may add to the window a text box, in which you want the message "Hello from Visual Basic." to appear when the user clicks the button marked Click Me. In that case, your program might appear in the following way:

```
Sub ClickMe_Click ()Message.text = "Hello from Visual Basic."
End Sub
```

This code is specifically designed to handle one type of event—clicking the button marked Click Me. Your programs will typically be collections of code sections like this, one after the other. That is how event-driven programming works: you will largely be designing your code around the interface—that is, around the way you have set up the window, at least in the early part of this book. Your programs will not have "modes," in the way an editor can have modes (insert mode, marking mode, and so on); instead, all the options available at one time will be represented on the screen, ready to be used. You will see how this works soon.

Besides being event-driven, Windows programming is also *object-oriented*. That means easy enough to see on the screen: just pick up an object such as an icon or paintbrush and move it around. This corresponds closely to what is called *object-oriented programming* (although it is not strictly object-oriented programming, because Visual Basic does not support classes and inheritance). This type of programming breaks a program up into discrete objects, each of which has its own code and data associated with it. In this way, each of the objects can be somewhat independent from the others.

Using object-oriented programming is a natural for event-driven software, because it breaks the program up into discrete, modular objects. That is the way you will be treating your windows and all the buttons, text boxes, etc., that you put in them, such as objects. Each of these objects can have data and code associated with it. You may have heard of object-oriented programming, and you may suspect that it is difficult to do, but it turns out that Visual Basic takes care of all of the details for you. In fact, you will look into that process in Visual Basic next; now that you have gotten your background down, you are ready to look at the programming tools you will be using in this book.

About Visual Basic Programming

Under Windows, the user is king—and until recently, the programmer paid the price. Programming Windows was often an excruciating task—until now. Now, the programmer is finally benefitting from some of the same ease of use the user has enjoyed for so long under Windows. Now, the computer itself is being enlisted as an aid for the programmer, not just the user.

This is a revolutionary step, and a welcome one. If you have programmed for Windows before, you will love the way this package works. On the other hand, if you have never created an actual Windows application, you will find that this kind of programming is like nothing you have ever seen. In the same sense that Windows may be thought of as a new operating environment, Visual Basic is the new BASICA or GW-BASIC.

There are three major steps to writing an application in Visual Basic, and you will follow them throughout this book. They are as follows:

▼ Draw the window(s) you want

▼ Customize the properties of buttons, text boxes, and so on

▼ Write the code for the associated events

The first step—drawing the window you want, complete with buttons and menus—is where Visual Basic really shines. Before, it was a tedious process to design the appearance of windows, where the buttons would go, how large they would be, and all types of other considerations. Adding or removing features was also very difficult. Under Visual Basic, however, this whole process has become extraordinarily easy. VB enables you to simply draw—just like a paint program—the window(s) you want, as well as all the buttons, boxes, and labels you want. In other words, you see the actual appearance of your application at design time.

Adding or removing buttons or boxes works just as it would in a paint program, as you will see; no difficult programming is involved at all. The next step involves customizing the properties of what you have drawn—for example, you might give a window or button a certain caption, or change its color (or even whether or not it is visible). Finally, you write the code that responds to the events you consider significant. That is an outline of how it works; now you will see it in practice.

Your First Window

Now you are going to put together a one-window application that simply has one button and one text box. When the user clicks or chooses the button, the message "Welcome to Visual Basic." should appear in the text box, as shown in figure 1.4.

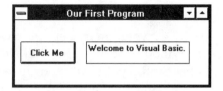

Figure 1.4. Your first program.

Start programming by starting Visual Basic under Windows. The VB display appears in figure 1.5. As with any new software, there are new terms and concepts to learn here. (In fact, there are only about 10 major terms to learn in Visual Basic.) Now you will work through the parts of the Visual Basic display.

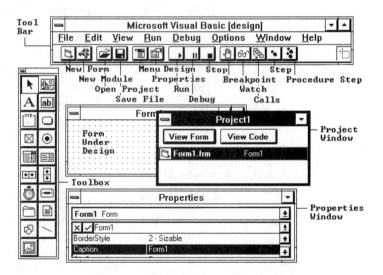

Figure 1.5. The Visual Basic display.

The Form

First, a window (labelled Form1) appears in the center of the screen. This is the window you are designing; Visual Basic refers to windows that you customize as *forms*. As you can see, the form you begin with has the appearance of a normal window. In fact, this is the way your window will look when the application you are writing starts. Notice that Form1 already has a system menu box, a title bar, both minimize and maximize boxes, a border, and a client area.

The client area is filled with dots at regular intervals. These dots form a grid that will help you to align buttons and boxes when you are designing your window (and they disappear at run time). In fact, your window is already viable as it stands; as a program it will work, but it will not do much. If you tell Visual Basic to run this program, a window labelled Form1 will appear on the screen. The parts of the window that you already see, including the system menu and the maximize and minimize boxes, will all be active. This is part of what Visual Basic provides for you. To give this a shot, move up to the menu bar in the VB display and select the Run menu (see figure 1.6).

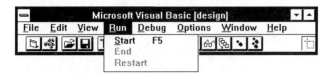

Figure 1.6. Visual Basic's Run menu.

Choose the Start option in this menu. When you do, the screen changes, and Form1 appears just like a normal window, as in figure 1.7.

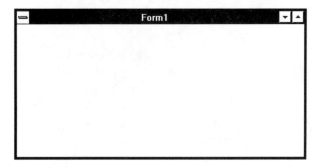

Figure 1.7. Form1 running.

Your program already is running, although it is not very spectacular. You can move the window Form1 around the screen and resize it just like a normal window. The minimize and maximize buttons work as you would expect, minimizing Form1 down to an icon or expanding it so that it takes up the whole page. In addition, note that the grid of dots that was present in the window when you started Visual Basic is now gone; these dots are present only at design time, to help you align objects in the window (in fact, you can remove the grid altogether with the Grid Settings... menu item in the Edit menu). End the program now by opening the system box in the window you have designed and selecting the Close option, or by selecting the End option in Visual Basic's Run menu.

Properties

The window—that is, the form—you have been designing is pretty plain. So far, all you have is a single window named Form1; now you will start customizing it. Visual Basic treats windows under design—forms—as well as boxes and buttons as *objects*, and each different type of object can have certain *properties*. The object named Form1, for example, has properties associated with it that are normal for a window, such as the title or caption, color, visibility (that is, whether or not it is visible on the screen), a certain screen position, and so on. A text box might have a different set of properties, including, for example, what text is currently displayed in it. In other words, an object's properties represent all the data that is normally associated with that object.

To change the caption property of Form1 so that the caption reads "Our First Program" instead of Form1, you have to use the *properties window* on the screen (see figure 1.5). Note that the properties window is separate from the menu bar—the properties window is present only when you are designing your programs, not when you are running them.

A Visual Basic improvement.
In Visual Basic 1.0, properties were displayed in a properties bar, which appeared right under the main menu bar. There you could work with one property at a time. However, the new properties window makes it much easier to see all the properties of a particular object at once.

As you work through the design process, you will place more and more objects on the screen; objects such as buttons, list boxes, radio buttons, and labels. Each of these objects has a specific set of properties—that is, data (such as color and size) that can be associated with it. As you work on the different objects, the properties window lets you change the properties of the object you are working on. For example, you are working on Form1 now, so the properties window holds the properties connected with this object.

Properties that are not there at design time.
Note, however, that not all the properties of a certain object may be available at design time. For example, one of the properties associated with a filename list box is the name of the file currently selected—but because no file is selected at design time, that property will not appear in the properties window for you to work on.

Currently, the properties window reads Caption and Form1; this is the first property associated with this window—that is, the caption of this window is Form1. If you move to the properties window, you will see an entire list of properties connected with this window, as in figure 1.8.

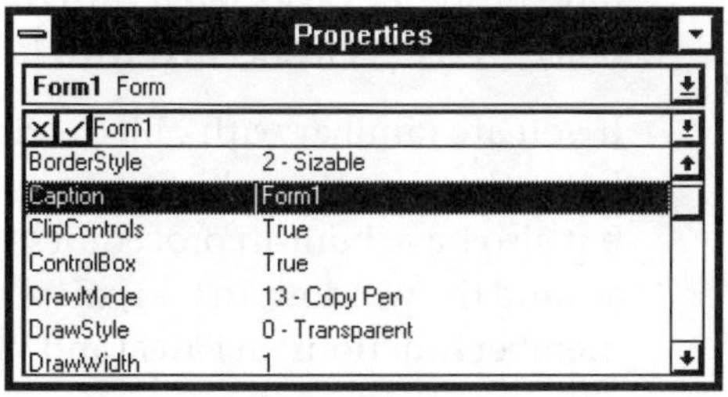

Figure 1.8. The Properties window.

You will explore these options thoroughly later; for now, just make sure that Caption is selected and appears in the top text box of the properties window (as in figure 1.8). This text box gives the current value of the selected property, which is Form1. You can change that now simply by selecting (highlighting with the mouse cursor) that text and then entering the new text so that it reads "Our First Program." That is, change the text Form1 in the text box (next to the x and the check mark in figure 1.8) to "Our First Program."

As you change the text, note that the caption of the window changes accordingly. At this point, you have renamed the window as Our First Program, which means that running it will produce that caption in the caption bar. That is fine as far as it goes (you will see that you can change a window's color also)—but now it is time to press on to more interesting topics, as you add a text box to your window.

Controls

So far, you have seen how to work on the elementary properties of a form. There are two types of objects in Visual Basic, however: forms and controls. *Controls* are all the graphical objects you can design and place on a form, such as list boxes, buttons, labels, and timers (timers tell you how much time has elapsed; they are represented graphically at design time in Visual Basic). In other words, a control is any object the user can manipulate which is not itself a window. The window you are designing and creating is a form; a control is used for I/O with the user (boxes and buttons are examples). Together, forms and controls are called *objects* in Visual Basic, because they both are treated like graphical objects. Objects have properties associated with them, which is the same as saying that an object has data associated with it.

If you are familiar with object-oriented programming, then you already know that objects such as these not only have data associated with them, but also have built-in procedures that can be used to, say, move a button around the window. In C++, these object-connected procedures are called member functions; in Pascal and Visual Basic, they are called *methods*. You will meet them soon.

The next section shows you an example of a control—how to add a text box to your first window by using the Visual Basic toolbox.

The Toolbox

Because this is Visual Basic, you are going to draw the controls you want right on the form you are designing. This process works in much the same way as it does in a paint program in which you select a drawing tool and then draw with it. In this example, you select a control tool and then paint controls with it. You do that by selecting a tool from the Visual Basic toolbox, which is shown in figure 1.9.

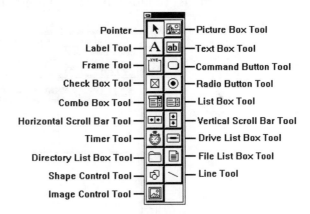

Figure 1.9. The Visual Basic toolbox.

The toolbox plays a big part in this book because it enables you to draw all of the controls you need. To draw a text box, select the text box tool—the second tool down on the right in figure 1.9. There are two ways to draw controls in Visual Basic. The first way is to select a tool from the tool box (click once on it); when you do, the Visual Basic pointer changes from an arrow to a cross when you move over to a form under design. You can position the cross anywhere on the form, click once to anchor that end of the control (the top left end), then move the pointer to the other end of the control (the bottom left end), and click again; the control appears. The second method, which you will use more often, is simply to click twice on the tool in the toolbox; when you do, the control you want appears in the center of the form, ready to be moved and shaped.

Your goal now is to create a text box. Double-click on the text box tool; a default-sized text box appears in the middle of the form, as shown in figure 1.10.

Note that the properties window now displays "Text1" (the name of the text box). The Name property holds the name of a control, and that is the way you will refer to it in your program. That is, the Name is the name of your control as far as Visual Basic is concerned. In this case, the default name for your text box is Text1. As you can also see, eight small black squares are on the periphery of your new text box. These squares, called *sizing handles*, allow you to manipulate the size of the controls you are designing. By using them, you can stretch a control in any of the eight directions. To move the control itself, simply click and drag it.

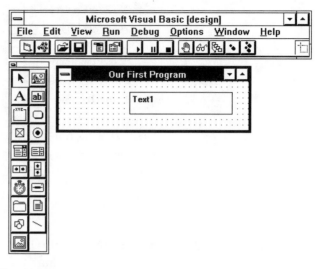

Figure 1.10. Default text box.

A Visual Basic improvement.
In Visual Basic 1.0, controls and forms both had name properties, but a control's name was referred to as a CtlName and a form's property as a FormName. In Visual Basic 2.0 and 3.0, however, you can treat forms with much the same flexibility as you treat controls, and both now have a Name property instead. You will see more about this in Chapter 11.

Move the text box and resize the window until it corresponds roughly to figure 1.11. Because the text box is selected, the properties window is ready to display the text box properties you can set.

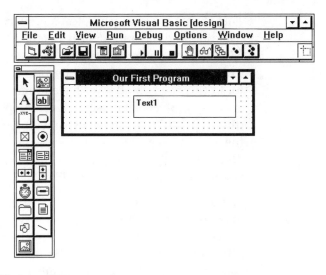

Figure 1.11. A text box moved.

Now take a look at the properties—for example, the data items—in the properties window (see figure 1.12). This list presents all of an object's properties that you can set at design time. You can scroll through the list to see what is available, such as BackColor (the background color behind the text), FontName, Left and Top (the position of the top left corner of the text box), and Width and Height. If you select a property such as Width, the current width of the text box appears in the top text box in the properties window.

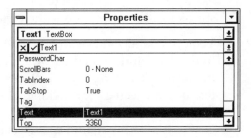

Figure 1.12. A Properties list.

That is how it works; you select a property of the object you are dealing with first, and the current setting of the property appears in the properties window. The downwards pointing arrow on the right of that box opens to display a list of all the possible options you can set the current property to. In this way, you do not have to remember long lists of numbers or codes—just select an object. Select a property in the top drop-down box (the list provided if you forget what properties are available), and then set the property as you want it to be when your program starts. In fact, if you do check the Width property, you may be surprised to find that your text box has a width of something like 2295.

The obvious next question is 2295 what? Meaning, what is the unit of measurement here? You might first assume that measurements on the screen would be in terms of pixels—the individual dots on the screen. Although measurements can be in pixels if you like (you will learn more about this topic later), the default measuring system for a Windows application should apply to all possible display devices, not just to the screen. For example, a laser printer typically prints 300 dots to the inch, so you would need some unit of measurement finer than that. Visual Basic uses *twips*, and there are 1440 of them to the inch for the display on the corresponding device. You will see more about such measurements later. In the meantime, you will simply use the toolbox tools to design your interface, rather than concern yourself with the actual location of controls on your forms. However, you might notice that you can change the Width property, like all the properties available at design time, simply by editing the text in the middle box of the properties window. For example, if you changed it to 1440, you would see your text box grow or shrink to 1440 twips, or one inch wide.

You can take advantage of this flexibility to change the text that appears in the text window. Right now, it simply reads Text1, which is not very interesting. To change it to "Welcome to Visual Basic," make sure that the text box is selected—for example, the sizing handles appear around it— and then move to the properties window. The property you want to change is called Text; find and select it. When you do, the text box in the properties window displays the word Text, and the box next to it displays the current setting of that property, which is Text1 (see figure 1.13).

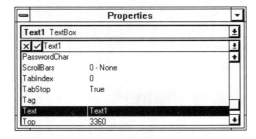

Figure 1.13. Setting text in a text box.

Now just edit the text matching the Text property in the top text box (i.e., "Text1"), changing it to "Welcome to Visual Basic." As you type, the text in the text box automatically changes, following each keystroke. Now you have changed a property of the text box—that is, you have changed the text in it from "Text1" to "Welcome to Visual Basic." This new data becomes part of the object, and, when you make this into a program, the new text will appear in the text box. As you will see in a few pages, you can also reach the properties of controls like this text box from your programs. In the meantime, select the Start option in the Run menu; at run time, the window you have been creating looks like the one in figure 1.14.

Figure 1.14. An initialized text box.

Note that when you run your program, the caption bar of Visual Basic itself, which has been displaying "Microsoft Visual Basic [design]," becomes "Microsoft Visual Basic [run]," indicating that the program is now running. In addition, you might notice two other windows that appear on the screen, one labelled PROJECT1.MAK, and the other labelled Debug Window (these windows are discussed later). As you can see, the new text appears in the text box: "Welcome to Visual Basic."

So far, your program is a success—you have displayed your own message—but it is still not very interesting. Now you are going to add a command button that you can click to display the text in the text box, instead of having the text present immediately when you run the program.

Command Buttons

Stop the program, either by choosing the Close option in the System menu of the window you created or by choosing the End option in Visual Basic's Run menu. The Visual Basic design screen reappears. Now choose the command button tool—the tool with a button shape in the toolbox, third tool down on the right side. When you double-click this tool, a command button appears in the center of your form, as shown in figure 1.15.

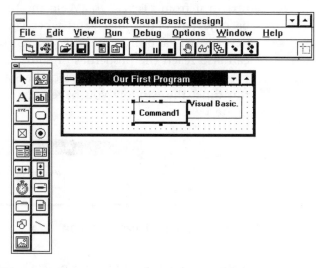

Figure 1.15. Creating command buttons.

Move the command button to the left side of the form so that it does not obscure the text box. Because the command button is selected, the properties window contains all of its properties that you can work with at design time. As you can see by looking through the properties list, this includes the Name of the control displayed at the top; the name of the properties control; Left, Top, Height, and Width as before; FontName and other properties having to do with fonts; and a number of other properties you have not seen before, such as TabStop.

20

In this case, you will change the caption of this button so that it says "Click Me." Just select the Caption property for this command button in the properties window and edit the text to "Click Me," as shown in figure 1.16. As you do, "Click Me" appears on the new command button. Next, erase the text in the text box by selecting it, choosing the Text property in the Properties List Box, and deleting all the characters there so that the text box is blank.

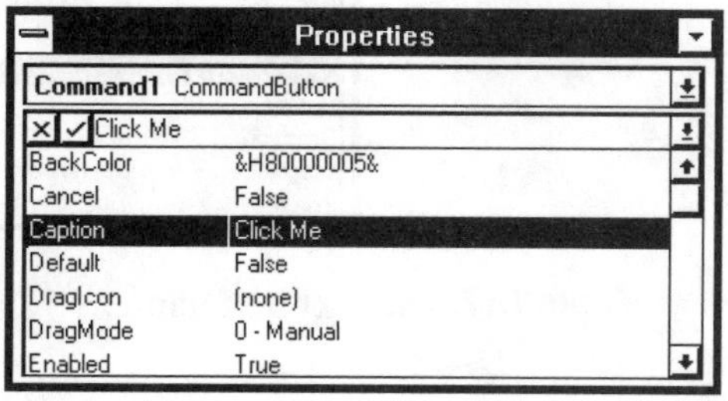

Figure 1.16. An empty text box.

Somehow you have to connect the command button to the text box so that when you click the button, the text "Welcome to Visual Basic" appears in the text box. This is where you will start writing your first lines of actual Basic code. Your goal is to reach the text property of the text box from inside your program. To do that, you have to know how Visual Basic refers to the properties of the different controls in your program.

It turns out that if you have a text box whose name (that is, whose Name) is Text1, then you can simply refer to the text in it (its Text property) as Text1.Text. In other words, the usual way to refer to a property in a Visual Basic program is Object.Property, where Object is the Name of the object—form or control—that has this property, and Property is the name of the property itself.

When you start dealing with the code routines that are built in for many of your screen objects—called methods—you will find that you access them like this: Object.Method, much like accessing a property.

Note that it is important not to get a control's caption or some other text confused with its actual Name. The Name is the internal name of that control in Visual Basic, and the default Name for your text box is Text1 (a second text box would automatically be named Text2, and so on). You can see this by checking the Name property of the text box, as in figure 1.17.

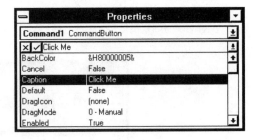

Figure 1.17. The text box name.

You can set Text1's Text property in your program in a Basic statement when the Click Me button is pushed, as follows:

```
Text1.Text = "Welcome to Visual Basic."
```

If you delete the text in the text box at design time, when the program starts, the text box will be empty. When you execute the preceding statement, however, the text "Welcome to Visual Basic." will appear in it.

As you know, your programs are going to be event-driven—that is, broken into sections specifically written to handle certain events, such as button pushes. This means that you have to connect your single line of code to the correct event; in this case, when the user clicks the command button. To find the events associated with any object, just click on that object twice while designing your program. A new window, called the *code window*, opens (see figure 1.18).

Using the Code Window

The code window has a template for every event procedure (i.e., connected with a specific object) you can write. This is exceptionally handy for two reasons—one is that it will save you some time setting up the outlines of the procedures you want to write; the other is that the Code

Window indicates what kind of events you can respond to. As you can see in figure 1.18, the following outline is already prepared for you:

```
Sub Command1_Click ()
End Sub
```

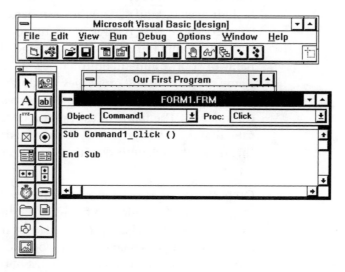

Figure 1.18. The code window.

There are two types of procedures in Visual Basic: Sub procedures and Function procedures. The two differ in that Function procedures can return values, and Sub procedures cannot, just as in normal Basic. INKEY$, for example, is a popular Basic function (which, incidentally, is not supported in Visual Basic) that you have already seen; it returns a value you can check as follows:

```
WHILE INKEY$ = "": WEND
PRINT "Hello from Basic."
```

Just as in standard Basic, Sub procedures and Function procedures take arguments passed to them in Visual Basic:

```
Sub MySub (A As Integer, B As Integer)
    :
    :
End Sub
```

```
Function MyFunc (C As Integer, D As Integer)
    :
    :
End Function
```

You will see how to set up your own Sub procedures and Functions later, including what kind of data they can handle. For now, take a look at the Sub procedure that is already set up for you, in outline, in the code window: Command1_Click(). Command1 is actually the default control name of your command button Click Me (as you can see by checking its Name property in the properties window)—just as the default Name of your text box was Text1, so the default Name of a command button is Command1. The name of the Sub procedure Command1_Click() indicates that this event procedure is connected with button Command1, and that this is the Sub procedure that gets executed when the user clicks that button.

Other events are associated with command buttons as well. Take another look at the code window in figure 1.18. The box on the right, below the caption bar, is called the *procedure box*; it indicates what procedures are available for a particular object. If you click the down arrow next to the procedure box, you will see a useful list of the available procedures, as in figure 1.19.

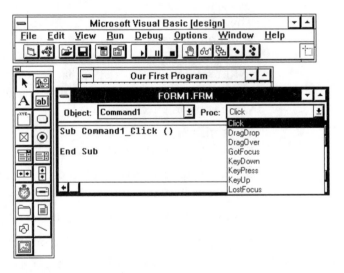

Figure 1.19. A Procedure box in the code window.

The code window also lists—in the leftmost box just under the caption bar, the *object box*—all the objects you have created so far. Clicking on the object box reveals the names of the objects you can attach event procedures to, as in figure 1.20.

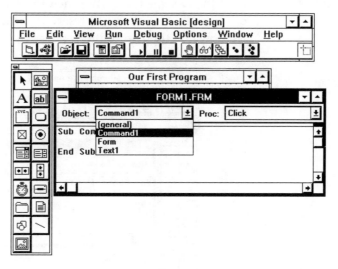

Figure 1.20. An object box in the code window.

You can see that Text1 is there, as are Command1, your text box, and command button. In addition, the form itself is listed, because there are several events that can take place with forms—for example, when a form is first used by a program, it is considered an event (Form_Load( )), as it is when the user clicks on the form during run time (Form_Click( )). In addition, there is another entry in the object list called (general). This is where your internal procedures will go when you write them—that is, the Sub and Function procedures you might write to do the real work of a program, where the rest is largely connected to I/O.

In this case, however, your code is entirely I/O related—for example, connected to a control—and consists of the following single line:

```
Text1.Text = "Welcome to Visual Basic."
```

You can place that line in the Command1_Click( ) Sub procedure as follows:

```
Sub Command1_Click ()
Text1.Text = "Welcome to Visual Basic."
End Sub
```

To do that in Visual Basic, you just have to position the insertion point (in Windows, the place where new text will go is called the *insertion point*, or *caret*; the term *cursor* is reserved for the mouse cursor) in the code window and then enter the text (see figure 1.21).

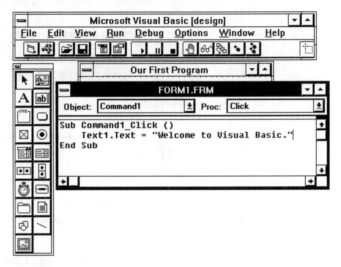

Figure 1.21. Entering Basic code.

Making your programs easier to read.
Note that you indented your single code line by pressing the tab key first. Although not necessary, it is good programming practice to indent code lines like this. When your code gets more complex and includes multiple levels of control, you will see that indenting helps make the code much easier to understand.

That's it as far as the code necessary for Command1_Click() is concerned. Close the code window by choosing the Close option in the system menu. Clear the text from the text box by selecting the text box and editing its text property in the properties window—for example, deleting the text there now.

Now you are ready to run. To begin, simply choose the Start option in
Visual Basic's Run menu. The window you have been creating appears on
the screen along with the command button (labelled Click Me) and the
text box (now empty). Just click the button, and the text "Welcome to
Visual Basic." will appear in the text box, as shown in figure 1.22.

Figure 1.22. Running your first program.

In fact, you do not have to run your program under Visual Basic; you can
make it into a stand-alone Windows application. All you need to do is to
choose the Make Exe File... option in Visual Basic's File menu, as shown
in figure 1.23.

When you choose this option, a dialog box opens (see figure 1.24). Click
on the OK button; Visual Basic creates a file called Project1.Exe, which you
can run under Windows directly, and which will produce your fully
functioning window. Congratulations; you have created your first complete Windows application.

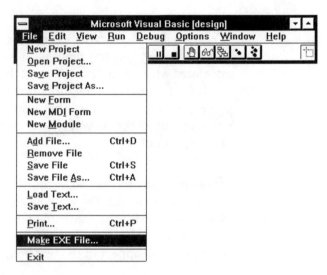

Figure 1.23. Visual Basic's file menu.

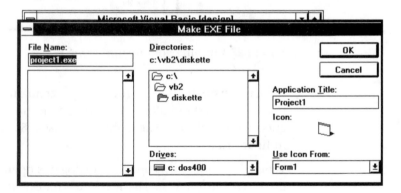

Figure 1.24. The Make Exe File dialog box.

Visual Basic Projects

You may wonder why Visual Basic gave the name Project1.Exe to your application. The reason is that VB organizes tasks by *projects*, not by forms. An application can have a number of forms associated with it—for example, multiple windows—and collecting everything together into a single project wraps it up into one easily managed package. Visual Basic allows only one project to be open at one time, and each project can have three different parts. Now that you have run your first program, it is time to explore what makes up a Visual Basic project.

Visual Basic Forms

You already know that a form is a window you design in Visual Basic. Applications usually have at least one form (but it is not technically necessary, as you will see later).

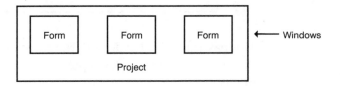

Visual Basic Modules

A Visual Basic *module* is made up of Basic code—but it is code that is not directly associated with a particular form. The procedures in a module can be reached from anywhere in the application. For example, you might want to define a Sub procedure that sorts data. This procedure is not directly concerned with input or output, but it can be vital to some applications. To avoid the necessity of having all code tied to some form, Visual Basic introduced the idea of a module, designed only to hold code. To create a module, as you will do later, use the New Module... item in Visual Basic's File menu. Usually, larger applications use modules to store procedures that are used throughout the application, as follows:

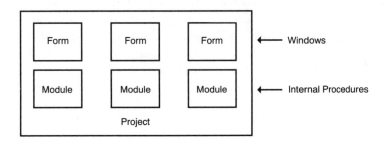

You can also declare items in a module to be global; that is, making them global makes them accessible to the rest of the application, as follows:

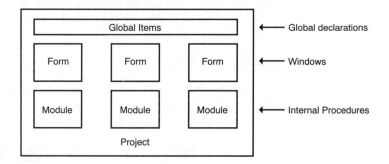

This has a great deal to do with the scope of constants and variables (that discussion is in the next chapter, when the variable types available are discussed).

Using Visual Basic Projects

When you start Visual Basic, it automatically starts or creates Project1. To rename the project, select the Save Project As... item in the File menu. To work on some project that already exists, you can use the Open Project... item in the File menu (see figure 1.25). To keep track of the current project, Visual Basic maintains the *project window*; the contents of the project window for your application are shown in figure 1.26.

The project window is useful when you have multiple forms or code modules. Here, because you have only one form, you have not made much use of it.

You might also notice in the project window that the default name of your form is Form1.Frm; the .Frm extension is normal for forms, just as the .Bas extension is normal for Basic files. When Form1.Frm is selected in the project window, you can jump back and forth between looking at the form and looking at the code window (which holds all the code associated with the objects in this project) by choosing the buttons in the project window: View Form or View Code. (However, it is just as easy to double-click an object to open up the code window.)

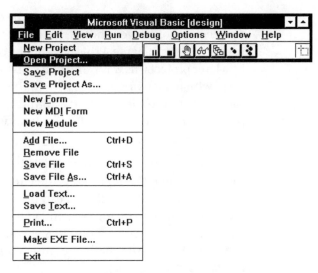

Figure 1.25. The File Menu with the Open Project Item.

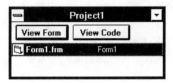

Figure 1.26. The Project window.

Projects themselves are saved as .Mak files (with the associated .Frm and .Bas files are stored separately). Initially, when you create a new project, including new forms and even modules, Visual Basic does not automatically create the corresponding files on disk. Instead, it is up to you to save the files you want (although Visual Basic will prompt you to save files when you leave, if you have not already done so). Now that you have created your own project, you need to make sure that you can save it to disk so that nothing is lost.

Saving Your Work on Disk

There are five Save items in the Visual Basic File menu: Save Project, Save Project As..., Save File, Save File As..., and Save Text.... The Save Project item saves all the files associated with the current project on disk. To save a project, however, you should first give it a name (unless you do not mind using the default name, Project1—but be careful that it is not overwritten by a later project this way), and you can do that with the Save Project As... item, which opens a dialog box. With this option, you can choose a name for the current project and save all the associated files on disk. After the project is named, the Save Project item will save your work under that name as well.

In addition, you can use the Save File item to save the currently selected form or module (as opposed to the current project). Again, you should give it a name first, which you can do with the Save File As... item. This menu item opens a dialog box, and you must specify the name of the file you want to save. Storing files this way usually makes them inaccessible to you outside Visual Basic, because VB stores them in its own binary format by default.

Saving your program files as text.
Visual Basic now offers you the option of saving your .Bas and .Frm files as text as opposed to its proprietary binary format. To do that,click the Save As Text box in the Save File As... dialog box.Also, .Mak files are stored in text by default.

Importing Basic code from DOS.
If you have Basic code—for example, if you are moving over from QuickBasic or the Microsoft Basic Professional Development System—the best two options for importing and checking it are the Load Text... and Save Text... pair in VB's Code menu.

Saving Your Project

To save your current project, give names to and save the file in the project window, the file currently named Form1.Frm. It is best to use new names for such files, because these are the Visual Basic defaults, and they might easily be overwritten by later projects. Next, use the Save Project As... item in the File menu to save the whole project, again selecting some name other than the default Project1.Mak (such as TheProg.Mak). That's it. The next time you start Visual Basic, you can reload this project by using the Open Project... item in the File menu and opening TheProg.Mak. To help you do this, Visual Basic 3.0 includes a Most Recently Used (MRU) file list. This list of the most recently opened projects is added to the File menu. When you want to reopen one of the projects, just select the matching menu item.

Adding More Power to Your Text Box

Before you finish with your first application, you might notice that, because the text ("Welcome to Visual Basic.") appears in a text box, the user is free to edit it, even after you have displayed your message—for example, just like a normal Windows text box. However, you can modify your program so that you are informed if any change is made to the text. It turns out that changing the text in a text box is one of the events you can write code for.

> **Read-only "text boxes."**
> If you do not want the user to change the text you display on a form, use a label instead. As you will see, you can write to a label at run time, but the user cannot change the displayed text. This means that labels can act as read-only text boxes.

When the text in a text box is edited, a *text box change* event occurs. Because your text box is named Text1, this event will be called Text1_Change(). You can intercept that change by going back to the Visual Basic design screen and clicking twice on the text box. The code window for the text box opens (see figure 1.27). The text change event is already selected, so you are ready to write code, as follows:

```
Sub Text1_Change()
End Sub
```

For example, if the text is edited, a text box change event is generated, and you might want to give the user the option of restoring it to the original welcome message. You can do that by changing the caption of the command button from "Click Me" to, say, "Restore Msg." This is easy because the caption of the command button is simply a property of the command button, which you can reach from your program. In particular, because the button's Name is Command1, you can simply make this Basic assignment: Command1.Caption = "Restore Msg," where you assign the string "Restore Msg" to the button's caption property. You do that by making this change to the Sub procedure Text1_Change(), as follows:

```
Sub Text1_Change()
    Command1.Caption = "Restore Msg"
End Sub
```

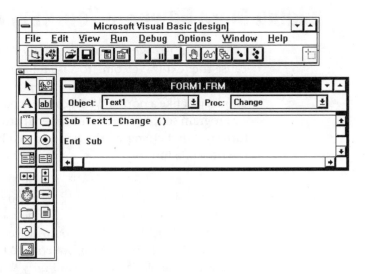

Figure 1.27. Text box's code window.

Now, when you run the program, the usual window appears, along with the Click Me button and the empty text window. However, as soon as the user changes the text in the text box, the caption of the button changes to "Restore Msg," as shown in figure 1.28, indicating that the original message can be restored by pressing this button.

Figure 1.28. The Restore Msg button.

That's it for this chapter. You have gotten down the fundamentals of Visual Basic. In the next chapter, you will start to dig into Visual Basic in depth. In particular, you will explore all there is to know about two of its most popular objects—in fact, two objects you have already been introduced to: buttons and text boxes.

Summary

In this chapter, you learned about the parts of a window, windows events, how to design and run a Visual Basic program, and how to save work on disk. You learned about the terms form, control, object, module, project, and others, as well as the elements of designing programs in Windows. You put together your first working Windows program—a program that uses text boxes and command buttons.

New Properties	Description
BackColor	Holds the background color value of the control or form (see Chapter 6 for a discussion of how colors are represented).
Caption	Holds the control's caption (title) on screen.
Height	Holds the height of object or form (default: in twips).
Left	Holds the distance of left edge to left edge of form (for controls) or screen (for forms) (default: in twips).
Name	Holds the name you use for form or control in code (for example, the text property of the text box named Text1 is Text1.Text).
Text	Holds text associated with the text-oriented control.
Top	Holds the distance of top edge to top edge of form (for controls) or screen (for forms) (default: in twips).

New Properties	Description
Width	Holds the width of control or form (default: in twips).

New Events	Description
Change	Occurs when the contents (usually text) of a control change.
Click	Occurs when a form or control is clicked with the mouse.
Load	Occurs when a form is first loaded; use it for initialization.

Buttons, Text Boxes, and an Alarm Clock Program

This chapter explores two of the most popular Windows controls: buttons and text boxes. These two controls provide the most fundamental methods of receiving input and displaying output in your programs. They can take the place of DOS Basic instructions like INKEY$ and PRINT, so they are very important. In particular, this chapter covers:

▼ Reading numbers into your programs

▼ Using labels

▼ Storing data in variables

▼ Changing fonts

▼ Formatting text output

▼ How to cut and paste text

▼ Enabling and disabling buttons

▼ Quick access keys

▼ Option (radio) buttons

▼ Reading individual keystrokes

▼ The Visual Basic Beep statement

The programs you will develop here include a Windows calculator, a notepad (which will allow you to mark, cut, and paste text), and an alarm clock. The alarm clock will show you how to work with fonts in Visual Basic, an asset to any program that uses text. You will also start to interpret and store the data you receive, which means that you will see how to use variables in Visual Basic. In other words, you are not only going to develop your I/O skills in this chapter—you will also learn how to manipulate data in your programs.

Two of the most common Windows controls are certainly text boxes and buttons. In fact, you used both of these controls in the first chapter. Text boxes are the important text I/O controls in Visual Basic, and buttons are one of the chief command I/O controls (the other being, of course, menus, which you will see in Chapter 3). For those reasons, you will see how to use both text and buttons in this chapter in some depth.

It is important to realize that text boxes are the primary means of character string input in Visual Basic. They take the place of the standard Basic instructions INKEY$, LINE INPUT, INPUT$, and INPUT, which can be used to read from the keyboard in other Basics. Here, you have to use the Windows method of reading text—which is with text boxes. In addition, text boxes are a primary means of character string output, which means they can take the place of other Basic instructions, such as PRINT or PRINT USING. Given the importance of both user character input and output, they make up the first topics this book should cover.

The whole idea of text I/O—that is, character string input and output—brings you closer to the heart of programming in Visual Basic. To understand handling text and how to display data from your programs, you will have to examine how to store it in the first place. That will bring you to the topic of variables. In fact, your first application in this chapter will be a simple calculator that operates in its own window so that you can learn how to accept and display numeric values in text boxes.

In addition, you will learn about the difficulties of displaying graphic text characters in Windows (for example, because the width of each character can be different, it is difficult to know exactly how far you have printed on the screen, and other concerns). Text boxes also have some pretty advanced capabilities you should look into. For example, you can set up text boxes with more than one line—what Visual Basic calls multiline text boxes—which include word wrap and scroll bars, and you can also retrieve specific text the user has marked. Later on, in the file handling chapter, you will put together a small file-editing program. You can get that started by writing a notepad application that takes keystrokes and lets you store text. That is the plan for this chapter. You will also handle all kinds of character string input and output with text boxes and get commands from the user with command buttons. You begin now with the calculator example.

A Calculator Example

The calculator is going to be remarkably simple, because you are focusing on text boxes and not on how to write larger applications. You will just have two text boxes—one for the first operand and one for the second—a button marked with an equal sign, and a text box to hold the result of adding the two operands together. When the user clicks on the equal button, the result of the addition will appear in the result text box.

To begin, start Visual Basic and change the caption property of the default window (which now reads Form1) to Calculator by editing its Caption property in the properties window—for example, the property that is selected there when Visual Basic starts. Next, save this form as, say, Calc.Frm by choosing the Save File As... item in the File menu. Now save the whole project as Calc.Mak, using the Save Project As... item, also in the File menu. These are the typical beginning steps of writing a new application, because the only way to name files in Visual Basic is with the Save options (Visual Basic does not even create files for the form and project until you save them). It is also a good idea to periodically save your work, which you can do now with the Save Project item.

Next, choose (double-click) the text box tool. A text box appears in the center of the form; move it up to the top of the form and change its Name—for example, its Name property in the properties window) to Operand1, as shown in figure 2.1.

This text box, Operand1, is going to receive the first operand; the next text box will receive the second, then there will be a button marked with an equal sign (=), and a result text box. For simplicity's sake, this calculator will only perform addition, adding Operand1 + Operand2 to get a result, but it is a simple matter to add buttons for subtraction, multiplication, and division.

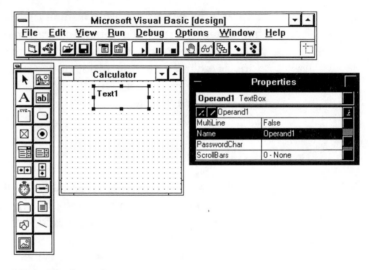

Figure 2.1. A calculator form.

Next, double-click on the text box tool again, and place the second text box under the first one, changing its Name to Operand2, as shown in figure 2.2. (Note that Visual Basic gives it the default Name Text1, just like the first text box, because you have renamed the first box Operand1.) Now place a command button under the two boxes, and give it an equal sign for a caption.Finally, place one last text box under the command button, and give it a Name of Result, as shown in figure 2.3.

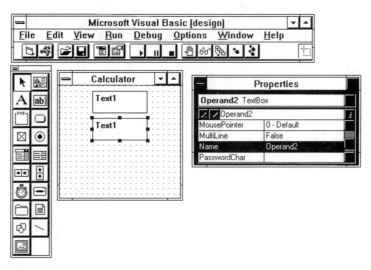

Figure 2.2. A calculator with a second text box.

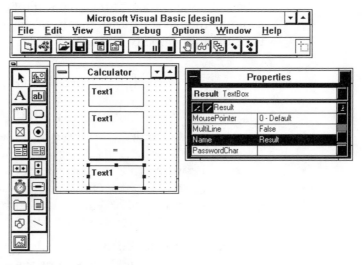

Figure 2.3. A calculator template.

There are two more things to do, and you will have designed the calculator's appearance completely. First, remove the text from each text box—for example "Text1"—by selecting their Text properties and deleting what is there. You should also add a plus sign (+) in front of the second text box (Operand1) to indicate what operation you are performing, as follows:

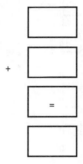

To do that, you can place a *label* on the form.

Labels

Labels are usually used, as their name implies, to label other controls on a form. Although your program can change the text in a label by referring to its Caption property, the user cannot.

> **Making a label look like a text box.**
> While labels often appear only as text, you can also put a box around them, making them look just like a text box. You do that by setting the BorderStyle option to 1. (Recall that all possible settings for a property are displayed in the settings box in the properties window.) However, you should note that it is only possible to set the value of this property at design time; that is, a program cannot add or remove a label's border at run time.

The label you want to add to your calculator is a very simple plus sign. You can do that by choosing the label tool, the second tool down on the left side of the toolbox (it is marked with a large uppercase A). A label appears in the middle of the form; change its Caption property from "Label1" to "+" in the properties window, and move it next to the Operand2 text box, as shown in figure 2.4.

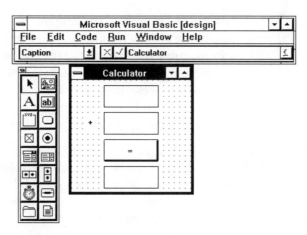

Figure 2.4. A completed calculator template.

> **Another way of placing text directly on a form.**
> You can also print directly to a form (as opposed to printing to a label), as you will see later when graphics are discussed.

Now the calculator template is complete; all that remains is to write the code. The action here is simple; when the user clicks the command button marked =, you want to take Operand1, add it to Operand2, and place the result in Result (the bottom text box). However, to do this poses a problem: so far, you have dealt only with text in text boxes. How do you display numbers? And how do you store them in your program?

This is going to be very important for you. How can you manipulate the input you receive from the user in your text boxes, especially if that input is supposed to represent numbers and not just text? In other words, your job now is to translate the text in the text boxes Operand1 and Operand2 into numbers, add them in your program, and then display the result. All this internal handling of data brings up the next topic, variables, which you need to explore before you proceed.

Variables in Visual Basic

The types of variables Visual Basic uses are much like the variables in QBasic, Quick Basic, or in the Basic Professional Development System.

Like those compilers, variable names can be up to 40 characters long (including letters, numbers, and underscores), and they have only two naming rules: the first character must be a letter (so that Visual Basic does not assume this is a numeric value), and you cannot use Visual Basic reserved words (such as Sub or Function) as variable names. The data types that are built in to Visual Basic are shown in table 2.1, along with their ranges of allowed values.

> **You are not restricted to the built-in data types.**
> Besides the built-in data types, you can also define your own aggregate data types with Type, which defines data structures, as you will see when you work with files.

Table 2.1. Visual Basic Data Types

Type	Number of bytes	Character	Range
Integer	2	%	–32,768 to 32,767
Long	4	&	–2,147,483,648 to 2,147,483,647
Single	4	!	–3.37E+38 to 3.37E+38
Double	8	#	–1.67D+308 to 1.67D+308
Currency	8	@	–9.22E+14 to 9.22E+14
String	varies	$	[Not applicable]

Type Conventions for Variables

If you are a QuickBasic user, you might not have seen the currency type before. Although originally designed to hold currency values, it is attractive for other reasons as well—it stores numbers with 15-place accuracy to the left of the decimal place and 4 places to the right. These numbers are fixed-point numbers; that is, they always have four places to the left of the decimal point.

Like other Basic compilers, there are certain characters for example—! or %, as indicated in table 2.1—you can use to indicate what type of variable you intend when you first use it. For example, if you want to use an integer value named my_int, you can indicate to Visual Basic that my_int is an integer by adding a % character to the end of it like this: my_int%. Similarly, if you want to use a single precision floating-point number called my_float, you can call it my_float!. In fact, you can even leave it as my_float, because the default type for variables is single in Visual Basic (as it is in QBasic, QuickBasic, and the Basic Professional Development System).

> **How to change the default data types.**
> You can change default data types with a Deftype statement like this: DefInt A-Z indicates that you want all variables beginning with letters A-Z to be integers. Other options include DefLng, DefSng, DefDbl, DefCur, and DefStr.

In fact, there are two ways of indicating to Visual Basic that you want to use a certain name as a variable name. The first is simply to use the name where you want it, as follows:

```
my_int% = 5
```

If Visual Basic has not seen my_int% before, this becomes an *implicit declaration*. As you have seen, the last character of the variable can determine the variable's type; if the last character is not a special type-declaraction character—for example, %, &, !, #, @, or $—then the default type is Single.

The other way (and more proper from a programming point of view) is to use the Dim statement to specifically declare a variable at the beginning of a procedure (you will see how to declare variables globally later), as in the following examples:

```
Dim my_int As Integer
Dim my_double As Double
Dim my_variable_string As String
Dim my_fixed_string As String * 20
```

Note in particular the last two variables: my_variable_string and my_fixed_string. The first one, my_variable_string, is a string with variable length (up to 65,535 characters in Visual Basic). The second one is explicitly declared a fixed length by adding "* 20" to the end of the declaration, which makes it a string of exactly 20 characters, just as in other Basic compilers. (You will take a closer look at strings later in this chapter, when you deal with the built-in string statements and functions in Visual Basic.)

There are several places to put such declarations, and the placement of a variable's declaration affects the variable's *scope*—which refers to the portion of the program that the variable is visible to. You look into that next, and then you will be ready to complete the calculator example.

Scope of Variables in Visual Basic

As mentioned, a variable's scope refers to the regions in the application that can access it. There are four different levels of variable scope because there are four different places to declare variables.

The first place to declare variables, either with the Dim statement or implicitly (for example, just by using it), is at the procedure level. There are two kinds of procedures in Visual Basic, Sub procedures and Function procedures, and each can have variable declarations. When you declare a variable in a procedure, however, that variable is *local* to that procedure; in other words, its scope is restricted to the procedure in which it is declared. Such variables are called *local variables* in Visual Basic, as follows:

```
+-----------+  +-----------+
| Procedure |  | Procedure |
|           |  |           |
| Local     |  | Local     |
| Variables |  | Variables |
+-----------+  +-----------+
```

One important note is that local variables do not outlast the procedure they are defined in; that is, every time you enter the procedure, the local variables are reinitialized. In other words, do not count on retaining the value in a local variable between procedure calls.

> **How to make local variables retain their data.**
> You can, however, make local variables permanent by declaring them *static*. Visual Basic will not reinitialize a static variable at any time. To make a variable static, declare it with the keyword Static instead of Dim—for example, Static my_int As Integer).

The next two places where you declare variables are the form and module levels (recall that a module can hold the general, non-I/O code associated with an application). If you declare a form-level variable, that variable is accessible to all procedures in that form. The same goes for code modules: if you declare a module-level variable, that variable is accessible to all procedures in that module, as follows:

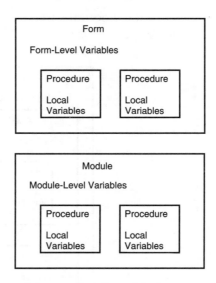

In particular, you might notice that this lets you share information between procedures. The way to declare a variable at the form or module level is to place it into the declarations part of the (general) object you saw before, in the code window (you will see this later). The way you create new modules is simply by selecting the New Module... item in Visual Basic's File menu (as you will also see later). These new variables are static by default—that is, although procedure-level variables are reinitialized each time the procedure is entered, variables at the form and module (and global variables as well) are static.

The final level, of course, is the global level. Every procedure or line of code in an application has access to these variables—for example, these variables are application-wide. To declare a variable global, place it in the section of a module named (general), using the keyword Global, not Dim. The (general) section of a module is the section you first see when you open a module in the code window. In the Objects box it will say (general) and in the Procedures box it will say (declarations). Place the following declarations there:

```
Global my_int As Integer
Global my_double As Double
Global my_variable_string As String
Global my_fixed_string As String * 20
```

Then at the procedure, form, module, or global levels, the structure is as follows:

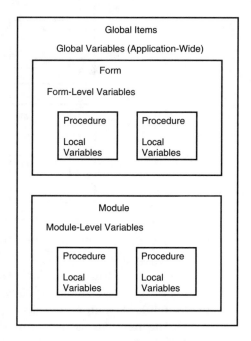

In the calculator example, you will be able to use procedure level—for example, local—variables. Now it is time to get back to that application.

Storing the Calculator's Data

If you want to, you can store the calculator's data—that is, the numbers typed by the user and the result—as single-precision numbers. You have designed things so that all action takes place when the user clicks the = button, so why not take a look at that procedure. Double-click on the command button you have labelled =, bringing up the code window and displaying the Sub procedure for a click event associated with it (note that Visual Basic's default name for it is Command1), as follows:

```
Sub Command1_Click()
End Sub
```

So far, there is nothing in this procedure. Begin by reading the text in the text box Operand1 (for example, Operand1.Text) and storing it in a single-precision variable named Op1, which you can declare as follows:

```
Sub Command1_Click()
    Dim Op1 As Single
        :

End Sub
```

To convert the text Operand1.Text into a number, Visual Basic provides the Val( ) function, which works in the following way:

```
Sub Command1_Click()
    Dim Op1 As Single

    Op1 = Val(Operand1.Text)
        :

End Sub
```

Creating a password textbox control.

Another handy way of processing input from a text box is as a password control—you can specify a character for the text box property PasswordChar, such as $pr*$pr, which will allow the text box to print out only a string of *s, no matter what is typed. Even so, the actual text there will be stored in the text box's Text property.

Val( ) will take a string and, starting from the left and working towards the right, convert as much of it as it can into a numeric value (if it reaches illegal characters, it simply stops converting the text into a number). Next, you do the same for Operand2, calling the resulting variable Op2, as follows:

```
Sub Command1_Click()
    Dim Op1 As Single
```

```
      Dim Op2 As Single

      Op1 = Val(Operand1.Text)
      Op2 = Val(Operand2.Text)
         :
End Sub
```

Besides the Val( ) function, Visual Basic also has the Str$( ) function, which goes the other way, converting a number into a text string. In other words, you can add the two numbers and display the results in Result.Text as follows:

```
Sub Command1_Click()
      Dim Op1 As Single
      Dim Op2 As Single

      Op1 = Val(Operand1.Text)
      Op2 = Val(Operand2.Text)

      Result.Text = Str$(Op1 + Op2)
End Sub
```

That is all the code you will need; your calculator is ready (if not powerful). Just select the Start item in the Run menu, and the calculator will function, as in figure 2.5. You can type in floating-point numbers for the first two operands, and, when you click the = button, the two will be added (it might even be a good idea to make the Result text window into a label so that the user cannot modify it). In fact, the user can even modify the two operands after typing them—for example, to correct mistakes—because you are using text boxes.

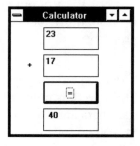

Figure 2.5. A calculator running.

As is usual in Windows, the user can switch from text box to text box by pressing Tab (not Enter), in addition to using the mouse. However, this includes the Result box—that is, the user can Tab to the Result box. Because that is not convenient for data entry, one change you might make to the program is to make sure that the Tab key will not move the focus to the Result box. When a control has the insertion point in Windows, it is called *having the focus*. The way to make sure that the Result box no longer gets the focus by tabbing around the text boxes is to set its TabStop property to False. (The default for text boxes and command buttons is True).

You can do that by selecting the TabStop property for the Result text box in the properties window and by setting it to False, as in figure 2.6. (Note that the two options offered by the settings list are True or False, so the choice is easy.)

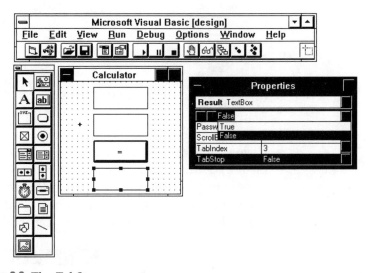

Figure 2.6. The TabStop property.

There is one more change you might make here—one that will indicate another capability of command buttons. Because the user will not use the Enter key for anything else here, you can make the equal button the *default button*. In other words, when the user presses Enter, it will be the same as clicking on the equal button. As is standard in Windows, the default button is surrounded by a thick black border so that the user knows exactly which button is the default.

You can make the equal button into the default button simply by setting its Default value to True at design time, as in figure 2.7. Now when the user runs the program, the equal button may be selected simply by pressing Enter.

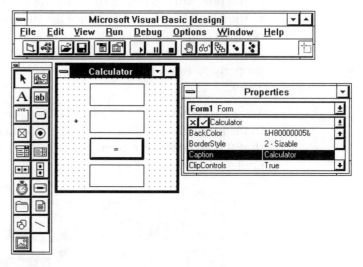

Figure 2.7. The calculator button design.

The full version of the calculator, then—complete with default equal button (note the thick black border)—appears in figure 2.8. You have made a good deal of progress as far as numeric I/O is concerned, but there is more to come. In particular, because text boxes are so important for displaying data (in addition to reading it), and this is the text box chapter, you will explore some of that added capability next.

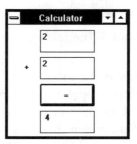

Figure 2.8. A calculator application.

Formatting Text

As you have seen, one way to display numbers as text in a text box is to use the Str$( ) function, as follows:

```
Sub Command1_Click()
    Dim Op1 As Single
    Dim Op2 As Single

    Op1 = Val(Operand1.Text)
    Op2 = Val(Operand2.Text)

    Result.Text = Str$(Op1 + Op2)
End Sub
```

Here, you set the Text property of the Result object to Str$(Op1 + Op2). The Str$( ) does a good job of formatting numeric data in most cases; that is, it adds a space before and after the number it is to print out, and it even handles floating-point numbers—for example, if numbers get too big, it will print them out with an exponent, such as: 1.2E+07 . However, this is essentially unformatted output—you have no real control over the format of the text in your Result text box.

To give you more control, Visual Basic includes the Format$( ) function. With Format$( ), you can indicate the number of decimal places a number must have, the number of leading or trailing zeros, as well as the capability of formatting currency values. The following is the way to use Format$( ) (square brackets indicate that the format string is optional), as follows:

```
text$ = Format$(number [, format_string$])
```

The format string here can be made up of any of the characters in table 2.2. Take a look at the following examples to get an idea of how Format$( ) works, as follows:

```
Format$(1234.56, "######.#")   =   1234.5
Format$(1234.56, "00000.000")  =   01234.560
Format$(1234.56, "###,###.0")  =   1,234.56
Format$(1234.56, "$#,000.00")  =   $1,234.56
```

As you can see, the # symbol is a placeholder, telling Format$( ) how many places you want to retain around the decimal point. The 0 symbol acts the same way, except that if no actual digit is to be displayed at the corresponding location, a 0 is printed. In addition, you can specify other characters, such as $ or commas to separate thousands.

Table 2.2. Format String Characters

Character	Means
0	Digit placeholder; print a digit or a 0 at this place
#	Digit placeholder; do not print leading or trailing zeros
.	Decimal placeholder; indicates position of the decimal point
,	Thousands separator
-+$( )Space	A literal character—displayed literally

To add thousands separators to your calculator, you simply change the Str$( ) statement to a Format$( ) statement, as follows:

```
Sub Command1_Click()
    Dim Op1 As Single
    Dim Op2 As Single

    Op1 = Val(Operand1.Text)
    Op2 = Val(Operand2.Text)

    Result.Text = Format$(Op1 + Op2, "###,###,###.#####")
End Sub
```

The resulting change to the calculator is shown in figure 2.9.

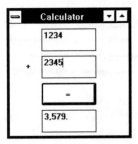

Figure 2.9. A calculator with a Thousands Separator.

Displaying Date and Time

Visual Basic also makes it easy to display the time and date with the Format$( ) function. In fact, you can use the built-in Visual Basic function named Now to return the current time and date in numeric form, and use Format$( ) to display that date and time. In this case, you can use special formatting characters: h, m, s and m, d, y. Format$( ) is capable of producing text strings from Now in many different ways, depending on how you use these characters and how many you use. Some examples are as follows:

```
Format$(Now, "m-d-yy")             =  "4-5-92"
Format$(Now, "m/d/y")              =  "4/5/92"
Format$(Now, "mm/dd/yy")           =  "04/05/92"
Format$(Now, "ddd, mmmm d, yyyy")    =  "Thursday, April 5, 1992"
Format$(Now, "d mmm, yyyy")        =  "5 Apr, 1992"
Format$(Now, "hh:mm:ss mm/dd/yy")     =  "16:00:00 04/05/92"
Format$(Now, "hh:mm:ss AM/PM mm-dd-yy") =  "4:00:00 PM 04-05-92"
```

As you can see, a variety of formats is available. In fact, if you use "ddddd" for the day and "ttttt" for the time, you will get the day and time in an appropriate format for the country the computer is in (as set in the Windows control panel). For example, Format$(Now, "ttttt ddddd") might be "4:00:00 PM 04-05-92" in the United States, but in some European countries, it would be "92-04-05 16.00.00".

At this point, you have had a good introduction to the use of text boxes and control buttons with your calculator, but you can move on to even more powerful applications. For example, your next project is to build a windowed notepad, complete with text boxes that include scroll bars.

A Notepad Example—Complete with Cut and Paste

Putting together a functioning notepad application might be easier than you think in Visual Basic. In fact, a notepad is really a multiline text box—and Visual Basic supports multiline text boxes automatically. To see how this works, start a Visual Basic project and give the form that appears the caption Pad in the properties window. Next, save the form as Pad.Frm (using Save File As...) and the project as Pad.Mak (using Save Project As...).

To produce your multiline text box, simply double-click on the text box tool and stretch the resulting text box until it takes up most of the form (leaving room for a row of buttons at the bottom), as shown in figure 2.10. Now find the Multiline property in the properties window; two settings— True and False—are allowed for this property, as indicated by the settings list (which drops down from the arrow next to the settings box). The default is False, which means that text boxes can handle only a single line of text by default. Set this property to True to give your pad multiline capability.

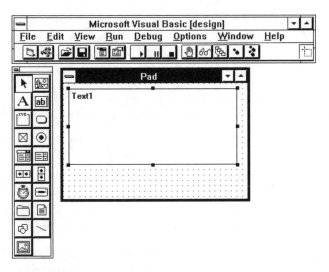

Figure 2.10. A pad prototype.

At this point, your pad is already functional; just delete the text in the text box—for example, "Text1"—using the properties window, and run the program. The pad appears, as in figure 2.11, and you can write to it. In fact, it comes complete with word wrap—when you get to the end of a line, the current word gets "wrapped" whole to the next line instead of being broken in the middle.

However, you can do a great deal more here; for example, you can add a vertical scroll bar to the text box just by changing its Scrollbars property. In fact, you can add horizontal scroll bars as well, but if you add horizontal scroll bars to a multiline text box, the word wrap is automatically turned off, so you are not going to add them. Unlike the scroll bars you will see later in this book, multiline text box scroll bars are managed entirely by

Visual Basic; adding them is easy. To add vertical scroll bars, just find the Scrollbars property in the properties window.

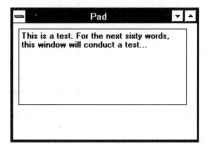

Figure 2.11. A pad at run time.

The settings list indicates what is available: horizontal scroll bars, vertical scroll bars, or both, as indicated in figure 2.12. To add vertical scroll bars to the text box in your notepad, just select the Vertical option; a vertical scroll bar appears, as in figure 2.13. Now you can scroll through a much larger document in your new notepad—up to 64K in fact, which is the maximum length of strings in Visual Basic. So far, all you have done has been quite easy. Now press on and add more capabilities to the pad; specifically, you will add cut and paste, where the user can select text, cut it, and paste it back in somewhere else.

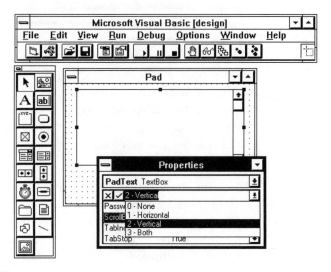

Figure 2.12. Scroll bar options.

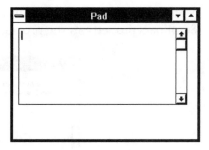

Figure 2.13. A pad with a vertical scroll bar.

Using Selected Text in Text Boxes

As is usual for a text box, the user can mark or select text in Visual Basic text boxes; for example, he can simply place the (mouse) cursor at some location, hold down the left button, move the cursor to another location, and release it. In that case, the text between the two points is highlighted automatically—for example, Windows has already given this capability to your text boxes. You already know that you can refer to the text in a text box as, say TheText.Text—for example, TheText is the Name you gave to the text box control—but how can you refer to selected text?

This is also easy under Visual Basic. Three properties associated with text boxes keep track of selected text: SelStart, SelLength, and SelText. The first of these, SelStart, is the location in the TheText.Text string at which the selected string starts. If no text is selected (which you can check with the next property, SelLength), this property indicates where the insertion point is. If SelStart is 0, the selected text starts just before the first character in the text box; if SelStart is equal to the length of the text in the text box, then it is indicating a position just after the last character in the text box. Note that SelStart is a long integer (because it has to be able to handle numbers up to 64K).

The next property, SelLength, is also a long integer; it indicates the number of characters selected. Finally, SelText is a string that contains the selected characters from the text box (if no characters are selected, this is the empty string, ""). In fact, your program can set these properties at run time—for example, SelStart = 0 : SelLength = 5 would highlight the first five characters.

You will use these properties to add cutting and pasting to your notepad by adding some command buttons. In particular, you can add three specific functions: Clear All, which deletes everything in the notepad's text box; Cut, which cuts the selected text; and Paste, which pastes the selected text at the insertion point.

The first button, Clear All, is easy. All you have to do is to set the Text property of the text box to the empty string, "". To start, change the name of the pad's text box to PadText in the properties window. (You will find that as programs get longer and longer, it is advisable to end an object's name with an indication of what type of object it is.) Now add a command button with the caption "Clear All" and the name—for example, ClearButton. Position the button in the lower right corner of the form and click on it twice to open the code window. The code window opens, displaying a template for the click event—for example, ClearButton_Click( )—which is exactly what you want, so add the following line:

```
Sub ClearButton_Click()
    PadText.Text = ""
End Sub
```

Changing the name of a control at design time.
If you change the name of a control part way through the design process, you should know that Visual Basic does *not* go through the code and change the names of the procedures you have already written to match—*you* are responsible for doing that.

Now you can run the program. When you do, the button becomes active and clicking on it deletes the text in the text box. However, after you have selected an object in Windows—by clicking on it, for example—the focus—for example, the active control, and the location of the insertion point is transferred to that object. This is the default action in Windows—if you click on an object, that object gets the focus. In this example, the Clear All button retains the focus even after clearing the pad (and it is surrounded by a thick black border to indicate that it still has the focus). To get back to the pad, the user has to press the Tab key or click on the text window, which seems less than professional.

You can fix that problem, however, with the SetFocus *method*. Programmers familiar with object-oriented languages know that you can associate two types of programming constructions with an object—both data and procedures. In Visual Basic, an object's data items are referred to as properties, and the procedures connected with it are called its *method*. You will see more about methods throughout this book. In the meantime, what concerns you here is the SetFocus method that is built into most controls. With it, you can give the focus back to the text box simply with the statement PadText.SetFocus.

That is, you refer to methods the same way you refer to properties— with the dot (.) operator. (Later on, you will see that some methods take arguments.) When you transfer the focus back to the text box, the insertion point appears there again and starts blinking. ClearButton_CLick( ) should appear as follows:

```
Sub ClearButton_Click()
  PadText.Text = ""
  PadText.SetFocus
End Sub
```

That's all there is to it; your pad should look like the one in figure 2.14. Now it is time to move on to cutting selected text in a text box.

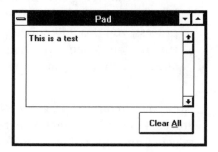

Figure 2.14. A pad with a clear all button.

How To Cut Selected Text

To start the process of cutting text, add another command button in the lower left corner of the form—you can name the button CutButton—and give it the caption Cut. When the user presses this button, he or she wants the text that is selected in the text box to be cut; actually, you place it in a temporary buffer so that you can paste it later if you need to. Begin by creating this temporary buffer, which should be a String type and which you can call CutText. Because you want both the Cut and Paste procedures to have access to this buffer, you make CutText a global variable, making it accessible from all parts of your notepad application.

To make a global declaration, you have to open a module, which you can do by selecting New Module in the File menu. The name that appears for this module in the Project window is Module1.Bas—change it to, say, Pad.Bas. Now click on Pad.Bas to open it. When you do, the module window opens (see figure 2.15). Declare CutText as follows:

```
Global CutText As String
```

Recall that you use the Global keyword to declare variables globally, not Dim.

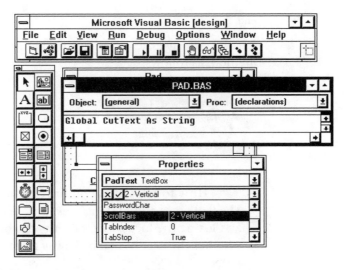

Figure 2.15. The pad's global declaration.

Now that your buffer, CutText, is ready, you are prepared to cut the string itself in the pad's text box. Before you do, however, you should save the selected text to the CutText string. To do that, click on the Cut button to open the Sub procedure template in the code window, as follows:

```
Sub CutButton_Click()
End Sub
```

Then save the cut text as follows:

```
Sub CutButton_Click()
   CutText = PadText.SelText
      :

End Sub
```

The next step is to cut the selected string itself. That turns out to be surprisingly easy; all you have to do is to replace PadText.SetText, the selected text, with an empty string, "" (if no text was selected, no text is cut), as follows:

```
Sub CutButton_Click()
   CutText = PadText.SelText
   PadText.SelText = ""
      :

End Sub
```

Finally, you give the focus back to the text window, using the SetFocus method, as follows:

```
Sub CutButton_Click()
   CutText = PadText.SelText
   PadText.SelText = ""
   PadText.SetFocus
End Sub
```

How to tell when you have gotten or lost the focus. The GotFocus and LostFocus events are connected with getting and losing the focus. These events can be useful to check whether the user has tabbed away from a text box or pressed Enter.

The cut button is now functional. At this point, you can make a stand-alone application out of your pad by choosing the Make Exe File... item in the File menu; when you run it under Windows, the pad appears. The user can select text and cut it with the Cut button. However, that is only half the story of a full notepad application; the next step is to allow the user to paste the text back in.

This can happen in two ways. First, the user can select some additional text in the text box, and the program should paste over that text. Second, the user might simply position the insertion point at a particular location, and then the program is supposed to insert the text there. As it happens, Visual Basic takes care of these two cases almost automatically.

To begin, you will have to introduce another button, which you can call PasteButton (give it the caption, Paste). Place this button between the other two and double-click on it to open the code window. You can see that PasteButton_Click( ) is already selected. All you have to do here is replace the selected text in the text window, PadText.SelText, with CutText (the global string that holds the cut text). Visual Basic handles the details: if some text is selected, it is replaced with CutText; if no text was selected, then CutText is inserted at the insertion point, exactly as it should be. The code for PasteButton_Click( ) (note that you return the focus to the text box here, too), is as follows:

```
Sub PasteButton_Click()
    PadText.SelText = CutText
    PadText.SetFocus
End Sub
```

You are almost done with the Paste button; the working pad application so far appears in figure 2.16. There are still a few problems, however. One problem occurs when the application is first started. Although there is nothing to paste yet, the Paste button can still be pushed. Even though it does nothing, it would be better still if you could gray the button caption—that is, disable the Paste button in the standard Windows fashion before there is something to paste.

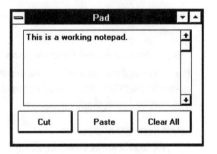

Figure 2.16. A pad application with a paste button.

In fact, you can do this. One of the properties associated with a command button is the Enabled property. When this property is set to True, the button is enabled and can be clicked; when set to False, the button does not respond to the user, and its caption is grayed. You can take advantage of this immediately. First, set the Enabled property of the Paste button to False in the properties window. You want to enable this button only when text has been placed in the CutText buffer. Because that is done only when the Cut button has been clicked, you can simply add a line to CutButton_Clicked( ), as follows:

```
Sub CutButton_Click()
    CutText = PadText.SelText
    PadText.SelText = ""
    PasteButton.Enabled = -1 'Set to True
    PadText.SetFocus
End Sub
```

Now, when you start the application, the pad appears as in figure 2.17, with the Paste button grayed and disabled. As soon as you cut some text with the Cut button, however, Paste becomes active again.

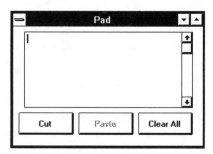

Figure 2.17. Pad with a paste button grayed.

Notice that you set PasteButton.Enabled to -1, which is the value Visual Basic uses for True. On the other hand, the constant True is already defined in Visual Basic, which means that you are free to use the constant True instead of -1, as follows:

```
Sub CutButton_Click()
    CutText = PadText.SelText
    PadText.SelText = ""
    PasteButton.Enabled = True
```

Peter Norton's Visual Basic for Windows, Third Edition, Covering Release 3.0

```
    PadText.SetFocus
End Sub
```

In fact, having gone this far, you might as well enable the Cut and Clear All buttons only when it makes sense. In particular, you can enable these buttons after the user has started typing something into the pad (i.e., at which time text is available to cut or clear). In this case, you can work with the text box's Change event—one of the primary programming events of a text box, as you saw in the last chapter. Whenever the contents of a text box change—for example, when characters are typed in it, or if your program affects the text box's Text property—a corresponding Change event is generated. You can take advantage of that here to enable the Cut and Clear All buttons in your pad after text has been typed for the first time.

To begin, set the Enabled property for both CutButton and ClearButton to False at design time; now, when the notepad first appears, all three buttons (Cut, Paste, and Clear All) will be grayed. Next, click the text box twice to open the code window. The following Sub procedure appears as follows:

```
Sub PadText_Change()
End Sub
```

Now just put the following code in as follows:

```
Sub PadText_Change()
    CutButton.Enabled = True
    ClearButton.Enabled = True
End Sub
```

That's it; the first time the user types, the two buttons will be enabled. Your notepad is getting to be quite a polished application. While on the topic of command buttons, note that you can supply your buttons with access keys.

Using Access Keys

An *access* key is used in a menu or command button as a key you can press along with the Alt key to select that option or button. For example, if you made C the access key for your Cut button, the user could press Alt-C to click the button. Each access key should be unique among the currently available buttons or menu items.

Adding access keys is very easy; all you have to do is to specify which letter you want to have stand for the access key by placing an ampersand (&) in front of it in the control's caption. For example, to make C the access key for the Cut button, change the button's caption to &Cut. To make P the access key for the Paste button, change the Paste button's caption to &Paste. Finally, to change the Clear All Button's access key to A (because you have already used C with the Cut button), change its caption to Clear &All. When you do, Visual Basic changes the caption of each button, underlining the access key (see figure 2.18). It is that easy to set access keys in Visual Basic.

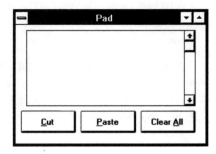

Figure 2.18. A pad with Access keys.

That's it for the pad for now (you will come back to it later); the code, event by event, appears in listing 2.1 (Pad.Mak on the Disk). Now it is time to turn to another application: a windowed alarm clock.

Listing 2.1. Pad Application (Pad.Mak on the Disk)

```
Form Form1
   Caption   =    "Pad"

TextBox PadText
   MultiLine       =   -1   'True
   ScrollBars      =   2    'Vertical

CommandButton CutButton
   Caption    =    "&Cut"
   Enabled    =    0    'False

CommandButton Pastebutton
```

```
    Caption       =   "&Paste"
    Enabled       =   0      'False


CommandButton ClearButton
    Caption       =   "Clear &All"
    Enabled       =   0      'False


Pad.Bas -------------------------------------------------
  Global CutText As String


Pad.Frm -------------------------------------------------

  Sub ClearButton_Click ()
    PadText.Text = ""
    PadText.SetFocus
  End Sub


  Sub CutButton_Click ()
    CutText = PadText.SelText  PadText.SelText = ""
    PasteButton.Enabled = True
    PadText.SetFocus
  End Sub


  Sub Pastebutton_Click ()
    PadText.SelText = CutText
    PadText.SetFocus
  End Sub


  Sub PadText_Change ()
    CutButton.Enabled = True
    ClearButton.Enabled = True
  End Sub
```

An Alarm Clock Example

There is still a good deal to learn about text boxes and buttons. For example, you can actually read keystrokes as they are typed in a text box, or even change display fonts. For that matter, you can use an entirely different kind of button: option buttons (the small round buttons that are also called *radio buttons*). You will take advantage of some of those capabilities with a new application: a digital alarm clock that lets you display the time and will notify you when a certain amount of time is up. The application you are aiming for appears in figure 2.19.

Figure 2.19. An alarm clock application.

Start a new Visual Basic project, give the caption Alarm to the default form, create a module, and then save the form, module, and project as Alarm.Frm, Alarm.Bas, and Alarm.Mak, respectively. Now you are ready to start; the first thing you can do is to set up the text box that will accept the alarm setting (for example, the alarm setting in figure 2.19 is 09:30:00). Double-click on the text box tool in Visual Basic's toolbox and place the text box in a position corresponding roughly to the one in figure 2.19—for example, the lower left corner of the form.

You can call this text box, say, AlarmSetting. In addition, you should clear the default text from the text box ("Text1") so that the text box is clear when the user starts the application. To keep this example relatively simple, you are only going to accept the time in this box in a restricted format, like this: "hh:mm:ss," the same way that the Time$ function of Basic will return it. (In a professional application, of course, you would have to be more forgiving.) You have not restricted user input before, but Visual Basic allows you to do so by reading each keystroke as it is typed.

Interpreting Individual Keystrokes

Three events occur each time the user types a key in a control or form that has the focus: KeyDown, KeyUp, and KeyPress. The KeyPress event is the one you will be using here, because it returns the standard type of character values you are used to dealing with in Basic. The KeyDown and KeyUp events are generated when the user presses and releases a key, and each event procedure receives two arguments: *KeyCode* and *Shift*. The key code here is the *ANSI* code (not ASCII) for the key that was pressed or released, and Shift holds the state of the Shift, Alt, and Ctrl keys. It turns out that ANSI, not ASCII, is the standard Windows character set. Although the two character sets have considerable overlap, they are not the same—however, they *are* the same for letters (like "a") and numbers (like "5").

In addition, KeyDown and KeyPress do not differentiate between lowercase ("z") and uppercase ("Z") except in the Shift argument; that is, the only way to tell whether a character is lower- or uppercase is to look at Shift. This argument has a value of 1 if the Shift key is down, 2 if the Ctrl key is down, 4 if the Alt key is down, or a sum of those values if more than one of those keys are down—for example, Shift+Alt would give a value of 5 in the Shift argument.

The reason KeyDown and KeyUp are useful is that they can read keys which have no standard ASCII value, such as the arrow keys or the function keys. For example, when the user presses the F1 key, KeyCode is equal to Key_F1 as defined in the Visual Basic file Constant.Txt; when the user presses F2, KeyCode equals Key_F2, and so forth. However, because KeyDown and KeyUp are advanced events, you will stick with KeyPress here.

Your intention is to restrict the user's keystrokes to those allowed in the AlarmSetting text box. Those characters are "0" through "9" and ":"; you will check to make sure that the typed key is in that range. To set up your procedure, double-click on the text box to open the code window, then select the KeyPress event from the procedures box. The following procedure template appears as follows:

```
Sub AlarmSetting_KeyPress (KeyAscii As Integer)
End Sub
```

As you can see, Visual Basic passes one argument to a KeyPress eventKeyAscii, the typed key's ASCII value. Although KeyDown and KeyUp use ANSI key codes, KeyPress uses the ASCII set most programmers are used to. In other words, this is just like a normal Sub procedure with one argument passed to youKeyAscii. You can make use of it immediately, checking the value of the just-typed key, as follows:

```
Sub AlarmSetting_KeyPress (KeyAscii As Integer)
    Key$ = Chr$(KeyAscii)
```

```
        If((Key$ < "0" OR Key$ > "9") AND Key$ <> ":") Then
        :
End Sub
```

First, you convert the ASCII code in KeyAscii to a character—for example, a string of length one—using the Basic Chr$( ) function like this: Key$ = Chr$(KeyAscii). Then you check the value of that character against the allowed range—the < and > operators work for string comparisons as well as numeric comparisons in Basic; that is, they compare strings in alphabetic order, so "0" is less than "1" and "c" is greater than "b."

Although you are restricting the user to the characters "0"-"9" and ":," it is a good idea in practice to allow text-editing characters as well, such as the backspace and delete keys (just get their ASCII codes from the Visual Basic documentation). Also, you need to be aware that the opposite of Chr$( ) is Asc( ); that is, Asc( ) returns the ASCII value of the first character of its argument string and is also useful when you check whether characters are in a certain range.

If the key that was typed is not in the allowed range, you should delete it and beep to indicate an error. You can beep with the Basic Beep statement, and deleting the key is easy—you just have to set KeyAscii to 0, as follows:

```
Sub AlarmSetting_KeyPress (KeyAscii As Integer)
    Key$ = Chr$(KeyAscii)
    If((Key$ < "0" OR Key$ > "9") AND Key$ <> ":") Then
        Beep
        KeyAscii = 0
    End If
End Sub
```

That's it for checking the typed keys and for AlarmSetting_KeyPress( ); in addition, you should place the label "Alarm Setting:" above the text box to indicate what it is for. To do that, just click the label tool (the uppercase A) in Visual Basic's tool box, and place the label above the text box, setting its caption to "Alarm Setting:" (see figure 2.19). Now you are set as far as recording and storing the alarm setting goes; your program will be able to read the alarm setting directly from the text box's Text property.

> **The masked edit control allows easy input filtering.**
> Visual Basic Professional Edition includes a Masked Edit control that lets you restrict input with a *mask*: like a format string that the input has to match—for example, #,##0.

Displaying the Time

The next step in assembling the alarm clock is to set up the clock's display. Because you do not want the clock display to be edited from the keyboard (it will use system time), you can use a label, not a text box here. Click on the label tool again and enlarge the label until it is roughly the size of the one in figure 2.20. Delete the characters in the Caption property and then take a look at the BorderStyle property in the properties window.

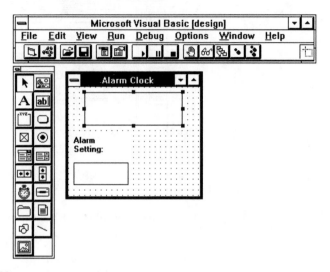

Figure 2.20. The clock template.

Normally, labels do not have a border, but they can have the same type of border text boxes have. If you open the settings list next to the settings box, you will see that the two options for BorderStyle are None and Fixed Single. Select Fixed Single to give the clock's display a border. In addition, you can give this label a name; call it Display. To display the time, then, you just use the Basic function Time$ like this: Display.Caption = Time$.

The question, however, is how to keep the time updated. In other words, what kind of event occurs often enough and regularly enough to make sure that the time in Display.Caption is current? Visual Basic has another type of control for exactly this kind of use: timers.

Visual Basic Timers

A timer is just that: it can produce a specific event, called a Timer event, at a predetermined interval. Its control symbol is a small clock, both on

71

the form (although it is not visible at run time) and in the toolbox. Double-click on the timer tool now and position the timer roughly in the same position as in figure 2.21. Visual Basic gives the timer the default name of Timer1.

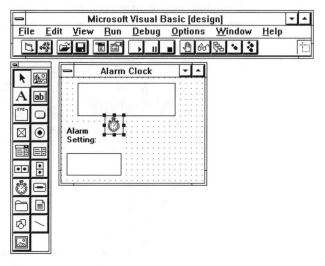

Figure 2.21. The clock template with a timer.

The next step is to set the timer's Interval property that is, how often the Timer event occurs. Make sure that the timer is selected, open the properties list in the properties window, highlight the Interval property, and then move over to the settings box. The Interval property is measured in milliseconds—that is, in thousandths of a second. Because you do not want to put a significant burden on the rest of the system, you will update the clock only once a second, so choose 1000 for the Interval property of the timer.

Be careful not to use timers too much.
Although there is a temptation to use timers to make sure that your code gets control as often as possible, you should avoid using them unless necessary (as with a clock, for example). Overuse goes against the spirit of event-oriented processing. That is, continual use of a timer can come very close to sequential (non-Windows) processing, where one application uses all the available computing time.

Now you are ready to write the actual procedure that will be run every time the timer ticks—for example, once a second. Double-click on the timer to open the code window. The procedure that is already displayed in outline—Timer1_Timer( )—is the one you want, as follows:

```
Sub Timer1_Timer()
End Sub
```

You can start by checking whether the time is up—that is, whether the string returned by the Basic function Time$ is the same as the time the alarm is set for (in other words, whether Time$ equals AlarmSetting.Text). If the time is up, you should sound an alarm. In fact, this is not a safe thing to do—if Windows is performing some action, or if the clock's window is being moved, the timer may not be called for a while. For that reason, you should actually check whether Time$ is greater than or equal to AlarmSetting.Text, as follows:

```
Sub Timer1_Timer()
    If (Time$ >= AlarmSetting.Text) Then
      :
End Sub
```

If the condition is true, then you can just use the Beep statement as follows:

```
Sub Timer1_Timer()
    If (Time$ >= AlarmSetting.Text) Then
      Beep
    End If
End Sub
```

That's it; when the time has elapsed, this procedure will make the clock beep—and because it is called once a second, the clock will keep beeping, once a second. However, this is incomplete as it stands; alarm clocks usually have two settings: alarm on and alarm off—for example, now that the alarm is on, you have to shut it off.

For that reason, you can add two option buttons labelled Alarm On and Alarm Off (refer to figure 2.19). The procedure connected with those buttons can communicate with the current procedure, Timer1_Timer( ), through a global variable, which you might call AlarmOn. In other words, if AlarmOn is True *and* Time$ >= AlarmSetting.Text, then the program should beep, which you can do in the following way:

```
Sub Timer1_Timer()
   If (Time$ >= AlarmSetting.Text AND AlarmOn) Then
      Beep
   End If
End Sub
```

The last thing to do here is to update the display (because this procedure is called when the time changes). You can do that as follows:

```
Sub Timer1_Timer()
   If (Time$ >= AlarmSetting.Text AND AlarmOn) Then
      Beep
   End If
   Display.Caption = Time$
End Sub
```

As mentioned, because this procedure is called once a second, the beeping will continue until the Alarm Off button is clicked (which will make AlarmOn False). Now set up AlarmOn itself; you can make it global (making it shared by the whole application) by double-clicking on Alarm.Bas in the project window. The (general) section of Alarm.Bas opens; declare AlarmOn as follows:

```
Global AlarmOn As Integer
```

You declare it an integer because both True and False are integers in Visual Basic.

> **The Boolean type becomes an integer in Visual Basic.**
> If you are familiar with the *Boolean* type in other languages, then you should know that the Boolean type becomes the integer type in Visual Basic.

At this point, then, the timer is ready and the clock is ready to function (that is, a clock display will appear on the screen, although in a smaller font than the one in figure 2.19). Compare the alarm setting to the current time and update the display on the screen: everything is ready—except for the AlarmOn variable. The last step is to design the two option buttons that make AlarmOn active; without them, the alarm part of the clock cannot work.

Using Option (Radio) Buttons

Option buttons—often called radio buttons—work in a group; that is, only one of the option buttons that appear on a form can be selected at one time. You use option buttons to select one option from among several mutually exclusive choices—for example, choices where it is either one or the other, such as male or female.

> **More on grouping option buttons together.**
> Another way to make option buttons work as a group is to enclose them in a *frame*, by using the frame tool in the Visual Basic toolbox. (The frame tool has a frame with xyz drawn on it; it is the third tool down on the left.) The option buttons in such a frame are separate from the rest of the option buttons on the form.

Visual Basic takes care of the details of turning option buttons on and off; if one of a group of option buttons is clicked, the one that was on—for example, with a black dot in the center—is turned off automatically. You can add two option buttons to the alarm clock easily; just double-click on the option button tool (fourth down on the right in the toolbox), and position the two option buttons under the Display label, giving them the captions Alarm Off and Alarm On, as in figure 2.22.

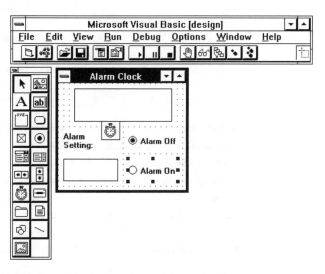

Figure 2.22. An alarm clock template with option buttons.

Together, these two make up an option button group. Because they are part of the same form (and not enclosed in separate frames), Visual Basic will turn them on and off so that only one is selected at a time. Note that you should have the Alarm Off option selected when the user starts the clock. A Value property is associated with each option button, indicating whether the button is selected—True if selected—for example, with a black dot in the center—False if not. You can set the Value property at design time and at run time, so set the Alarm Off button's Value to True in the properties window now.

In addition, you need names for these new buttons. You can give them their own names, such as AlarmOnButton and AlarmOffButton, and then write the corresponding procedures when one of them is clicked—that is, you can set the variable AlarmOn to True or False by checking the values of AlarmOnButton.Value and AlarmOffButton.Value. However, groups of buttons (in fact, groups of controls) like this are usually handled in a different way in Visual Basic—by making the group of buttons into a *control array*.

Arrays of Controls

Control arrays are the way to handle groups of controls in Visual Basic. For example, imagine that you have a number of buttons as follows:

[ ]	ButtonA
[ ]	ButtonB
[ ]	ButtonC
[ ]	ButtonD

In this case, you would have to write a separate event handler for each button. For example, if you were interested in the Click event, you would have ButtonA_Click( ), ButtonB_Click( ), ButtonC_Click( ), and ButtonD_Click( ). This can be awkward if the buttons perform essentially the same action with a few variations (as groups of controls usually do). The easier way to handle such groups of buttons is to give them all the same name. If you do, Visual Basic automatically gives them separate *Index* numbers (you might have noticed the Index property associated with most controls in the properties window). For example, if you call each button MyButton, Visual Basic gives the first one an index of 0, the next an index of 1, and so on, as follows:

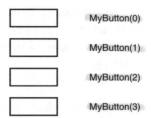

MyButton(0)

MyButton(1)

MyButton(2)

MyButton(3)

Now, instead of four separate event procedures—like ButtonA_Click( ) to ButtonD_Click( )—there is only one procedure for each event, and Visual Basic automatically passes the Index corresponding to the button that was clicked: MyButton_Click(Index As Integer).

To see this in action, make the Name of the top option button (Alarm Off) OnOffButton. Next, do the same for the other option button (Alarm On). When you do, Visual Basic pops up a box with the message: You already have a control named OnOffButton. Do you want to create a control array? (see figure 2.23). Answer yes, then double-click on either option button to open the code window.

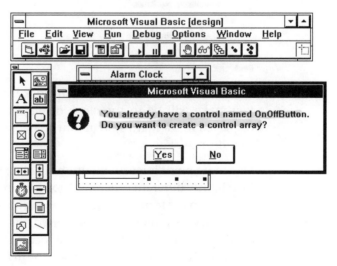

Figure 2.23. A control array box.

The following procedure template appears in the code window:

```
OnOffButton_Click(Index As Integer)
End Sub
```

Notice the first line—because you have set up OnOffButton as a control array, Visual Basic passes the Index of the button pushed. That is, because you named the Alarm Off button as OnOffButton first, it has Index 0; the Alarm On button has Index 1. (If you wonder what a control's Index value is, just check it in the properties window).

If you check the value of Index, you can determine which button was pushed, letting you write one procedure for both buttons—which is precisely the idea behind creating groups of controls; when a set of controls handles similar functions, you should try to make them into a group and create a control array. (It is easy to do because Visual Basic handles all the details.) All the current procedure has to do is determine which button was clicked by checking Index (0 —> Alarm Off, 1 —> Alarm On) and then correctly set the global variable AlarmOn—for example, that is the job of these option buttons: to set the global variable AlarmOn. You can do that as follows:

```
OnOffButton_Click(Index As Integer)
    If (Index = 1) Then
      AlarmOn = True
    Else
      AlarmOn = False
    End If
End Sub
```

That's all there is to it. The alarm clock is almost done. The last change you make will be to the clock display itself; as it stands, the time is displayed in standard system font characters—but you can improve that significantly.

One more point is worth mentioning here; if you had designed the clock in a slightly different order than you have here, and put the alarm setting text box on the form after the option buttons, then there would be a small problem; when the application started, the option button that was placed on the form first would have the focus (rather than the alarm settings box). To give the alarm settings box the default focus, set it first in the *tab order*. That is, one of the properties of controls that can get the focus is called TabIndex. The control with a TabIndex of 0 gets the default focus, and you can tab around the form to the other controls at will (the other controls have tab indices of 1, 2, 3, and so on). In fact, using the TabIndex, you can rearrange the way the user tabs from control to control on the form (you will learn about this later).

Selecting Fonts

Some of the properties associated with labels and text boxes have to do with fonts; they are as follows:

FontName	Name of font to use for text (such as "Courier")
FontSize	Font size in points (72nds of an inch)
FontBold	Make text bold
FontItalic	Make text italic
FontStrikeThrough	Overstrike text with dashes
FontUnderline	Underline the text

By selecting these properties at design time, you can set the type of font in the clock's display. For this example, you will just use the standard font (although eight fonts are available, including Helvetica, Modern, Roman, System, and others), except that you will expand the font size from 8.25 to 24 points (a point is 1/72 of an inch). To do that, select the Display label and then open the settings list for the FontSize property (see figure 2.24).

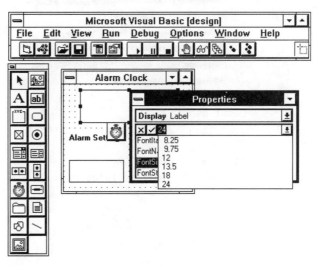

Figure 2.24. FontSize settings.

Change the value of the FontSize setting from 8.25 to 24 points. That will change the display size to 24 points, filling the Display label with the clock display. And that's it for the alarm clock; the working application appears in figure 2.19, and the code, event by event, appears in listing 2.2 (Alarm.Mak on the Disk).

 Listing 2.2. Alarm Application (Alarm.Mak on the Disk)

```
Form Form1
    Caption     =    "Alarm Clock"

Timer Timer1
    Interval    =    1000

OptionButton OnOffButton
    Caption     =    "Alarm Off"
    Index       =    0
    Value       =    -1  'True

OptionButton OnOffButton
    Caption     =    "Alarm On"
    Index       =    1
    Value       =    0   'False

Label Display
    BorderStyle =    1   'Fixed Single
    Caption     =    ""
    FontBold    =    -1  'True
    FontItalic  =    0   'False
    FontName    =    "MS Sans Serif"
    FontSize    =    24

Label Label1
    Caption     =    "Alarm Setting:"

Alarm.Bas ------------------------------------------
    Global AlarmOn As Integer

Alarm.Frm ------------------------------------------

    Sub Timer1_Timer ()
```

```
      If (Time$ > AlarmSetting.Text And AlarmOn) Then
          Beep
      End If
      Display.Caption = Time$
  End Sub

  Sub OnOffButton_Click (Index As Integer)
    If (Index = 1) Then
        AlarmOn = True
    Else
        AlarmOn = False
    End If
  End Sub

  Sub AlarmSetting_KeyPress (KeyAscii As Integer)
    Key$ = Chr$(KeyAscii)
    If ((Key$ < "0" Or Key$ > "9") And Key$ <> ":") Then
        Beep
        KeyAscii = 0
    End If
  End Sub
```

Next, you will continue your exploration of I/O with the user under Visual Basic in the next chapter, when you start really digging in—by using menus in your programs.

Summary

In this chapter, you put to work not only buttons and textboxes, but also a wide variety of Visual Basic techniques and methods. You have seen how to read in numbers and store them, what variable scope means and how to take advantage of it, how to make buttons into default buttons, how to enable and disable buttons, and how to let the user tab from one control to the next in your programs. Another big topic covered here is the use of alternate fonts—including font properties like FontSize, FontBold, FontItalic, and so on. You have also seen some more advanced techniques like how to add access keys to buttons, how to interpret individual keystrokes, and how to set up entire arrays of controls. Control arrays are useful when you have several similar controls that can be handled in similar ways—for example, you might make a chess board out of an array of command buttons, and the Index value will let you know which one has been clicked. (This saves you from writing a separate procedure for each button.)

New Property	Description
BorderStyle	Sets type of border for control or form from the available options (single-width border, double-width border, etc.)
Default	If true, makes this control the default control (gets focus when the form opens)
Enabled	If True, the control is enabled; if False, disabled (grayed)
FontBold	Holds the text bold setting (True or False)
FontItalic	Holds the text italic setting (True or False)
FontName	Holds the name of font to use for text (such as "Courier")
FontSize	Holds the font size in points (72nds of an inch)
FontStrikeThrough	Holds the overstrike text (with dashes) setting (True or False)
FontUnderline	Holds the underline text setting (True or False)
Index	Sets a control's index value; used in control arrays (When a control in a control array is clicked or chosen, the value in its Index property is passed to the event procedure.)
Multiline	If available, allows a text control to support multiple lines of text (True or False)
Scrollbars	Determines whether text-oriented control will have scroll bars on the side(s) (True or False)
SelStart	The starting location of text selected in the text-oriented control

New Property	Description
SelLength	The length of the selected text in a text-oriented control
SelText	String holding the selected text from a text-oriented control
TabIndex	Sets the control's place in the tab order (e.g., the control with TabIndex 3 follows the control with TabIndex 2)
TabStop	Determines whether this control may be tabbed to (True or False)

New Event	Description
KeyDown	Occurs when a key is pressed; passes only the ANSI value of the struck key (use the Shift parameter to determine whether letters are uppercase)
KeyPress	Occurs when a key is interpreted into ASCII (from ANSI); the preferred event for most keystroke-reading programs in Visual Basic
KeyUp	Occurs when a key is released; passes only the ANSI value of the struck key (use the Shift parameter to determine whether letters are uppercase)

Menus

This chapter examines how to work with one of the most popular features of Windows: menus. You will see that it is easy to design and add menus to your programs. This chapter covers the following topics:

▼ Designing menus and adding them to your programs

▼ Enabling and disabling menu items and menus

▼ Menu Access keys

▼ Menu Shortcut keys

▼ Separator bars

▼ How to end a Visual Basic program

▼ Adding check marks to menu items

▼ Adding menu items at *run time*

▼ Creating a font menu that lets you select fonts

▼ Giving programs their own icon in Windows

In addition, you will write a demonstration tic-tac-toe game (the idea here is to see control arrays at work—it does not include the code to play tic-tac-toe, although you can click the buttons, making them display "x" or "o") and a phone book application in which you will add people's names to a menu. You will also start the Editor application. When finished, the Editor will let you read in files up to 64K, edit them, and write them back out. Menus are a big part of any Windows application, and creating them is a skill you should not be without.

The next step in creating useful Windows applications is to add menus. If you are a Windows user, you are certainly familiar with menus; in fact, you have already used many menus in Visual Basic. For example, Visual Basic's File menu appears in figure 3.1, with the various parts labelled.

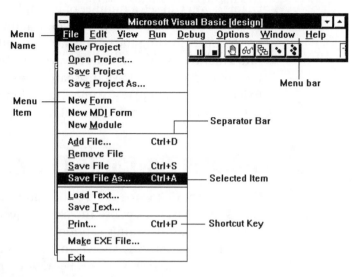

Figure 3.1. Visual Basic's file menu.

There are a number of elements in a menu that you should be familiar with before you read about how to build menus. The first of these elements, of course, is the *menu bar*, which indicates all the menus currently available in an application. Selecting a name in the menu bar pops down (or up, if you are at the bottom of the screen) the associated menu. Each line in a menu lists a unique *menu item*; if that item is highlighted, it is selected.

Releasing the mouse button while an item is selected chooses that item; if the item is followed by an *ellipsis* (...), it opens a dialog box that can read more information from the user. In addition, items can be *grayed* (disabled), or *checked* (a check mark next to them) indicating that a certain option has been turned on (for example, making text bold in a word processor). Finally, menu items can be grouped together with a *separator bar*, as shown in figure 3.1. In other words, all the menu items having to do with text color can fit into one group and all the items having to do with font size can appear in another. You will see most of these parts—

menu bars, menu items, disabled items, checked items, separator bars, etc.—in this chapter. (Because the ellipsis items usually open a dialog box, they are discussed in Chapter 4, the dialog box chapter.)

Designing and implementing menus in Visual Basic is not difficult. In this chapter, you will see a number of examples. In particular, you will start a small file-editing program that you will finish later, after you learn the mechanics of loading and saving files. You will also update the alarm clock into a menu-driven program. However, the first example will be a tic-tac-toe game. You do not have the space here to develop the code necessary to let the computer play— games can be long programs to write—so this will be a game for two (human) players.

A Menu-Driven Tic-Tac-Toe Game

You begin the tic-tac-toe game by beginning a new project—for example, start Visual Basic or choose the New Project item in Visual Basic's File menu. Change the form's caption to Tic-tac-toe, and place nine command buttons on it as shown in figure 3.2. (You will use command buttons rather than text boxes because there is no click event for text boxes, which means the user would have to type "x" or "o.")

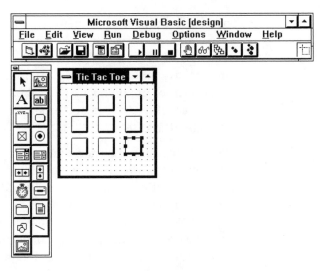

Figure 3.2. The Tic-Tac-Toe template.

Clear the Caption property of each command button, and name them all—for example, TTT for Tic-tac-toe. When Visual Basic asks whether you want to set up a control array, answer yes; writing one click procedure is going to be easier than writing nine. In fact, you can write that procedure immediately—double-click on a command button, and the code window opens, displaying this Sub procedure template, as follows:

```
Sub TTT_Click(Index As Integer)
End Sub
```

Because you have put the TTT buttons together into an array, Visual Basic passes an Index argument as well. If you have arranged the buttons in random order on the form, do not worry. It doesn't matter which index belongs to which button, because you can set the caption of a button like this: TTT(Index).Caption = "x". This is the way you can change the text or caption of a control when you are working with a control array—simply refer to the name of the array and add the index in parentheses afterwards. In this case, you can refer to the caption of each button as TTT(Index).Caption.

You have to know whether you should put an x or an o at the current place, however. Declare a global variable named XTurn. When it is True, it is x's turn; when False, it is o's turn. You can declare that variable by adding a module—call it TicTac.Bas—and making the following declaration:

```
Global XTurn As Integer
```

You should also save the form as TicTac.Frm, and the project itself as TicTac.Mak. At this point, setting the button's caption to x or o is easy; you can do it as follows:

```
Sub TTT_Click(Index As Integer)
   If (Xturn) Then
      TTT(Index).Caption = "x"
      XTurn = False
   Else
      TTT(Index).Caption = "o"
      XTurn = True
   End If
End Sub
```

This will alternate the characters that appear when the user clicks the different command buttons. Notice that in this simple program you did not check whether the button had been clicked already or whether someone had won the game. These are two things you should do if you intend to develop this into a tournament-level tic-tac-toe game.

Now you have to provide the user with some way of starting over—that is, adding a New Game option, which involves initializing the XTurn variable and clearing all the command buttons that make up the places on the tic-tac-toe board. This is where you will start working with menus, because New Game is exactly the kind of item you might find in a menu. In addition, you will add an Exit item to the menu because all applications that have menus should have an Exit item.

Adding A Menu to the Tic-Tac-Toe Game

Designing menus in Visual Basic is not as hard as you might expect. In fact, each menu item is a control itself, and the primary event associated with it is the Click event. To get these new types of controls onto the form, however, you have to design them first, using the Menu Design Window (you cannot just paint them with toolbox tools).

To pop that window onto the screen, open the Visual Basic Window menu and select the Menu Design Window item. That window appears (see figure 3.3).

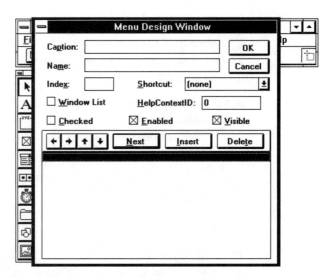

Figure 3.3. The Visual Basic menu design window.

You can start by specifying the caption of the menu. You can call it File, because applications often have a File menu and because that is where the user expects to find the Exit item. (After you learn about file handling, you can modify the tic-tac-toe game to save the current game to a file.) To create a File menu—for example"File" will appear in the menu bar), type **File** in the Caption text box at the top of the Menu Design Window (see figure 3.4). In addition, each menu has to be given a Name so that the program can refer to it. (This enables you to switch menus around in the menu bar, or change them altogether, as you will see later.) In this case, type the name **FileMenu** in the Name text box.

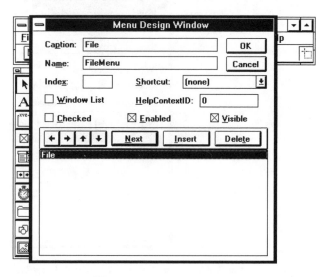

Figure 3.4. The Menu design window with a file caption.

You might have noted that as you typed File in the Caption box, the same word appeared in the main list box below it. (As you can see, File is highlighted in the main list box at the bottom of figure 3.4.) This is where the menu(s) you are designing will appear. So far, you only have the caption of one menu: File. The next step is to add the New Game and Exit items.

The insertion point should be right after the last name you typed—FileMenu in the Name text box. Press Enter to end this item and to move the highlight bar in the list box down one line; the Caption and Name text boxes are cleared in preparation for receiving the new menu item. Type

New Game in the Caption text box, and, say, **NewItem** (meaning the New Game item in this menu) in the Name text box. Again, the text—New Game—appears in the list box at the bottom of the window. If you were to leave it this way, however, New Game would be a menu name just like File and would appear in the menu bar. Instead, because you want this to be the first menu item in the File menu, click the right arrow in the bar above the list box, the second arrow from the left in the group of four. When you do, the New Game entry is indented four spaces in the list box (see figure 3.5).

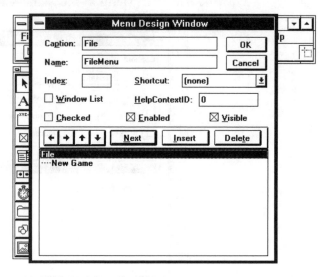

Figure 3.5. Menu Design Window, New Game Indented.

This means that New Game is an *item* in the File menu, not a menu itself; in fact, New Game is the first item. Next, press Enter again so that the highlight bar in the list box moves down one more line. Once again, the Caption and Name text boxes are cleared.

What about menus within menus?

Visual Basic enables you to have menus within menus so that selecting a menu item will pop open a new menu. You do this by successive levels of indentation—and you can have five such levels.

The next item in the File menu is Exit. Type **Exit** as the Caption and, say, **ExitItem** as the Name. Notice that you did not have to click the right arrow again to indent Exit in the list box; it was indented automatically, now that you are adding names to the File menu. (To remove the automatic indentation, click on the left arrow above the list box). The menu design is now complete, as shown in figure 3.6.

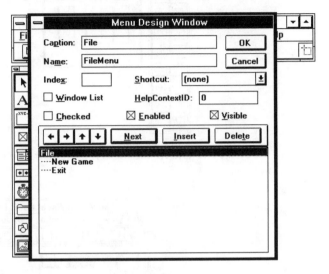

Figure 3.6. The completed menu design window.

Close the Menu Design Window by clicking on the OK button; when you do, you will see that a File menu has been added to the tic-tac-toe game template, as in figure 3.7.

As mentioned earlier, the design process primarily adds controls to the template; now that you have added the controls, you can treat them like any others—that is, you can attach code to them as easily. To see how this works, click on the File menu in the tic-tac-toe menu bar. The menu opens, showing the two items you have put in it, New Game and Exit (see figure 3.8).

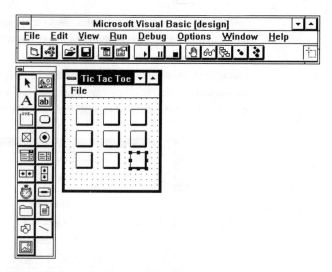

Figure 3.7. The tic-tac-toe template with file menu.

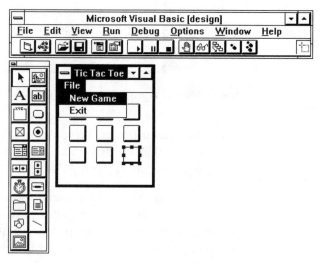

Figure 3.8. File menu open on tic-tac-toe template.

These two items are now simply controls, like buttons or text boxes. To open the code window, for example, just double-click on the New Game item. The code window opens, holding a Sub procedure template like this (recall that you gave the New Game item a Name of NewItem), as follows:

```
Sub NewItem_Click()
End Sub
```

When the user chooses this item, this Sub procedure is executed. In other words, you will be using the Click event for menu items, just as you did for buttons. In this case, the user wants to start a new tic-tac-toe game, so you will have to reset the variable you have called XTurn like this—for example, "o" will go first as follows:

```
Sub NewItem_Click()
        XTurn = 0      'Set XTurn False
   :
End Sub
```

In addition, you need to set the Caption property of all the command buttons to "". As an added touch, you can set the focus (that is, the thick black outline that appears around a command button) to the top left button, although this is not necessary, as follows:

```
Sub NewItem_Click()
     XTurn = 0
     For loop_index = 0 To 8
     TTT(loop_index).Caption = ""
     Next loop_index
     TTT(0).SetFocus
End Sub
```

Here, you are using the Basic *for loop* to loop over the caption of each button. In general, the for loop works in the following way:

```
for loop_index = begin To end [, Step stepsize]
   :
       [body of for loop]
   :
Next loop_index
```

(Basic syntax like this is presented throughout the book as a review only.)

The variable loop_index is originally set to the value *begin* and tested against the value *end*; if it is less than *end*, the body of the loop is executed and loop_index is incremented by 1—unless you include the Step keyword and a stepsize value (which can be negative). In that case, stepsize is added to loop_index instead (if stepsize is negative, the loop ends when the value in loop_index is less than *begin*). In this example, you are simply setting the caption of buttons TTT(0) to TTT(8) to the empty string, "", in the body of the loop, as follows:

```
Sub NewItem_Click()
     XTurn = 0
For loop_index = 0 To 8
TTT(loop_index).Caption = ""
Next loop_index
TTT(0).SetFocus
End Sub
```

Now the New Game option in the File menu is active. Making the Exit option active is even easier. Open the File menu on the tic-tac-toe form again and double-click on the Exit item; a new Sub procedure template appears as follows:

```
Sub ExitItem_Click()
End Sub
```

All you want to do here is to end the application if the user selects this item; you can do that with the Basic End statement, in the following way:

```
Sub ExitItem_Click()
     End
End Sub
```

When Visual Basic executes the End statement, it ends the program and removes the window from the screen, just like selecting Close in the system menu. And that's it for the tic-tac-toe game; everything is ready to go— it was that quick. The full, operating version appears in figure 3.9; the code is in listing 3.1 (Tictac.Mak on the Disk).Every time the user clicks on a command button, an x or an o (in alternating sequence) appears. To start over, select the New Game item in the File menu; to stop completely, select Exit. Note that this is a demonstration program only; as mentioned earlier, the program allows you to click a command button that has already been clicked and does not stop, even when someone wins— the idea here is to demonstrate menus, and you have already put them to work. (The disk version does, however, tell you whether x or o won.)

Figure 3.9. A tic-tac-toe application.

Listing 3.1. Tic-Tac-Toe Game (Tictac.Mak on the Disk)

```
Form Form1
      Caption           =     "Tic-tac-toe "

CommandButton TTT
      Caption           =     ""
      Index             =     0

CommandButton TTT
      Caption           =     ""
      Index             =     1

CommandButton TTT
      Caption           =     ""
      Index             =     2

CommandButton TTT
      Caption           =     ""
      Index             =     3

CommandButton TTT
      Caption           =     ""
      Index             =     4

CommandButton TTT
      Caption           =     ""
      Index             =     5

CommandButton TTT
      Caption           =     ""
      Index             =     6
```

continues

Listing 3.1. continued

```
CommandButton TTT
        Caption          =     " "
        Index            =     7

CommandButton TTT
        Caption          =     " "
        Index            =     8

Menu FileMenu
        Caption          =     "File"

Menu NewItem
        Caption          =     "New Game"

Menu ExitItem
        Caption          =     "Exit"

TicTac.Bas------------------------------------------------------
Global XTurn As Integer

TicTac.Frm------------------------------------------------------
    Sub TTT_Click(Index As Integer)
      If (Xturn)
        TTT(Index).Caption = "x"
        XTurn = False
      Else
        TTT(Index).Caption = "o"
        XTurn = True
      End If
    End Sub
    Sub NewItem_Click()
      XTurn = 0
      For loop_index = 0 To 8
      TTT(loop_index).Caption = ""
      Next loop_index
      TTT(0).SetFocus
    End Sub
    Sub ExitItem_Click()
    End
    End Sub
```

At certain times you should use command buttons for options; at other times, you should use menus instead. Generally, you use command buttons when the options they represent are so frequently used that it is acceptable to have them continually presented to the user. On the other hand, commands such as the ones you used in the notepad in the last chapter—Cut, Paste, and Clear All—are usually part of a menu and are not displayed as command buttons. In fact, why not modify the notepad so that it uses menus instead of command buttons; it will point out how close command buttons and menus are from a Visual Basic programming point of view, and get you started on an application you will complete when you learn more about files—a file editor.

Beginning the Editor Example

There is nothing wrong with the notepad you developed, but it is of very limited use. In particular, the contents of the notepad disappear when you close the application. It would be much better if you could save your work on disk and read in preexisting files to modify them.

Towards that end, you are going to modify the Pad project to start working with menu selections. Later, you will be able to add the actual mechanics of Visual Basic's file handling. To begin, read in the Pad project and save it as, say, Editor.Mak. Change the Caption of the form from Pad to Editor, and the save the other files as Editor.Bas and Editor.Frm, respectively. Now to design the Editor's menu system.

Select the Menu Design Window from the Window menu in Visual Basic to open the Menu Design Window. Because the leftmost menu in Windows applications is usually the File menu, type **File** first, as the Caption of that menu. Give this menu a Name of, say, FileMenu. After you have entered these two names, press Enter to move down to the first entry that will go in this menu. To make the first item Load File..., type that as the Caption. Indent it by clicking on the right arrow in the group of four arrows above the main list box. In addition, give this Menu item the Name LoadItem. You can also make a provision to save files with a Save File... item. Add that next, giving it the Name SaveItem. After that, you need a final menu item of Exit, which is expected in the File menu.

Because Exit does not fit in with Load File... and Save File..., however, you can set it off as its own group by placing a menu separator in the menu.

A separator in a menu is a horizontal line that divides menu items into groups (refer to figure 3.1). Note that Exit is set off from the rest of the menu items with a separator in Visual Basic's File menu as well. To specify that you want a menu separator, simply type a hyphen (-). Type a hyphen as the Caption now, and type anything (Separator, for example) as the Name. Finally, enter Exit as the last item in the File menu. At this point, the Menu Design Window should look like figure 3.10. Close the Menu Design Window by clicking on Done; the Editor should look like figure 3.11.

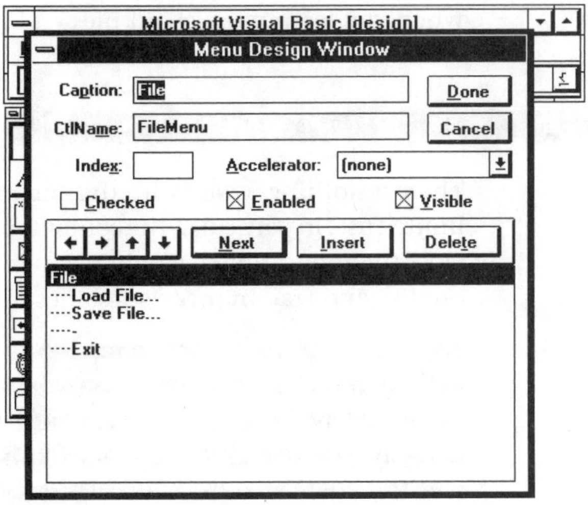

Figure 3.10. The Menu Design Window for Editor, stage 1.

As you can see, the separator was inserted, setting the Exit option off from the others. Grouping menu items in this way is often a good idea because the user can more easily find commands that are connected with each other.

Unfortunately, the only File menu item you can make active at this time is the Exit item. (You have to wait until you have expertise with files before you can handle Load File... and Save File....) Double-click on the Exit item to make this template appear as follows:

```
Sub ExitItem_Click()
End Sub
```

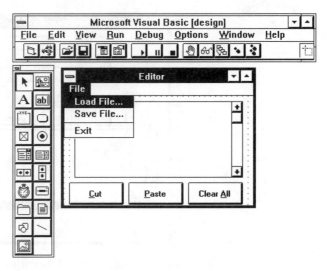

Figure 3.11. An Editor template with File Menu.

Just add the End statement here, so that the user can quit the application if he or she chooses to.

```
Sub ExitItem_Click()
    End
End Sub
```

The Edit menu usually follows the File menu in word processors and editors, so add that menu now. Open the Menu Design Window again, and click on the blank line in the main list box below the last entry—for exampleExit—to highlight it. Now move up to the Caption box and type **Edit**. Note that because you left the Menu Design Window and came back, the automatic indentation was turned off—for exampleEdit is made a menu bar item.

Because you will be supplanting the notepad's command buttons with menu items here, the three items in the Edit menu should be Cut, Paste, and Clear All. Enter them one at a time; make sure that they are indented and give them the Names CutItem, PasteItem, and ClearItem, respectively. At this point, the Menu Design Window should look like figure 3.12. Close the window. The Editor template should look like figure 3.13.

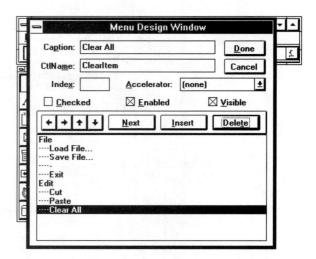

Figure 3.12. The Menu design window with the Edit menu.

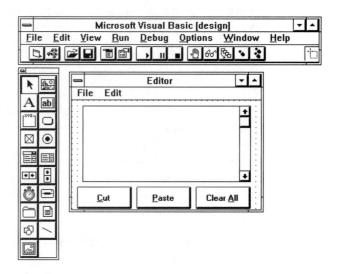

Figure 3.13. The Editor template with the Edit menu.

The only work remaining is to transfer the procedures from the command buttons Cut, Paste, and Clear All to the menu items. Because each of them is a click event, they can be transfered whole. This is also easy to do in

Visual Basic; just double-click on the first button, Cut, to open the code window (see figure 3.14).

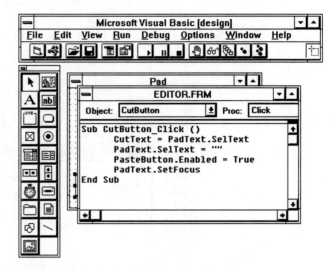

Figure 3.14. The CutButton_Click( ) code window.

Because you called this control CutButton, the Sub procedure that appears as follows:

```
Sub CutButton_Click()
    CutText = PadText.SelText
    PadText.SelText = ""
    PasteButton.Enabled = True
    PadText.SetFocus
End Sub
```

Much of this will be the same under the menu system; just change the name to CutItem_Click( ) (the name of the Cut item in the Edit menu) instead of CutButton_Click( ), as follows:

```
Sub CutItem_Click()
    CutText = PadText.SelText
    PadText.SelText = ""
    PasteButton.Enabled = True
    PadText.SetFocus
End Sub
```

As soon as you make this change and switch to another line, Visual Basic checks the object list to see whether this new name corresponds to an object that already exists. In this case it does, so Visual Basic assigns this procedure to the CutItem menu control. Note that this is indicated by the object box in the upper left of the code window, which now reads CutItem (see figure 3.15).

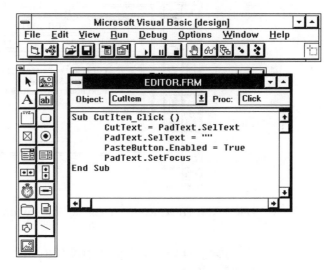

Figure 3.15. The CutItem_Click( ) code window.

How Visual Basic treats unfamiliar procedures.
If Visual Basic did not recognize the new name of the procedures, it would put them in the form object named (general), assuming that it is not directly connected with an already existing object.

Next, you can do the same thing for the other buttons. The Paste button procedure, PasteButton_Click( ), looks like this now:

```
Sub PasteButton_Click()
    PadText.SelText = CutText
End Sub
```

You might recall that you save the cut text in a global string named CutText; here you are just pasting it back in. You can change this to

PasteItem_Click( ) easily enough; just edit the name of the Sub procedure until you have the following:

```
Sub PasteItem_Click()
    PadText.SelText = CutText
End Sub
```

That's it; you can handle the Clear All button the same way. Click on it—you do not have to close the code window first; the code in it simply changes to display ClearButton_Click( )—to pop up this procedure in the code window, as follows:

```
Sub ClearButton_Click()
    PadText.Text = ""
    PadText.SetFocus
End Sub
```

Change the preceding code to Sub ClearItem_Click( ), as follows:

```
Sub ClearItem_Click()
    PadText.Text = ""
    PadText.SetFocus
End Sub
```

Now you have made the menu items active and can start making the changes to the code itself. First, you no longer need to set the focus to other objects because, in the absence of buttons, the text box will always have it. For that reason, remove the PadText.SetFocus line in all the procedures, until they appear as follows:

```
Sub CutItem_Click()
    CutText = PadText.SelText
    PadText.SelText = ""
    PasteButton.Enabled = True
End Sub

Sub PasteItem_Click()
    PadText.SelText = CutText
End Sub

Sub ClearItem_Click()
    PadText.Text = ""
End Sub
```

Next, you might recall that you started the pad with all three buttons grayed and that you enabled the Cut and Clear All buttons only after the user typed something. In other words, after there was a change in PadText, these lines were executed in the following way:

```
Sub PadText.Change()
    CutButton.Enabled = True
    ClearButton.Enabled = True
End Sub
```

Menu items have an Enabled property just as buttons do. You are probably more accustomed to seeing grayed menu items than grayed button captions. All you have to do is change the references from button Enabled properties to menu item Enabled properties. In other words, what was CutButton.Enabled becomes CutItem.Enabled and what was ClearButton.Enabled becomes ClearItem.Enabled, as follows:

```
Sub PadText.Change()
    CutItem.Enabled = True
    ClearItem.Enabled = True
End Sub
```

In addition, you might recall that you enabled the Paste button only after some text had been cut—for example in the procedure CutButton_Click(). You can change that reference also from PasteButton.Enabled to PasteItem.Enabled, as follows:

```
Sub CutItem_Click()
    CutText = PadText.SelText
    PadText.SelText = ""
    PasteItem.Enabled = True
End Sub

Sub PasteItem_Click()
    PadText.SelText = CutText
End Sub

Sub ClearItem_Click()
    PadText.Text = ""
End Sub
```

Now all the references to buttons in the code have been replaced by references to menu items. Cut the buttons to remove them from the form. To do that, click on the buttons and then select the Cut item in the Edit menu, readjusting the size of the form to absorb the space left by their absence.

At this point, you are almost done. The final step is to make sure that all the menu items in the Edit menu (Cut, Paste, Clear All) are grayed when the application starts—for example before the user starts typing. As you might expect, you can do that at design time in the Menu Design Window. Open that window by selecting it in the Window menu. Move the highlight bar in the main list box until the Cut item is highlighted. Then click on the Enabled check box—the middle check box in the row of three—to turn it off. (The x in the box disappears, as shown in figure 3.16).

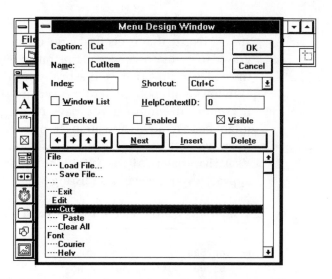

Figure 3.16. A Menu design box with the Enabled option off.

Next, do the same for the other two menu items in the Edit menu, Paste and Clear All, and click on the Done button. Now, when you run the Pad application, the Edit menu items originally appear grayed out (see figure 3.17). When you start typing, however, the Cut and Clear All items are made active. When you actually do cut something, the Paste item is enabled as well.

That is the way to enable or disable menu items—with the Enabled property. Setting it to True enables the menu item, whereas setting it to False disables the item. This capability is often extremely valuable for ensuring that the user does not choose an impossible option—attempting to save a file before any text is in the text window, for example.

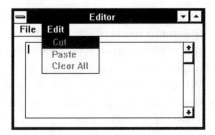

Figure 3.17. Pad with the Edit menu grayed out.

You must keep track of the items you have disabled, however. And you should realize that users find large menus in which almost all items are grayed to be unattractive and frustrating. (This has the flavor of operating in modes again—that is, drastically restricting the user's options, and Windows is all about presenting every possible option so that the user has maximum freedom.) If you have many grayed items, a better option might be to remove those items from your menus altogether and replace them when they become enabled again (you will see how to do this in Visual Basic later). All the code in the Editor so far (Editor.Mak on the Disk) appears, event by event, in listing 3.2.

Listing 3.2. Editor Version 1 (Final version is Editor.Mak on the Disk)

```
Editor.Bas ----------------------------------------------------------
    Global CutText As String

Editor.Frm ----------------------------------------------------------
    Sub ExitItem_Click()
        End
    End Sub


    Sub CutItem_Click()
        CutText = PadText.SelText
        PadText.SelText = ""
        PasteItem.Enabled = True
    End Sub
```

```
Sub PasteItem_Click()
    PadText.SelText = CutText
End Sub

Sub ClearItem_Click()
    PadText.Text = ""
End Sub

Sub PadText.Change()
    CutItem.Enabled = True
    ClearItem.Enabled = True
End Sub
```

However, there are still some ways to improve the editor. One is to add another menu to it so that the user can select the actual font used in the text. Because this operation will expose you to more of what menus are all about from a programmer's point of view, you look into it next.

Selecting Fonts from Menus

If you have worked with word processors that allow you to switch fonts, you know that such alternative fonts are exactly the kind of option you should put in a menu, not into a set of command buttons. You usually do not change fonts often enough to make it worthwhile to have all the font options in front of you at all times. Some of the fonts available to use in Windows are shown in figure 3.18.

You can change the text in the editor text box to any one of these fonts simply by changing the FontName property of the text box. However, there is a drawback. When you change the font in a text box, all the text is automatically changed to that font. In other words, you can use only one font in a text box. With that restriction, add a font menu to to the editor.

```
Courier   abcdefg
   Helv    abcdefg
 Modern    obcdefg
  Roman    abcdefg
  Script   abcdefg
 Symbol    abcdefg
 System    αβχδεφγ
Terminal   abcdefg
```

Figure 3.18. Some Windows fonts.

Using different fonts in one document.
If you want to use different fonts in a single document, use the
Print method, which applies to forms and picture boxes. In fact,
Print is the general-purpose way to display text in Visual Basic.
You can use it, for example, if you want to write an editor that
can handle more than 64K of text (which is the limit for text
boxes). In that case, however, you are responsible for such
operations as scrolling and selecting text. You will see how to use
Print later in this book, when graphics are covered.

To add a Font menu, open the Menu Design Window and add a new
menu, Font (with the Name FontMenu). Give the Font menu eight
items—Courier, Helv, Roman, Modern, Script, Symbol, System, and
Terminal—as shown in figure 3.19. You could write a separate Click event
procedure for each menu item, but now that you have eight of them,
setting up a control array is easier. (You want Visual Basic to pass an Index
to the event procedure, as you did earlier for buttons.)

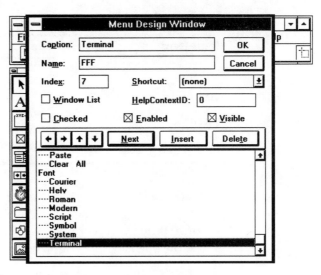

Figure 3.19. A Menu Design window with a Font menu.

In fact, it is just as easy to have Visual Basic pass an Index to a menu-event procedure as it is to pass an Index to a button-event procedure. To do this, give each menu item—Courier, Helv, Roman, Modern, Script, Symbol, System, and Terminal—the same control name of, say, FFF in the Name text box (under the Caption text box). As far as Visual Basic is concerned, each menu item has the same name. To distinguish between them, it needs an Index. Unfortunately, Visual Basic does not automatically assign indices to menu items as it did to the buttons earlier. You have to use the Index text box (refer to figure 3.19) to set an Index for each menu item. In this case, you can simply give the Index 0-7 to the eight fonts, as shown in table 3.1. To do that, just select each menu item in turn and fill in the Index text box.

Table 3.1. Font Menu Items

Menu Item	Name	Index
Courier	FFF	0
Helv	FFF	1
Roman	FFF	2
Modern	FFF	3

continues

Table 3.1 continued

Menu Item	Name	Index
Script	FFF	4
Symbol	FFF	5
System	FFF	6
Terminal	FFF	7

Close the Menu Design Window. Now you are ready to write some code. As you can see in figure 3.20, a new menu, Font, has been added to the Editor form. When you click on any of the menu items in this menu, the code window opens with a template for FFF_Click( ), as follows:

```
Sub FFF_Click (Index As Integer)
End Sub
```

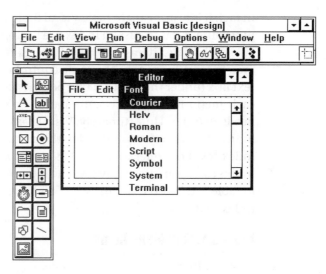

Figure 3.20. The Editor Form with a Font menu.

Your goal here is to select the appropriate font, depending on which selection was made. Because the menu item's index was passed to you, you can use it to set the font. The name of the text window in the Editor is PadText, so the property you want to set is PadText.FontName. You can do that with a Select Case statement. In general, that statement works the following way:

```
Select Case test_variable
    Case constant1
  [Statements...]
     [Case constant2]
  [Statements...]
     :
    [Case Else]
  [Statements...]
End Select
```

Here, the action taken is determined by the value in test_variable. If that value matches one of the constants in a Case statement, the statements corresponding to that case are executed. If no case matches, the statements in the Else case are executed (if there is an Else case; it is optional). In FFF_Click( ), that code will appear, as follows:

```
Sub FFF_Click (Index As Integer)
    Select Case Index
    Case 0
       PadText.FontName = "Courier"
    Case 1
       PadText.FontName = "Helv"
    Case 2
       PadText.FontName = "Roman"
    Case 3
       PadText.FontName = "Modern"
    Case 4
       PadText.FontName = "Script"
    Case 5
       PadText.FontName = "Symbol"
    Case 6
       PadText.FontName = "System"
    Case 7
       PadText.FontName = "Terminal"
End Select
End Sub
```

That's all there is to selecting a font, and we've made the Font menu active. When you run the Editor, you can select the font from this menu (and all the text will change at once). However, there is no easy way to tell from the font menu which font is the current one (the default in Visual

Basic is Helv). This usually is indicated in Windows applications with a check mark—that is, applications often indicate which option is currently active by putting a check mark next to the menu item in the menu. As you might expect, you can do this too. In the next section, you will add this capability to the Editor.

Marking Menu Items with Check Marks

Open the Menu Design Window again. To make sure that the Helv option appears checked when the Editor first starts, click on the Checked box for the Helvetica font (see figure 3.21). This is the property you will use to add check marks to menu items: the Checked property. When True, the item appears checked; when False, it appears without a check mark.

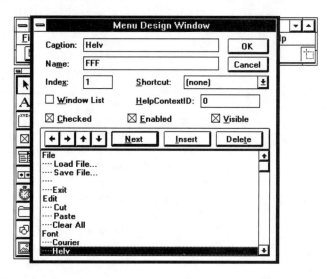

Figure 3.21. A Menu design window with Helvetica checked.

When you select a new font, you should first remove the check mark from the Font menu. You can do this by looping over each menu item and setting the Checked property (FFF(0-7).Checked) to False, as follows:

```
Sub FFF_Click (Index As Integer)
    Select Case Index
    Case 0
    PadText.FontName = "Courier"
```

```
   Case 1
     PadText.FontName = "Helv"
   Case 2
     PadText.FontName = "Roman"
   Case 3
     PadText.FontName = "Modern"
   Case 4
     PadText.FontName = "Script"
   Case 5
     PadText.FontName = "Symbol"
   Case 6
     PadText.FontName = "System"
   Case 7
     PadText.FontName = "Terminal"
   End Select
 For (loop_index = 0 To 7)
     FFF(loop_index).Checked = False
 Next loop_index
     :
End Sub
```

Finally, you should check the new font, which is simply menu item FFF(Index), as follows:

```
Sub FFF_Click (Index As Integer)
   Select Case Index
    Case 0
     :
     :
   For (loop_index = 0 To 7)
     FFF(loop_index).Checked = False
   Next loop_index

     FFF(Index).Checked = True
End Sub
```

Now the Font menu is fully functional; when the user clicks on a new font— not Helv—the check mark is removed from Helv and placed in front of the new font (see figure 3.22). In this way, the user can keep track of which font is currently selected. The code for the Editor so far (Editor.Mak on the Disk) appears in listing 3.3.

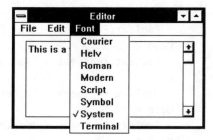

Figure 3.22. Check marks in the Editor's Font menu.

Listing 3.3. Editor Version 2 (Final version is Editor.Mak on the Disk)

```
Editor.Bas ------------------------------------------------------------
CutText As String
Editor.Frm ------------------------------------------------------------
Sub ExitItem_Click()
    End
End Sub

Sub CutItem_Click()
    CutText = PadText.SelText
    PadText.SelText = ""
    PasteItem.Enabled = True
End Sub

Sub PasteItem_Click()
    PadText.SelText = CutText
End Sub

Sub ClearItem_Click()
    PadText.Text = ""
End Sub

Sub PadText.Change()
    CutItem.Enabled = True
    ClearItem.Enabled = True
End Sub
```

```
Sub FFF_Click (Index As Integer)
    Select Case Index
    Case 0
      PadText.FontName = "Courier"
    Case 1
      PadText.FontName = "Helv"
    Case 2
      PadText.FontName = "Roman"
    Case 3
      PadText.FontName = "Modern"
    Case 4
      PadText.FontName = "Script"
    Case 5
      PadText.FontName = "Symbol"
    Case 6
      PadText.FontName = "System"
    Case 7
      PadText.FontName = "Terminal"
    End Select

    For (loop_index = 0 To 7)
      FFF(loop_index).Checked = False
    Next loop_index

    FFF(Index).Checked = True
End Sub
```

The Editor application is looking better, but a number of features are still missing from it (besides its obvious inability to work with files yet). In most complete Windows applications that use menus, you can also use access keys—for example one letter of a menu name or item is underlined, indicating that typing that letter will select the corresponding option—and shortcut keys (like Ctrl+A). Naturally, you can add those options to your Visual Basic programs, too.

Adding Access Keys to Menus

Adding an access key—the underlined letter in a name or caption—to menus is as easy as adding buttons. Just place an ampersand (&) in front of the letter you want to use. For example, you can change Cut to &Cut to make C the access key for the Cut item in the Edit menu. Note again that the access keys should be unique on their level—that is, no two menu names in the menu bar should have the same access key, nor should two menu items in the same menu have the same access key.

In fact, you will use the first letter in the name of each item or menu name as its access key, with a few exceptions: because two menu names begin with F—File and Font—you can use F for the File menu access key and o for the Font menu. In addition, because both Cut and Clear All appear in the Edit menu, you can use C for the Cut item's access key and A for Clear All (as you did when you designed the notepad). You will not give access keys to the fonts because you do not expect to switch fonts often enough to need them. Finally, even though the Exit option begins with E, you give it the access key x; this is unique in the File menu. (The Windows convention is to give Exit x as an access key; many users are accustomed to using it that way, and few menu items are likely to begin with x.) All the access keys you will use for Editor are marked with an ampersand (see figure 3.23).

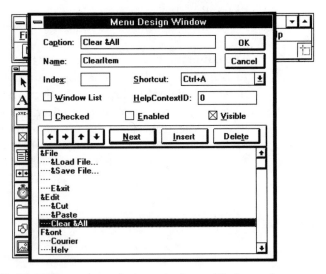

Figure 3.23. The Editor menu design window with Access keys.

Now when you run the Editor, you will see the access keys underlined, as in figure 3.24. The Editor looks more professional, but there is one last change still to be made—adding shortcut keys.

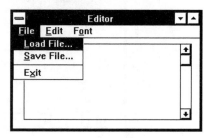

Figure 3.24. An Editor template Access keys.

Adding Shortcut Keys to Menus

You probably have seen shortcut keys in menus already. For example, the Visual Basic File menu in figure 3.1 has four shortcut keys for handling file operations. Ctrl+D is a shortcut for adding a file; Ctrl+S, a shortcut for saving a file; Ctrl+A is the shortcut for the Save File As... menu item; and Ctrl+P is a shortcut for the Print... item. You can add shortcuts like this to the Editor as well.

To do that, open the Menu Design Window again. Select shortcut keys with the Shortcut box that appears on the right side. As in most cases, Visual Basic is capable of presenting you with all the options available here (that is, instead of having to look them up, the options are displayed on the screen for your immediate use). When you click on the arrow next to the Shortcut box, a list of the possible shortcut keys appears (see figure 3.25).

The first menu item you might give a shortcut key to is the Load File item in the File menu. Because you will have no use for the Ctrl-key combinations (like Ctrl+A or Ctrl+B) in your application, you can use them as shortcut keys—Ctrl+Letter key combinations are often easier for the user to remember than function-key combinations (those are available also in the Shortcut drop-down list box). To connect Ctrl+L with the Load File item, just highlight that item in the main list box (as shown in figure 3.25) and select Ctrl+L from the Shortcut list box. When you do, Ctrl+L appears in the main list box on the same line as the Load File... item.

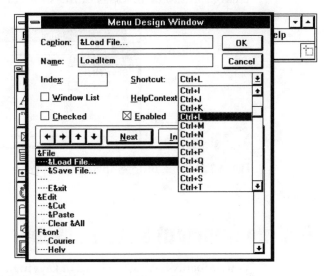

Figure 3.25. Shortcut Keys in the Menu design window.

In this way, you can keep going by choosing Shortcut keys for most of the items (see figure 3.26). To make these shortcut keys active, just click on the Done box in the Menu Design Window and run the Editor application. As you can see in figure 3.27, the shortcut keys are now displayed in the menus themselves, next to the items they represent.

> **About the scope of shortcut keys.**
> Keep in mind that a menu has to be open for you to use the access keys in that menu, shortcut keys like Ctrl+X or Shift-F3 are valid even when the menu is closed. For this reason, the keys should be unique over all menus, not just the one they are defined in.

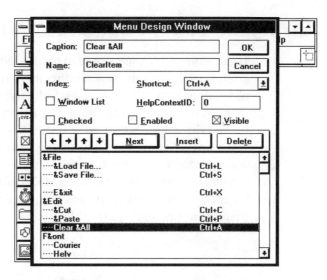

Figure 3.26. Shortcut keys for the Editor application.

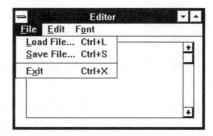

Figure 3.27. Editor with Shortcut keys.

For the time being, that's it for developing the Editor. It has shown you a great deal about menu design, including how to gray items in a menu to show that they are inactive, how to mark menu items with a check mark, how to use access keys and separator bars, and now how to use shortcut keys. In fact, the Editor application is the closest you have come to producing a polished application; for that reason, you should give it its own icon. As it turns out, this is easy enough to do—Visual Basic has a library of some 400 icons, ready for you to use.

Giving the Editor Application an Icon

These icons, which are stored in the ICONS directory, are broken into 13 groups, each with its own subdirectory: arrows, communications, computer, dragdrop, elements, flags, industry, mail, miscellaneous, msicons, office, traffic signs, and writing. The writing category sounds appropriate for an Editor application, so you should explore those icons for the one you want. A complete copy of the icon library is in the Visual Basic documentation. Figure 3.28 shows some of the icons from the writing library. Note that the icon labelled Default is Visual Basic's default icon for applications—the icon each of the .Exe files has had until now—and that it is not actually part of the Visual Basic icon library.

Figure 3.28. Some Visual Basic writing icons.

The Pencil01 icon looks good for your purposes. To use it, you must associate the icon with the Editor application's form. Click on the form itself and look at the Icon property in the properties window. An ellipsis (three dots) appears in the button next to the settings window; click on it to open the Load Icon dialog box (see figure 3.29).

Use the Directories box in this dialog box to switch to Visual Basic's Icons\Writing directory. Then load the Pencil01 icon by highlighting Pencil01 and clicking on the OK button. At this point, the Pencil01 icon is associated with the Editor application's form, which still has the default name Form1. This is where Visual Basic takes the icon it will associate with the .Exe file (again, by default). Select the Make EXE File... item in Visual Basic's File menu; the Make EXE File dialog box opens (see figure 3.30).

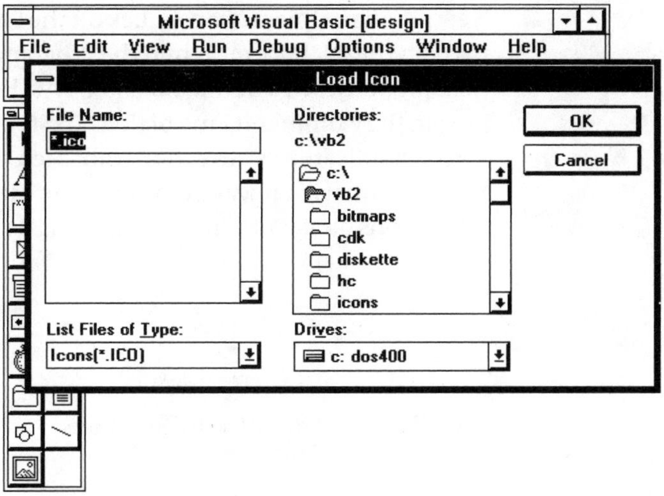

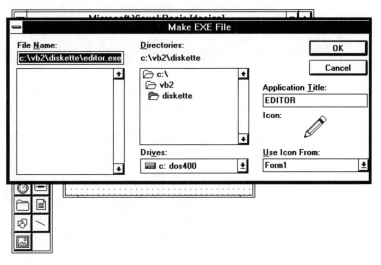

Figure 3.29. The Load Icon dialog box.

Figure 3.30. The Make EXE File dialog box.

As you can see, Pencil01 has become the icon for the Editor application. After you create Editor.Exe, you can add it to the applications displayed in Windows' Program Manager window by selecting the New... item in the Program Manager's File menu. When you do, a dialog box labelled

New Program Object opens. Click on the Program Item option button and then on the OK button. When the Program Manager asks for the program item properties in a new dialog box, type **Editor** in the Description dialog box; in the Command Line dialog box, type the location and name of the Editor application's .Exe file, and then click on the OK button. The Editor's icon will appear in the Program Manager window, along with the other icons already there (see figure 3.31). When you click it, the Editor will start.

Paintbrush - (Untitled)   Editor   Solitaire

Figure 3.31. The Editor Icon with others.

That's it for the Editor for now. You will return to it later when you are able to add file support. Meanwhile, there is more to learn about menus. For example, you can change menu items at run time. To see how to do this, you are going to adapt one of your old programs—the alarm clock.

Changing Menu Items at Run Time

As you may recall, the alarm clock program has two option buttons—Alarm Off and Alarm On. You can convert this application to use a menu, just as you did for the editor. In particular, your goal here is to have one menu—Alarm—with one item in it. At first, that item will be Alarm Off; when you select it at run time, it will change to Alarm On, and so on, toggling back and forth as necessary.

To do that, open the Alarm project and the Menu Design Window in that project. All you need here is a single menu named Alarm, with a Name of, say, AlarmMenu, and with one item, Alarm Off, in it. You can give this item the Name of OnOffItem—for example the option buttons were named OnOffButton. Now double-click on one of the option buttons to open the code window and display this code, as follows:

```
Sub OnOffButton_Click (Index As Integer)
    If (Index = 1) Then
    AlarmOn = True
    Else
```

```
        AlarmOn = False
    End If
End Sub
```

As you may recall, AlarmOn was a global variable that determined whether the program would beep when the allotted time elapsed. You can change this Sub procedure code, rewriting it in the following way:

```
Sub OnOffItem_Click()
    If (AlarmOn) Then
    AlarmOn = False        'Toggle alarm
    OnOffItem.Caption = "Alarm Off"
    Else
    AlarmOn = True   'Toggle alarm
    OnOffItem.Caption = "Alarm On"
    End If
End Sub
```

That's it; you can delete the option buttons now (using the Visual Basic Edit menu) because all reference to them in the code has been removed. By changing the Caption property of the single menu item, you are able to change that menu item at run time. When you run the clock now, you will see the menu name Alarm in the menu bar; opening it will reveal the Alarm Off item. Clicking on that item closes the menu and changes it to Alarm On (see figure 3.32). In this way, you can toggle the caption of the Alarm On/Off item to match the alarm setting.

Figure 3.32. Alarm Clock with Menu.

The other way to do this is to use the Visible property of menu items instead. If you had two menu items, AlarmOnItem (Alarm On) and AlarmOffItem (Alarm Off), for example, setting the AlarmOnItem.Visible property to True would display the Alarm On menu item, and setting the AlarmOffItem.Visible property to False would hide it, as follows:

```
Sub OnOffItem_Click()
    If (AlarmOn) Then
    AlarmOn = False        'Toggle alarm
    AlarmOnItem.Visible = False
    AlarmOffItem.Visible = True
    Else
    AlarmOn = True         'Toggle alarm
    AlarmOnItem.Visible = True
    AlarmOffItem.Visible = False
    End If
End Sub
```

This is the way you can hide options in the menus when you need to (to avoid presenting too many grayed options, for example). Setting the Visible property this way can be an important part of menu design.

You also can make the alarm clock function with check marks—for examplecheck marks are designed for cases where you toggle options on and off. To put a menu with check marks into the alarm clock, open the Menu Design Window and again set up a menu with the Caption Alarm and Name AlarmMenu. Then put one item into this menu— OnItem, with the caption Alarm On—for example when this item is checked, the alarm will be on. Close the Menu Design Window and click on the Alarm On menu item to open the code window with this Sub procedure template, as follows:

```
Sub OnItem_Click()
End Sub
```

You can check the Alarm On item and set AlarmOn appropriately as follows:

```
Sub OnItem_Click()
If (AlarmOn) Then
AlarmOn = False
OnItem.Checked = False
Else
AlarmOn = True
OnItem.Checked = True
End If
End Sub
```

This way, the Alarm On item toggles between being checked and un-checked, corresponding to the state of the alarm, as in figure 3.33.

(Alternatively, you can have two items, Alarm On and Alarm Off, and place a check mark in front of the appropriate one.)

Figure 3.33. The Alarm Clock application with check marks.

As you have seen, then, it is possible to change a menu item's caption at run time, as well as make it visible or invisible. However, this does not take care of all possibilities. What if you wanted to add or delete entirely new menu items at run time? You will look into this possibility next.

Adding and Deleting Menu Items

Suppose that you want to write a menu-driven phone book application—a program you can use to keep track of your friends' phone numbers. Such an application might have two text boxes in it: one holding a name and the other one holding the corresponding phone number. If all the stored names appear in a menu, selecting among them will be easy. When you chose a name, it will appear in the name text box; the corresponding phone number will appear in the phone number text box. However, you will have to take into account that such a list of names (as displayed in the menu) can grow or shrink.

In Visual Basic, you can add menu items with the *Load* statement and remove them with the *Unload* statement. (As you will see, Load and Unload can be used for many Visual Basic controls.) To do this, however, the menu items must be part of a control array and must use the same click procedure, although their indices will be different). (The reason for this is that you cannot add entirely new code for a new click procedure at run time—for example when you want to add a new item to a menu.) Rather, Visual Basic must already have the code necessary to handle the new menu item.

Using Load and Unload is not difficult. For example, if you had a menu item named, say, TheItem, whose index was 0, you could add another item named TheItem(1) in the following way:

```
Load TheItem(1)
```

This adds another item right below the last item; to add a new item to the menu itself, you can load a string into TheItem(1)'s Caption property, in the following way:

```
Load TheItem(1)
TheItem(1).Caption = "Load File..."
```

Similarly, you can unload items using Unload. Say, for example, that you added these file-handling items to a menu in the following way:

```
Load TheItem(1)
TheItem(1).Caption = "Load File..."
Load TheItem(2)
TheItem(2).Caption = "Check Spelling"
Load TheItem(3)
TheItem(3).Caption = "Format Text"
Load TheItem(4)
TheItem(4).Caption = "Save File As..."
```

Now say that you wanted to remove the Load File... item. Visual Basic allows you to remove only the last item in a control array with Unload, so you would have to do that by moving all the other items up and then deleting the last item, as follows:

```
Load TheItem(1)
TheItem(1).Caption = "Load File..."
Load TheItem(2)
TheItem(2).Caption = "Check Spelling"
Load TheItem(3)
TheItem(3).Caption = "Format Text"
Load TheItem(4)
TheItem(4).Caption = "Save File As..."
For loop_index = 1 To 3
    TheItem(loop_index).Caption = TheItem(loop_index + 1).Caption
Next loop_index
Unload TheItem(4)
```

Note that in this case, the indices of each surviving item are decremented by one; you would have to account for that in code. Note also that you did nothing with the first item in the array, TheItem(0). This is a defect of using Load and Unload for menu items. You cannot set up a control array unless you have at least one element in place at design time, and you cannot unload items created at design time. No matter what you do, you must always have one element of the control array in the menu—but because you do not know before run time which items you want to place in the menu—for example, the names of your friends—what Caption should you give it at design time?

When designing a menu, the usual solution to this problem is to give the 0th item—the one that starts the control array—an invisible menu item as a caption. That way, all subsequent menu items that you add will come after this invisible 0th item. Now you will see how this works in practice.

You can start a new project named, say, Phone.Mak (with Phone.Bas and Phone.Frm in it). Add two text boxes and labels (Name: and Number:) as shown in figure 3.34 and then open the Menu Design Window. Because the menu in the phone book application can conceivably be expanded to save phone directories on disk, you can give it the name File.

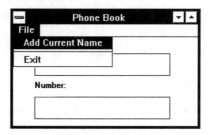

Figure 3.34. The phone project template.

Give the first item in that menu the Caption Add Current Name and a Name of AddNameItem. Next, put in a separator bar by typing a hyphen (-) and give it the control name of, say, Separator. After that, add another item with any caption (except a null string, "")—even a space. Give this dummy item— the first item in the control array—a Name of, say, NNN. In addition, give it an Index of 0 (by putting 0 in the box marked Index), and make it invisible (by clicking on the Visible box so that the X disappears). In other words, the control array will be named NNN( ), and you can refer to specific items in it as NNN(1), NNN(2), and so on. (Note that because NNN(0) will always remain invisible, you can give it any caption you like.) Finally, add the last item of any File menu, Exit, with a Name of ExitItem.

If you run the program, you will see a menu, as in figure 3.34. This is how you want the program to work: You should be able to type a name in the name text box and a phone number in the number text box and then, when you select the Add Current Name menu item, the program should add that name to the menu (it should appear right below the separator bar). After you finish entering names this way, select a name from the menu. That name, along with the corresponding phone number, should appear in the text boxes.

You can start with the Add Current Name item in the menu; click on that item twice to open the code window, which displays this Sub procedure template, as follows:

```
Sub AddNameItem_Click()
End Sub
```

Because the first thing you want to keep track of is the number of menu items you have, declare a variable named NumberNames as Static—for example its value will not change between successive calls, as follows:

```
Sub AddNameItem_Click()
    Static NumberNames
    :
End Sub
```

Because you are adding a name in this procedure, your first action might be to simply increment NumberNames by one (static variables are initialized to 0) and Load a new menu item, in the following way:

```
Sub AddNameItem_Click()
    Static NumberNames
    NumberNames = NumberNames + 1
    Load NNN(NumberNames)
    :
End Sub
```

Next, you can load the name now in the name text box into the new menu item's Caption property this way (assuming that you left the name text box's Name as Text1), as follows:

```
Sub AddNameItem_Click()
    Static NumberNames
```

```
    NumberNames = NumberNames + 1
    Load NNN(NumberNames)
    NNN(NumberNames).Caption = Text1.Text
    :
End Sub
```

Now, to store the names and numbers, you can set up two string arrays named Names( ) and Numbers( ). These arrays have to have broader scope than just the current procedure, because when the user clicks on a name in the menu to retrieve data, the corresponding Click procedure will have to read from these arrays to fill the name and number text boxes. For that reason, you can declare Names( ) and Numbers( ) as form-level arrays (or you could declare them globally). To do that, click the (general) item in the object box of the code window and make sure that the (declarations) item is showing in the procedure box (the box on the right). Then add the following declarations, as shown in figure 3.35.

```
Dim Names(0 To 10) As String
Dim Numbers(0 To 10) As String
```

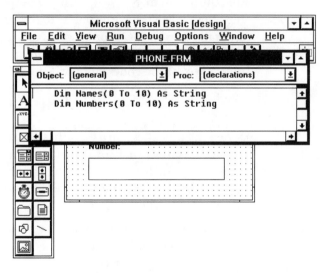

Figure 3.35. A Form's general object.

Placing these arrays in the general object makes them form-level arrays, accessible to all procedures in the form. Now you can go back to AddName_Click( ) and complete it like this to store the current name and number, as follows:

```
Sub AddNameItem_Click()
    Static NumberNames
    NumberNames = NumberNames + 1
    Load NNN(NumberNames)
    NNN(NumberNames).Caption = Text1.Text
    Names(NumberNames) = Text1.Text     'Data from name text box
    Numbers(NumberNames) = Text2.Text   'Data from number text box
End Sub
```

With AddName_Click( ) now complete, you can add your friends' names to the File menu at run time. The next step after adding names is to retrieve them on demand; that occurs when the user clicks on a name in the menu. When that happens, an NNN_Click( ) event occurs—for exampleNNN( ) is the name you have given to the menu item array). Note that the first item, NNN(0), is simply the place-holding invisible item. The next item, NNN(1), corresponds to the first name in the menu under the separator bar; NNN(2) corresponds to the next name, and so on. To write the NNN_Click( ) Sub procedure, then, find and click on NNN in the object box of the code window. This Sub procedure appears as follows:

```
Sub NNN_Click(Index As Integer)
End Sub
```

When the user clicks on a name in the menu, this procedure is called with an index number that corresponds to the item chosen. Because you have stored the names and numbers with the same index as the menu items themselves, you can display the requested name and number on the screen, in the following way:

```
Sub NNN_Click(Index As Integer)
    Text1.Text = Names(Index)
    Text2.Text = Numbers(Index)
End Sub
```

That's all there is to it. If you add an End statement to make the Exit item active, you are finished. The complete code is in listing 3.4 (in Phone.Mak on the Disk).

Listing 3.4. Phone Book Application (Phone.Mak on the Disk)

```
Form Form1
    Caption    =   "Phone Book"

TextBox Text1
    TabIndex   =   0

TextBox Text2
    TabIndex   =   1

Label Label1
    Caption    =   "Number:"

Label Label2
    Caption    =   "Name:"

Menu FileMenu
    Caption    =   "File"

Menu AddNameItem
    Caption    =   "Add Current Name"

Menu NNN
    Caption    =   " "
    Index      =   0
    Visible    =   0'False

Menu ExitItem
    Caption    =   "Exit"

Phone.Frm ------------------------------------------------
    Dim Names(1 To 10) As String    'Form-level array -- General object
    Dim Numbers(1 To 10) As String  'Form-level array -- General object

Sub AddNameItem_Click ()
    Static NumberNames
    NumberNames = NumberNames + 1
    Load NNN(NumberNames)
    NNN(NumberNames).Caption = Text1.Text
    NNN(NumberNames).Visible = true
```

continues

Listing 3.4. continued

```
    Names(NumberNames) = Text1.Text
    Numbers(NumberNames) = Text2.Text
End Sub

Sub ExitItem_Click ()
    End
End Sub

Sub NNN_Click (Index As Integer)
    Text1.Text = Names(Index)
    Text2.Text = Numbers(Index)
End Sub
```

Run the phone application; you can store names and numbers by typing them in the text boxes and selecting the Add Current Name item. Each time you do, another name is added to the menu (see figure 3.36). To retrieve the number for any name, just select that menu item.

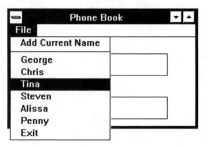

Figure 3.36. Functioning Phone Book Application.

You have come far in your work with menus in this chapter, but there is one significant thing you did not do: make items like Load File... and Save File... active. Usually, selecting a menu item with an ellipsis like this pops open a dialog box—for that reason, you will learn about dialog boxes next.

Summary

You have learned how work with menus in this chapter—in fact, you have seen just about all that is possible with menus. In particular, you have seen how to design menus with the Menu Design Window, how to incorporate them into your programs and add code to specific menu items, how to enable and disable menu items, how to add and use menu access and shortcut keys, as well as how to add separator bars, menus within menus, and check marks. You have also created a font menu that will allow you to switch fonts. And you have developed a phone book application that lets you add menu items to a menu at run time—for examplefrom inside your program—note that the new menu items have to be members of a control array). Two other useful topics in this chapter were how to end a Visual Basic program with the End statment, and how to give an .Exe file an icon in Windows.

New Property	Description
Checked	Indicates whether a menu item appears with a check mark in front of it or not (True or False)
Icon	Holds the path and filename of the icon that Visual Basic will associate with the program's .Exe file (Use Visual Basic's Make EXE File menu item.)
Visible	Indicates whether a control or form is visible on the screen (True or False)

New Statement	Description
End	Ends a Visual Basic program
Load	Loads a form or control into memory
Unload	Unloads a form or control from memory

Dialog Boxes and a Database Program

In this chapter, you will see how to work with multiple windows—specifically, dialog boxes. You will add dialog boxes to your programs, popping them on the screen when required. In fact, this chapter covers all these topics:

▼ Visual Basic programs without any windows

▼ Message boxes

▼ Input boxes

▼ Creating and using dialog boxes

▼ Connecting dialog boxes to menu items

▼ How the Multiple Document Interface (MDI) works

▼ "About" boxes

▼ How scroll bars work

▼ Combo boxes

▼ List boxes

You will develop some good programs in this chapter—a Windows shell program that will start Windows applications and a control panel application that will show how a dialog box can adjust the properties of the main window—and you will start your database application (like the editor, the database program will extend over a few chapters, and you will pick up skills like file handling as they are covered). You will also update your tic-tac-toe program to use message boxes. And you will add some other skills, such as how to run a Visual Basic program without any windows at all, how to set colors in Visual Basic, and how to use the Multiple Document Interface (MDI), which can maintain a number of windows inside a larger one, just like the Windows Program Manager. Dialog boxes are an important part of almost any Windows program, and the knowledge you pick up here will be handy when you set up almost any Windows application.

So far, all of your programs have involved a single window; that is, a single form. However, it is common for applications to use many windows—dialog boxes, message boxes, warning boxes, help windows, and all sorts of other windows. Probably the most common types of such windows are dialog boxes (that is exactly what they are—windows). However, you will learn a lot about other types of multiple form applications in this chapter.

In fact, Visual Basic provides some built-in windows that you can use for just this purpose: MsgBox( ) and InputBox$( ). These two Visual Basic statements display a message and get string input from the user, respectively. Using them is easy, so you will start with them first. Next, you will see how to work with multiple forms in general—how to create a second form when designing your application, how to display it, how to address the properties of other forms, and how to hide them again.

After that, you will see how to create and use dialog boxes in general. If you have used Windows, you know that dialog boxes play an integral part in getting information from the user. So far, you have handled tasks like numeric input, string input, and option selection by using buttons and menus. In real applications, these same tasks are often handled with dialog boxes. You will also spend a good deal of time in this chapter with some of the controls that are often associated with dialog boxes—combo boxes and list boxes. You will also see how the Multiple Document Interface works (MDI—many windows inside one major window). With all that in mind, you will start by seeing that sometimes no windows are needed. Then you will move on with MsgBox( ) and InputBox$( ), the two simplest types of dialog boxes available.

No Windows Needed

It may surprise you to learn that you do not need any windows in a Visual Basic program. To see how this works, start Visual Basic and remove the default form—Form1 (use the Remove File item in Visual Basic's File menu). Add a module (use the New Module... item, also in Visual Basic's File menu) that will have the default name Module1. As you may recall, you store code that is not associated with any form in Visual Basic modules. If you add a Sub named Main( ) to the module's (general) object, Visual Basic will execute it—no forms are needed. For example, put the following code in the (general) object of Module1:

```
Sub Main()
        Beep
End Sub
```

When you run the program, it will simply execute the Visual Basic Beep statement and then exit. It is as simple as that to write a windowless program in Visual Basic. Of course, it is more interesting when there are windows; so you can start to add more windows to your programs now.

More uses for a windowless program in Windows.
Note that you can do much more with Windows programs that do not display windows—especially those that can communicate with other Windows programs with Dynamic Data Exchange (see the chapter on DDE). You will also see later that you can use the Load( ) and Show( ) methods to load and display windows, even from a program that does not have any originally.

Displaying a Message Box with MsgBox()

The first function covered here, MsgBox( ), really allows only a restricted dialog. You place a message on the screen in a window, and the user is restricted to communicating back through buttons. The way you use MsgBox( ) is as follows:

```
RetVal% = MsgBox (message$ [,type [,title$]])
```

In this line of code, message$ is the message you want to display—for example, Error Number 5 or That button is already selected—*type* indicates what buttons and/or icons you want in the message box, and *title$* is the string you want placed in the message box window's caption (this string is truncated after the 255th character).

The type argument lets you select from a number of options, such as displaying OK buttons, Abort, Retry, or Ignore buttons, Cancel buttons, or even icons, such as a Stop sign, an information symbol (a lowercase i in a circle), or others, as indicated in table 4.1. The values in that table can be added together; for example, to display Yes, No, and OK buttons along with a Stop sign, you would use a type value of $4 + 16 = 20$. Note that even if you do not specify a value for type, Visual Basic still places an OK button in the message box so that the user can close it. The return values for this function (which allow you to determine what button the user pushed) are in table 4.2.

Table 4.1. Type Argument for MsgBox() Function

Value	Means
0	OK button only
1	OK button and Cancel button
2	Abort, Retry, Ignore buttons
3	Yes, No, Cancel buttons
4	Yes, No buttons
5	Retry, Cancel buttons
16	Stop sign
32	Query sign (question mark in a circle)
48	Warning sign (exclamation point in a circle)
64	Information icon ("i" in a circle)
0	First button has default focus
256	Second button has default focus
512	Third button has default focus

Table 4.2. MsgBox() Return Values

Value	Means
1	OK button was pressed
2	Cancel button was pressed
3	Abort button was pressed
4	Retry button was pressed
5	Ignore button was pressed
6	Yes button was pressed
7	No button was pressed

Now to put all this to use. Some common uses for message boxes are: help messages, About boxes (describing the application and the application's authors), and error messages. You begin with a help message. Start Visual Basic, put a command button in the middle of the default form (Form1) with the caption Help, and double-click on it. The following Sub procedure template appears as follows:

```
Sub Command1_Click ()
End Sub
```

You can use MsgBox to display a simple help message: "This button displays Help." along with an information symbol—an "i" inside a circle (type = 64)—as well as an OK button and a Cancel button (type = 1), as follows:

```
Sub Command1_Click ()
        MsgBox"This button displays Help.", 65, "Help"
End Sub
```

Notice that you can also use MsgBox( ) as a statement, not a function, which you do here because you are not interested in its return value. When clicked, the Help button puts your message box on the screen (see figure 4.1). That's it; you are using elementary dialog boxes already.

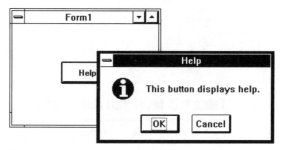

Figure 4.1. A trial Help message box.

You can see an example of an error message box if you modify your tic-tac-toe game; you may recall that the user could click any button, changing it to an x or an o whether or not something was already there. You can fix that by checking the clicked button's caption and displaying an error message if the button had already been clicked. You called the control array that handles the button clicks TTT, and this was the corresponding event procedure, as follows:

```
Sub TTT_Click (Index As Integer)
If (Xturn) Then
TTT(Index).Caption = "x"
Xturn = False
Else
TTT(Index).Caption = "o"
Xturn = True
End If
End Sub
```

You can add an error message with a warning symbol (an exclamation point inside a circle—type = 48), and leave the Sub procedure if the button was already clicked, in the following way:

```
Sub TTT_Click (Index As Integer)
    If(TTT(Index).Caption <> "") Then
  MsgBox "That button was already clicked.", 48, "Error"
    Exit Sub
    End If
    If (Xturn) Then
TTT(Index).Caption = "x"
Xturn = False
    Else
TTT(Index).Caption = "o"
Xturn = True
    End If
End Sub
```

This way, if the user clicks on a button that already had an x or an o displayed, an error box is displayed (see figure 4.2) and the button is not changed. Now the user can simply click on the OK button and click on another button in the game instead.

Figure 4.2. An error message box.

Because the icons and general appearance of message boxes like these look like standard message boxes in normal Windows applications, using MsgBox( ) in your programs can make them seem more professional. And, as indicated, you can receive a limited amount of information back from MsgBox—which button a user clicked. However, that limits the user's input options to: Yes, No, Cancel, Abort, Retry, Ignore, and OK. On the other hand, the next function you will explore, InputBox$( ), has no such restriction.

An InputBox$() Application—a Windows Shell

To see how InputBox$( ) functions, you are going to create an application that uses it; in this case, you will use Visual Basic's Shell( ) function, with which you can start Windows applications. The following is how you use Shell( ):

```
RetVal = Shell (command$ [, windowtype$])
```

Here, command$ is the command string, just as you might type after the command Win when you start Windows—for example, Win Sol.Exe starts the Windows solitaire game; in particular, command$ must be the name of a file that ends in .Exe, .Bat, .Com, or .Pif. The windowtype$ argument indicates the startup options you want for the application's window—for example, minimized or maximized—(see table 4.3). If the shell function was able to execute the program, it returns the program's task ID (a unique number that identifies the program, but which you will not use here).

Table 4.3. Shell Function's Window Types

Value	Means
1	Normal window, with focus
2	Minimized, with focus
3	Maximized, with focus
4	Normal window, without focus
7	Minimized, without focus

You can create your own application called, say, Windows Shell, which will start applications on request. To get the name and path of the application to start, you can use the InputBox$( ) function. That function appears as follows, in general:

```
RetString$ = InputBox$(prompt$ [,title$ [,default$ [,x% [,y%]]]])
```

Here, RetString$ is the string you typed—for example, the input from the input box), prompt$ is the prompt you display to indicate what type of input is desired, title$ is the caption you want to give the input box, default$ is the default string that first appears in the input box's text box—for example, if you type no other response, default$ is returned), and the optional x% and y% arguments indicate the position of the input box as measured from the upper left corner of the screen (in twips, 1/1440th of an inch).

To see all of this in action, start a new Visual Basic project called Windows Shell and open the Menu Design Window. Create one menu named File, with two items in it: Run... and Exit, giving them the Names RunItem and ExitItem (see figure 4.3).

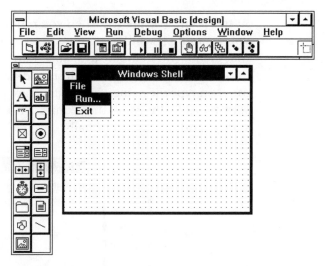

Figure 4.3. A file menu for the Windows Shell application.

Now click on the Run... menu item, opening the code window, which displays the template for RunItem_Click( ) like this:

```
Sub RunItem_Click()
End Sub
```

You want to get a string for input here, so that you can use InputBox$( ). In fact, because the menu item here has an ellipsis (Run...), you expect a dialog box to appear. When you get a string back from InputBox$( ), you can just pass it on to Shell( ) like this:

```
Sub RunItem_Click()
    RetVal = Shell(InputBox$("Application to run:", "Run..."), 1)
End Sub
```

In this case, you are asking for an input box that has the prompt "Application to run:" and the caption "Run..." in the title bar. You can then pass the string that was typed back to the Shell( ) function, along with a windowtype% argument of 1, requesting a normal window. In addition, you should make the Exit item in your File menu active as well, by placing the End statement in the ExitItem_Click( ) Sub procedure as follows:

```
Sub ExitItem_Click()
    End
End Sub
```

At this point, you are set; when you run the Windows Shell application, you see a simple window on the screen with a File menu; when you open that menu, two items are available: Run... and Exit. When you click on Run..., a dialog box opens—as it should—and as shown in figure 4.4. You can then type the name of a Windows application to run—say, Sol.Exe to start the solitaire game that comes with Windows. The application is started, and functions normally.

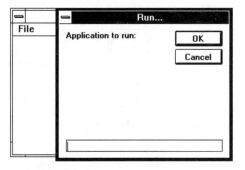

Figure 4.4. Windows shell application.

However, the appearance of your dialog box is less than optimal, which can be a problem unless you can design your windows explicitly yourself. As you can see, the prompt appears in the top of the dialog box, and the text box is some distance away, at the bottom. In other words, although InputBox works, you may be surprised at the results. A better option is to design the dialog box you want to use yourself. You will learn how in the next section.

Creating Applications with Multiple Windows

As you might expect, it is not difficult to create multiple-form programs under Visual Basic. You are going to revise the Windows Shell program to use a dialog box of your own creation. To do that, you need a new form, which is easily created—just select the New Form item in the File menu, and a new form, called Form2, appears on the screen (see figure 4.5).

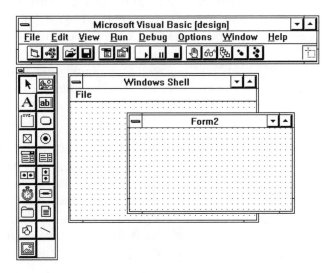

Figure 4.5. Visual Basic with a second form.

The Name of this form is Form2; until now, you have not paid much attention to the Names of forms, but now that you are using multiple forms, Names become important. For example, now you will be able to switch between forms using the project window—just click on the name of the form you want to work on.

The First Form

When multiple forms are involved, a natural question is—which one does Visual Basic start first when the application starts? It would be awkward if Visual Basic decided to place your dialog box on the screen by itself. The default here is that the first form created when you create an application is the first form started when the application runs.

> **Choosing the window a program should display first.**
> Use Visual Basic 2.0 or 3.0 if you want to indicate specifically which of a number of windows to place on the screen first, you can use the Set Startup Form... item in the dialog box connected to the Project... item in Visual Basic's Options menu (Visual Basic 1.0: use the Set Startup Form... item in the Run menu).

When the first form is started, a Form_Load event is generated for that form. As you have seen, this is a special event that occurs when a form is about to appear; you can often do initialization of your entire application here. In particular, if your application depends on a number of windows being on the screen at the same time, you can use the Form_Load event of the first window—for example, the one Visual Basic displays first) to display the others. (You will see a great deal about the Form_Load event later.)

The question now is—how do you display other windows? After you have designed the dialog box, how will you be able to place it on the screen when you want it? Visual Basic has several ways of handling this task. For example, the two statements Load and Unload load and unload forms into and out of memory. In this way, Load and Unload work in much the same way they did with menu items in the last chapter. Here, however, you can load and unload forms by using their Name properties like this:

```
Load Form2
UnLoad Form2
```

Note, however, that simply loading a form does not display it; display is handled by the Show method. As you have seen before (with the SetFocus method), a *method* is like a procedure, except that it is tied to an object (a control or form), just like a property. In other words, a property is made up of data attached to the object, and a method is a procedure attached to the object.

To show a form named Form2, then, you just have to execute this statement: Form2.Show [modal%], where the optional argument modal% can take on two values: 0 or 1. If it is 0, the user is free to use other forms even when this form (Form2 here) is on the screen; if it is 1, all other forms in the application become inactive, and the user cannot switch to them. In the latter case, the form is said to be *modal*—for example, the user's course of action is restricted). Dialog boxes are mostly modal—for example, InputBox$( ) places a modal dialog box on the screen. Note that if you omit the form's Name, the reference is assumed to be to the current form.

One more important point to mention is Show. You must have loaded a form before you can display it, but if a form is not loaded, Show loads it before displaying it. For that reason, you can display forms by using the Show method alone (not Load followed by Show). In fact, if you simply execute any code that uses a property or method of a form not loaded into memory, Visual Basic automatically loads it before executing that statement.

Besides the Show method, there is the *Hide* method, which, predictably, hides the form from the screen once again. Together, Show and Hide are the two methods that handle dialog box appearances and disappearances. For example, you can change the name of your dialog box's form from Form2 to, say, RunDialog. To load and display this form, you only have to execute the RunDialog.Show 1 statement (where you are making this dialog box modal by passing an argument of 1 to the Show method).

When a number of forms are on the screen, you may wonder how to refer to the controls and properties of a specific one. The solution to that is simply to use the form as part of that control or property's name, like this: Form1.ExitItem or Form2.Text2. Until now, when you have been dealing with only one form, you did not have to specify the form name when referring to a control—Visual Basic simply assumed that the current form was the one you wanted. With multiple forms, however, all you need to do is to specify the form's Name along with the property or method you want to access.

In other words, you used to refer to a control's set of properties like this: control.property. Now, however, you might have a number of forms to choose among, so you can specify the same thing like this: form.control.property. In addition, now that you know a little about methods, you can refer to them by form as well, like this: form.method. Now you will see some of this at work.

Creating Custom Dialog Boxes

The first step is to design your dialog box the way you want it. That is, you can start working on the second form, RunDialog, in the Visual Basic environment. To begin, change its Name property from Form2 to RunDialog, using the Name property in the properties window (click on the second form first if you have to). Also, give it the caption Run..., just as you earlier labelled the InputBox$( ) dialog box.

The job of this dialog box is to accept a string—for example, the name of a Windows application to run), so you will need a text box in it. For that reason, place a text box in the upper half of the form (see figure 4.6) and remove the default text in it so that it appears blank. Also, you do not need minimizing or maximizing buttons here, because this is a modal dialog box—for example, users cannot do anything else in your application until they deal with this box), so find the MinButton and MaxButton properties of the Run... dialog box and set them to False. When you do, the buttons will disappear from the form at run time.

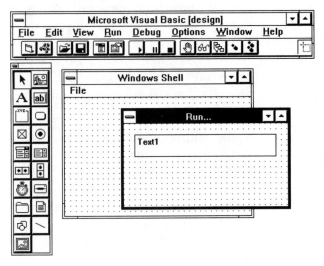

Figure 4.6. The Text box position in the Run... dialog box.

In addition, just like most dialog boxes, this dialog box need not be resized, so change its BorderStyle property to Fixed Single—that is, a fixed-size, single-width border. (When you select a fixed border type, Visual

Peter Norton's Visual Basic for Windows, Third Edition, Covering Release 3.0

Basic also removes the Size option in that form's system menu.) You also want two buttons here: OK and Cancel. In particular, note that most dialog boxes should have Cancel options (especially if the dialog box is modal). This option gives the user a way out if the choices he or she has made until now were in error or were unintentional. For that reason, double-click on the command button tool twice, once for each new button, and position the buttons below the text box, labelling one OK and the other Cancel. You can give Names to these buttons of, say, OKButton and CancelButton.

Now that you have designed the dialog box's appearance, it is time to go back and start working on the code that will make this box active. In particular, the event that should make the dialog box appear is the RunItem_Click( ) event (where RunItem is the Name of the Run... item in the application's File menu). Double-click on that option in the File menu, and open up that procedure:

```
Sub RunItem_Click()
    RetVal = Shell(InputBox$("Application to run:", "Run...") ,1)
End Sub
```

This is the actual Shell statement that you put in earlier, but is now going to be used only if the user presses the OK button in the dialog box. In other words, this procedure should be changed to simply display the dialog box, in the following way:

```
Sub RunItem_Click()
    RunDialog.Show 1
End Sub
```

Recall that even if the RunDialog form is not in memory when the Show method is executed, Visual Basic will automatically load it. In fact, you can run the program right now. When you click on the Run... item in the File menu, your Run... dialog box will appear. On the other hand, there is no way to get rid of it now, because it is modal. If you try to switch to other windows in the same application, you will get a beep, although you can switch to other Windows applications.

End the program (using the Visual Basic End item in the Run menu, not the menus in the Windows Shell form) and bring up the second form so that you can work on it—for example, click on Form2.Frm in the project window), as shown in figure 4.7. The real action here takes place in the click procedures associated with the buttons. When the user clicks on the OK button, the program is supposed to execute the Windows application whose path and name were typed in the text box.

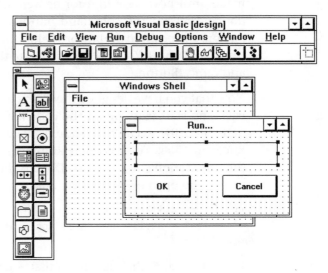

Figure 4.7. The Run... dialog box.

Click on the OK button to bring up the code window. The following Sub procedure template appears:

```
Sub OKButton_Click()
End Sub
```

Because this is the procedure connected with the OK button, you are supposed to run the application here. Because the path and name of that application are presumably in the dialog box's text box, which is still named Text1, you can simply put this line in the following procedure:

```
Sub OKButton_Click()
    RetVal = Shell(Text1.Text, 1)
End Sub
```

However, before doing so, you should hide the dialog box. That way, when the Windows application finishes, you will return to the original Windows Shell application, not to the dialog box, as follows:

```
Sub OKButton_Click()
    RunDialog.Hide
    RetVal = Shell(Text1.Text, 1)
End Sub
```

Immediately after you click on the OK button, the dialog box disappears and the application the user wanted to start begins. In addition, while you are here, you should make the OK button the default—for example, display it with a thick black border) so that the user only has to type the name of the application he or she wants to start and press Enter (because pressing Enter clicks the default button). To do that, set the button's Default property to True in the properties window.

> **Determining whether a window is visible.**
> You can check whether a form is hidden or visible with the Visible property. If Form.Visible is True, the form is visible; if False, the form is hidden.

The other button in the dialog box is the Cancel button. If it is clicked, you should just hide the dialog box and return to the original form, the Windows Shell application. That procedure can appear as follows:

```
Sub CancelButton_Click()
    RunDialog.Hide
End Sub
```

This returns you to the original form and restores the focus to it—nothing else is required. That's all there is to it; the complete code for the whole program appears in listing 4.1.

 Listing 4.1. Windows Shell Application

```
Shell.Frm — — — — — — — — — — — — — — — —
   Sub RunItem_Click ()
     RunDialog.Show 1
   End Sub

   Sub ExitItem_Click ()
     End
   End Sub
```

continues

Listing 4.1. continued

```
Form2.Frm  — — — — — — — — — — — — — — —
   Sub OKButton_Click ()
     RunDialog.Hide
     RetVal = Shell(Text1.Text, 1)
   End Sub

   Sub CancelButton_Click ()
     RunDialog.Hide
   End Sub
```

As you can see, it is quite short—only five lines of actual code, each line tied to its own event. In this way, event-driven programming can save you a good deal of work when it comes to I/O handling. (So far, you have been dealing mostly with I/O, but in the next chapter, when you start working with files, you will start adding more code to your programs for internal processing of data behind the scenes.) Earlier in this chapter, you saw how to use InputBox$( ) as a dialog box of sorts, but now you have seen that it is almost as easy to create your own dialog boxes, and the result is usually worth the trouble in Visual Basic (compare figure 4.7 to figure 4.4).

In fact, there are many types of controls you can find in dialog boxes—buttons and text boxes are only two of them. For example, your next application will include a control panel, which will let you set different aspects of the main window with various controls, including scroll bars (control panels are very popular in large-scale Windows applications). You will look into that next.

Adding a Control Panel to Your Applications

You can start a new application to demonstrate how control panels work in Windows applications. As you probably know, a control panel is used to customize certain aspects of an application; in this example, you will use it to set some properties of the main window: the background color, the height and width of the window, and the main window's caption. You will call this application Panel.Mak. This program will give you experience with changing the properties of another window from the current one, as well as a new type of control, scroll bars.

You can leave the Name of the main window as Form1 so that the control panel you develop is quite generic. Start this project and create a new form—for example, select the New Form item in the File menu), give it the name—for example, Name) ControlPanel, with a Caption of Control Panel. At this point, you should also save all files as Panel.* so that your project does not inadvertently write over earlier files. Put a text box, which you might name NewCaption, into the control panel, with the label "Application Caption:" (see figure 4.8).

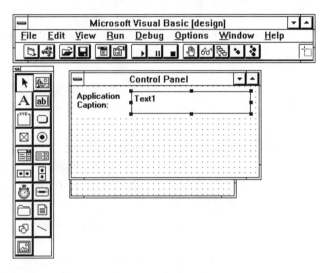

Figure 4.8. Starting the control panel application.

Labels have word wrap too.
Do not worry if the text you want to put into a label is too long for the label's width. Like multiline text boxes, labels have automatic word wrap.

Delete the text now in the text box—for example, "Text1"). This will be where you can change the name of the main window if you want to. These kinds of changes will go into effect when you click the OK button, to which you can give the Name OKButton. Add that at the bottom of the control panel, along with a Cancel button, which you can call CancelButton. As an added touch, you can give the OK button the focus (which is usually the case in control panels) by setting its Default property to true in the properties window.

As you might expect, the code for CancelButton does nothing more than hide the control panel, in the following way:

```
Sub CancelButton ()
    ControlPanel.Hide
End Sub
```

On the other hand, you will do more work in the OKButton procedure because of the way your control panel will work. Rather than keep track of the changes you made, you will just set the relevant properties of the main window, Form1, after you click the OK button. For example, the following way is how to set the main window's new caption in OKButton_Click( ).

```
Sub OKButton_Click ()
    Form1.Caption = NewCaption.Text
    ControlPanel.Hide
End Sub
```

Notice the first line here: Form1.Caption = NewCaption.Text. In general, the way you refer to the properties of another form is by using the form's Name first. If you wanted to change the properties of one of Form1's controls, you could refer to it as Form1.Control.Property.

Note that you should also load the current settings of the main window's properties into the control panel's controls when you open it (e.g., when you start the control panel the first time, the text box should say: "Form1", which is the current caption of the main window), because that is the way a control panel usually works. Next, you will manipulate the size of the main window.

Using Scroll Bars

The default measuring unit in Visual Basic is twips, or 1/1440th of an inch. This means that the two properties you are interested in changing, the main window's height and width, are measured in twips. You could just use a text window in the control panel and set new sizes in terms of twips, which means that you could read in the values using Val( ) and set the two appropriate Form1 properties, Form1.Height and Form1.Width, directly.

However, it is not so easy to get a feel for 1/1440th of an inch; instead, you can use a popular Windows control for converting a numerical value into a smooth range that is easily manipulated graphically—scroll bars.

You have seen scroll bars many times in Windows applications. In fact, you used them yourself when you developed the multiline text box for the Editor application. However, Visual Basic took care of all the details there. Now it is up to you. You are interested here in five primary properties of scroll bars: Min, Max, Value, LargeChange, and SmallChange.

Min is the numerical value you assign to the top or left of a scroll bar (all of these properties can go from 0 to 32,767), Max is the value you assign to the right or bottom, and Value is the current value corresponding to the position of the thumb—the box that moves inside the scroll bar, also called the scroll box. You set Min and Max yourself; the scroll bar then indicates the position of the thumb by placing a value in its Value property, which you can read directly (Min <= Value <= Max). For example, if the thumb were all the way to the left in a horizontal scroll bar, the scroll bar's Value property would be equal to the value you put in the Min property.

The LargeChange property indicates the amount that Value should change each time the user clicks the bar above or below the thumb in the scroll bar—for example, how far the thumb moves. SmallChange is the amount that Value should change when the user clicks on one of the arrows at the top and bottom of the scroll bar. With the exception of Value, you can set all these properties at design time.

The main event with scroll bars is the Change event, which occurs every time the thumb is moved. However, because you do not want your changes to take effect unless the user clicks the OK button, you will not read the value of your scroll bars until then. Now you will see how this works in practice. Click on the vertical scroll bar tool in the Visual Basic toolbox—for example, the sixth tool down on the right); a scroll bar appears in the control panel. You will be using a total of five scroll bars in the control panel (corresponding to the height and width of the main window, and the three colors, RGB, to use for its background color). Place this first scroll bar over to the left in the control panel.

Next, you have to decide the Min and Max values for this scroll bar. Because there are 1440 twips to an inch, you can design your window size in inches. For example, you can have a minimum window size of 1" x 2" (height x width) and a maximum of 5" x 7", which translates into a twip range of 1440 x 2880 to 7200 x 10080. This first scroll bar (you might call it NewHeight) can set the main window's height. This means that the properties you should set at design time are NewHeight.Min = 1440 and NewHeight.Max = 7200. (Similarly, when you design a scroll bar to change the main window's width, you can call it NewWidth; NewWidth.Min will be 2880, and NewWidth.Max will be 10080.)

To set those properties, click on the Min property in the property window. The default value is 0; set it to 1440. Next, click on the Max property. Its default value is 32767; set it to 7200. In addition, you have to specify values for LargeChange (when the user clicks on the scroll bar above or below the thumb) and SmallChange (when the user clicks on the arrows at the end of the scroll bar). For the purposes of this demonstration, you can use NewHeight.LargeChange = 1000, and NewHeight.SmallChange = 500. Now the scroll bar will be active when you run the program (that is, you will be able to read its setting simply by reading NewHeight.Value), so you should label the scroll bar. Put a label above it that says "New Height" (see figure 4.9).

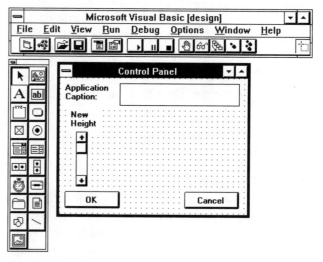

Figure 4.9. Your first scroll bar.

Next, create a new vertical scroll bar. Give it the Name NewWidth and put a label above it that says "New Width." Place it next to the first scroll bar, and give it the Min and Max properties of 2880 and 10080, respectively. For the LargeChange and SmallChange values, you can use 1000 and 500 again. Now you will add the necessary code to the OK button. When the user clicks on the OK button, he or she wants the main window properties Height and Width set to NewHeight.Value and NewWidth.Value, respectively, so you can just add these lines to OKButton_Click ( ), as follows:

```
Sub OKButton_Click ()
    Form1.Caption = NewCaption.Text
    Form1.Height = NewHeight.Value
    Form1.Width = NewWidth.Value
    ControlPanel.Hide
End Sub
```

To see this code in action, you have to add code to the main window to pop up the control panel in the first place. Go back to the main window, Form1, and open the Menu Design Window. In this case, you can create a single menu, named File (menu name: FileMenu), which has two items in it: Control Panel... (Name: ControlPanelItem) and Exit (Name: ExitItem).

In fact, while you are here, you can add access keys and shortcut keys to the menu (say, Ctrl+C for the control panel and Ctrl+X to exit). After creating the menu, close the Menu Design Window and open the ControlPanelItem_Click( ) in the code window, as follows:

```
Sub ControlPanelItem_Click()
End Sub
```

When the user selects this item, you should load the control panel's controls with the current settings of the main window and then display the control panel on the screen. In other words, you want to do the following:

Load ControlPanel.NewCaption.Text with Form1.Caption

Load ControlPanel.NewHeight.Value with Form1.Height

Load ControlPanel.NewWidth.Value with Form1.Width

The thumb in the scroll bars will move, matching the number you place in their Value property, as follows:

```
Sub ControlPanelItem_Click()
    ControlPanel.NewCaption.Text = Form1.Caption
    ControlPanel.NewHeight.Value = Form1.Height
    ControlPanel.NewWidth.Value = Form1.Width
     :
End Sub
```

After loading the defaults, you want to display (show) the control panel, which you can do as follows (note that the control panel does not have to be on the screen for you to change its properties), as follows:

```
Sub ControlPanelItem_Click()
    ControlPanel.NewCaption.Text = Form1.Caption
    ControlPanel.NewHeight.Value = Form1.Height
    ControlPanel.NewWidth.Value = Form1.Width
    ControlPanel.Show
End Sub
```

The way to refer to the properties of another form is by referring to the properties' full name, including form. In addition, before starting the application, you should make the Exit item in the File menu active, which you can do with the End statement as follows:

```
Sub ExitItem_Click()
    End
End Sub
```

Now start the application and click on the Control Panel... item in the File menu. When you do, the control panel opens and displays the current defaults for the main window's caption and size. You might try changing the size to see whether the program works. If you change the text in the text box and then click on the OK button, the control panel disappears and the caption in the main window will change to match the new caption. If you use the scroll bars, you can reset the size of the window. This is really no great savings, because the main window can be resized just as easily by dragging its edges; it is still impressive to see as an example.

In fact, you should really give some indication of the new size of the main window as you manipulate the scroll bars. It is always best to give as much visual feedback in a Windows application as possible because you do not want to actually change the size of the main window while you are using the scroll bars. (If you do change the size by mistake, you can still click on the Cancel button.) A good idea here might be to draw one rectangle in the control panel to represent the screen and another to represent the main window, to show their relative sizes. You will learn how to draw rectangles in Chapter 6.

Now you will work on changing the color of the main window. The background color—the color behind the text—is kept in the BackColor property and is the color you want to manipulate. The foreground color—the color of the text itself—is kept in the ForeColor property.

Note, however, that colors in Windows are determined by three independent settings: a red setting, a green setting, and a blue setting. To take care of all three, you need three vertical scroll bars. You can create them by clicking on the vertical scroll bar tool. Position them next to the two you already have. Label the first one Red (place the label above it), the second one Green, and the third one Blue. For control names, you can call them NewRed, NewGreen, and NewBlue.

In addition, you can actually provide some direct visual feedback, indicating the color you are selecting. Doing so will introduce you to the scroll bar change event at the same time. Create a label named NewColor and place it in the space between the OK and Cancel buttons at the bottom of the control panel. Give it a fixed single border by changing its BorderStyle property (by default, labels do not have a border), as shown in figure 4.10. This is where you will display the color selected with the scroll bars. Now you will explore how to actually deal with colors in Visual Basic.

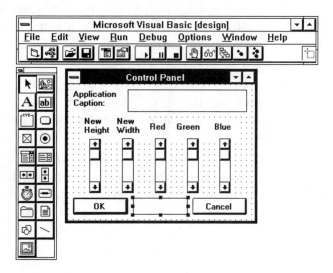

Figure 4.10. A complete control panel template.

Setting Colors in Visual Basic

As mentioned, there are three color settings in a color value under Visual Basic. Each can range from 0 to 255 and they can be put together to form a long integer. This is what you can place in properties like Form1.BackColor or NewColor.BackColor, where NewColor is the Name of the label you have added to show the color combination represented by the scroll bar values. In fact, Visual Basic provides a special function, the RGB( ) function, to combine these values. For example, you can set the background color of the NewColor label like this, where NewRed.Value, etc., are the names of the Value properties of the scroll bars:

```
NewColor.BackColor = RGB(NewRed.Value, NewGreen.Value, NewBlue.Value)
```

In other words, you just need to pass the three color values red, green, and blue, in order, to RGB( ); it will return a setting you can use in the BackColor (and ForeColor) properties. For that reason, you should give each color value scroll bar a Min property of 0 and a Max property of 255. You can also use SmallChange and LargeChange values of, say, 10 and 20. After setting these values in the scroll bars, click on the first scroll bar (which sets the amount of red in the color you are designing) to open this Sub procedure template:

```
Sub NewRed_Change()
End Sub
```

This is the event procedure called whenever NewRed.Value is changed. Although you could simply read this value when the OK button is clicked and change Form1.BackColor accordingly, you can use this event to keep track of the currently selected color and display it in the NewColor label, as follows:

```
Sub NewRed_Change()
    NewColor.BackColor = RGB(NewRed.Value, NewGreen.Value, NewBlue.Value)
End Sub
```

Now, whenever the user changes the setting of the Red scroll bar, the color in the NewColor label changes to match. In fact, you can do the same thing in the change event procedures of all three color scroll bars, as follows:

```
Sub NewRed_Change()
    NewColor.BackColor = RGB(NewRed.Value, NewGreen.Value, NewBlue.Value)
End Sub


Sub NewGreen_Change()
    NewColor.BackColor = RGB(NewRed.Value, NewGreen.Value, NewBlue.Value)
End Sub


Sub NewBlue_Change()
    NewColor.BackColor = RGB(NewRed.Value, NewGreen.Value, NewBlue.Value)
End Sub
```

Make these changes and run the program. When you do, you will be able to manipulate the color in the NewColor label simply by moving the scroll bars around, adjusting the color components in it. In addition, you need to make the color you have designed this way into the background color of the main window when the user clicks on the OK button. You can do that by adding the following line to the OK_Button_Click event:

```
Sub OKButton_Click ()
    Form1.Caption = NewCaption.Text
    Form1.Height = NewHeight.Value
    Form1.Width = NewWidth.Value
    Form1.BackColor = RGB(NewRed.Value, NewGreen.Value, NewBlue.Value)
    ControlPanel.Hide
End Sub
```

Now you can select the color of the main window and see what color you are selecting at the same time. When you click the OK button, the change is made instantly to the main window's BackColor property, turning it into whatever color you choose. That's almost it for your control panel application. At this point, most of it is functional. The last step is to load the original background color from the main window into the control panel when it first starts. To do that, you can load the original color, Form1.BackColor, into ControlPanel.NewColor.BackColor. (Because this is only a demonstration program, you are not going to dissect this color into separate settings for each color scroll bar.) Because the control panel pops up when the Control Panel... item is selected in the File menu, you can do that as follows:

```
Sub ControlPanelItem_Click()
    ControlPanel.NewCaption.Text = Form1.Caption
    ControlPanel.NewHeight.Value = Form1.Height
    ControlPanel.NewWidth.Value = Form1.Width
    ControlPanel.NewColor.BackColor = Form1.BackColor
    ControlPanel.Show
End Sub
```

That's it. You have completed the control panel application, which lets you customize your main window through the use of scroll bars. Its code (Panel.Mak on the Disk) appears in listing 4.2.

 Listing 4.2. Control Panel Application (Panel.Mak on the Disk)

```
Form Form1 — — — — — — — — — — — — — —
            Caption      =      "Form1"

Menu FileMenu
            Caption      =      "&File"

Menu ControlPanelItem
            Caption      =      "&Control Panel..."
            Shortcut     =      ^C

Menu ExitItem
            Caption      =      "E&xit"
            Shortcut     =      ^X

Form ControlPanel — — — — — — — — — — — — —
            Caption      =      "Control Panel"

TextBox NewCaption
            TabIndex     =      0

VScrollBar newHeight
            LargeChange  =      1000
            Max    =    7200
            Min    =    1440
            SmallChange  =      500
            Value  =    1440
```

```
VScrollBar NewWidth
    LargeChange   =     1000
    Left    =    1320
    Max     =    10080
    Min     =    2880
    Value   =    2880


    VScrollBar NewRed
    LargeChange   =     20
    Max     =    255
    SmallChange   =     10

VScrollBar NewGreen
    LargeChange   =     20
    Max     =    255
    SmallChange   =     10

VScrollBar NewBlue
    LargeChange   =     20
    Max     =2   55
    SmallChange   =     10

CommandButton OKButton
    Caption   =     "OK"

CommandButton CancelButton
    Caption   =     "Cancel"

Label Label1
    Caption   =     "Application Caption:"

Label Label2
    Caption   =     "New Height"

Label Label3
    Caption   =     "New Width"

Label Label4
    Caption   =     "Red"
```

continues

Listing 4.2. continued

```
Label Label5
    Caption      =      "Green"

Label Label6
    Caption      =      "Blue"

Label NewColor
    BorderStyle    =    1        'Fixed Single
    Caption    =        ""

Form1 — — — — — — — — — — — — — — — — — — — —

    Sub ControlPanelItem_Click()
    ControlPanel.NewCaption.Text = Form1.Caption
    ControlPanel.NewHeight.Value = Form1.Height
    ControlPanel.NewWidth.Value = Form1.Width
    ControlPanel.NewColor.BackColor = Form1.BackColor
    ControlPanel.Show
    End Sub

    Sub ExitItem_Click()
    End
    End Sub

ControlPanel — — — — — — — — — — — — — — — — — —

    Sub NewRed_Change()
    NewColor.BackColor = RGB(NewRed.Value, NewGreen.Value, NewBlue.Value)
    End Sub

    Sub NewGreen_Change()
    NewColor.BackColor = RGB(NewRed.Value, NewGreen.Value, NewBlue.Value)
      End Sub

    Sub NewBlue_Change()
    NewColor.BackColor = RGB(NewRed.Value, NewGreen.Value, NewBlue.Value)
    End Sub

    Sub OKButton_Click ()
    Form1.Caption = NewCaption.Text
```

```
Form1.Height = NewHeight.Value
Form1.Width = NewWidth.Value
Form1.BackColor = RGB(NewRed.Value, NewGreen.Value, NewBlue.Value)
ControlPanel.Hide
End Sub

Sub CancelButton ()
ControlPanel.Hide
End Sub
```

Scroll bars are not the only controls you find in dialog boxes. Other common controls include list boxes and combo boxes. You will take a look at them next, starting with list boxes.

Creating List Boxes

You use list boxes when you have a number of choices to present and you want to limit the choices. By contrast, a combo box is used more for suggested choices—that is, you can enter your own choice in the combo box's text box if you want to. Say, for example, that you have a list of customized Windows applications your program is capable of starting— you can present the choices in a list box. Or you might want to present the different file attribute options —plain file, read-only, hidden, etc.— when writing to a file. In general, list boxes can be useful wherever there are a number of choices to choose from. Because list boxes can have scroll bars, you can present a greater number of choices in them than you in a menu (which makes list boxes popular in dialog boxes).

As an example, you will put together a mini-database program. Databases usually sort their data records according to some key. You can do that here with a list box. Say that this database program is meant to keep track of stock inventory in a pharmacy or even in your own medicine cabinet. You might want to keep track of the following things:

Name of the product

Number of the product

Comments

For example, if you had seven bottles of aspirin, each of which had 100 tablets, the data might appear as follows:

Name of the product: "Aspirin"

Number of the product: "7"

Comments: "Sell by Thursday."

Each of these data items ("Aspirin", "7", and "Bottles of 100 each.") is called a *field* in a database. Together, they make up a *record*. To set up your application, you can add to the main window a menu with an item named Find Record.... When selected, a dialog box will open with a list box that lists the names associated with each record—for example, Aspirin, Bandages, Cold cream, and so on.:

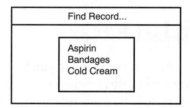

By double-clicking on one of these names, you can bring up the corresponding record—for example, the dialog box will disappear and the record's data will be placed into text boxes in the main window). One of the properties of list boxes that will help you here is the Sorted property. If True, Visual Basic keeps all the items in the list box sorted alphabetically—in other words, Visual Basic automatically sorts the products.

To design this application, start Visual Basic. Call this project Database.Mak and give the form the caption "Database." You will need three text boxes on this main form; label the text boxes Name:, Number:, and Comment:, and give them the Names NameField, NumberField, and CommentField. In fact, you can make the comment box a multiline text box so that a considerable amount of text can be stored there. Next, add a menu named File with the following items in it: Add Item, Find Item..., Save File..., Load File..., and Exit. At this point, the main window should look like the one in figure 4.11.

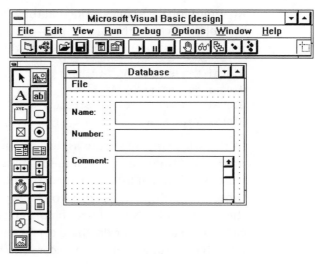

Figure 4.11. The database template window.

For the first menu choice, Add Item, use the Name AddAnItem (AddItem is a reserved word, as you are about to see); this item is available so that the user can fill the database with data. After editing the three text boxes, you can select Add Item to add this data to a new record in the database. Use the Name FindItem for the next menu choice, Find Item...; this item is the one that will open the dialog box (the dialog box will contain the list box that holds the product names of each record, sorted alphabetically). When the user double-clicks on an item in the list, the dialog box will disappear and the correct record will appear in the main window. You will learn how to add the code for the next two menu items, Save File... and Load File..., in the chapter about files. In the meantime, give them the Names SaveItem and LoadItem.

First, you will write the AddAnItem_Click( ) procedure. Click on the Add Item menu choice, opening the following Sub procedure template:

```
Sub AddAnItem_Click()
End Sub
```

When the user clicks on Add Item, he or she wants the current contents of the text boxes to be stored in the database. You can do that by setting up some global variables (note that they should be global, not form-level, variables, because the dialog box—an entirely separate form—has to reach them as well) in a module named Database.Bas, as follows:

```
Global Names(100) As String
Global Numbers(100) As String
Global Comments(100) As String
Global TotalRecords As Integer
```

In this way, you are setting aside enough space to hold records for 100 products. Also note that you are keeping track of the total number of records in a global integer named TotalRecords. Now you are free to fill those arrays with data because you have placed the data you will need in the main window's text boxes before clicking on Add Item. That is, you can store data in your database arrays this way in AddAnItem_Click( ). Note that you increment TotalRecords first, because you are adding a new record, as follows:

```
Sub AddAnItem_Click()
    TotalRecords = TotalRecords + 1
    Names(TotalRecords) = NameField.Text
    Numbers(TotalRecords) = NumberField.Text
    Comments(TotalRecords) = CommentField.Text
    :
End Sub
```

Suppose, for example, that you are about to create the first record, and the main window's text boxes hold the following data:

```
Name of the product: "Aspirin"
Number of the product: "7"
Additional space for comments: "Bottles of 100 each."
```

You would set Names(1) to "Aspirin," Numbers(1) to "7," and Comments(1) to "Bottles of 100 each." Having stored the data, you have to add the name of this product (Aspirin) to the automatically alphabetized list box so that the user can select records easily. You do that with the *AddItem* method. Note that this is a method, which means that you have to attach it to the name of the list box you want to change. For example, you can call the list box that holds all the products' names NameList, which means that you would include this line in AddAnItem_Click( ), as follows:

```
Sub AddAnItem_Click()
    TotalRecords = TotalRecords + 1
    Names(TotalRecords) = NameField.Text
    Numbers(TotalRecords) = NumberField.Text
    Comments(TotalRecords) = CommentField.Text
    Form2.NameList.AddItem NameField.Text
End Sub
```

Form2 is the name of the second form, which appears when you want to select a record. In general, you use AddItem in Visual Basic the following way:

```
form.listbox.AddItem string$ [, index]
```

The optional argument named index specifies the new entry's position in the list box—0 (at the top of the list box) is the first position, the next down is 1, and so on. Because the list box will be sorted automatically, you will not specify an index for your entries. Correspondingly, to remove an item, you can use the RemoveItem method, as follows:

```
form.listbox.RemoveItem index
```

Here, the index is not optional. You must use it to specify which item you want to remove from the list. That's it for adding an item. The next step is to find items on demand. Click on the Find Item... menu choice to bring up this template, as follows:

```
Sub FindItem_Click()
End Sub
```

The actual work of finding a record is done by the second form, Form2. You can pop that up on the screen now.

```
Sub FindItem_Click()
    Form2.Show
End Sub
```

That's it for FindItem_Click( ). Now you can design the dialog box named Form2. Create Form2 by clicking on the New Form item in Visual Basic's File menu and giving it a caption of Find Item.... Remove the Min and Max buttons and give it a fixed border by selecting the BorderStyle property. Next, create a list box by clicking on the list box tool in the toolbox (fifth tool down on the right). Give this list box the Name you have already used, NameList. Set the Sorted property to True so that the entries in it will appear in alphabetical order. Note that the Name, NameList, appears in the list box; it will be gone at run time. There are no scroll bars on this list, but they will appear automatically if the list is too long for the list box.

Now add the two normal control buttons for a dialog box—OK and Cancel (see figure 4.12), giving them the Names OKButton and CancelButton. It is a good idea to make the OK button the default—for example, set its default property to True as well. As before, it is easy to write the Cancel Button procedure—all you have to do is to hide Form2, like this:

```
Sub CancelButton_Click()
    Form2.Hide
End Sub
```

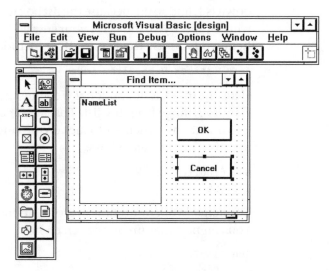

Figure 4.12. The Find Item... dialog box template.

Now you can work on the dialog box's OKButton_Click( ) procedure, as follows:

```
OKButton_Click()
End Sub
```

When the user clicks on the OK button, or double-clicks on an item in the list box, he or she has selected an item in the list box, and you should display the corresponding record. Say, for example, that this is your dialog box:

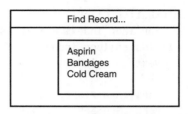

Find Record...

Aspirin
Bandages
Cold Cream

Clicking on Aspirin should fill the text boxes in the main window with the data you already have stored by using Add Item, as follows:

Name of the product: "Aspirin"

Number of the product: "7"

Additional space for comments: "Bottles of 100 each."

In general, you can determine which item is selected in a list box (one item is always selected in list boxes) by using the following list box properties:

Text   The currently selected item

List   Array of string containing all the items

ListIndex   The index of the selected item (0 based)

ListCount   Total number of items in the list

The most commonly used property is Text—the string that holds the currently selected item. However, the others are very useful too (and you might notice that Text = List(ListIndex)). In this case, you have to find the record corresponding to the selection and display it. You can find the correct record with a loop in OKButton_Click( ), as follows:

```
Sub OKButton_Click()
    For loop_index% = 1 To 100
    If Names(loop_index%) = NameList.Text Then Exit For
Next loop_index%
    :
```

Here, you are just comparing the selected product name with the product name of each record. When you find the product name you want (it must be in the list, because the list box simply displays these names), you leave the record for the loop with the Visual Basic Exit For statement. At this point, you can fill the fields on the main form correctly and hide Form2, as follows:

```
Sub OKButton_Click()
    For loop_index% = 1 To 100
  If (Names(loop_index%) = NameList.Text) Then Exit For
    Next loop_index%

    Form1.NameField.Text = Names(loop_index%)
    Form1.NumberField.Text = Numbers(loop_index%)
    Form1.CommentField.Text = Comments(loop_index%)

    Form2.Hide
End Sub
```

Note that the important events for list boxes are Click—when the user makes a selection—and DblClick, when the user makes a choice. Double-clicking on an item is the same as clicking on the OK button, so you can add the same procedure there, as follows:

```
Sub NameList_DblClick()
    For loop_index% = 1 To 100
  If (Names(loop_index%) = NameList.Text) Then Exit For
    Next loop_index%
    Form1.NameField.Text = Names(loop_index%)
    Form1.NumberField.Text = Numbers(loop_index%)
    Form1.CommentField.Text = Comments(loop_index%)
    Form2.Hide
End Sub
```

The only remaining thing to do is to make the Exit item active in the main window's menu, which you do in the usual way, with the Visual Basic End statement, as follows:

```
Sub ExitItem ()
    End
End Sub
```

The completed program appears in figure 4.13, ready to run. You use it by typing data into the text boxes in the main window. When you want to read a record back, you can select Find Item... in the File menu to pop your dialog box on the screen. When you select the item in the list box and click on the OK button, or double-click on the item in the list box, that item's records appear in the main window. The database is a success.

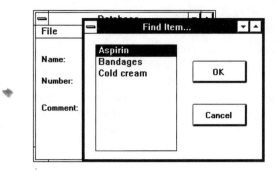

Figure 4.13. A database application.

Note, however, that you had to duplicate the same code in both NameList.DblClick( ) and OKButton_Click( )—for example, both display the selected product's records. One way to avoid this is to place this code into a module and call it from these two procedures. For example, if you create a Sub procedure which contains all this code called GetItem( ), you can change both NameList.DblClick( ) and OKButton_Click( ) to the following:

```
Sub NameList.DblClick()
     Call GetItem
End Sub


Sub OKButton_Click()
     Call GetItem
End Sub
```

That is, you use a *Call* statement to reference GetItem( ). To create a module, select the New Module item in Visual Basic's File menu. A code window opens; the code you put here can be reached from anywhere in the entire application. You can place GetItem( ) in this module very simply: just type the following code into the code window. Visual Basic takes the name of this new procedure, GetItem, from the declaration in the first line: Sub GetItem( ). Note, however, that each time you refer to a control on some form, you have to include the form's name because this code is not attached to any form. For example, note the reference to NameList, which now becomes Form2.NameList:

```
Sub GetItem()
    For loop_index% = 1 To 100
  If (Names(loop_index%) = Form2.NameList.Text) Then Exit For
    Next loop_index%

    Form1.NameField.Text = Names(loop_index%)
    Form1.NumberField.Text = Numbers(loop_index%)
    Form1.CommentField.Text = Comments(loop_index%)
    Form2.Hide
End Sub
```

The global arrays Names( ), Numbers( ), and Comments( ) are not attached to any form, of course. This module is just like any other file associated with the current project; that is, it is saved and loaded along with the others. That's it. The code for the entire database program, form by form (recall that you have not yet added any code for the Save File... or Load File... items), appears in listing 4.3 (Database.Mak on the Disk).

> **Connecting to external database systems.**
> If you are an advanced Visual Basic programmer interested in databases, the new Visual Basic Open Database Connectivity (ODBC) dynamic link libraries enable you to connect to many external database systems, such as Microsoft SQL.

Listing 4.3. Database Program (Database.Mak on the Disk)

```
Global Names(100) As String
Global Numbers(100) As String
Global Comments(100) As String
Global TotalRecords As Integer


Form1 — — — — — — — — — — — — — — — — — — — — —


Sub AddAnItem_Click ()
TotalRecords = TotalRecords + 1
Names(TotalRecords) = NameField.Text
Numbers(TotalRecords) = NumberField.Text
Comments(TotalRecords) = CommentField.Text
```

```
        Form2.NameList.AddItem NameField.Text
        End Sub

        Sub FindItem_Click ()
        Form2.Show
        End Sub

        Sub ExitItem_Click ()
        End
        End Sub

Form2  — — — — — — — — — — — — — —

        Sub OKButton_Click ()
        Call GetItem
        End Sub

        Sub NameList_DblClick ()
        Call GetItem
        End Sub

        Sub CancelButton_Click ()
        Form2.Hide
        End Sub

Module1  — — — — — — — — — — — — — — — —

        Sub GetItem ()
        For loop_index% = 1 To 100
        If (Names(loop_index%) = Form2.NameList.Text) Then Exit For
        Next loop_index%
        Form1.NameField.Text = Names(loop_index%)
        Form1.NumberField.Text = Numbers(loop_index%)
        Form1.CommentField.Text = Comments(loop_index%)

        Form2.Hide
        End Sub
```

There is one more important point here, which has to do with data organization.

Creating Your Own Data Types

The way the database program stands, you are maintaining three arrays of data:

```
Global Names(100) As String
Global Numbers(100) As String
Global Comments(100) As String
```

In fact, fields like this usually are gathered together into their own *type* (and that introduces a powerful Visual Basic concept). In general, such a type declaration appears as follows:

```
Type typename
    elementname As variabletype
    [elementname As variabletype]
    [elementname As variabletype]
    :
End Type
```

For example, you can make a Record type for your database, as follows:

```
Type Record
    Name As String * 50
    Number As String * 20
    Comment As String * 200
End Type
```

This code defines a new data type, Record, which contains the individual fields shown previously. Note that you are giving each string a definite size here—the * 50, *20, and * 200 mean that many characters. Name As String * 50 means that the string called Name will be exactly 50 characters long. You can declare an array of this type called, TheData( ), as follows:

```
Type Record
    Name As String * 50
    Number As String * 20
    Comment As String * 200
End Type

Global TheData(100) As Record
```

You can reach any one of them by using the dot (.) operator (just as you
do to reach a Visual Basic property), as follows:

```
TheData(3).Name = "Carrots"
TheData(3).Number = "287"
TheData(3).Comment = "Price too high?"
```

Now you will use this new array in your database application to combine
the three separate arrays—Names( ), Numbers( ), and Comments( )—into
one—TheData( ). After setting up the new record type, Record, and the
array of that type, TheData( ), you have to change the matching references in the program. For example, Names(TotalRecords) becomes
TheData(TotalRecords).Name. There are only two Sub procedures to
change—the procedure in which you store the data, and the procedure in
which you retrieve it. In Form1, the procedure for adding an item should
be changed from the following:

```
Sub AddAnItem_Click ()
     TotalRecords = TotalRecords + 1
     Names(TotalRecords) = NameField.Text
     Numbers(TotalRecords) = NumberField.TextComments(TotalRecords)
     Comments(TotalRecords) = CommentField.Text
     Form2.NameList.AddItem NameField.Text
End Sub
```

To the following:

```
Sub AddAnItem_Click ()
     TotalRecords = TotalRecords + 1

     TheData(TotalRecords).Name = NameField.Text
     TheData(TotalRecords).Number = NumberField.Text
     TheData(TotalRecords).Comment = CommentField.Text
     Form2.NameList.AddItem NameField.Text
End Sub
```

Here, you just change Names(TotalRecords) to TheData(TotalRecords) .Name, and so on. Also, in your module, you should change the procedure for looking up an item, GetItem( ), from the following:

```
Sub GetItem ()
      For loop_index% = 1 To 100
   If (Names(loop_index%) = Form2.NameList.Text) Then Exit For
      Next loop_index%

      Form1.NameField.Text = Names(loop_index%)
      Form1.NumberField.Text = Numbers(loop_index%)
      Form1.CommentField.Text = Comments(loop_index%)

    Form2.Hide
End Sub
```

To this:

```
Sub GetItem ()
      For loop_index% = 1 To 100
      If (Rtrim$(TheData(loop_index%).Name) =
          Rtrim$(Form2.NameList.Text)) Then Exit For
      Next loop_index%

      Form1.NameField.Text = TheData(loop_index%).Name
      Form1.NumberField.Text = TheData(loop_index%).Number
      Form1.CommentField.Text = TheData(loop_index%).Comment

      Form2.Hide
End Sub
```

Note that you are using a fixed-length string for all fields. Because Visual Basic pads such strings with spaces to the right, you had to remove those spaces with the Basic function Rtrim$( ); its counterpart for trimming spaces off the left side is Ltrim$( ). The Rtrim$( ) function simply trims any spaces off the right side of strings before comparing them to the item in the list box, as follows:

```
For loop_index% = 1 To 100
      If (Rtrim$(TheData(loop_index%).Name) =
      Rtrim$(Form2.NameList.Text)) Then Exit For
Next loop_index%
```

That's it. The revised database program, complete with its own data type— for example, Record, appears in listing 4.4 (Database.Mak on the Disk).

Listing 4.4. Revised Database Program (Database.Mak on the Disk)

```
Form Form1 — — — — — — — — — — — — — — —
          Caption      =      "Database"

TextBox NameField
     TabIndex     =     0

TextBox NumberField
     TabIndex     =     1

TextBox CommentField
     MultiLine     =     -1        'True
     ScrollBars    =     2         'Vertical
     TabIndex      =     2

Label Label1
     Caption     =     "Name:"

Label Label2
     Caption     =     "Number:"

Label Label3
     Caption     =     "Comment:"

Menu FileMenu
     Caption     =     "File"

Menu AddAnItem
     Caption     =     "&Add Item"

Menu FindItem
     Caption     =     "&Find Item..."

Menu SaveItem
     Caption     =     "&Save File..."

Menu LoadItem
     Caption     =     "&Load File..."

Menu ExitItem
     Caption     =     "E&xit"
```

continues

Listing 4.4. continued

```
Form Form2 — — — — — — — — — — — — — —
                    Caption      =      "Find Item..."

ListBox NameList
    Sorted           =           -1        'True

CommandButton OKButton
    Caption          =        "OK"

CommandButton CancelButton
    Caption          =        "Cancel"

Global — — — — — — — — — — — — — — — — — —
    Type Record
        Name As String * 50
        Number As String * 20
        Comment As String * 200
    End Type

    Global TheData(100) As Record
    Global TotalRecords As Integer

Form1 — — — — — — — — — — — — — — — — — — —

    Sub AddAnItem_Click ()
    TotalRecords = TotalRecords + 1
    TheData(TotalRecords).Name = NameField.Text
    TheData(TotalRecords).Number = NumberField.Text
    TheData(TotalRecords).Comment = CommentField.Text
    Form2.NameList.AddItem NameField.Text
    End Sub

    Sub FindItem_Click ()
    Form2.Show
    End Sub

    Sub ExitItem_Click ()
    End
    End Sub
```

```
Form2  — — — — — — — — — — — — — —

    Sub OKButton_Click ()
  Call GetItem
    End Sub

    Sub NameList_DblClick ()
  Call GetItem
    End Sub

    Sub CancelButton_Click ()
  Form2.Hide
    End Sub

Module1  — — — — — — — — — — — — — — — —

    Sub GetItem ()
  For loop_index% = 1 To 100
    If (Rtrim$(TheData(loop_index%).Name) =
        Rtrim$(Form2.NameList.Text)) Then Exit For
  Next loop_index%

  Form1.NameField.Text = TheData(loop_index%).Name
  Form1.NumberField.Text = TheData(loop_index%).Number
  Form1.CommentField.Text = TheData(loop_index%).Comment
  Form2.Hide
    End Sub
```

That's it for the database program and list boxes. Next, you look at combo boxes.

Creating Combo Boxes

The difference between combo boxes and list boxes is that combo boxes combine a list box with a text box (which is why they are called combo boxes) so that users can type their own text if they do not want to select one of the choices offered. The three styles of combo boxes appear in figure 4.14. The first, style 0, is a standard combo box, with the arrow detached from the text box. When the user clicks on the arrow, the list of items to choose from drops down. The second style, style 1, is the same, except that the list box is always displayed. In the third style, style 2, the arrow is attached; this is actually a list box (called a drop-down list box). It is the same as a normal list box (that is, users cannot edit the selections as they can in a combo box), except that the list is hidden until the user clicks on the arrow.

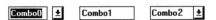

Figure 4.14. Combo Box Styles.

Because style 2 combo boxes are really list boxes, they are covered first, before you start working with straight combo boxes.

It is easy to adapt your database application to use drop-down list boxes instead of normal list boxes. All you have to do is to delete the list box named NameList on Form2 and replace it with a combo box, style 2, named NameList. To do that, click the original list box and select Cut in the Edit menu. Next, click on the combo box tool in the toolbox (next to the list box tool), select style 2, and position it correctly. As you can see from figure 4.15, using a drop-down list box enables the Find Item... dialog box to be considerably more compact. Using a drop-down list box is that easy.

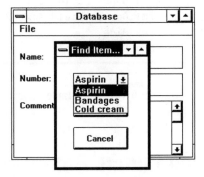

Figure 4.15. Database with a Drop Down List Box.

Now to get into combo boxes. Because you can change or edit the item in the text box which forms part of the combo box, the two important events connected with combo boxes are Click and Change (the Change event occurs when the text in the text box is changed). In addition, a simple combo box—style 1, no drop down box—recognizes the DblClick event;

the other combo box—style 0—does not. The following properties are associated with combo boxes:

Text	The currently selected item
List	Array of String containing all the items
ListIndex	The index of the selected item (0 based; -1 if the user entered text rather than selected this item)
ListCount	Total number of items in the list

In fact, the properties of a combo box are similar to the properties of a list box, with one difference—if you type the current selection instead of selecting it from the available list (an option which does not exist with list boxes), then the ListIndex property is set to -1. As for the rest of the details of combo boxes—maintaining the selected text, marking text, and so on—Visual Basic performs them for you.

To see how this works, you need to alter your database program to display its product names in a combo box instead of a list box. The advantage of this is that you can simply type the name of the product you are looking for instead of searching through what might be a long list. Unfortunately, this introduces the possibility that the selected entry might not correspond to a record at all—for example, in case the user mistypes the product name.

That is something you will have to check for when you click on the OK button. In the meantime, open the database application in Visual Basic again and select the drop-down list box you just put in. Because Visual Basic treats it as a combo box of style 2, you can change it to another type of combo box without replacing it. For this exercise, use combo box style 1, which is the same as style 0, except that the list of selected choices is always visible—for example, this is the style of the middle box in figure 4.14. Although you should rename it from NameList to NameCombo, leaving the name as NameList is more convenient because the code already refers to it that way. In fact, because this is the style that recognizes double-click events (combo box style 0 does not), you can leave the code in NewList_DblClick( ) (as well as in OKButton_Click( )) alone.

Now you have to make sure that the selection actually corresponds to one of the records. To do that, add this code in your Sub procedure GetItem( ), as follows:

```
Sub GetItem ()

    Matched = False
    For loop_index% = 1 To 100
    If (Rtrim$(TheData(loop_index%).Name) =
    Rtrim$(Form2.NameList.Text)) Then
    Matched = True
    Exit For
    End If
    Next loop_index%

    If (Matched) Then
    Form1.NameField.Text = TheData(loop_index%).Name
    Form1.NumberField.Text = TheData(loop_index%).Number
    Form1.CommentField.Text = TheData(loop_index%).Comment
    Form2.Hide
Else
MsgBox "Sorry, I cannot find that record.", 48, "Database"
End If

End Sub
```

Here, if you cannot find the record that was typed, you pop up an error message box and let the user start over. After this change, the program functions as before, except that now users can type the name of the record they are looking for as a shortcut (see figure 4.16). However, if the user enters the name of a record that does not match one of the existing records, an error box appears (see figure 4.17).

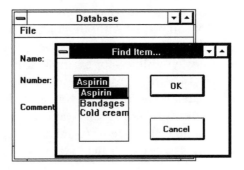

Figure 4.16. A database application.

Figure 4.17. A database application with an error box.

That's it for your database application in this chapter. Before you finish with multiple-window applications, however, you will look at another kind of program: MDI applications.

Multiple Document Interface (MDI) Programs

It is often convenient for one Windows application to manage a number of smaller windows, all of which are present on the screen at the same time. The Multiple Document Interface (MDI) gives you one way of doing that. For example, the Windows Program Manager is an MDI program— you can move the windows around in the main window, but they will not leave it. When you minimize the Program Manager, all the windows in it are wrapped up in the Program Manager icon. That is the way MDI programs work.

Creating such a program is easy. First, start Visual Basic (Form1 will appear). Next, select the New MDI Form item in Visual Basic's File menu; a form named MDIForm1 will appear (only one MDI Form is allowed per application). Now set the first form's—for example, Form1) MDIChild property to True in the properties window and run the program. The result is something like that in figure 4.18, where Form1 is confined to the larger MDIForm1.

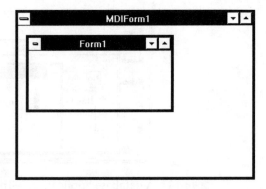

Figure 4.18. MDI Form with one internal form.

To add another form, select the New Form item in Visual Basic's File menu. When Form2 appears, set its MDIChild property to True as well. When you run the program, only the default Form1 will appear at first—for example, just like a normal Visual Basic program—but now all the action is confined to MDIForm1. To display Form2, add this code to Form1_Click( ):

```
Sub Form1_Click()
      Form2.Show
End Sub
```

In other words, you work with multiple windows in an MDI application as you normally work with multiple windows. It is that simple to use MDI. Now when you click on Form1, Form2 appears (see figure 4.19).

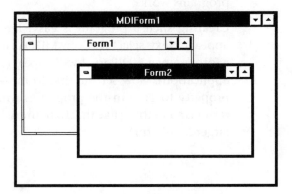

Figure 4.19. The MDI Form with two internal forms.

That's it for your MDI application—and for this chapter on dialog boxes and multiple window applications. You have covered dialog boxes and many of the controls commonly used in them. There are, however, some other types of controls that you often find in dialog boxes—directory boxes and file list boxes. You will see how they work in the next chapter, when you start working with files.

Summary

In this chapter you learned about message boxes and input boxes; then you moved on to multiple forms, to design your own dialog boxes. You also covered the typical kinds of controls found in dialog boxes: scroll bars, list boxes, and combo boxes. You also saw Visual Basic programs without any windows, how to connect dialog boxes to menu items, and how the Multiple Document Interface (MDI) works. In general, then, you are no longer restricted to a single form. You have seen how to create and use multiple-window programs in Windows. That is useful for almost anything you write—for example, almost all programs use dialog boxes), including database programs (as you have seen), word processors, file-handling programs, programs with control panels, even graphics paint programs. Using dialog boxes is a necessary skill for the Windows programmer and now it is one you are familiar with.

New Property	Description
Forecolor	Foreground (drawing) color of forms and controls; set with the RGB( ) function
LargeChange	Holds the amount the Value of a scroll bar changes when user clicks on area between scroll box and scroll arrow
List	An array of type String containing all the items in a list-oriented control
ListCount	The total number of items in the list for a list-oriented control
ListIndex	The index of the selected item (0 based) in a list-oriented control

continues

189

New Property	Description
Max	Holds maximum amount a scroll bar's Value property can be
MDIChild	Indicates whether this form is an MDI child of an MDIform; if True, this form is displayed inside the MDI form (True or False)
Min	Holds minimum amount a scroll bar's Value property can be
SmallChange	Holds the amount the Value property of a scroll bar changes when user clicks on a scroll arrow
Sorted	Indicates whether list-oriented controls should keep their lists sorted (True or False)
Value	The current value of a scroll bar control

New Event	Description
DblClick	Occurs when a form or control is double-clicked

New Method	Description
Hide	Hides a form or control
Show	Displays a form or control; use with the parameter 1—for example, Form2.Show 1—to display a modal dialog box

What About Files?

I n this chapter, you will see how to work with files in Visual Basic. The most common way to keep data around after a program ends is to store it in files. This chapter discusses this important skill as well as the following topics:

▼ Creating, opening, and closing files

▼ Reading and writing files

▼ The End of file (EOF) and Length of file (LOF) functions

▼ Sequential files

▼ Random-access files

▼ Directory list boxes

▼ File list boxes

▼ Drive list boxes

▼ The Seek statement

▼ The Get and Put statements

▼ How to handle file errors

You will also add file-handling capabilities to some of the programs you have already developed, specifically your Editor and Database programs. Most Windows programs use files of some sort, so the skills you pick up here will be important for all types of programs: graphics programs, word processors, database programs, and so on.

You may recall that your Editor program had two menu choices you never supported: Load File... and Save File.... Until now, all the data your programs have handled has been very temporary: when the application ended it was gone. Files, of course, are the most common way to store data in the PC, so they are vitally important to most computer applications.

The file-manipulation statements system in Visual Basic is very similar to the system in other Basics, so if you are familiar with Open, Close, Input$, and Seek, you already have a considerable head start. As you might expect, however, things are very different when it comes to interacting with the user. For example, the user usually picks file names to load data from or save to using dialog boxes in Windows applications (which, incidentally, is why dialog boxes were covered before files). You will see how to do that in this chapter as you set up your own file dialog boxes.

Two of these dialog boxes will be for the Save File... and Load File... items from your Editor application. In addition, you will see how to work with structured files, where the data is broken into specific records as it was in the database application in the last chapter. In fact, you will be able to modify that application in this chapter so that it can save its data to disk. With this and other topics coming up, why not get started immediately?

> **The new common dialog boxes.**
> The Visual Basic Professional Edition also supports a set of common dialog boxes for the purpose of opening and closing files. See Chapter 13 for details.

Saving Data in a File

If you want to add file support to your editor application, you might start with the Save File... item (after all, you have to create and save files before reading them back in). When you select the Save File... item, you could pop a dialog box onto the screen with a list box and two buttons: OK and Cancel. You could then type the name of the file you wanted to save your document to, and your program would create the file with that name (if necessary), and then store the document there. To put this into practice, start Visual Basic and open the Editor project. If you look at the File menu, you will see that the Save File... menu item already exists. Click on it to bring up the following template:

```
Sub SaveItem_Click ()


End Sub
```

To save the current document, you have to place the Save File... dialog box on the screen. Name that dialog box SaveForm. To display it, you need to do the following:

```
Sub SaveItem_Click ()
        SaveForm.Show
End Sub
```

Next, you put together that dialog box (still in the Editor project), naming it SaveForm, giving it a caption that reads Save File..., and saving your work as, say, SaveForm.Frm. In addition, you should add a text box to this new form, place a label above the text box with the caption Save File As... (to let the user know that a file name is expected), and add an OK button, a default property of True, and a Cancel button (see figure 5.1). Finally, because this is a dialog box, you can remove the Min and Max buttons.

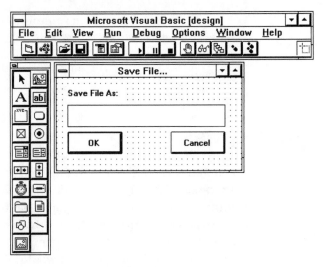

Figure 5.1. A Save File... dialog box.

The Cancel button procedure is easy, so you can do that first. If the user cancels, all you want to do is conceal the form again, so put this in CancelButton_Click( ), as follows:

```
Sub CancelButton_Click ()
     SaveForm.Hide
End Sub
```

The real work is done when the user clicks on the OK button. Click on that button now to open the OK button's click procedure, as follows:

```
Sub OKButton_Click ()


End Sub
```

When you reach this point in the program, you might suppose that the text in FilenameBox holds a file name, and that you are supposed to save the current document—that is, the string named Form1.PadText.Text—to this file. Three steps are involved in this process: opening the file (or creating it if it does not exist), writing the data to the file, and closing it. You can look at each of these steps in order as you build OKButton_Click( ); each step tells you something about the Visual Basic file system.

Opening Files in Visual Basic

To open or create a file in Visual Basic, simply use the Open statement. You have to give some consideration to the way you open or create that file, however. In particular, there are five ways to open files in Visual Basic, corresponding to the five ways you can use them. A list of the available file modes is as follows:

Sequential Input

Sequential Output

Sequential Append

Random Input/Output

Binary Input/Output

The Types of Visual Basic Files

The first three file modes are associated with sequential files. Sequential files are usually used for text files, where you write the file from beginning to end and read it the same way; that is, you do not jump around in the file. Working with sequential files is like using cassette tapes; if you want to hear something at the end of the tape, you have to pass by everything in front of it first. In the same way, if you want some of the text at the end of a file opened for sequential access, you have to read all the text that precedes it.

If sequential files are like cassette tapes, then random files are like compact discs. Unlike a cassette, you can simply move around at will on a CD without going through all the intervening tracks. You can move around in a random-access file in the same way, taking data from whatever location you want. The price you pay is that the data in a random-access file must be carefully sectioned into records so that you know exactly where the data you want is. For example, if the records you developed for your database application were all the same size, they would work perfectly in a random-access file; when you wanted the 20th record, you could simply skip over the first 19 and then start reading. Because text—such as the text you are storing in the Editor application—is not neatly sectioned into records of the same size, however, you will place the text you are about to save into a sequential file.

The third type of files are binary files; here, Visual Basic does not interpret the contents of the file at all. For example, executable (.Exe) files are binary files, and you treat them on a byte-by-byte basis in Visual Basic. To copy such a file over, you would read in every byte of the original file (the source file) and then send them to the new file (the destination or target file). Although you can set the amount of data you want to read under sequential or random access, binary files are always dealt with byte-by-byte.

Each of these three types of file access has its own set of Visual Basic statements, as you will see later in this chapter. Because that can get confusing, a collection of the most common Visual Basic file-handling statements, organized by file type, is in table 5.1.

Table 5.1. Visual Basic File Statements

Access	Common Visual Basic Statements
Sequential	Open, Line Input #, Print #, Write #, Input$, Close
Random	Type...End Type, Open, Put #, Len, Close, Get #
Binary	Open, Get #, Put #, Close, Seek, Input$

Your job here is to save the Editor's current document. You will do that by opening a sequential file (although it could actually be treated as a binary file). There are three ways to open sequential files: for Input, for Output, and for Append. You open a file for input if you want to read from it, for output if you want to write to it, and for append if you want to add to the end of it. These three modes are consistent with the idea of opening the file and then working with the data from beginning to end. For example, if you open a file for sequential output, write a string to it, and then follow it with a second string, the second string goes directly after the first, and so on for any subsequent strings, one after the other. To read them in again, you have to close the file and open it for input; then you can read the data back from beginning to end. Random files, where you can move around in the file at will, do not have any such restrictions. When you open a file for random access, it is for both input and output (but you have to section the data into records in random files). In this case, where you are writing your Editor document to disk, you will open your file for sequential output. In general, Visual Basic's file Open statement appears as follows:

```
Open fff$ [For mmm] [Access aaa] [lll] As [#] nnn% [Len = rrr%]
```

The following is a list of the arguments:

fff$	The filename (including an optional path).
mmm	Mode: can be Append, Binary, Input, Output, or Random.
aaa	Access: can be Read, Write, or Read Write.

lll	Lock: restricts access of other applications to this file to: Shared, Lock Read, Lock Write, Lock Read Write.
nnn%	Filenumber (1-255): The number you will use to refer to this file from now on.
rrr%	Record length for random files, or size of the buffer you want Visual Basic to use for sequential files.

In this case, the user wants to write to the file name now in FilenameBox.Text, so you can use the folowing Open statement to open that file.

```
Open FilenameBox.Text For Output As # 1
```

In fact, this file might not even exist—the user might want you to create it. That is actually handled automatically by the Open statement: If the file does not exist and you are trying to open it for anything but Input, Visual Basic will create the file for you. Note that when you open an existing file for output and then write to it, the original contents of the file are destroyed. (If you want to add to the end of a sequential file while retaining what was there before, open the file for Append.) Now you can start the Editor's Save File... dialog box with this line in the OK button's click procedure, as follows:

```
Sub OKButton_Click ()
        Open FilenameBox.Text For Output As # 1        'Open file
    :
End Sub
```

As in standard Basic, you will be able to refer to this file as file # 1 when you want to write to it or close it. Note, however, that there is the possibility of error when you open a file this way: the user may have specified an invalid path, for example, or misspelled the file name. To handle such errors, you can include an On Error GoTo statement, in the following way:

```
Sub OKButton_Click ()
    On Error GoTo FileError
    Open FilenameBox.Text For Output As # 1        'Open file
    :
    :
```

Now, if an error occurs, the program control will jump automatically to the label FileError where you can place a message box on the screen and execute a Resume statement to bring you back to the erroneous line so that you can try again.

```
Sub OKButton_Click ()
    On Error GoTo FileError
    Open FilenameBox.Text For Output As # 1        'Open file
  :
  :

    Exit Sub

FileError:
    MsgBox "File Error", 48, "Editor"    'MsgBox for file error.
    Resume
End Sub
```

How "untrapped" errors are handled.

If you had not placed this statement in your code, you would not have caught these "trappable" errors. Visual Basic notifies the user of trappable errors directly with a message box, which is undesirable in most applications.

More about errors.

The chapter on error-handling and debugging goes into more depth about the specific kinds of errors that can occur in this and other situations. That chapter tells you a great deal more about the On Error GoTo and Resume statements.

In other words, if the file name was legal, and the corresponding file can be opened or created, you do so. If there was a problem, you indicate that fact and let the user change the file specification for another attempt. At this point, then, the file is open; the next step is to write your document to it.

Writing to Files in Visual Basic

The usual way to write to a sequential file is by using either the Print # or Write # statements, as follows:

```
Print # nnn%, expressionlist
Write # nnn%, expressionlist
```

Here, nnn% is the file number (1, in this example), and expressionlist is a list of the variables (including strings) you want to write to the file. The two statements, Print # and Write #, are different; Write # inserts commas between the separate items in the expressionlist as it writes them to the file, places quotation marks around strings, and inserts a new (blank) line at the end of the file. Because you do not want any of these added characters, you will use Print # instead. In fact, because you only want to send a single string—Form1.PadText.Text—to the file, your Print # statement should appear as follows:

```
Sub OKButton_Click ()
      On Error GoTo FileError
      Open FilenameBox.Text For Output As # 1     'Open file
      Print # 1, Form1.PadText.Text                'Write document
      :
      :
      Exit Sub


FileError:
      MsgBox "File Error", 48, "Editor"    'MsgBox for file error.
      Resume
End Sub
```

That's all there is to writing the text into the file. Closing the file is not much harder; use the Close statement in the following way:

```
Sub OKButton_Click ()
      On Error GoTo FileError
      Open FilenameBox.Text For Output As # 1    'Open file
      Print # 1, Form1.PadText.Text          'Write document
      Close # 1        'Close file
      :
      Exit Sub


FileError:
      MsgBox "File Error", 48, "Editor"    'MsgBox for file error.
End Sub
```

Close # 1 closes file number 1, the file you are working on. After closing the file, exit the Sub procedure with an Exit Sub statement. At this point, the file has been successfully written to disk—or if not, you have alerted the user to that fact. (You would then jump to the FileError label and pop your message box on the screen as before.)

> **Closing all the files at once.**
> If you use the Close statement without a file number, Visual Basic closes all the open files in your application.

If the file handling has gone smoothly, the final step is to hide the Save File... dialog box—for example, SaveForm—in the following way:

```
Sub OKButton_Click ()
     On Error GoTo FileError
     Open FilenameBox.Text For Output As # 1     'Open file
     Print # 1, Form1.PadText.Text            'Write document
     Close # 1        'Close file
     SaveForm.Hide
     Exit Sub


FileError:
     MsgBox "File Error", 48, "Editor"     'MsgBox for file error.
     Resume
End Sub
```

To see this in action, make the preceding changes and then try typing some lines of text into the Editor and saving them, as shown in figure 5.2. When you do, you will find that the text is indeed saved to disk in the file you choose.

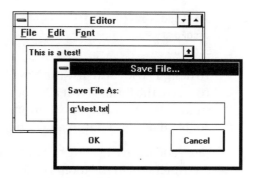

Figure 5.2. Saving a file with the Editor application.

Note that the text in the file is stored as one long string without carriage returns (unless they were present in the original document) because the main text box stores it that way. That's it for your Save File... item. You have been able to write a sequential text file to disk; you have polished your Editor application. The next step is to read files back in to the Editor's Load File... item. You will look into that process next.

Using the Visual Basic File Controls

The first step in reading the contents of a file is to get the name of that file. However, that is not just a simple matter of asking the user to type the name in a text box. You have to be able to search the disk (like other, similiar Windows applications) and let the user select from what is already there. Visual Basic provides three special controls for doing exactly that: disk list boxes, directory list boxes, and file list boxes.

The tools for creating these file controls are near the bottom of the Visual Basic toolbox. These controls will do much of the work for you. The toolbox will search the disks and directories automatically, and you will be able to work with various properties associated with them.

You start this process by designing a dialog box for the Load File... option, which you can call LoadForm and save as Loadform.Frm. First, connect it to the Load File... menu item by clicking on that item in the Editor's File menu, as follows:

```
Sub LoadItem_(Click)
End Sub
```

To display the Load File... dialog box (LoadForm), you can simply show it in the following way:

```
Sub LoadItem_(Click)
LoadForm.Show
End Sub
```

To design LoadForm, use the New Form item in Visual Basic's File menu. To create the form, give it a Name of LoadForm, a caption of Load File..., remove the Min and Max buttons, change the BorderStyle property to double fixed, and put in an OK button and a Cancel button.

Next, add a drive list box by double-clicking on the drive list tool next to the Timer tool in the toolbox. Note that the drive list box is a drop-down list box, which will save you some space. You will also need a directory list box and a file list box, so double-click on those tools too (the tools at the very bottom of the toolbox), and arrange them as you want them in the dialog box. See figure 5.3 for an idea (notice that all three list boxes are already active, showing the current drive, directory, and file list, respectively).

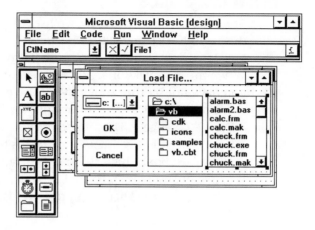

Figure 5.3. The Load File... dialog box template.

The user will be able to load any existing file this way, through the combination of the drive, directory, and file list boxes. He or she can use the drive list box to specify the drive, the directory list box to specify the directory in that drive, and the file list box to indicate the actual file to open. That file can be opened in two ways: by double-clicking on the file name in the file list box, or by selecting (highlighting) it in the file list box and then clicking on the OK button.

As usual, making the Cancel button active is easy; you can just hide the dialog box when this button is clicked, as follows:

```
Sub CancelButton_Click()
        LoadForm.Hide
End Sub
```

Now turn to the file controls. At this point, the three list boxes—drive, directory, and file—are not communicating with each other; that is, they are just showing independent information for the current directory on disk. If you were to run this program and change the disk in the disk box list, the other two boxes would not respond to the change. To get them to communicate, you have to know a little more about what the important events are for each of them. That is what you look into next.

Drive List Boxes

The drive list box is a drop-down list box (refer to figure 5.3). The current drive is indicated in it; when the user clicks on the attached arrow, the list box drops down, showing what other drives are available to choose from. When the user picks one, a Change event occurs in the list box. Because you have not set the name of your drive list box, it still has the default name of Drive1 (the default for drive list boxes), so the event procedure is Drive1_Change( ). The property of your Drive1 box that holds the drive is simply Drive1.Drive. Your next task is to pass this new drive on to the directory list box, which still has its default name of Dir1 (as is standard for directory list boxes). To do that, you just need to pass the Drive1.Drive property on to the Dir1.Path property, as follows:

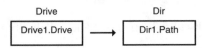

You can do that by clicking on the drive list box, which brings up the Drive1_Change procedure, as follows:

```
Sub Drive1_Change ()


End Sub
```

Just assign the Drive property of Drive1 to the Path property of Dir1, in the following way:

```
Sub Drive1_Change ()
      Dir1.Path = Drive1.Drive
End Sub
```

That's all it takes to connect the drive and directory boxes together. In fact, you can run the program at this point. When you do, you can click on the Load File... item of the Editor's File menu. The dialog box you have been designing, LoadForm, appears, displaying the current drive, directory, and the files in that directory. If you click on the drive box, the drop-down list of all drives in the system appears. Clicking on one of those changes you to that drive, causing a ripple through to the directory list box, which also changes to list the directories on that new disk. The next step in your program now is to connect the directory list box with the file list box, so that when the directory is changed, the files displayed will be the files in that directory.

Directory List Boxes

The directory list box displays the directories available on a certain drive. It is a simple list box—that is, it is always displayed, not a drop-down list box. The working drive is displayed in the top line, with that drive's directories below it. If there are more directories than you have allowed space for, a vertical scroll bar appears on the right side of the box. The current directory appears as a shaded open folder; its subdirectories appear as nonshaded closed folders, just below it (refer to figure 5.3). When the user changes the directory by clicking on a new directory, a Dir1_Change event occurs and the new path is placed in Dir1.Path. The way you have set things up, when the user changes drives, Drive1.Drive is loaded into Dir1.Path, which also generates a Dir1_Change event. In other words, the only event you need to be concerned about here is Dir1_Change, which now handles both drive and directory changes.

When such an event occurs, you need to communicate the news to the file list box, which you can do by passing on the Dir1.Path property to the Path property of the file list box. Because the file list box is still named File1 (the default for file list boxes), you can do that in the following way:

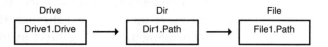

To do this in code, click on the directory list box to bring up this Sub procedure template in the code window, as follows:

```
Sub Dir1_Change ()


End Sub
```

Your goal here is to ripple any changes in the Dir1.Path property down to File1.Path, and you can do that in the following way:

```
Sub Dir1_Change ()
      File1.Path = Dir1.Path
End Sub
```

This way, every time a change occurs in the working directory—or the working drive—the file list box will know about it. If you make this change and then start the program, you will find that the list boxes are all connected together. For example, when you click on the drive list box to change the drive, the change is automatically communicated to the directory list box, which changes to display the new set of directories. That change in turn is also communicated to the file list box, which then displays the files in the new working directory.

On the other hand, if you change the working directory in the directory list box, that change is also communicated to the file list box, which then displays the files in the new directory. In other words, the important events here are Drive1_Change and Dir1_Change, and the important properties to be transferred are Drive1.Drive —> Dir1.Path and Dir1.Path —> File1.Path. The way you actually read the filename that the user wants to load will be from the FileName property of File1— File1.FileName—in the following way:

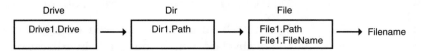

You might note also that, although you can select a new drive with a single click, it takes two clicks to select a new directory in the directory list box. This difference has to do with the difference between drop-down and straight list boxes. You need two clicks in the directory list box so that users can move up and down through the list, using the arrow keys, without changing the working directory to each highlighted entry along the way; that is, the change is postponed until they reach the directory they want.

Your next task is to integrate the file list box into the program; when the user double-clicks on a file's name, you should open that file and load it into the Editor. Next, you will look at file list boxes.

File List Boxes

The file list box shows the files in the current working directory. Like the directory list box, it is a simple list box, with its list always displayed; if the list is too long for the box, a vertical scroll bar appears. The files shown in the list box correspond to two properties—Path and Pattern. The Path property holds the path name of the directory whose files you want to display; the Pattern property holds the file specification, such as "*.Exe" (the default pattern is "*.*").

Although you are not going to do it in this demonstration program, you can include a text box to get a file specification from the user, transferring the appropriate text from the text box to the Pattern property of a file list box. Try something like this: File1.Pattern = Text1.Text. (Note that you might have to separate the pattern string from a longer string if the user specifies both path and pattern in the same text box—for example, "C:\TheData\Thesis.Phd.") A line of code like this can be put into the text box's Change event procedure.

File list boxes can respond to click or double-click events. In particular, because it is normal to let the user select a file from a file list box and close the current dialog box by double-clicking on a file's name, you should add code to the File1_DblClick( ) procedure. Note that this is the same as selecting a file and then clicking on the OK button, so you should write one procedure that can be used by both events. You did that before by placing a procedure in a code module and then calling that general procedure from two event procedures. You could do that again here. However, there is another way of doing the same thing, which you might try here. First, click on the file list box and select the File1_DblClick ( ) Sub procedure in the following code window, as follows:

```
Sub File1_DblClick ()

End Sub
```

You want to make this the same as the OKButton_Click ( ) procedure, but because that is also a procedure, you can simply call it, in the following way:

```
Sub File1_DblClick ()
    OKButton_Click
End Sub
```

(Note that if OKButton were part of a control array, you would have to pass an index, like this: OKButton(3).) That's all there is to it; now you will write OKButton_Click ( ), which is where all the action is going to be. Click on the OKButton to bring up this Sub procedure template in the code window, as follows:

```
Sub OKButton_Click ()

End Sub
```

At this point, the user is trying to open a file—the correct drive is in Drive1.Drive and the correct path is Dir1.Path. Now you need the actual file name from the file list box. As mentioned earlier, the current selected file name is kept in the file list box's FileName property, so you have the file's complete specification. You are ready to open the file.

> **Drive, directory, and file controls are still lists.**
> Because the drive, directory, and file list boxes are still list boxes, you can use their List, ListCount, and ListIndex properties as well.

> **Setting drive, directory, and file at the same time.**
> Your program can change the FileName property of a file list box to set the drive, path, and pattern of the files displayed in the file list box all at once.

One way of opening the required file is to actually change to the new drive (Drive1.Drive) with the Basic ChDrive statement, change to the new path with (Dir1.Path) with the Basic ChDir statement, and then open the file itself (File1.FileName). There is no need to change the default drive and directory at operating system level, however; instead, you can assemble the complete file specification yourself.

What if a program requires support files?
Changing the drive and directory like this is useful if you are about to run a program in that directory (with the Shell statement, for example). The program itself will search for some supporting files (like .Dll or .Dat files) it might need.

The Path property of the directory list box, Dir1.Path, usually represents a complete path, including the drive letter—for example, "C:\vb2\icons\arrows". You can add that to your file name, File1.FileName, if you add a backslash after the path—using Basic's standard method of joining strings together with a + sign—as follows:

```
Filename$ = Dir1.Path + "\" + File1.FileName
```

Here, Filename$ is a local variable you can use in your OKButton_Click( ) procedure. However, this is not quite good enough; if you happen to be in the root directory of a drive, such as d:\, then Dir1.Path would be "d:\"; if the current file were Novel.Txt, then Filename$—equal to Dir1.Path + "\" + File1.FileName—would be "d:\\Novel.Txt." In other words, you would have one backslash too many. To avoid this, check the last character of Dir1.Path; if it is already a backslash, you do not have to add one yourself, as follows:

```
If (Right$(Dir1.Path, 1) = "\") Then
     Filename$ = Dir1.Path + File1.FileName
Else
     Filename$ = Dir1.Path + "\" + File1.FileName
End If
```

Now Filename$ holds the complete file specification of the file you are supposed to open, and you can open it with an Open statement. Because you are using sequential file access, and you want to read the file, you can open it for Input in the following way:

```
If (Right$(Dir1.Path, 1) = "\") Then
     Filename$ = Dir1.Path + File1.FileName
Else
     Filename$ = Dir1.Path + "\" + File1.FileName
End If
Open Filename$ For Input As # 1
```

Once again, there is the possibility of errors here (for example, the disk with the file might have been removed inadvertently), so you should put in some error-handling code. That might appear as follows in the OKButton_Click( ) Sub procedure:

```
Sub OKButton_Click ()
        On Error GoTo FileError
        :
        Exit Sub


FileError:
        MsgBox "File Error", 48, "Editor"    'MsgBox for file error.
        Resume
End Sub
```

If there were any file errors, you simply display a message box, allowing the user to try again after the problem has been fixed. Now you can add your file opening statements, as follows:

```
Sub OKButton_Click ()
        On Error GoTo FileError
  If (Right$(Dir1.Path, 1) = "\") Then
        Filename$ = Dir1.Path + File1.FileName
  Else
        Filename$ = Dir1.Path + "\" + File1.FileName
  End If
        Open Filename$ For Input As # 1
         :
  Exit Sub


FileError:
        MsgBox "File Error", 48, "Editor"    'MsgBox for file error
        Resume
End Sub
```

At this point, you no longer need to use the file controls; the file has been selected and opened. The next step is to read in the data.

Reading from Files in Visual Basic

The standard ways to read a sequential file in Visual Basic are Input #, Line Input #, and Input$ (refer to table 5.1). You should use them in the following way:

```
Input # nnn%, expressionlist
Line Input # nnn%, stringvariable
Input$ (bbb%, [#] nnn%)
```

Here, nnn% is a file number (1, for this exercise), bbb% is the number of bytes to read, stringvariable is the name of a string variable to place data into, and expressionlist is a list of expressions the data will be placed into.

For example, if you used Input # to fill Form1.PadText.Text, it might look like this: Input # 1 Form1.PadText.Text. The problem with Input #, however, is that it expects the items in the file to be separated by commas, spaces, or the ends of lines—for example, a carriage return. For numbers, this means that when Input # encounters the first comma, space, or end of line, it assumes that the current number is finished. For strings, Input # terminates the string when it reaches a comma or end of line. This is unacceptable here, because the text of the document you are reading in may contain many commas. In fact, the user may have put carriage returns in the document deliberately (although they are not required, because the Editor's multiline text box has automatic word wrap) or may be trying to read in another application's document that has carriage returns in it.

Similarly, the Line Input # function reads strings from files until it encounters a carriage return, when it quits. That means that you would have to read in each line of the file (if it is divided into lines) separately. One way to do that would be as follows:

```
Do Until EOF(1)
      Line Input # 1, Dummy$
      Form1.PadText.Text = Form1.PadText.Text + Dummy$ + Chr$(13) +Chr$(10)
Loop
```

Here, you are using several capabilities of Visual Basic that you have not used before, including the Do Until loop, EOF( ), and Chr$( ). These all function as in standard Basic. The Do Until loop has the following general form:

```
Do Until condition
      [statements]
Loop
```

Any statements in this loop are executed repeatedly until condition becomes true, at which point execution stops. (Note that if the condition is true at the beginning, the statements in the body of the loop are not even executed once.) In the example, you are using the EOF( ) function to make up the condition for your loop. This function takes a file number as its argument (for you, that would be EOF(1)), and returns a value of True when you reach the end of the file. In the preceding loop, then, you keep reading lines from the file until you reach the end of that file. In addition, each time you read a line, you add carriage return and line feed characters to the end of the line, in the following way:

```
Do Until EOF(1)
    Line Input # 1, Dummy$
    Form1.PadText.Text = Form1.PadText.Text + Dummy$ + Chr$(13) +Chr$(10)
Loop
```

Here, you are using the Chr$( ) function, which returns the ANSI character corresponding to the ANSI code passed to it. For example, Chr$(13) returns a carriage return. The reason you have to add a carriage-return-line-feed pair at the end of each line is that Line Input # treats these two characters purely as delimiters between strings, and deletes them. Because they are actually part of the file, however, you can simply put them back.

A better option than either Input # or Line Input # is the Input$ function, which is specially made to read strings and which does not supress carriage returns of line feeds. To use this function, however, you have to indicate the exact number of bytes you want to read; when you do, Input$ returns a string (which you can assign to Form1.PadText.Text). The number of bytes you want to read is simply the length of the file in bytes; you can use another file function, LOF( ), to get that for you. Like EOF( ), LOF( ) takes a file number as an argument. LOF( ), however, returns the length of the indicated file in bytes (the file must be open for LOF( ) to work), so you can read in the whole thing like this, with the Input$( ) statement.

```
Form1.PadText.Text = Input$(LOF(1), # 1)
```

> **Limitations of Input$( ).**
> The Input$( ) function is limited to reading files of 32,767 bytes if you open the file for sequential or binary access. However, if you want to use longer files, you can simply check the length of the file, LOF( ), and then read from the file several times in succession until you get all the data you need.

In fact, because you specify the number of bytes to read, you can also use this statement to read data from binary files. You can add your Input$ statement to OKButton_Click( ) this way, placing the string that is read in—for example, the entire contents of the file—directly into the Editor's text box (Form1.PadText.Text), as follows:

```
Sub OKButton_Click ()
    On Error GoTo FileError
    If (Right$(Dir1.Path, 1) = "\") Then
Filename$ = Dir1.Path + File1.FileName
    Else
Filename$ = Dir1.Path + "\" + File1.FileName
    End If
    Open Filename$ For Input As # 1
    Form1.PadText.Text = Input$(LOF(1), # 1)


    Exit Sub


FileError:
    MsgBox "File Error", 48, "Editor"    'MsgBox for file error.
    Resume
End Sub
```

All that remains now is to close the file and, of course, to hide the dialog box (LoadForm) at the same time. You can do that like this, ending OKButton_Click( ), as follows:

```
Sub OKButton_Click ()
    On Error GoTo FileError

    If (Right$(Dir1.Path, 1) = "\") Then'Get file name
        Filename$ = Dir1.Path + File1.FileName
    Else
        Filename$ = Dir1.Path + "\" + File1.FileName
    End If

    Open Filename$ For Input As # 1     'Open file
    Form1.PadText.Text = Input$(LOF(1), # 1)     'Read file in

    Close # 1    'Close file
    LoadForm.Hide           'Hide dialog box
```

```
        Exit Sub

FileError:
        MsgBox "File Error", 48, "Editor"    'MsgBox for file error.
        Resume
End Sub
```

Now the Load File... dialog box is complete. To use it, simply start the program and select the Load File... item in the File menu. The Load File... dialog box opens, as shown in figure 5.4. As you can see, the file list box presents the file names in alphabetical order. To open one of them, just double-click on it or select it and click on the OK button. When you do, the OKButton_Click( ) procedure is executed, the file is opened and read into the Editor. At that point, you can edit it and save it to the disk again with the Save File... option.

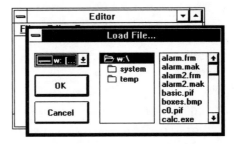

Figure 5.4. Editor with the Load File... dialog box.

That's the end of the entire Editor application; you have made all the parts operational. All the code, form by form, appears in listing 5.1 (and as Editor.Mak on the Disk).

Listing 5.1. Editor Application's Code (Editor.Mak on the Disk)

```
Form Form1
        Caption =    "Editor"


TextBox PadText
        MultiLine       =    -1   'True
        ScrollBars      =    2    'Vertical
        TabIndex=       0
```

```
Menu FileItem
        Caption =    "&File"

Menu LoadItem
        Caption =    "&Load File..."
        Shortcut=    ^L

Menu SaveItem
        Caption =    "&Save File..."
        Shortcut=    ^S

Menu Separator

Menu ExitItem
        Caption =    "E&xit"
        Shortcut=    ^X

Menu EditMenu
        Caption =    "&Edit"

Menu CutItem
        Caption =    "&Cut"
        Enabled =    0    'False
        Shortcut=    ^C

Menu PasteItem
        Caption =    "&Paste"
        Enabled =    0    'False
        Shortcut=    ^P

Menu ClearItem
        Caption =    "Clear &All"
        Enabled =    0    'False
        Shortcut=    ^A

Menu FontMenu
        Caption =    "F&ont"

Menu FFF
        Caption =    "Courier"
        Index   =    0
```

continues

Listing 5.1. continued

```
Menu FFF
     Caption =   "Helv"
     Checked =   -1   'True
     Index   =   1

Menu FFF
     Caption =   "Roman"
     Index   =   2

Menu FFF
     Caption =   "Modern"
     Index   =   3

Menu FFF
     Caption =   "Script"
     Index   =   4

Menu FFF
     Caption =   "Symbol"
     Index   =   5

Menu FFF
     Caption =   "System"
     Index   =   6

Menu FFF
     Caption =   "Terminal"
     Index   =   7

Form LoadForm ------------------------------------------
     BorderStyle    =   3   'Fixed Double
     Caption =   "Load File..."

DriveListBox Drive1
     TabIndex=   1

DirListBox Dir1
     TabIndex=   4
```

```
FileListBox File1
      TabIndex=   3

CommandButton OKButton
      Caption =   "OK"
Default =   -1  'True
      TabIndex=   0

CommandButton CancelButton
      Caption =   "Cancel"

Form SaveForm - - - - - - - - - - - - - - - - - - - - - - - - - - - - - - - - - - - - - -
      BorderStyle    =   3  'Fixed Double
      Caption =   "Save File..."

TextBox FilenameBox
      TabIndex=   0

CommandButton OKButton
      Caption =   "OK"
      Default =   -1  'True

CommandButton CancelButton
      Caption =   "Cancel"

Label Label1
      Caption =   "Save File As:"

Form1 - - - - - - - - - - - - - - - - - - - - - - - - - - - - - - - - - -
      Sub Command1_Click ()
      PadText.SelText = CutText
      PadText.SetFocus
      End Sub

      Sub PadText_Change ()
      CutItem.Enabled = True
      ClearItem.Enabled = True
      End Sub
```

continues

Listing 5.1. continued

```
Sub CutItem_Click ()
    CutText = PadText.SelText
    PadText.SelText = ""
    PasteItem.Enabled = True
    PadText.SetFocus
End Sub

Sub ExitItem_Click ()
    End
End Sub

Sub ClearItem_Click ()
PadText.Text = ""
PadText.SetFocus
End Sub

Sub PasteItem_Click ()
PadText.SelText = CutText
End Sub

Sub FFF_Click (Index As Integer)
Select Case Index
  Case 0
      PadText.FontName = "Courier"
  Case 1
      PadText.FontName = "Helv"
  Case 2
      PadText.FontName = "Roman"
  Case 3
      PadText.FontName = "Modern"
  Case 4
      PadText.FontName = "Script"
  Case 5
      PadText.FontName = "Symbol"
  Case 6
      PadText.FontName = "System"
  Case 7
      PadText.FontName = "Terminal"
End Select
```

```
    For loop_index = 0 To 7
        FFF(loop_index).Checked = False
    Next loop_index

        FFF(Index).Checked = True
    End Sub

    Sub SaveItem_Click ()
SaveForm.Show
    End Sub

    Sub LoadItem_Click ()
LoadForm.Show
    End Sub
```

SaveForm ------------------------------------

```
    Sub CancelButton_Click ()
SaveForm.Hide
    End Sub

    Sub OKButton_Click ()
On Error GoTo FileError
Open FileNameBox.Text For Output As #1
Print #1, Form1.PadText.Text
Close #1
SaveForm.Hide
    Exit Sub

    FileError:
MsgBox "File Error", 48, "Editor"
Resume
    End Sub
```

LoadForm ------------------------------------

```
    Sub CancelButton_Click ()
LoadForm.Hide
    End Sub
```

continues

Listing 5.1. continued

```
   Sub Drive1_Change ()
Dir1.Path = Drive1.Drive
   End Sub

   Sub Dir1_Change ()
File1.Path = Dir1.Path
   End Sub

   Sub OKButton_Click ()
On Error GoTo FileError
If (Right$(Dir1.Path, 1) = "\") Then
   Filename$ = Dir1.Path + File1.Filename
Else
   Filename$ = Dir1.Path + "\" + File1.Filename
End If
Open Filename$ For Input As #1
Form1.PadText.Text = Input$(LOF(1), #1)
Close #1
LoadForm.Hide
   Exit Sub

   FileError:
MsgBox "File Error" + Str$(Err), 48, "Editor"
Resume
   End Sub

   Sub File1_DblClick ()
OKButton_Click
   End Sub
```

At this point, you have opened sequential files for Input and for Output. And, as mentioned earlier, if you want to add to the end of a sequential file, you can open it for Append. In that case, everything you write to the file goes at the end of the contents already in the file.

That's it for sequential files. Now you are going to move on to the next type: random files.

Using Random Files in Visual Basic

You are ready to move past sequential files to random-access files. These kinds of files usually break their data up into records, all of which have the same format but (usually) different data. As you may remember, in the last chapter you set up the data in your database program in exactly those kinds of records, in the following way:

```
Type Record
     Name As String * 50
     Number As String * 20
     Comment As String * 200
End Type

Global TheData(100) As Record
```

In other words, each record, TheData(n), appears in the following way:

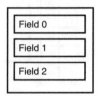

You can make well-organized files from such records, in the following way:

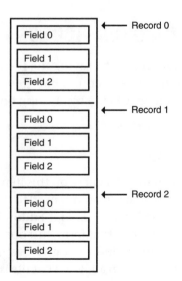

As you may recall, the database application had five items in its menu (see figure 5.5)—Add Item (which added the current item to the database), Find Item... (which opened the Find Item... dialog box), Save File..., Load File..., and Exit. Everything works in this menu except the two file items, which you will complete now, because the database application is exactly where you should use random-access files.

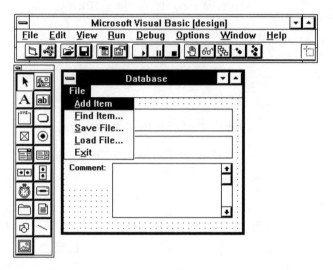

Figure 5.5. A Database application with the menu open.

Writing Random-Access Files

You can start by saving the file after the user selects the Save File... item in the File menu. That item's Name is SaveItem. You can open SaveItem_Click( ) by clicking on the item in the menu, as follows:

```
Sub SaveItem_Click ()

End Sub
```

When the user clicks on this item, he or she wants to save the database in a particular file, so you need to pop up a dialog box much like the one you designed earlier for your Editor. In fact, you can use the same dialog box here. To load that form, just open Visual Basic's File menu, select the Add File... item, and then give the name of the Save File... form (you used Saveform.Frm above). That file is loaded automatically—in this way, you can swap forms like dialog boxes between projects, saving you a great deal of design time and making your applications more uniform. Now you can pop that dialog box onto the screen this way in SaveItem_Click( ), as follows:

```
Sub SaveItem_Click ()
        SaveForm.Show
End Sub
```

Next, you have to make some changes to SaveForm's code, because it is set up to store sequential files. Just switch to that form, using the project window, and click on the main Sub procedure, OKButton_Click( ), which currently appears as follows:

```
Sub OKButton_Click ()
        On Error GoTo FileError
        Open FilenameBox.Text For Output As # 1        'Open file
        Print # 1, Form1.PadText.Text        'Write document
        Close # 1        'Close file
        SaveForm.Hide
        Exit Sub


FileError:
        MsgBox "File Error", 48, "Editor"        'MsgBox for file error.
        Resume
End Sub
```

Because you are using a random file of records this time, not a sequential file of text, you open the file as Random.

```
Sub OKButton_Click ()
        On Error GoTo FileError
        Open FilenameBox.Text For Random As # 1 Len = Len(TheData(1))
        Print # 1, Form1.PadText.Text                        'Write document
        Close # 1                        'Close file
        SaveForm.Hide
        Exit Sub
FileError:
        MsgBox "File Error", 48, "Editor"        'MsgBox for file error.
        Resume
End Sub
```

Here, you are indicating that the record length you will be using is Len(TheData(1)), which returns the length (in bytes) of your record size. Next, you want to write the entire array of records, TheData( ), out to that file, so you should look into the options for writing random-access files.

The most common I/O statements for both binary and random-access files are Get # and Put #; these statements can get or put records from or to a file. In this case, you will use Put #, whose syntax is as follows:

```
Put [#] nnn% , [rrr%], vvv%
```

Here, nnn% is a file number, rrr% is the record number you want to put into the file, and vvv% is the variable you want to put there. If you do not specify a record number, Visual Basic simply places one record after the last into the file. The total number of records is stored in the global integer TotalRecords, so you can write that many records out, as follows (note that no records are written if TotalRecords is 0):

```
Sub OKButton_Click ()
    On Error GoTo FileError
    Open FilenameBox.Text For Random As # 1 Len = Len(TheData(1))
  For loop_index = 1 To TotalRecords
    Put # 1, , TheData(loop_index)
    Next loop_index
            Close # 1                              'Close file
    SaveForm.Hide
Exit Sub

FileError:
    MsgBox "File Error", 48, "Database"    'MsgBox for file error.
    Resume
End Sub
```

That's it; now you can use the database's Save File... option (see figure 5.6).

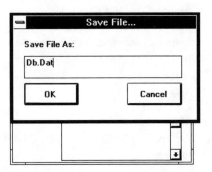

Figure 5.6. The Database application's Save File... box.

At this point, the file is written to disk. (Note that the error message box in the FileError section of the code was changed also; its title was changed to "Database" instead of "Editor.") Had you wanted to, you could have written any given record instead of all of them by specifying a particular record number, in the following way:

```
Put # 1, 5, TheData(23)
```

This writes record 5 in the file, filling it with the record TheData(23). In this way, random access is truly random as you have access to all records in the file. In other words, you can move around in the file at will, writing records in the order you want them. This works in a similiar way with Get #, as you will see next, when you read the file of records back in.

Reading Random Access Files

You copied the Save File... dialog box from the Editor application to your database, and you can copy the Load File... dialog box as well. Once again, select the Add File... item in Visual Basic's File menu, and then add the .Frm file containing the Load File... dialog box (you named it Loadform.Frm above). Next, make the Load File... item in the Database's File menu active in the following way:

```
Sub LoadItem_Click()
        LoadForm.Show
End Sub
```

Now click on the OK button in that new form, LoadForm, to bring up the important procedure there—OKButton_Click( )—which currently appears as follows:

```
Sub OKButton_Click ()
    On Error GoTo FileError

    If (Right$(Dir1.Path, 1) = "\") Then'Get file name
   Filename$ = Dir1.Path + File1.FileName
    Else
   Filename$ = Dir1.Path + "\" + File1.FileName
    End If

    Open Filename$ For Input As # 1     'Open file
    Form1.PadText.Text = Input$(LOF(1), # 1)    'Read file in
```

```
        Close # 1    'Close file
        LoadForm.Hide          'Hide dialog box

        Exit Sub

FileError:
        MsgBox "File Error", 48, "Editor"    'MsgBox for file error.
        Resume
End Sub
```

Once again, you open the file for random access in the following way:

```
Sub OKButton_Click ()
        On Error GoTo FileError
        :
        :
         Open Filename$ For Random As # 1 Len       = Len(TheData(1))
        Form1.PadText.Text = Input$(LOF(1), # 1) 'Read file in

        Close # 1    'Close file
        LoadForm.Hide          'Hide dialog box

        Exit Sub

FileError:
        MsgBox "File Error", 48, "Editor"    'MsgBox for file error.
        Resume
End Sub
```

Now you have to get records from the file by using Get #, which you use to read from random and binary files, and whose syntax is as follows:

```
Get [#] nnn% , [rrr%], vvv%
```

As with Put #, nnn% is a file number, rrr% is the record number you want to get from the file, and vvv% is the variable you want to place the data in. If you do not specify a record number, Visual Basic simply gets the next record from the current position in the file. Your first job here is to find out how many records are in the file. You can do that simply by dividing the length of the file by the size of each record. Then you can read the data in like this, record by record, as follows:

```
Sub OKButton_Click ()
        On Error GoTo FileError
      :
      :
```

```
    Open Filename$ For Random As # 1 Len = Len(TheData(1))
     NumberFileRecords = LOF(1) / Len(TheData(1))
     For loop_index = 1 To NumberFileRecords
   Get # 1, , TheData(loop_index)
    Next loop_index

    Close # 1    'Close file
    LoadForm.Hide         'Hide dialog box

    Exit Sub

FileError:
    MsgBox "File Error", 48, "Database"    'MsgBox for file error.
    Resume
End Sub
```

Note that, once again, you changed the name of the error box title in the FileError section of the code from "Editor" to "Database."

Simply loading a file does not make the database active, however. You also have to load the record names you read into the database's sorted list box, where they can be selected by the user. That list box is maintained in the database's Find Item... dialog box. To load the record names into that list box, you must first erase all the current entries (using Visual Basic's RemoveItem method). Then you can load the new entries from TheData( ), using the following AddItem method:

```
Sub OKButton_Click ()
     On Error GoTo FileError

    If (Right$(Dir1.Path, 1) = "\") Then'Get file name
   Filename$ = Dir1.Path + File1.FileName
    Else
   Filename$ = Dir1.Path + "\" + File1.FileName
    End If

    Open Filename$ For Random As # 1 Len = Len(TheData(1))
    NumberFileRecords = LOF(1) / Len(TheData(1))
    For loop_index = 1 To NumberFileRecords
   Get # 1, , TheData(loop_index)
    Next loop_index

    Close # 1    'Close file
```

```
     For loop_index = 1 To TotalRecords
    Form2.NameList.RemoveItem 0
    Next loop_index

    TotalRecords = NumberFileRecords'After safely reading file


    For loop_index = 1 To TotalRecords
    Form2.NameList.AddItem TheData(loop_index).Name
    Next loop_index

    Form1.NameField.Text = TheData(1).Name
    Form1.NumberField.Text = TheData(1).Number
    Form1.CommentField.Text = TheData(1).Comment

    LoadForm.Hide          'Hide dialog box

    Exit Sub

FileError:
    MsgBox "File Error", 48, "Database"     'MsgBox for file error.
    Resume
End Sub
```

That's it, then; you have read in the file and filled the program variables correctly. The database Load File... dialog box is now functional (see figure 5.7).

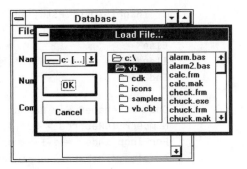

Figure 5.7. The database Load File... dialog box.

Note that you did not have to read in the whole array of records at once; in fact, you could have read in only one record at a time if you had wanted to (saving a significant amount of memory). For example, if you always stored your data in a file named Db.Dat, you could change the Sub procedure that looks up records, GetItem( ), from this—which retrieves the data from the array TheData( )—as follows:

```
Sub GetItem ()
    For loop_index = 1 To 100
    If (Rtrim$(TheData(loop_index).Name) =
        Rtrim$(Form2.NameList.Text)) Then Exit For
    Next loop_index

    Form1.NameField.Text = TheData(loop_index).Name
    Form1.NumberField.Text = TheData(loop_index).Number
    Form1.CommentField.Text = TheData(loop_index).Comment

    Form2.Hide
End Sub
```

The following list retrieves the data from the Db.Dat file directly.

```
Sub GetItem ()
    For loop_index = 1 To 100
    If (Rtrim$(TheData(loop_index).Name) =
        Rtrim$(Form2.NameList.Text)) Then Exit For
    Next loop_index

    Open "Db.Dat" For Random As # 1 Len = Len(TheData(1))
    Get # 1, loop_index, TheData(loop_index)
     Close # 1

    Form1.NameField.Text = TheData(loop_index).Name
    Form1.NumberField.Text = TheData(loop_index).Number
    Form1.CommentField.Text = TheData(loop_index).Comment

    Form2.Hide
End Sub
```

In this way, you can move around in the file, retrieving the specific records you want. At this point, your file expertise is almost complete. Note, however, that you do not have to specify the record number in the Get # statement if you do not want to; you can use Seek instead. The next section covers Seek, the last file topic.

Using the Seek Statement

This statement can be extremely useful, because it allows you to specify which record will be read from or written to next. Its syntax is as follows:

```
Seek [#] nnn%, ppp&
```

Here, nnn% is the file number and ppp& (a long integer) is the new position in the file; for sequential files, ppp& is measured in bytes, for random files, in record numbers. In other words, the following line:

```
Get # 1, loop_index, TheData(loop_index)
```

The previous line is the same as the following one:

```
Seek # 1, loop_index
Get # 1, , TheData(loop_index)
```

Using Get, Put, and Seek together, you have a great deal of control over your files; in particular, with these statements you can work byte-by-byte in binary files.

A Visual Basic improvement.
If you simply want to copy files, you can use Visual Basic's FileCopy command.

That completes the coverage of files. In the next chapter, you will see another exciting aspect of Visual Basic: graphics. This topic is extremely important in Windows because everything is graphically oriented. You will see how to start designing your own displays in Chapter 6.

Summary

You have seen Visual Basic's file-handling statements, you have seen how they work in practice, and now you have added file-handling capabilities to two of your major applications—the Database (random file access) and Editor (sequential file access).

As you have seen, working with files in Visual Basic is similar to working with files in standard Basic, except that Visual Basic has the added advantage of three new types of file controls: directory list boxes, drive list boxes, and file list boxes—to make selecting files easier. Visual Basic works just like standard Basic, except when it comes to communicating with the user. In addition, you have seen how to use the EOF( ), Get, Put, and Seek statements. You have even started dealing with file errors (which you will see more of in Chapter 9).

In general, then, you have seen how to create, open, work with, and close files in Visual Basic. As mentioned at the beginning of this chapter, file handling is part of any major Windows program, so the skills you have learned can be put to use over and over again.

New Property	Description
Drive	Determines the selected drive in a drive list box control.
FileName	This property holds the name of the file currently selected in a File list box.
Path	The Path property holds the path name of the directory whose files you want to display in file-oriented controls.
Pattern	The Pattern property holds the file specification in file-oriented controls; "*.Exe", for example (the default pattern is "*.*").

New Statement	Description
Close	Closes an open file. Use it like this: Close [fff%]
fff%	The filenumber
Get	Gets data from an open file. Use it like this: Get [#] nnn% , [rrr%], vvv%
nnn%	Filenumber (1-255): The file's number.
rrr%	Record length for random files, or size of the buffer you want Visual Basic to use for sequential files.
vvv%	The variable you want to fill with data.

continues

231

New Statement	Description
Input$	Reads a string from an open (sequential) file. Use it as follows: Input$ (bbb%, [#] nnn%)
nnn%	Filenumber (1-255): The file's number.
bbb%	Number of bytes
Open	Opens disk files for read or write access. Use it as follows: Open fff$ [For mmm] [Access aaa] [lll] As [#] nnn% [Len = rrr%]
fff$	The filename (including an optional path)
mmm	Mode: can be Append, Binary, Input, Output, or Random
aaa	Access: can be Read, Write, or Read Write
lll	Lock: restricts access of other applications to this file to: Shared, Lock Read, Lock Write, Lock Read Write
nnn%	Filenumber (1-255): The number you will use to refer to this file from now on.
rrr%	Record length for random files, or size of the buffer you want Visual Basic to use for sequential files.
Put	Puts data into an open file. Use it as follows: Put [#] nnn% , [rrr%], vvv%
nnn%	Filenumber (1-255): The file's number.
rrr%	Record length for random files, or size of the buffer you want Visual Basic to use for sequential files.
vvv%	The variable you want to put into the file.
Write	Writes data to an open (sequential) file. Use it like this: Write # nnn%, expressionlist.
nnn%	Filenumber (1-255): The file's number.
expressionlist	Variable(s) to write.

Graphics

This chapter begins this book's coverage of one of the most exciting parts about Visual Basic: graphics. In this chapter, you will see how to display (colorful) output beyond simply filling text boxes with text. In particular, it covers these topics:

▼ Animation

▼ Drawing individual points in different colors

▼ Drawing lines in different styles

▼ Drawing circles

▼ Drawing rectangles

▼ Loading graphics images on disk into graphics controls

▼ Filling figures with patterns and colors

▼ Designing your own icons

▼ Using the printer in Visual Basic

▼ Changing graphics coordinate systems to plot data easily

▼ How to draw text (outside text boxes)

The programs developed in this chapter include an animation example that sends a small rocket ship flying smoothly up the window, and an example showing how to plot data in a graph that will be tailored to the size of your window. The main graphics program is in the next chapter, where you design and write a fully functional Windows paint program. The skills you learn in this chapter are applicable every time you want to draw in a window, and that's not only in paint programs. You could have drawn a small rectangle in the earlier control panel application, for example, to give users some visual feedback about the size they were setting for the main window. You will draw a rectangle on the screen (and outside your window) later in this book, when you write a screen-capture program. Plenty of examples of graphics are used in Visual Basic applications—from game boards to puzzles to screen savers, and you learn how to draw these types of figures in this chapter. You will see that you can display text outside a text box (on a form itself, for example, as a word processor program might)—to do that, you must "draw" that text by using graphics techniques.

Peter Norton's Visual Basic for Windows, Third Edition, Covering Release 3.0

This is the chapter on graphics and graphical text output. You may not have been expecting to see the subject of handling text in a chapter on graphics; in an environment such as Windows (a graphical user interface, or GUI), however, everything is presented as graphics, including text (except in text boxes, lists, and labels). If you have read standard books about programming, you probably are used to seeing text treated differently than graphics; in this chapter, however, you will see that Visual Basic treats it the same. If text is not in a specifically text-oriented control, such as a text box, label, or list box, it simply is treated the same as any other graphics.

In addition to text, of course, this chapter explores the rest of Visual Basic's graphics capabilities—and they are extensive. You will draw points, lines, rectangles, circles, ellipses, and other graphical objects, for example, and learn how to change their color and width—even the pattern they are filled with. You will see how you can protect drawings in case they are covered temporarily by other windows (a risk you don't have in standard Basic), and how to load pictures from files. In addition, you will learn how to send your graphics (including text) to the printer, which is easier than you might imagine. With all this in store, let's begin immediately.

Drawing with Visual Basic

There are two main types of objects you can draw on in Visual Basic: forms and picture boxes. You are already familiar with forms; you have not seen picture boxes yet, however. Picture boxes are simply boxes like any other (text boxes, for example), which you can place on forms (except that they have one primary function you have not seen yet: to display graphics). In fact, let's start immediately with a picture box and some elementary graphics by drawing a single point.

Drawing Points

The Visual Basic graphics functions that draw on forms or in picture boxes are much like the matching QuickBasic functions. The first graphics function you look at, for example, is PSet( ), which sets a pixel on the screen.

To use PSet( ), start Visual Basic, name this project Graphics.Mak, and change the caption of the default form, Form1, to Graphics. Next, find the AutoRedraw property in the properties window and set it to True. This property indicates that Visual Basic should redraw the graphics on the form if part or all of it is covered temporarily by another window.

The coordinate system in Visual Basic uses *twips* (1/1440th of an inch) by default. You may have wondered why a twip rather than a screen pixel is the default measurement. The answer is that the Visual Basic environment is intended to operate in a manner that's as device-independent as possible—you can draw on the printer as easily as on the screen. Because printers can have a considerably higher resolution than screens, however (laser printers typically have a resolution of 300 dots per inch), you need a measuring system that's even more precise than the best any of your devices can give you. As a programmer, of course, you may be used to other units, such as pixels, centimeters, or even points. (A *point*, often used in measuring the dimensions of a font, is 1/72nd of an inch, and a twip is 1/20th of a point.) You will see later that you can switch the basic unit of measurement to pixels, centimeters, or other units.

The coordinate system starts at (0, 0) in a form or picture box; x and y increase to the right and down, as follows:

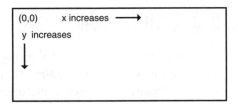

Let's make use of this fact in drawing a pixel, which you can place in the exact center of the form. To do that, you can get the size of the form from the properties window. For example, you might have a form that's 4320 twips high × 7200 twips wide (3 inches by 5 inches). In that case, the PSet( ) statement might appear as follows:

```
Pset (4320 / 2, 7200 / 2)
```

This statement sets the pixel in the center of the form—the syntax of PSet( ) is as follows:

```
PSet (x , y)
```

There is another way, however, to center the pixel without knowing the size of the form beforehand, by using the ScaleWidth and ScaleHeight properties.

Four built-in properties can tell you the dimensions of a form or picture box: Height, Width, ScaleHeight, and ScaleWidth. It might seem that the natural properties to use to determine how to center a pixel are Width and Height, but these properties correspond to the outer width and height of the window (including title bar, menu bar, and so on). The dimensions of the client area (the area you have control of) is ScaleWidth wide and ScaleHeight tall (in twips), as shown in figure 6.1. For that reason, your PSet( ) statement might appear as follows:

```
PSet (ScaleWidth / 2, ScaleHeight / 2)
```

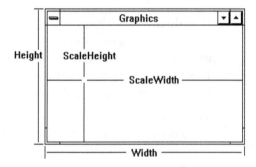

Figure 6.1. Height and width properties of forms.

Because you want to execute this line as soon as the form appears on the screen, you will put it in the Form_Load ( ) Sub procedure, which is run when the form is first displayed. Click the form and find the Form_Load( ) procedure in the code window, as follows:

```
Sub Form_Load()

End Sub
```
Next, place your PSet() statement there:
```
Sub Form_Load()
  PSet (ScaleWidth / 2, ScaleHeight / 2)
End Sub
```

When you run the program, the pixel appears in the center of the form, as shown in figure 6.2. Note that you could have used other events also to display this pixel, such as the Form_Click( ) event, which means that the dot would appear when you clicked any client area location on the form.

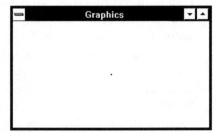

Figure 6.2. A graphics application with Dot.

Now do the same thing in a picture box. Double-click the picture box tool (in the upper right corner of Visual Basic's toolbox), size the picture box until it takes up most of the window, and set its AutoRedraw property to True. The default name for picture boxes is Picture1, so you can add this line to Form_Load( ), as follows:

```
Sub Form_Load()
  PSet (ScaleWidth / 2, ScaleHeight / 2)
  Picture1.PSet (Picture.ScaleWidth / 2, Picture1.ScaleHeight / 2)
End Sub
```

In other words, PSet( ) is a Visual Basic method—it is connected to the object on which you want to draw. (This statement is true also for the other graphics routines in this chapter, such as the line-drawing routine, Line.) When you do not use it with an object name, the current form is assumed; if you do use an object's name, that object is PSet( )'s target. Now run the program. You can see the picture box with a dot in its center, as shown in figure 6.3. Note that the picture box obscures the dot on the form; this is true in general: Any controls placed on a form are placed on top of graphics already on the form, which covers them.

So far, nothing exciting has happened; you have just drawn a single point in black. You can change the color of that point also, however, and you learn how to do that next.

238

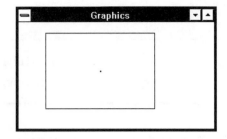

Figure 6.3. A picture box with Dot.

Selecting Colors

There are several ways to set your own colors in Visual Basic. The easiest way is to use the predefined values in the file Constant.Txt. Every color value in Visual Basic is a long integer, and many such values are ready to use, such as the constants named RED and BLUE, as shown in table 6.1. In addition, you can find out how the user has set the system colors (by using the Windows control panel) and tailor your application to match by using the system color constants, as defined in table 6.2. You can set a form's background color property (BackColor), for example, to the current system-wide standard by setting it equal to WINDOW_BACKGROUND. To load the definitions in Constant.Txt into the declarations section of a module, use Visual Basic's Load Text... menu item. Because the items in that file are declared globally, they are available everywhere in your program. (You have to load them into a module because you cannot have global declarations in a form.)

Table 6.1. Visual Basic Predefined Colors

BLACK	&H0&
RED	&HFF&
GREEN	&HFF00&
YELLOW	&HFFFF&
BLUE	&HFF0000
MAGENTA	&HFF00FF

continues

Table 6.1. continued

CYAN	&HFFFF00
WHITE	&HFFFFFF

Table 6.2. Visual Basic System Colors

SCROLL_BARS	&H80000000
DESKTOP	&H80000001
ACTIVE_TITLE_BAR	&H80000002
INACTIVE_TITLE_BAR	&H80000003
MENU_BAR	&H80000004
WINDOW_BACKGROUND	&H80000005
WINDOW_FRAME	&H80000006
MENU_TEXT	&H80000007
WINDOW_TEXT	&H80000008
TITLE_BAR_TEXT	&H80000009
ACTIVE_BORDER	&H8000000A
INACTIVE_BORDER	&H8000000B
APPLICATION_WORKSPACE	&H8000000C
HIGHLIGHT	&H8000000D
HIGHLIGHT_TEXT	&H8000000E
BUTTON_FACE	&H8000000F
BUTTON_SHADOW	&H80000010
GRAY_TEXT	&H80000011
BUTTON_TEXT	&H80000012

Let's have your program print a red dot. The general syntax of PSet( ) is shown in the following line:

```
[object.]Pset [Step] (x!, y!)[,color&]
```

(x!, y!) represents the location of the pixel with which you want to work. You should note that these variables are measured with respect to the object (form or picture box) in which you are drawing. In other words, when you are setting pixels in a picture box, (x! y!) represents the location of the pixel with respect to the picture box's upper left corner (which is (0, 0)). In addition, the color value, color&, is always a long integer.

The Step keyword is one you will see in many of the drawing methods. It indicates that the coordinates specified are with respect to the current graphics position, whose coordinates are stored in the CurrentX and CurrentY properties of forms and picture boxes. As you will see, you can draw lines or other graphics figures by using the current graphics position. To set that position, set the CurrentX and CurrentY properties. Also, using graphical methods like PSet( ) can set the current graphics position. When you set a pixel with PSet( ) in some objects, the current graphics position is set to that pixel. You don't use Step here, however. To make your pixel red, you can simply use the predefined constant RED, as in the following example:

```
Sub Form_Load()
  PSet (ScaleWidth / 2, ScaleHeight / 2)
  Picture1.PSet (Picture.ScaleWidth / 2, Picture1.ScaleHeight / 2), RED
End Sub
```

In addition, you must load Constant.Txt into a module because the constant RED is defined there. Running this program changes the pixel in the center of the picture box to red, so your program is a success. There are other ways, however, to indicate the color you want in Visual Basic.

For example, you can use the RGB function, which you have seen already, to specify the color. This function takes three arguments (a red color value, a green color value, and a blue color value) as follows:

```
RGB (RedVal%, GreenVal%, BlueVal%)
```

Each of these color values can go from a minimum of 0 (when the color is excluded entirely) to a maximum of 255 (when it's at its strongest). For a pure red dot, you can use RedVal = 255, GreenVal = 0, and BlueVal = 0, in the following way:

```
Sub Form_Load()
  PSet (ScaleWidth / 2, ScaleHeight / 2)
  Picture1.PSet (Picture.ScaleWidth / 2,
  Picture1.ScaleHeight / 2), RGB(255, 0, 0)
End Sub
```

There are even more options for setting colors. You can set the actual bytes in a long integer directly, for example, and pass that as your color value. A long integer is made up of four bytes, with the three colors taking the bottom three bytes. It is easiest to look at it in hexadecimal, where a color value is represented like this: &H00rrggbb&, where rr is the (hex) value of the red setting, gg is the green setting, and bb is the blue setting. (The reason that this method is most convenient in hex is that, in hex, each byte takes up exactly two hex digits). To turn on red, therefore, you can give it the highest value a byte can have—&HFF (255), as follows:

```
Sub Form_Load()
  PSet (ScaleWidth / 2, ScaleHeight / 2)
  Picture1.PSet (Picture.ScaleWidth / 2,
  Picture1.ScaleHeight / 2), &H00FF0000&
End Sub
```

This example works as well, by displaying a red dot in your picture box. The last way to specify colors in Visual Basic is with the QBColor( ) function. QuickBasic has 16 predefined colors, and you can access them in Visual Basic also (which makes it easier to move graphics code over to Visual Basic from QuickBasic) by using the QBColor( ) function. This function returns a long integer that corresponds to the correct Visual Basic RGB value. You use QBColor( ) like this: QBColor(nnn%), where nnn% is the QuickBasic color number from 0 to 15 associated with the color you want, as shown in table 6.3.

Table 6.3. QuickBasic Colors for the QBColor() Function

Color Number	Color
0	Black
1	Blue
2	Green

Color Number	Color
3	Cyan
4	Red
5	Magenta
6	Yellow
7	White
8	Grey
9	Light Blue
10	Light Green
11	Light Cyan
12	Light Red
13	Light Magenta
14	Light Yellow
15	Bright White

For example, you can turn your dot red in the following way:

```
Sub Form_Load()
  PSet (ScaleWidth / 2, ScaleHeight / 2)
  Picture1.PSet (Picture.ScaleWidth / 2,
  Picture1.ScaleHeight / 2), QBColor(4)
End Sub
```

Finding the color at a particular screen location.
If you ever want to determine the color of a particular position on the screen, you can use the Point method—[object].Point (x!, y!), which returns the corresponding long integer color value.

That's it for drawing points. This is just the beginning of Visual Basic's graphics capabilities, of course; let's move on to drawing lines.

Drawing Lines

A new tool in the Visual Basic toolbox lets you draw lines at design time: the Line control tool (see figure 1.9). Using it is easy; when you double click it, a small line appears with two sizing handles. Just size the line the way you want it to appear on your form. This procedure makes it easy to add underlines or other emphasis to the design of your windows. Here, however, you are interested in drawing lines in code (in preparation for your paint program); to draw lines in code, you can use the Line method, whose syntax is shown in the following line:

```
[object.]Line [[Step](x1!, y1!)]-[Step](x2!, y2!)[,[color&],B[F]]]
```

A Visual Basic improvement.
Beginning with version 2.0, Visual Basic includes three new graphics controls: the line control, the shape control, and the image control. They are discussed later in this chapter.

Again, notice that this is a method, which means that you can specify on which object you want to draw lines. (As usual, if you do not specify an object, Visual Basic assumes that you intend to use the current form.) As before, you can use the Step keyword here, if you want. To draw a line, two points usually are involved: the beginning and end of the line—(x1!, y1!) and (x2!, y2!), respectively. When you use Step in front of either of them, it indicates that that point is to be taken with respect to the current graphics position, as specified by (CurrentX, CurrentY). In addition, you can specify the line's color with the color& argument. The next section discusses the last two arguments, B and F, used to draw rectangles (boxes).

This means that if you want to draw a single line diagonally across a form, you can use Line, as follows:

```
Line (0, 0) - (ScaleWidth, ScaleHeight)
```

That is all that's required—just the two endpoints of the line (Visual Basic draws the line so that the first endpoint, not the second, is included). Let's remove the picture box from the Graphics application temporarily, for example, and change the Form_Load Sub procedure to the following:

```
Sub Form_Load()
  Line (0, 0) - (ScaleWidth, ScaleHeight)
End Sub
```

Running the program now results in a window like the one shown in figure 6.4. You can make that line a blue line by specifying a color as shown in the following example (as long as Constant.Txt has been loaded).

```
Sub Form_Load()
  Line (0, 0) - (ScaleWidth, ScaleHeight), BLUE
End Sub
```

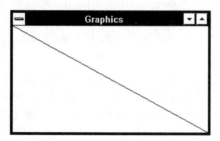

Figure 6.4. A Graphics window with a diagonal line.

Another way to specify that this line should be blue without passing a color value to the Line method is by first setting the object's ForeColor property. All forms and picture boxes have this property, which you can think of as the drawing color. All controls that can display text also have this property, in fact, which determines the color of the text (except for command buttons, which have only a BackColor property). When you draw text or other graphics figures and do not specify a color, the foreground color is used as the default. You can specify that color for a particular object as shown in the following example (if you do not specify an object for a graphical method, the current form is used).

```
Sub Form_Load()
  ForeColor = BLUE
  Line (0, 0) - (ScaleWidth, ScaleHeight)
End Sub
```

Until this object's drawing color is changed again, it will be blue. In other words, text and so on will be blue when you place it here. You should note that changing the foreground color, however, does not change the color of text or other graphics already in graphical objects. By specifying the ForeColor property, therefore, you can have a number of different forms or picture boxes in your application, all with a different drawing color. In the same way, other drawing properties are associated with these types of objects, and some of them are explored next.

A graphics pen, for example, is associated with each object that can display graphics. One of the properties associated with a graphics pen is the DrawWidth property, with which you can change the width of the line you draw (or the size of the dot the PSet( ) draws). The default value for this graphics property is 1, which corresponds to the thinnest line, as shown in figure 6.4. This line is 1 pixel wide on the screen. You can make this line thicker, however, by specifying a higher value—DrawWidth = 2 results in a line 2 pixels wide, and so on. To see some of these lines, you might set up a loop in the Form_Load( ) Sub procedure, as shown in the following example:

```
Sub Form_Load()
  For i = 1 To 9
  DrawWidth = i
  Line (0, i * ScaleHeight / 10) - (ScaleWidth, i * ScaleHeight / 10)
  Next i
  DrawWidth = 1
End Sub
```

This example displays a window in which the line across the form grows steadily thicker as you go downward (see figure 6.5).

You can affect the style of the line in addition to the width. In other words, you can specify whether the line is solid (the default) or is broken up into dots or dashes. There are seven different styles of lines, from solid to dotted to transparent (see table 6.4).

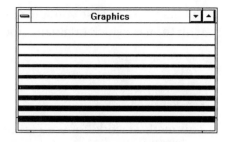

Figure 6.5. A Graphics window with thickening lines.

Table 6.4. Line Styles—The DrawStyle Property

DrawStyle	Result
0	Solid line (default DrawStyle value)
1	Dashed line
2	Dotted line
3	Dash-dot line
4	Dash-dot-dot line
5	Transparent line (does not appear)
6	Inside line

An inside line (DrawStyle 6) deserves some special mention. When you draw a box with a thick line, the line is normally centered on the edge of the box. The box then ends up slightly larger than intended because the thick line is half in and half out of the box. On the other hand, an inside line is drawn so that it is entirely inside the box, even for thick lines. Let's look at these line styles in the Graphics application, this time by modifying the Form_Click ( ) Sub procedure. Go to the form and bring up the Form_Click ( ) Sub procedure, as follows:

```
Sub Form_Click ()

End Sub
```

By the time this Sub procedure is invoked (by clicking the form), Form_Load ( ) has already put the thickening lines on the form, as shown in figure 6.5. Because you want to get rid of that pattern first, you begin with the Cls (which originally stood for *clear screen*) method, as follows:

```
Sub Form_Click ()
  Cls
  :
End Sub
```

This method works for both forms and picture boxes to clear the object and blank whatever graphics (including text) were already there. Next, you simply want to draw the seven line styles on the form, which you can do by looping, as follows:

```
Sub Form_Click()
  Cls
  For i = 1 To 7
  DrawStyle = i - 1
  Line (0, i * ScaleHeight / 8) - (ScaleWidth, i * ScaleHeight / 8)
  Next i
End Sub
```

The result of this program is that the window first appears as shown in figure 6.5; then, when you click on it, it changes as shown in figure 6.6, with all the different line styles displayed.

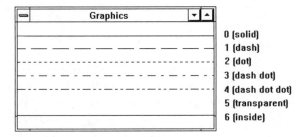

Figure 6.6. A Graphics window that shows line styles.

> **Using a width of greater than 1 alters line styles.**
> You should note, however, that using a drawing width (DrawWidth) of greater than 1 makes line styles 1 through 4 produce solid lines rather than series of dashes or dots.

So far, you have been able to change the thickness and style of lines. You can go even further, in fact, and specify how what you draw affects what's already there. This DrawMode property affects which type of pen you use to draw.

As mentioned, you can think of each graphics object having a pen. This pen can draw in different styles. If you have set DrawWidth to 6, for example, the pen draws lines or circles that are six pixels wide, or draws dots that are six pixels wide with PSet( ) because the default for the pen is simply to draw in the foreground color (ForeColor), which corresponds to a DrawMode of 13. If you change DrawMode to 4, on the other hand, the pen changes into a Not Pen and draws in the inverse of the foreground color. If the foreground color is black, for example, a Not Pen draws in white. Altogether, DrawMode can take values from 1 to 16; the most common settings are shown in table 6.5.

Table 6.5. Visual Basic Pen Styles

DrawMode	Name	Means
4	Not Pen	Draws the inverse of the pen
6	Invert Pen	Inverts what is on-screen
7	Xor Pen	Xors pen and screen
11	No Pen	Draws nothing
13	Copy Pen	Draws pen directly (default)

Some of these pens deserve mention. The Invert Pen (DrawMode = 6), for example, color-inverts what is on the screen when it draws. If you are drawing over a black area, white appears, and if you are drawing over green, red appears (the color inverse of green). This capability can create some striking visual effects. Let's make this change to Form_Click( ) in your Graphics application so that, when it is clicked on, two broad diagonal bands appear on the form and invert what is underneath them, as follows:

```
Sub Form_Click ()
  DrawMode = 6
  DrawWidth = 9
  Line (0, 0) - (ScaleWidth, ScaleHeight)
```

```
   Line (0, ScaleHeight) - (ScaleWidth, 0)
End Sub
```

When you run the application, the window first appears as shown in figure 6.5. When you click the window, however, the two diagonal bands appear and invert whatever they draw over, as shown in figure 6.7.

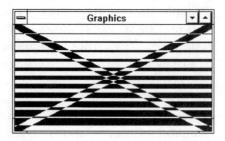

Figure 6.7. An invert pen example.

The Xor Pen also deserves mention because it is commonly used in animation. Xor—Exclusive Or—is a bit-wise operator much like And and Or, which you probably are already familiar with in Basic. These operators compare the individual bits of two operands and produce a result based on a bit-by-bit comparison. Oring two bits that are both 1 produces 1, for example; Oring two bits that are both 0 produces 0. The general action of these operators is shown in table 6.6; if you are working with two bytes, for example, the results, bit by bit, might look like the following:

```
     01010101              11111111              11111111
Or   10101010      And     10101010      Xor     10101010
     ————————              ————————              ————————
     11111111              10101010              01010101
```

Table 6.6. Visual Basic's Logical Operators

And	0 1	Or	0 1	Xor	0 1
————————	————————	————————
0	0 0	0	0 1	0	0 1
1	0 1	1	1 1	1	1 0

When you use the Xor Pen, the drawing color and the colors being overwritten on the screen are Xored together. If you are drawing on a white screen, for example, this color-inverts the drawing color (green becomes red, and so on). That's because the color value of the drawing color is Xored with white, which has a color value of &HFFFFFF&—all 1s; when you Xor anything with all 1s, you get its inverse (and therefore invert the color), as follows:

```
        11111111
Xor     10101010
        01010101
```

If you Xor the result with the same pen again, on the other hand, you always get the original value back (white, in this case), as follows:

```
        11111111
Xor     10101010

        01010101
Xor     10101010
        11111111
```

You can draw anything on the screen by using the Xor Pen to make it appear—and when you draw it a second time with the same pen, what you have drawn disappears (the original display is restored). Animation often works in this way. On a white screen, for example, you can draw in white by using the Xor Pen, and the result is black; drawing the same figure again erases it and restores the white screen (because any value Xored with another value twice is restored to its original value).

Using Xor to encrypt data.
Because Xoring a value twice restores the original value, the logical Xor operator also can be used to encrypt data. Just Xor the data, byte by byte, with some value or values (such as the characters in a password) to encrypt it, and then Xor it again with the same value or values to reproduce the original exactly. This process is called *Xor encryption*.

Let's move on to a new capability of the Line method: drawing boxes.

Drawing Rectangles

You have seen that the Line control lets you draw lines at design time. Another graphics control, the Shape Control (see figure 1.9), enables you to draw a number of shapes, including rectangles, ovals, squares, circles, rounded rectangles, and rounded squares. You select which shape you want to draw at design time by setting the Shape control's Shape property. Because these shapes are controls, you can set their Top, Left, Width, Height, Bottom, and Right properties in a program. Suppose that you draw a rectangle as Shape1; to double the width of that rectangle when the user clicks the form, you can execute the following code:

```
Sub Form_Click()
   Shape1.Width = 2 * Shape1.Width
End Sub
```

The Shape controls usually are not used for producing program output, however; instead, they are used to enhance the design and visual appeal of your windows (you can set a group of controls off if you bound them with a shape, for example). To produce normal graphics rectangles, you use the Line method again. It might seem odd that you have to use the Line method only once to draw a box, but that's exactly what the B option lets you do:

```
[object.]Line [[Step](x1!, y1!)]-[Step](x2!, y2!)[,[color&],B[F]]]
```

When you specify a line in Visual Basic, you specify the endpoints. Similarly, when you specify a rectangle, it makes sense that you need to specify only two points—the upper left and lower right corners, as follows:

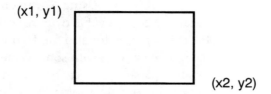

Because both patterns are uniquely specified by two points, Visual Basic (and many other types of Basic, including QuickBasic) lets you draw rectangles and lines with Line. You can see how this works by modifying the Graphics application to draw a few rectangles, as in the following example:

```
Sub Form_Load()
  DrawWidth = 8
  Line (0, 0) - (ScaleWidth / 2, ScaleHeight / 2), , B
  Line (ScaleWidth/4, ScaleHeight/4)-(3*ScaleWidth/4, 3*ScaleHeight/4),,B
  Line (ScaleWidth / 2, ScaleHeight / 2) - (ScaleWidth, ScaleHeight), , B
End Sub
```

This example generates the window, as shown in figure 6.8. The thick lines at the edges are half inside and half outside the client area. You can fix this by using the Inside Line drawing style in the following way:

```
Sub Form_Load()
  DrawWidth = 8
  DrawStyle = 6
  Line (0, 0) - (ScaleWidth / 2, ScaleHeight / 2), , B
  Line (ScaleWidth/4, ScaleHeight/4)-(3*ScaleWidth/4, 3*ScaleHeight/4),,B
  Line (ScaleWidth / 2, ScaleHeight / 2) - (ScaleWidth, ScaleHeight), , B
End Sub
```

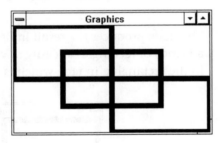

Figure 6.8. Graphics rectangles.

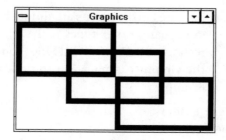

Figure 6.9. Graphics rectangles with inside lines.

Now the rectangles are drawn so that the thick border is inside the boundaries, as shown in figure 6.9. That's the way inside lines work—they do not overlap the figure's boundaries. You can also change the drawing mode (use a different pen setting); you can use an Invert Pen, for example, which inverts what it draws over (DrawMode = 6), as follows:

```
Sub Form_Load()
  DrawWidth = 8
  DrawStyle = 6
  DrawMode = 6
  Line (0, 0) - (ScaleWidth / 2, ScaleHeight / 2), , B
  Line (ScaleWidth/4, ScaleHeight/4)-(3*ScaleWidth/4, 3*ScaleHeight/4),,B
  Line (ScaleWidth / 2, ScaleHeight / 2) - (ScaleWidth, ScaleHeight), , B
End Sub
```

This code produces the result in figure 6.10. Generally, you can produce all kinds of rectangles as easily as you might draw lines. You can also fill in the rectangles, in fact, which is discussed in the next section.

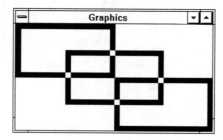

Figure 6.10. Rectangles.

Filling Figures with Patterns

You now have drawn enclosed graphics figures for the first time, but Visual Basic lets you go further than that. You can specify a fill pattern so that your boxes are filled in automatically. Your boxes have automatically been filled in already, in fact, but the default fill pattern is transparent. That's only one of the eight fill patterns available, however—the other ones include horizontal or vertical lines, diagonal lines, or, of course, filling your figures with solid color. These options appear in table 6.7.

Table 6.7. Fill Options—The FillStyle Property

FillStyle Value	Resulting Fill Pattern
0	Solid
1	Transparent (the default)
2	Horizontal lines
3	Vertical lines
4	Upward diagonals
5	Downward diagonals
6	Cross-hatch
7	Diagonal cross-hatch

You select one of the fill patterns from table 6.7 with the FillStyle property. Let's see this in action. You can draw eight rectangles on the main form of the Graphics application and then fill them, one by one, with the different patterns corresponding to different FillStyle property settings. Again, let's use the Form_Load ( ) Sub procedure to see this process work. You can change that procedure to the following one, in which you draw two rows of four rectangles and fill each one with a different fill pattern.

```
Sub Form_Load()
  SX = ScaleWidth
  SY = ScaleHeight
  For i = 0 To 3
  FillStyle = i
  Line ((2*i+1) * SX/9, SY/5) - ((2*i+2) * SX/9, 2*SY/5), ,B
  FillStyle = i + 4
```

```
    Line ((2*i+1) * SX/9, 3*SY/5) - ((2*i+2) * SX/9, 4*SY/5), ,B
    Next i
End Sub
```

As you can see, all the eight fill patterns appear, as shown in figure 6.11. You can use these built-in patterns to create visual effects in your Visual Basic programs. Again, you are using the B option to draw boxes—if you are familiar with QuickBasic, you may have expected to use the F option so that the rectangles were filled, as follows:

```
Line (0, 0) - (1000, 1000), , BF
```

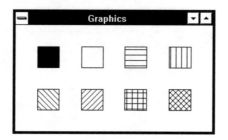

Figure 6.11. The different FillStyle options.

The F option—for *fillcolor*—is used only to specify that the fill pattern will be made the same color as the rectangle. If you do not specify F (F can be specified only if you have already specified B), the current FillColor is used. This color is just like BackColor and ForeColor, except that it is used exclusively as the color of the fill pattern. Like ForeColor and BackColor, it is a property of graphical objects such as picture boxes and forms, and, like other properties, it remains set until you change it again. You learn how to use the fill color later in this chapter, when you draw circles.

Before finishing a discussion of rectangles, however, it is worth noting something important: Drawing solid white rectangles—with white borders—is a standard way to delete text on forms and picture boxes. Because text is treated as graphics in both of these objects, you cannot just erase it by selecting text and then deleting it. Instead, you have to remove it from the screen as you would do with any graphics. You will see more about text soon. Let's move on to drawing circles.

Drawing Circles

Drawing circles is very easy with the Circle method, as follows:

```
[object].Circle [Step] (x!, y!), radius! [,[color&][,[start!]
  [,[end!][, aspect!]]]]
```

In this example, (x!, y!) represents the center of the circle, and radius! represents its radius (all in twips). In addition, you can draw arcs by specifying a start angle and an end angle (in radians). You can see this at work by drawing a few circles. You can start with a fill style of downward diagonals and a simple red circle, as in the following example:

```
Sub Form_Load()
  FillStyle = 5          'Downward diagonals
  ForeColor = RGB(255, 0, 0)     'Red
  Circle (ScaleWidth/4, ScaleHeight/4), ScaleHeight/5
End Sub
```

This code produces a red circle filled with downward diagonals and a black fill pattern, not a red one. If you were drawing boxes, you could fix that with the F option, but there is no F option here; instead, you can set the FillColor property to match the current ForeColor, as follows:

```
Sub Form_Load()
  FillStyle = 5          'Downward diagonals
  ForeColor = RGB(255, 0, 0)     'Red
  FillColor = ForeColor
  Circle (ScaleWidth/4, ScaleHeight/4), ScaleHeight/5
End Sub
```

Now both the circle and the fill pattern inside are red. The Circle method is more powerful; you can draw ellipses and arcs with it also. To draw ellipses, you use the aspect argument with Circle; the *aspect ratio* indicates the vertical to horizontal ratio for ellipses. When you are drawing a circle, this is set to its default value of 1; you can draw an ellipse as easily, however. To draw a circle and then an ellipse that's twice as high as it is wide, for example, you can use an aspect ratio of 2, as follows:

```
Sub Form_Load()
  Circle (ScaleWidth/4, ScaleHeight/4), ScaleHeight/5
  FillStyle = 2
  Circle (ScaleWidth/2, ScaleHeight/2), ScaleHeight/3,,,,2     'Ellipse
End Sub
```

The resulting graphics display appears in figure 6.12. You can also draw arcs (partial circles) by specifying start! and end! angles. These angles are measured in radians, which go from 0 to 2 pi. Let's add an arc that goes, for example, from 0 (the 3 o'clock position) to pi (moving counterclockwise to the 9 o'clock position), as in the following example:

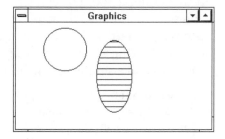

Figure 6.12. An ellipse.

```
Sub Form_Load()
  Circle (ScaleWidth/4, ScaleHeight/4), ScaleHeight/5
  FillStyle = 2
  Circle (ScaleWidth/2, ScaleHeight/2), ScaleHeight/3,,,,2    'Ellipse
  Circle (3*ScaleWidth/4, 3*ScaleHeight/4), ScaleHeight/5,,0,3.1415
'Arc
End Sub
```

The resulting figures appear in figure 6.13. Even though you specified a fill pattern, the arc is not filled because it is not a closed figure.

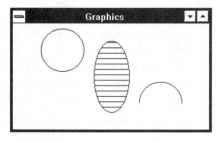

Figure 6.13. A circle, an ellipse, and an arc.

That's it for the primary, built-in drawing methods—PSet, Line, and Circle. You have seen that you can produce some interesting effects with them. Visual Basic also enables you to do many other things with graphics, however; you can load predrawn pictures, for example, into either forms or picture boxes, which is discussed in the following section.

Loading Pictures

You can load pictures into picture boxes, image controls, or forms by using the LoadPicture( ) function and by assigning them to the object's Picture property. In particular, you can use LoadPicture( ) with three types of files: .ICO files (icons), .BMP files (bitmap files produced by such applications as Windows Paintbrush), and .WMF (Windows metafiles). You can also load these types of files into picture boxes, Image controls, or forms at design time by setting their Picture properties to the correct file name.

The Image control (see figure 1.9) is a new control in Visual Basic 2+ (version 2.0 and higher) and functions much like a picture box when you load and display images (it does not have the standard graphics methods, such as Line or Circle, however). It differs from a picture box in two ways: It automatically changes its size to fit the picture loaded into it and, by setting its Stretch property to True, you can even adjust the size of the Image control after a picture has been loaded into it. The picture inside it is stretched to match (a picture box does not do this).

> **Saving pictures on disk.**
> Just as you can load pictures with LoadPicture( ), you can also save them with SavePicture( ) (see Chapter 7).

Let's give this procedure a try by loading an icon into a picture box. Visual Basic already has many icons set up for you to use. The icon you want might be the stoplight icon, for example, that is stored in "Icons\Traffic\Trffc10a.Ico" (see the Visual Basic documentation for a complete listing of its icon library). To "read in" that icon, you can place a picture box on the Graphics application's form and then execute the following line:

```
Sub Form_Click ()
  Picture1.Picture = LoadPicture("..\ICONS\TRAFFIC\TRFFC10A.ICO")
End Sub
```

In this way, you assign the icon to the picture property of Picture1. The result is shown in figure 6.14. Note that the icon is placed in the upper left corner of the picture box. You can make the picture box grow or shrink to fit the image you have loaded into it by setting its Autosize property to True. Remember that an Image control does this automatically. When you do, the picture box shrinks around the icon, as shown in figure 6.15. If the icon had been larger than the picture box, it would have grown to fit it. Image controls also enable you to resize the picture after they are loaded, but picture boxes do not.

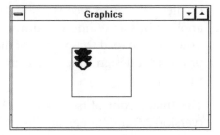

Figure 6.14. Loading a Stoplight icon.

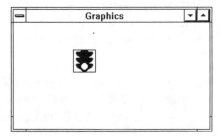

Figure 6.15. Loading a Stoplight icon with AutoSize set to true.

You can also load .BMP files as are produced by Windows Paintbrush this way (.WMF files are not discussed here). This capability can be valuable if you want to customize the appearance of a window. First, draw the figure you want in an application such as Windows Paintbrush and then save it in bitmap (.BMP) format. Next, read it in with a line like the following one:

```
Sub Form_Click ()
  Picture = LoadPicture("C:\WINDOWS\IMAGE.BMP")
End Sub
```

The window in figure 6.16, for example, was produced by loading a .BMP file directly with LoadPicture( ). At this point, because you know how to use graphics in Visual Basic relatively well—not to mention how to load graphics files—into your programs directly, you are ready to begin exploring how to deal with text.

Figure 6.16. A LoadPicture example.

Before ending this discussion of nontext graphics, however, a point deserves to be made here. In your Graphics application, you have been setting the Form's AutoRedraw property to true. This means that, when the graphics in your application's forms or picture boxes are obscured temporarily by other windows and then restored, Visual Basic takes charge of restoring the graphics. To do this, however, it needs to store the entire graphics image, which is costly in terms of memory.

There is another way to do the same thing, by restoring graphics images yourself. You must redraw the image every time a form Paint event occurs. This event is generated when an obscured part of your client area is uncovered—and then you are supposed to "repaint" the image you want. (The easiest way to do that is simply to redraw everything in the client area.) That's easy enough to do if you put the correct code in the Form_Paint( ) event, as you do later in this chapter. If you are going to use Paint events, however, you should know two more things: Paint events do not occur if AutoRedraw is True, and if AutoRedraw is False, you cannot draw graphics in the Form_Load ( ) Sub procedure. The next section discusses text.

Displaying Text in Visual Basic

In Visual Basic, graphical text (text that does not appear in text-oriented controls) can be printed in three places: on forms, in picture boxes, and on the printer. This chapter takes a look at the use of all three.

Before you begin, however, it is important to understand that, here, text is indeed treated as graphics. That means that the ANSI code of each character is not stored—when you print a character on a form, a picture of that character appears, and that's all; the text itself is not somewhere in memory, as a text or list box is. To write your own editor that doesn't use a text box as a base (and therefore can go beyond the 64K limit), you would have to handle all the screen details yourself.

You have already seen the Visual Basic fonts that were available when you designed your notepad application; now it's important to concentrate on how to print when it comes to graphical text. Printing text can be more involved than you might think, because most fonts in Windows do not have characters of the same width. Fonts in which all characters have the same width (called *monospace* fonts) exist in Windows, but fonts with different character widths (called *variable-width* fonts) are much more common. Because Windows normally uses the latter, you have to be careful about printing. To add more text to the end of a printed string, for example, you will have to figure out just where that string ends.

To print graphical text, then, you simply use the Print method (defined only for the types of objects to which you can print directly: forms, picture boxes, and the printer). Because it is a method, you use it together with the name of an object (or, if you omit the object name, Visual Basic assumes that you are referring to the current form). For example, you can print a string of text, as in the following example:

```
Form1.Print "No worries."
```

To see the result of this line, you can put it in the Form_Load Sub procedure of your Graphics application and then run that application, as follows:

```
Sub Form_Load()
  Form1.Print "No worries."
End Sub
```

The result appears in figure 6.17. The text appears in the upper left corner of the form—the upper left corner of the text appears at (0, 0). The reason is that text is printed at the current graphics output position, as set by the properties (CurrentX, CurrentY), where both quantities are measured in twips. To begin the text in the exact middle of the form, you can use the following example instead:

```
Sub Form_Load()
  CurrentX = ScaleWidth / 2
  CurrentY = ScaleHeight / 2
  Form1.Print "No worries."
End Sub
```

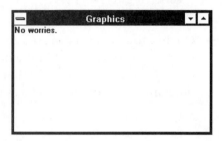

Figure 6.17. Graphics application with First Text String.

The result appears in figure 6.18. In general, the following line is the way you can use the Print method:

```
[object.]Print [expressionlist][{;¦,}]
```

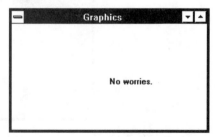

Figure 6.18. Text String Origin at Form Center.

Here, expressionlist is a list of the strings you want to print. Notice that you can use either a comma or a semicolon at the end of the expressionlist. Which one you use, if you use either one, determines where you leave the text cursor when you finish printing. If you use a semicolon, the text cursor is placed immediately after the text you print (so that future text immediately follows it); this program produces the same result as the one you just ran, as follows:

```
Sub Form_Load()
  CurrentX = ScaleWidth / 2
  CurrentY = ScaleHeight / 2
  Form1.Print "No ";
  Form1.Print "worries."
End Sub
```

On the other hand, if you use a comma, a tab is inserted, which means that the text cursor is placed in the next print zone. The default length for a tab is the width of 14 average characters of the current font. The following program, for example, produces the output in figure 6.19.

```
Sub Form_Load()
  Form1.Print "No ", "worries."
End Sub
```

This way, you can print tables of data in neat columns. In fact, you can set up your own tab widths with the Tab( ) function. For example, Tab(20) tabs over to a print zone that starts 20 average character widths rather than 14.

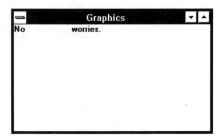

Figure 6.19. Tabbed text output.

For example, you might want to print the following table:

Region	Product
East	Apples
West	Tomatoes
North	Wheat
South	Oranges

You can print it with the Print method. To begin, let's move down a few lines. Because you move to the next line every time you use Print without an argument, you can skip three lines, as in the following example:

```
Sub Form_Load()
   Print
   Print
   Print
   :
End Sub
```

Next, you can place customized tabs in your table, in the following way:

```
Sub Form_Load()
   Print
   Print
   Print
   Print Tab(10); "Region"; Tab(30); "Product"
   Print
   Print Tab(10); "East"; Tab(30); "Apples"
   Print Tab(10); "West"; Tab(30); "Tomatoes"
   Print Tab(10); "North"; Tab(30); "Wheat"
   Print Tab(10); "South"; Tab(30); "Oranges"
   :
End Sub
```

You can even draw a box around your table, in the following way:

```
Sub Form_Load()
   Print
   Print
   Print
   Print Tab(10); "Region"; Tab(30); "Product"
   Print
```

```
       Print Tab(10); "East"; Tab(30); "Apples"
       Print Tab(10); "West"; Tab(30); "Tomatoes"
       Print Tab(10); "North"; Tab(30); "Wheat"
       Print Tab(10); "South"; Tab(30); "Oranges"
       DrawWidth = 2
       Line(650, 400)-(3600, 2000), , B
       Line (650, 930)-(3600, 930)
End Sub
```

The final table appears in figure 6.20, printed (as with all text) in the object's ForeColor. Of course, you can also print to picture boxes by double-clicking the picture box tool and changing the code in Form_Load( ) to the following:

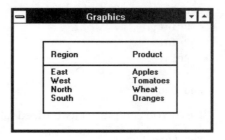

Figure 6.20. Tabbed tabular text output.

```
Sub Form_Load()
  Picture1.Print "This is a very long string for such a small picture box."
End Sub
```

Now set the picture box's AutoRedraw property to true (if you do not, you cannot put graphics in it from the Form_Load Sub procedure). As you can see in figure 6.21, because the string is too long for the picture box to hold, the text is cut off on the right. To fix this problem, you would have to know when to skip to the next line and, to know that, you would have to know the length of your text string as it will appear on the screen. You can determine the length by using the TextWidth method.

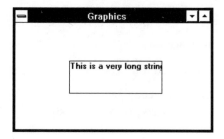

Figure 6.21. Truncated text in a picture box.

Determining the Length of the String on the Screen

You can use two methods to determine the dimensions of a text string as it will appear on the screen. (In an environment that uses variable-width fonts, these methods can be invaluable.) The two methods are called TextHeight and TextWidth. For example, the length of the string Now is the time. in your picture box is equal to the following line:

```
StringLength% = Picture1.TextWidth("Now is the time.")
```

Let's say that your picture box is not big enough to print this string on one line and that you have to break it up into two lines. To check where to break it up, you can use the TextWidth method.

> **Determining the height of a string of text.**
> Although TextWidth is the most commonly used method, you can use TextHeight to determine the height of a line of text by asking for the height of a string, as shown in the following line:
>
> Height% = TextHeight("ABCDEFGHIJK")
>
> Then, to position yourself down five lines, you only have to add 5 * Height% to CurrentY.]

Let's start this example by setting up an array of type String, as follows:

```
Sub Form_Load
  Static My_Text(4) As String
```

```
      :

End Sub
```

Next, you load each word into the string array, as follows:

```
Sub Form_Load
  Static My_Text(4) As String

  My_Text(1) = "Now "
  My_Text(2) = "is "
  My_Text(3) = "the "
  My_Text(4) = "time."
    :
End Sub
```

Then you loop over each word, adding it to a string to print and checking whether it is too long, as follows:

```
Sub Form_Load
  Static My_Text(4) As String

  My_Text(1) = "Now "
  My_Text(2) = "is "
  My_Text(3) = "the "
  My_Text(4) = "time."

  Temp$ = ""
  First_Line$ = ""

  For Word% = 1 To 4
  Temp$ = Temp$ + My_Text(Word%)
  If Picture1.TextWidth(Temp$) > Picture1.ScaleWidth Then Exit For
  First_Line$ = Temp$
  Next Word%
    :
End Sub
```

If the string is too long, you have to create a second line, in the following way:

```
Sub Form_Load
  Static My_Text(4) As String
```

```
My_Text(1) = "Now "
My_Text(2) = "is "
My_Text(3) = "the "
My_Text(4) = "time."

Temp$ = ""
First_Line$ = ""
Second_Line$ = ""

For Word% = 1 To 4
Temp$ = Temp$ + My_Text(Word%)
If Picture1.TextWidth(Temp$) > Picture1.ScaleWidth Then Exit For
First_Line$ = Temp$
Next Word%

FirstWordSecondLine% = Word%

For Word% = FirstWordSecondLine% to 4
Second_Line$ = SecondLine$ + My_Text(Word%)
Next Word%
:
End Sub
```

Finally, you can print the text, as follows:

```
Sub Form_Load
  Static My_Text(4) As String

  My_Text(1) = "Now "
  My_Text(2) = "is "
  My_Text(3) = "the "
  My_Text(4) = "time."

  Temp$ = ""
  First_Line$ = ""
  Second_Line$ = ""

  For Word% = 1 To 4
  Temp$ = Temp$ + My_Text(Word%)
  If Picture1.TextWidth(Temp$) > Picture1.ScaleWidth Then Exit For
  First_Line$ = Temp$
```

```
    Next Word%

    FirstWordSecondLine% = Word%

    For Word% = FirstWordSecondLine% to 4
    Second_Line$ = SecondLine$ + My_Text(Word%)
    Next Word%

    Picture1.Print First_Line$
    Picture1.Print Second_Line$

End Sub
```

The result of all this work appears in figure 6.22. Word-wrap is a common problem in printing with variable-width fonts. You can vary other font properties when you are printing, including underlining text or making it bold or italicized, which can make string widths even more unpredictable. As a recap from Chapter 2, these properties appear in table 6.8.

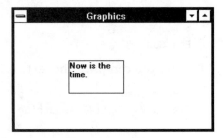

Figure 6.22. A word-wrap example.

Table 6.8. Font Properties in Visual Basic

Property	Means
FontName	Name of font, such as Courier or Modern
FontSize	Size of font in points (1/72nd of an inch)
FontBold	Makes font bold if true
FontItalic	Makes font italic if true

Property	Means
FontStrikethru	Strikes through characters with a dash if true
FontTransparent	Determines whether background shows around characters
FontUnderline	Characters are underlined if true

More uses for TextHeight and TextWidth.
TextHeight and TextWidth have many other uses, of course. For example, you can center text on a form by using them together with the ScaleWidth and ScaleHeight properties. Or, you can find the width of an average character by finding the width of a long string and dividing by the number of characters in it.

Because formatting text for output in a restricted space is a common problem, let's develop some code to help, beginning with the Form_Load event and assuming that you are printing to a picture box whose Name is Picture1. In other words, you want to break the print string PString$ into lines that fit in the picture box. You might set up a function named GetWord$( ) (which you write later in this chapter) to return the next word in PString$. Also, you can loop as long as it doesn't return "" (if it does, you have exhausted the print string), as follows:

```
Sub Form_Load()
  PString$ = "Now is the time for all good men..."

  PrintLine$ = ""
  NextWord$ = GetWord$()

  Do While NextWord$ <> ""
  :
  :
  Loop

End Sub
```

The following example uses a BASIC Do While loop. You assemble the line to print—PrintLine$—until it gets too long, and then you print it and start over on the next line. You can check its length by creating a temporary string, which you might name Temp$; that is, Temp$ equals PrintLine$ + NextWord$, and if Temp$ is too long for the picture box, it's time to print the following:

```
Sub Form_Load()
  PString$ = "Now is the time for all good men..."

  PrintLine$ = ""
  NextWord$ = GetWord$()

  Do While NextWord$ <> ""
  Temp$ = PrintLine$ + NextWord$
  If Picture1.TextWidth(Temp$) > Picture1.ScaleWidth Then
  Picture1.Print PrintLine$    'Print before too long
  Else
  :
  :
  End If
  Loop

End Sub
```

If you are printing "Now is the time for all good men...", then, the first time through, PrintLine$ equals "", and Temp$ (which equals PrintLine$ + NextWord$) equals "Now ". The next time through the loop, Temp$ equals "Now is ", and so on, until Temp is too long to fit on the line. If the line wasn't too long, on the other hand, you want to add the current word to PrintLine$, get the next word from GetWord$( ) (if there is one), and start over, as follows:

```
Sub Form_Load()
  PString$ = "Now is the time for all good men..."

  PrintLine$ = ""
  NextWord$ = GetWord$()
  Do While NextWord$ <> ""
  Temp$ = PrintLine$ + NextWord$
  If Picture1.TextWidth(Temp$) > Picture1.ScaleWidth Then
  Picture1.Print PrintLine$    'Print before too long
```

```
    Else
    PrintLine$ = Temp$
    End If
    NextWord$ = GetWord$()
    Loop

End Sub
```

That's it, except for one last thing. You have been printing lines when they get too long, but you have not yet printed the leftover words that make up the last line. After you print that remainder as shown in the following code, you are finished.

```
Sub Form_Load()
  PString$ = "Now is the time for all good men..."

  PrintLine$ = ""
  NextWord$ = GetWord$()

  Do While NextWord$ <> ""
  Temp$ = PrintLine$ + NextWord$
  If Picture1.TextWidth(Temp$) > Picture1.ScaleWidth Then
  Picture1.Print PrintLine$    'Print before too long
  Else
  PrintLine$ = Temp$
  End If
  NextWord$ = GetWord$()
  Loop

    Picture1.Print PrintLine$          'Print remainder
End Sub
```

The final step is to write the function GetWord$( ), (the function that returns the next word in the string PString$). This function needs a copy of PString$ from which to get the successive words, but you cannot just pass it a copy of the string PString$ every time, because it would keep chopping off and return the first word over and over. Instead, you can add a global string, StringToPrint, and let GetWord$( ) chop successive words off that. To do that, you declare StringToPrint global in a module that you can add, as in the following example:

```
Global StringToPrint As String
```

Or, you can make it a form-wide string by placing it in the declarations section of the general object, in the following way:

```
Dim StringToPrint As String
```

You can fill StringToPrint immediately in Form_Load( ), as shown in the following example (which gives GetWord$ access to it), as follows:

```
Sub Form_Load()
  PString$ = "Now is the time for all good men..."
  StringToPrint = PString$

  PrintLine$ = ""
  NextWord$ = GetWord$()

  Do While NextWord$ <> ""
  Temp$ = PrintLine$ + NextWord$
  If Picture1.TextWidth(Temp$) > Picture1.ScaleWidth Then
  Picture1.Print PrintLine$    'Print before too long
  Else
  PrintLine$ = Temp$
  End If
  NextWord$ = GetWord$()
  Loop

  Picture1.Print PrintLine$        'Print remainder
End Sub
```

Now let's write GetWord$( ). Your task is to chop off the first word of the string StringToPrint—in other words, to find the first space in that string and return everything up to and including it. If this was StringToPrint, then GetWord$( ) should return "Now " and leave StringToPrint as "is the time for all good men...", as follows:

```
"Now is the time for all good men..."
```

Let's begin with the easy case, in which StringToPrint has no spaces in it; that is, it is an empty string ("") or a single word. In that case, you can just return that single word or empty string. And, because you are chopping off words from StringToPrint, you make StringToPrint an empty string, indicating that there is nothing left, as follows:

```
Function GetWord$ ()
  If InStr(StringToPrint, " ") = 0 Then
```

```
    GetWord$ = StringToPrint
    StringToPrint = ""
    :
    :
```

In the following example, you are using the Visual Basic InStr( ) function
to determine whether there is a space in StringToPrint. As in other BASICs,
this function returns the place number of a substring in a string; in this
case, if InStr(StringToPrint, " ") equals 0, there is no space in StringToPrint.
Notice that you must return a value from the GetWord$ function—assign
the value you want to return to the name of the function, as follows:

```
Function GetWord$ ()                               'No words
  If InStr(StringToPrint, " ") = 0 Then
  GetWord$ = StringToPrint
  StringToPrint = ""
  :
  :
```

On the other hand, if there is a space in StringToPrint, that string has at
least two words in it; you should return the first one and cut it off the
string to prepare for the next time GetWord$ is called. You can do that as
shown in the following example, by using the Left$(String$, n) and
Right$(String$, n) Visual Basic string functions, which return the leftmost
or rightmost *n* characters in a string, as follows:

```
Function GetWord$ ()
  If InStr(StringToPrint, " ") = 0 Then       'No words
  GetWord$ = StringToPrint
  StringToPrint = ""
  Else
  GetWord$ = Left$(StringToPrint, InStr(StringToPrint, " "))
  StringToPrint = Right$(StringToPrint, Len(StringToPrint) -
  InStr(StringToPrint, " "))
  End If
End Function
```

That's it for GetWord$( )—and that's it for your string-printing routine.
Now you can use it to print to picture boxes, with the result appearing in
figure 6.23. In this case, you are asking PrintString( ) to print "Now is the
time for all good men..." in picture box Picture1, and the result appears
in figure 6.23. That's it for your Sub procedure PrintString( ); its code
appears in listing 6.1 (Prnstrg.Mak on the diskette).

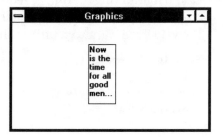

Figure 6.23. A tight text squeeze.

Listing 6.1. PrintString Sub Procedure (Prnstrg.Mak on the diskette)

```
Form Form1
  Caption      =         "Print String Example"

Picture box  Picture1
  TabIndex     =         0
Form1 General Declarations — — — — — — — — — — — — — — — —

  Dim StringToPrint As String          'Form-wide variable

Form1 — — — — — — — — — — — — — — — —

  Sub Form_Load ()
  PString$ = "Now is the time for all good men..."

  StringToPrint = PString$
  PrintLine$ = ""
  NextWord$ = GetWord$()
```

```
Do While NextWord$ <> ""
Temp$ = PrintLine$ + NextWord$
If Picture1.TextWidth(Temp$) > Picture1.ScaleWidth Then
Picture1.Print PrintLine$     'Print before too long
PrintLine$ = NextWord$
Else
PrintLine$ = Temp$
End If
NextWord$ = GetWord$()
Loop

Picture1.Print PrintLine$     'Print remainder.
End Sub

Function GetWord$ ()
If InStr(StringToPrint, " ") = 0 Then
GetWord$ = StringToPrint
StringToPrint = ""
Else
GetWord$ = Left$(StringToPrint, InStr(StringToPrint, " "))
StringToPrint = Right$(StringToPrint, Len(StringToPrint) - InStr(StringToPrint, " "))
End If
End Function
```

Next, let's turn to the topics of animation and designing your own icons.

Creating Your Own Animation

Visual Basic unfortunately does not handle pixel-by-pixel manipulations fast enough to be capable of doing true animation. Suppose that you want to animate a picture of a small rocket ship moving up the screen (see figure 6.24). You can address any pixel in your window or picture box with the PSet( ) method, which sets pixels one by one. To form a two-dimensional image, such as your rocket ship, however, you have to use PSet( ) inside a loop within a loop, as in Listing 6.2. But, as expected, the actual result (like most BASICs) is so slow that you can see the rocket ship being redrawn as it moves ponderously up the screen.

Figure 6.24. An animated rocket ship on the first try.

Listing 6.2. The Rocket Ship Sprite—First Try

```
Sub Command1_Click ()
  Static SpriteArray(1 To 16) As String
  Static Sprite(16, 16) As Long

  SpriteArray(1)  = "00000000E0000000"
  SpriteArray(2)  = "00000000E0000000"
  SpriteArray(3)  = "0000000EEE000000"
  SpriteArray(4)  = "000000EE3EE00000"
  SpriteArray(5)  = "000000EE3EE00000"
  SpriteArray(6)  = "00000EE333EE0000"
  SpriteArray(7)  = "00000EE333EE0000"
  SpriteArray(8)  = "00E00EE333EE00E0"
  SpriteArray(9)  = "00EE00EE3EE00EE0"
  SpriteArray(10) = "00EEE0EE3EE0EEE0"
  SpriteArray(11) = "00EEEEEE3EEEEEE0"
  SpriteArray(12) = "00EEE00E3E00EEE0"
  SpriteArray(13) = "00EE004444400EE0"
  SpriteArray(14) = "00E00004440000E0"
  SpriteArray(15) = "0000000444000000"
  SpriteArray(16) = "0000000040000000"

  DrawMode = 7
  BackColor = 0

  GoSub MakeSprite
```

```
    X = Int(ScaleWidth / 3)
    Y = ScaleHeight - UBound(SpriteArray, 1)

    GoSub DrawSprite
    Stepsize% = Int(ScaleHeight / 10)

    For i = (ScaleHeight - UBound(Sprite, 1)) To Stepsize% Step -Stepsize%
    Y = i
    GoSub DrawSprite
    Y = i - Stepsize%
    GoSub DrawSprite
    Next i

    Exit Sub

MakeSprite:
    For i = 1 To UBound(SpriteArray, 1)
    For j = 1 To Len(SpriteArray(i))
    CurrentColor% = Asc(UCase$(Mid$(SpriteArray(i), j, 1)))
    If CurrentColor% <= Asc("9") Then
    CurrentColor% = CurrentColor% - Asc("0")
    Else
    CurrentColor% = CurrentColor% - Asc("A") + 10
    End If
    Sprite(j, i) = QBColor(CurrentColor%)
    Next j
    Next i
Return

DrawSprite:
    For ii = 1 To UBound(Sprite, 1)
    For jj = 1 To UBound(Sprite, 2)
    PSet (X + ii - 1, Y + jj - 1), Sprite(ii, jj)
    Next jj
    Next ii
Return

End Sub
```

It would be best if Visual Basic gave you bitmap support (two-dimensional arrays of screen or printer bits) because then you could move your bit maps around the way you want. It doesn't, however (although you can interface to the underlying Windows system calls for bitmap support—or any kind of Windows system calls, as you will see later). Even so, you can cheat.

Visual Basic supports picture box controls, which are your best bet for animation. You can easily move picture boxes around the screen (Visual Basic moves the associated bitmap around for you almost instantaneously), and you can even switch between them rapidly to create animation.

The rocket ship is referred to in graphics as a *sprite*, which is a simple bitmap that doesn't change but that can be moved around the screen. To move it around the screen, you first must load it in a picture box or Image control: You can do that with the LoadPicture function. First, you can draw the figure you want in an application such as Windows Paint, and then save it in bitmap (.BMP) format. Next, you can read it in with a line like the following:

```
Sub Form_Click ()
  Image1.Picture = LoadPicture("C:\WINDOWS\IMAGE.BMP")
End Sub
```

The window in figure 6.25, for example, was produced in this way, by loading in a .BMP file directly with LoadPicture( ). You can create images of any size (up to full-screen size), in fact, by cutting sections from a larger picture (with the Paint program's Copy To... item in the Edit menu). You can therefore easily create your rocket as a small .BMP file, load it in a picture box or Image control, and send it around the screen with the Move method, which moves Visual Basic objects (forms or controls).

Figure 6.25. A LoadPicture bit-map file example.

Copying the screen to the clipboard and Windows Paint.
You can even load copies of what has appeared on the screen into forms or picture boxes. If you press Print Screen while you are in Windows, Windows pastes a copy of the complete screen to the clipboard. From there, you can paste it into Windows Paint, work on it, and then save it as a .BMP file that you can load into Visual Basic graphics objects.

Let's create the rocket ship as an icon, to give you some experience in creating .ICO files. This experience is useful because a) the rocket ship is small enough to be an icon and b) you will learn how to produce custom icons for your applications. In fact, you can even use the same icon as the icon for the program as a whole; that is, if you call this program sprite2 (assuming that the slow program in listing 6.2 is sprite1), you can use the rocket ship as Sprite2.exe's icon.

Setting the mouse cursor to an icon.
You can also change the mouse cursor into various icons as it moves around the window by using the MousePointer property of controls and forms. As the mouse cursor passes over that form or control, it changes into the corresponding icon (which you can also change at run-time). If you design your own icons, you can produce some interesting results.

Creating Customized Icons in Visual Basic

Visual Basic provides you with an extensive icon library in the subdirectories of the ICONS directory. Some of the writing icons appear in figure 6.26. Because a careful search of all these icons does not turn up any rocket ships, however, you have to design your own.

To design your own icons, Visual Basic provides the IconWorks application. It is a Visual Basic program, much as you might write yourself, but you can design icons with it. Load this program (buried deep in Samples\Iconwrks\Iconwrks.Mak) into Visual Basic now and run it. Its display looks something like figure 6.27.

Note02

Pencil01

Book02

Note16

Default

Figure 6.26. Sample Visual Basic Library icons.

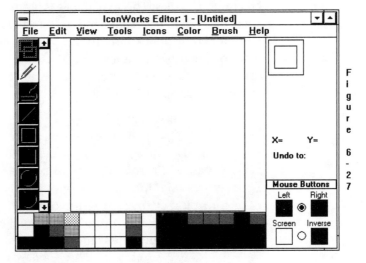

Figure 6.27. Visual Basic's IconWorks at work.

IconWorks is almost a full-power paint program, and it includes such tools as pixel-by-pixel drawing (with the pen-shaped tool in the upper left), color filling (with the roller-shaped tool), line drawing, and more. A complete help system is built right in (in the Help menu). You can use IconWorks now to draw your rocket ship, as shown in figure 6.28. Make sure that the background color is black, because this icon appears against the black background of Sprite2.exe's window. Save this icon as Sprite2.ico by using the Save As... menu item in IconWorks' File menu.

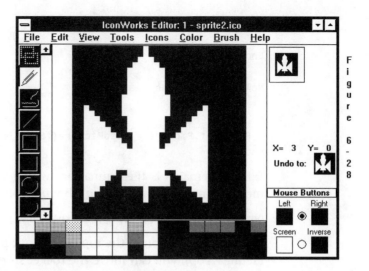

Figure 6.28. The rocket ship icon in IconWorks.

Now you are ready to put your new icon to work in animation. Start a new project in Visual Basic and set the form's BackColor property to black (an RGB value of RGB(0, 0, 0), or black), and its Caption to Animation. Next, add a command button and a picture box, as shown in figure 6.29.

Figure 6.29. The animation example's template.

Give the command button the caption "Click Me". Click the form and bring up the Form_Load( ) subprocedure, as follows:

```
Sub Form_Load ()

End Sub
```

Now add this line:

```
Sub Form_Load ()
  Picture1.Picture = LoadPicture("SPRITE2.ICO")
End Sub
```

All that remains is the animation, which you can do with the Move method. In general, it works in the following way:

```
Object.Move left![, top![, width![, height!]]]
```

Because the location of the top left of your picture box is (Picture1.Left, Picture1.Top), you can move the rocket ship picture box up the screen by changing the top! value you pass to Move successively in a loop, as follows:

```
Sub Command1_Click ()
  For loop_index% = Picture1.Top To 0 Step -50
  Picture1.Move Picture1.Left, loop_index%
  Next loop_index%
End Sub
```

That's it; now the rocket ship flies smoothly up the window when you click the Click Me button. Because the internal functions of Visual Basic (actually, Windows) handle the bit manipulations on the screen, everything happens quickly. The entire program appears in Listing 6.3 (Sprite2.Mak on the diskette).

 Listing 6.3. Sprite2, Animation—Second Try (Sprite2.Mak on the diskette)

```
Sub Form_Load ()
  Picture1.Picture = LoadPicture("SPRITE2.ICO")
End Sub

Sub Command1_Click ()
  For loop_index% = Picture1.Top To 0 Step -50
  Picture1.Move Picture1.Left, loop_index%
  Next loop_index%
End Sub
```

There is one last thing to do here—associate the rocket ship icon, Sprite2.ico, with Sprite2.exe so that the user can simply double-click that icon in the Windows Program Manager to start the program. You can do that at design-time simply by simply setting the form's Icon property to Sprite2.ico. Now when you select the Make EXE File... item in Visual Basic's File menu, you see that the rocket ship icon is the one Visual Basic will use for the .exe file (see figure 6.30). Then, after you create the .exe file, you can add Sprite2.exe to the Program Manager (by using the Program Manager's New... menu item in its File menu), as shown in figure 6.31.

Figure 6.30. Adding a custom icon to your program.

Figure 6.31. Using a custom icon for your program.

If someone double-clicks sprite2's icon, the program begins. That's it for animation, and that's it for your study of screen graphics for this chapter; next, you will learn about printer graphics.

Using a Printer from Visual Basic

It turns out that, when it comes to graphics, you use the printer much as you might use a picture box or form. In particular, you can simply use the Print method as before, except that now you use it with the Printer object, which corresponds to the default printer that was loaded with the Windows control panel. To print "Now is the time for all good men..." on the printer in underlined Courier text, for example, you can do it as shown in the following example:

```
Sub Form_Load ()
    Printer.FontName = "Courier"
    Printer.FontUnderline = True
    Printer.Print "Now is the time for all good men..."
End Sub
```

Similarly, you can use CurrentX and CurrentY to position printer output on the page (as measured in twips), as follows:

```
Sub Form_Load ()
    Printer.CurrentX = 1440
    Printer.CurrentY = 2880
    Printer.FontName = "Courier"
    Printer.FontUnderline = True
    Printer.Print "Now is the time for all good men..."
End Sub
```

This code doesn't move the printer head, but it does indicate where graphics should go on the next page. You can skip to the next page, in fact, with the NewPage method, as follows:

```
Sub Form_Load ()
    Printer.CurrentX = 1440
    Printer.CurrentY = 2880
    Printer.FontName = "Courier"
    Printer.FontUnderline = True
    Printer.Print "Now is the time for all good men..."
    Printer.NewPage
End Sub
```

In fact, because Visual Basic is designed to be device independent, there is little more to learn here. For example, the Printer object supports the other graphics methods you saw earlier (PSet, Line, and Circle), and it includes the normal graphical properties, such as ScaleHeight and ScaleWidth, so you can draw a circle in the following way:

```
Sub Form_Load ()
  Printer.CurrentX = 1440
  Printer.CurrentY = 2880
  Printer.FontName = "Courier"
  Printer.FontUnderline = True
  Printer.Print "Now is the time for all good men..."
  Printer.NewPage
  Printer.Circle (ScaleWidth/4, ScaleHeight/4), ScaleHeight/5
End Sub
```

One method you have not seen before, however, is the PrintForm method, which lets you print an entire form, as shown in the following example (if the form has graphics in it, set the AutoRedraw property to True so that the graphics also print).

```
Sub Form_Load ()
  Form1.PrintForm
End Sub
```

Note, however, that this code prints with only pixel resolution (as though it were a direct transcription from the screen); if you want higher-resolution graphics, use the Print method. That's it for printing, which is easy in Visual Basic; let's turn next to tailoring the Visual Basic graphics coordinate system.

Changing Coordinate Systems

Sometimes the default coordinate system in your windows, which looks like the following figure, is not optimal for what you want to present.

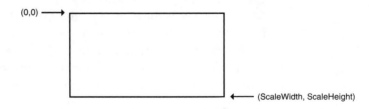

Suppose that you want to display the following data for your telephone bills by month (note that month 3 is missing from the study), as follows:

Month of Study	Phone Bill ($)
1	200
2	95
4	350
5	425

By using these data values, it is much better if the window is set up something in the following way:

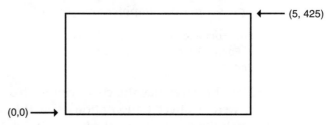

You can set up your window in exactly this way, in fact, with the Scale method, which you use like this:

```
Scale (xtop!, yleft!) - (xright!, ybottom!)
```

This method sets the new coordinates of the top left of the client area of your window to (xtop!, yleft!) and the new bottom right corner to (xright!, ybottom!). To do this in your program, you need to execute only a single statement, in the following way:

```
Scale (0, YBiggest)-(XBiggest, 0)  'Assume (0, 0) origin
```

where YBiggest is the biggest y value you have to plot and XBiggest is the biggest x value. To find those values, you can put the following code into the Form_Paint( ) Sub procedure—that is, the Paint event, which is called every time Windows has to redraw the form (leave the AutoRedraw property False)—of a new project named, Plotter.Mak, as follows:

```
Dim XVal(4), YVal(4) As Single      'Form-level variables
Dim XBiggest, YBiggest As Single
```

```
Sub Form_Paint ()
   'Plotting program. Assumes origin is (0, 0)

   Cls

   XVal(1) = 1
   YVal(1) = 200
   XVal(2) = 2
   YVal(2) = 95
   XVal(3) = 4
   YVal(3) = 350
   XVal(4) = 5
   YVal(4) = 425

   XBiggest = 0
   For loop_index% = 1 To UBound(XVal)
   If XVal(loop_index%) > XBiggest Then
   XBiggest = XVal(loop_index%)
   End If
   Next loop_index%

   YBiggest = 0
   For loop_index% = 1 To UBound(YVal)
   If YVal(loop_index%) > YBiggest Then
   YBiggest = YVal(loop_index%)
   End If
   Next loop_index%

   Scale (0, YBiggest)-(XBiggest, 0)'Assume (0, 0) origin
   :
```

Now you have set up the window the way you want it, as shown in the
following figure (your coordinates are scaled to your data):

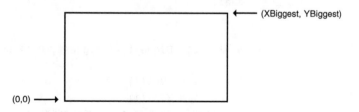

All that remains is to plot your values directly; you can do that as shown in the following example:

```
Dim XVal(4), YVal(4) As Single        'Form-level variables
Dim XBiggest, YBiggest As Single

Sub Form_Paint ()
  'Plotting program. Assumes origin is (0, 0)

  Cls

  XVal(1) = 1
  :
  :
  Scale (0, YBiggest)-(XBiggest, 0)'Assume (0, 0) origin

  CurrentX = XVal(1)
  CurrentY = YVal(1)
  For loop_index% = 1 To UBound(XVal)
  Line -(XVal(loop_index%), YVal(loop_index%))
  Next loop_index%
  :
```

You can also add a Form_Resize event. It occurs when the form is resized, and you can put code in the event so that the data is replotted as follows:

```
Dim XVal(4), YVal(4) As Single        'Form-level variables
Dim XBiggest, YBiggest As Single

Sub Form_Paint ()
  'Plotting program. Assumes origin is (0, 0)

  Cls

  XVal(1) = 1


  Scale (0, YBiggest)-(XBiggest, 0)'Assume (0, 0) origin

  CurrentX = XVal(1)
  CurrentY = YVal(1)
  For loop_index% = 1 To UBound(XVal)
  Line -(XVal(loop_index%), YVal(loop_index%))
  Next loop_index%
```

```
End Sub

Sub Form_Resize ()
  Call Form_Paint
End Sub
```

In it, you call Form_Paint( ), which you can call as though it were any other Sub procedure, of course. The result of all this appears in figure 6.32 and in Listing 6.4 (Plotter.Mak on the diskette). (Note that, because you set the origin to (0, 0), the points do not begin there). Your plotter is a success.

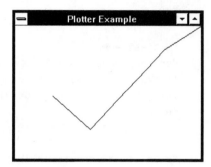

Figure 6.32. The Plotter application.

 Listing 6.4. Plotter.Mak

```
Form Form1
  Caption      =        "Plotter Example"

  Dim XVal(4), YVal(4) As Single      'Form-level variables
  Dim XBiggest, YBiggest As Single

Sub Form_Paint ()
  'Plotting program. Assumes origin is (0, 0)

  Cls

  XVal(1) = 1
  YVal(1) = 200
  XVal(2) = 2
  YVal(2) = 95
```

continues

Listing 6.4. continued

```
    XVal(3) = 4
    YVal(3) = 350
    XVal(4) = 5
    YVal(4) = 425

    XBiggest = 0
    For loop_index% = 1 To UBound(XVal)
    If XVal(loop_index%) > XBiggest Then
    XBiggest = XVal(loop_index%)
    End If
    Next loop_index%

    YBiggest = 0
    For loop_index% = 1 To UBound(YVal)
    If YVal(loop_index%) > YBiggest Then
    YBiggest = YVal(loop_index%)
    End If
    Next loop_index%

    Scale (0, YBiggest)-(XBiggest, 0)'Assume (0, 0) origin

    CurrentX = XVal(1)
    CurrentY = YVal(1)
    For loop_index% = 1 To UBound(XVal)
    Line -(XVal(loop_index%), YVal(loop_index%))
    Next loop_index%

End Sub

Sub Form_Resize ()
  Call Form_Paint
End Sub
```

That's it for coverage of graphics in this chapter. Let's move on now to Chapter 7, where you write a mouse-driven Paint program to incorporate the mouse with your graphics abilities.

Summary

In this chapter, you have learned a great deal about graphics handling in Visual Basic. The chapter has described how to draw points, lines, rectangles, circles, and ellipses, and how to draw them in different colors, in different ways (DrawMode and DrawStyle) and fill them with a variety of patterns (FillPattern and FillColor). It explored loading pictures from files directly into picture boxes, Image controls (which can stretch the pictures they hold), and forms. The chapter presented an easy and quick method of designing your own icons in addition to creating your own graphics animation with the Move method. It described the AutoRedraw property and its capability to preserve a copy of graphics on a form and redraw it when necessary. It also described how to print text in a picture box or in a form—as well as on the printer. Finally, the chapter explained how to change the graphics coordinate system in Visual Basic to fit your data better. Graphics methods such as these can add much visual appeal to your program, and bring both color and pizazz to your applications. Use these methods whenever possible.

New Properties	Description
AutoRedraw	When it is set for a form, it stores a copy of the form and redraws it automatically when needed (if the form is covered up and then uncovered, for example, or if the form was resized)
AutoSize	If True, lets a picture box grow or shrink to fit the picture it displays
CurrentX	Holds the current graphics x coordinate position, which you can define lines, boxes, circles, and printed text with respect to
CurrentY	Holds the current graphics y coordinate position, which you can define lines, boxes, circles, and printed text with respect to.

New Properties	Description
DrawMode	Sets the way the graphics pen affects the original screen data when it draws (see table 6.5).
DrawStyle	Sets the style of the graphics pen you want to use (see table 6.4)
DrawWidth	Sets the width (in pixels) of the graphics pen
FillColor	Sets the color to be used when filling graphics figures
FillStyle	Sets the fill pattern used when filling graphics figures (see table 6.7)
ScaleHeight	The height of a form's client area
ScaleWidth	The width of a form's client area

New Methods	Description
Circle	Draws a circle; use it in the following way:
	[object].Circle [Step] (x!, y!), radius! [,[color&][,[start!] [,[end!][, aspect!]]]]
Line	Draws a line; use it in the following way:
	[object.]Line [[Step](x1!, y1!)]-[Step](x2!, y2!)[,[color&],B[F]]]
Move	Moves a control in a form; use it in the following way:
	Object.Move left![, top![, width![, height!]]]
Point	Returns the color of a point in a form
Print	Prints in picture boxes, the printer, or forms; use it in the following way: [object.]Print [expressionlist][{;|,}]

New Methods	Description
PSet	Sets a pixel; use it in the following way:
	[object.]Pset [Step] (x!, y!)[,color&]
Scale	Sets the graphics coordinate scale; use it in the following way:
	Scale (xtop!, yleft!) - (xright!, ybottom!)
TextHeight	Returns the height of a string of text for the associated form or control
TextWidth	Returns the width of a string of text for the associated form or control

1	2	3	4	5	6		8	9	10
11	12	13	14	A		C	D	E	

7

The Mouse and a Mouse-driven Paint Program

In this chapter, you will see how to use the mouse and read mouse events (including location and mouse button push information). You will also use the graphics skills you learned in Chapter 6 to write a fully functional Windows paint program. In addition, you will learn about the following topics:

▼ Drawing with the mouse

▼ The MouseDown and MouseUp events

▼ "Stretching" graphics images

▼ Saving graphics images in disk files

▼ Using the Windows clipboard

▼ Changing the graphics scale used (from twips to pixels)

▼ The MouseMove event

The major program in this chapter is the Paint program, which lets you draw points, lines, boxes, and circles, and fill them in. You can print the graphics images you create and store them on disk, and write them out and read them back in whenever you want. This program is pretty large, and teaches you a few things about program design (such as the need for making larger programs modular). The skills you learn in this chapter can be applied when you write large programs of your own, or when you need to set up a user interface of some kind. It goes without saying that, if you want to include a painting capability in your program, the information here will be useful. In addition, you will pick up the skills to let you handle the mouse, which is invaluable in all kinds of programs, particularly in word processors, spreadsheets, business form-design programs, and many others.

Chapter 6 explored the Visual Basic graphics system. In this chapter, you study the mouse and learn how to put them together by creating a mouse-driven paint program at the same time. You have already been using the mouse, one of the two most important user interface tools in Windows (the other is the keyboard) throughout this book by responding to the Click event for various controls. There is much more information in this chapter, however, than you have been using: You can get the precise location of the mouse pointer (called the cursor or pointer in Windows) when the user clicks or releases a button. You can watch, in fact, as users move the mouse around the screen. Let's begin by investigating one of the basic mouse events, the MouseDown event.

MouseDown Events

A MouseDown event is generated when the user positions the mouse cursor on a form and presses a mouse button. This event is not the same as a Click event. In a Click event, the user must press and release the mouse button; a MouseDown event occurs when the user simply presses a mouse button. These kinds of events are recognized by forms, picture boxes, labels, and any control that includes a list. Note that controls such as buttons respond only to Click events, not to MouseDown events.

In a MouseDown event, you get considerably more information than you did with the Click event. To see this, let's begin putting together the Paint program. Start Visual Basic and create a new project. Give the default form (Form1) the Caption Paint and set its AutoRedraw property True. Now click the form, bring up the code window, and find the Form_MouseDown( ) event procedure in it. That procedure already has the following template:

```
Sub Form_MouseDown (Button As Integer,Shift As Integer,X As Single,Y As Single)

End Sub
```

You have not seen a number of arguments that are passed to this procedure: Button, Shift, X, and Y. The Button and Shift arguments pass mouse button and keyboard shift state information to you, and the X and Y arguments report the position of the mouse cursor. You can make use of that information by reporting the cursor's position when you press a mouse button. To do that, create two new text boxes, Text1 and Text2, and place them on the form. You can report the position, (X, Y), as shown in the following example:

```
Sub Form_MouseDown (Button As Integer,Shift As Integer,X As Single,Y As Single)
    Text1.Text = Str$(X)
    Text2.Text = Str$(Y)
End Sub
```

Now run the program and press a mouse button (the MouseDown event occurs when any mouse button is pressed); when you do, the mouse cursor's position is reported (in twips) in the two text boxes. In this way, you can read direct information about the mouse cursor's position. Now let's look at the two other arguments passed to you, Button and Shift, which both are integers. The Button argument describes which mouse button is pressed by encoding that information in its lowest three bits. It looks like the following figure (recall that an integer is 2 bytes, or 16 bits, long).

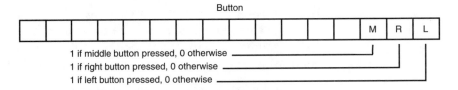

You can test for only one button being pushed, not two or three at a time; that is, Button reports only which button was pushed first—right, left, or middle (not many mouse devices have middle buttons anymore, although some do). The event examined next, the MouseMove event, does report when two or more buttons are pressed simultaneously. Here, however, the Button argument can take only one of three values (see table 7.1).

Table 7.1. Values for the Button Argument (MouseDown, MouseUp)

Button Value	Binary	Means
1	0000000000000001	Left button was pushed
2	0000000000000010	Right button was pushed
4	0000000000000100	Middle button was pushed

Note in particular that Button cannot be 0 because at least one button must have been pushed to cause the MouseDown event. Let's make use of this information in your program; you can add another text box, Text3, to report which button caused the MouseDown event with a Select Case statement, as follows:

```
Sub Form_MouseDown (Button As Integer,Shift As Integer,X As Single,Y As Single)
    Text1.Text = Str$(X)
    Text2.Text = Str$(Y)
    Select Case Button
    Case 1
    Text3.Text = "Left Button"
    Case 2
    Text3.Text = "Right Button"
    Case 4
    Text3.Text = "Middle Button"
    End Select
End Sub
```

Now when you run the program, it reports not only the position of the mouse cursor when the MouseDown event occurred but also which button caused it. If you use the left mouse button, for example, you may see something like the window in figure 7.1.

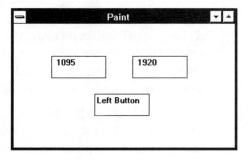

Figure 7.1. A MouseInfo window.

Besides X, Y, and Button, the Shift argument also returns some useful information. This integer indicates whether the Ctrl or Shift keys on the keyboard were pressed when the mouse button was clicked (some programs distinguish between Click and Shift-Click, and Visual Basic has no ShiftClick event). This information is encoded in the last two bits of Shift like this:

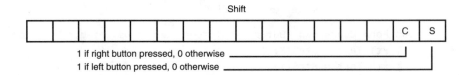

In other words, Shift can take on three values: 0 (neither key was pressed), 1, or 2, as shown in table 7.2.

Table 7.2. Values for the Shift Argument

Shift Value	Binary	Means
0	0000000000000000	Neither Shift nor Ctrl was down
1	0000000000000001	Shift key was down
2	0000000000000010	Ctrl key was down

So far, you have seen that the MouseDown event reports four things: the X position of the mouse cursor, the Y position of the mouse cursor, which one of the buttons was pushed, and which (if either) of the keyboard's Shift or Control keys was pushed. MouseDown also has an important use in paint programs: It usually is used to begin a drawing operation.

If you want to draw a line in a paint program, for example, you might press the left mouse button once to indicate where you want the line to begin, move to the other end of the line, and release the button. You then expect the program to draw a line between the two locations. In Visual Basic terms, you can translate that into saving the point where the MouseDown event occurred, which you can call the Anchor point (AnchorX, AnchorY), setting the current graphics position to the same point, and then performing the drawing operation when the mouse button goes up. In other words, when the user presses a mouse button, you record that position; when the user releases it, you can draw a line or a box, or whatever figure was required. That means that you should remove the three text boxes from the form and change Form_MouseDown( ) to the following:

```
Sub Form_MouseDown (Button As Integer,Shift As Integer,X As Single,Y As Single)
    If Button = 1 Then          'Left button
    AnchorX = X
    AnchorY = Y
    CurrentX = X
    CurrentY = Y
    End If
End Sub
```

You should also make AnchorX and AnchorY into global variables so that any routine in the application can tell where the MouseDown event occurred. This process is useful if, for example, you are supposed to draw a line from the anchor point to the current location when the mouse button goes up. To make these variables global, declare them the following way in a module:

```
Global AnchorX As Integer
Global AnchorY As Integer
```

Now you can tell, from anywhere in the application, where the anchor point is. Let's put this to work and begin drawing.

MouseMove Events

One capability of a paint program should be to draw continuously when the user moves the mouse cursor; in other words, the user should be able to press the mouse button and move the mouse to create a freehand drawing by leaving a trail of pixels. To do that, you need to know where the mouse cursor is at any particular time. You can do that with the MouseMove event. Every time the mouse is moved across a form or selected controls (file list boxes, labels, list boxes, or picture boxes), a MouseMove event is generated. MouseMove events usually are not generated for each pixel over which the mouse cursor moves; instead, Windows generates only a certain number of such events per second. Still, you will see that it will be good enough for your application.

In addition, the Button argument in a MouseMove event reports the complete state of the mouse buttons (it can report whether more than one button is being pressed). The values that it can report for Button are shown in table 7.3.

303

Table 7.3. Values for the Button Argument (MouseMove)

Button Value	Binary	Means
0	0000000000000000	No button is pushed
1	0000000000000001	Only left button is pushed
2	0000000000000010	Only right button is pushed
3	0000000000000011	Right and left buttons are pushed
4	0000000000000100	Only middle button is pushed
5	0000000000000101	Middle and left buttons are pushed
6	0000000000000110	Middle and right buttons are pushed
7	0000000000000111	All three buttons are pushed

Let's make use of the MouseMove event to begin drawing in your paint application. In particular, when the user presses the left mouse button, you set the anchor point (AnchorX, AnchorY) and set that location as the current graphics location. Next, when the user moves and still holds down the left mouse button, you want to draw on the screen, following the mouse cursor's movements. To do that, find the Form_MouseMove ( ) Sub procedure in the following code window:

```
Sub Form_MouseMove (Button As Integer,Shift As Integer,X As Single,Y As Single):
End Sub
```

Because you want to make sure that you draw only when the left mouse button is down, you can check the value of button as follows:

```
Sub Form_MouseMove (Button As Integer,Shift As Integer,X As Single,Y As Single)
  If Button = 1 Then          'Left button
  :

  End If
End Sub
```

Now you should draw on the form, following the mouse cursor. When you enter this procedure, the user has already moved from the original MouseDown location. Because you set the graphics position to that position already, however, you only need to draw from the graphics position to the current position. You can do that with the following Line method:

```
Sub Form_MouseMove (Button As Integer,Shift As Integer,X As Single,Y As Single)
   If Button = 1 Then          'Left button
   Line -(X, Y)
   End If
End Sub
```

If you do not specify the first point with the Line method, it uses the current graphics position, which you were smart enough to set when the mouse originally went down. Now you are free to draw on the form as much as you want, simply by holding the left mouse button down, as shown in figure 7.2.

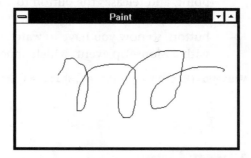

Figure 7.2. Freehand drawing with the Paint application.

So far, you have used only two event procedures, MouseMove and MouseDown, but you have already been able to draw on the following form:

```
Sub Form_MouseMove (Button As Integer,Shift As Integer,X As Single,Y As Single)
   If Button = 1 Then          'Left button
   Line -(X, Y)
   End If
End Sub
```

```
Sub Form_MouseDown (Button As Integer,Shift As Integer,X As Single,Y As Single)
   If Button = 1 Then          'Left button
   AnchorX = X
   AnchorY = Y
   CurrentX = X
   CurrentY = Y
   End If
End Sub
```

Paint programs, however, are expected to draw all sorts of objects, such as lines and rectangles. For these items, you need to determine the position where the mouse button went up.

MouseUp Events

To draw a line, the user moves the mouse cursor to the first endpoint (the anchor point), presses the left mouse button, moves to the other endpoint, and releases the button to complete the line. You already set the anchor point (AnchorX, AnchorY) when the user presses the left mouse button, so now you have to watch where it is released. You can do that with a MouseUp event, which appears in the following way:

```
Sub Form_MouseUp (Button As Integer,Shift As Integer,X As Single,Y As Single)


End Sub
```

Drawing Lines

In the following procedure, you just check whether the left mouse button was the button released and, if so, draw the line from (AnchorX, AnchorY) to the current position (X, Y).

```
Sub Form_MouseUp (Button As Integer,Shift As Integer,X As Single,Y As Single)
   If Button = 1 Then
   Line (AnchorX, AnchorY) - (X, Y)
   End
End Sub
```

This leaves you with a problem, however: Although the line is drawn, you are still drawing over all the intermediate positions with the MouseMove( ) Sub procedure, as follows:

```
Sub Form_MouseMove (Button As Integer,Shift As Integer,X As Single,Y As Single)
    If Button = 1 Then          'Left button
    Line -(X, Y)
    End If
End Sub
```

In other words, you are drawing freehand and lines at the same time. Usually, paint applications solve this problem by letting the user select only one drawing tool at a time. You can do the same thing by setting up a toolbox from which the user can select tools. To do that, you can create a toolbox of command buttons, as shown in figure 7.3, that correspond to the painting operations you will support in this program: Draw, Line, Box, Circle, Text, and Clear. Give each one a name to match its caption.

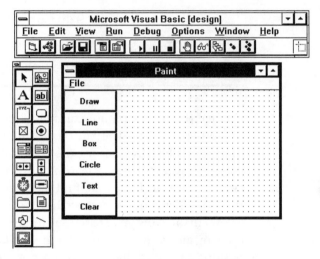

Figure 7.3. A Paint application template with buttons.

Changing the color of command buttons.
If you prefer not to have a toolbox full of gray buttons (the default color) in your Paint application, you can change their color by changing their BackColor property.

Paint applications often have a different mouse cursor in the drawing area (a cross rather than an arrow) from the cursor with which you select tools from the toolbox. You can do that here too. Forms and most controls have a MousePointer property, which enables you to specify the mouse cursor style as it passes over that form or control. You can change the cursor to any of those shown in table 7.4 by using the properties window.

Table 7.4. Mouse Cursor Styles

Default	Use Form's Default Cursor
Arrow	Use arrow
Cross	Use a cross
I-Beam	Use an I-beam (the insertion-point cursor)
Icon	Use an icon
Size	Use a sizing arrow
Size NE SW	Use northeast-southwest arrow
Size N S	Use north-south arrow

Change the form's mouse cursor to a cross, for example, by using the properties window. The buttons in the toolbox, however, will use the same cursor because they use the default mouse cursor (the form's mouse cursor) unless you change it. You can switch them back to using an arrow cursor, however. To do that, find each button's MousePointer property in the properties window, display the list of available cursors, and choose the arrow cursor. Now you are set; the mouse cursor switches to a cross in the drawing area and to an arrow in the toolbox. You can make one of these buttons in the toolbox active immediately—the Clear button, which simply clears the drawing area. Because that's done with the Cls statement in Visual Basic, just add this line to ClearButton_Click( ), as follows:

```
Sub ClearButton_Click()
  Cls
End Sub
```

In addition, you can have each button set a flag to indicate to the rest of the application which drawing tool is in use; that is, a MouseUp event means something different if you are drawing lines or rectangles. Because these flags should be global, add them to the (declarations) section of the module that holds AnchorX and AnchorY—Paint.Bas, as follows:

```
Global AnchorX As Integer
Global AnchorY As Integer
Global DrawFlag As Integer
Global LineFlag As Integer
Global BoxFlag As Integer
Global CircleFlag As Integer
Global TextFlag As Integer
```

In other words, you now have two kinds of data available to you anywhere in the program: the anchor point (AnchorX, AnchorY), and a set of flags that tell you which drawing tool is active. To set the flags, you can make each button in your toolbox set the corresponding flag while you reset the rest. This way, you can tell (from anywhere in the Paint program) which drawing operation is being used. This lets you cut up your program into smaller event procedures rather than handle everything in one giant procedure; doing so makes your program more modular, and that is very important in larger programs. To set these flags, you need to put the following code in the button's Sub procedures:

```
Sub DrawButton_Click()
   DrawFlag = True        'Turn drawing on
   LineFlag = False
   BoxFlag = False
   CircleFlag = False
   TextFlag = False
End Sub

Sub LineButton_Click()
   DrawFlag = False
   LineFlag = True        'Turn line drawing on
   BoxFlag = False
   CircleFlag = False
   TextFlag = False
End Sub

Sub BoxButton_Click()
   DrawFlag = False
   LineFlag = False
   BoxFlag = True         'Turn box drawing on
   CircleFlag = False
   TextFlag = False
End Sub
```

```
Sub CircleButton_Click()
  DrawFlag = False
  LineFlag = False
  BoxFlag = False
  CircleFlag = True      'Turn circle drawing on
  TextFlag = False
End Sub

Sub TextButton_Click()
  DrawFlag = False
  LineFlag = False
  BoxFlag = False
  CircleFlag = False
  TextFlag = True        'Turn text drawing on
End Sub
```

Now the buttons are done and your toolbox is finished; the only thing that remains is to use these flags with the mouse events. In other words, from now on, you can just check the global variables DrawFlag, LineFlag, BoxFlag, CircleFlag, and TextFlag to find out which drawing tool is active. You can check, for example, whether the DrawFlag is True in the MouseMove event; if it is, you draw the following:

```
Sub Form_MouseMove (Button As Integer,Shift As Integer,X As Single,Y As Single)
  If Button = 1 Then         'Left button

  If DrawFlag Then
  Line -(X, Y)
  End If
  End If
End Sub
```

This code solves the problem of drawing lines and freehand at the same time. Now, if the user selects the Line tool, he can tack down one end of the line by pressing the mouse button and then move to the other end, releasing it to create the line.

Paint programs usually do more than this. They usually display the line after one end has been tacked down at the anchor point, giving the impression of stretching a line into a shape, which becomes permanent when you release the mouse button. You can do that here too, by checking whether LineFlag is True in the MouseMove event Sub procedure, as follows:

```
Sub Form_MouseMove (Button As Integer,Shift As Integer,X As Single,Y As Single)
   If Button = 1 Then              'Left button
   If DrawFlag Then
   Line -(X, Y)
   End If

   If LineFlag Then
   :

   End If
   End If
End Sub
```

The way to create the illusion of stretching (or dragging) a graphic object is with the Xor pen. To use that pen, you have to change the ForeColor and DrawMode properties, so you can save them first. Then you set ForeColor to BackColor (the reason is explained in a moment) and set DrawMode to 7, the Xor Pen, as follows:

```
Sub Form_MouseMove (Button As Integer,Shift As Integer,X As Single,Y As Single)
   If Button = 1 Then              'Left button
   If DrawFlag Then
   Line -(X, Y)
   End If

   If LineFlag Then
   TempFore& = ForeColor
   TempMode% = DrawMode
   ForeColor = BackColor
   DrawMode = 7                    'Xor mode
   :

   End If
   End If
End Sub
```

When you use the Xor Pen, the ForeColor is Xored with what is already on the screen. Because you want the line to show up as you stretch it, you will want it to be a different color from the background; if you temporarily make the foreground color the same as the background color, in fact, Xoring the two displays black, so you end up with a black line on the standard white foreground. To erase that line and restore the background, you only need to draw it on the screen with the Xor pen again (and in the

311

same place). In MouseMove, then, the plan is to erase the last line drawn from the anchor point to the mouse cursor and draw a new line from the anchor point to the new mouse cursor's position. You can do that in the following way:

```
Sub Form_MouseMove (Button As Integer,Shift As Integer,X As Single,Y As Single)
   If Button = 1 Then          'Left button
   If DrawFlag Then
   Line -(X, Y)
   End If

   If LineFlag Then
   TempFore& = ForeColor
   TempMode% = DrawMode
   ForeColor = BackColor
   DrawMode = 7                 'Xor mode
   Line (AnchorX, AnchorY)-(CurrentX, CurrentY)
   Line (AnchorX, AnchorY)-(X, Y)
   :
   End If
   End If
End Sub
```

Finally, you just replace the original values in the ForeColor and DrawMode properties to finish the MouseMove event, as follows:

```
Sub Form_MouseMove (Button As Integer,Shift As Integer,X As Single,Y As Single)
   If Button = 1 Then          'Left button
   If DrawFlag Then
   Line -(X, Y)
   End If

   If LineFlag Then
   TempFore& = ForeColor
   TempMode% = DrawMode
   ForeColor = BackColor
   DrawMode = 7                    'Xor mode
   Line (AnchorX, AnchorY)-(CurrentX, CurrentY)
   Line (AnchorX, AnchorY)-(X, Y)
   ForeColor = TempFore&
   DrawMode = TempMode%
   End If
   End If
End Sub
```

312

That's it—now the user can tack down one end of a line by pressing the left mouse button, move around while stretching a line from that point, and then release the mouse button to make the line permanent. Note that you also have to update your other event procedures to take the new flags into account. The MouseDown event procedure is not going to change because it sets only the anchor point and the current graphics location. You will have to update the MouseUp event procedure, however, so that it draws lines only if LineFlag is True, as in the following example:

```
Sub Form_MouseUp (Button As Integer,Shift As Integer,X As Single,Y As Single)
   If Button = 1 Then

   If LineFlag Then
   Line (AnchorX, AnchorY) - (X, Y)
   End If

   End
End Sub
```

That's it for lines and freehand drawing; all the code so far appears in listing 7.1, and the application at run-time appears in figure 7.4. You have made a good deal of progress: You have set up a Paint program that lets you draw freehand or create lines. As you know, however, it is as easy to draw rectangles or boxes as it is to draw lines, so let's do that next.

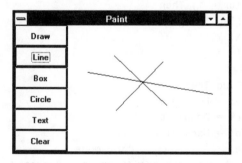

Figure 7.4. Line-drawing Paint application.

Listing 7.1. Paint Program with Drawing and Lines

```
Paint Module— — — — — — — — — — — — — — — — — — — — — — — —

  Global AnchorX As Integer
  Global AnchorY As Integer
  Global DrawFlag As Integer
  Global LineFlag As Integer
  Global BoxFlag As Integer
  Global CircleFlag As Integer
  Global TextFlag As Integer


Form Form1 — — — — — — — — — — — — — — — — — — — — — — — —

Sub Form_MouseDown (Button As Integer,Shift As Integer,X As Single,Y As Single)
  If Button = 1 Then      'Left Button
  AnchorX = X
  AnchorY = Y
  CurrentX = X
  CurrentY = Y
  End If
End Sub

Sub Form_MouseMove (Button As Integer,Shift As Integer,X As Single,Y As Single)
  If (Button = 1) Then
  If DrawFlag Then
  Line -(X, Y)
  End If

  If LineFlag Then
  TempFore& = ForeColor
  TempMode% = DrawMode
  ForeColor = BackColor
  DrawMode = 7               'Xor mode
  Line (AnchorX, AnchorY)-(CurrentX, CurrentY)
  Line (AnchorX, AnchorY)-(X, Y)
  ForeColor = TempFore&
  DrawMode = TempMode%
  End If
  End If
End Sub
```

```
Sub Form_MouseUp (Button As Integer, Shift As Integer, X As Single, Y As Single)
   If Button = 1 Then

   If LineFlag Then
   Line (AnchorX, AnchorY)-(X, Y)
   End If

   End If
End Sub

Sub DrawButton_Click ()
   DrawFlag = True
      LineFlag = False
   BoxFlag = False
   CircleFlag = False
   TextFlag = False
End Sub

Sub LineButton_Click ()
   DrawFlag = False
   LineFlag = True
   BoxFlag = False
   CircleFlag = False
   TextFlag = False
End Sub

Sub BoxButton_Click ()
   DrawFlag = False
   LineFlag = False
   BoxFlag = True
   CircleFlag = False
   TextFlag = False
End Sub

Sub CircleButton_Click ()
   DrawFlag = False
   LineFlag = False
   BoxFlag = False
   CircleFlag = True
   TextFlag = False
End Sub
```

continues

Listing 7.1. continued

```
Sub TextButton_Click ()
  DrawFlag = False
  LineFlag = False
  BoxFlag = False
  CircleFlag = False
  TextFlag = True
End Sub


Sub ClearButton_Click ()
  Cls
End Sub
```

Drawing Boxes

You can draw boxes by using the Line method as long as you specify the B parameter. It will be simple, in fact, to add this capability to your code: Wherever you drew lines before, you can do the same thing for boxes (after testing BoxFlag, which is set by the Box drawing tool). The two places where you have used Line already are the MouseMove and MouseUp procedures, as follows:

```
Sub Form_MouseMove (Button As Integer,Shift As Integer,X As Single,Y As Single)
  If (Button = 1) Then
  If DrawFlag Then
  Line -(X, Y)
  End If

  If LineFlag Then
  TempFore& = ForeColor
  TempMode% = DrawMode
  ForeColor = BackColor
  DrawMode = 7                'Xor mode
  Line (AnchorX, AnchorY)-(CurrentX, CurrentY)
  Line (AnchorX, AnchorY)-(X, Y)
  ForeColor = TempFore&
  DrawMode = TempMode%
  End If
  End If
End Sub
```

```
Sub Form_MouseUp (Button As Integer, Shift As Integer, X As Single, Y As Single)
  If Button = 1 Then

  If LineFlag Then
  Line (AnchorX, AnchorY)-(X, Y)
  End If
  End If
```

All you need to do is repeat the line code for boxes, by using the B parameter and checking for BoxFlag, as in the following example:

```
Sub Form_MouseMove (Button As Integer,Shift As Integer,X As Single,Y As Single)
  If (Button = 1) Then
        If DrawFlag Then
            Line -(X, Y)
        End If

        If LineFlag Then
            :
            :
        End If

        If BoxFlag Then
            TempFore& = ForeColor
            TempMode% = DrawMode
            ForeColor = BackColor
            DrawMode = 7                'Xor mode
            Line (AnchorX, AnchorY)-(CurrentX, CurrentY), , B
            Line (AnchorX, AnchorY)-(X, Y), , B
            ForeColor = TempFore&
            DrawMode = TempMode%
        End If

  End If
End Sub


Sub Form_MouseUp (Button As Integer, Shift As Integer, X As Single, Y As Single)
  If Button = 1 Then

        If LineFlag Then
            Line (AnchorX, AnchorY)-(X, Y)
        End If
```

```
If BoxFlag Then
     Line (AnchorX, AnchorY)-(X, Y), , B
End If
```

That's it—that's the only change you have to make. Now your Paint application can draw freehand as well as draw lines and boxes. There are still other drawing routines in Visual Basic, however, that you can make use of—for example, circles.

"Stretching" graphics figures on the screen.
You can use this code to "stretch" rectangles on the screen; in fact, you can make the rectangle dotted as it is being stretched by setting its DrawStyle property to 1 and then resetting it back to its original value when you finish. You can even let users select portions of the drawing in this way, by letting them stretch a rectangle into place and reading all the enclosed pixels with the Point( ) method; you can then transfer those pixels to other locations by using PSet( ).

Drawing Circles

Drawing circles using the Circle method is not very difficult. You can use the anchor point as the center of the circle and draw the circle out to the mouse pointer's location when the user releases the button. To begin, you check whether the CircleFlag (set by clicking the Circle tool) is set this way in the MouseUp event procedure, which is where you are supposed to draw the circle, as follows:

```
Sub Form_MouseUp (Button As Integer, Shift As Integer, X As Single, Y As Single)
  If Button = 1 Then

    If LineFlag Then
        Line (AnchorX, AnchorY)-(X, Y)
    End If

    If BoxFlag Then
    Line (AnchorX, AnchorY)-(X, Y), , B
    End If
```

```
    If CircleFlag Then

    End If
```

Next, you draw the circle, by using (AnchorX, AnchorY) as the center point and the distance from (AnchorX, AnchorY) to the current location, (X, Y), as the radius.

```
Sub Form_MouseUp (Button As Integer, Shift As Integer, X As Single, Y As Single)
  If Button = 1 Then

    If LineFlag Then
        Line (AnchorX, AnchorY)-(X, Y)
    End If

    If BoxFlag Then
        Line (AnchorX, AnchorY)-(X, Y), , B
    End If

    If CircleFlag Then
        Radius! = Sqr((AnchorX - X)^2 + (AnchorY - Y)^2)
        Circle (AnchorX, AnchorY), Radius!
    End If
```

In this example, you are using the standard Basic Sqr( ) function to find square roots, and the ^ operator to square quantities. The result is that now you can draw circles, as shown in figure 7.5.

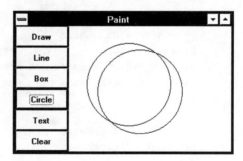

Figure 7.5. Drawing circles with the Paint application.

You can draw the intermediate circles as the user is moving the mouse cursor, in fact, as you did for lines and boxes. To do that, you have to modify the MouseMove event procedure. The code you add has to check whether the CircleFlag is set first, as follows:

```
If CircleFlag Then
     :
End If
```

Next, you save the foreground color and the current drawing mode, restoring them at the end:

```
If CircleFlag Then
   TempFore& = ForeColor
   TempMode% = DrawMode
   ForeColor = BackColor
   DrawMode = 7                    'Xor mode
        :
   ForeColor = TempFore&
   DrawMode = TempMode%
End If
```

As before, giving the appearance of stretching a graphics figure is really a matter of erasing the old figure and drawing the new one. To do that, you use the Xor Pen and draw the old circle; assuming that you stored the last mouse position in (CurrentX, CurrentY), it appears as follows:

```
If CircleFlag Then
   TempFore& = ForeColor
   TempMode% = DrawMode
   ForeColor = BackColor
   DrawMode = 7                    'Xor mode
   Radius! = Sqr((AnchorX - CurrentX)^2 + (AnchorY - CurrentY)^2)
   Circle (AnchorX, AnchorY), Radius!
        :

   ForeColor = TempFore&
   DrawMode = TempMode%
End If
```

Next, you draw the new circle and store the mouse cursor's position in (CurrentX, CurrentY) for the next time, as follows:

```
If CircleFlag Then
   TempFore& = ForeColor
```

```
        TempMode% = DrawMode
        ForeColor = BackColor
        DrawMode = 7                    'Xor mode
        Radius! = Sqr((AnchorX - CurrentX)^2 + (AnchorY - CurrentY)^2)
        Circle (AnchorX, AnchorY), Radius!
        Radius! = Sqr(AnchorX - X)^2 + (AnchorY - Y)
        Circle (AnchorX, AnchorY), Radius!
        CurrentX = X
        CurrentY = Y
        ForeColor = TempFore&
        DrawMode = TempMode%
    End If
```

That's it—the entire MouseMove event procedure looks like the following example now, where you have broken it up into specific drawing actions, depending on which drawing tool is being used, as follows:

```
Sub Form_MouseMove (Button As Integer,Shift As Integer,X As Single,Y As Single)
  If (Button = 1) Then
      If DrawFlag Then
          Line -(X, Y)
      End If

      If LineFlag Then
          TempFore& = ForeColor
          TempMode% = DrawMode
          ForeColor = BackColor
          DrawMode = 7              'Xor mode
          Line (AnchorX, AnchorY)-(CurrentX, CurrentY)
          Line (AnchorX, AnchorY)-(X, Y)
          ForeColor = TempFore&
          DrawMode = TempMode%
      End If

      If BoxFlag Then
          TempFore& = ForeColor
          TempMode% = DrawMode
          ForeColor = BackColor
          DrawMode = 7              'Xor mode
          Line (AnchorX, AnchorY)-(CurrentX, CurrentY), , B
          Line (AnchorX, AnchorY)-(X, Y), , B
          ForeColor = TempFore&
          DrawMode = TempMode%
```

```
        End If

    If CircleFlag Then
        TempFore& = ForeColor
        TempMode% = DrawMode
        ForeColor = BackColor
        DrawMode = 7                    'Xor mode
        Radius! = Sqr((AnchorX - CurrentX)^2 + (AnchorY - CurrentY)^2)
        Circle (AnchorX, AnchorY), Radius!
        Radius! = Sqr(AnchorX - X)^2 + (AnchorY - Y)
        Circle (AnchorX, AnchorY), Radius!
        CurrentX = X
        CurrentY = Y
        ForeColor = TempFore&
        DrawMode = TempMode%
    End If

  End If
End Sub
```

The last of the tools is Text, which lets you draw text directly in the graphics area.

Drawing Text

You can draw text if you make use of the fact that, when the user clicks the Text button in your toolbox, that button gets the focus. From then on, you can read each key struck (until another tool is selected) by placing code in the TextButton_KeyPress ( ) Sub procedure, as follows:

```
Sub TextButton_KeyPress (KeyAscii As Integer)

End Sub
```

In fact, because text is printed at the current graphics position and the user sets that position with a MouseDown event, all you need to do is to let the user select the Text tool, click somewhere in the graphics area, and then print whatever they type, in the following way:

```
Sub TextButton_KeyPress (KeyAscii As Integer)
  Print Chr$(KeyAscii);
End Sub
```

That's all there is to it; everything the user types is sent to the current paint document as long as the Text toolbox button retains the focus, as it does until the user selects a new tool (which is when you should stop printing characters). Now you can use text in addition to figures, as shown in figure 7.6. You can even add a text cursor (an insertion point) to this program with a little more work. The entire program so far appears in listing 7.2.

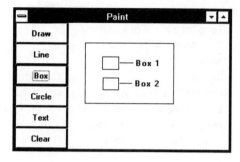

Figure 7.6. A Paint application with text.

Listing 7.2. Paint Program: Drawing, Lines, Boxes, Circles, and Text

```
Paint Module — — — — — — — — — — — — — — — — — — — —

Global AnchorX As Integer
Global AnchorY As Integer
Global DrawFlag As Integer
Global LineFlag As Integer
Global BoxFlag As Integer
Global CircleFlag As Integer
Global TextFlag As Integer


Form1 — — — — — — — — — — — — — — — — — — — — — — —

Sub Form_MouseDown (Button As Integer,Shift As Integer,X As Single,Y As Single)
  If Button = 1 Then      'Left Button
      AnchorX = X
      AnchorY = Y
      CurrentX = X
      CurrentY = Y
  End If
End Sub
```

continues

Listing 7.2. continued

```
Sub Form_MouseMove (Button As Integer,Shift As Integer,X As Single,Y As Single)
  If (Button = 1) Then
        If DrawFlag Then
            Line -(X, Y)
            End If

        If LineFlag Then
            TempFore& = ForeColor
            TempMode% = DrawMode
            ForeColor = BackColor
            DrawMode = 7             'Xor mode
            Line (AnchorX, AnchorY)-(CurrentX, CurrentY)
            Line (AnchorX, AnchorY)-(X, Y)
            ForeColor = TempFore&
            DrawMode = TempMode%
        End If

        If BoxFlag Then
            TempFore& = ForeColor
            TempMode% = DrawMode
            ForeColor = BackColor
            DrawMode = 7             'Xor mode
            Line (AnchorX, AnchorY)-(CurrentX, CurrentY), , B
            Line (AnchorX, AnchorY)-(X, Y), , B
            ForeColor = TempFore&
            DrawMode = TempMode%
        End If

        If CircleFlag Then
            TempFore& = ForeColor
            TempMode% = DrawMode
            ForeColor = BackColor
            DrawMode = 7             'Xor mode
            radius! = Sqr((AnchorX - CurrentX) ^ 2 + (AnchorY - CurrentY) ^ 2)
            Circle (AnchorX, AnchorY), radius!
            radius! = Sqr((AnchorX - X) ^ 2 + (AnchorY - Y) ^ 2)
            Circle (AnchorX, AnchorY), radius!
            CurrentX = X
            CurrentY = Y
```

```
              ForeColor = TempFore&
              DrawMode = TempMode%
          End If

  End If
End Sub

Sub Form_MouseUp (Button As Integer, Shift As Integer, X As Single, Y As Single)
  If Button = 1 Then
      If LineFlag Then
          Line (AnchorX, AnchorY)-(X, Y)
      End If

      If BoxFlag Then
          Line (AnchorX, AnchorY)-(X, Y), , B
      End If

      If CircleFlag Then
          radius! = Sqr((AnchorX - X) ^ 2 + (AnchorY - Y) ^ 2)
          Circle (AnchorX, AnchorY), radius!
      End If
  End If
End Sub

Sub ClearButton_Click ()
  Cls
End Sub

Sub DrawButton_Click ()
  DrawFlag = True
  LineFlag = False
  BoxFlag = False
  CircleFlag = False
  TextFlag = False
End Sub

Sub LineButton_Click ()
  DrawFlag = False
  LineFlag = True
  BoxFlag = False
  CircleFlag = False
  TextFlag = False
End Sub
```

continues

Listing 7.2. continued

```
Sub BoxButton_Click ()
  DrawFlag = False
  LineFlag = False
  BoxFlag = True
  CircleFlag = False
  TextFlag = False
End Sub

Sub CircleButton_Click ()
  DrawFlag = False
  LineFlag = False
  BoxFlag = False
  CircleFlag = True
  TextFlag = False
End Sub

Sub TextButton_Click ()
  DrawFlag = False
  LineFlag = False
  BoxFlag = False
  CircleFlag = False
  TextFlag = True
End Sub

Sub TextButton_KeyPress (KeyAscii As Integer)
  Print Chr$(KeyAscii);
End Sub
```

That's it for your toolbox. The next step is to add a File menu, which lets you undertake such operations as saving your image to disk, reading it back in again, printing an image, and selecting drawing colors. Let's begin by saving the image to disk.

Saving Your Paint Image on Disk

You need a File menu in your Paint application, so bring up the Menu Design Window and create a menu with that caption (Name: FileMenu). Add three items to the menu: Save File... (Name: SaveItem), Load File... (Name: LoadItem), and Exit (Name: ExitItem). As before, the Exit item is easy to complete; you just need to use the End statement, as in the following example:

```
Sub ExitItem_Click ()
  End
End Sub
```

> **Adding an Undo item.**
> You can even add an Undo item to the Paint application's menu by adding another form that is never shown. Whenever the user chooses a drawing tool, for example, copy the current Picture from Form1 to that form; when the user selects Undo, copy it back to restore the image.

Now let's make the Save File... item active. Find the SaveItem_Click( ) Sub procedure in the code window, as follows:

```
Sub SaveItem_Click ()

End Sub
```

When the user selects this item, you want to get a file name, and then you can save the image you have been working on. In fact, you have already developed two forms that deal with the problems of saving and loading files for you: LoadForm and SaveForm from your Editor application. To save files, add the SaveForm.Frm file to the Paint application by using the Add File... item in the Visual Basic File menu. After loading the file, save it with a new name (Savpaint.Frm) so that you do not overwrite the Editor's dialog box. After the user types the name of the file, he wants to save the image in the text box you named FileNameBox, you can save the image using the SavePicture statement when they click the OK button. Originally, OKButton_Click ( ) looks like this in SaveForm, as follows:

```
Sub OKButton_Click ()
  On Error GoTo FileError
  Open FileNameBox.Text For Output As #1
  Print #1, Form1.PadText.Text
  Close #1
  SaveForm.Hide
  Exit Sub
```

```
FileError:
  MsgBox "File Error", 48, "Editor"
  Resume
End Sub
```

You want to use SavePicture instead, however, whose syntax is the following:

```
SavePicture [Object.]Image, FileName$
```

In this example, Image is the name of a special property of the form, which stands for the picture. You can use SavePicture like this in your program (note that you also change the name in the error message from "Editor" to "Paint".), as follows:

```
Sub OKButton_Click ()
  On Error GoTo FileError
  SavePicture Form1.Image, FileNameBox.Text
  Exit Sub

  FileError:
  MsgBox "File Error", 48, "Paint"
  Resume
End Sub
```

All that remains is to make the Save File... item active in the File menu; you can do that by clicking it and adding the following line to SaveItem_Click( ):

```
Sub SaveItem_Click()
  SaveForm.Show
End Sub
```

Now when users decide to save their graphics work, they can click the Save File... item (Name: SaveItem), which pops up SaveForm. The user then types a file name, which you read out of the text box and pass on the SavePicture. And, that's it. Next, let's make sure that you have saved the file correctly, by reading it back in.

Reading the Image Back from Disk

To read files from the disk, you can use the LoadForm dialog box from your Editor application. Add that file, LoadForm.Frm, to the Paint application and bring up the OKButton_Click ( ) Sub procedure in the code window. This button is clicked after a user has selected the file to read in. You spend a little time in the procedure making sure that the pathname is correct, and then you read in files as follows:

```
Sub OKButton_Click ()
  On Error GoTo FileError
  If (Right$(Dir1.Path, 1) = "\") Then
    Filename$ = Dir1.Path + File1.Filename
  Else
      Filename$ = Dir1.Path + "\" + File1.Filename
  End If
  Open Filename$ For Input As #1
  Form1.PadText.Text = Input$(LOF(1), #1)
  Close #1
  LoadForm.Hide
  Exit Sub

FileError:
  MsgBox "File Error", 48, "Editor"
  Resume
End Sub
```

In the Paint application, of course, you change this code to read in a picture rather than a text file. In particular, you use the LoadPicture function, which appears as follows:

```
[Object.]Picture = LoadPicture(Filename$)
```

In other words, you have to assign the return value from LoadPicture( ) to the Picture property of an object (a Form or Picture Box). You can modify OKButton_Click ( ) to that this way (again, you also change the name in the error message from Editor to Paint).

```
Sub OKButton_Click ()
  On Error GoTo FileError
  If (Right$(Dir1.Path, 1) = "\") Then
      Filename$ = Dir1.Path + File1.Filename
  Else
      Filename$ = Dir1.Path + "\" + File1.Filename
  End If
  Form1.Picture = LoadPicture(Filename$)
  LoadForm.Hide
  Exit Sub
```

```
FileError:
  MsgBox "File Error", 48, "Paint"
  Resume
End Sub
```

Finally, to make this form appear on the screen when the user clicks the Load File... item (Name: LoadItem) in your File menu, you can place a line like the following in LoadItem_Click ( ).

```
Sub LoadItem_Click ()
  LoadForm.Show
End Sub
```

Now you can save images to disk and retrieve them also, as shown in figure 7.7. You can add more power to your application, however, relatively easily. For example, you can change the drawing (foreground) color. Let's look into that subject next.

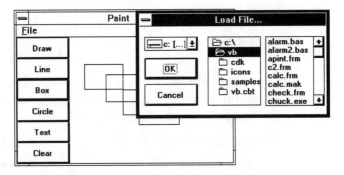

Figure 7.7. A Paint application with a Load File... box.

About the format of your graphics image file.
You can even exchange images with Microsoft Paintbrush for Windows this way. The disk format created by the SavePicture statement is a bit-map format, the same as is created by Paintbrush when it saves files in its .BMP format. That means also that you can read your files into Paintbrush and save them in another format, such as .PCX.

Changing the Drawing Color

Earlier, you designed a Control Panel application complete with a control panel that let you change a number of properties of the main window, including its color. To do that, you had a number of scroll bars the user could manipulate while watching the result in a box in the control panel. It is easy to modify that form for use, to enable you to set the drawing color. (After you have created some general-purpose forms in Visual Basic, the usual thing to do is to use them over and over again.) Just load it into the Paint application with the Add File... item in Visual Basic's File menu (you called this file Panel.Frm a while ago). The panel appears, as shown in figure 7.8.

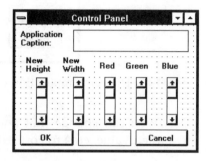

Figure 7.8. A customized control panel.

This control panel has a number of items you do not need: the scroll bars for the main window's height and width, and a text box for that window's new name. You can remove those controls, however, and move around the color controls to fill up the box, as shown in figure 7.9. In particular, notice that you enlarged the label that displays the new color (you called this label NewColor), and also labeled it New Drawing Color, as follows:.

Now you have scroll bars for color and a box to indicate that color to users. When users move the scroll bars (called NewRed, NewGreen, and NewBlue), the new drawing color is indicated in the box named NewColor. After the drawing color is set, the user clicks the OK button to make it active; at that point, you want to set the new drawing color (the ForeColor property of

Form1). Originally, OKButton_Click ( ) appeared the following way:

```
Sub OKButton_Click ()
  Form1.Caption = NewCaption.Text
  Form1.Height = NewHeight.Value
  Form1.Width = NewWidth.Value
  Form1.BackColor = RGB(NewRed.Value, NewGreen.Value, NewBlue.Value)
  ControlPanel.Hide
End Sub
```

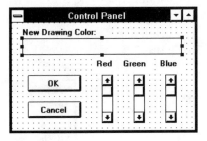

Figure 7.9. The Paint application control panel's template.

Now you can change that and transfer the values of the scroll bars (NewRed.Value, etc.) to Form1.ForeColor, as in the following example:

```
Sub OKButton_Click ()
  Form1.ForeColor = RGB(NewRed.Value, NewGreen.Value, NewBlue.Value)
  ControlPanel.Hide
End Sub
```

The new control panel is set; all that remains is to make it active when the user selects an item in the File menu. Go back to the paint application's main window and bring up the Menu Design Window. Move the highlight bar in the list box at the bottom to the last item, Exit, and click the button labeled Insert. A new line appears above Exit; type New Drawing Color... as the name of the menu item that will bring up the new color control panel, and give this item the name DrawingItem, for example. Then close the Menu Design Window by clicking Done, and click the new menu item to bring up this Sub procedure template, as follows:

```
Sub DrawingItem_Click ()

End Sub
```

You want to do two things here—load the current drawing color into the color-displaying label in the control panel (ControlPanel.NewColor), and show the color control panel. You can do those things in the following way:

```
Sub DrawingItem_Click ()
  ControlPanel.NewColor.BackColor = ForeColor
  ControlPanel.Show
End Sub
```

Now you can design the drawing color in your Paint application. Give it a try: When you select the Drawing Color... item in the File menu, the color control panel pops up. Manipulate the scroll bars until you have a new drawing color you like, and then select the OK button. When you draw again, you will see that the drawing color has been switched to the new color. The new program, including the code for changing colors, loading and saving files, and all the drawing tools, appears in listing 7.3.

Listing 7.3. Paint Application with File Capability and Color Selection

```
Paint Module — — — — — — — — — — — — — — — — —

Global AnchorX As Integer
Global AnchorY As Integer
Global DrawFlag As Integer
Global LineFlag As Integer
Global BoxFlag As Integer
Global CircleFlag As Integer
Global TextFlag As Integer


Form1 — — — — — — — — — — — — — — — — — — — — —

Sub Form_MouseDown (Button As Integer,Shift As Integer,X As Single,Y As Single)
  If Button = 1 Then      'Left Button
      AnchorX = X
      AnchorY = Y
      CurrentX = X
      CurrentY = Y
```

continues

Listing 7.3. continued

```
   End If
End Sub

Sub Form_MouseMove (Button As Integer,Shift As Integer,X As Single,Y As Single)
  If (Button = 1) Then
       If DrawFlag Then
            Line -(X, Y)
    End If

       If LineFlag Then
            TempFore& = ForeColor
            TempMode% = DrawMode
            ForeColor = BackColor
            DrawMode = 7               'Xor mode
            Line (AnchorX, AnchorY)-(CurrentX, CurrentY)
            Line (AnchorX, AnchorY)-(X, Y)
            ForeColor = TempFore&
            DrawMode = TempMode%
        End If

       If BoxFlag Then
            TempFore& = ForeColor
            TempMode% = DrawMode
            ForeColor = BackColor
            DrawMode = 7               'Xor mode
            Line (AnchorX, AnchorY)-(CurrentX, CurrentY), , B
            Line (AnchorX, AnchorY)-(X, Y), , B
            ForeColor = TempFore&
            DrawMode = TempMode%
        End If

    If CircleFlag Then
            TempFore& = ForeColor
            TempMode% = DrawMode
            ForeColor = BackColor
            DrawMode = 7               'Xor mode
            radius! = Sqr((AnchorX - CurrentX) ^ 2 + (AnchorY - CurrentY) ^ 2)
            Circle (AnchorX, AnchorY), radius!
            radius! = Sqr((AnchorX - X) ^ 2 + (AnchorY - Y) ^ 2)
            Circle (AnchorX, AnchorY), radius!
            CurrentX = X
```

```
                CurrentY = Y
                ForeColor = TempFore&
                DrawMode = TempMode%
            End If

    End If
End Sub

Sub Form_MouseUp (Button As Integer, Shift As Integer, X As Single, Y As Single)
    If Button = 1 Then
        If LineFlag Then
            Line (AnchorX, AnchorY)-(X, Y)
        End If

        If BoxFlag Then
            Line (AnchorX, AnchorY)-(X, Y), , B
        End If

        If CircleFlag Then
            radius! = Sqr((AnchorX - X) ^ 2 + (AnchorY - Y) ^ 2)
            Circle (AnchorX, AnchorY), radius!
        End If
    End If
End Sub

Sub ClearButton_Click ()
    Cls
End Sub

Sub DrawButton_Click ()
    DrawFlag = True
    LineFlag = False
    BoxFlag = False
    CircleFlag = False
    TextFlag = False
End Sub

Sub LineButton_Click ()
    DrawFlag = False
    LineFlag = True
    BoxFlag = False
    CircleFlag = False
```

continues

Listing 7.3. continued

```
    TextFlag = False
End Sub

Sub BoxButton_Click ()
  DrawFlag = False
  LineFlag = False
  BoxFlag = True
  CircleFlag = False
  TextFlag = False
End Sub

Sub CircleButton_Click ()
  DrawFlag = False
  LineFlag = False
  BoxFlag = False
  CircleFlag = True
  TextFlag = False
End Sub

Sub TextButton_Click ()
  DrawFlag = False
  LineFlag = False
  BoxFlag = False
  CircleFlag = False
  TextFlag = True
End Sub

Sub TextButton_KeyPress (KeyAscii As Integer)
  Print Chr$(KeyAscii);
End Sub

Sub ExitItem_Click ()
  End
End Sub

Sub SaveItem_Click ()
  SaveForm.Show
End Sub

Sub LoadItem_Click ()
  LoadForm.Show
End Sub
```

```
Sub DrawingItem_Click ()
  ControlPanel.NewColor.BackColor = ForeColor
  ControlPanel.Show
End Sub


SaveForm — — — — — — — — — — — — — — — — —


Sub CancelButton_Click ()
  SaveForm.Hide
End Sub


Sub OKButton_Click ()
  'On Error GoTo FileError
  SavePicture Form1.Image, FileNameBox.Text
  SaveForm.Hide
  Exit Sub

FileError:
  MsgBox "File Error", 48, "Paint"
  Resume
End Sub


LoadForm — — — — — — — — — — — — — — — —


Sub CancelButton_Click ()
  LoadForm.Hide
End Sub


Sub Drive1_Change ()
  Dir1.Path = Drive1.Drive
End Sub


Sub Dir1_Change ()
  File1.Path = Dir1.Path
End Sub


Sub OKButton_Click ()
  On Error GoTo FileError
  If (Right$(Dir1.Path, 1) = "\") Then
          Filename$ = Dir1.Path + File1.Filename
  Else
```

continues

Listing 7.3. continued

```
            Filename$ = Dir1.Path + "\" + File1.Filename
    End If
    Form1.Picture = LoadPicture(Filename$)
    LoadForm.Hide
    Exit Sub

FileError:
    MsgBox "File Error", 48, "Editor"
    Resume
End Sub

Sub File1_DblClick ()
    OKButton_Click
End Sub

Sub CancelButton_Click ()
    ControlPanel.Hide
End Sub

ControlPanel — — — — — — — — — — — — — — — — — —

Sub OKButton_Click ()

    Form1.ForeColor = RGB(NewRed.Value, NewGreen.Value, NewBLue.Value)
    ControlPanel.Hide
End Sub

Sub NewRed_Change ()
    NewColor.BackColor = RGB(NewRed.Value, NewGreen.Value, NewBLue.Value)
End Sub

Sub NewGreen_Change ()
    NewColor.BackColor = RGB(NewRed.Value, NewGreen.Value, NewBLue.Value)

End Sub

Sub NewBlue_Change ()
    NewColor.BackColor = RGB(NewRed.Value, NewGreen.Value, NewBLue.Value)
End Sub
```

As polished as your Paint application is becoming, it is not very useful unless you can print the results on the printer. That is not difficult, however, so let's examine how to do so next.

Printing the Paint Program's Graphics

You have already seen the Printer object in Chapter 6. With it, you can use any of the graphics methods you have already seen: Line, Circle, Print, and so on. However, there is a very simple way that will let you print all the predrawn graphics in your Paint document: the PrintForm method. As you learned in Chapter 6, this method prints all that is in the client area of a window (excluding menu bar, borders, and so on). This includes all the controls, however, such as buttons, that are on the form too. Because you don't want to print them also, you can make them disappear temporarily by setting their Visible property to False.

Let's begin by adding a Print item to your Paint program's File menu. Bring up the Menu Design Window and highlight the Exit item, clicking the Insert button as before. Add an item with the caption Print and the Name PrintItem, and then close the Menu Design Window. Next, click the new menu item to bring up this Sub procedure template, as follows:

```
Sub Print Item_Click ()

End Sub
```
First, you hide all the buttons in your toolbox:

```
Sub PrintItem_Click ()
  DrawButton.Visible = False
  LineButton.Visible = False
  BoxButton.Visible = False
  CircleButton.Visible = False
  TextButton.Visible = False
  ClearButton.Visible = False
            :

End Sub
```

Then you can print the form with PrintForm and show the buttons again, in the following way:

```
Sub PrintItem_Click ()
  DrawButton.Visible = False
  LineButton.Visible = False
  BoxButton.Visible = False
  CircleButton.Visible = False
  TextButton.Visible = False
  ClearButton.Visible = False
  PrintForm
  DrawButton.Visible = True
  LineButton.Visible = True
  BoxButton.Visible = True
  CircleButton.Visible = True
  TextButton.Visible = True
  ClearButton.Visible = True
End Sub
```

When you print using PrintForm, Visual Basic even pops a small window on the screen, as shown in figure 7.10, indicating that it is printing; this window even includes a button that lets the user cancel at any time. That's it for printing from the Paint application. The next, and last, capability you give to this program is to let it interact with the Window's clipboard.

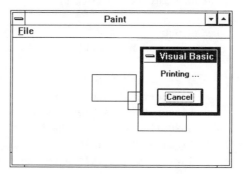

Figure 7.10. Visual Basic's Print window.

Using the Windows Clipboard

The clipboard is a means of passing data back and forth between applications in Windows. You can press the Print Screen key in Windows, for example, to take a snapshot of the screen and paste it automatically in the clipboard. When you use Windows Paintbrush, you can then paste the snapshot of the screen into the current document.

Let's add this kind of power to your Paint application. Visual Basic supports a clipboard object with the methods indicated in table 7.5. There are two usual ways of using the clipboard object: to pass text or to pass graphics. Because you are designing a Paint application, you will be interested in graphics; the two clipboard methods you will use are GetData and SetData.

Table 7.5. Clipboard Object Methods

Clear	Clears the clipboard
GetText	Gets the text in the clipboard
GetData	Gets the graphics data in the clipboard
SetData	Pastes graphics data to the clipboard
GetFormat	Gets clipboard format (text or graphics)
SetText	Pastes text to the clipboard

To use the clipboard, just add two items to the File menu: Paste From Clipboard and Paste To Clipboard, with Names FromItem and ToItem. You can make those items active by adding the appropriate lines to their procedures. To begin, let's look at GetData, whose syntax is as follows:

```
Clipboard.GetData ([format%])
```

In the following example, format% can take the following values (defined with Const in Constant.Txt):

```
CF_BITMAP        'Bitmap
CF_METFILE       'Metafile
CF_DIB           'Device Independent bitmap
```

If you omit format%, CF_BITMAP is assumed, which is the format you want here. You can get the current picture, therefore, from the Clipboard and paste it into your Paint application the following way, in the Sub procedure FromItem:

```
Sub FromItem_Click ()
  Picture = Clipboard.GetData()
End Sub
```

Now let's look at the process of pasting data into the Clipboard. To do that, you use the Clipboard.SetData method, whose syntax is as follows:

```
Clipboard.SetData (data, [format%])
```

In your case, data refers to the Image property of your form, Form1.Image, and format% can be one of the following, as before:

```
CF_BITMAP          'Bitmap
CF_METFILE         'Metafile
CF_DIB             'Device Independent bitmap
```

You can paste your form's picture to the Clipboard in the following way:

```
Sub ToItem_Click ()
  Clipboard.SetData Form1.Image
End Sub
```

Now you can paste to and from the clipboard, which enables you to communicate with other Windows applications. That's it for the Paint application; the entire listing appears in Listing 7.4 (Paint.Mak on the diskette). You have come far with this program: You have learned how to use the mouse to draw freehand; to draw lines, boxes, and circles; to position text with the mouse; to save and retrieve graphics images to and from disk; to print graphics, and to use the clipboard.

> **Adding more to the Paint program.**
> You can add further capabilities to the Paint application, of course, and even add vertical and horizontal scroll bars. The possibilities are endless.

Listing 7.4. Complete Paint Application (Paint.Mak on the diskette)

```
Form Form1 — — — — — — — — — — — — — — — — —
   AutoRedraw      =    -1  'True
```

```
   Caption          =    "Paint"
   MousePointer     =    2   'Cross

CommandButton DrawButton
        Caption          =    "Draw"
        MousePointer     =    1   'Arrow
        TabIndex         =    0

CommandButton LineButton
        Caption          =    "Line"
        MousePointer     =    1   'Arrow
        TabIndex         =    1

CommandButton BoxButton
        Caption          =    "Box"
        MousePointer     =    1   'Arrow
        TabIndex         =    2

CommandButton CircleButton
        Caption          =    "Circle"
        MousePointer     =    1   'Arrow
        TabIndex         =    3

CommandButton TextButton
        Caption          =    "Text"
        MousePointer     =    1   'Arrow
        TabIndex         =    4

CommandButton ClearButton
        Caption          =    "Clear"
        MousePointer     =    1   'Arrow
        TabIndex         =    5

Menu FileMenu
        Caption          =    "&File"

Menu SaveItem
            Caption          =    "&Save File..."

Menu LoadItem
            Caption          =    "&Load File..."
```

continues

343

Listing 7.4. continued

```
Menu DrawingItem
        Caption          =    "&Drawing Color..."

Menu PrintItem
        Caption          =    "&Print"

Menu FromItem
        Caption          =    "Paste &From Clipboard"

Menu ToItem
        Caption          =    "Paste &To Clipboard"

Menu ExitItem
        Caption          =    "E&xit"

Begin Form SaveForm — — — — — — — — — — — — — — — —
   BorderStyle     =    3   'Fixed Double
   Caption         =    "Save File..."
   MaxButton       =    0   'False
   MinButton       =    0   'False

TextBox FilenameBox
     TabIndex       =    0

CommandButton OKButton
        Caption          =    "OK"
        Default          =    -1  'True
        TabIndex         =    1

CommandButton CancelButton
        Caption          =    "Cancel"
        TabIndex         =    2

Label Label1
        Caption          =    "Save File As:"

Begin Form LoadForm — — — — — — — — — — — — — — — —
   BorderStyle     =    3   'Fixed Double
   Caption         =    "Load File..."
   MaxButton       =    0   'False
   MinButton       =    0   'False
```

```
DriveListBox Drive1
        TabIndex        =    1


DirListBox Dir1
        TabIndex        =    4


FileListBox File1
        TabIndex        =    3


CommandButton OKButton
        Caption         =    "OK"
        Default         =    -1    'True
        TabIndex        =    0


CommandButton CancelButton
        Caption         =    "Cancel"
        TabIndex        =    5


Begin Form ControlPanel  — — — — — — — — — — — — — — — — — —
   Caption          =    "Control Panel"


CommandButton OKButton
        Caption         =    "OK"
        TabIndex        =    0


VScrollBar NewRed
        LargeChange     =    20
        Max             =    255
        Min             =    0
        SmallChange     =    10
        TabIndex        =    3


VScrollBar NewGreen
        LargeChange     =    20
        Max             =    255
        Min             =    0
        SmallChange     =    10
        TabIndex        =    3


VScrollBar NewBlue
        LargeChange     =    20
        Max             =    255
```

continues

Listing 7.4. continued

```
        Min             =   0
        SmallChange     =   10
        TabIndex        =   3

CommandButton CancelButton
        Caption         =   "Cancel"
        TabIndex        =   1

Label Label1
        Caption         =   "New Drawing Color:"

Label NewColor
        BorderStyle     =   1   'Fixed Single
        Caption         =   " "

Label Label4
        Caption         =   "Red"

Label Label5
        Caption         =   "Green"

Label Label6
        Caption         =   "Blue"

Paint Module — — — — — — — — — — — — — — — — —

Global AnchorX As Integer
Global AnchorY As Integer
Global DrawFlag As Integer
Global LineFlag As Integer
Global BoxFlag As Integer
Global CircleFlag As Integer
Global TextFlag As Integer


Form1 — — — — — — — — — — — — — — — — — — — —

Sub Form_MouseDown (Button As Integer,Shift As Integer,X As Single,Y As Single)
    If Button = 1 Then      'Left Button
        AnchorX = X
        AnchorY = Y
```

```
        CurrentX = X
        CurrentY = Y
    End If
End Sub


Sub Form_MouseMove (Button As Integer,Shift As Integer,X As Single,Y As Single)
    If (Button = 1) Then
        If DrawFlag Then
            Line -(X, Y)
        End If

        If LineFlag Then
            TempFore& = ForeColor
            TempMode% = DrawMode
            ForeColor = BackColor
            DrawMode = 7               'Xor mode
            Line (AnchorX, AnchorY)-(CurrentX, CurrentY)
            Line (AnchorX, AnchorY)-(X, Y)
            ForeColor = TempFore&
            DrawMode = TempMode%
        End If

        If BoxFlag Then
            TempFore& = ForeColor
            TempMode% = DrawMode
            ForeColor = BackColor
            DrawMode = 7               'Xor mode
            Line (AnchorX, AnchorY)-(CurrentX, CurrentY), , B
            Line (AnchorX, AnchorY)-(X, Y), , B
            ForeColor = TempFore&
            DrawMode = TempMode%
        End If

        If CircleFlag Then
            TempFore& = ForeColor
            TempMode% = DrawMode
            ForeColor = BackColor
            DrawMode = 7               'Xor mode
            radius! = Sqr((AnchorX - CurrentX) ^ 2 + (AnchorY - CurrentY) ^ 2)
            Circle (AnchorX, AnchorY), radius!
            radius! = Sqr((AnchorX - X) ^ 2 + (AnchorY - Y) ^ 2)
            Circle (AnchorX, AnchorY), radius!
```

continues

347

Listing 7.4. continued

```
                CurrentX = X
                CurrentY = Y
                ForeColor = TempFore&
                DrawMode = TempMode%
        End If

    End If
End Sub

Sub Form_MouseUp (Button As Integer, Shift As Integer, X As Single, Y As Single)
    If Button = 1 Then
        If LineFlag Then
        Line (AnchorX, AnchorY)-(X, Y)
        End If

        If BoxFlag Then
            Line (AnchorX, AnchorY)-(X, Y), , B
        End If

        If CircleFlag Then
            radius! = Sqr((AnchorX - X) ^ 2 + (AnchorY - Y) ^ 2)
            Circle (AnchorX, AnchorY), radius!
        End If
    End If
End Sub

Sub ClearButton_Click ()
    Cls
End Sub

Sub DrawButton_Click ()
    DrawFlag = True
    LineFlag = False
    BoxFlag = False
    CircleFlag = False
    TextFlag = False
End Sub

Sub LineButton_Click ()
    DrawFlag = False
    LineFlag = True
```

```
   BoxFlag = False
   CircleFlag = False
   TextFlag = False
End Sub

Sub BoxButton_Click ()
  DrawFlag = False
  LineFlag = False
  BoxFlag = True
  CircleFlag = False
  TextFlag = False
End Sub

Sub CircleButton_Click ()
  DrawFlag = False
  LineFlag = False
  BoxFlag = False
  CircleFlag = True
  TextFlag = False
End Sub

Sub TextButton_Click ()
  DrawFlag = False
  LineFlag = False
  BoxFlag = False
  CircleFlag = False
  TextFlag = True
End Sub

Sub TextButton_KeyPress (KeyAscii As Integer)
  Print Chr$(KeyAscii);
End Sub

Sub ExitItem_Click ()
  End
End Sub

Sub SaveItem_Click ()
  SaveForm.Show
End Sub

Sub LoadItem_Click ()
```

continues

Listing 7.4. continued

```
   LoadForm.Show
End Sub

Sub DrawingItem_Click ()
  ControlPanel.NewColor.BackColor = ForeColor
  ControlPanel.Show
End Sub

Sub PrintItem_Click ()
       DrawButton.Visible = False
       LineButton.Visible = False
       BoxButton.Visible = False
       CircleButton.Visible = False
       TextButton.Visible = False
       ClearButton.Visible = False
       PrintForm
       DrawButton.Visible = True
       LineButton.Visible = True
       BoxButton.Visible = True
       CircleButton.Visible = True
       TextButton.Visible = True
       ClearButton.Visible = True
End Sub

Sub FromItem_Click ()
       Picture = Clipboard.GetData()
End Sub

Sub ToItem_Click ()
       Clipboard.SetData Form1.Image
End Sub

SaveForm — — — — — — — — — — — — — — — — —

Sub CancelButton_Click ()
  SaveForm.Hide
End Sub

Sub OKButton_Click ()
  'On Error GoTo FileError
```

```
    SavePicture Form1.Image, FileNameBox.Text
    SaveForm.Hide
    Exit Sub

FileError:
    MsgBox "File Error", 48, "Paint"
    Resume
End Sub


LoadForm  — — — — — — — — — — — — — — — — —

Sub CancelButton_Click ()
    LoadForm.Hide
End Sub


Sub Drive1_Change ()
    Dir1.Path = Drive1.Drive
End Sub


Sub Dir1_Change ()
    File1.Path = Dir1.Path
End Sub


Sub OKButton_Click ()
    On Error GoTo FileError
    If (Right$(Dir1.Path, 1) = "\") Then
        Filename$ = Dir1.Path + File1.Filename
    Else
        Filename$ = Dir1.Path + "\" + File1.Filename
    End If
    Form1.Picture = LoadPicture(Filename$)
    LoadForm.Hide
    Exit Sub

FileError:
    MsgBox "File Error", 48, "Editor"
    Resume
End Sub


Sub File1_DblClick ()
    OKButton_Click
End Sub
```

continues

Listing 7.4. continued

```
Sub CancelButton_Click ()
  ControlPanel.Hide
End Sub


ControlPanel — — — — — — — — — — — — — — — — — —


Sub OKButton_Click ()

  Form1.ForeColor = RGB(NewRed.Value, NewGreen.Value, NewBLue.Value)
  ControlPanel.Hide
End Sub

Sub NewRed_Change ()
  NewColor.BackColor = RGB(NewRed.Value, NewGreen.Value, NewBLue.Value)
End Sub

Sub NewGreen_Change ()
  NewColor.BackColor = RGB(NewRed.Value, NewGreen.Value, NewBLue.Value)

End Sub

Sub NewBlue_Change ()
  NewColor.BackColor = RGB(NewRed.Value, NewGreen.Value, NewBLue.Value)
End Sub
```

Before leaving the subject of drawing graphics, however, there is one more consideration that you should examine—the scale you use.

Graphics Scaling

So far, you have used twips, the default unit of measurement in Visual Basic. You do not have to use twips forever, however. In fact, if you do a lot of graphics programming with Visual Basic, there are times you will want to use other units. If you want to draw a grid on the screen, for example, you have to specify where your lines go. If you use twips, your measurements are converted to pixels, which can cause problems—if you specify a twip spacing between gridlines that turns out to be 36.7 pixels, those lines are not always the same distance apart on the screen. (If the grid spacing is small, this effect is very noticeable.) Instead, the best thing is to use a pixel scale and work in pixels from then on. To do that, set the form's ScaleMode property, as shown in table 7.6 (the ScaleMode property is available for picture boxes, forms, and the Printer object).

Table 7.6. ScaleMode Values

ScaleMode	Means
0	User-defined; ScaleHeight, ScaleWidth already set
1	Twips (1440 twips per inch)
2	Points (72 points per inch)
3	Pixels (dot on monitor screen)
4	Character (120 twips on x axis, 240 twips on y axis)
5	Inches
6	Millimeters
7	Centimeters

Finding the pixel dimensions of the user's screen.
To find the size of the current screen in pixels, use the Screen object and check the Screen.Width and Screen.Height properties.

Besides these predefined scales, you can design your own scale. For example, this capability can make drawing graphs very easy if you set up a system of units so that both x and y directions are exactly 100 units. To plot a point at (56, 93) on your graph, you would just have to use PSet(56, 93). You can set such a scale by simply setting the ScaleWidth and ScaleHeight properties of the form or picture box yourself; to make the form or picture box 100 x 100 units, for example, set both ScaleWidth and ScaleHeight to 100.

This capability has another use too: If you have set up a custom scale and the user resizes the window, you do not have to make any changes in the way you send graphics to the screen. For instance, if you have made your window 100×100 units and the user doubles the size of the window, it is still 100×100 units.

That's it for graphics, your Paint application, and the mouse. It's time to move on now for some behind-the-scenes (non-I/O) work. Chapter 8 begins to look at some advanced data handling.

Summary

In this chapter, you have seen how to use the mouse by adding code to the mouse events: MouseDown, MouseUp, and MouseMove. Using these events gives you control over the mouse in your programs. This skill is useful because you cannot always use controls (which have a Click procedure to handle the mouse) for everything you want to do.

In addition, you have learned how to write a Windows Paint program, how to save graphics images to disk and read them back in, and how to use the Windows clipboard. Developing a large-scale program like this one is useful because it points out the need to cut large programs into manageable chunks; this process is called making the program modular. It is much easier to debug and maintain a modular program than a nonmodular one, and making big programs modular is part of good programming practice. You have also seen a few other techniques in this chapter, such as stretching a graphics figure on the screen, changing the mouse cursor for a control or form, and changing the graphics scale (pixels or twips) that Visual Basic uses. These graphics techniques will come in handy in many of your programs, especially when you use the mouse.

New Events	Description
MouseDown	Occurs when a mouse button goes down and the mouse cursor is in the form or control. Use it like this: Sub Form_MouseDown (Button As Integer,Shift As Integer,X As Single,Y As Single).
	The Button parameter is defined in table 7.1.
	The Shift parameter is defined in table 7.2.

New Events	Description
MouseMove	Occurs when the mouse moves over a control or form. Use it like this: Sub Form_MouseMove (Button As Integer,Shift As Integer,X As Single,Y As Single). Button is defined in table 7.3. Shift is defined in table 7.2.
MouseUp	Occurs when a mouse button goes up and the mouse cursor is in the form or control. Use it like this: Sub Form_MouseDown (Button As Integer,Shift As Integer,Sub Form_MouseUp (Button As Integer,Shift As Integer,X As Single,Y As Single). The Button parameter is defined in table 7.1. The Shift parameter is defined in table 7.2.

New Methods	Description
Cls	Clears the graphics in a form or picture.
GetData	Gets data from the Windows clipboard; use it like this: Clipboard.GetData ([format%]). The format% parameter can take these values (from Constant.Txt): CF_BITMAP for a bit map; CF_METFILE for a Metafile; CF_DIB for a Device-independent bit map.
SetData	Sets data in the Windows clipboard: Clipboard.SetData (data, [format%]). The format% parameter can take these values (from Constant.Txt): CF_BITMAP for a bit map; CF_METFILE for a Metafile; CF_DIB for a Device-independent bit map.
New Properties	Description
MousePointer	Sets the mouse cursor for the control or form; the available ones are listed in table 7.4.

8

Advanced Data Handling, Sorting, and Storing a Spreadsheet Program

In this chapter, you will see how Visual Basic lets you organize data for maximum power in your programs. These are techniques all Visual Basic programmers should be familiar with. They include the following:

▼ Determining which variable types are available

▼ Learning how to use arrays

▼ Organizing data with the shell sort

▼ Organizing data with the Quicksort

▼ Creating a working spreadsheet program

▼ Looking at how binary trees can help

▼ Getting the most from data structures

▼ Understanding a linked list

▼ Understanding a circular buffer

This chapter develops some useful programs, including working examples of a shell sort, a Quicksort, and a fast data-search algorithm. In addition, you will put the Grid control that comes with Visual Basic to work in a functioning spreadsheet program. In general, you will find that organizing your data for easy access can be crucial in program development for speed in both program coding and execution.

Because organizing your data at the beginning, in fact, may help you win more than half the battle of writing a program, it's an important topic. The way you set up the data in a database program, for example, can make the difference between programming failure and success. If you have to keep track of 31 uncoordinated data arrays with different indices, there is a higher probability of failure than if you can condense them into one array of data structures. You don't have to write a database program, of course, to take advantage of these techniques. Almost all programs use and manipulate data of some kind, and organizing it for maximum ease of use is a skill no programmer should be without. For instance, you might have a program that asks ask yes-or-no questions of the user (as do some artificial intelligence *expert systems*). This method cries out for binary trees, a fact you might not know if you have never heard of binary trees. You will soon find that the skills you learn in this chapter come to you naturally as you begin to expect more from your Visual Basic programs.

In this chapter, you will work through almost all the ways of organizing data in Visual Basic (and then you will add a few of your own). You will work through the most helpful methods of arranging data, including arrays, data structures, linked lists, circular buffers, and binary trees.

Programmers should be familiar with these common methods of organizing data and not have to continually re-invent the wheel. Also examined are two fast sorting methods to get the most out of your data, in addition to a fast searching algorithm to search through sorted arrays. The end of the chapter even shows you how to use the Grid control now supplied with Visual Basic to create a working spreadsheet program.

Variables

The most elementary method of organizing data is by storing it in simple variables. The following table shows the standard types used in Visual Basic.

Type	Symbol	Bytes	Range
Integer	%	2	—32,768 to 32,767
Long	&	4	—2,147,483,648 to 2,147,483,647
Single	!	4	—3.402823E38 to —1.40129E-45
Double	#	8	—1.79769313486232D308 to —2.2250738585072D-308
Currency	@	8	—$922337203685477.5808 to $922337203685477.5807
String	$	6	4K strings can range up to 32K characters (bytes)

You are familiar with all of these types, except perhaps the Currency type. You use it to store amounts of money. In the following example, the results are printed to the nearest cent, as follows:

```
Sub Form_Load ()
Savings@ = 6000.00
Rent@ = 775.00
Food@ = 124.50
Bills@ = 513.72

Savings@ = Savings@ - Rent@
Savings@ = Savings@ - Food@
Savings@ = Savings@ - Bills@

Print "Money left: $"; Savings@
End Sub
```

This example prints the amount of your savings that remains after paying rent and the bills. For most purposes, you can think of a Currency variable as a more accurate Long variable with four decimal places added to it, although the last two decimal places are for internal accuracy only.

In many versions of Basic, the next step up in data handling is the Data statement, which you are probably familiar with. You calculate the sum and product of the numbers 1 through 10 as stored in a Data statement, in the following way:

```
Sum& = 0
Product& = 1

For i = 1 To 10
   Read Number&
   Sum& = Sum& + Number&
Next i

Print "The sum of your data is:"; Sum&

Data 1, 2, 3, 4, 5, 6, 7, 8, 9, 10
```

There are a number of Basic statements, however, that Visual Basic does not support, and Data (largely considered obsolete) is one of them. Instead, the next step up in data handling in Visual Basic is working with something you are already familiar with: arrays.

360

Arrays

We are all familiar with arrays, such as the one in this example. Set the form's AutoRedraw property to True so that you can draw text from the following Form_Load() procedure:

```
Sub Form_Load()
  Static Array(10, 2) As Currency

  'Fill Array(n,1) with today's sales:

  Array(1, 1) = 10.00
  Array(2, 1) = 53.00
  Array(3, 1) = 7.17
  Array(4, 1) = 9.67
  Array(5, 1) = 87.99
  Array(6, 1) = 14.00
  Array(7, 1) = 91.19
  Array(8, 1) = 12.73
  Array(9, 1) = 1.03
  Array(10, 1) = 5.04


  'Fill Array(n,2) with yesterday's sales:

  Array(1, 2) = 9.67
  Array(2, 2) = 3.5
  Array(3, 2) = 8.97
  Array(4, 2) = 10.00
  Array(5, 2) = 78.33
  Array(6, 2) = 17.00
  Array(7, 2) = 91.36
  Array(8, 2) = 12.73
  Array(9, 2) = 16.12
  Array(10, 2) = 7.98


  Print "     SALES (in $)"
  Print "Yesterday" ; Tab(20) ; "Today"
  Print "————" ; Tab(20) ; "——"
  For loop_index = 1 To 10
  Print Array(loop_index, 1) ; Tab(20) ; Array(loop_index, 2)
  Next loop_index
  Print "————" ; Tab(20) ; "——"
```

```
      Sum1@ = 0
      Sum2@ = 0
      For loop_index = 1 To 10
      Sum1@ = Sum1@ + Array(loop_index, 1)
      Sum2@ = Sum2@ + Array(loop_index, 2)
      Next loop_index

      Print Sum1@ ; Tab(20) ; Sum2@ ; " = Total"

End Sub
```

In this program, you set up an array of ten rows and two columns to hold sales values for the past two days, and then you fill it with the following data:

Static Array(10, 2) As Currency

```
'Fill Array(n,1) with today's sales:
```

Array(1, 1) = 10.00
```
Array(2, 1) = 53.00   :
Array(3, 1) = 7.17    :
Array(4, 1) = 9.67
Array(5, 1) = 87.99
Array(6, 1) = 14.00
Array(7, 1) = 91.19
Array(8, 1) = 12.73
Array(9, 1) = 1.03
Array(10, 1) = 5.04
```

```
'Fill Array(n,2) with yesterday's sales:
```

Array(1, 2) = 9.67
```
Array(2, 2) = 3.5     :
Array(3, 2) = 8.97    :
Array(4, 2) = 10.00
Array(5, 2) = 78.33
Array(6, 2) = 17.00
Array(7, 2) = 91.36
Array(8, 2) = 12.73
Array(9, 2) = 16.12
Array(10, 2) = 7.98
   :
   :
```

The following array is the one that is produced:

	Col 1	Col 2	
	10.00	9.67	← Row 1
	53.00	3.5	← Row 2
	7.17	8.97	
	9.67	10.00	
	87.99	78.33	
	14.00	17.00	
	91.19	91.36	
	12.73	12.73	
	1.03	16.12	
	5.04	7.98	

The reason you declare this array with Static rather than with Dim is that, in Visual Basic, you must use Static to declare a fixed-size array in non-Static procedures. If you declare the entire procedure Static, you can use either Dim or Static. Declaring an array Static in this way means that the values in this array don't change between calls to this procedure. Now you can reach each day's column of sales just by incrementing the column index. In this format, you can perform parallel operations on parallel sets of data, such as adding the columns of sales to produce sums, as in the following example program:

```
Sub Form_Load()
   Static Array(10, 2) As Currency

   'Fill Array(n,1) with today's sales:

   Array(1, 1) = 10.00
   :
   :
   Array(10, 1) = 5.04

   'Fill Array(n,2) with yesterday's sales:
```

```
Array(1, 2) = 9.67
:
:
Array(10, 2) = 7.98

Print "    SALES (in $)"
Print "Yesterday" ; Tab(20) ; "Today"
Print "————" ; Tab(20) ; "——"
For loop_index = 1 To 10
Print Array(loop_index, 1) ; Tab(20) ; Array(loop_index, 2)
Next loop_index
Print "————" ; Tab(20) ; "——"

Sum1@ = 0
Sum2@ = 0
For loop_index = 1 To 10
Sum1@ = Sum1@ + Array(loop_index, 1)
Sum2@ = Sum2@ + Array(loop_index, 2)
Next loop_index

Print Sum1@ ; Tab(20) ; Sum2@ ; " = Total"
End Sub
```

The results of this program appear in figure 8.1.

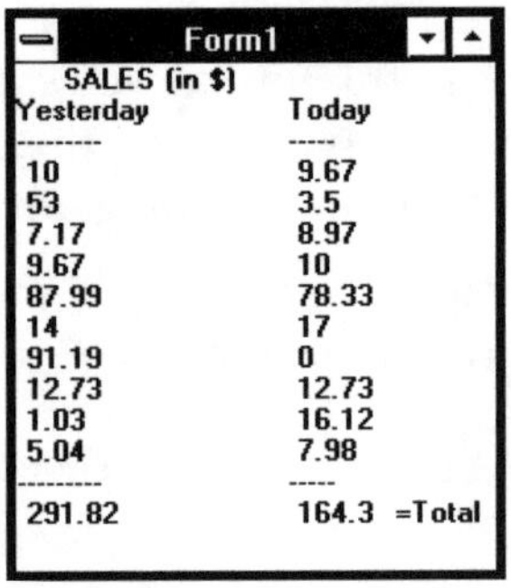

Figure 8.1. An array example.

In Visual Basic, you can also declare arrays as *dynamic*, which means that you can redimension them with the *ReDim* statement at run-time. To declare a dynamic array at the procedure level, use Dim with no arguments in the parentheses, as follows:

```
Sub Form_Load()
  Dim Array() As Currency
  :
```

Now you can redimension it whenever you want to and use it as you have before:

```
Sub Form_Load()
  Dim Array() As Currency

  ReDim Array(10, 2) As Currency

  'Fill Array(n,1) with today's sales:

  Array(1, 1) = 10.00
  :
  :
  Array(10, 1) = 5.04

  'Fill Array(n,2) with yesterday's sales:

  Array(1, 2) = 9.67
  :
  :
  Array(10, 2) = 7.98
  :


End Sub
```

The ReDim statement initializes all elements of the array to 0. In addition, you cannot use ReDim to create arrays with more than eight dimensions. There is a 64K limit on the size of dynamic or static arrays in Visual Basic.

That's it. Arrays don't get very complex in Visual Basic, unlike in C or C++, where array names are just pointers, and two-dimensional array names are just pointers to pointers. There, you can go wild and save both time and memory by converting all array references to pointer references. At the same time, you make your code extremely difficult to read.

As it is, we have gotten about as complex as arrays get in Visual Basic, so let's move on to the next most-advanced way to organize data after arrays: data structures.

Data Structures

As you have seen to some extent, you can group the standard data types together and come up with a new type of your own. To define a Type named Person, you can do the following:

```
Type Person
  FirstName As String * 20
  LastName As String * 20
End Type
  :
```

You can actually use variable-length strings in Type statements, except when you are using variables of this type as records in a random-access file, as you saw in the file handling chapter. The data structure created here just stores a person's first and last names. You can set up a variable of this type or, even more powerfully, an array of variables of this type, as follows:

```
Type Person
  FirstName As String * 20
  LastName As String * 20
End Type

Global People(10) As Person
  :
```

You can reference them in the following way in your procedures:

```
People(1).FirstName = "Al"
People(1).LastName = "French"

People(2).FirstName = "Frank"
People(2).LastName = "Reuben"

People(2).FirstName = "Charlie"
People(2).LastName = "Allen"

Print People(1).FirstName
  :
```

That is not the end to working with data structures. If there is some connection between the elements of your array, you can connect them in a *linked list*.

Linked Lists

Linked lists are good for organizing data items in sequential chains, especially if you have a number of such chains to manage and you want to use space efficiently.

They work this way: For each data item, there is also a *pointer* pointing to the next data item—that is, an index of some sort that references the next data item, as you will see. You find the next item in the list by referring to the pointer in the present item. You can add another data item to the list at any time, as long as you update the current pointer to point to the new data item, as follows:

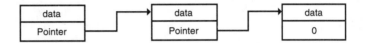

Because the last pointer in the chain is a null pointer with a value of 0, you know the list is finished when you reach it. A prominent example of a linked list in your computer is the File Allocation Table (FAT) on disks. This is a list of the clusters allocated to files for storage. Files are stored cluster by cluster, and, for each cluster on the disk, there is one entry in the FAT.

> **What is a disk cluster?**
> A cluster is the minimum size of disk storage allocation. On 360K diskettes, clusters are 2 sectors, or 1,024 bytes, long. This means that the amount of free space on 360K diskettes is always reported in units of 1,024 bytes.

To see which cluster a file is stored in, you get its first cluster number from the internal data in its directory entry; suppose that the number is 2. This means that the first section of the file is stored in cluster 2 on the disk. This number is also the key to the FAT. You can find the *next* cluster occupied by the file by looking in cluster 2's entry in the FAT, as follows:

FAT Entry #	2	3	4	5	6	7	8	9	10	11	12	13
	3	4	6	32	7	End	29	10	End	0	0	0

That cluster's entry in the FAT holds 3, which is the number of the next cluster the file occupies on the disk. To find the cluster after 3, check the entry in the File Allocation Table for that cluster, as follows:

FAT Entry #	2	3	4	5	6	7	8	9	10	11	12	13
	3	4	6	32	7	End	29	10	End	0	0	0

That entry holds 4, so the next section of the file is in cluster 4. To continue from there, check the number in the FAT entry for cluster 4, as follows:

FAT Entry #	2	3	4	5	6	7	8	9	10	11	12	13
	3	4	6	32	7	End	29	10	End	0	0	0

That number is 6, and you continue until you come to the end-of-file mark in the FAT:

FAT Entry #	2	3	4	5	6	7	8	9	10	11	12	13
	3	4	6	32	7	End	29	10	End	0	0	0

In other words, this file is stored in clusters 2, 3, 4, 6, and 7. Notice that 5 was already taken by another file, which is also weaving its own thread of clusters through the FAT at the same time. Linked lists such as this one are used when you want to use memory or disk space efficiently and you have to keep track of a number of sequential chains of data. When this file is deleted, for example, its entries in the FAT can be written over, and those clusters can be taken by another file.

Let's see an example of a linked list in Visual Basic. You might have these two distinct career paths to keep track of the following:

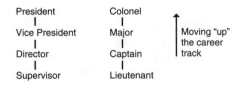

You can connect the various levels with a linked list. You start by setting up a variable of type Person in a module, as follows:

```
Type Person
   Rank As String * 20
   SuperiorPointer As Integer
End Type
```

Now you can fill the Rank fields in any order because the SuperiorPointers will keep them straight, as follows:

```
Sub Form_Load ()

   'Linked List Example

   Static People(10) As Person

   People(1).Rank = "Supervisor"
:  People(2).Rank = "Major"
:  People(3).Rank = "Director"
   People(4).Rank = "President"
   People(5).Rank = "Captain"
   People(6).Rank = "Vice President"
   People(7).Rank = "Colonel"
   People(8).Rank = "Lieutenant"
   :
```

For each entry in People( ), there is also a "superior" position. For example, the superior of the entry in People(1), Supervisor, is in People(3)—Director. To link the entries in each of the two chains, you have to point to the superior rank by filling the pointers in the array Person( ).SuperiorPointer, as follows:

```
Sub Form_Load ()
```

```
'Linked List Example

Static People(10) As Person

People(1).Rank = "Supervisor"
People(2).Rank = "Major"
People(3).Rank = "Director"
People(4).Rank = "President"
People(5).Rank = "Captain"
People(6).Rank = "Vice President"
People(7).Rank = "Colonel"
People(8).Rank = "Lieutenant"

People(1).SuperiorPointer = 3
: People(2).SuperiorPointer = 7
: People(3).SuperiorPointer = 6
People(4).SuperiorPointer = 0
People(5).SuperiorPointer = 2
People(6).SuperiorPointer = 4
People(7).SuperiorPointer = 0
People(8).SuperiorPointer = 5
:
```

Now that all the items in the two lists are linked, you can choose a number (1 or 2) and work your way through the first or second linked list, printing the various Rank names as you go. In the following example, let's choose life track 1.

```
Sub Form_Load ()

'Linked List Example

Static People(10) As Person

People(1).Rank = "Supervisor"
:
:
People(8).Rank = "Lieutenant"

People(1).SuperiorPointer = 3
:
:
People(8).SuperiorPointer = 5
```

```
Index = 1

Do
Print People(Index).Rank      'Print out results.
Index = People(Index).SuperiorPointer
Loop While Index <> 0
```

End Sub

When this program runs, it prints life track 1, and you see the following list on the form:

```
Supervisor
Director
Vice President
President
```

Note that you must know in advance that chain 1 starts with entry 1, and chain 2 with entry 8—you always need the first entry to use as a key to the first position in the linked list. After that, you can work your way up either chain of command. As you do so, you print the current Rank and get a pointer (the array index number) to the next Rank at the same time.

Circular Buffers

Another type of linked list programmers often use is a list in which the last item points to the first one so that the whole thing forms a circle. This is called a *circular buffer*. The most well-known circular buffer in your computer is the keyboard buffer.

While one part of the operating system is putting key codes in the keyboard buffer, another part of the operating system is taking them out. The location in the buffer where the next key code will be placed is called the *tail*. The location from which the next key code is to be read is called the *head*.

When characters are typed, the tail advances. When they are read, the head advances. As you write to and read from the keyboard buffer, the head and tail march around; each data location can be either the head or the tail. When the buffer is filled, the tail comes up behind the head, and the buffer-full warning beeps.

You can use circular buffers, but at different rates, when part of your program is writing data and another part is reading it. Store the location of the head and tail positions. After you put data in the buffer, advance the tail. When you take data out, advance the head. This way, you can use the same memory space for both reading and writing.

The primary problem with linked lists, however, is that all access to their data is sequential access. To find the last entry in a linked list, for example, you have to begin at the first one and work your way back. That method is fine for files tracked through the FAT (where you need every FAT entry before you can read the whole file), but it is a terrible method if you are looking for a specific record. A better way is to make a binary tree.

Binary Trees

Binary trees differ from linked lists in that the data is ordered. You can begin with a linked list, as follows:

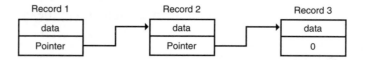

After that, you can make it a *doubly linked list*, as follows:

Now there are two pointers in each record; one scans up the chain; the other scans down. A doubly linked list has many uses, but it still is not a binary tree. Instead, let's put in some values for the data fields: —5, 0, and 2, as follows:

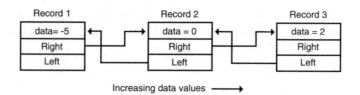

Notice that you have constructed a hierarchy based on data values, arranging them from left to right in increasing order (—5, 0, 2). The record with the data value closest to the median data value becomes the *root* of the binary tree, as follows:

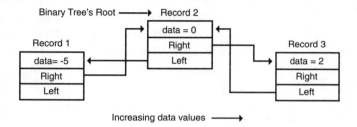

Record 2 is the root of your binary tree because it has the data value closest to the middle of all three records. To find a record with a data value of –5, for example, you start at the root—record 2, whose data value is 0. Because –5 is less than 0, next you search the record to its left because data values decrease to the left. This record is record 1, with a data value of –5, which means that you have found your target value. This gain might seem small, but imagine having a list like the following one:

```
First name = "Denise"
Age = 23

First name = "Ed"
Age = 46

First name = "Nick"
Age = 47

First name = "Dennis"
Age = 42

First name = "Doug"
Age = 33

First name = "Margo"
Age = 27

First name = "John"
Age = 41
```

```
First name = "Cheryl"
Age = 28
```

Let's say that it is your job to coordinate this list and find a person with a specified age. To construct a binary tree, you pick the person with an age as close as possible to the median (Doug) and then you might put the tree together as follows. There are many possible variations. Note that each successive node is the root of a binary tree.

```
                        Doug (33)
                       /         \
              Margo (27)          Dennis (42)
             /     \             /      \
   Denise (23)  Cheryl (28)  John (41)   Ed (46)
                                          \
                                          Nick (47)
```

Now you can start with Doug and keep working until you find the required age. To find the person who is 46 years old, for example, start at Doug, who is 33. Because 46 is greater than 33, continue moving to the right from Dennis to Ed, who is the person for whom you are searching. Let's put this example into code. You begin by defining a new Person Type that has two pointers—one to the next-older person, and one to the next-younger, as follows:

```
Type Person
  FirstName As String * 20
  Age As Integer
  NextYoungerPerson As Integer
  NextOlderPerson As Integer
End Type
```

Now you can use that type in a Form_Load() Sub procedure, as follows:

```
Sub Form_Load ()

  'Binary Tree example.

  Static People(10) As Person
  :
: People(1).FirstName = "Denise"
  People(1).Age = 23
  People(1).NextYoungerPerson = 0
```

```
People(1).NextOlderPerson = 0

People(2).FirstName = "Ed"
People(2).Age = 46
People(2).NextYoungerPerson = 0
People(2).NextOlderPerson = 3

People(3).FirstName = "Nick"
People(3).Age = 47
People(3).NextYoungerPerson = 0
People(3).NextOlderPerson = 0

People(4).FirstName = "Dennis"
People(4).Age = 42
People(4).NextYoungerPerson = 7
People(4).NextOlderPerson = 2

People(5).FirstName = "Doug"
People(5).Age = 33
People(5).NextYoungerPerson = 6
People(5).NextOlderPerson = 4

People(6).FirstName = "Margo"
People(6).Age = 27
People(6).NextYoungerPerson = 1
People(6).NextOlderPerson = 8

People(7).FirstName = "John"
People(7).Age = 41
People(7).NextYoungerPerson = 0
People(7).NextOlderPerson = 0

People(8).FirstName = "Cheryl"
People(8).Age = 28
People(8).NextYoungerPerson = 0
People(8).NextOlderPerson = 0
    :
    :
```

Next, you can search for the first person who is 46 years old. First, you begin at the root and check to see whether that person is 46 years old.

375

```
Sub Form_Load ()

  'Binary Tree example.

  Static People(10) As Person

  People(1).FirstName = "Denise"
  People(1).Age = 23
  People(1).NextYoungerPerson = 0
  People(1).NextOlderPerson = 0
    :
    :
    :
  People(8).FirstName = "Cheryl"
  People(8).Age = 28
  People(8).NextYoungerPerson = 0
  People(8).NextOlderPerson = 0

  BinaryTreeRoot% = 5      'Doug has about the median age
  :
: Print "Searching for a person 46 years old..."

  CurrentRecord% = BinaryTreeRoot%

  Do
  If People(CurrentRecord%).Age = 46 Then
  Print "That person is: "; People(CurrentRecord%).FirstName
  Exit Do
  End If
    :
    :
```

If not, you have to compare the current person's age to 46. If it is less, you want the NextOlderPerson; if it is greater, you want the NextYoungerPerson. That looks like the following in Form_Load():

```
Sub Form_Load ()

  'Binary Tree example.

  Static People(10) As Person

  People(1).FirstName = "Denise"
```

```
People(1).Age = 23
People(1).NextYoungerPerson = 0
People(1).NextOlderPerson = 0
:
:
People(8).FirstName = "Cheryl"
People(8).Age = 28
People(8).NextYoungerPerson = 0
People(8).NextOlderPerson = 0


BinaryTreeRoot% = 5     'Doug has about the median age


Print "Searching for a person 46 years old..."


CurrentRecord% = BinaryTreeRoot%


Do
If People(CurrentRecord%).Age = 46 Then
Print "That person is: "; People(CurrentRecord%).FirstName
Exit Do
End If
If People(CurrentRecord%).Age > 46 Then
: CurrentRecord% = People(CurrentRecord%).NextYoungerPerson
: Else
CurrentRecord% = People(CurrentRecord%).NextOlderPerson
End If
Loop While CurrentRecord% <> 0
```

End Sub

That is how to search through a binary tree. You just keep going until you find what you are looking for or you run out of branches. The results of this program appear in figure 8.2, and the program appears in Listing 8.1.

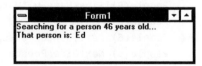

Figure 8.2. A binary tree example.

Listing 8.1. Binary Tree Example

```
Sub Form_Load ()

    'Binary Tree example.

    Static People(10) As Person

    People(1).FirstName = "Denise"
    People(1).Age = 23
    People(1).NextYoungerPerson = 0
    People(1).NextOlderPerson = 0

    People(2).FirstName = "Ed"
    People(2).Age = 46
    People(2).NextYoungerPerson = 0
    People(2).NextOlderPerson = 3

    People(3).FirstName = "Nick"
    People(3).Age = 47
    People(3).NextYoungerPerson = 0
    People(3).NextOlderPerson = 0

    People(4).FirstName = "Dennis"
    People(4).Age = 42
    People(4).NextYoungerPerson = 7
    People(4).NextOlderPerson = 2

    People(5).FirstName = "Doug"
    People(5).Age = 33
    People(5).NextYoungerPerson = 6
    People(5).NextOlderPerson = 4

    People(6).FirstName = "Margo"
    People(6).Age = 27
    People(6).NextYoungerPerson = 1
    People(6).NextOlderPerson = 8

    People(7).FirstName = "John"
    People(7).Age = 41
    People(7).NextYoungerPerson = 0
    People(7).NextOlderPerson = 0
```

```
People(8).FirstName = "Cheryl"
People(8).Age = 28
People(8).NextYoungerPerson = 0
People(8).NextOlderPerson = 0

BinaryTreeRoot% = 5     'Doug has about the median age

Print "Searching for a person 46 years old..."

CurrentRecord% = BinaryTreeRoot%

Do
If People(CurrentRecord%).Age = 46 Then
Print "That person is: "; People(CurrentRecord%).FirstName
Exit Do
End If
If People(CurrentRecord%).Age > 46 Then
CurrentRecord% = People(CurrentRecord%).NextYoungerPerson
Else
CurrentRecord% = People(CurrentRecord%).NextOlderPerson
End If
Loop While CurrentRecord% <> 0

End Sub
```

You have begun to order your data with binary trees. This statement means that you have established the relative position of a record with respect to its two neighbors. But, what if you want to sort all the data? Sorting data is a common task. It is the next, more advanced step in organizing data. You should explore it in some detail because it is so common. To do that, let's work through two of the fastest algorithms available—shell sorts and the Quicksort.

Shell Sorts

The standard shell sort is always popular among programmers. It works like this—suppose that you have a one-dimensional array with these values in it, as follows:

```
8 7 6 5 4 3 2 1
```

To sort this list in ascending order, divide it into two partitions, in the following way:

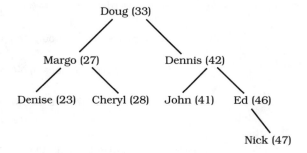

Then compare the first element of the first partition with the first element of the second partition, as follows:

8 7 6 5 4 3 2 1

In this case, because 8 is greater than 4, you switch the elements and go on to compare the next pair:

8 7 6 5 4 3 2 1

Again, because 7 is greater than 3, you switch and go on, as follows:

4 7 6 5 8 3 2 1

You also switch 6 and 2 and then look at the last pair, as follows:

4 3 6 5 8 7 2 1

After you switch them too, you get the following as the new list:

4 3 2 1 8 7 6 5

Although this is somewhat better than before, you are not finished. The next step is to change to smaller partitions and repeat the process, comparing 4 with 2, and 8 with 6. (This is not the most efficient shell sort, but it is the best way to see how they work):

4 3 2 5 8 7 6 1

You switch elements or a pair and move on to the next pair, as follows:

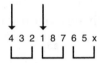

4 3 2 1 8 7 6 5 x

The elements or a pair are in order, so you proceed up the line and make only one more change (exchange 8 with 5). Note that, in the very last case, you are comparing 7 with nothing.

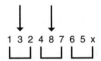

1 3 2 4 8 7 6 5 x

In this case, you make no switches (there is no later element that 7 should replace). Now go to the next smaller partition size and begin the process again, comparing 1 with 2, and 5 with 6, as follows:

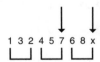

1 3 2 4 5 7 6 8 x

These are OK, so you go on, comparing 3 with 4, and 7 with 8, as follows:

That leaves you with the following:

1 3 2 4 5 7 6 8

This looks even closer to the desired ordering. Now the partition size is down to one element, the following result:

1 2 3 4 5 6 7 8

That is how the standard shell sort works. Now let's see this concept in code. You begin by dimensioning an array and filling it with values (which are as far from ascending order as they can be):

```
Sub Form_Load ()

  Static Array(9) As Integer

  Array(1) = 9
  Array(2) = 8
  Array(3) = 7
  Array(4) = 6
  Array(5) = 5
  Array(6) = 4
  Array(7) = 3
  Array(8) = 2
  Array(9) = 1
      :
      :
```

You can also print those values to the form so that they can be compared to the sorted list later.

```
Sub Form_Load ()

  Static Array(9) As Integer

  Array(1) = 9
  Array(2) = 8
```

```
Array(3) = 7
Array(4) = 6
Array(5) = 5
Array(6) = 4
Array(7) = 3
Array(8) = 2
Array(9) = 1

Print " i" ; Tab(20) ; "Array(i)"
Print "---" ; Tab(20) ; "--------"
For i = 1 To 9
Print i ; Tab(20) ; Array(i)
Next i
Print
Print "Sorting..."
    :
    :
```

Now you have to implement your shell sort. In this type of sorting routine, you loop over partition size (PartitionSize% in the case below), so let's set up that loop first, as follows:

```
Sub Form_Load ()

    Static Array(9) As Integer

    Array(1) = 9
    :
    :
    Array(9) = 1

    Print " i" ; Tab(20) ; "Array(i)"
    Print "---" ; Tab(20) ; "--------"
    For i = 1 To 9
    Print i ; Tab(20) ; Array(i)
    Next i
    Print
    Print "Sorting..."

    NumItems% = Ubound(Array, 1)
    PartitionSize% = Int((NumItems% + 1) / 2)
```

```
Do
   :
   :
Loop While PartitionSize% > 0
   :
   :
```

Notice in particular that, because you need the number of items to sort, you can use the Ubound() function, which returns the dimensions of an array as in Quick Basic or other Basics. This statement means that Ubound() returns an array's upper bound, and Lbound( ) returns its lower bound. In the loop, you loop over partition size and subtract 1 each time, as follows:

For every partition size, however, the list is broken up into a different number of partitions. You have to loop over those partitions so that you can compare elements in the current partition to the elements of the next one.

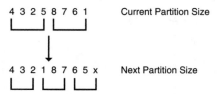

In the following loop over partitions, note that, when you are finished with each partition, you subtract one from the partition size, as follows:

```
Sub Form_Load ()

   Static Array(9) As Integer

   Array(1) = 9
      :
      :
```

```
Array(9) = 1
    :
    :
Print "Sorting..."

NumItems% = Ubound(Array, 1)
PartitionSize% = Int((NumItems% + 1) / 2)

Do
NumPartitions% = (NumItems% + 1) / PartitionSize%
Low% = 1
For i = 1 To NumPartitions% - 1
    :
    :
Next i
PartitionSize% = PartitionSize% - 1
Loop While PartitionSize% > 0
    :
    :
```

Finally, you have to loop over each element in the current partition and compare it to the corresponding element in the next partition:

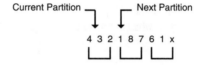

This is the element-by-element comparison. You go from Array(Low%) to Array(High%) in the current partition, where Low% is the array index at the beginning of this partition and High% is the index of the element at the end, and compare each element to the corresponding one in the next partition:

```
Sub Form_Load ()

  Static Array(9) As Integer

  Array(1) = 9
    :
    :
```

```
    Array(9) = 1
    :
    :
    Print "Sorting..."

    NumItems% = Ubound(Array, 1)
    PartitionSize% = Int((NumItems% + 1) / 2)

    Do
    NumPartitions% = (NumItems% + 1) / PartitionSize%
    Low% = 1
    For i = 1 To NumPartitions% - 1
    High% = Low% + PartitionSize% - 1
    If High% > NumItems% - PartitionSize% Then High% =
    NumItems% - PartitionSize%
    For j = Low% To High%
    If Array(j) > Array(j + PartitionSize%) Then
    :
    :
    End If
    Next j
    Low% = Low% + PartitionSize%
    Next i
    PartitionSize% = PartitionSize% - 1
    Loop While PartitionSize% > 0
    :
    :
```

If the element in the later partition is smaller than the element in the current one, you have to swap them by doing the following:

```
Sub Form_Load ()

    Static Array(9) As Integer

    Array(1) = 9
    :
    :
    Array(9) = 1
    :
    :
    Print "Sorting..."
```

```
NumItems% = Ubound(Array, 1)
PartitionSize% = Int((NumItems% + 1) / 2)

Do
NumPartitions% = (NumItems% + 1) / PartitionSize%
Low% = 1
For i = 1 To NumPartitions% - 1
High% = Low% + PartitionSize% - 1
If High% > NumItems% - PartitionSize% Then High% =
NumItems% - PartitionSize%
For j = Low% To High%
If Array(j) > Array(j + PartitionSize%) Then
Temp% = Array(j)
Array(j) = Array(j + PartitionSize%)
Array(j + PartitionSize%) = Temp%
End If
Next j
Low% = Low% + PartitionSize%
Next i
PartitionSize% = PartitionSize% - 1
Loop While PartitionSize% > 0
    :
    :
```

You loop over partition sizes, over each partition, and over each element in the current partition, and swap it with its counterpart in the next partition if necessary. At the end, you can print the newly sorted array. The entire program appears in Listing 8.2 (Ssort.Mak on the diskette).

Listing 8.2. Shell Sort (Ssort.Mak on the diskette)

```
Sub Form_Load ()

    Static Array(9) As Integer

    Array(1) = 9
    Array(2) = 8
    Array(3) = 7
    Array(4) = 6
    Array(5) = 5
    Array(6) = 4
    Array(7) = 3
```

continues

Listing 8.2. continued

```
   Array(8) = 2
   Array(9) = 1

   Print " i" ; Tab(20) ; "Array(i)"
   Print "---" ; Tab(20) ; "--------"
   For i = 1 To 9
   Print i ; Tab(20) ; Array(i)
   Next i
   Print
   Print "Sorting..."

   NumItems% = Ubound(Array, 1)
   PartitionSize% = Int((NumItems% + 1) / 2)

   Do
   NumPartitions% = (NumItems% + 1) / PartitionSize%
   Low% = 1
   For i = 1 To NumPartitions% - 1
   High% = Low% + PartitionSize% - 1
   If High% > NumItems% - PartitionSize% Then High% =
   NumItems% - PartitionSize%
   For j = Low% To High%
   If Array(j) > Array(j + PartitionSize%) Then
   Temp% = Array(j)
   Array(j) = Array(j + PartitionSize%)
   Array(j + PartitionSize%) = Temp%
   End If
   Next j
   Low% = Low% + PartitionSize%
   Next i
   PartitionSize% = PartitionSize% - 1
   Loop While PartitionSize% > 0

   Print
   Print " i" ; Tab(20) ; "Array(i)"
   Print "---" ; Tab(20) ; "--------"
   For i = 1 To 9
   Print i ; Tab(20) ; Array(i)
   Next i
End Sub
```

The results of this program are shown in figure 8.3.

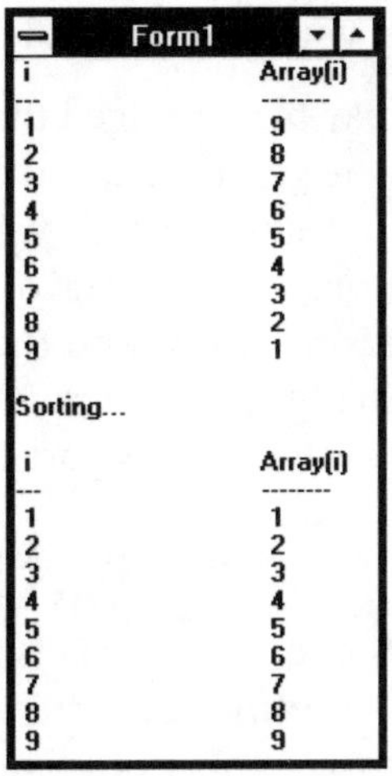

i	Array(i)
---	---------
1	9
2	8
3	7
4	6
5	5
6	4
7	3
8	2
9	1

Sorting...

i	Array(i)
---	---------
1	1
2	2
3	3
4	4
5	5
6	6
7	7
8	8
9	9

Figure 8.3. A shell sort example.

Quicksorts

In addition to shell sorts, another popular sorting algorithm is the Quicksort. That sorting routine works like this: first, you find a key, or test, value to which to compare values. The best value in this case would be the median value of the elements of the array; in practice, however, a random entry is usually chosen. In our discussion to follow, you will choose a value from the center of the array.

You divide the array into two partitions: those less than the test value, and those greater than the test value. You move upward in the array until you come to the first value that is greater than the test value. Then you move down the array, beginning from the end, until you find a number less than the test value and swap them. You keep going until all the numbers in the first partition are less than the test value, and all the numbers in the second partition are greater.

Do the same thing to each partition: Select a new test value from each partition and break that partition into two *new* partitions. One of those new partitions holds the numbers less than that test value, and the other holds those values that are greater. You continue in that way, and split partitions continuously until just two numbers are in a partition. At that point, you compare and switch them, if necessary.

You may have noticed that each subsequent step is a Quicksort. In other words, to get started, you divide the array into two partitions less than and greater than the test value, and then break *each* partition into two partitions, depending on a new test value, and so on. In this way, QuickSorts easily lend themselves to recursion, and this is the way they are usually coded. Because Visual Basic supports recursion, the Quicksort you develop in this part of the chapter is no exception.

What is recursion all about?

If the term *recursion* is new to you, you should know that it refers to a routine that calls itself. If a programming task can be divided into a number of identical levels, it can be dealt with recursively—every time the routine calls itself, it deals with a deeper level. After the final level is reached, control returns through each successive level back to the beginning.

Let's see how this looks in code. Because this routine is recursive, you set up a subprogram called SortQuick() to call from the main program (this subprogram calls itself repeatedly—or, recursively).

```
Call SortQuick(Array(), SortFrom%, SortTo%)
```

You just pass the array name to sort, the index from which to begin sorting (SortFrom%), and the index to sort to (SortTo%); working this way is useful when you have to sort a particular partition in the array. In SortQuick(), you first handle the final case—that is, a partition of only two elements, as follows:

```
Sub SortQuick (Array() As Integer, SortFrom%, SortTo%)

    If SortFrom% >= SortTo% Then Exit Sub
    If SortFrom% + 1 = SortTo% Then   'Final case
    If Array(SortFrom%) > Array(SortTo%) Then
    Temp% = Array(SortFrom%)
    Array(SortFrom%) = Array(SortTo%)
    Array(SortTo%) = Temp%
    End If
```

:
:

In this case, you just compare each element to its neighbor (the only other element in this partition) and swap them, if necessary. That's all there is to the final case in the Quicksort algorithm.

If the partition size is greater than two, however, you have to sort the values from Array(SortFrom%) to Array(SortTo%) according to a test value, divide the elements into two new partitions, and then call SortQuick() again on every new partition. Let's see how that process works. First, you pick a test value and then you divide the present partition into two partitions on the basis of it. Next, you start by moving up from the bottom of the partition and stop at any values that you find are greater than the test value, as follows:

```
Sub SortQuick (Array() As Integer, SortFrom%, SortTo%)

    If SortFrom% >= SortTo% Then Exit Sub
    If SortFrom% + 1 = SortTo% Then    'Final case
    If Array(SortFrom%) > Array(SortTo%) Then
    Temp% = Array(SortFrom%)
    Array(SortFrom%) = Array(SortTo%)
    Array(SortTo%) = Temp%
    End If


    Else    'Have to split problem
    AtRandom = (SortFrom% + SortTo%) \ 2
    Test = Array(AtRandom)
    Temp% = Array(AtRandom)
    Array(AtRandom) = Array(SortTo%)
    Array(SortTo%) = Temp%


    Do
    'Split into two partitions

    For i = SortFrom% To SortTo% - 1
    If Array(i) > Test Then Exit For
    Next i
    :
    :

    Loop...
```

You also scan from the top of the partition down in the same loop, looking for the first value that's smaller than the test value. If you find any numbers that should be swapped between partitions, you do so and then go on to the next values.

```
Sub SortQuick (Array() As Integer, SortFrom%, SortTo%)

  If SortFrom% >= SortTo% Then Exit Sub
  :
  :
  Do
  'Split into two partitions

  For i = SortFrom% To SortTo% - 1
  If Array(i) > Test Then Exit For
  Next i

  For j = SortTo% To i + 1 Step -1
  If Array(j) < Test Then Exit For
  Next j

  If i < j Then
  Temp% = Array(i)
  Array(i) = Array(j)
  Array(j) = Temp%
  End If

  Loop UNTIL i >= j
  :
  :
```

You continue until i and j meet, and then you have created your two new partitions. Next, you can call SortQuick() again for each of the resulting partitions (which may be of unequal size).

```
Sub SortQuick (Array() As Integer, SortFrom%, SortTo%)

  Do
  :
  :
  Loop Until i >= j

  Temp% = Array(i)
```

```
      Array(i) = Array(SortTo%)
      Array(SortTo%) = Temp%

      Call SortQuick(Array(), SortFrom%, i - 1)
      Call SortQuick(Array(), i + 1, SortTo%)

   End If
End Sub
```

That's all there is to it; the sort continues recursively until you get down
to the final case of a partition size of 1, the final swaps are done if
necessary, and then you're finished. The whole thing appears in Listing
8.3 (Qsort.Mak on the diskette).

 Listing 8.3. A Quicksort (Qsort.Mak on the diskette)

```
Sub Form_Load ()
   Static Array(9) As Integer

   Array(1) = 9
   Array(2) = 8
   Array(3) = 7
   Array(4) = 6
   Array(5) = 5
   Array(6) = 4
   Array(7) = 3
   Array(8) = 2
   Array(9) = 1

   Print " i" ; Tab(20) ; "Array(i)"
   Print "---" ; Tab(20) ; "--------"
   For i = 1 To 9
   Print i; Tab(20) ; Array(i)
   Next i

   Call SortQuick(Array(), 1, UBound(Array, 1))

   Print
   Print "Sorting..."
   Print
   Print " i" ; Tab(20) ; "Array(i)"
   Print "---" ; Tab(20) ; "--------"
```

continues

Listing 8.3. continued

```
   For i = 1 To 9
   Print i; Tab(20) ; Array(i)
   Next i


End Sub

Sub SortQuick (Array() As Integer, SortFrom%, SortTo%)

   If SortFrom% >= SortTo% Then Exit Sub
   If SortFrom% + 1 = SortTo% Then   'Final case
   If Array(SortFrom%) > Array(SortTo%) Then
   Temp% = Array(SortFrom%)
   Array(SortFrom%) = Array(SortTo%)
   Array(SortTo%) = Temp%
   End If

   Else'  Have to split problem
   AtRandom = (SortFrom% + SortTo%) \ 2
   Test = Array(AtRandom)
   Temp% = Array(AtRandom)
   Array(AtRandom) = Array(SortTo%)
   Array(SortTo%) = Temp%

   Do

   For i = SortFrom% To SortTo% - 1
   If Array(i) > Test Then Exit For
   Next i

   For j = SortTo% To i + 1 Step -1
   If Array(j) < Test Then Exit For
   Next j

   If i < j Then
   Temp% = Array(i)
   Array(i) = Array(j)
   Array(j) = Temp%
   End If

   Loop Until i >= j
```

```
    Temp% = Array(i)
    Array(i) = Array(SortTo%)
    Array(SortTo%) = Temp%

    Call SortQuick(Array(), SortFrom%, i - 1)
    Call SortQuick(Array(), i + 1, SortTo%)

  End If
End Sub
```

That's it for sorting. Both the shell sort and the Quicksort are pretty fast—the one you should use depends on your application; you might want to try them both and use the faster of the two.

Searching Your Data

Now that you have ordered your data, it becomes much easier to search through it. If the data is unordered, you would have no choice other than to simply check one value after another until you find a match, as in the following example program:

```
Sub Form_Load ()

  'Unordered Search

  Static Array(9) As Integer

  Array(1) = 9
  Array(2) = 7
  Array(3) = 8
  Array(4) = 3
  Array(5) = 5
  Array(6) = 4
  Array(7) = 6
  Array(8) = 2
  Array(9) = 1

  Print "Searching the unordered list for the value 1."

  For i = 1 To Ubound(Array,1)
```

```
    If Array(i) = 1 Then
    Print "Value of 1 in element";i
    End If
    Next i

End Sub
```

You just continue scanning up the list of values until you find what you're looking for. On the other hand, you can be more intelligent when you are searching a sorted list. For example, if your sorted array had the following values in it:

1 2 3 4 5 6 7 8 9 10 11 12 13 14 15

You were searching for the entry with 10 in it; begin in the center of the list, as follows:

Because 10 is greater than 8, you divide the *upper* half of the array in two and check the midpoint again.

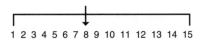

Because the value you are looking for, 10, is less than 12, you move *down* and cut the remaining distance in half.

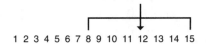

In this way, you have zeroed in on the number, cutting down the number of values you have to check. Let's see how this looks in a program. First, you set up your array. In this example, let's search an array of nine elements for the entry with 8 in it, as follows:

```
Sub Form_Load()
```

```
'Ordered Search

Static Array(9) As Integer

Array(1) = 1
Array(2) = 2
Array(3) = 3
Array(4) = 4
Array(5) = 5
Array(6) = 6
Array(7) = 7
Array(8) = 8
Array(9) = 9

SearchValue% = 8
Print "Searching the ordered list for the value 8."
  :
  :
```

Now you cut the array into two partitions and check the test value, which is right between them, at position TestIndex%. Then you need to begin searching. You continue looping over partition size—if the partition size becomes 0 without success, the value you are looking for isn't in the array.

```
Sub Form_Load ()

  'Ordered Search

  Static Array(9) As Integer

  Array(1) = 1
  :
  :
  Array(9) = 9

  SearchValue% = 8
  Print "Searching the ordered list for the value 8."

  Partition% = (Ubound(Array, 1) + 1) \ 2
  TestIndex% = Partition%

  Do
: Partition% = Partition% \ 2
```

```
:
:
: Search this partition
:
:

Loop While Partition% > 0
```

First, you check to see whether you have found your target. If so, you can quit. If you haven't found your target, you have to go on to the next iteration of the loop, set TestIndex% to the middle of either the higher or lower partition, and then divide that partition into two new partitions. If the target is bigger than the value at your current location in the array, you need to move to the partition at higher values, as follows:

```
Sub Form_Load ()

  'Ordered Search

  Static Array(9) As Integer

  Array(1) = 1
  :
  :
  Array(9) = 9

  SearchValue% = 8
  Print "Searching the ordered list for the value 8."

  Partition% = (Ubound(Array, 1) + 1) \ 2
  TestIndex% = Partition%

  Do
  Partition% = Partition% \ 2
  If Array(TestIndex%) = SearchValue% Then
  Print "Value of"; SearchValue%; "in element"; TestIndex%
  Exit Do
  End If
  If Array(TestIndex%) < SearchValue% Then
  TestIndex% = TestIndex% + Partition%
  :
  :
  Loop While Partition% > 0
```

If the search value is smaller, on the other hand, you want to move to the lower partition (which holds lower values), as follows:

```
Sub Form_Load ()

  'Ordered Search

  Static Array(9) As Integer

  Array(1) = 1
  :
  :
  Array(9) = 9

  SearchValue% = 8
  Print "Searching the ordered list for the value 8."

  Partition% = (Ubound(Array, 1) + 1) \ 2
  TestIndex% = Partition%

  Do
  Partition% = Partition% \ 2
  If Array(TestIndex%) = SearchValue% Then
  Print "Value of"; SearchValue%; "in element"; TestIndex%
  Exit Do
  End If
  If Array(TestIndex%) < SearchValue% Then
  TestIndex% = TestIndex% + Partition%
  Else
  TestIndex% = TestIndex% - Partition%
  End If
  Loop While Partition% > 0
```

That's almost all there is. You just continue until you find what you are looking for, or until the partition size becomes 0, in which case it's not there. If you were unsuccessful, however, you should apply two last tests: Check the value you are searching for against the first and last entries in the array. Your algorithm demands that all numbers it checks be *straddled* by two other values. That is true of every element in the array except for the first and last ones. If you didn't find what you were looking for, therefore, you have to check these last two values explicitly. You do that in the final version, which appears in Listing 8.4.

Listing 8.4. Ordered Search Program

```
Sub Form_Load ()

 'Ordered Search

 Static Array(9) As Integer

 Array(1) = 1
 Array(2) = 2
 Array(3) = 3
 Array(4) = 4
 Array(5) = 5
 Array(6) = 6
 Array(7) = 7
 Array(8) = 8
 Array(9) = 9

 SearchValue% = 8
 Print "Searching the ordered list for the value 8."

 Partition% = (Ubound(Array, 1) + 1) \ 2
 TestIndex% = Partition%

 Do
 Partition% = Partition% \ 2
 If Array(TestIndex%) = SearchValue% Then
 Print "Value of"; SearchValue%; "in element"; TestIndex%
 Exit Do
 End If
 If Array(TestIndex%) < SearchValue% Then
 TestIndex% = TestIndex% + Partition%
 Else
 TestIndex% = TestIndex% - Partition%
 End If
 Loop While Partition% > 0

 'Can only find straddled numbers, so add these tests:

 If Array(1) = SearchValue% Then
```

```
    Print "Value of"; SearchValue%; "in element 1"
    End If

    If Array(Ubound(Array, 1)) = SearchValue% Then
    Print "Value of"; SearchValue%; "in element"; Ubound(Array, 1)
    End If
End Sub
```

You have completed the ordered search. The result of this program appears in figure 8.4.

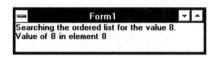

Figure 8.4. An ordered search example.

A Spreadsheet Example

Another example of advanced data handling might be a spreadsheet program. Creating such a program is easy with the Grid control, which comes in the file Grid.Vbx and is automatically loaded into Visual Basic. Start a new program now and give it the name Spread.Mak. Save the form as Spread.Frm. Next, click the Grid tool (the one with a small grid in its button), and draw a grid covering most of the form. Use the properties window to set the *Rows* property of this new Grid, Grid1, to 7, and set the *Cols* property to the same value. Also, give the form the caption *Spreadsheet*. The result should look something like figure 8.5.

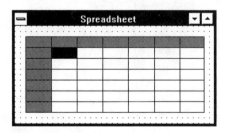

Figure 8.5. Beginning your spreadsheet.

Now you can refer to the individual cells in your spreadsheet by making a cell the *current* cell. You only need to set the Grid1.Row and Grid1.Col properties to do that. Suppose that you want to keep track of expenses, as follows:

$400 Rent

$100 Food

$80 Car

$15 Phone

$10 Gas

? Total

You can track by first labeling the cells in your spreadsheet in the Form_Load() event. All you want to do is label the rows with numbers and the columns with letters (the standard way to label spreadsheets), and enter the preceding item labels. That process, which is simple enough, appears as follows:

```
Sub Form_Load ()
  Static Items(6) As String
  Items(1) = "Rent"
  Items(2) = "Food"
  Items(3) = "Car"
  Items(4) = "Phone"
  Items(5) = "Gas"
  Items(6) = "Total"
  Grid1.Row = 1
  For loop_index% = 1 To 6
  Grid1.Col = 0
  Grid1.Row = loop_index%
  Grid1.Text = Str$(loop_index%)
  Grid1.Col = 2
  Grid1.Text = Items(loop_index%)
```

```
    Next loop_index%
    Grid1.Col = 1
    Grid1.Row = 0
    For loop_index% = 1 To 6
    Grid1.Col = loop_index%
    Grid1.Text = Chr$(Asc("A") - 1 + loop_index%)
    Next loop_index%
    Grid1.Row = 1
    Grid1.Col = 1
End Sub
```

The result of this code appears in figure 8.6.

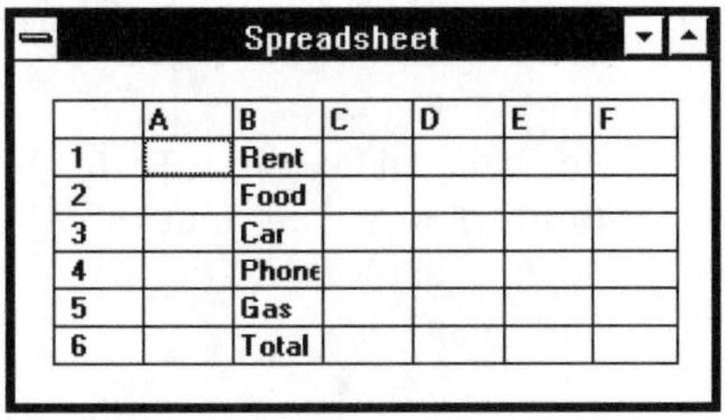

Figure 8.6. A completed spreadsheet template.

Now you can read numbers as they are entered in the data cells (all those you have labeled except the cell marked Total) and keep a running total in the bottom box, called Total. You do that with Grid1's KeyPress() event; whenever a KeyPress() event occurs, you can place the typed number in the appropriate cell and update the running total at the bottom of the column.(The Grid control does not do this automatically.) First, you add the typed key to the current cell, in the following way:

```
Sub Grid1_KeyPress (KeyAscii As Integer)
  Grid1.Text = Grid1.Text + Chr$(KeyAscii)
    :
End Sub
```

As you type, the values appear in the current cell. You can change them by using the mouse or pressing the arrow keys. Next, you should update the running total in column 1. First, save the Row and Col values of the current cell, as follows:

```
G
Sub Grid1_KeyPress (KeyAscii As Integer)
```

```
    Grid1.Text = Grid1.Text + Chr$(KeyAscii)
    OldRow = Grid1.Row
    OldCol = Grid1.Col
    :
End Sub
```

Then you add all of the numbers in column 1, and loop over them, in the
following way:

```
Sub Grid1_KeyPress (KeyAscii As Integer)
Grid1.Text = Grid1.Text + Chr$(KeyAscii)
    OldRow = Grid1.Row
    OldCol = Grid1.Col
    Grid1.Col = 1    'Add numbers in first column
    Grid1.Row = 0
    Sum% = 0
    For row_index% = 1 To 5
    Grid1.Row = row_index%
    Sum% = Sum% + Val(Grid1.Text)
    Next row_index%
    :
End Sub
```

All that remains is to place the value that is now in Sum% into the Total
cell and restore the original current cell. That process appears as follows:

```
Sub Grid1_KeyPress (KeyAscii As Integer)
    Grid1.Text = Grid1.Text + Chr$(KeyAscii)
    OldRow = Grid1.Row
    OldCol = Grid1.Col
    Grid1.Col = 1    'Add numbers in first column
    Grid1.Row = 0
    Sum% = 0
    For row_index% = 1 To 5
    Grid1.Row = row_index%
    Sum% = Sum% + Val(Grid1.Text)
    Next row_index%
    Grid1.Row = 6
    Grid1.Text = Str$(Sum%)
    Grid1.Row = OldRow
    Grid1.Col = OldCol
End Sub
```

Now the spreadsheet is working. As the user types values in the first
column, a running total appears in the Total cell. The resulting program

appears in figure 8.7. As you can imagine, this program is easily adaptable for many applications—anywhere you can use a spreadsheet. Note, however, that connecting cells together, as you have done by keeping a running total in the Total cell, has to be programmed into your code, unless you write a program smart enough to read spreadsheet formulas as the user types them directly. The entire code appears in Listing 8.5 (and in Spread.Mak on the diskette).

	A	B	C	D	E	F
1	400	Rent				
2	100	Food				
3	80	Car				
4	15	Phone				
5	10	Gas				
6	605	Total				

Figure 8.7. Your spreadsheet at work.

Listing 8.5. Spread.Mak (Spread.Mak on the diskette)

```
Form Form1 — — — — — — — — — — — — — — — — — — —
  Caption =    "Spreadsheet"

Grid Grid1
  Cols=    7
  Rows=    7
  ScrollBars  =   0  'None

Sub Form_Load ()
  Static Items(6) As String
  Items(1) = "Rent"
  Items(2) = "Food"
  Items(3) = "Car"
  Items(4) = "Phone"
  Items(5) = "Gas"
  Items(6) = "Total"
  Grid1.Row = 1
  For loop_index% = 1 To 6
  Grid1.Col = 0
```

continues

Listing 8.5. continued

```
    Grid1.Row = loop_index%
    Grid1.Text = Str$(loop_index%)
    Grid1.Col = 2
    Grid1.Text = Items(loop_index%)
    Next loop_index%
    Grid1.Col = 1
    Grid1.Row = 0
    For loop_index% = 1 To 6
    Grid1.Col = loop_index%
    Grid1.Text = Chr$(Asc("A") - 1 + loop_index%)
    Next loop_index%
    Grid1.Row = 1
    Grid1.Col = 1
End Sub

Sub Grid1_KeyPress (KeyAscii As Integer)
    Grid1.Text = Grid1.Text + Chr$(KeyAscii)
    OldRow = Grid1.Row
    OldCol = Grid1.Col
    Grid1.Col = 1      'Add numbers in first column
    Grid1.Row = 0
    sum% = 0
    For row_index% = 1 To 5
    Grid1.Row = row_index%
    sum% = sum% + Val(Grid1.Text)
    Next row_index%
    Grid1.Row = 6
    Grid1.Text = Str$(sum%)
    Grid1.Row = OldRow
    Grid1.Col = OldCol
End Sub
```

That's it for advanced data handling and sorting and for the spreadsheet example. You have seen in this chapter most of the popular ways of handling numeric data. When you design code, it is always important to organize your data correctly—as mentioned earlier, that can be half the battle of writing a program. Next, let's see how to debug your programs and handle errors.

Summary

Many data-handling techniques have been covered in this chapter, including how to use arrays, data structures, linked lists, doubly linked lists, binary trees, and circular buffers. You have learned how to use the Grid control to quickly create a functioning spreadsheet program. You have seen some useful algorithms, including the shell sort and the recursive Quicksort. You have even developed your own ordered search program. As you might imagine, it is much easier to search through ordered data than through unordered data. If your program maintains long lists of data, you might keep it sorted by using one of the sorting techniques and then search through it by using an ordered search.

The skills you have learned in this chapter are applicable in any program that maintains more than a rudimentary amount of data. This is clear for database programs, of course, but it also applies to data-entry programs, disk-optimizing programs (which maintain linked lists of the various parts of files on a disk), mail-merge programs, arcade-style games, and many others. Binary trees, for example, are very common when you can distinguish between data items on the basis of a yes-no answer (for example, is the age of A greater than the age of B?). All the skills that have been discussed can be found in intermediate and advanced programs— and now they are your skills also.

New Properties	Description
Col	The column number of the current cell in a Grid control
Row	The row number of the current cell in a Grid control

New Functions	Description
LBound	Returns the minimum value an array index can take; use it like this: LBound(array [,dimension])
UBound	Returns the maximum value an array index can take; use it like this: UBound(array [,dimension])

Error Handling and Debugging

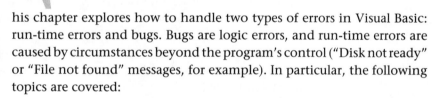

his chapter explores how to handle two types of errors in Visual Basic: run-time errors and bugs. Bugs are logic errors, and run-time errors are caused by circumstances beyond the program's control ("Disk not ready" or "File not found" messages, for example). In particular, the following topics are covered:

▼ Handling run-time errors without crashing

▼ Using Visual Basic's Debugger

▼ How to use breakpoints

▼ The Debug window

▼ Trappable errors

▼ All about error codes

▼ Converting error codes into English messages

409

▼ How to test your programs

▼ The Err and Erl functions

▼ How to write working error handlers

▼ How the Resume statement can get you out of trouble

You will see only a few demonstration programs in this chapter, although you will see how to add error handling to a few programs written earlier. When it comes to debugging, however, the programs we write (such as an investment calculator) will have a few bugs in them. We will have to find and eliminate these bugs. Mostly what we learn in this chapter are new skills: error handling and debugging. These skills are invaluable to programmers, of course, and you will find that you will use them time and time again if you develop programs that are longer than two dozen lines or so.

Any program that handles files—and that you let other people use—should include some file error handling because that's probably the most common type of run-time error. Such errors include a diskette that gets filled up or not placed in a drive, a file that is not being found, or a nonexistent record that is being requested. Rather than let Visual Basic handle errors like these (by default, Visual Basic displays error information that is useful only to the programmer), your program should be capable of handling them. Visual Basic has some excellent ways to handle errors—your programs don't have to simply crash. Even more important, you should make sure that your programs have no logic errors because users may be able to fix run-time errors, but not bugs. For these reasons, the skills you develop in this chapter are necessary ones for the programmer to cultivate and use.

Even the best programmers make errors. The longer the program, in fact, the more complex the code, and the more likely errors are to appear. Errors come in several different types: those that cause design-time errors, those that cause run-time errors, and those that make your programs produce incorrect or unexpected results (bugs). Visual Basic handles the first type, design-time errors, by refusing to run programs until they are fixed, and it usually offers some assistance in the form of help and help messages. The second two types, run-time errors and bugs, are left up to you to fix. They are the subject of this chapter.

Visual Basic refers to a run-time error as a *trappable error*, that is, Visual Basic recognizes that an error occurred and allows you to trap it and take some corrective action. (Untrappable errors usually occur only at design-time.) Bugs are different because Visual Basic usually doesn't recognize that there's a problem, but the code still doesn't operate as intended. For example, if you have a function called Counter that was supposed to increase an internal counter and return its current value every time it was called, it might appear as follows:

```
Function Counter()
  Dim counter_value As Integer

  counter_value = counter_value + 1

  Counter = counter_value
End Function
```

This code has a bug: counter_value is not declared Static. Every time this function is called, therefore, counter_value begins at 0. Because the function then adds 1 to counter_value, 1 is returned every time. A function that returns 1 every time it is called does not generate a run-time error, but, in light of its intended purpose, it is a bug.

You can find trappable errors without difficulty because Visual Basic generates them, it knows exactly when they occur, and it enables you to take some action. Bugs, however, are another story. In their case, you have to use Visual Basic's debugging capabilities to find out what went wrong and slowly work your way through the program, possibly even statement by statement. These kinds of skills are necessary tools for programmers, however, especially if you want to produce real applications subject to strict testing. That is our first topic—how to test the programs you write.

How to Test Programs

When programs run, they usually operate on ranges of data. For example, a program may read the value of an integer ranging from –32,768 to 32,767 from the user. (*Remember:* If the value could not vary, there would be no point in reading it.) The limits of that value, –32,768 and 32,767, are called its *bounds*. When you are trying to check your programs for potential problems, it is important to cover the entire range of such values. That doesn't normally mean checking every value between –32,768 and 32,767, but it does mean checking values at the bounds of this range, as well as some mid-range values and any other values likely to give you problems.

This value may represent the number of students in a class, for example. Perhaps after summing all the students' test scores, you want to divide by this value to find the class average. This is no problem for 15 or 20 students, but what if the user enters 0? Even though it is in the allowed range for unsigned integers, dividing by this value results in an error. Or, what if you stored the students' test scores in another unsigned integer and found that, as you went toward higher numbers of students, the division didn't give you the accuracy you want? Checking your program's bounding values like this is vitally important: Generally, there will be bounds for every crucial variable, and you should check all combinations of these values when you run your program to see how they interact (this is particularly important when it comes to array indices).

Of course, you should check midrange values also. It may turn out that some combination of such values also gives you unexpected errors. The longer you test your program under usual and unusual operating circumstances, the more confidence you have in it. As programs get more complex, the testing period normally gets longer and longer, which is why major software companies often send out hundreds of preliminary versions of their software (called *beta* versions) for testing by programmers (the final software package is usually the *gamma* version).

In addition, you should attempt to duplicate every run-time problem that may occur to see how your program reacts. File operations are great at generating such errors: What if the disk is full, for example, and you try to write to it? What if the specified input file doesn't exist? What if the specified file to write is already read-only? What if the diskette has been

Peter Norton's Visual Basic for Windows, Third Edition, Covering Release 3.0

removed? What if the user asks you to write record –15 in a file? It is difficult to generate every conceivable set of problematic circumstances, of course, but the closer you come, the more polished your application is.

Visual Basic gives you a hand when it comes to certain types of errors, however, called trappable errors. Let's look first at how to handle them.

Handling Run-time Errors

You may remember that you already placed some error checking in your Editor program because file handling is such a notorious source of possible errors (as is handling input from the keyboard). For example, if you asked the Editor to read a file on a diskette that has been removed, you would get a message box like the one in figure 9.1, informing you that a file error has occurred. You were able to intercept that kind of error, so let's reexamine how you did it.

Figure 9.1. The Editor application's file error message.

The On Error GoTo Statement

The way you trap trappable errors is with an On Error GoTo statement. For example, the following list is how we did it in the Editor application:

```
Sub OKButton_Click ()
  On Error GoTo FileError
  If (Right$(Dir1.Path, 1) = "\") Then    'Get file name
      Filename$ = Dir1.Path + File1.FileName
  Else
```

```
        Filename$ = Dir1.Path + "\" + File1.FileName
    End If

    Open Filename$ For Input As # 1  'Open file
    Form1.PadText.Text = Input$(LOF(1), # 1)      'Read file in

    Close # 1 'Close file
    LoadForm.Hide  'Hide dialog box

    Exit Sub

FileError:
    MsgBox "File Error", 48, "Editor"  'MsgBox for file error.
    Resume
End Sub
```

When Visual Basic generates a trappable error after executing a statement like this one in a procedure, control jumps to the specified label—in this case, that's FileError. That is exactly what the GoTo statement does: It transfers control to a new location in the program. The general form for such a procedure looks like the following:

```
Sub Name ()
    On Error GoTo ErrorLabel
    :
    :
    Exit Sub
ErrorLabel:
    :
    :
End Sub
```

Here, you execute the On Error GoTo statement first and set up your error-handling routine. Note that, because you exit from the Sub procedure before reaching that routine, you do not inadvertently execute the error-handling code. In this way, the procedure is set up much like a procedure that has subroutines, which are handled with the GoSub statement in Visual Basic just as they are handled in other forms of BASIC—that is, like the following:

```
Sub Name ()
    :
    GoSub Label1
```

414

```
    :
  Exit Sub

Label1
  :
  :
  Return
End Sub
```

Note that, because the code in an error-handling routine (as well as the code in a GoSub subroutine) is in the same Sub or Function procedure, this code shares all the variables of the rest of the Sub or Function procedure. That means that you will have access to variables that may be of value in fixing the error.

You should also note that you can override On Error GoTo statements with later statements of the same kind. This capability is useful if you have entered a different part of the code, with different potential errors, and you want to use a different error handler. Not much has been done here, however; we have only recognized the fact that an error occurred. The next step must be to find out what the error was and to then take action if possible.

> **Turning error handling off.**
> You can even turn error-handling off. Just execute the statement On Error GoTo 0 in your program.

The Err and Erl Functions

To determine what kind of error occurred, you can use the Err( ) function, which returns an error number. These error numbers are predefined in Visual Basic; the most common ones appear in table 9.1. Note that Err( ) includes such items as array subscripts out of bounds, division by zero, file not found, disk full (a very common file-writing error), and other errors that all represent trappable errors you can catch. And, if you can catch these errors, there is some possibility of fixing them.

Table 9.1. Common Trappable Errors

Error Number	Meaning
5	Illegal function call
6	Overflow
7	Out of memory
9	Subscript out of range
10	Duplicate definition
11	Division by zero
13	Type mismatch
14	Out of string space
19	No RESUME
20	RESUME without error
28	Out of stack space
51	Internal error
52	Bad file name or number
53	File not found
54	Bad file mode
55	File already open
57	Device I/O error
58	File already exists
59	Bad record length
61	Disk full
62	Input past end of file
63	Bad record number
64	Bad file name
65	File previously loaded
66	Tried to load file with duplicate procedure definition

Error Number	Meaning
67	Too many files
68	Device unavailable
70	Permission denied
71	Disk not ready
72	Disk-media error
75	Path/file access error
76	Path not found
323	Incompatible version created
340	Control array element does not exist
341	Illegal control array index
342	Not enough room to allocate control array
343	Object is not an array
344	Must specify index when using control array
360	Object is already loaded
361	Only forms and control array elements can be loaded or unloaded
362	Controls created at design-time cannot be unloaded
380	Illegal property value
381	Illegal property array index
384	Property cannot be modified when form minimized or maximized
420	Invalid object reference
421	Method not applicable for this object
422	Property not found
423	Property or control not found
424	Object required
425	Illegal object use

continues

417

Table 9.1. continued

Error Number	Meaning
427	Object is not the Printer object
428	Object is not a control
429	Object is not a form
430	There is no currently active control
431	There is no currently active form
461	Specified format does not match format of data
480	Unable to create AutoRedraw bit map
481	Invalid picture

Let's update your Editor program so that it can at least indicate which error occurred. To do that, you can use the following statement:

```
Sub OKButton_Click ()
  On Error GoTo FileError

  If (Right$(Dir1.Path, 1) = "\") Then  'Get file name
  :
  :
  LoadForm.Hide  'Hide dialog box
  Exit Sub

FileError:
  MsgBox "File Error" + Str$(Err), 48, "Editor"
  Resume
End Sub
```

We can do this for both saving and loading files. Now, if you select a file from a diskette, remove the diskette, and then try to read it, you see that your former error box now displays the message "File Error 68," as shown in figure 9.2. When you check table 9.1, you see that this error means that the device is unavailable.

418

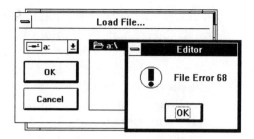

Figure 9.2. The Editor application with an error number.

In fact, you can report more information here also; in particular, you can report the line number in which the error occurred by using the Erl( ) function. This function returns a number that stands for the line number in the current procedure of the statement that caused the error. To use Erl(), you have to use line numbers (which is no longer standard in BASIC). That might appear like the following:

```
Sub OKButton_Click ()
1      On Error GoTo FileError

2      If (Right$(Dir1.Path, 1) = "\") Then     'Get file name
3      Filename$ = Dir1.Path + File1.FileName
4 Else
5      Filename$ = Dir1.Path + "\" + File1.FileName
6      End If

7      Open Filename$ For Input As # 1     'Open file
8      Form1.PadText.Text = Input$(LOF(1), # 1)      'Read file in

9      Close # 1 'Close file
10     LoadForm.Hide  'Hide dialog box

11     Exit Sub

FileError:
12     MsgBox "File Error"+Str$(Err)+" in line "+Str$(Erl), 48,
"Editor"
13     Resume
End Sub
```

If you cause the same error as before, removing the diskette with the file on it, you see a message informing you that the error occurred in line 7, the line in which you try to open the file. On the other hand, that information is of very little use to the user; why does it matter in which line the error occurred? The user would much rather know what the error was. You can, of course, print the error number, as above, but that is not necessarily more helpful. If the user has no knowledge of Visual Basic or doesn't have the information in table 9.1, the simple explanation that error 68 occurred will not be well received. there is a way, however, to translate that explanation into English from your program with a simple function, which is explored in the next section.

The Error$ Function

The Error$( ) function is a very useful function when you are handling errors because it can translate into English the error number you get from Err( ). You can therefore change your procedure to the following:

```
Sub OKButton_Click ()
  On Error GoTo FileError

  If (Right$(Dir1.Path, 1) = "\") Then      'Get file name
  :
  :
  LoadForm.Hide   'Hide dialog box
Exit Sub


FileError:
  MsgBox Error$(Err), 48, "Editor"
  Resume
End Sub
```

When you run the Editor application with this new error handler (but the same error), you get a message that the device is unavailable, as shown in figure 9.3. This is a considerable improvement over "File Error 68." In fact, it resembles having table 9.1 built into your program and ready to use. In general, this way of handling errors is much better than printing the error number, which may be meaningless and frustrating to the user. Even this message leaves something to be desired, however: What action are you requiring of the user? Does the user know which device you are talking about? Indicating the next step is still up to you, and you should design your error handler around such contingencies.

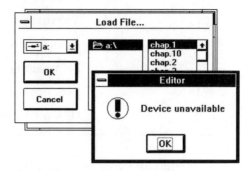

Figure 9.3. The Editor application with an English Error message.

Creating Customized Error Handlers

When you are creating your own error handler, you might anticipate that some errors will occur more frequently than others, and you might want to make special provisions for handling them. If you were writing files, for example, you might anticipate error 61—disk full. If that error occurred, you could place the following message in a message box:

```
The disk is full—please delete some files and click the OK
Button
```

The user then could switch to the Windows File Manager and clear some more disk space. (In cases like this one, you should also include a Cancel button in case the user wants to cancel the file-writing operation.) Then, after the user clicks the OK button, he can go back and try the operation again, as you will soon see. Let's see an example of a custom error handler in code. The following table shows some of the errors and messages you might expect Error$( ) to give when you load in the files.

Error Number	Meaning
7	Out of memory
55	File already open
57	Device I/O error

continues

Error Number	Meaning
61	Disk full
67	Too many files
68	Device unavailable
70	Permission denied
71	Disk not ready
72	Disk media error

You might write your own error handler like the following list:

```
Sub OKButton_Click ()
  On Error GoTo FileError

  If (Right$(Dir1.Path, 1) = "\") Then     'Get file name
  :
  :
  LoadForm.Hide   'Hide dialog box

Exit Sub
FileError:
  Msg$ = Error$(Err)
  Select Case Err       'Display our own message?
      Case 7
          Msg$ = "File is too big to open."
      Case 57, 68, 71, 72
          Msg$ = "Please check the disk and try again."
      Case 67
          Msg$ = "Too many files open. Close some and try again."
  End Select
  MsgBox Msg$, 48, "Editor"
  Resume
End Sub
```

Now, if you produce the same error as before, you see the message to check the disk and try again, as shown in figure 9.4. Generally, the more information you can provide to the user, the better. (It is usually better to handle the error internally, of course, if at all possible.) Often, you want the user to take some action and then click the OK button. When she does, you should retry the operation, such as trying to read in the file again. Let's see how to do that next.

Figure 9.4. A customized error message.

> **Other error-handling additions to your editor.**
> Two very useful places to add error handling to your Editor application are when the user is about to write over an already existing file ("Overwrite existing file NOVEL.TXT?") and when the file the user requested doesn't exist and you are about to create it ("File doesn't exist—create it?").

The Resume Statement

Note the line at the end of your error handler, as follows:

```
Sub OKButton_Click ()
  On Error GoTo FileError
  :
  :
FileError:
  Msg$ = Error$(Err)
  Select Case Err   'Display our own message?
      Case 7
            Msg$ = "File is too big to open."
      Case 57, 68, 71, 72
            Msg$ = "Please check the disk and try again."
      Case 67
```

```
                  Msg$ = "Too many files open. Close some and try again."
    End Select
    MsgBox Msg$, 48, "Editor"
    Resume
End Sub
```

This simple statement, Resume, lets you retry the operation that caused the error after the user took some corrective action. When Visual Basic encounters a Resume statement in an error handler—after an On Error GoTo type of routine has been set up and entered (the error trap is said to be active at this point)—it leaves the error handler and returns to the statement that caused the error. In other words, Resume enables you to retry an operation. When the Resume statement is encountered, the program jumps back to the highlighted line.

```
Sub OKButton_Click ()
  On Error GoTo FileError
  If (Right$(Dir1.Path, 1) = "\") Then      'Get file name
       Filename$ = Dir1.Path + File1.FileName
  Else
       Filename$ = Dir1.Path + "\" + File1.FileName
  End If

  Open Filename$ For Input As # 1      'Open file
  Form1.PadText.Text = Input$(LOF(1), # 1)      'Read file in

  Close # 1 'Close file
  LoadForm.Hide   'Hide dialog box
  Exit Sub

FileError:
  Msg$ = Error$(Err)
  Select Case Err       'Display our own message?
       Case 7
             Msg$ = "File is too big to open."
       Case 57, 68, 71, 72
             Msg$ = "Please check the disk and try again."
       Case 67
             Msg$ = "Too many files open. Close some and try again."
  End Select
  MsgBox Msg$, 48, "Editor"
  Resume
End Sub
```

If you had a problem trying to open the file, you display an error message, let the user take some corrective action, and then try opening the file again. Note, however, that this is a potential problem. If the user decides not to open the file, you should provide some way of exiting from this Sub procedure. You can do that by using a message box that has two buttons rather than one—both OK and Cancel. You can also read the response in the same statement with the MsgBox( ) function (you might recall that MsgBox has two forms: It can be used as a statement if you expect no reply and as a function if you want input from the user).

```
Response% = MsgBox(Msg$, 49, "Editor")
```

You are passing a message-box type parameter of 40—48 ! + 1 (include both OK and Cancel buttons) and placing the user's response in the variable Response%. If she selects the OK button, this response will equal 1; if she selects the Cancel button, it will equal 2. You can modify your code as shown in the following code to retry the problematic operation if the user selected the OK button, as follows:

```
Sub OKButton_Click ()
  On Error GoTo FileError
  :
  :
FileError:
  Msg$ = Error$(Err)
  Select Case Err   'Display our own message?
      Case 7
          Msg$ = "File is too big to open."
      Case 57, 68, 71, 72
          Msg$ = "Please check the disk and try again."
      Case 67
          Msg$ = "Too many files open. Close some and try again."
  End Select
  Response% = MsgBox(Msg$, 49, "Editor")
  If Response% = 1 Then Resume
End Sub
```

In this case, if the user chose OK, you move back to the same line that caused the error (probably the Open statement) and try it again. If the user chose the Cancel button, on the other hand, you want to exit from the Sub procedure entirely. To do that, however, it isn't enough to rely on the End Sub statement at the end of the procedure, as shown in the preceding example. If Visual Basic is in an error handler and reaches the end of the procedure without finding a Resume, it stops everything and helpfully points out that you have no Resume statement in your error handler. (It even does this in complied code, by placing a special No Resume window on the screen.)

You really don't want to use Resume, however, if the user chose Cancel because there are some errors a user cannot fix at this level. If the error occurred because the file was too big to fit into memory, for example, the user has to leave this procedure (OKButton_Click( )), select a new file, and then select the OK button again. To leave this procedure without messages about your lack of a Resume statement, you need to use Exit Sub, as follows:

```
Sub OKButton_Click ()
  On Error GoTo FileError
  :
  :
FileError:
  Msg$ = Error$(Err)
  Select Case Err        'Display our own message?
       Case 7
            Msg$ = "File is too big to open."
       Case 57, 68, 71, 72
            Msg$ = "Please check the disk and try again."
       Case 67
            Msg$ = "Too many files open. Close some and try again."
  End Select
  Response% = MsgBox(Msg$, 49, "Editor")
  If Response% = 1 Then
       Resume
  Else
       Exit Sub
  End If
End Sub
```

This code avoids the "No Resume" messages from Visual Basic and fixes the problem. In fact, there are other ways also of handling Resume statements. Visual Basic supports two variations of Resume: Resume Next and Resume Line #.

Resume Next and Resume Line

Sometimes you don't want to keep retrying the operation that caused the error. You have seen that one alternative method is simply to leave the procedure entirely and let the user select some other action. Two other methods are Resume Next and Resume Line #. The Resume Next statement causes Visual Basic to resume with the statement following the one that caused the error—in effect, skipping the statement that produced the problem. This can be useful, but it is not usually good to simply skip a line and then continue executing the rest of the code. If you used Resume Next rather than Resume, for example, and the Open statement had caused the error, you would continue with the next statement, which tries to read from the file you haven't been able to open, as follows:

```
Sub OKButton_Click ()
  On Error GoTo FileError

  If (Right$(Dir1.Path, 1) = "\") Then      'Get file name
       Filename$ = Dir1.Path + File1.FileName
  Else
       Filename$ = Dir1.Path + "\" + File1.FileName
  End If

  Open Filename$ For Input As # 1      'Open file
  Form1.PadText.Text = Input$(LOF(1), # 1)      'Read file in

  Close # 1 'Close file
  LoadForm.Hide  'Hide dialog box

  Exit Sub

FileError:
  Msg$ = Error$(Err)
  Select Case Err      'Display our own message?
       Case 7
             Msg$ = "File is too big to open."
       Case 57, 68, 71, 72
             Msg$ = "Please check the disk and try again."
       Case 67
             Msg$ = "Too many files open. Close some and try again."
  End Select
  MsgBox Msg$, 48, "Editor"
  Resume Next
End Sub
```

There are times, however, when Resume Next is exactly what you need. Let's see an example of this in code. One common Visual Basic method of

427

Chapter 9: Error Handling and Debugging

determining whether a file exists on disk is to create a deliberate, trappable error. You may recall that, in almost all Open modes (For Random and For Binary, for example), the file is created automatically if it doesn't already exist. On the other hand, if you open a file For Input, Visual Basic generates a trappable error if the file doesn't exist (it doesn't make sense to create the file from scratch if you are about to read from it). You can use that error to indicate whether the file exists.

Let's write a function called Exist( ), which takes a file name as its argument and returns True if the file exists, or False otherwise. In other words, you might use it in the following way:

```
Sub Form_Load ()
  If Exist("C:\AUTOEXEC.BAT") Then Print "Boot batch file exists."
End Sub
```

To add this function at the form level, click (general) in the Object box of the code window, click New Procedure... in the View menu, click the Function option button, and give it the name Exist. The following template appears:

```
Function Exist ()

End Function
```

Give this function the argument FileName As String and set up the error handler in the following:

```
Function Exist (FileName As String)
  On Error GoTo DoesNotExist
  :
  :
  Exit Function

DoesNotExist:
  :
  :
End Function
```

If there is no error, you should return a value of True, so you set Exist to True and try to open the file.

```
Function Exist (FileName As String)
  On Error GoTo DoesNotExist
  Exist = True    'Set to True
  Open (FileName) For Input As #200   'Unlikely to conflict
  :
  :
  Exit Function

DoesNotExist:
  :
  :
End Function
```

In this example, you open the file as #200 because that file number is unlikely to conflict with other file numbers used elsewhere in the program.

> **Finding the next unused file number.**
> In a real application, it is better to use the Visual Basic FreeFile function to find the next available (unused) file number rather than a fixed value, such as 200.

If the file does not exist, you go to the location DoesNotExist, where you want to set Exist to False. Then you want to use Resume Next, not Resume (which would cause you to try to open the file again), as follows:

```
Function Exist (FileName As String)
  On Error GoTo DoesNotExist
  Exist = True    'Set to True
  Open (FileName) For Input As #200   'Unlikely to conflict
  :
  :
  Exit Function

DoesNotExist:
  Exist = False   'Set to False
  Resume Next
End Function
```

At this point, Exist holds the correct value, True or False. All that remains is to close the file and exit from the function, which you can do as in the following example:

```
Function Exist (FileName As String)
  On Error GoTo DoesNotExist
  Exist = True   'Set to True
  Open (FileName) For Input As #200   'Unlikely to conflict
  Close #200
  Exit Function

DoesNotExist:
  Exist = False   'Set to False
  Resume Next
End Function
```

And that's it. Exist() is ready to go, which gives you a good use for Resume Next. It is usually better, however, to move to an entirely different part of the code and take some alternative action (and let the user know that you are doing so). That is what the Resume Line # statement enables you to do. With it, you can specify the line number at which to resume execution. You might decide, for example, that your Editor application should always try to open and load a default file named File.Txt when you start the application. To do that, you can put this code in the Form_Load( ) Sub procedure, as follows:

```
Sub Form_Load()
   Open "File.Txt" For Input As # 1    'Open file
   Form1.PadText.Text = Input$(LOF(1), # 1)      'Read file in
   Close # 1 'Close file
End Sub
```

If an error occurred, on the other hand, you might want to pop the Load File... dialog box on the screen. First, you set up your error handler in the following way:

```
Sub Form_Load ()
   On Error GoTo FileError

   Open "File.Txt" For Input As # 1    'Open file

   Form1.PadText.Text = Input$(LOF(1), # 1)      'Read file in
   Close # 1 'Close file
   Exit Sub

FileError:
   :
   :
End Sub
```

Then you can resume to another part of the procedure entirely with a Resume Line # statement like the following, in which you pop up the Load File... dialog box.

```
Sub Form_Load()
   On Error GoTo FileError

   Open "File.Txt" For Input As # 1    'Open file

   Form1.PadText.Text = Input$(LOF(1), # 1)      'Read file in
   Close # 1 'Close file
   Exit Sub

10 LoadForm.Show
   Exit Sub

FileError:
   Resume 10
End Sub
```

That's almost all there is for Resume, Resume Next, and Resume Line #. You must consider only one more point. Suppose that Proc1 calls Proc2:

Next, assume that an error occurs while you are in Proc2, but that it has no error handler. Instead, Visual Basic works its way back up the calling ladder, searching for an error handler. In this case, that error handler is Proc1.

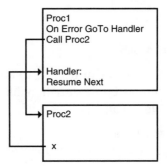

In other words, Proc1 is handling Proc2's error. If you leave an error handler out of Proc2, you should be aware of this. That is, statements such as Resume Next in Proc1's error handler may cause unexpected or even disastrous results.

That's it for this chapter's coverage of trappable errors in Visual Basic. As you can see, you can do a lot with the On Error GoTo statement, especially when it is coupled with the Resume statement. There's more to finding and eliminating errors than this, however—now it's time to turn to debugging.

Debugging

As you type your program in Visual Basic, you may have errors in syntax—that is, you may type something like the following:

```
Circle (ScaleWidth/2, ScaleHeight/2)
```

When you try to move to the next line, Visual Basic puts on the screen a warning box indicating that something more is expected. In this case, you need to indicate the circle's radius (at least). In this way, Visual Basic catches syntax errors at design-time. On the other hand, you may end up with errors at run-time that are impossible to avoid at design-time, such as out-of-memory or disk-full errors—in other words, trappable errors. You have just learned that, if you can anticipate such errors, you can trap and deal with them.

The kinds of errors discussed next, logic errors in the program, usually are more difficult to find—in a word, they are bugs. An error may be buried deep in a long chain of complex statements. Fortunately, Visual Basic provides some debugging tools you can use to locate and even fix errors.

> ### Using text boxes in debugging.
> Even text boxes can make excellent debugging tools, in fact, if you use them to print intermediate results in your programs. To use them, simply add a few extra text boxes to your application and print crucial values in them as your program is running. You might want to see, for example, what is happening to a variable that is supposed to be counting keystrokes: Is it increased every time you press a key? Or, you might want to make sure that you are reading mouse cursor coordinates correctly in a MouseDown( ) event by displaying them in text boxes also. Temporary text boxes generally can provide a window into what's happening behind the scenes in your program. That's what debugging is all about.

For the purposes of exploring debugging, let's alphabetize ten or so names, like the following:

```
John
```

```
Tim
Edward
Samuel
Frank
Todd
George
Ralph
Leonard
Thomas
```

You can start by setting up an array to hold all the names in the Form_Click() Sub procedure, as follows:

```
Sub Form_Click ()
  Static Names(10) As String

  Names(1) = "John"
  Names(2) = "Tim"
  Names(3) = "Edward"
  Names(4) = "Samuel"
  Names(5) = "Frank"
  Names(6) = "Todd"
  Names(7) = "George"
  Names(8) = "Ralph"
  Names(9) = "Leonard"
  Names(10) = "Thomas":
```

Then you arrange them in alphabetical order with the following BASIC instructions (this part of the code has three very common bugs in it).

```
Sub Form_Click ()
  Static Names(10) As String

  Names(1) = "John"
  Names(2) = "Tim"
  Names(3) = "Edward"
  Names(4) = "Samuel"
  Names(5) = "Frank"
  Names(6) = "Todd"
  Names(7) = "George"
  Names(8) = "Ralph"
  Names(9) = "Leonard"
  Names(10) = "Thomas"
```

```
    For i = i To 10
        For j = i To 10
            If Names(i) > Names(j) Then
                Temp$ = Names(i)
                Names(j) = Names(j)
                Names(j) = Tmp$
            End If
        Next j
    Next i
```

Note that you are using the > logical operator to compare strings; this is
perfectly legal in Visual Basic and enables you to determine the alphabetical order of such strings. Finally, you can print the result, name by name,
as follows:

```
Sub Form_Click ()
  Static Names(10) As String

  Names(1) = "John"
   :
   :
  Names(10) = "Thomas"

  For i = i To 10
      For j = i To 10
          If Names(i) > Names(j) Then
              Temp$ = Names(i)
              Names(j) = Names(j)
              Names(j) = Tmp$
          End If
      Next j
  Next i

  For k = 1 To 10
          Print Names(k)
  Next k
End Sub
```

Unfortunately, this is the result of the program when you execute the
Form_Click( ) procedure by clicking the form.

```
John
```

```
Tim
```

```
Todd
```

This result looks a little incomplete; it's time to debug. In fact, you can start debugging without even stopping the program. To do that, select the View Code item in Visual Basic's View menu. The Form_Click( ) Sub procedure pops up, as shown in figure 9.5.

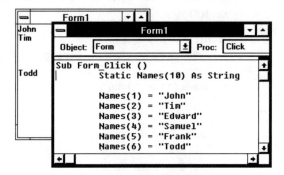

Figure 9.5. Editing code when running a program.

Visual Basic gives you the chance to scan the code for possible errors while the program is running. When you do that, you might spot one error immediately by just reading the code. In particular, when you switch elements around in the array, you load them temporarily into a variable named Temp$; when you load them back into the array, however, you use a (misspelled) variable named Tmp$, as follows:

```
Sub Form_Click ()
  Static Names(10) As String

  Names(1) = "John"
  :
  :
  Names(10) = "Thomas"
```

```
    For i = i To 10
        For j = i To 10
            If Names(i) > Names(j) Then
                Temp$ = Names(i)
                Names(j) = Names(j)
                Names(j) = Tmp$
            End If
        Next j
    Next i

    For k = 1 To 10
        Print Names(k)
    Next k
End Sub
```

Misspelling a variable's name is probably the most common type of Visual Basic logic error. Visual Basic does not complain about such errors because it assumes that you are implicitly declaring a new variable, tmp$, and it sets that new variable to the empty string ("").

You can actually fix this problem without ending the program. Just open Visual Basic's Run menu, where three choices are highlighted: Break, End, and Restart. Select Break to stop the program temporarily. Now you can change the code (to a certain extent) and then continue with program execution (Visual Basic usually allows you to make changes up to the level of declaring new variables). Here, you just edit the code to change Tmp$ to Temp$, as shown in figure 9.6.

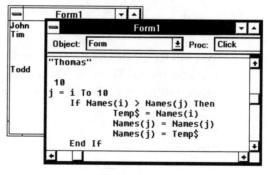

Figure 9.6. Editing code in a running application.

Now the program appears as follows:

```
Sub Form_Click ()
  Static Names(10) As String

  Names(1) = "John"
  :
  :
  Names(10) = "Thomas"

  For i = i To 10
      For j = i To 10
          If Names(i) > Names(j) Then
              Temp$ = Names(i)
              Names(j) = Names(j)
              Names(j) = Temp$
          End If
      Next j
  Next i

  For k = 1 To 10
      Print Names(k)
  Next k
End Sub
```

You can let the program continue now by selecting the Continue item in the Run menu. Then, you can click the form to see whether you have made a difference. The list appears as follows:

```
John
Tim
Tim
Tim
Tim
Todd
```

```
Todd
Todd
Todd
Todd
```

There has been a change, but the result is clearly not yet correct. The obvious problem in your program is that the entries in the Names( ) array are being filled incorrectly. To check what is happening, you should watch the array elements as they are filled. You can do that by setting a breakpoint. A *breakpoint* halts program execution when it is reached. You can set a breakpoint, for example, by moving the cursor on the screen down to the line that reads "If Names(i) > Names(j) Then".

```
Sub Form_Click ()
  Static Names(10) As String

  Names(1) = "John"
  :
  :
  Names(10) = "Thomas"

  For i = i To 10
      For j = i To 10
            If Names(i) > Names(j) Then
                  Temp$ = Names(i)
                  Names(j) = Names(j)
                  Names(j) = Temp$
            End If
      Next j
  Next i

  For k = 1 To 10
      Print Names(k)
  Next k
End Sub
```

Now you press F9 or select Toggle Breakpoint in the Debug menu. The statement you have selected appears in bold to indicate that a breakpoint has been set, as shown in figure 9.7.

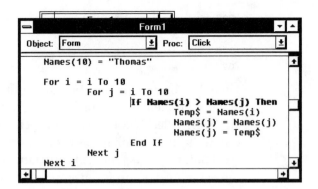

Figure 9.7. A Breakpoint set.

Next, you run the program by selecting Start in the Run menu. Program execution continues until you reach the breakpoint. The breakpoint line ("If Names(i) > Names(j) Then") is outlined with a border, as shown in figure 9.8. You can check the values of Names(i) and Names(j) in Visual Basic's *Debug window* (which was called the Immediate window in Visual Basic 1.0).

The Debug window lets you check the values of a program while you are in a break state (which happens when you select Break in the Run menu or the program reaches a breakpoint). To check the value of Names(i), you only need to type ?Names(i) in the Debug window (or Print Names(i)) and press Enter. When you check the values of Names(i) and Names(j), you see that nothing is in them, as shown in figure 9.8.

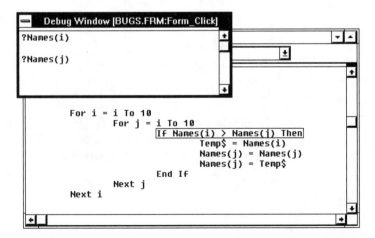

Figure 9.8. The Debug window.

In other words, the line "If Names(i) > Names(j) Then" is comparing nothing; the values in Names(i) and Names(j) are not valid. At this point, both i and j are supposed to point at the first element in the array. That is, both i and j should be 1. You can check the value of i by simply executing ?i (or Print i) in the Debug window. When you do, you see that i = 0, which is a problem. This line in the code must be changed to For i = 1 To 10 because you need to initialize i before using it.

```
Static Names(10) As String

Names(1) = "John"
:
:
Names(10) = "Thomas"

For i = i To 10
  For j = i To 10
      If Names(i) > Names(j) Then
            Temp$ = Names(i)
            Names(j) = Names(j)
            Names(j) = Temp$
      End If
  Next j
Next i

For k = 1 To 10
  Print Names(k)
Next k
```

When you make the change, however, and run the program (note that you can use F9 to toggle off the breakpoint you set or you can remove all breakpoints by selecting the Clear All Breakpoints in the Run menu), you still see the following:

```
John
Tim
Tim
Tim
Tim
Todd
Todd
Todd
Todd
Todd
```

Obviously, a problem still exists. Let's examine the part of the program in which the actual elements are switched—the only other part of the program. You can put a breakpoint at the end of the element-switching section, as in the following example:

```
Static Names(10) As String

Names(1) = "John"
    :
    :
Names(10) = "Thomas"

For i = i To 10
  For j = i To 10
      If Names(i) > Names(j) Then
            Temp$ = Names(i)
            Names(j) = Names(j)
            Names(j) = Temp$
      End If
  Next j
Next i

For k = 1 To 10
  Print Names(k)
Next k
```

Now when you execute the program, you stop at the breakpoint and you can determine whether the elements really were switched. In fact, you don't need to evaluate elements in the Debug window with the ? command: You can print directly to the Debug window from the program. To do that, you use the Print method of the Debug object, the object responsible for maintaining the Debug window.

```
Static Names(10) As String

Names(1) = "John"
    :
    :
Names(10) = "Thomas"

For i = i To 10
  For j = i To 10
      If Names(i) > Names(j) Then
```

```
        Temp$ = Names(i)
        Names(j) = Names(j)
        Debug.Print Names(i), Names(j)
        Names(j) = Temp$
    End If
  Next j
Next i

For k = 1 To 10
  Print Names(k)
Next k
```

Now run the program. Execution halts at the breakpoint (the line that reads: Names(j) = Temp$), and you examine Names(i) and Names(j) in the Debug window, as shown in figure 9.9. One is John, and the other is Edward.

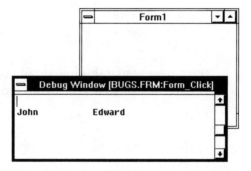

Figure 9.9. A Debug window with Names(i) and Names(j).

The exchange of array elements is supposed to go as follows: You place the value that is in Names(i) in Temp$. Then you copy the element in Names(j) and place it in Names(i). Finally, you move Temp$ into Names(j). At the breakpoint shown in figure 9.9, all but the final step has been taken. You are about to move the value in Temp$ into Names(j).

In other words, you would expect Names(i) and Names(j) to hold the same value, but they do not. Names(i) holds "John" and Names(j) holds "Edward." Something is wrong. If you look back one line in your code, you see the following in blue:

```
Static Names(10) As String

Names(1) = "John"
:
:
Names(10) = "Thomas"

For i = 1 To 10
  For j = i To 10
      If Names(i) > Names(j) Then
            Temp$ = Names(i)
            Names(j) = Names(j)
            Names(j) = Temp$
      End If
  Next j
Next i

For k = 1 To 10
  Print Names(k)
Next k
```

It is apparent that this line should be Names(i) = Names(j). You make the change, which yields the debugged program, as follows:

```
Static Names(10) As String

Names(1) = "John"
Names(2) = "Tim"
Names(3) = "Edward"
Names(4) = "Samuel"
Names(5) = "Frank"
Names(6) = "Todd"
Names(7) = "George"
Names(8) = "Ralph"
Names(9) = "Leonard"
Names(10) = "Thomas"

For i = 1 To 10
  For j = i To 10
      If Names(i) > Names(j) Then
            Temp$ = Names(i)
            Names(i) = Names(j)
            Names(j) = Temp$
```

```
        End If
    Next j
Next i

For k = 1 To 10
    Print Names(k)
Next k
```

The following list is the final result when you run it:

```
Edward
Frank
George
John
Leonard
Ralph
Samuel
Thomas
Tim
Todd
```

The program has been debugged. As you can see, you have some powerful debugging tools available to you in Visual Basic, including the Debug window and breakpoints. These tools have still more capabilities, in fact. You can execute a program line by line, for example, and even change the values of variables while the program is running. Let's see how this works with an example.

Debugging an Investment Calculator

You might decide, for instance, to write a small investment calculator program to tell you what an investment will be worth in a certain number of years. Suppose that you invest $1,000 at 7 percent for 12 years. Compounded annually, that investment would be worth the following:

$$(\$1,000.00) \times (1.07)12 = \$2,252.19$$

Let's put this calculator together. Start Visual Basic and place three text boxes on the form to hold the three values: Investment ($1,000), InterestRate (7%), and Years (12). You want to perform the following calculation:

Result = Investment × (1 + InterestRate / 100) Years

Label the boxes as shown in figure 9.10 and give them the names (from the top) of InvestmentText, InterestRateText, and YearsText. Next, place a button with the caption Yields and Name YieldsButton under them and a label at the bottom (set its BorderStyle to Fixed Single so that it looks like the text boxes) with the Name ResultLabel, as shown in figure 9.11.

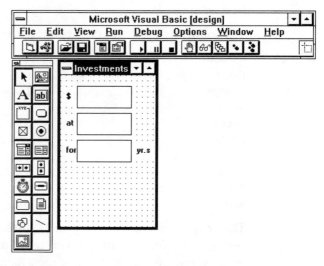

Figure 9.10. An Investment Calculator template.

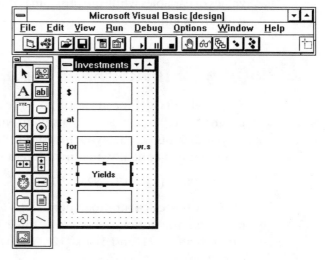

Figure 9.11. A completed Investment Calculator template.

Our investment calculator template is set; all that remains is the code. To use the calculator, the user places the investment amount in the top text box, the interest rate in the next box, and the number of years the investment will last in the third text box. Then he clicks the Yields button to see the result in the bottom box. All the action takes place in YieldsButton_Click ( ). Click that button to bring up the following code window:

```
Sub YieldsButton_Click()
End Sub
```

You can start by converting the text in the text boxes into numeric values, as in the following example:

```
Sub YieldsButton_Click()
    Investment = Val(InvestmentText.Text)
    InterstRate = Val(InterestRateText.Text)
    Years = Val(YearsText.Text)
    :
    :
End Sub
```

Next, you can perform the following calculation:

```
Sub YieldsButton_Click()
    Investment = Val(InvestmentText.Text)
    InterstRate = Val(InterestRateText.Text)
    Years = Val(YearsText.Text)
    Result = Investments * (1 + InterestRate / 100) ^ Years
    :
    :
End Sub
```

Finally, you display the result in the following way:

```
Sub YieldsButton_Click()
    Investment = Val(InvestmentText.Text)
    InterstRate = Val(InterestRateText.Text)
    Years = Val(YearsText.Text)
    Result = Investments * (1 + InterestRate / 100) ^ Years
    ResultLabel.Caption = Format$(Result, "###,###,##0.00")
End Sub
```

Let's give it a try; for example, $1,000 at 7 percent for 12 years. The result is $0.00, however, as shown in figure 9.12. Obviously, there's a problem; it's time to debug.

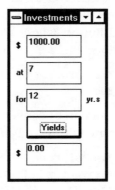

Figure 9.12. An Investment Calculator; first attempt.

You can begin by placing a breakpoint (by using F9 or Toggle Breakpoint in the Run menu) in the first line of the YieldsButton_Click ( ) procedure, as follows:

```
Sub YieldsButton_Click()
  Investment = Val(InvestmentText.Text)
  InterstRate = Val(InterestRateText.Text)
  Years = Val(YearsText.Text)
  Result = Investments * (1 + InterestRate / 100) ^ Years
  ResultLabel.Caption = Format$(Result, "###,###,##0.00")
End Sub
```

When you reach this point, the program automatically breaks. Start the program again, place the same values in the text boxes, and click the Yields button. When you do, the program reaches the break point and stops. Now you can single-step through the code one line at a time by using the F8 key or selecting the Single Step item in the Debug menu. Press F8 once to execute the first line. The box around the first line (as is usual for a breakpoint) moves to the second line, indicating where you are, as shown in figure 9.13. Note that the text of the first line stays bold, indicating that a breakpoint still is there.

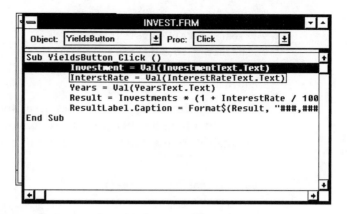

Figure 9.13. Single-Stepping in the Investment Calculator.

After executing the first line, you can check the value of Investment in the Debug window with a ? command, as shown in figure 9.14. You can see that Investment holds 1000.00, as it should.

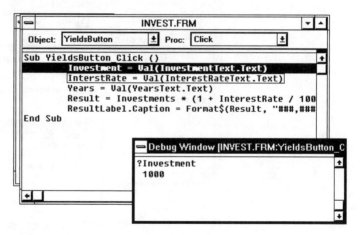

Figure 9.14. The Debug window with Investment's value.

The next step is to set the interest rate; you execute the following line by pressing F8 again and then check the value of InterestRate in the Debug window by typing ?InterestRate, as follows:

```
Sub YieldsButton_Click()
  Investment = Val(InvestmentText.Text)
```

449

```
      InterstRate = Val(InterestRateText.Text)
    Years = Val(YearsText.Text)
    Result = Investments * (1 + InterestRate / 100) ^ Years
    ResultLabel.Caption = Format$(Result, "###,###,##0.00")
End Sub
```

This value should be 7, but the result, as shown in figure 9.15, is 0. This is clearly a bug. By checking the code, you can see that InterestRate is misspelled (InterstRate) in the second line. Fixing that yields the following code:

```
Sub YieldsButton_Click()
  Investment = Val(InvestmentText.Text)
  InterestRate = Val(InterestRateText.Text)
  Years = Val(YearsText.Text)
  Result = Investments * (1 + InterestRate / 100) ^ Years
    ResultLabel.Caption = Format$(Result, "###,###,##0.00")
End Sub
```

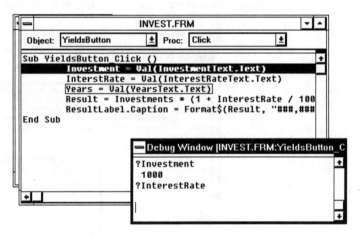

Figure 9.15. The Debug window showing InterestRate.

You can also fix the problem without stopping the program by placing a value directly in InterestRate—that is, Visual Basic enables you to load values into your variables even when the program is running. In particular, you want to load a value of 7 into InterestRate. To do that, simply type the line InterestRate = 7 in the Debug window. You can then check the new value of InterestRate by typing ?InterestRate. As shown in figure 9.16, InterestRate does indeed hold 7 now.

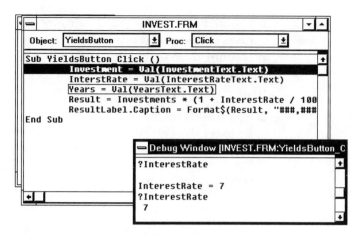

Figure 9.16. Debugging the Investment Calculator.

Pressing F8 again executes the third line in the code and sets the value of the variable Years, as follows:

```
Sub YieldsButton_Click()
  Investment = Val(InvestmentText.Text)
  InterestRate = Val(InterestRateText.Text)
  Years = Val(YearsText.Text)
  Result = Investments * (1 + InterestRate / 100) ^ Years
  ResultLabel.Caption = Format$(Result, "###,###,##0.00")
End Sub
```

Checking that variable in the Debug window verifies that it holds 12, as it should. The next line does the actual calculation, and pressing F8 a fourth time executes it in the following way:

```
Sub YieldsButton_Click()
  Investment = Val(InvestmentText.Text)
  InterestRate = Val(InterestRateText.Text)
  Years = Val(YearsText.Text)
  Result = Investments * (1 + InterestRate / 100) ^ Years
  ResultLabel.Caption = Format$(Result, "###,###,##0.00")
End Sub
```

This line assigns the results of the calculation to a variable named Result. You can check the value of Result in the Debug box. When you do, however, you find that it is 0. Again, you check the code, and find that you are using in the fourth line a variable named Investments, not

Investment. Because you have already executed that line, however, you cannot execute it again without reentering the YieldsButton_Click() procedure. Even so, because you have isolated that problem, you can fix the code. Change that line so that it uses the variable Investment rather than Investments, as follows:

```
Sub YieldsButton_Click()
  Investment = Val(InvestmentText.Text)
  InterestRate = Val(InterestRateText.Text)
  Years = Val(YearsText.Text)
  Result = Investment * (1 + InterestRate / 100) ^ Years
  ResultLabel.Caption = Format$(Result, "###,###,##0.00")
End Sub
```

Now you can rerun the program by using the same values. When you do, you see that the following line is indeed true.

$(\$1,000.00) \times (1.07)12 = \$2,252.19$

The program now is debugged, as you can see in figure 9.17.

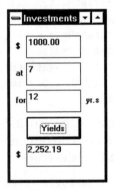

Figure 9.17. A working Investment Calculator.

As you can see, single-stepping like this can be a powerful debugging tool to give you a picture of what your program is doing line by line. In general, then, you should have a good idea of Visual Basic's considerable debugging capabilities. If you suspect errors in a program's logic, you can set breakpoints inside it and stop it at strategic locations and check what is happening. In addition, you can print values to the Debug object and see them appear in the Debug window when your program runs in the Visual

Basic environment. To further locate the problem, you can even work through the code line by line.

> **About debugging and mouse or keyboard input.**
> One problem should be mentioned before we finish with debugging and move on to the next chapter. Because Visual Basic programs are event driven, you must take into account a few considerations. If you place a breakpoint in a MouseDown or KeyPress event procedure and then release the mouse button or key while the program is in a break state, you may never get a MouseUp or KeyUp event when you continue. In other words, keep in mind that Visual Basic programs respond to the computer environment and that, if you change that environment while you are debugging, it may result in unexpected consequences.

That's it for this chapter's coverage of debugging and error handling. Let's move on to the next topic: communicating between Windows applications.

Summary

In this chapter, you have learned how to handle two types of errors that may occur: run-time errors (trappable errors) and logic errors (bugs). You have seen how to inform the user of an error by using the Erl( ), Err( ), and Error$() functions together with message boxes. You have been able to conquer many trappable errors with the statements On Error GoTo and Resume. When you use these statements along with error-handling code, your program doesn't have to come to a halt when unforeseen circumstances cause problems. Instead, you can fix the problem or inform the user of the problem and let here fix it. This ability is especially important when you send out your programs for others to use (programs that can handle errors are called *robust*), as is making sure that all logic errors are removed.

You have seen that debugging a program's logic is made easier by the debugging tools and techniques available in Visual Basic, including the

Debug window, breakpoints, and single stepping. In particular, you have used the Debug window to watch variables as you execute a program, set breakpoints to halt program execution at a specific line of code, and single-stepped through a program under development to watch the effect of every line of code. These powerful tools and techniques are now available for you to use.

New Functions	Description
Erl	Reports the line number at which the last error occurred
Err	Reports the error code of the last error that occurred
Error$	Translates error codes (see Err( )) into English strings

New Statements	Description
On Error GoTo	Sets error handling. Use it like this to jump to the label ErrorOccurred: On Error GoTo ErrorOccurred.
Resume	Used at the end of an error handler, Resume enables you to retry an operation or resume program execution after a problem has been fixed. Simply using Resume causes control to exit from an error handler (error handlers are set up with On Error GoTo) and resume execution beginning with the line of code that caused the problem. To skip that line, you can use Resume Next; to jump to some other line, you can use Resume #, where # is a line number, or Resume label, where label is a line label.

454

Connecting to Other Windows Applications (DDE and OLE)

I n this chapter, you will learn how to connect your programs to other (prewritten) Windows applications (both those written in Visual Basic and others) by transferring data and commands to and from them. The following topics are discussed in this chapter:

▼ Using Windows Dynamic Data Exchange (DDE)

▼ Exchanging numeric data between programs

▼ Exchanging graphics between programs

▼ Copying and pasting links

- ▼ Handling DDE errors

- ▼ Using Object Linking and Embedding (OLE)

- ▼ Sending Microsoft Excel commands to Excel

- ▼ Adding a Paste Link menu item to a Visual Basic program

- ▼ Embedding part of a Microsoft Excel spreadsheet

Now we are beginning to cover material that is slightly more advanced. In this chapter, you will learn how to communicate and exchange data, in addition to commands, with other Windows programs. This process is called *Dynamic Data Exchange (DDE)*. You also will learn how to use *Object Linking and Embedding (OLE)*. In particular, you will be able to "embed" a section of a Microsoft Excel for Windows worksheet in one of your Visual Basic forms, and be able to use it just as though you were in Excel. This ability can be very useful if you want to coordinate the use of several applications into one. Your program can have, for example, a few sections of Excel worksheets on the same master form as a few documents from Microsoft Word for Windows and some graphs from the Visual Basic Professional Edition Graph control (see Chapter 13).

DDE is also a very useful technique, relying on "links" between your program and others. You will learn that there are a number of ways of setting up such links. You can link a text box to a WinWord document, for example, or to a few cells in an Excel spreadsheet. It is very easy to add a link between a text box on your Visual Basic form and a few cells in Excel. You also will learn how you can do it at design-time by using Visual Basic's Paste Link menu item. Then you learn how to set up DDE links between your programs and others, and end up creating a Paste Link menu item and adding it to your programs.

After you finish with DDE, you will see how easy it is to use the new OLE control to embed objects in your Visual Basic forms.

What Is DDE?

One of the benefits of the Windows operating environment is that it is *multitasking:* It can run several different applications at a time, which makes it substantially different from DOS. This Windows capability raises some interesting possibilities for program interaction. What if two programs could communicate in some way, for example, by passing data and instructions back and forth? In this way, each one could handle the tasks it was best at. A spreadsheet could manipulate data in cells, a word processor could format data into documents, and the power of both would be increased by being capable of working together. All this is possible, in fact, under Windows, in a process called *Dynamic Data Exchange,* or *DDE.*

Using DDE, you can coordinate the transfer of data between a number of Windows applications. Word for Windows can talk with Excel for Windows, for example, by enabling the user to design something of an integrated program environment. DDE is also available in Visual Basic, however, and the possibilities are richer there because you can design your own programs from scratch. You might be interested, for example, in modeling some complex financial or scientific model beyond a spreadsheet's capabilities, even though the spreadsheet is useful for entering and examining data points. By using DDE, you can connect the spreadsheet's individual cells, or a range of those cells to a Visual Basic form or control where you can manipulate the data as you want.

You will see DDE at work in this chapter and explore its possibilities. You will use two popular Windows software packages—Word for Windows and Excel for Windows—to see how DDE works by setting up conversations with both of them. You have to have these packages, however. Many applications support Windows DDE (in fact, you will write Visual Basic programs that will be capable of communicating).

You begin by establishing a DDE link between your program and these packages at design-time, and then move on to establishing such links when your programs run through the use of built-in Visual Basic properties. Next, you learn how to let users set up their own DDE links between the controls in your programs and other applications (DDE links you didn't design into the program originally), as well as how to start the application you are supposed to be communicating with, if it isn't already running.

Finally, you will learn some advanced DDE topics, such as how to send actual commands to other applications (closing or saving Excel spreadsheets, for example) and how to handle DDE errors. With all this information coming up, let's begin immediately by examining what makes DDE tick.

How DDE Works

There are two ways to open a link between programs: as an automatic link or as a manual link. In an automatic link, for example, data is updated in your Visual Basic program whenever it is changed in a spreadsheet. This kind of communication is impressive. Imagine entering a value in a spreadsheet cell and seeing it appear simultaneously in some text box in a program you have written. A manual link functions in much the same way, except that you have more control over when the exchanged data is updated. In a manual link, data updates are made only on request, not whenever the data itself changes.

In addition, there are two different types of links, called *client links* and *source links*, or *server links* in Visual Basic version 1.00, depending on which role your application is taking—that of a DDE client, or that of a DDE source. Data generally flows from a DDE source to the DDE client, although it is possible for the DDE client also to send data back.

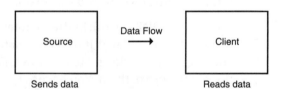

If you want to read data, you will set up as a client by establishing a client link. To supply data, you will set yourself up as a source and establish a source link. To read some cells in an Excel spreadsheet, for example, you would be the client, and Excel the source.

In Visual Basic, three types of controls can act as clients—that is, can get DDE data (picture boxes, text boxes, and labels). In other words, you can read text and place it in text boxes or labels, and read pictures and place them in picture boxes. Only forms can act as sources—that is, can send DDE data. The controls on the form, however, can be the sources of that data. If Form1 is the source, for example, a control such as Text1 can be the actual source of the data. Depending on what the client asks for, it will supply the actual name of the control it wants to read from.

You should note that DDE works through the clipboard: The data and DDE requests are passed back and forth in the clipboard object. This capability is valuable to you if you will do a lot of DDE programming, because you need to see what is in the clipboard only by clicking the clipboard icon in the Windows' Program Manager's Main window to see what is being passed back and forth. With all this preparation, let's get started with some design-time DDE links.

Design-time Client Links

Establishing DDE links at design-time is very easy in Visual Basic. For example, let's say that you had a document in Word for Windows named Document1 (Word's default document name). You might want to establish a link between the text in that document and a text box, Text1, in a program you are designing. If you do establish such a link, it will remain as part of the program when it runs. You should note, however, that you can establish automatic links only at design-time, not manual links (data is transferred to the client immediately after being changed in the source).

In this case, because you want the text box to mirror what is in the Word document, Word is the source and Text1 is the client. To establish this link, start Visual Basic and Word for Windows (WinWord), if you have it. Select all the text in Document1, as shown in figure 10.1, and then copy it by using the Copy item in WinWord's Edit menu. This action transfers the text to the clipboard (as you can see in the clipboard) and establishes WinWord as the source of the data—that is, as the source.

The next step is to set up the link with Text1: Select Text1 in Visual Basic and select the Paste Link item in Visual Basic's Edit menu. This item is active only if data in the clipboard conforms to the DDE link standards (as you will see later in this chapter). After you select Paste Link, the link is formed and immediately the text in Document1 appears in Text1, as shown in figure 10.2. You will see that editing the text in Document1 produces similar changes in Text1.

Figure 10.1. Selecting text in WinWord.

Congratulations—you have just set up your first DDE link (in this case, a design-time client link). If you write a program by using Text1, the link is preserved; when the program starts, it attempts to reestablish that link.

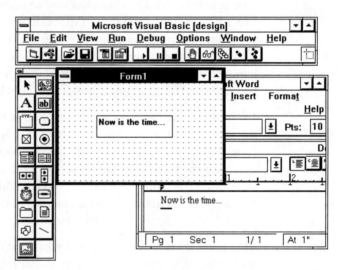

Figure 10.2. A design-time DDE client link.

> **Design-time links are briefly cut when you run.**
> If you run a program with a design-time link in the Visual Basic environment, Visual Basic has to cut the link temporarily when it switches from design- to run-time. Most, but not all, applications, such as WinWord or Excel, attempt to reestablish the link.

> **Linking to a specific section of a WinWord document.**
> If you want to link to only a certain part of the text in a WinWord document, you can do that by only selecting and then copying that part of the text. From then on, only that range of text, and changes to that range of text, appear in Text1.

Because you are dealing with Visual Basic, you might expect that information about this link (whether it is automatic or manual, what you are linking to, and so on) might be stored in Visual Basic properties. In fact, this information is indeed stored in a special set of Text1's properties: its Link properties (LinkMode, LinkTopic, LinkItem, and LinkTimeout). Because Visual Basic already has set up these properties automatically, it is easy to see what they hold.

DDE's LinkMode

Select Text1 and find the link properties in the properties window; these properties are available even if you are not linked to anything (if you don't have WinWord, for example). Next, find the LinkMode property. This property has a value of Automatic, which corresponds to a LinkMode setting of 1. A LinkMode setting of 2 is a Manual link, and a setting of 0 means that there is no DDE link (the default).

In other words, this control (Text1) has an automatic DDE client link with some external data source (recall that individual controls cannot function as DDE sources (only forms can do that). To find out what the other end of the link is, let's look next at the LinkTopic property.

DDE's LinkTopic

Find the LinkTopic property in the properties window. It is set to
WinWord|Document1. This is the normal form for a LinkTopic to take:
Application|File. In other words, you have already found that there is an
automatic link with another application. Now you can find what the
actual link is to. It is not enough to know the name of the application, but
you also have to know the name of the file that holds the data item you
are linked to. The process is a little like tracking down someone you want
to talk to who's staying in a hotel somewhere—it's not enough to know
the town, you also should know the name of the hotel.

Specific DDE application names are given to Windows programs that
support DDE. The two dealt with here, Excel and Word for Windows, for
example, have the DDE names Excel and WinWord, which is why
LinkTopic is set to WinWord|Document1. Document1 is the name of the
file that the data you want is in. If you saved it as Doc1.Doc (.Doc is
WinWord's normal extension), for example, the LinkTopic could be
WinWord|Doc1.Doc or even WinWord|C:\WinWord\Doc1.Doc. If you
have questions about an application's DDE name or the way it names files,
check its documentation, which usually addresses such problems.

Now we have narrowed the link to an application and a file. You need
more than that, however—you need the name or names of the data item
or items in which you are interested. That is, you may have the name of
the town in which your friend's hotel is located and the name of the hotel,
but you still need a room number. That kind of information is stored in
LinkItem.

DDE's LinkItem

If you check the LinkItem property next, you see that it is set to DDE_LINK, which is a generic name for a link item. The source application, therefore, determines which particular data item you are linked to (the text you selected). If you were dealing with an application that had many discrete data items, such as the cells in a spreadsheet, LinkItem would hold the name of the cell or cells you are linked to. In Microsoft Excel, for example, if you want to link to Row 1, Column 1 in the spreadsheet, you set LinkItem to R1C1 (as you will see later in this chapter). In this way, Excel names its cells for DDE purposes. Usually, then, LinkTopic holds both the name of the application and the file that holds the data item in which you are interested. LinkItem holds the name of that item if it has a name, or DDE_LINK.

The last client Link property you can set at design-time is LinkTimeout, which indicates the time you allow for the DDE link to be established.

DDE's LinkTimeout

The LinkTimeout property is measured in tenths of a second, and the default value is 50, which corresponds to five seconds. In other words, if you put a link in your program at design-time, the program attempts to establish that link as soon as it is run. If it cannot do so before the time-out period, however, it quits by placing an error message box on the screen and asking you whether it should start the application that makes up the other end of the link. If you answer yes, the program attempts to run the other application and set up the link.

If you check Text1's LinkTimeout value, you find that it is set to 50, which corresponds to the default value of five seconds. This number is usually more than adequate, but you should keep in mind that, because this means five real-time seconds, you might want to extend it on slower computers if tests show that your program's DDE attempt is timing out before the DDE link is established.

As you can see, it is not at all difficult to establish a client link at run-time (where you read data from another application). Let's move on and see whether you can do the same for establishing a source link (where you provide data to another application).

Design-time Source Links

Start Visual Basic over again or select New Project in the File menu, and start Microsoft Excel also, if you have it. This time, we go the other way; your application is the source, and the other application (Microsoft Excel, for example) is the client.

To set up this link at design-time, place a text box, Text1, on the default form (Form1), and make sure that it is selected. Next, select the copy command in Visual Basic's Edit menu and place the string in Text1 (which is simply "Text1" at the moment) in the clipboard. Next, move to Excel and select one of the cells in the spreadsheet—the top left cell, R1C1, for example. Now move to Excel's Edit menu and open it; the Paste Link item should be enabled. When you select it, a link is established between Text1 and cell R1C1, and the string in Text1 ("Text1") appears in R1C1, as shown in figure 10.3.

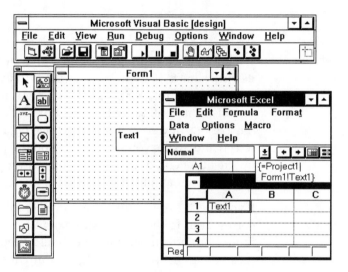

Figure 10.3. A design-time DDE Source Link.

That's it; the source link is established as an automatic link. Now whatever you type in Text1 appears in R1C1 also. You should note, however, that this is not a source link between Text1 and R1C1. If you check the Link properties of Text1, you find that LinkMode = 0 (no link). Instead, because only forms can have source links, the link has been

464

established between Form1 and R1C1. If you check Form1's LinkMode property, you see that it is set to Source (LinkMode = 1; the only other possibility is None: LinkMode = 0). In addition, Form1's LinkTopic property is set to Form1 because that is the current name of your application; therefore, it is DDE's name also.

When other applications try to establish a link with your new source application, they should try to contact Form1 (rather than WinWord or Excel) because that is your default application name. In addition, the controls on Form1, like Text1, can be the source of the data they read. From Excel's point of view, it now has a link to Form1|Text1. The source link is in place. If you create a program by using this form, the link is preserved and anything you type in Text1 (in the source application Form1) is communicated instantly to R1C1 (in the client application Excel).

At this point, you have set up both client and source links at design-time. They will be preserved when your programs run. You can do the same thing at run-time, however, and you can set up and maintain manual links also. Let's look into this subject in the next section.

Run-time Client Links

Let's put together a program (a client application) that can read data from an Excel spreadsheet by setting up an automatic link at run-time. Start a new project in Visual Basic by adding a text box, Text1, and a check box by double-clicking the check box tool. A check box appears in the center of the form. This button acts just as any command button might, except that, when it is clicked, it stays clicked (indicated by an x) until you click it again (when the x disappears). Change the caption of this check box, Check1, to "Check to start link" (see figure 10.4).

When the user clicks this check box, a Click event is generated. You can set up the link from an Excel spreadsheet to Text1 at that time (the spreadsheet is the source, and you are the client; that is, data is sent from Excel to Text1). Click the check box now to bring up the Check1_Click() template, as follows:

```
Sub Check1_Click ()

End Sub
```

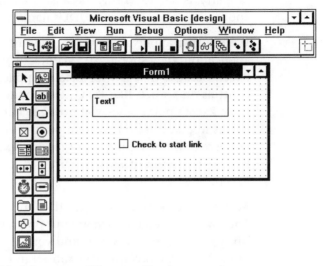

Figure 10.4. A Run-time Client application template.

Here, you set the appropriate link properties. To begin, you set Text1's LinkMode to NONE, as follows:

```
Sub Check1_Click ()
  Text1.LinkMode = NONE
        :

End Sub
```

Because DDE constants such as NONE and the one you are about to use, LINK_AUTOMATIC, are defined in Constant.Txt, you have to make sure that you have loaded that file into one of your program's modules also. Setting the LinkMode property in Visual Basic is the important thing when you establish or break DDE links. By setting Text1's LinkMode property to NONE, which equals 0, you break any links it has now.

Automatic and manual links in Visual Basic 1.0.
In Visual Basic Version 1.0, LINK_AUTOMATIC was referred to as HOT, and LINK_MANUAL was referred to as WARM.

Next, you can set Text1's LinkTopic property. This property has the format "Application|File." Suppose that you have open in Excel a spreadsheet named Sheet1 (the default name for a spreadsheet); you can set LinkTopic in the following way:

```
Sub Check1_Click ()
  Text1.LinkMode = NONE
  Text1.LinkTopic = "Excel¦Sheet1"
      :

End Sub
```

The next step is setting the LinkItem. For example, you can link to Row 1 Column 1 (R1C1) of the spreadsheet, as shown in the following example:

```
Sub Check1_Click ()
  Text1.LinkMode = NONE
  Text1.LinkTopic = "Excel¦Sheet1"
  Text1.LinkItem = "R1C1"
      :

End Sub
```

Now you are set. All you need to initiate a DDE link are the two properties, LinkTopic and LinkItem. To start the link, you simply set LinkMode to LINK_AUTOMATIC and you are finished.

```
Sub Check1_Click ()
  Text1.LinkMode = NONE
  Text1.LinkTopic = "Excel¦Sheet1"
  Text1.LinkItem = "R1C1"
  Text1.LinkMode = LINK_AUTOMATIC
End Sub
```

At this point, as soon as LinkMode becomes Automatic, Visual Basic attempts to form the link with the target application by sending out the LinkTopic and LinkItem and waiting to see whether an application answers. If the correct application answers, the link is established. In this case, Excel should answer and link Text1 to R1C1, as shown in figure 10.5. Because everything you type in R1C1 also appears now in Text1, it is accessible to your program as Val(Text1.Text). You now can read data directly from Excel and manipulate it.

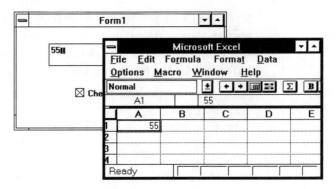

Figure 10.5. A Run-time Client Link.

Now that the link is established, you also can change the LinkItem (the cell in the spreadsheet, in this case) at run-time without breaking it. Let's examine that process next.

Changing the LinkItem at Run-time

Let's put a counter into the program that will let you keep track of how many times the check box has been clicked. You can call this variable First (so that it indicates whether you are in Check1_Click () for the first time) and declare it Static, as follows:

```
Sub Check1_Click ()
  Static First As Integer
      Text1.LinkMode = NONE
      Text1.LinkTopic = "Excel¦Sheet1"
      Text1.LinkItem = "R1C1"
      Text1.LinkMode = LINK_AUTOMATIC
End Sub
```

When the program starts, First is set to 0; you can increment the value in First by adding 1; if First = 1 after that operation, the check box was clicked for the first time and you want to establish the link, as follows:

```
Sub Check1_Click ()
  Static First As Integer
  First = First + 1
```

```
    If First = 1 Then
        Text1.LinkMode = NONE
        Text1.LinkTopic = "Excel¦Sheet1"
        Text1.LinkItem = "R1C1"
        Text1.LinkMode = LINK_AUTOMATIC
    Else
    :

End Sub
```

You can change the LinkItem the next time the check box is clicked. You can change it to R2C1 (Row 2 Column 1), for example, in the spreadsheet, as shown in the following example:

```
Sub Check1_Click ()
    Static First As Integer
    First = First + 1
    If First = 1 Then
        Text1.LinkMode = NONE
        Text1.LinkTopic = "Excel¦Sheet1"
        Text1.LinkItem = "R1C1"
        Text1.LinkMode = LINK_AUTOMATIC Else
        Text1.LinkItem = "R2C1"
    End If
End Sub
```

In this way, you don't have to break the link with the external application before switching your attention to other data items. That's it. Now you have seen how to establish a run-time automatic link (where data is updated automatically every time it is changed in the source). Let's look now at the other option: run-time manual links.

Manual Run-time Client Links

A manual link differs from an automatic link in one respect: In an automatic link, data is automatically updated in the client (in this case, it goes into the control Text1) whenever it changes in the source (Excel, in the example). Your program may not be ready for new data so quickly, however. If you are carrying out some complex calculation with a number of links, for example, it might be inadvisable to have the data in some of those links fluctuate before the entire calculation is finished, because it can lead to misleading results. Instead, you can create a manual link. With

469

manual links, data is not sent to the client as soon as it changes in the source. Instead, the client must specifically request updates when it wants new data.

You do this with the LinkRequest method. After a manual link to some control has been set up, it takes a LinkRequest statement to update the data in it. Because LinkRequest is a method, it is associated with the control you want to update, like this: Text1.LinkRequest. To set up your manual link, you begin as before, in your check box Sub procedure, as follows:

```
Sub Check1_Click ()
  Text1.LinkMode = NONE
  Text1.LinkTopic = "Excel¦Sheet1"
  Text1.LinkItem = "R1C1"
        :
        :
End Sub
```

When you define the LinkMode, however, you use Manual rather than Automatic (the constant LINK_MANUAL has a value of 2, LINK_AUTOMATIC equals 1, and NONE equals 0), as follows:

```
Sub Check1_Click ()
  Text1.LinkMode = NONE
  Text1.LinkTopic = "Excel¦Sheet1"
  Text1.LinkItem = "R1C1"
  Text1.LinkMode = LINK_MANUAL
End Sub
```

This code sets up your manual link. When the link is established, nothing visible occurs because you have not specifically asked for an update. You can do that, however, whenever the form is clicked. Open the Form_Click() Sub procedure in the following way:

```
Sub Form_Click ()

End Sub
```

Now all we have to do is to execute Text1.LinkRequest this way:

```
Sub Form_Click ()
  Text1.LinkRequest
End Sub
```

When the program runs, the manual link is set up with Excel R1C1, Sheet1. You can do the next step, getting some data, by simply clicking

Peter Norton's Visual Basic for Windows, Third Edition, Covering Release 3.0

the form. At that point, Text1.LinkRequest is executed and the data now in R1C1 appears in Text1 also.

You might notice the two stubby, upright bars in Text1 that appear after you have established a link (look in figure 10.5, for example), and you might wonder why they are there. Those bars are sent as delimiters when you interact with Excel, and they are meant to separate the data from different cells in the spreadsheet. Does this mean that you can send the data from more than one cell to Text1? The answer is yes. In particular, you can specify a range of cells to read. If you want the data from the first two cells of column 1 in spreadsheet Sheet1, for example, you specify the appropriate range like this: R1C1:R2C1 (from Row 1 Column 1 to Row 2 Column 1).

```
Sub Check1_Click ()
  Text1.LinkMode = NONE
  Text1.LinkTopic = "Excel¦Sheet1"
  Text1.LinkItem = "R1C1:R2C1"
  Text1.LinkMode = LINK_AUTOMATIC
End Sub
```

The result of this program appears in figure 10.6 and shows that both the values you want, R1C1 and R2C1, appear in Text1, separated by the cell delimiter. In this way, you can pack an entire range of Excel cells into a single control.

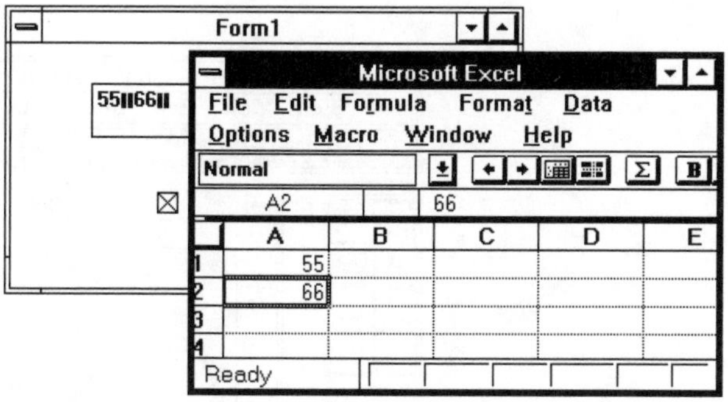

Figure 10.6. A Client Link to a range of Excel cells.

So far, then, you have examined how to set up automatic run-time client links and manual run-time client links. Let's explore the process of setting up run-time source links next.

Run-time Source Links

Now you get a chance to see how setting up a source application works. As it turns out, Visual Basic handles most of the details here; all you have to do is to set the correct Link properties, and Visual Basic handles the transfer of data.

For an added twist, let's send pictures rather than text this time because DDE links can be established for bit maps as well as for text (and you don't need Excel or WinWord for this example). To start, open the Windows Paintbrush program and draw some figure with the drawing tools. Next, choose the Selection tool from Paintbrush's toolbox (the upper left tool in the toolbox) and stretch a dotted rectangle around the figure you have drawn to select it. You will transfer this figure between applications in your client-source link.

Because the first step is to move the figure into a picture box, select the Copy item in Paintbrush's Edit menu and place a copy of the figure in the clipboard. Now you have to display that figure in a Visual Basic application, so start a new project in Visual Basic and double-click the picture box tool by creating a picture box on the form. To paste the figure now in the clipboard into that picture box, simply make sure that the picture box is selected and choose the Paste item in Visual Basic's Edit menu. The figure should appear in the picture box, something like figure 10.7 (in addition, you should set the picture box's AutoRedraw property to True).

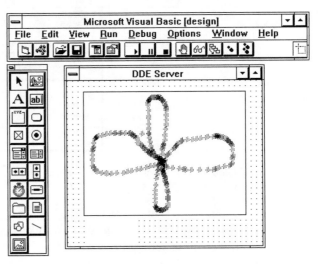

Figure 10.7. A Source application template.

Because this application already has the figure in a picture box, Picture1, this becomes your source application. As you may recall, because only forms, not individual controls, can be sources, click the form to bring up the Form_Click() template, as follows:

```
Sub Form_Click()

End Sub
```

The first thing you can do to make this application into a source is to set the form's LinkMode property to LINK_SOURCE, as follows:

```
Sub Form_Click()
  LinkMode = LINK_SOURCE        'Default = NONE
        :
        :
End Sub
```

To make this code meaningful, load Constant.Txt into a module belonging to the source (Source.Bas) because constants such as LINK_SOURCE are defined there. Note that, although LinkMode could be Automatic or Manual before, there is no such option here because the client determines whether the link is automatic or manual. As far as forms go, there are only two settings for LinkMode: LINK_SOURCE (the form is a source) or NONE (it is not a source).

Having made this application a source, let's give it a name as well. For example, you can call it Source.Exe when you create the .Exe file. To do that, save the form you are designing as Source.Frm and the project itself as Source.Mak. By doing this, you set the program's DDE application name also; it is now Source. That is, the name given to the .Exe file when you create it using Visual Basic's Make Exe File... window is the application's DDE name also. In addition to a name, this application needs a Topic to respond to DDE attempts. The default Topic is the name of the form, which is Form1 here, but you can change it by setting the LinkTopic property in the following way:

```
Sub Form_Click()
  LinkTopic = "Figure"     'Default = Name of form
  LinkMode = LINK_SOURCE   'Default = NONE
End Sub
```

If applications want to use your Source application as a source, they have to look for an application with the link topic of Source|Figure. In fact, let's put together a client application, also in Visual Basic, that reads the figure in Source's Picture1 control. Now that you have set up the current application as a source, the controls on it are suitable items for a DDE conversation. In other words, if "Source|Figure" is the DDE topic this source will support, "Picture1" is the DDE item.

The last step in creating the source is making and running the .Exe file. To do that, simply select Make Exe File... in the File menu, and then switch to the Windows Program Manager and run Source. The Source window appears with the figure in its Picture1 control. Now you are all set to use that application as a source for the client application you can write next.

There is no such thing as an automatic or manual DDE source.
It is worth emphasizing, again, that there are no automatic or manual sources. The selection of automatic or manual links is up to the client (although the source may elect not to grant such a link).

You already have seen how to write client applications that establish links in code as opposed to at design-time. To do that, you can start a new project in Visual Basic and create a picture box (set the picture box's AutoRedraw property to True), named Picture1, about the same size as the picture box in the source application. Next, bring up the Form_Load Sub procedure in the following way:

```
Sub Form_Click ()

End Sub
```

Accounting for differences in DDE picture box sizes.
You can set Picture1's AutoSize property to True in the client application to account for any difference in sizes between the picture boxes in the client and source applications. If the source picture is smaller, for example, the client picture box shrinks to fit it when it is transferred.

This is where you add the code to create the link. When you click the form, the picture is transferred from the source to your client application. First, you turn off any current links to the client application's Picture1, as follows:

```
Sub Form_Click ()
  Picture1.Linkmode = NONE
    :

End Sub
```

Next, you have to specify the LinkTopic. Because the name of the application you are trying to link to is Source, and the LinkTopic property is set to Figure (rather than the default, which is the name of the form acting as a source), you set LinkTopic in the following way:

```
Sub Form_Click ()
  Picture1.Linkmode = NONE
  Picture1.LinkTopic = "Source¦Figure"
    :

End Sub
```

Now you are ready for the LinkItem. In Visual Basic, that is the name of the actual control: Any of the controls on a form can be LinkItems. In this case, that's Picture1, which is the name of the picture in the source application that holds the figure you want. You can set LinkItem like the following in your client application:

```
Sub Form_Click ()
  Picture1.Linkmode = NONE
  Picture1.LinkTopic = "Source¦Figure"
  Picture1.LinkItem = "Picture1"
    :

End Sub
```

Finally, you initiate the automatic link, as follows:

```
Sub Form_Click ()
  Picture1.Linkmode = NONE
  Picture1.LinkTopic = "Source¦Figure"
  Picture1.LinkItem = "Picture1"
  Picture1.LinkMode = LINK_AUTOMATIC
End Sub
```

Now the code is set. Run this application in Visual Basic and a window appears (your client application) that looks much like the source application, except that the figure is only in the source's picture box. Next, click the client application's window to execute the preceding code and establish the link. When you do, the picture is copied from the picture box in the source to the picture box in the client, as shown in figure 10.8. In this way, it's just as easy to link pictures as it is to link text.

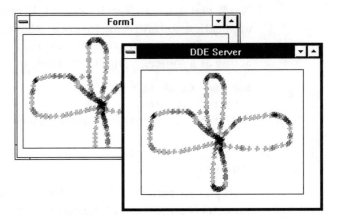

Figure 10.8. Custom Source-Client applications.

Or, it is *almost* as easy. The initial link is as easy to make, in fact, but maintaining that link is a little more difficult when you are working with picture boxes rather than with text. The reason is that changes in text boxes are usually very small-scale compared to changes in figures and pictures. When you start changing a picture, you may change hundreds or thousands of pixels at a time. In an automatic link, data is transferred from source to client whenever there's any change in the data, which means that the source would have to send the entire picture to the client whenever you change even a pixel.

Needless to say, this requirement can be disastrous if you do any kind of graphics. The way Visual Basic handles it is by sending updates to pictures only when the source specifically requests that updates be sent (as opposed to text box or label changes, which are sent instantaneously in automatic links or when the client requests updates in manual links). The source does that with the LinkSend method.

Maintaining a Picture Box Link

Suppose that you modify your source application so that, the first time you click it, it sets itself up as a source. If you click it again, however, let's have it draw some additional graphics figures in the picture box, Picture1. You might draw randomly sized rectangles, for example. To do that, you modify the source application's Form_Click() Sub procedure so that it knows when it has been clicked more than once.

```
Sub Form_Click()
  Static First
  First = First + 1
  If First = 1 Then
      LinkTopic = "Figure"     'Default = Name of form
      LinkMode = LINK_SOURCE   'Default = NONE
  Else
      :

  End If
End Sub
```

You can determine the coordinates (x1, y1) and (x2, y2) of the randomly sized rectangles by using the size of the picture box (that is, Picture1.ScaleWidth and Picture1.ScaleHeight) and the Visual Basic Rnd function, which returns a random floating-point number from 0 to 1, as follows:

```
Sub Form_Click()
  Static First
  First = First + 1
  If First = 1 Then
      LinkTopic = "Figure"     'Default = Name of form
      LinkMode = LINK_SOURCE   'Default = NONE
  Else
      x1 = Picture1.ScaleWidth * Rnd
      y1 = Picture1.ScaleHeigth * Rnd
      x2 = Picture1.ScaleWidth * Rnd
      y2 = Picture1.ScaleHeigth * Rnd
      :

  End If
End Sub
```

477

Finally, you just draw the box, by using Picture1's Line method (and specifying the B argument for a box), as follows:

```
Sub Form_Click()
  Static First
  First = First + 1
  If First = 1 Then
      LinkTopic = "Figure"     'Default = Name of form
      LinkMode = LINK_SOURCE   'Default = NONE
  Else
      x1 = Picture1.ScaleWidth * Rnd
      y1 = Picture1.ScaleHeigth * Rnd
      x2 = Picture1.ScaleWidth * Rnd
      y2 = Picture1.ScaleHeigth * Rnd
      Picture1.Line (x1, y1) .. (x2, y2), , B
  End If
End Sub
```

The result is something like that shown in figure 10.9; the first time you click the Source window when it's running, it sets itself up as a DDE source; every time you click it thereafter, it draws a random rectangle in the picture box and overlaps the figure that is already there.

Now when you run Source, click it once to make it respond as a DDE source; run the client to get the figure into the client's picture box, and then begin generating random rectangles. You will see that the rectangles do not appear in the client application's picture box, only in the source's picture box.

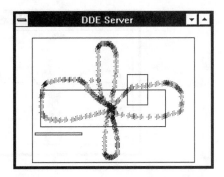

Figure 10.9. A Source application with random rectangles.

You can fix this with the LinkSend method. Close the source application and exit from the client application in Visual Basic as well. Next, bring up Source in Visual Basic one more time and add a command button, Command1, with the caption "Send figure" (see figure 10.9). Click the command button to bring up this template:

```
Sub Command1_Click ()

End Sub
```

This is where you can use the LinkSend method to send an updated version of the picture to your clients. You do that like the following (note that, because LinkSend is a method, it is associated with the control Picture1):

```
Sub Command1_Click ()
  Picture1.LinkSend
End Sub
```

Now you are all set. Make the Exe file Source.Exe and run it. Again, the source application appears on the screen. Next, click it once to make it active as a source. Now bring up the client application in Visual Basic again and run it. Click it once to establish the link and send over the original version of the figure in the source's picture box.

Next, you can generate some random rectangles; click the source's window a few times to generate them, as shown in figure 10.9. Again, they do not appear in the client window. You can change that, however, by clicking the "Send figure" button; click it, and you will see the entire figure transferred—rectangles and all—to the picture box in the client application, similar to figure 10.10. That's how to maintain a graphics DDE link.

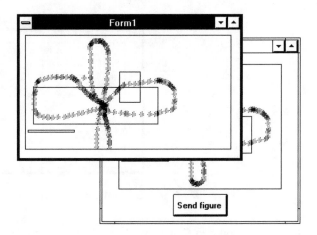

Figure 10.10. Source-Client graphics link with Update.

Now you are familiar with the idea of clients and sources, and how to set them up in your programs. It may surprise you, however, to learn that there are times when a client can act as a source and send data itself. Now that you have set up your own source application, let's check into this.

Sending Data Back to a DDE Source

Usually, of course, data goes from a DDE source to the client—automatically if there is an automatic link between them, or on request if the link is manual. However, you can reverse the direction of data flow in a link with the LinkPoke method. In other words, for each link you have set up between applications, you can send data two ways if required; to send data from the client to the source, however, you have to take specific steps. There is no such thing as a two-way automatic DDE link.

Let's see this concept in action. Currently, this is the way the Form_Click() Sub procedure looks in your client application, as follows:

```
Sub Form_Click ()
  Picture1.Linkmode = NONE
  Picture1.LinkTopic = "Source¦Figure"
  Picture1.LinkItem = "Picture1"
  Picture1.LinkMode = LINK_AUTOMATIC
End Sub
```

You can change this so that the first time the client form is clicked, it establishes the following link:

```
Sub Form_Click ()
  Static First
  First = First + 1
  If First = 1 Then
      Picture1.Linkmode = NONE
      Picture1.LinkTopic = "Source¦Figure"
      Picture1.LinkItem = "Picture1"
      Picture1.LinkMode = LINK_AUTOMATIC Else   :
              :
  End If
End Sub
```

When the link is established like this with the source, the figure is transferred to the client's picture box. The next time the client is clicked, however, let's draw a circle in that picture box and change the figure you got from the source, as follows:

```
Sub Form_Click ()
  Static First
  First = First + 1
  If First = 1 Then
      Picture1.Linkmode = NONE
      Picture1.LinkTopic = "Source¦Figure"
      Picture1.LinkItem = "Picture1"
      Picture1.LinkMode = LINK_AUTOMATIC
  Else
      x = Picture1.ScaleWidth/2
      y = Picture1.ScaleHeight/2
      r = Picture1.Width/4
      Picture1.Circle (x, y), r
              :
  End If
End Sub
```

At this point, the circle appears in the client and not in the source. You can reverse the direction of a DDE link temporarily, however, with the LinkPoke method, as follows:

```
Sub Form_Click ()
  Static First
  First = First + 1
```

```
    If First = 1 Then
        Picture1.Linkmode = NONE
        Picture1.LinkTopic = "Source¦Figure"
        Picture1.LinkItem = "Picture1"
        Picture1.LinkMode = LINK_AUTOMATIC
    Else
        x = Picture1.ScaleWidth/2
        y = Picture1.ScaleHeight/2
        r = Picture1.Width/4
        Picture1.Circle (x, y), r
        Picture1.LinkPoke
    End If
End Sub
```

Because this statement temporarily reverses the roles of client and source, the picture in the client's picture box is sent to the source, as shown in figure 10.11. Your attempt to send data back to the source is a success.

It turns out that this method can be very useful not only for sending data to the source but also for sending commands. An additional way to do this with DDE is by sending commands explicitly.

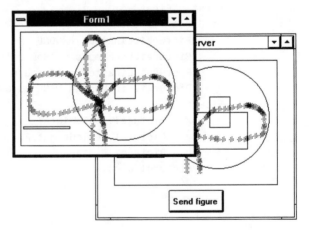

Figure 10.11. Poking data back to the Source.

Sending Commands through DDE

Some applications let you send commands to them through a DDE channel. For example, Excel accepts any of its legal macro commands, such as OPEN(), AVERAGE, and CLOSE() (see the Excel Function Reference for additional commands) through DDE. To see how this works, set up an automatic link with Excel:

```
Sub Check1_Click ()
  Text1.LinkMode = NONE
  Text1.LinkTopic = "Excel¦Sheet1"
  Text1.LinkItem = "R1C1"
  Text1.LinkMode = LINK_AUTOMATIC
  :

End Sub
```

This code connects Excel to a text box named Text1. To send the commands, you need to use the LinkExecute method. You can open a file named C:\Excel\Sheet1.Xls—for example—in the following way:

```
OPEN(""C:\EXCEL\SHEET1.XLS"")
```

Next, you can have Excel beep with BEEP, close the file with FILE.CLOSE(), and then quit with QUIT(). Excel also lets you pass a number of these types of macro commands at one time if you enclose them in square brackets in the following manner:

```
Sub Check1_Click ()
  Text1.LinkMode = NONE
  Text1.LinkTopic = "Excel¦Sheet1"
  Text1.LinkItem = "R1C1"
  Text1.LinkMode = LINK_AUTOMATIC
  Text1.LinkExecute
  "[OPEN(""C:\EXCEL\SHEET1.XLS"")][BEEP][FILE.CLOSE()][QUIT()]"
End Sub
```

Give this method a try. After the link is set up, Excel opens Sheet1.Xls, beeps, closes the file, and quits. Not all Windows applications that support DDE can take commands this way (WinWord cannot, for example), but some (like Excel) can.

> **An easy way to send keystrokes to another program.**
> You also can use the SendKeys statement to send keystrokes to the window (any window) with the focus. You can give another program's window the focus with the Shell or AppActivate statements.

This raises one of the conventional problems of DDE, however: What if the other application is not running? As things stand now, you would get a Visual Basic error message in a message box indicating that the other application is not running and asking whether you want to start it. It turns out that this error is trappable, and that you often can take care of errors like this yourself.

Handling DDE Errors

The trappable DDE errors appear in table 10.1. You can make use of these errors in the same way as you did in Chapter 9. If the other application isn't running, for example, you get a No Foreign Application error, number 282, and you can make use of it in your programs.

Table 10.1 DDE Errors

Error	Means
280	The DDE channel has not been fully closed and waits for a response
281	No more DDE channels
282	No foreign application responded to a DDE initiate
283	Multiple applications responded to a DDE initiate
284	DDE channel locked
285	Received negative DDE acknowledgment from foreign application
286	Time-out occurred while waiting for DDE response
287	User Hit DDE Attention Key
288	Destination is busy

Error	Means
289	No data for DDE data message
290	Data in wrong format
291	Foreign application terminated
292	An invalid DDE channel has been referenced
293	A DDE method was invoked with no channel open
294	Invalid DDE Link format
295	The message queue was filled and a DDE message was lost
296	A PasteLink has been executed on a channel with an existing PasteLink

If Excel is not running, for example, you can start it. To begin, you can set up an error handler:

```
Sub Check1_Click ()
  On Error GoTo ErrorHandler
  Text1.LinkMode = NONE
  Text1.LinkTopic = "Excel¦Sheet1"
  Text1.LinkItem = "R1C1"
  Text1.LinkMode = LINK_AUTOMATIC
  Text1.LinkExecute
  "[OPEN(""C:\EXCEL\SHEET1.XLS"")][BEEP][FILE.CLOSE()][QUIT()]"
ErrorHandler:
    :

End Sub
```

Next, you check to make sure that the error was number 282. In that case, you can start Excel by using Visual Basic's Shell function, which starts a Windows application in the following way:

```
Sub Check1_Click ()
  On Error GoTo ErrorHandler
  Text1.LinkMode = NONE
  Text1.LinkTopic = "Excel¦Sheet1"
  Text1.LinkItem = "R1C1"
```

```
Text1.LinkMode = LINK_AUTOMATIC
Text1.LinkExecute
"[OPEN(""C:\EXCEL\SHEET1.XLS"")][BEEP][FILE.CLOSE()][QUIT()]"
ErrorHandler:
  If Err = 282 Then    'No foreign application error.
  temp = Shell("C:\Excel\Excel.Exe")
      :

End Sub
```

After Excel is started, you can execute a Resume statement so that Visual Basic goes back and tries to reestablish the link, as follows:

```
Sub Check1_Click ()
  On Error GoTo ErrorHandler
  Text1.LinkMode = NONE
  Text1.LinkTopic = "Excel¦Sheet1"
  Text1.LinkItem = "R1C1"
  Text1.LinkMode = LINK_AUTOMATIC
  Text1.LinkExecute
  "[OPEN(""C:\EXCEL\SHEET1.XLS"")][BEEP][FILE.CLOSE()][QUIT()]"
ErrorHandler:
  If Err = 282 Then    'No foreign application error.
  temp = Shell("C:\Excel\Excel.Exe")
  Resume
  Else
    :

End Sub
```

On the other hand, if this was not the error you can handle, you place a message box on the screen to indicate which error occurred.

```
Sub Check1_Click ()
  On Error GoTo ErrorHandler
  Text1.LinkMode = NONE
  Text1.LinkTopic = "Excel¦Sheet1"
  Text1.LinkItem = "R1C1"
  Text1.LinkMode = LINK_AUTOMATIC
  Text1.LinkExecute
  "[OPEN(""C:\EXCEL\SHEET1.XLS"")][BEEP][FILE.CLOSE()][QUIT()]"
ErrorHandler:
  If Err = 282 Then    'No foreign application error.
  temp = Shell("C:\Excel\Excel.Exe")
```

```
      Resume
      Else
      MsgBox "Error number" + Str$(Err)
      Exit Sub
      End If
End Sub
```

That's it, then. If Excel is not running, you intercept the error and start it yourself so that you can set up the link. This DDE technique is extraordinarily powerful. You are no longer dependent on linking only to Windows applications that are already running. Instead, you can start the other Windows application, a valuable use for DDE errors. If the other application accepts commands with LinkExecute as Excel does, in fact, you can terminate it also.

Because two applications are involved here, however, you should note that DDE errors do not occur only when you are handling events in one of them. If the link is automatic and the source application sends data in the wrong format, for example, a DDE error is generated even if nothing is happening in the client. Nonetheless, the client should have some way of noticing that such errors are occurring and should be able to either fix or report the problem. For this reason, when there is a DDE error, a LinkError event is generated.

This kind of event is associated with the objects that can support DDE: forms, picture boxes, text boxes, and labels. For instance, two common DDE errors are too many DDE links (LinkError = 7) and running out of memory (LinkError = 11). If you were using a text box, Text1, you would find the following template for the associated LinkError event in the code window:

```
Sub Text1_LinkError (LinkError As Integer)


End Sub
```

Note that an argument is passed to this Sub procedure: LinkError. You can test that argument and check to see what kind of error occurred.

```
Sub Text1_LinkError (LinkError As Integer)

    If LinkError = 7 Then 'Wrong format for data
        MsgBox "Too many DDE Links"
    End If
```

```
    If LinkError = 11 Then    'Out of memory
        MsgBox "Out of memory for DDE"
    End If
```

```
End Sub
```

Note that if your application was a source and not a client, you would have to intercept DDE errors like this in the Form_LinkError( ) Sub procedure because only forms can act as sources.

The LinkOpen and LinkClose Events

LinkError is one of three DDE events that exist: The other two are LinkOpen and LinkClose. As you might imagine, the LinkOpen event occurs when a link is established with the current application as a participant, and LinkClose occurs when such a link is terminated. Both kinds of events occur for source or client applications (forms can have LinkOpen and LinkClose events in source applications, as well as have picture boxes, text boxes and labels in client applications).

The LinkOpen event also offers an important option: You can refuse the link if you want. For example, if you have a form that can act as a source (its LinkMode is set to Source), other applications may try to establish conversations with it, depending on its LinkTopic and LinkMode. If you look through the code window, you will find this Sub procedure template:

```
Sub Form_LinkOpen (Cancel As Integer)
```

```
End Sub
```

Notice in particular that an argument is passed to this procedure: Cancel. If you set this argument to True in your procedure, the link is refused; if you leave it False, the link is accepted. In this way, you can restrict the number of such links you allow, or refuse links until your data is ready. In a similar way, you can use the LinkClose event to indicate when a link is broken (note that it takes no arguments):

```
Sub Form_LinkClose()
```

```
End Sub
```

This is fine as far as it goes, but you are operating in the dark. Who is trying to establish or break DDE links with you—that is, how is that information encoded? And to which controls is Visual Basic connecting the foreign application? To find the answers to these and other questions, you can turn next to some advanced DDE topics.

Pasting Links in Code

Let's say that you have a window with two text boxes and that you want to let the user connect them, as clients, to an application of their choice. In other words, you do not know ahead of time to which application they want to link. You have seen that this can be done at design-time in Visual Basic by copying an item in another application and then using Paste Link in Visual Basic. The user usually is not present at design-time, however, so that capability is not useful here. Instead, you can provide in your programs a Paste Link option that can be used at run-time. This way, the user can paste links to the controls of their choice (you cannot program the target control name into your code while writing the program).

Let's see how this concept works. Start Visual Basic and place two text boxes, Text1 and Text2, on the default form. Then add an Edit menu with one item in it: Paste Link, with the Name PasteItem, as shown in figure 10.12. Next, click Paste Link in the menu to open the associated procedure:

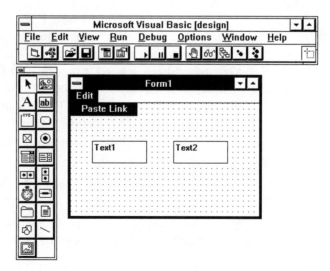

Figure 10.12. A Paste Link application template.

```
Sub PasteItem ()

End Sub
```

When the you select this menu choice, you want to paste a link into your application from another application. First, you must copy an item in that other application, which now resides in the clipboard. Your task now is to decipher the information there and connect it to the correct control in your application.

Applications generally provide link information in the clipboard like this: Application|Topic!Item. This is stored in the part of the clipboard reserved for DDE link information; when the user tries to paste a link in your application, you assume that it is waiting for you there. You can retrieve this text by using the clipboard's GetText() method and specify that you want DDE link information with CF_LINK, as follows:

```
Sub PasteItem ()
  DDEData$ = Clipboard.GetText(CF_LINK)
        :
        :
  End Sub
```

The constant CF_LINK, which indicates that you want DDE format data from the clipboard, is defined in Constant.Txt, so you should include that in one of your application's modules. Next, you have to decipher the name of the DDE topic and item from the string you received, DDEData$.

You can do that with some Visual Basic string manipulations. After you get the LinkTopic and LinkItem, you can connect them to the control you have selected. In other words, suppose that you have selected a cell in an Excel spreadsheet, copied it, and placed it in the clipboard. Next, you might select a text box in your application (giving it the focus), open your Edit menu, and paste the link. That means that you have to determine which of the two text boxes now is active (has the focus). You can do that by using the ActiveControl property of the Screen object. That is, if the user selects Text1, Screen.ActiveControl equals Text1.

First, you set the control's LinkMode to NONE, as follows:

```
Sub PasteItem ()
  DDEData$ = Clipboard.GetText(CF_LINK)
  Screen.ActiveControl.LinkMode = NONE
```

```
              :
              :
    End Sub
```

Next, you can cut the LinkTopic from the string DDEData$ this way (that string looks like this now: "Application|Topic!Item").

```
Sub PasteItem ()
  DDEData$ = Clipboard.GetText(CF_LINK)
  Screen.ActiveControl.LinkMode = NONE
  Screen.ActiveControl.LinkTopic = Left$(DDEData$,
InStr(DDEData$, "!")--1)
    :
    :
End Sub
```

After that, you can cut the LinkItem from DDEData$ in the following way:

```
Sub PasteItem ()
  DDEData$ = Clipboard.GetText(CF_LINK)
  Screen.ActiveControl.LinkMode = NONE
  Screen.ActiveControl.LinkTopic = Left$(DDEData$, InStr(DDEData$, "!")--1)
  Screen.ActiveControl.LinkItem = Right$(DDEData$, Len(DDEData$) -- InStr(DDEData$, "!"))
      :
      :
End Sub
```

The last step is to set the active control's LinkMode to LINK_AUTOMATIC, and you are finished.

```
Sub PasteItem ()
  DDEData$ = Clipboard.GetText(CF_LINK)
  Screen.ActiveControl.LinkMode = NONE
  Screen.ActiveControl.LinkTopic = Left$(DDEData$, InStr(DDEData$, "!")--1)
  Screen.ActiveControl.LinkItem = Right$(DDEData$, Len(DDEData$) -- InStr(DDEData$, "!"))
  Screen.ActiveControl.LinkMode = LINK_AUTOMATIC
End Sub
```

At this point, the link is established with the other application. You can select two cells, R1C1 and R2C1, for example, in an Excel spreadsheet and copy them by using the Excel Copy menu. This process places the string

"Excel|Sheet1!R1C1:R2C1" in the clipboard. If Text1 is the active control when the user selects the Paste item in your Edit menu, you can then use that data and set Text1's LinkTopic to "Excel|Sheet1" and its LinkItem to "R1C1:R2C1". Next, you establish the link, as shown in figure 10.13. In this way, you enable the user to select which links they want to set up with which of your controls they choose.

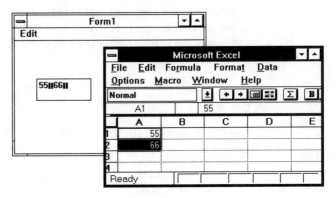

Figure 10.13. A run-time Paste Link operation.

That is one side of the story. So far, you have formed client links with specific controls. You also can set up your application as a source, however, by placing a Copy command in your Edit menu. In other words, you let the user set up a source link in the same way as you did in the beginning of this chapter: By simply using the Copy command. Here, however, you use your own application's Copy command, not Visual Basic's. Later, users can use Paste Link in another application and form the link with any application that supports DDE. Let's look into this subject in the next section.

Customized Source Applications

The goal in this section is to add a Copy item to your application's Edit menu so that users can set up a link, which they can then paste into another application. To begin, add a Copy item to the Edit menu, as shown in figure 10.14, and give it the name CopyItem.

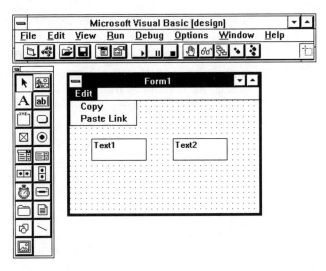

Figure 10.14. A Custom Source application with the copy item.

Next, open the CopyItem_Click () Sub procedure, as follows:

```
Sub CopyItem_Click ()

End Sub
```

You are going to load DDE data into the clipboard. Begin by clearing it of any data that might be in there now by using the Clipboard object's Clear method, as follows:

```
Sub CopyItem_Click ()
  Clipboard.Clear
      :
      :
End Sub
```

Now you can assemble the string you want to send to the clipboard; as you have seen, DDE strings generally look like this: "Application|Topic!Item". Let's give this project the name Custom.Mak and save the form as Custom.Frm, and the module as Custom.Bas so that your application name is Custom. Because this application is a source, the topic comes from the form's LinkTopic property, which now has the default value "Form1". The real problem here is the item name (the name of the control that provides the data) because names such as Text1 and Text2 are not stored when the program runs.

In other words, when a user selects the Copy item, she already has selected one of the controls in your application, making it the active control. The problem now is locating that item's Name so that you can copy it, because the actual Names are not present when the program runs. Visual Basic handles this problem by providing a Tag property for each object. The tag property is made up of a string that is preserved even when the program runs. A common use for the Tag property is to store the Names like Text1 and Text2. Click Text1 now, locate the Tag property in the properties window, and set it to "Text1". Then do the same for Text2, and set its tag to "Text2". Now you can make up your DDE string like the following:

```
Sub CopyItem_Click ()
  Clipboard.Clear
  DDEData$ = "Custom¦Form1!" + Screen.ActiveControl.Tag
      :
      :
End Sub
```

After that, you can place it in the clipboard by using the Clipboard.SetText method, indicating that it is a DDE string with the CF_LINK option, as follows:

```
Sub CopyItem_Click ()
  Clipboard.Clear
  DDEData$ = "Custom¦Form1!" + Screen.ActiveControl.Tag
  ClipBoard.SetText DDEData$, CF_LINK
      :
      :
End Sub
```

Technically, you are ready to go at this point; it is customary, however, for applications to store the data currently in the control in the clipboard at the same time so that the client application can read it immediately. If the control selected was a text box or label, for example, you want to place in the clipboard the text that is in it. If it were a picture, you would want to place that in the clipboard.

You can check the type of the active control with the TypeOf keyword in an If statement (see how this works in Chapter 11). You can check whether the active control is a text box, for example, like the following:

```
If TypeOf Screen.ActiveControl Is TextBox Then...
```

Note that you must use Is rather than an equals sign (=) in an If TypeOf statement like this. You can make use of this statement as shown in the following example:

```
Sub CopyItem_Click ()
  Clipboard.Clear
  DDEData$ = "Custom¦Form1!" + Screen.ActiveControl.Tag
  ClipBoard.SetText DDEData$, CF_LINK

  If TypeOf Screen.ActiveControl Is TextBox Then
      Clipboard.SetText Screen.ActiveControl.Text
  End If
      :
      :
End Sub
```

Send the text in the active text box into the clipboard. It remains separate from the DDEData$ string you placed in the clipboard earlier, because you specified that that was a DDE string with CF_LINK. In addition, you can check for other types of controls; the control type returned by TypeOf also can include Label or PictureBox. You can test whether the control is a label and, if so, send the caption to the clipboard. You also can check whether the active control is a picture box. If it is, send the picture by using the Clipboard object's SetData method.

```
Sub CopyItem_Click ()
  Clipboard.Clear
  DDEData$ = "Custom¦Form1!" + Screen.ActiveControl.Tag
  ClipBoard.SetText DDEData$, CF_LINK

  If TypeOf Screen.ActiveControl Is TextBox Then
      Clipboard.SetText Screen.ActiveControl.Text
  End If

  If TypeOf Screen.ActiveControl Is Label Then
      Clipboard.SetText Screen.ActiveControl.Caption
  End If

  If TypeOf Screen.ActiveControl Is PictureBox Then
      Clipboard.SetData Screen.ActiveControl.Picture
  End If

End Sub
```

495

Your new application, complete with Copy and Paste Link, is ready. You can use it, for example, to establish a source link with Excel. You might copy the text in Text2 with the Copy item and then move over to Excel and choose its Paste Link option. That establishes you as a DDE source, as shown in figure 10.15.

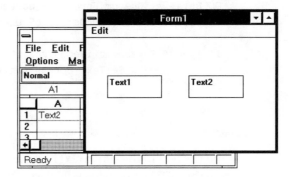

Figure 10.15. A Custom Source application in Action.

That's it for DDE coverage in this chapter. The next section turns to *Object Linking and Embedding (OLE)*.

How to Use Object Linking and Embedding (OLE)

One of the most exciting parts of Visual Basic is the OleClient control, which fits in with the discussion of DDE. Visual Basic supports OLE, which enables you to, among other things, *link* or *embed* objects into an OLE control. Rather than simply paste a range of Excel spreadsheet cells into your Visual Basic programs, for example, now you can paste in an entire spreadsheet. The following figure shows how the spreadsheet, Sheet1.Xls, might look in Excel.

Using an OLE control, you also can work with that spreadsheet or a section of it, like this (the spreadsheet cells appear just as they would in Excel).

If you link a file to your OLE control, the data is stored in that file (and displayed in your OLEClient control); if you embed an OLE object in your control, however, the data associated with it is connected to the control itself.

Microsoft Excel			

SHEET1.XLS			
	A	B	C
1	344	90	7
2	78	709	7
3	790	70	796

Visual Basic Application			

	A	B	C
1	344	90	7
2	78	709	7
3	790	70	796

You can even use multiple OLE controls in the same program—one with a spreadsheet from Excel, one with a document from WinWord, and so on. Let's see OLE in action. There are two versions of OLE: OLE1 (Visual Basic 2.0) and OLE2 (Visual Basic 3.0). The process of using them is similar, so let's examine how to use both OLE versions.

Object Linking and Embedding Version 1 (OLE1)

The first step in using OLE1 (or OLE2) is to create an OleClient control: Just select the OleClient tool and draw OleClient1 on a new program's form. To connect this control to c:\excel\sheet1.xls, you need to set these properties of OleClient1 in OLE1: Class, Protocol, ServerType, SourceDoc, SourceItem.

The class property depends on the kind of object you are connecting to. For an Excel worksheet, it is "ExcelWorksheet". You can leave the protocol setting to its default value of "StdFileEditing". The ServerType is set to 0 to indicate a linked OLE control. SourceDoc is your Excel spreadsheet: "c:\excel\sheet1.xls". Finally, you can indicate a range of

497

cells to link to in the SourceItem property, which you might set to "R1C1:R3C3". To sum up, OleClient1's properties are set like this:

```
OleClient1.Class      =    "ExcelWorksheet"
OleClient1.Protocol   =    "StdFileEditing"
OleClient1.ServerType =    0  'Linked
OleClient1.SourceDoc  =    "c:\excel\sheet1.xls"
OleClient1.SourceItem =    "R1C1:R3C3"
```

This is not all, however. To make the OLE link active, you have to set OleClient1's Action property to OLE_ACTIVATE. In general, the Action property's possible settings in OLE1 (from Constant.Txt) appear in table 10.2.

Table 10.2. OLE1 Action Settings

Global Const OLE_CREATE_NEW = 0

Global Const OLE_CREATE_FROM_FILE = 1

Global Const OLE_COPY = 4

Global Const OLE_PASTE = 5

Global Const OLE_UPDATE = 6

Global Const OLE_ACTIVATE = 7

Global Const OLE_EXECUTE = 8

Global Const OLE_CLOSE = 9

Global Const OLE_DELETE = 10

Global Const OLE_SAVE_TO_FILE = 11

Global Const OLE_READ_FROM_FILE = 12

Global Const OLE_CONVERT_TO_TYPE = 13

When you load the program, you can indicate that you want the OLE control to load the file c:\excel\sheet1.xls into Excel and display it in the following way:

```
Sub Form_Load ()
  OleClient1.Action = OLE_CREATE_FROM_FILE
```

```
    OleClient1.Action = OLE_ACTIVATE
End Sub
```

That's it. Now you create the Excel worksheet Sheet1.Xls in Excel, as shown in figure 10.16. Then you start your Visual Basic program—and the section of spreadsheet you want is loaded automatically into OLEClient1, as shown in figure 10.17. At this point, you can work with the displayed cells of the spreadsheet just as though you were in Excel. As you can see, this exceptionally powerful technique has been made very easy by the OLEClient control.

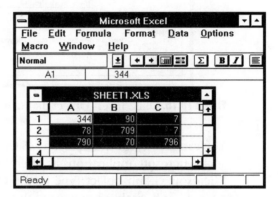

Figure 10.16. Excel's worksheet SHEET1.XLS.

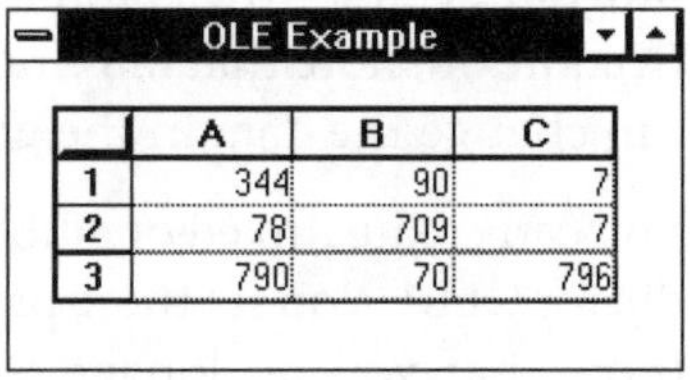

Figure 10.17. Your OLE1 program using SHEET1.XLS.

Now let's look at OLE2.

Object Linking and Embedding Version 2 (OLE2)

OLE2 (which comes with Visual Basic 3.0) has even more capabilities. For example, you can create and link or embed OLE objects at design-time by

499

using OLE2. To do that, draw a new OLE client control by using the OLE2 tool now. When you do, the Insert Object dialog box opens, as shown in figure 10.18.

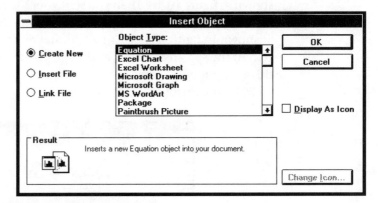

Figure 10.18. OLE2 Insert Object dialog box.

You can create, for example, an MS Graph object (MS Graph comes with such Microsoft applications as Microsoft Word) by simply selecting the Microsoft Graph object type in the Object Type list box. Visual Basic opens Graph, enabling you to put the data you want in a graph. When you finish with the graph, you will find an item marked Update in Graph's File menu; select it to see your graph appear in OleClient1. When you run the program, you see the graph in the OLE control, as shown in figure 10.19. In addition, note that MS Graph also is automatically opened so that you can change the data in the graph.

You can create linked or embedded objects at run-time, of course, as you did for OLE1. You set these properties for your Excel worksheet sheet1.xls (note that you no longer set the Protocol or ServerType properties—instead, you set ServerTypeAllowed), as follows:

```
OleClient1.Class =        "ExcelWorksheet"
OleClient1.ServerTypeAllowed    =      0  'Linked
OleClient1.SourceDoc     =        "c:\excel\sheet1.xls"
OleClient1.SourceItem    =        "R1C1:R3C3"
```

In addition, you set OleClient1.Action to one of the values in table 10.3 for OLE2.

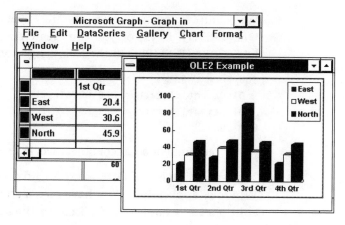

Figure 10.19. Your OLE2 graph example.

Table 10.3. OLE2 Action Settings

Global Const OLE_CREATE_EMBED = 0

Global Const OLE_CREATE_LINK = 1

Global Const OLE_COPY = 4

Global Const OLE_PASTE = 5

Global Const OLE_UPDATE = 6

Global Const OLE_ACTIVATE = 7

Global Const OLE_CLOSE = 9

Global Const OLE_DELETE = 10

Global Const OLE_SAVE_TO_FILE = 11

Global Const OLE_READ_FROM_FILE = 12

Global Const OLE_INSERT_OBJ_DLG = 14

Global Const OLE_PASTE_SPECIAL_DLG = 15

Global Const OLE_FETCH_VERBS = 17

Global Const OLE_SAVE_TO_OLE1FILE = 18

For example, you can link to the file sheet1.xls if you set the Action to OLE_CREATE_LINK, or you can create an embedded object if you use OLE_CREATE_EMBED in the following way:

```
Sub Form_Load ()
  OleClient1.Action = OLE_CREATE_EMBED
  OleClient1.Action = OLE_ACTIVATE
End Sub
```

Now your embedded Excel object works as it did in OLE1.

That's it for OLE and DDE—and for linking your applications to other Windows applications. You have seen a good deal of power here, which continues in Chapter 11. It discusses the advanced uses of Visual Basic controls.

Summary

In this chapter, you have learned about DDE and OLE techniques. You have seen how to set up DDE design-time source and client links, and how to do the same thing at run-time, in code. You have learned how to set up a manual link (use LinkRequest to receive data) and how to send graphics images along a DDE link. You also have used the LinkExecute method to send commands to another Windows application, and intercepted trappable DDE errors in the LinkError event. Finally, you saw how to enable Copy and Paste Link items in your own menus to support the copying and pasting of DDE links to and from your Visual Basic programs.

After DDE was covered, the discussion turned to OLE; handling OLE is made easy with the use of the OLEClient controls. To do this, you created an OLEClient control and set the following properties in OLE1: Class, Protocol, ServerType, SourceDoc, and SourceItem. In OLE2, you set Class, ServerTypeAllowed, SourceDoc, and SourceItem. Then, you set the Action property to OLE_ACTIVATE to make the object you were embedding appear. In this way, you were able to embed part of another Windows application (in this case, a section of an Excel spreadsheet) in your Visual Basic form, where you were able to use it just as though you were in Excel. In this way, DDE and OLE provide extremely powerful techniques for connecting applications in Windows, which is itself a multitasking environment.

New Methods	Description
LinkExecute	Sends commands to a DDE client. The format of the commands depends on the client; for example, you can open the Excel spreadsheet c:\Excel\Sheet1.Xls if Text1 has a link to Excel the following way: Text1.LinkExecute. "[OPEN(""C:\EXCEL\SHEET1.XLS"")]".
LinkPoke	Similar to LinkSend, it temporarily reverses the flow of data so that it goes from client to source (takes no parameters).
LinkSend	Sends data from source to client in a Manual or Notify DDE link (takes no parameters).

New Properties	Description
Action	Starts or sets OLE connection; see table 10.2 for settings.
Class	Sets OLE class of object to be embedded —for example, "ExcelWorksheet").
LinkItem	Document you want to have DDE with (WinWord|Document1, for example).
LinkMode	Sets the way in which you want to maintain a DDE link. Select from these options: None, Automatic, Manual, Notify.
LinkTimeout	Tenths of a second to allow for DDE connection to be made before timing out.
LinkTopic	Section of DDE document you want to link to or from—for example, R1C1 links you to row 1, column 1 in an Excel spreadsheet; also, sets LinkItem to correct spreadsheet document.

503

New Properties	Description
Protocol	Sets OLE1 protocol; usual is the default value: "StdFileEditing". OLE1 only.
ServerType	Sets OLE1 connection type; usual is 0 (meaning "Linked"). Read-only in OLE2.
ServerTypeAllowed	OLE2 only. Determines type of object you can create (linked, embedded, or either).
SourceDoc	The source OLE document (for example, "c:\excel\sheet1.xls"). Use together with the SourceItem property.
SourceItem	The source OLE item inside an OLE SourceDocument—for example, Excel cells "R1C1:R3C3". Use together with the SourceDocument property.

New Events	Description
LinkOpen	Occurs when an application attempts to open a DDE link. Receives one parameter, Cancel, like the following: Form_LinkOpen (Cancel As Integer).
LinkClose	Occurs when a DDE link is closed (no parameters).
LinkError	Occurs when a DDE error occurred. Receives LinkError as a parameter like the following: Text1_LinkError (LinkError As Integer).

Advanced Control and Form Handling

I n this chapter, we will see some exciting advanced and professional methods of handling controls and forms in Visual Basic. In particular, these are the topics we will cover:

▼ Passing controls to procedures

▼ Setting up arrays of forms

▼ How to determine a control's type at run time

▼ Finding a passed control's parent form

▼ The Visual Basic Screen object

▼ Dragging and dropping Visual Basic controls

▼ Determining which control on a form is active

▼ Determining which form is active

▼ Changing the tab order of controls

▼ Making sure a control can never get the focus

505

▼ Passing forms to procedures

▼ Using the "Me" keyword to identify forms

Here we will see a number of techniques, including how to drag and drop controls on a form; how to pass controls to a Sub procedure or Function; and how to pass forms themselves to a Sub procedure or Function. Visual Basic gives us a great deal of flexibility here that we haven't used before, but we will in this chapter. For example, you can write a single Sub procedure that fills list boxes with some data. But what if you have thirty list boxes across a dozen forms, some of which should be filled with this data and some of which shouldn't? Should they all call this Sub procedure? Clearly, it is much easier to be able to pass the list boxes you want filled to this one Sub procedure. The same can work for forms. In fact, we will even see how to create arrays of forms here, which is useful if you are writing, say, a cardfile application. In addition, we will see how to set the tab order of controls on a form. This is important, since the user is supposed to be able to use the keyboard as well as the mouse in Windows, and they use the tab key to move from control to control.

In Chapter 8, we saw a good deal about advanced data handling. There is another aspect of Visual Basic that comes naturally after advanced data handling, and that is advanced control handling. In this chapter, we will work through advanced control handling much as we did in the last chapter for data handling. We will see as far as we can go with controls in Visual Basic.

We will see how to pass controls as arguments to functions, and why you would want to. We will see the Screen object, which will let us learn about the graphical environment we are in; how set a control's tab order; how to make sure controls never receive the focus; how to determine which control (and which form) is active at any particular time; how to resize controls when the form they are on is resized; how to find a control's parent form; how our program can determine a control's type at run time (for example, label, text box, and so on); how to let the user drag controls around our windows, and even more topics.

You might think that dragging controls around a window is not terribly exciting—who'd want to drag a list box or text box around? Visual Basic controls include picture boxes and labels. So in this chapter we should be able to build a Desktop Organizer which acts a little like the Windows program manager, allowing us to organize executable files in Windows by dragging them around a window and placing them in one of two boxes, labelled Business and Home. We will also update some of our earlier programs in this chapter to take advantage of new techniques. For example, we will update our earlier alarm clock program to use a menu, and our earlier string printing Sub procedure so that it can print in picture boxes that we pass to it as arguments. With all this coming up, let's start by creating a small mock-up of the Windows Program Manager, even allowing us to drag filenames around the screen as we like. It will show us a great deal about advanced techniques in working with controls.

A Desktop Organizer Example

The program we are aiming for might look something like the following when it is completed:

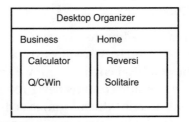

Here, the names like Reversi and Calculator refer to Windows applications, as they might in the Program Manager. Our goal here is to allow the user to click one such name and drag it into the other box—for example, from Business to Home or the other way around), as follows:

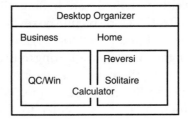

When they release the mouse button, the application name will stay where it is placed.

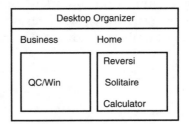

In this way, users can organize their applications. When they double click an application name, our program should start that application up (we will use the Shell( ) function to do that). Let's see how this will work.

To enable dragging and dropping of the filenames in our window, we will use the DragMode property that most controls have, and the form's DragDrop event. That is, we will store the names of the applications like "Calculator" and "Solitaire" in labels, and make it possible for the user to drag these labels around the window by setting their DragMode property correctly. In addition, when the user stops dragging them across the window and drops them, Visual Basic will generate a Form_DragDrop event, and we will be able to react to that. Note that we are going to use labels instead of text boxes to hold the application names because text boxes don't have Click or DblClick events, and we want to start the corresponding application when the user double clicks the application's name.

To start, let's draw the two boxes that we will label Business and Home. It will prove much easier to draw the boxes rather than to use frames, because frames are controls and each of them would have their own DragDrop event. In that case, we would have to coordinate three events: Label1_DragDrop, Label2_DragDrop, and Form_DragDrop. Simply draw the two boxes in the following way:

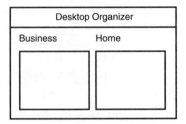

Then the only event we will have to worry about when the user drags an application name around is Form_DragDrop(). We can draw the two boxes in the Form_Load() event. After setting the form's AutoRedraw property to True, we can print the two labels like this, tying them to the size of the window. If we added this same code to the Form_Resize event, the user could resize our window as well.

```
Sub Form_Load ()
    CurrentY = ScaleWidth / 20
    CurrentX = ScaleWidth / 9
    Print "Business";
    CurrentX = 5 * ScaleWidth / 9
    Print "Home"
        :
```

In fact, since "Business" and "Home" are the names of the two boxes
themselves, we should do something to make them stand out from the
application names which will be inside the boxes. To do that, let's increase
the font size of these names from 8.25 points (a point is 1/72 of an inch,
and Visual Basic's default font size is 8.25 points) to, say 12 points using
the form's FontSize property. Next, we can draw the boxes themselves
using the Line method with the "B" option, also tailoring them to the size
of the form—whatever that is—in the following way:

```
Sub Form_Load ()
    CurrentY = ScaleWidth / 20
    CurrentX = ScaleWidth / 9
    Print "Business";
    CurrentX = 5 * ScaleWidth / 9
    Print "Home"
    Line (ScaleWidth / 9, 2 * ScaleHeight / 9)-
        (4 * ScaleWidth / 9, 8 * ScaleHeight / 9), , B
    Line (5 * ScaleWidth / 9, 2 * ScaleHeight / 9)-
        (8 * ScaleWidth / 9, 8 * ScaleHeight / 9), , B
End Sub
```

In addition, we can give our window the caption Desktop Organizer. At
this point, when our program runs, we will see something like that in
figure 11.1.

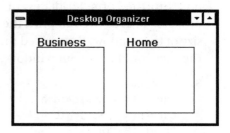

Figure 11.1. Beginning the Desktop Organizer.

What remains now is to add the labels holding the application names, to make it possible to drag them around the window, and to start the corresponding application when the user double clicks one of them. To do that, create four new labels, giving them each the name, say, LLL to create a control array. In addition, give each of them the names of Windows applications you have. As shown above, we will use Solitaire, Calculator, Reversi, and QC/Win (Microsoft QuickC for Windows) in this example. Now when we run the program, the Desktop Organizer looks something like that in figure 11.2 (depending on where you placed your labels).

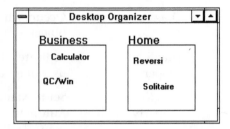

Figure 11.2. The Desktop Organizer.

Next, we should concern ourselves with the dragging process itself. The properties, events, and methods of dragging appear in table 11.1. One property of most controls is the DragMode property; this property indicates how controls will respond when the user attempts to drag them around with the mouse. If you set a control's DragMode property to Automatic—for example, DragMode = 1—then the user can drag the control around at any time. This sounds like what we want—except for one thing: when a control's DragMode is Automatic, it will not respond to any mouse events, except attempts to drag it. This is the defect of Automatic dragging mode—controls are useless except to be dragged. In our case, as in most programs, we want to use our controls for other things besides dragging them around; here, we want to be able to double click our labels and start the corresponding application.

Table 11.1. Control Dragging Methods, Properties, and Events

Drag Method	Controls dragging if control's DragMode is set to Manual (0); Control.Drag 0 cancels the drag operation, Control.Drag 1 starts it (moves the mouse cursor to the control and attaches the control to it) and Control.Drag 2 ends dragging. (Drag is only needed when a control's DragMode is manual, but you can use it if DragMode is Automatic (1) also).
DragDrop Event	Occurs when a control is dropped on an object
DragIcon Property	Indicates the icon you want used as the user drags a control around.
DragMode Property	Set to Manual (0—the default) or Automatic (1)to control dragging of controls. If a control's DragMode is automatic, the user can drag it at any time (and the control does not respond to normal mouse input like clicks). If you use manual dragmode, the dragging is under your control with the Drag method.
DragOver Event	Occurs when a control is dragged over an object—for example., form or control).

That means we want to use manual dragging—for example, DragMode is set to Manual (0—the default). When a user presses a mouse button while the mouse cursor is on top of a control whose DragMode is set to Manual, a MouseDown() event is generated. We can take advantage of that fact to enable dragging at that time, using the Drag method (whose job is exactly that—to enable dragging). In other words, the sequence of events will go like this: the user moves the mouse cursor on top of a label and presses a mouse button. At that point, a LLL_MouseDown() event is generated, where LLL is the name of the control array that we gave to our labels. In that event procedure, we can execute this statement: LLL(Index).Drag 1, which starts dragging (i.e. associates the label with the mouse cursor).

Here, Index is the index value of the selected label in the control array, and it is passed to us in LLL_MouseDown(). In code, that appears as follows:

```
Sub Form_Load ()
    CurrentY = ScaleWidth / 20
    CurrentX = ScaleWidth / 9
    Print "Business";
    CurrentX = 5 * ScaleWidth / 9
    Print "Home"
    Line (ScaleWidth / 9, 2 * ScaleHeight / 9)-
        (4 * ScaleWidth / 9, 8 * ScaleHeight / 9), , B
        Line (5 * ScaleWidth / 9, 2 * ScaleHeight / 9)-
            (8 * ScaleWidth / 9, 8 * ScaleHeight / 9), , B
End Sub
Sub LLL_MouseDown (Index As Integer, Button As Integer, Shift As Integer, X
As Single, Y As Single)
    LLL(Index).Drag 1
        :
End Sub
```

Now the user is able to drag the label around. When this happens, a shady outline is displayed connected to the mouse cursor, and it follows the mouse cursor around. The default outline shape is simply a fuzzy box the same size as the control itself, as shown in figure 11.3. In a true application, we could specify a DragIcon (one of the drag properties associated with most controls) instead of a fuzzy box. For example, here we might use one of the file icons in Visual Basic's icon library. In figure 11.3, we are dragging "Calculator"'s icon—but note that although we are dragging the control's outline, the control itself (that is, the label with the displayed name "Calculator") stayed behind. We should fix that by making the label invisible when we start dragging its outline, and we can do that in the MouseDown event, as follows:

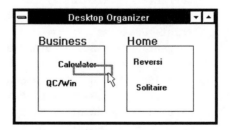

Figure 11.3. The Desktop Organzier dragging example.

```
Sub Form_Load ()
    CurrentY = ScaleWidth / 20
    CurrentX = ScaleWidth / 9
    Print "Business";
    CurrentX = 5 * ScaleWidth / 9
    Print "Home"
    Line (ScaleWidth / 9, 2 * ScaleHeight / 9)-
        (4 * ScaleWidth / 9, 8 * ScaleHeight / 9), , B
    Line (5 * ScaleWidth / 9, 2 * ScaleHeight / 9)-
        (8 * ScaleWidth / 9, 8 * ScaleHeight / 9), , B
End Sub


Sub LLL_MouseDown (Index As Integer, Button As Integer, Shift As Integer,
X As Single, Y As Single)
    LLL(Index).Drag 1
    LLL(Index).Visible = 0
End Sub
```

The next step is to respond when the user releases the mouse button,
dropping the label in its new position. When that happens, a DragDrop()
event will be generated. The information that Visual Basic passes to the
DragDrop event procedure must contain three items: the x coordinate of
the mouse cursor when the control was dropped, the y coordinate of the
cursor, and some indication of what control was actually dropped—for
example, this is a Form_DragDrop event, and forms can hold many
controls.

To indicate what control was dropped, Visual Basic passes a type of
argument that we haven't seen before—it actually passes the control itself
as an argument. That is, this is the way the DragDrop event Sub procedure
appears as follows:

```
Sub Form_Load ()
    CurrentY = ScaleWidth / 20
    CurrentX = ScaleWidth / 9
    Print "Business";
    CurrentX = 5 * ScaleWidth / 9
    Print "Home"
    Line (ScaleWidth / 9, 2 * ScaleHeight / 9)-
        (4 * ScaleWidth / 9, 8 * ScaleHeight / 9), , B
    Line (5 * ScaleWidth / 9, 2 * ScaleHeight / 9)-
        (8 * ScaleWidth / 9, 8 * ScaleHeight / 9), , B
End Sub
```

```
Sub LLL_MouseDown (Index As Integer, Button As Integer, Shift As Integer,
X As Single, Y As Single)
    LLL(Index).Visible = 0
    LLL(Index).Drag 1
End Sub
```

```
    Sub Form_DragDrop (Source As Control, X As Single, Y As Single) <--
            :
        End Sub
```

Note the first argument, Source, which is passed "As Control"; that is, as a Visual Basic control. Inside the Sub procedure Form_DragDrop(), we can use Source entirely as if it were a Visual Basic control like any other. For example, if the dropped control was a text box, we could examine its text property—Source.Text—and so on. In fact, this brings up an interesting point. How exactly are we to know what type of control was dropped? Now that we know we can pass controls to Sub procedures and Functions as part of our advanced control handling techniques, we will have to be able to know something about which control was passed. Names like Text1 or Label1 are not available at run time in Visual Basic. However, we can determine the type of control with the Typeof keyword, which we saw briefly in the last chapter. For example, if we wanted to make sure that the dropped control was a label, we could do the following:

```
Sub Form_DragDrop (Source As Control, X As Single, Y As Single)
    If TypeOf Source Is Label Then
        :
    End If
End Sub
```

Note the syntax here:

```
If TypeOf Source Is Label Then
        :
            'Perform actions  :
End If
```

Here, we use the TypeOf, Label, and Is keywords (note that you use Is, not =, with TypeOf) to check the type of the control named Source. Besides Label, the other keywords you can check passed controls against are: CheckBox, ComboBox, CommandButton, DirListBox, DriveListBox, FileListBox, Frame, HScrollBar, Label, ListBox, Menu, OptionButton, PictureBox, TextBox, Timer, or VScrollBar.

We should also note that only arguments can be of type Control—that is, we cannot have variables in programs of type Control, we can only pass controls to Sub procedures or to Functions. In this case, you dropped the label you were dragging when you saw a DragDrop event, so you can do two things here: make the original label visible again, and terminate dragging (disconnect the label outline from the mouse cursor) with the Drag method in the following way:

```
Sub Form_DragDrop (Source As Control, X As Single, Y As Single)
    If TypeOf Source Is Label Then
        Source.Drag 2
        Source.Visible = -1      'True
            :

            :

    End If
End Sub
```

You may be surprised to learn that Visual Basic does not move the label that was dragged to the new location when it was dropped. The reason is that this gives us, the programmers, more control over what happens in our programs. For instance, we might not want to reposition the control where it was dropped, since it might have been dropped in some illegal region of our application (perhaps we don't want command buttons on top of our picture boxes, for example). Instead, we are responsible for moving the control to its new location itself if we want it there, and we can do that with the Move method, which Visual Basic uses to move objects around, which we first saw in Chapter 6.

To use Move correctly, we should have saved the original location of the mouse cursor in the control that was dragged at the time of the MouseDown event so we could restore the control with respect to the cursor's new position. That is, we only get the mouse cursor's position in a DragDrop event and we have to figure out the control's new position from that. But the cursor could have been anywhere inside the control to drag it—upper left corner, center, etc.—which means it is hard to know how to position the control with respect to the cursor. For this example, however, we will just make the assumption that the mouse cursor was roughly in the middle of the label when dragging started, and position the label accordingly, as follows:

```
Sub Form_DragDrop (Source As Control, X As Single, Y As Single)
    If TypeOf Source Is Label Then
        Source.Drag 2
        Source.Visible = -1      'True
```

```
        Source.Move (X - Source.Width / 2), (Y - Source.Height / 2)
    End If
End Sub
```

That's almost it for this application. All that remains is making the four labels' DblClick() procedure active so that the user can start the applications by double clicking the label. Since we have left the labels' DragMode as Manual, the labels can still recognize mouse events like double clicks, and we can simply add the code necessary to the procedure LLL_DblClick(). Note that this would not be possible if we had permanantly enabled dragging by setting their DragModes to Automatic, because controls cannot respond to mouse events in that case.

However, there is a problem: what application do we start? As in the Program Manager, it is not necessarily the case that the names in the labels correspond to the actual names of the applications' executable files. When you add an application to the Program Manager, you have to specify both the name you want for its icon—say, "Reversi"—and the actual name of its executable file (path and filename): "c:\windows\reversi.exe". In addition to the name in the label, you need the path and filename information here too.

As mentioned, not even the Names of controls like Text1 or Picture1 are preserved at run time. However, the need to associate text information with a control like this is frequent, especially when you pass controls, in case you might want to know which control was passed. So Visual Basic provides the Tag property, which we saw in the last chapter and which is a property of all controls. The Tag property enables you to associate a text string with a control. A common use of the Tag property is to store the control's Name so that you can see which control you are working with at run time. Here, you will store the path and filenames of each application in the matching label's Tag property. To do that, simply place the correct text string in each label's Tag property, as shown in table 11.2.

Table 11.2. Our Desktop Organizer's Tag Properties

Label Name	Label Caption	Tag Property
LLL(1)	Calculator	"c:\windows\calc.exe"
LLL(2)	Reversi	"c:\windows\reversi.exe"
LLL(3)	QC/Win	"c:\qcwin\bin\qcw.exe"
LLL(4)	Solitaire	"c:\windows\sol.exe"

Now we are finished. All we have to do is add one line to the LLL_DblClick()
Sub procedure like this, completing the program (Desktop.Mak on the
diskette), which appears in listing 11.1, as follows:

```
Sub LLL_DblClick (Index As Integer)
    Resultval% = Shell(LLL(Index).Tag, 1)
End Sub
```

Listing 11.1. Desktop.Mak (Desktop.Mak on the diskette)

```
Form Form1 -----------------------------
    AutoRedraw          =    -1   'True
    Caption             =    "Desktop Organizer"

Label LLL
        Caption         =    "Calculator"
        Tag             =    "c:\windows\calc.exe"
        Index           =    1

Label LLL
        Caption         =    "Reversi"
        Tag             =    "c:\windows\reversi.exe"
        Index           =    2

Label LLL
        Caption         =    "Paintbrush"
        Tag             =    "c:\windows\pbrush"
        Index           =    3

Label LLL
        Caption         =    "Solitaire"
        Tag             =    "c:\windows\sol.exe"
        Index           =    4

Sub Form_Load ()
    CurrentY = ScaleWidth / 20
    CurrentX = ScaleWidth / 9
    Print "Business";
    CurrentX = 5 * ScaleWidth / 9
    Print "Home"
    Line (ScaleWidth / 9, 2 * ScaleHeight / 9)-
        (4 * ScaleWidth / 9, 8 * ScaleHeight / 9), , B
```

```
                    Line (5 * ScaleWidth / 9, 2 * ScaleHeight / 9)-
                        (8 * ScaleWidth / 9, 8 * ScaleHeight / 9), , B
            End Sub


Sub LLL_MouseDown (Index As Integer, Button As Integer, Shift As Integer,
X As Single, Y As Single)
            LLL(Index).Visible = 0
            LLL(Index).Drag 1
        End Sub


        Sub Form_DragDrop (Source As Control, X As Single, Y As Single)
            If TypeOf Source Is Label Then
                Source.Drag 2
                Source.Visible = -1
              Source.Move (X - Source.Width / 2), (Y - Source.Height / 2)
            End If
        End Sub


        Sub LLL_DblClick (Index As Integer)
            Resultval% = Shell(LLL(Index).Tag, 1)
        End Sub
```

And that's it. The second argument to Shell() indicates how we want the
application to start, and we pass a 1 so that it starts in an open window.
Now the Desktop Organizer is ready to launch applications, as in figure 11.4.

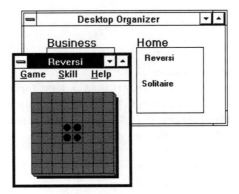

Figure 11.4. The Desktop Organizer at work.

Passing Controls to Procedures Ourselves

Of course, we can pass controls to Sub procedures and Functions ourselves. It is advisable to set up Sub procedures or Functions that can accept controls as arguments in two cases: 1) when you have a number of controls and you want to perform the same (but multiple) actions on each one, such as initializing them; or 2) when you don't know which control you will be expected to work on. An example of the second case might be the procedure that we developed back in Chapter 6 to print strings in picture boxes. That code appeared as follows:

```
Form1 General Declarations --------------------------------

    Dim StringToPrint As String          'Form-wide variable

Form1 --------------------------------

    Sub Form_Load () PString$ = "Now is the time for all good men..."

        StringToPrint = PString$ PrintLine$ = "" NextWord$ = GetWord$()
Do While NextWord$ <> ""
        Temp$ = PrintLine$ + NextWord$
        If Picture1.TextWidth(Temp$) > Picture1.ScaleWidth Then
Picture1.Print PrintLine$    'Print before too long
PrintLine$ = NextWord$
            Else
PrintLine$ = Temp$
            End If
            NextWord$ = GetWord$()
```

```
        Loop
Picture1.Print PrintLine$      'Print remainder.
End Sub

    Function GetWord$ ()
        If InStr(StringToPrint, " ") = 0 Then
            GetWord$ = StringToPrint
        StringToPrint = ""
        Else
            GetWord$ = Left$(StringToPrint, InStr(StringToPrint, " "))
            StringToPrint = Right$(StringToPrint, Len(StringToPrint) -
        InStr(StringToPrint, " "))
        End If
End Function
```

Here, we printed a text string in a picture box whose name was Picture1. This code would be much more useful if we could write a general Sub procedure called, PrintString() that would print text in any picture box. To let it print in any picture box, we can pass the picture box as an argument, as follows:

```
    Sub PrintString(PBox As Control, PString As String)

    End Sub
```

Inside PrintString(), you can refer to the picture box simply as PBox. For the actual body of the procedure, we can simply borrow code from above, like this—for example, everything after the first line of the Form_Load() procedure—just changing all references to Picture1 to PBox, as follows:

```
    Sub PrintString(PBox As Control, PString As String)

            StringToPrint = PString      PrintLine$ = ""
            NextWord$ = GetWord$()
        Do While NextWord$ <> ""
Temp$ = PrintLine$ + NextWord$
If PBox.TextWidth(Temp$) > PBox.ScaleWidth Then
    PBox.Print PrintLine$    'Print before it gets too long
Else
    PrintLine$ = Temp$
End If
NextWord$ = GetWord$()
```

```
                   Loop

                   PBox.Print PrintLine$          'Print remainder
                   End Sub
```

And that's it. Now we have set up PrintString(), a general word-wrapping routine for printing in picture boxes. We can call it with a single line in the Form_Load() procedure like this—for example, this line replaces the original line in the Form_Load() event which did the same thing.

```
Sub Form_Load ()
    Call PrintString(Picture1, "Now is the time for all good men...")
End Sub
```

The result appears in figure 11.5. The final listing appears in Listing 11.2 (Prnstrg.Mak on the diskette).

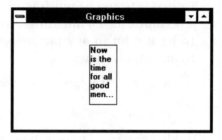

Figure 11.5. The PrintString() code at work.

Listing 11.2. The PrintString Sub Procedure (Prnstrg.Mak on the diskette).

```
Form Form1 ---------------------------
    AutoRedraw       =    -1   'True
    Caption          =    "Graphics"

PictureBox Picture1
        AutoRedraw       =    -1   'True

Form1 General Declarations -------------------------------

    Dim StringToPrint As String            'Form-wide variable
```

```
Form1 --------------------------------

    Sub Form_Load ()
        Call PrintString(Picture1, "Now is the time for all good men...")
    End Sub

Form1 General -------------------------------

    Sub PrintString (PBox As Control, PString As String)

        StringToPrint = PString PrintLine$ = "" NextWord$ = GetWord$()
        Do While NextWord$ <> ""
           Temp$ = PrintLine$ + NextWord$
          If PBox.TextWidth(Temp$) > PBox.ScaleWidth Then
PBox.Print PrintLine$    'Print before it gets too long
PrintLine$ = NextWord$
                Else
PrintLine$ = Temp$
                    End If
                  NextWord$ = GetWord$()
                  Loop
    PBox.Print PrintLine$    'Print remainder.
End Sub


Function GetWord$ ()
If InStr(StringToPrint, " ") = 0 Then
GetWord$ = StringToPrint
StringToPrint = ""
Else
GetWord$ = Left$(StringToPrint, InStr(StringToPrint, " "))
StringToPrint = Right$(StringToPrint, Len(StringToPrint) -
InStr(StringToPrint, " "))
End If
End Function
```

Passing Forms As Arguments to Procedures

You can actually pass forms to Sub procedures and Functions. This is very useful if you have a number of forms that you want to apply the same set of operations to, or to coordinate in some way. Because you can pass a form to a Sub or Function in one line, that Sub or Function might contain many lines of code. That is, the more windows you have to handle in the same way, the more economical it becomes to package the form-handling code in a single procedure. For example, let's say that we had a program that maintained four windows, named Form1 through Form4. With the click of one button, we should be able to arrange all these windows in a cascade, as well as to make them all the same size.

We might start by making sure that all windows appeared in the screen. Form1 is the startup form here; if you wanted another form to be the startup form, you can use the Set Startup Form... in Visual Basic's Run menu, as follows:

```
Sub Form_Load ()
    Form2.Show
    Form3.Show
    Form4.Show
End Sub
```

Now we can add a button labelled Cascade which, when clicked, will arrange the four windows in a cascade. That button might appear as in figure 11.6. Next, let's design a Sub procedure named, say, Cascade() that will arrange the windows for us. We will be able to pass forms using the As Form declaration in Cascade()'s definition, as we will see in a moment. We can use that Sub procedure like this when the Cascade button (whose Name is Command1) is clicked, as follows:

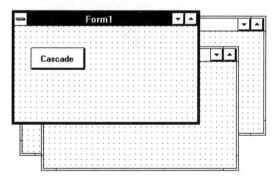

Figure 11.6. Our Cascade program template.

```
Sub Form_Load ()
    Form2.Show
```

```
        Form3.Show
        Form4.Show
End Sub

Sub Command1_Click ()
    Cascade Form1
    Cascade Form2
    Cascade Form3
    Cascade Form4
End Sub
        :
```

Note that we are passing the four forms, Form1 to Form4, to Cascade().
We can start Cascade() like this (here we are associating it with the startup
form, Form1, but we could put it in a module as well).

```
Sub Cascade (TheForm As Form)


End Sub
```

The form is passed as TheForm; now we are able to refer to it in Cascade()'s
code as TheForm. First, let's work on positioning the form. Because we
want to cascade the forms, we have to retain the upper left position of each
form between calls, so we can make those coordinates Static, as follows:

```
Sub Cascade (TheForm As Form)
    Static TopX, TopY As Integer
        :
End Sub
```

Now we can position TheForm like the foillowing:

```
Sub Cascade (TheForm As Form)
    Static TopX, TopY As Integer
    TheForm.Move TopX, TopY
        :
End Sub
```

Then we update the top left coordinates for the next form. To do that, we
need the height and width of the screen, which we can find with the
Screen object. The width of the screen is held in Screen.Width, and the
height in Screen.Height, so we can use them in the following way:

```
Sub Cascade (TheForm As Form)
    Static TopX, TopY As Integer
    TheForm.Move TopX, TopY
```

```
      TopX = TopX + Screen.Width / 10
      TopY = TopY + Screen.Height / 10
                :
End Sub
```

Finally, we change the form's size so that they will all be uniform, as follows:

```
Sub Cascade (TheForm As Form)
    Static TopX, TopY As Integer
    TheForm.Move TopX, TopY
    TopX = TopX + Screen.Width / 10
    TopY = TopY + Screen.Height / 10
    TheForm.Width = Screen.Width / 4
    TheForm.Height = Screen.Height / 4
End Sub
```

When you click the button labelled Cascade, the four windows will arrange themselves as in figure 11.7 because we are passing these forms, one after the next, to Cascade(), which moves and resizes them. Note that Form1 appears on top because it receives the focus when the Cascade() Sub procedure finishes, you can give another window the focus with the SetFocus method.

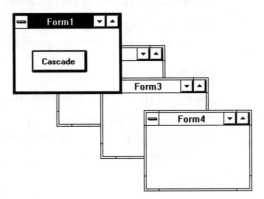

Figure 11.7. The Cascade example at work.

That's it for our cascade application, which appears in Listing 11.3 (Cascade.Mak on the diskette).

Listing 11.3. Cascade Program (Cascade.Mak on the diskette)

```
Form Form1 - - - - - - - - - - - - - - - - - - - - - - - - - - - - -
    Caption          =    "Form1"

CommandButton Command1
    Caption          =    "Cascade"

Form Form2 - - - - - - - - - - - - - - - - - - - - - - - - - - - - -
    Caption          =    "Form2"

Form Form3 - - - - - - - - - - - - - - - - - - - - - - - - - - - - -
    Caption          =    "Form3"

Form Form4 - - - - - - - - - - - - - - - - - - - - - - - - - - - - -
    Caption          =    "Form4"

Sub Cascade (TheForm As Form)
    Static TopX, TopY As Integer
    TheForm.Width = Screen.Width / 4
    TheForm.Height = Screen.Height / 4
    TheForm.Move TopX, TopY
    TopX = TopX + Screen.Width / 10
    TopY = TopY + Screen.Height / 10
End Sub

Sub Command1_Click ()
    Cascade Form1
    Cascade Form2
    Cascade Form3
    Cascade Form4
End Sub

Sub Form_Load ()
    Form2.Show
    Form3.Show
    Form4.Show
End Sub
```

Let's take a look at another example now. Let's say that we wanted a Sub procedure in a module that would change the Title of a form to "Hello." We might call this Sub procedure CallHello(), and start in the following way:

```
Sub CallHello ()
    :
```

We have to indicate what type of argument is passed to CallHello, and that type is Form, which appears as follows:

```
Sub CallHello (TheForm As Form)
    :
```

Now we are free to refer to the form that was passed to us as TheForm. If we want to change TheForm's Caption property to "Hello.", we could do it in the following way:

```
Sub CallHello (TheForm As Form)
    TheForm.Caption = "Hello."
End
```

At this point, we have to pass a form to CallHello(), and we might do that in a Form_Click() event, as follows:

```
Sub Form_Click()

End
```

Here, we want to pass the current form to CallHello() —but how do we do that? We cannot use a line like CallHello Form1, where Form1 is the name of our form, since many copies of Form1 may be running and Visual Basic won't know which one we mean. Instead, we can use a special keyword that comes with every form, which is Me, and which refers to the current form (in this sense, it acts like the this keyword in C++). To change the current form's Caption to "Hello." when it is clicked, then, we can do the following:

```
Sub Form_Click()
    CallHello Me
End
```

That is all there is to it. Now we can pass forms and refer to the current form as well.

A Visual Basic improvement.
The Me keyword was first introduced in Visual Basic 2.0.

Creating An Array of Forms

It may surprise you to learn that you can even set up an array of forms in Visual Basic. Let's say that we want to create such an array in Form1's Form_Click() event:

```
Sub Form_Click()

End
```

First, we set up an array of forms called TheForms() (using Static so they will stay around after we leave this event procedure), as follows:

```
Sub Form_Click()
    Static TheForms(5) As Form
:
End
```

In the case of forms, having declared the array does not mean they actually exist. We have to set aside memory and actually create them with the Set and New keywords, which allocate space for the elements in this array.

Now that we are about to create a new form, the question here is: what kind of type of form shall it be? We can't just give it type Form since there are so many types, sizes, colors, and so on of forms that Visual Basic wouldn't know what we mean. Instead, we can specify a type of form that already exists, such as Form1, and we do that in the following way:

```
Sub Form_Click()
    Static TheForms(5) As Form
        Set TheForms(1) = New Form1
:
End
```

Now TheForms(1) exists and it is a perfect copy of Form1. To display it, although it will overlap the current Form1 on the screen, as follows:

```
Sub Form_Click()
    Static TheForms(5) As Form
    Set TheForms(1) = New Form1
        TheForms(1).Show
End
```

That's it for advanced form handling for the moment. Let's go back to controls; there is more to advanced control handling to come. For example, we can also determine what the active control—for example, the one with the focus—is at any time.

Determining Which Control is Active

We have seen the Screen object before. The width and height of the screen are stored in the Screen.Width and Screen.Height properties. However, there is another useful property of the Screen object that we can look at here: Screen.ActiveControl. We saw this property briefly in the last chapter, but we will go into more detail here. This property holds the currently active control and we can refer to the properties of that control in the normal way. For example, if the active control was a text box, we can refer to its Text property like this: Screen.ActiveControl.Text.

Using Screen.ActiveControl is useful if you have a number of similar controls and have to make use of them outside their event procedures. For example, let's say that we had a number of text boxes in a window, as follows:

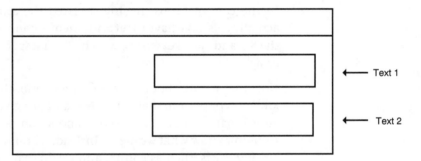

Next, we could add a File menu with two items in it: Copy—for example, Copy selected text to the clipboard—and Paste—for example, Paste text from the clipboard—in the following way:

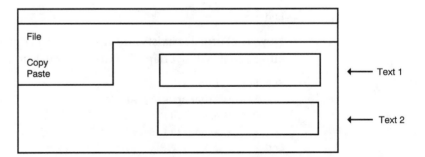

When the user marks text in one of the text boxes and selects, say, Copy from the file menu, they want to copy the selected text to the clipboard. However, we are not in an event procedure connected with either text box when the user selects the Copy item in the File menu, so we have to determine which text box the user wants us to select text from. That is done by checking which text box is currently active—which one has the focus. We can do that by checking Screen.ActiveControl.

This program might be, for example, part of a data input form for a hospital, keeping track of patient insurance, as follows:

```
┌─────────────────────────────────────────────────────┐
│                  Patient Data Form                    │
├─────────────────────────────────────────────────────┤
│    File                                               │
├─────────────────────────────────────────────────────┤
│                                                       │
│   Patient's        ┌──────────────────────────────┐  │
│   Name:            │                              │  │
│                    └──────────────────────────────┘  │
│                                                       │
│                                                       │
│   Insured's        ┌──────────────────────────────┐  │
│   Name             │                              │  │
│                    └──────────────────────────────┘  │
│                                                       │
└─────────────────────────────────────────────────────┘
```

Here we are keeping track of the name of the patient and the person whose name the insurance is in. Since that is frequently the same person, the Cut and Paste menu items can come in handy here—the user can clip the name from one box and copy it to the other.

To start, set up the window as shown in figure 11.8. Place a File menu in the window with two items in it: Copy and Paste, and with the Names CopyItem and PasteItem.

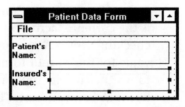

Figure 11.8. The patient data form example.

Now we can make these two menu items active. To make the CopyItem active, we only have to copy the text selected in the active text box to the clipboard using the SetText method as follows:

```
Sub CopyItem_Click ()
    Clipboard.SetText Screen.ActiveControl.SelText
End Sub
```

Next, we can make the Paste item active. When the user selects Paste, they want to paste the text now in the the clipboard into the active text box—for example, Screen.ActiveControl—and we can do that like this with the clipboard's GetText method, as follows:

```
Sub CopyItem_Click ()
    Clipboard.SetText Screen.ActiveControl.SelText
End Sub

Sub PasteItem_Click ()
    Screen.ActiveControl.SelText = Clipboard.GetText()
End Sub
```

Now we can cut and paste names in our Patient Data Form as in figure 11.9. That is all the effort it took—now our data entry form works (Clipper.Mak on the diskette).

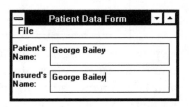

Figure 11.9. The patient data form at work.

Determining which form is active.

Besides Screen.ActiveControl, we can also determine which form is the currently active one—that is, which form has the focus—by checking Screen.ActiveForm. Screen.ActiveForm holds the Me value for the current form. In addition, you can check how many forms the current application has by checking the Forms objects like this: Forms.Count. The number of controls in a given form, say Form1, is stored in Form1.Count.

Affecting Tab Order

Another topic that we saw only briefly before concerns the tab order of the controls in a window. For example, let's say that we had three command buttons in a window, as follows:

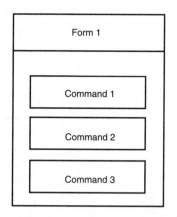

Because these controls were added in the order—Command1, Command2, Command3—they are arranged in a certain tab order. We have left Command1 as the default button (which you can change by setting another button's Default property to True), so when the program starts, Command1 will have the focus (and be surrounded by a thick black border). As is normal in Windows, the user can move to the next control in the tab order by pressing the Tab key; in this case, that's Command2. Pressing the Tab key again will move the focus to Command3, as in figure 11.10.

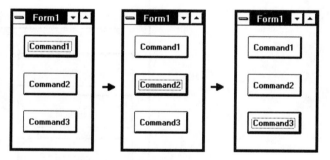

Figure 11.10. The normal Tab Order example.

Visual Basic keeps track of the order with the TabIndex property. In this example, the command buttons have these values for the TabIndex property, as follows:

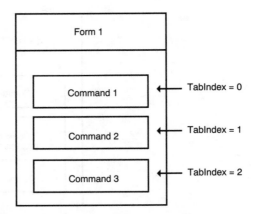

We can change this at run time by placing new values in the TabIndex properties. For example, when the user clicks Command1, we might execute the following code:

```
Sub Command1_Click()
    Command2.TabIndex = 2
    Command3.TabIndex = 1
End Sub
```

This changes the TabIndex properties in the following way:

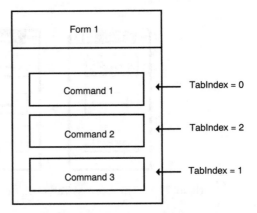

As we press the Tab key, the focus moves this way: from Command1 to Command3, then from Command3 to Command2 (then back to Command1 if the Tab key is pressed again), as in figure 11.11.

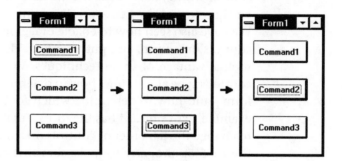

Figure 11.11. The new Tab Order example.

It is also worth noticing that if you want to remove one of the buttons (or any control) from the tab order—which means that it cannot receive the focus—you can set its TabStop property to False. Another way of doing this is to set its Enabled property to False, which grays out the button's caption, as shown in figure 11.12, and makes sure that the button can't receive the focus (we saw how to do this in Chapter 2).

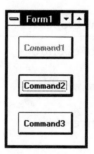

Figure 11.12. A disabled button.

That's it for our coverage of advanced control and form handling. In the next chapter, we will start connecting various Visual Basic programs to C and to the Windows libraries themselves—which will extend Visual Basic far beyond what is possible using Basic alone. Let's look into that now.

Summary

Here we have become familiar with some advanced methods of working with forms and controls. We have seen how to pass both forms and controls to procedures, and how to work with them in those procedures. We have also seen how to set up an array of forms (much like our earlier control arrays), how to use the Me keyword to refer to the current form, and how to find a passed control's parent form (with the Parent keyword). We have also seen how to enable dragging and dropping of Visual Basic controls on a form, and put together a desktop organizer program that took advantage of these techniques. We learned how to determine a control's type at run time, how to determine which control is active in a form—and how to determine which form is active on the screen—for example, active means has the focus. Finally, we finished by seeing how to change the tab order of controls on a form, and by seeing how to use the TabStop property to make sure that certain controls never get the focus.

New Events	Description
DragDrop Event	Occurs when a control is dropped on an object
DragOver	Occurs when a control is dragged over an object—for example, form or control).

New Properties	Description
ActiveControl	This property holds a form's curently active control—for example, the one with the focus. You can refer to its properties like this: Form1.ActiveControl.Text.
ActiveForm	Holds the currently active form on the screen or in an MDIForm. You can refer to its properties like this: Screen.ActiveForm.Caption.
DragIcon	Indicates the icon you want used as the user drags a control around.

New Properties	Description
DragMode	Set to Manual (0—the default) or Automatic (1) to control dragging of controls. If a control's DragMode is automatic, the user can drag it at any time (and the control does not respond to normal mouse input like clicks). If you use manual dragmode, the dragging is under your control with the Drag method.
TabStop	If true, means this control can receive the focus; if false, it cannot (True or False only).
Zorder	Determines the position of a control on or under overlapping controls. Setting a control's Zorder to 0 places it on top of the other controls it overlaps.

New Methods	Description
Drag Method	Controls dragging if control's DragMode is set to Manual (0); Control.Drag 0 cancels the drag operation, Control.Drag 1 starts it (moves the mouse cursor to the control and attaches the control to it) and Control.Drag 2 ends dragging. (Drag is only needed when a control's DragMode is manual, but you can use it if DragMode is Automatic (1) also).

12

Linking to C and to Windows Directly

I n this chapter, you will see how to connect your programs directly to C and to the Windows library functions. In particular, this chapter covers the following topics:

▼ Creating C library functions

▼ Declaring external functions in Visual Basic

▼ A screen-capture program

▼ Drawing on the screen outside a window

▼ Getting a Windows handle to the entire screen

▼ Copying sections of the screen outside a window

▼ Capturing mouse events, no matter where they occur in Windows

▼ How to write a dynamic link library

▼ Calling C code directly from Visual Basic

▼ Passing parameters to C functions

Here you will see a new program that extends Visual Basic by using the Windows library functions. As you will see, these library functions are available to all Windows programs, which means that they are available to your Visual Basic programs too. All you have to do is inform Visual Basic about the characteristics of the Windows library function(s) you will be using; then you are free to call them. You will use these functions to extend Visual Basic considerably. For example, you will write a screen-capture program here to do three things that normally are impossible in Visual Basic: capture mouse events that occur outside your window, draw on the screen outside your window, and copy graphics from areas outside your window. By developing these methods of interfacing to the Windows library functions, your programs can be extended immeasurably. In other words, if it can be done in Windows, your program will be able to do it. In addition, you will see how to connect your Visual Basic code to code you have written in C. Many people who program in C would like to use Visual Basic because developing programs is so easy, but they have great amounts of C code they would have to rewrite. Using the skills developed here, they will be able to interface Visual Basic directly to their C code.

You have gone far with Visual Basic—about as far as the language itself permits, in fact. At this point, you have seen almost all the keywords in action. The actual language is not designed to get extraordinarily complex. However, there is a great deal more to come. You can go beyond the language itself, extending it through its own external interface system.

You will look at two ways of using that interface system in this chapter: connecting to Windows system calls (that is, the system calls Visual Basic uses for creating programs), and connecting to your own C routines. You will not need any additional software to connect to Windows system calls, but you will need some additional software to connect your code to C. Visual Basic can link to external code as long as it is in .dll format—or dynamic link library format.

You will see more about this special Windows file format later in this chapter; it can become quite complex. Dynamic link libraries are especially set up so that Windows programs can call the routines inside them. They are called dynamic link libraries because these links between Windows programs and library routines are made at run time, not at the time the program's .exe file is made, as is the case with DOS programs. Many routines (about 2,000) are already in dynamic link libraries that come with Windows, and you can make use of them to extend Visual Basic. After you do that, you will see how to create your own dynamic link libraries, containing your own code (written in C) so that you can link your own external routines into Visual Basic.

No extra software is required to work with Windows system calls. Although you should have the documentation for those calls, it helps to have the Visual Basic Control Development Kit (CDK) because that kit includes the file Winapi.Txt, which will be very useful. The CDK—which comes with Visual Basic Professional Edition—also contains documentation for all Windows system calls. However, to create dynamic link libraries, as you will do in this chapter, you need a programming package capable of creating them. For clarity, we will use Microsoft QuickC for Windows—perhaps the easiest package to use these days to create dynamic link libraries. To follow along, you also need a knowledge of C and, preferably, experience in Windows programming. Note that if you use the Visual Basic CDK, you are expected to use C.

Linking to Windows System Calls

Visual Basic is surprisingly useful for a relatively simple language, primarily because its I/O capabilities (forms and controls) are so well developed and easy to use. However, general Windows programs can do some things that Visual Basic cannot do because of built-in limitations. For example, there is no provision in Visual Basic to receive mouse messages (MouseDown, for example) when the mouse clicks outside your program's window, but it is possible to do so in a general Windows program. However, it turns out that you can call the same Windows routines that Visual Basic calls, and through this mechanism, you can do (almost) anything a general Windows program can do.

A Screen-Capture Program

Now you will see an example of this, an example that goes beyond the bounds of conventional Visual Basic programming and does something useful at the same time. For instance, you can develop a screen-capture program that enables you not only to capture the whole Windows screen, but also to capture only a certain piece of it if you prefer. That is, you can move the mouse cursor to a location on the screen (inside or outside your program's window), and press and hold down the left mouse button, and stretch a rectangle around the region of the screen you want to capture. When you release the mouse button, that section of the screen should then appear inside your form. From there it can be transferred to disk with SavePicture or to the clipboard with Clipboard.SetData.

To do this, you have to do three things that normally are impossible in Visual Basic:

▼ Receive mouse input when the mouse cursor is outside your program's window.

▼ Stretch—draw—a rectangle anywhere on the screen, including stretching it wholly or partly outside your program's window.

▼ Copy an image—a bitmap—from any location on the screen into your form.

You might not be able to do that in standard Visual Basic, but by taking the initiative, you can extend it.

For example, a simple way to make sure that your program gets all mouse messages, even if the mouse is outside your program's window, is by calling the Windows SetCapture() function. This is the first external function you will see, so we will look at how to link it into your programs.

> **About available Windows documentation.**
> If you want to link to Windows system calls like this yourself, you should get a complete set of documentation that lists them all. The Windows interface is referred to as the Windows Application Programming Interface—the Windows API—and documentation covering it is available from many sources.

Declaring External Code

Say, for example, that you start with the modest goal of making the computer emit a beep whenever a mouse button goes down—no matter where the mouse cursor is on the screen. You can begin, as follows:

```
Sub Form_MouseDown (Button As Integer, Shift As Integer, X As
Single, Y As Single)

    Beep

End Sub
```

This certainly will get the computer to beep when a mouse button is pressed if the mouse cursor is inside your program's window. The next step is to capture mouse events even when they occur outside the window. You can do that with the Windows API function SetCapture(). This function takes one argument—hWnd, the Windows handle of your program's main window. Anticipating your use of such handles, Visual Basic provides them to you as properties. That is, your main window has a hWnd property; you just need to pass it to SetCapture() in the following Form_Load() procedure:

```
Sub Form_Load ()

    Dummy% = SetCapture(hWnd)

End Sub
```

This Windows handle, hWnd, is one of three types of handles available to Visual Basic programmers; it applies only to forms. The next one, hDC, is a handle to a device context. Whenever Windows produces graphics, it does so in a device context. Because Windows is expected to handle a large number of devices (screens, printers, memory bitmaps, and so on), it maintains information about each of them in a device context. Whenever you want to produce graphics using the Windows system calls, you have to set up a device context (using Windows calls) and get a device context handle. When you want to draw in that device context, you have to pass the handle to the Windows calls that do the drawing. Visual Basic objects designed expressly to handle graphics—forms, picture boxes, the printer—already have a predefined hDC (handle to a device context) property, and you can use that if you need to. In addition, the Image property of forms and picture boxes is actually the handle to the bitmaps contained in them. In Windows programming, this handle is usually given the name hBitmap, and you can pass that handle to Windows functions, if necessary.

So far, you are just passing the hWnd handle to SetCapture( ). After you do that, all mouse messages come to you, no matter where the mouse event took place. You might wonder about the x and y values that are passed to you in a MouseDown event when the following occurs:

```
Sub Form_MouseDown (Button As Integer, Shift As Integer, X As
Single, Y As Single)

    Beep

End Sub
```

It turns out that x and y are still defined with respect to the upper left corner of your program's client area, which means that you can get values larger than Form.ScaleWidth or Form.ScaleHeight. They can go negative as well when the mouse cursor is above or to the left of your window. To release the mouse cursor, you will use ReleaseCapture( ) later.

As it stands, however, you cannot run your program because Visual Basic has never heard of the SetCapture( ) function. If you try to run the program, it will tell you so. You have to indicate that SetCapture( ) is in one of the Windows dynamic link libraries, and further indicate which one. Three primary Windows dynamic link libraries come with Windows: User, GDI (Graphics Device Interface), and Kernel. You can determine which library holds what routines by checking the Windows documentation. Set Capture() is in the User dynamic link library, so you indicate that to Visual Basic with a declaration in a module you add to your program. It might begin in the following way:

```
Declare Function SetCapture Lib "User"
```

Next, you have to indicate that this function takes a Windows handle, hWnd, as an argument. Handles like this are integers, so you will be passing an integer argument. In addition, you will be passing arguments to routines that expect you to pass by value, not by reference. That is, the Windows routines you are interfacing to expect you to pass everything except arrays and structures by value (Windows uses the Pascal calling convention). The Visual Basic convention is to pass by reference, which means that you usually will have to place the ByVal keyword before arguments when you declare them, so that VB passes them by value, as follows:

```
Declare Function SetCapture Lib "User" (ByVal hWnd As Integer)
```

Finally, you have to indicate the return value of the function you are declaring. Because it is a function, it will have a return value; if it were a Sub procedure, it would have none. SetCapture returns the handle of the previous window that received all mouse input—an integer—or NULL (meaning zero, 0%) if there was none. The complete declaration appears as follows:

```
Declare Function SetCapture Lib "User" (ByVal hWnd As Integer) As Integer
```

Now you can run the program. When you do, you get a beep when the mouse button goes down, whether or not it is in your program's window. You have successfully captured the mouse. Declarations like the preceding one can get a little tedious to write, especially when they are long like the following one—for BitBlt()—which you will use later:

```
Declare Function BitBlt Lib "GDI" (ByVal hDestDC As Integer,
ByVal X As Integer, ByVal Y As Integer, ByVal nWidth As Integer,
ByVal nHeight As Integer, ByVal hSrcDC As Integer, ByVal XSrc As
Integer, ByVal YSrc As Integer, ByVal dwROP As Long) As Integer
```

Fortunately, the Windows system calls already are declared for us in a file named Winapi.Txt that comes with the VB Control Development Kit, the CDK. You can take the declaration of any Windows routine you want out of that file and place it into a module. If you do not have that file, you will have to create your own declarations from Windows programming documentation.

Starting the Screen-Capture Program

To implement your screen-capture program, give the program the name Screen Capture, as in figure 12.1. You will have to wait until the mouse goes down somewhere. When it does, you will want to store that location as an anchor point, as you did in your Paint program.

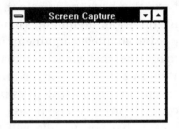

Figure 12.1. The screen-capture template.

You can set up a structure to hold this and other points in the module, like this (some Windows routines expect you to pass a point structure like the following, as you will see in a minute):

```
'Module -------------------------------

Type ApiPoint
   X As Integer
   Y As Integer
End Type


Declare Function SetCapture Lib "User" (ByVal hWnd As Integer) As Integer
```

Next, you set up a form-level variable of that type in the (declarations) part of Form1's (general) object, as follows:

```
'Form1 Form-level Declarations --------------------------------

Dim Anchor As ApiPoint
```

Now when the mouse button goes down like this in the MouseDown event, you can store the anchor point (that is, one corner of the screen section that you want to capture) like this:

```
Sub Form_MouseDown (Button As Integer, Shift As Integer, X As
Single, Y As Single)
```

```
                    Anchor.X = X
                    Anchor.Y = Y
                         :

        End Sub
```

Note, however, that these coordinates are with respect to the upper left corner of Form1's client area. To work with the whole screen, you will have to use screen coordinates, which are required by the Windows functions you will be calling. In addition, because most Windows screen manipulation uses pixel measurements, not twips, change Form1's ScaleMode to 3 (pixels). X and y will be reported to you in pixels, not twips, which is what you will need to pass to Windows.

Now that you are using pixels, there is an easy way to change from client area coordinates (called client coordinates) to screen coordinates. You can use the Windows ClientToScreen Sub procedure to pass the Anchor point structure (which is what ClientToScreen requires—a point structure), as follows:

```
Sub Form_MouseDown (Button As Integer, Shift As Integer, X As Single, Y As Single)

     Anchor.X = X
     Anchor.Y = Y
—    ClientToScreen hWnd, Anchor
             :

End Sub
```

> **Winapi.Txt has all the structures Windows requires.**
> The structures required by Windows calls—like the preceding Point structure—are defined in Winapi.Txt.

This converts the point stored in the Anchor structure to screen coordinates. Note that you also have to declare ClientToScreen in your module, as follows:

```
'Module ---------------------------------

Type ApiPoint
     X As Integer
     Y As Integer
End Type
```

```
Declare Function SetCapture Lib "User" (ByVal hWnd As Integer) As Integer
Declare Sub ClientToScreen Lib "User" (ByVal hWnd As Integer, lpPoint As ApiPoint)
```

You also might note that Windows routines expect you to pass structures to them by reference, not by value, so you omit the ByVal keyword when you declare the point structure here. You want to stretch a rectangle around the screen when the user moves the mouse cursor. To do that, you will have to draw a box from the Anchor point to the mouse cursor's current location, which you will store in a point structure named Current, as follows:

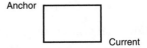

After you draw the box, you should store the current location in another structure, which you can call OldCurrent. In other words, the box you just drew extends from Anchor to OldCurrent, as follows:

When the mouse cursor moves, there will be a new Current position, so you want to redraw the box from Anchor to OldCurrent, erasing it, as follows:

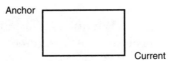

Next, you want to redraw the box from Anchor to the new Current, giving the impression of stretching it:

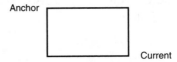

To begin, you can store the Anchor point in the OldCurrent structure when the mouse goes down, so that when you erase the box from Anchor to OldCurrent, you will have values to work with.

```
Sub Form_MouseDown (Button As Integer, Shift As Integer, X As Single, Y As Single)

        Anchor.X = X
        Anchor.Y = Y
        ClientToScreen hWnd, Anchor
        OldCurrent.X = Anchor.X
        OldCurrent.Y = Anchor.Y
                :

End Sub
```

You can define OldCurrent and Current as form-level variables, in the following way:

```
'Form1 Form-level Declarations ---------------------------------

        Dim Anchor As ApiPoint
        Dim Current As ApiPoint
        Dim OldCurrent As ApiPoint
        Dim CapFlag As Integer
```

Finally, now that the mouse button has gone down, you can start the capture process. Until now, the user could move the cursor freely around the screen; now you have to start stretching a rectangle from the anchor point. You indicate that by setting a flag named CapFlag, as follows:

```
Sub Form_MouseDown (Button As Integer, Shift As Integer, X As Single, Y As Single)

        Anchor.X = X
        Anchor.Y = Y
        ClientToScreen hWnd, Anchor
        OldCurrent.X = Anchor.X
        OldCurrent.Y = Anchor.Y
        CapFlag = -1          'True

End Sub
```

That flag is also a form-level variable, which you can store in the following way:

```
'Form1 Form-level Declarations ---------------------------------

        Dim Anchor As ApiPoint
        Dim Current As ApiPoint
```

```
Dim OldCurrent As ApiPoint
Dim CapFlag As Integer
```

Note that you should also initialize CapFlag to 0 when the form is first loaded, as follows:

```
Sub Form_Load ()

     Dummy% = SetCapture(hWnd)
     CapFlag = 0

End Sub
```

At this point, you have the mouse cursor in your control and you have started the capture process, which means that when you move the cursor around, you are supposed to stretch a rectangle around the screen. We will work on the MouseMove event first. To do that, you have to learn how to draw anywhere on the screen in Windows.

Accessing the Screen Directly in Windows

To stretch a rectangle around the screen, you will use the following MouseMove event:

```
Sub Form_MouseMove (Button As Integer, Shift As Integer, X As Single, Y As Single)

End Sub
```

Note that you should draw the rectangle only if you are capturing (that is, if the mouse button went down), which you can check with CapFlag, as follows:

```
Sub Form_MouseMove (Button As Integer, Shift As Integer, X As Single, Y As Single)

    If CapFlag Then
          :
    End If

End Sub
```

You begin by storing the current location of the mouse cursor in the Current point structure, and by converting it to screen coordinates with ClientToScreen, as follows:

```
Sub Form_MouseMove (Button As Integer, Shift As Integer, X As Single, Y As Single)
```

```
        If CapFlag Then
              Current.X = X
              Current.Y = Y
              ClientToScreen hWnd, Current
                    :
        End If

End Sub
```

Next, you have to draw the rectangle. To do any drawing with the Windows system calls, you need a device context handle. You cannot use the device context handle of your program's main window, because you would only be able to draw inside it. (That is why you are restricted to drawing inside it in VB.) Instead, you actually can get a device context handle to the entire screen by using the CreateDC() function, which works in the following way:

```
Declare Function CreateDC Lib "GDI" (ByVal lpDriverName As String, ByVal
lpDeviceName As Any, ByVal lpOutPut As Any, ByVal lpInitData As Any) As
Integer
```

The first argument, lpDriverName, of type String, is supposed to carry the DOS filename of the device driver for the new device you are trying to create a device context for. Actually, it is a long pointer to a string (in C, a pointer holds the address of the object pointed to, not the object itself). It turns out that when you use ByVal with a string argument, VB automatically passes the string, using conventions appropriate for a C-style string, so you are set: all you have to do is put the name of a device driver into a string and pass that. Ordinarily, you use CreateDC() to create device contexts for devices not originally designed into Windows if the manufacturer supplies a Windows device driver file. However, Windows already has a few default device drivers here, one of which is "Display." If you pass "Display" as lpDriverName, you will get a device context handle to the entire screen, which is exactly what you want. When you have a device context to the screen (call it hDCScreen), you can draw anywhere on it.

The remaining arguments are these: lpDeviceName is normally a pointer to a string that holds the name of the device ("AllPro LaserWriter," for example); lpOutPut is normally a pointer to a string that specifies the output device (a DOS filename or a physical device); lpInitData is a long pointer to a device initialization data structure. Because you are using a default device name ("Display"), you will pass NULL pointers (that is, 0&, because long pointers are two words long), as indicated by the Windows documentation for these three arguments. When you need to pass a pointer to a Windows function, it will often accept a NULL pointer instead, which usually means that you want to use a default value or that the argument does not apply. All this means that you want to use CreateDC() as follows:

```
hDCScreen = CreateDC("Display", NULL, NULL, NULL)
```

You have to be a little careful when passing NULL pointers; to see why, let's take a look at each of the arguments. You might notice that the first argument, lpDriverName, is of type String. The Windows routines expect strings to be passed in ASCIIZ format—that is, as ASCII strings with a terminating 0 byte (the last byte is simply 0, not Chr$(0)). As mentioned, the ByVal argument, used with As String, indicates to Visual Basic that it should pass the string as an ASCIIZ (C style) string.

> **About .dll files written for Visual Basic.**
> If you come across a .dll file specially written for Visual Basic (not C) that accepts strings, you do not have to pass them using the ByVal keyword. Just declare them As String and Visual Basic will pass them as Visual Basic strings.

And you might notice that the remaining arguments are passed As Any. This special declaration removes type restrictions on those arguments and enables you to pass NULL pointers. Originally, these arguments were all declared As String (which is the way you will find them in Winapi.Txt).

```
Declare Function CreateDC Lib "GDI" (ByVal lpDriverName As String,
ByVal lpDeviceName As String, ByVal lpOutPut As String, ByVal
lpInitData As String) As Integer
```

However, if you want to pass a pointer as a NULL pointer, you have to declare the corresponding argument As Any in Visual Basic (if you left it As String and passed a 0 value, then VB, expecting a string, would generate an error).

```
Declare Function CreateDC Lib "GDI" (ByVal lpDriverName As String,
ByVal lpDeviceName As Any, ByVal lpOutPut As Any, ByVal lpInitData As
Any) As Integer
```

That is the way to handle NULL pointers. In addition, you have to pass the actual argument—0&—with ByVal when you use it so that the 0& argument is passed directly. Now that you have removed the type restrictions, you can use CreateDC() in the following way:

```
Sub Form_MouseMove (Button As Integer, Shift As Integer, X As Single, Y
As Single)

    Dim hDCScreen As Integer

    If CapFlag Then
        Current.X = X
        Current.Y = Y
        ClientToScreen hWnd, Current
        hDCScreen = CreateDC("DISPLAY", ByVal 0&, ByVal 0&, ByVal 0&)
            :
```

The only other data item to be careful of when passing to Windows calls are arrays. In Visual Basic, you can pass an entire array to a Sub procedure or Function by including a set of empty parentheses after the array name, but you cannot do that when calling a Windows procedure. In C, you pass a pointer to an array, not the whole thing. VB allows you to do this by passing the first element of the array by reference (do not use ByVal), like this: WinResult% = WinFunc(my_array(1)). In other words, the Windows routine will get what it needs (a pointer to the array) if you pass the first element of the array by reference instead of by value. (Passing by reference means passing by pointer—that is, by address.) You can pass properties by value (declare the argument with ByVal), but note that you cannot pass forms or controls. Having covered strings, handles, and NULL pointers, you are in good shape. A summary is in table 12.1. Note that if you have the file Winapi.Txt, you will not need to worry about declarations because they are all supplied for you.

Table 12.1. Window API Declaration Conventions

To Pass	Use this Declaration
Arrays	Pass first array element
Controls	Cannot be passed to the Win API
Forms	Cannot be passed to the Win API
Handles	ByVal Integer
Numbers	ByVal NumberType (ByVal Integer/Long/ Single/Etc)
NULL Pointers	As Any (And pass ByVal &0 in the call)
Properties	ByVal PropertyName
Strings	ByVal String
Win Structs	As StructName (defined in Winapi.Txt: for example, As ApiPoint)

At this point, then, you also should add CreateDC() to your module, as follows:

```
'Module ---------------------------------

Type ApiPoint
     X As Integer
     Y As Integer
End Type


Declare Function SetCapture Lib "User" (ByVal hWnd As Integer) As Integer
Declare Sub ClientToScreen Lib "User" (ByVal hWnd As Integer, lpPoint As ApiPoint)
Declare Function CreateDC Lib "GDI" (ByVal lpDriverName As String,
          ByVal lpDeviceName As Any, ByVal lpOutPut As Any,
          ByVal lpInitData As Any) As Integer
```

Now you have your handle to the screen, hDCScreen. Windows functions that draw or manipulate graphics images demand that you pass a device context handle to them every time you use them (because you can have many such device contexts open in Windows). In fact, you will use hDCScreen right away. Here, in the MouseMove event, you are supposed to allow the user to stretch a rectangle across the screen, enclosing the area you capture.

As you know, to draw such a rectangle you must first erase the previous rectangle (from the Anchor point to the OldCurrent point) and then draw a new one (from the Anchor point to the new Current point). To make sure that you can erase the previous lines simply by drawing over them, you can make the drawing mode Not Pen. (As defined in Chapter 6, Not Pen makes the pen draw the inverse of what is on the screen.) There is one pen per device context. As you might suspect, all Visual Basic objects that have pens are really Windows device contexts. You can change the one in your screen device context to the Not Pen with SetROP2(), whose name means "set binary raster operation." By passing a value of 6 (this and other values may be found in the Windows documentation) to SetROP2(), you indicate that you want to use the Not Pen for this device context, as follows:

```
Sub Form_MouseMove (Button As Integer, Shift As Integer, X As Single, Y As Single)

    Dim hDCScreen As Integer

    If CapFlag Then
        Current.X = X
        Current.Y = Y
        ClientToScreen hWnd, Current
        hDCScreen = CreateDC("DISPLAY", ByVal 0&, ByVal 0&, ByVal 0&)
        Dummy% = SetROP2(hDCScreen, 6)
                :
    End If
End Sub
```

Then you add SetROP2() to your module, as follows:

```
'Module --------------------------------

Type ApiPoint
        X As Integer
        Y As Integer
End Type
```

```
Declare Function SetCapture Lib "User" (ByVal hWnd As Integer) As Integer
Declare Sub ClientToScreen Lib "User" (ByVal hWnd As Integer, lpPoint As ApiPoint)
Declare Function CreateDC Lib "GDI" (ByVal lpDriverName As String, ByVal
lpDeviceName As Any, ByVal lpOutPut As Any, ByVal lpInitData As Any) As Integer
Declare Function SetROP2 Lib "GDI" (ByVal hDC As Integer,
    ByVal nDrawMode As Integer) As Integer
```

SetROP2() returns the current value of the device context's pen. It is usually a good idea to save that value before changing to a new pen, so that you can change back afterwards (that is, some other part of the program may not expect a Not Pen here). Here, however, because you are going to destroy this device context before leaving this event procedure, you just place the old pen value in a dummy variable and continue. Next, you should erase the old box that goes from (Anchor.X, Anchor.Y) to (OldCurrent.X, OldCurrent.Y). To do that, you move to the anchor point with the Windows function MoveTo(), which works like setting the CurrentX and CurrentY properties of an object (in fact, when you set those properties, that is exactly what Visual Basic is doing). Because all your points are already stored in screen coordinates, you can move to the anchor point in the following way:

```
Sub Form_MouseMove (Button As Integer, Shift As Integer, X As Single, Y As Single)

    Dim hDCScreen As Integer

    If CapFlag Then
        Current.X = X
        Current.Y = Y
        ClientToScreen hWnd, Current
        hDCScreen = CreateDC("DISPLAY", ByVal 0&, ByVal 0&, ByVal 0&)
        Dummy% = SetROP2(hDCScreen, 6)
        Dummy2& = MoveTo(hDCScreen, Anchor.X, Anchor.Y)
            :
    End If

End Sub
```

And you add MoveTo() to the module, as follows:

```
'Module ---------------------------------

Type ApiPoint
```

```
        X As Integer
        Y As Integer
    End Type


    Declare Function SetCapture Lib "User" (ByVal hWnd As Integer) As Integer
            :
            :
    Declare Function MoveTo Lib "GDI" (ByVal hDC As Integer,
            ByVal X As Integer, ByVal Y As Integer) As Long
```

MoveTo() returns a long value—two 16-bit words—whose upper word holds the old y coordinate and whose lower word holds the previous x coordinate. Again, you place that value in a dummy variable and continue. The next step is to erase the box, which you do simply by drawing it with Not Pen, using the Windows LineTo() function, as follows:

```
Sub Form_MouseMove (Button As Integer, Shift As Integer, X As Single, Y As Single)

    Dim hDCScreen As Integer

    If CapFlag Then
        Current.X = X
        Current.Y = Y
        ClientToScreen hWnd, Current
        hDCScreen = CreateDC("DISPLAY", ByVal 0&, ByVal 0&, ByVal 0&)
        Dummy% = SetROP2(hDCScreen, 6)
        Dummy2& = MoveTo(hDCScreen, Anchor.X, Anchor.
        Dummy% = LineTo(hDCScreen, OldCurrent.X, Anchor.Y)
        Dummy% = LineTo(hDCScreen, OldCurrent.X, OldCurrent.Y)
        Dummy% = LineTo(hDCScreen, Anchor.X, OldCurrent.Y)
        Dummy% = LineTo(hDCScreen, Anchor.X, Anchor.Y)
            :
    End If

End Sub
```

And you add LineTo() to your module, as follows:

```
    'Module --------------------------------

    Type ApiPoint
        X As Integer
        Y As Integer
    End Type
```

```
Declare Function SetCapture Lib "User" (ByVal hWnd As Integer) As Integer
        :
        :
Declare Function LineTo Lib "GDI" (ByVal hDC As Integer,
        ByVal X As Integer, ByVal Y As Integer) As Integer
```

Now that the old box from Anchor to OldCurrent has been erased, you update the OldCurrent point (so that the next time the mouse moves, you will erase the box you are about to draw) in the following way:

```
Sub Form_MouseMove (Button As Integer, Shift As Integer, X As Single, Y As Single)

    Dim hDCScreen As Integer

    If CapFlag Then
        Current.X = X
        Current.Y = Y
        ClientToScreen hWnd, Current
        hDCScreen = CreateDC("DISPLAY", ByVal 0&, ByVal 0&, ByVal 0&)
        Dummy% = SetROP2(hDCScreen, 6)
        Dummy2& = MoveTo(hDCScreen, Anchor.X, Anchor.Y)
        Dummy% = LineTo(hDCScreen, OldCurrent.X, Anchor.Y)
        Dummy% = LineTo(hDCScreen, OldCurrent.X, OldCurrent.Y)
        Dummy% = LineTo(hDCScreen, Anchor.X, OldCurrent.Y)
        Dummy% = LineTo(hDCScreen, Anchor.X, Anchor.Y)
        OldCurrent.X = Current.X
        OldCurrent.Y = Current.Y
            :
    End If

End Sub
```

And now you can draw the new box from Anchor to Current in the following way:

```
Sub Form_MouseMove (Button As Integer, Shift As Integer, X As Single, Y As Single)

    Dim hDCScreen As Integer

    If CapFlag Then
            :
            :
```

```
            OldCurrent.X = Current.X
            OldCurrent.Y = Current.Y
            Dummy2& = MoveTo(hDCScreen, Anchor.X, Anchor.Y)
            Dummy% = LineTo(hDCScreen, Current.X, Anchor.Y)
            Dummy% = LineTo(hDCScreen, Current.X, Current.Y)
            Dummy% = LineTo(hDCScreen, Anchor.X, Current.Y)
            Dummy% = LineTo(hDCScreen, Anchor.X, Anchor.Y)
                :
        End If
    End Sub
```

The final step is to destroy the screen device context, now that you no longer need it; you can do that with DeleteDC(), as follows:

```
Sub Form_MouseMove (Button As Integer, Shift As Integer, X As Single, Y As Single)

    Dim hDCScreen As Integer

    If CapFlag Then
        Current.X = X
        Current.Y = Y
        ClientToScreen hWnd, Current
        hDCScreen = CreateDC("DISPLAY", ByVal 0&, ByVal 0&, ByVal 0&)
        Dummy% = SetROP2(hDCScreen, 6)
        Dummy2& = MoveTo(hDCScreen, Anchor.X, Anchor.Y)
        Dummy% = LineTo(hDCScreen, OldCurrent.X, Anchor.Y)
        Dummy% = LineTo(hDCScreen, OldCurrent.X, OldCurrent.Y)
        Dummy% = LineTo(hDCScreen, Anchor.X, OldCurrent.Y)
        Dummy% = LineTo(hDCScreen, Anchor.X, Anchor.Y)
        OldCurrent.X = Current.X
        OldCurrent.Y = Current.Y
        Dummy2& = MoveTo(hDCScreen, Anchor.X, Anchor.Y)
        Dummy% = LineTo(hDCScreen, Current.X, Anchor.Y)
        Dummy% = LineTo(hDCScreen, Current.X, Current.Y)
        Dummy% = LineTo(hDCScreen, Anchor.X, Current.Y)
        Dummy% = LineTo(hDCScreen, Anchor.X, Anchor.Y)
        Dummy% = DeleteDC(hDCScreen)
    End If

End Sub
```

> **It is important to deallocate Windows handles.**
> If your Windows programs crash, one reason may be that you are
> not deallocating handles. If you do not delete the device context
> with DeleteDC() at the end of MouseMove() and keep allocating
> new device context handles when you enter the MouseMove
> event, Windows soon will run out of handle space in memory
> and everything will come to a halt.

And, of course, you add DeleteDC() to your module as well.

```
'Module --------------------------------

Type ApiPoint
     X As Integer
     Y As Integer
End Type

Declare Function SetCapture Lib "User" (ByVal hWnd As Integer) As Integer
        :
        :
Declare Function DeleteDC Lib "GDI" (ByVal hDC As Integer) As Integer
```

At this point, you can draw rectangles on the screen just by running your
program, pressing the mouse button at some screen location, and dragging the resulting rectangle, as shown in figure 12.2.

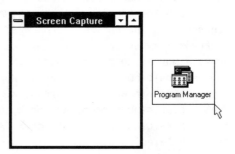

Figure 12.2. How to draw anywhere on the screen.

Now you are prepared to start work on the MouseUp event. When the user
releases the mouse button, he or she wants to capture the screen image
that appears in the rectangle bounded by Anchor and Current. To do that,
you use the BitBlt() function, which enables you to copy bitmaps.

The first thing in the MouseUp event is to check whether you are capturing screen data—that is whether CapFlag is True. You check that in the following way:

```
Sub Form_MouseUp (Button As Integer, Shift As Integer, X As Single, Y As Single)

    If CapFlag Then
        :
    End If

End Sub
```

If CapFlag is True, you are expected to capture the image, ending the capture process. You can set CapFlag to False and release the mouse cursor (you won't need mouse events any longer) using ReleaseCapture( ), in the following way:

```
Sub Form_MouseUp (Button As Integer, Shift As Integer, X As Single, Y As Single)

    If CapFlag Then
        ReleaseCapture
        CapFlag = 0
        :
    End If

End Sub
```

You also have to add ReleaseCapture() to your module, as follows:

```
'Module ----------------------------------

Type ApiPoint
        X As Integer
        Y As Integer
End Type
Declare Function SetCapture Lib "User" (ByVal hWnd As Integer) As Integer
        :
        :
Declare Sub ReleaseCapture Lib "User" ()
```

Next, you update the current point and get a device context handle to the screen again, as follows:

```
Sub Form_MouseUp (Button As Integer, Shift As Integer, X As Single, Y As Single)
```

```
        Dim hDCScreen As Integer

    If CapFlag Then
        ReleaseCapture
        CapFlag = 0
        Current.X = X
        Current.Y = Y
        ClientToScreen hWnd, Current
        hDCScreen = CreateDC("DISPLAY", ByVal 0&, ByVal 0&, ByVal 0&)
            :
    End If

End Sub
```

Now you have to erase the last rectangle left on the screen as a result of the last MouseMove event, in the following way:

```
Sub Form_MouseUp (Button As Integer, Shift As Integer, X As Single, Y As Single)

    Dim hDCScreen As Integer

    If CapFlag Then
        ReleaseCapture
        CapFlag = 0
        Current.X = X
        Current.Y = Y
        ClientToScreen hWnd, Current
        hDCScreen = CreateDC("DISPLAY", ByVal 0&, ByVal 0&, ByVal 0&)
        Dummy% = SetROP2(hDCScreen, 6)
        Dummy2& = MoveTo(hDCScreen, Anchor.X, Anchor.Y)
        Dummy% = LineTo(hDCScreen, OldCurrent.X, Anchor.Y)
        Dummy% = LineTo(hDCScreen, OldCurrent.X, OldCurrent.Y)
        Dummy% = LineTo(hDCScreen, Anchor.X, OldCurrent.Y)
        Dummy% = LineTo(hDCScreen, Anchor.X, Anchor.Y)
            :
    End If

End Sub
```

Now you are ready to copy the screen image to your form, using BitBlt(). To use BitBlt(), you have to know the width of the bitmap you want to copy—Abs(Anchor.X - Current.X)—and the height—Abs(Anchor.Y - Current.Y). In addition, you have to know its upper left coordinate in screen coordinates. That appears as follows:

```
Sub Form_MouseUp (Button As Integer, Shift As Integer, X As Single, Y As Single)
```

Peter Norton's Visual Basic for Windows, Third Edition, Covering Release 3.0

```
    Dim hDCScreen As Integer

If CapFlag Then
    ReleaseCapture
    CapFlag = 0
    Current.X = X
    Current.Y = Y
    ClientToScreen hWnd, Current
    hDCScreen = CreateDC("DISPLAY", ByVal 0&, ByVal 0&, ByVal 0&)
    Dummy% = SetROP2(hDCScreen, 6)
    Dummy2& = MoveTo(hDCScreen, Anchor.X, Anchor.Y)
    Dummy% = LineTo(hDCScreen, OldCurrent.X, Anchor.Y)
    Dummy% = LineTo(hDCScreen, OldCurrent.X, OldCurrent.Y)
    Dummy% = LineTo(hDCScreen, Anchor.X, OldCurrent.Y)
    Dummy% = LineTo(hDCScreen, Anchor.X, Anchor.Y)
    MapWidth% = Abs(Anchor.X - Current.X)
    MapHeight% = Abs(Anchor.Y - Current.Y)
    If Anchor.X < Current.X Then
        UpperLeftX% = Anchor.X
    Else
        UpperLeftX% = Current.X
    End If
    If Anchor.Y < Current.Y Then
        UpperLeftY% = Anchor.Y
    Else
        UpperLeftY% = Current.Y
    End If
    :
End If

End Sub
```

The last thing to do is to use BitBlt(), which takes arguments in the following way:

```
Declare Function BitBlt Lib "GDI" (ByVal hDestDC As Integer, ByVal X
As Integer, ByVal Y As Integer, ByVal nWidth As Integer, ByVal nHeight
As Integer, ByVal hSrcDC As Integer, ByVal XSrc As Integer, ByVal YSrc
As Integer, ByVal dwROP As Long) As Integer
```

In order, these arguments refer to the destination device context handle for the copied bitmap (which will simply be the hDC property of your form, so that the bitmap will appear there); the new (x, y) location of the bitmap in the destination (which you can make (0, 0)—that is, the upper left of the form); the width and height of the bitmap; the source device context handle (hDCScreen); the location of the bitmap in the source device context; and a final argument that indicates what you want done with the bitmap (you will pass a value of &HCC0020, which indicates that you want the bitmap copied from the source to the destination—this value also is stored as the constant SRCCOPY in Winapi.Txt). Finally, you delete the screen device context, as follows:

```
Sub Form_MouseUp (Button As Integer, Shift As Integer, X As Single, Y As Single)

    Dim hDCScreen As Integer

    If CapFlag Then
        ReleaseCapture
        CapFlag = 0
        Current.X = X
        Current.Y = Y
        ClientToScreen hWnd, Current
        hDCScreen = CreateDC("DISPLAY", ByVal 0&, ByVal 0&, ByVal 0&)
        Dummy% = SetROP2(hDCScreen, 6)
        Dummy2& = MoveTo(hDCScreen, Anchor.X, Anchor.Y)
        Dummy% = LineTo(hDCScreen, OldCurrent.X, Anchor.Y)
        Dummy% = LineTo(hDCScreen, OldCurrent.X, OldCurrent.Y)
        Dummy% = LineTo(hDCScreen, Anchor.X, OldCurrent.Y)
        Dummy% = LineTo(hDCScreen, Anchor.X, Anchor.Y)
        MapWidth% = Abs(Anchor.X - Current.X)
        MapHeight% = Abs(Anchor.Y - Current.Y)
        If Anchor.X < Current.X Then
            UpperLeftX% = Anchor.X
        Else
            UpperLeftX% = Current.X
        End If
        If Anchor.Y < Current.Y Then
            UpperLeftY% = Anchor.Y
        Else
            UpperLeftY% = Current.Y
        End If
        Dummy% = BitBlt(hDC, 0, 0, MapWidth%, MapHeight%, hDCScreen,
          UpperLeftX%, UpperLeftY%, &HCC0020)
        Dummy% = DeleteDC(hDCScreen)
    End If

End Sub
```

The final listing appears in listing 12.1 (Capture.Mak on the Disk). Figure 12.3 shows your screen-capture program in operation. It is a success. You can capture any rectangular region of the screen with it.

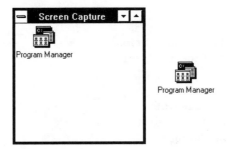

Figure 12.3. The screen-capture program at work.

Listing 12.1. Screen-capture Program (Capture.Mak on the Disk)

```
Form Form1 --------------------------------
Caption          =            "Screen Capture"


Capture.Bas -----------------------------


Type ApiPoint
     X As Integer
     Y As Integer
End Type


Declare Function SetCapture Lib "User" (ByVal hWnd As Integer) As Integer
Declare Sub ClientToScreen Lib "User" (ByVal hWnd As Integer, lpPoint As ApiPoint)
Declare Function CreateDC Lib "GDI" (ByVal lpDriverName As String, ByVal
lpDeviceName As Any, ByVal lpOutPut As Any, ByVal lpInitData As Any) As Integer
Declare Function SetROP2 Lib "GDI" (ByVal hDC As Integer, ByVal nDrawMode As
Integer) As Integer
Declare Function MoveTo Lib "GDI" (ByVal hDC As Integer, ByVal X As Integer, ByVal
Y As Integer) As Long
Declare Function LineTo Lib "GDI" (ByVal hDC As Integer, ByVal X As Integer, ByVal
Y As Integer) As Integer
Declare Function DeleteDC Lib "GDI" (ByVal hDC As Integer) As Integer
Declare Sub ReleaseCapture Lib "User" ()
Declare Function BitBlt Lib "GDI" (ByVal hDestDC As Integer, ByVal X As Integer,
ByVal Y As Integer, ByVal nWidth As Integer, ByVal nHeight As Integer, ByVal
```

continues

Listing 12.1. continued

```
hSrcDC As Integer, ByVal XSrc As Integer, ByVal YSrc As Integer, ByVal dwROP As
Long) As Integer


    'Form1 Form-level Declarations --------------------------------------
    'Set Form ScaleMode to Pixel

    Dim Anchor As ApiPoint
    Dim Current As ApiPoint
    Dim OldCurrent As ApiPoint
    Dim CapFlag As Integer

    'Form1 ---------------------------------------

    Sub Form_Load ()

        Dummy% = SetCapture(hWnd)
        CapFlag = 0

    End Sub

    Sub Form_MouseDown (Button As Integer, Shift As Integer, X As Single, Y As Single)

        Anchor.X = X
        Anchor.Y = Y
        ClientToScreen hWnd, Anchor
        OldCurrent.X = Anchor.X
        OldCurrent.Y = Anchor.Y
        CapFlag = -1          'True

    End Sub

    Sub Form_MouseMove (Button As Integer, Shift As Integer, X As Single, Y As Single)

        Dim hDCScreen As Integer

        If CapFlag Then
            Current.X = X
            Current.Y = Y
            hDCScreen = CreateDC("DISPLAY", ByVal 0&, ByVal 0&, ByVal 0&)
            ClientToScreen hWnd, Current
            Dummy% = SetROP2(hDCScreen, 6)
```

Peter Norton's Visual Basic for Windows, Third Edition, Covering Release 3.0

```
        Dummy2& = MoveTo(hDCScreen, Anchor.X, Anchor.Y)
        Dummy% = LineTo(hDCScreen, OldCurrent.X, Anchor.Y)
        Dummy% = LineTo(hDCScreen, OldCurrent.X, OldCurrent.Y)
        Dummy% = LineTo(hDCScreen, Anchor.X, OldCurrent.Y)
        Dummy% = LineTo(hDCScreen, Anchor.X, Anchor.Y)
        OldCurrent.X = Current.X
        OldCurrent.Y = Current.Y
        Dummy2& = MoveTo(hDCScreen, Anchor.X, Anchor.Y)
        Dummy% = LineTo(hDCScreen, Current.X, Anchor.Y)
        Dummy% = LineTo(hDCScreen, Current.X, Current.Y)
        Dummy% = LineTo(hDCScreen, Anchor.X, Current.Y)
        Dummy% = LineTo(hDCScreen, Anchor.X, Anchor.Y)
        Dummy% = DeleteDC(hDCScreen)
    End If

End Sub

Sub Form_MouseUp (Button As Integer, Shift As Integer, X As Single, Y As Single)

    Dim hDCScreen As Integer

    If CapFlag Then
        ReleaseCapture
        CapFlag = 0
        Current.X = X
        Current.Y = Y
        ClientToScreen hWnd, Current
        hDCScreen = CreateDC("DISPLAY", ByVal 0&, ByVal 0&, ByVal 0&)
        Dummy% = SetROP2(hDCScreen, 6)
        Dummy2& = MoveTo(hDCScreen, Anchor.X, Anchor.Y)
        Dummy% = LineTo(hDCScreen, OldCurrent.X, Anchor.Y)
        Dummy% = LineTo(hDCScreen, OldCurrent.X, OldCurrent.Y)
        Dummy% = LineTo(hDCScreen, Anchor.X, OldCurrent.Y)
        Dummy% = LineTo(hDCScreen, Anchor.X, Anchor.Y)
        MapWidth% = Abs(Anchor.X - Current.X)
        MapHeight% = Abs(Anchor.Y - Current.Y)
        If Anchor.X < Current.X Then
            UpperLeftX% = Anchor.X
        Else
            UpperLeftX% = Current.X
        End If
        If Anchor.Y < Current.Y Then
            UpperLeftY% = Anchor.Y
```

continues

Listing 12.1. continued

```
    Else
            UpperLeftY% = Current.Y
        End If
        Dummy% = BitBlt(hDC, 0, 0, MapWidth%, MapHeight%, hDCScreen,
        UpperLeftX%, UpperLeftY%, &HCC0020)
        Dummy% = DeleteDC(hDCScreen)
    End If

End Sub
```

That's it for our exploration of connecting VB to the Windows system calls. Next, you will see how to connect Visual Basic to C.

Connecting Visual Basic to C

You can, of course, create your own dynamic link libraries. This is especially useful because it enables you to link C code you already have into Visual Basic. In the remainder of this chapter, you will see how to do this by constructing a sample C function named Cinterface() (because you can use it as a C interface template, replacing its code with your own). To do that, you will use Microsoft's QuickC for Windows and keep the C programming to a minimum. Accordingly, the function CInterface() will only do something minimal. You will have it accept a long integer argument and return the same long integer after incrementing it by one. After the C interface is all set up, of course, you can use your own C code for the body of this function.

To create a dynamic link library file, the C source file needs only three parts: a LibMain() function (note that in C, unlike Visual Basic, all procedures are functions) that performs whatever initialization you need; the externally callable functions that make up the library itself (here, just the function CInterface(); and, a Windows exit procedure, whose name must be WEP(). In fact, a default WEP() function is already in the Windows library; later, you will specify that you want to use that function. That leaves you with only two functions to write: WinMain() and CInterface(). You can put them in a file named Cuser.C and work on that file in QuickC for Windows.

To start creating Cuser.C (and therefore your .dll file, Cuser.Dll), you must include the C header file, Windows.H. You can do that with the C preprocessor statement, as follows:

```
#include <Windows.H>
```

Next, the LibMain() function accepts these arguments, as follows:

```
#include <Windows.H>

int FAR PASCAL LibMain(HANDLE hModule, WORD wDataSeg,
        WORD cbHeapSize, LPSTR lpszCmdLine)
{

}
```

In LibMain(), you can perform initialization for the rest of the functions in your dynamic link library (treat it something like a Form_Load event), because it is called when the library is first loaded. To indicate that the initialization went successfully, you return a value of TRUE (which has the value 1 in QuickC for Windows, not -1). Because you do not have to perform any initialization here, you will just return a value of TRUE.

```
#include <Windows.H>

int FAR PASCAL LibMain(HANDLE hModule, WORD wDataSeg,
        WORD cbHeapSize, LPSTR lpszCmdLine)
{
    return TRUE;
}
```

Next, you have to set up your function CInterface(). This function is supposed to take a long argument (call it arg1) and pass a long back, so we set it up in the following way:

```
#include <Windows.H>

int FAR PASCAL LibMain(HANDLE hModule, WORD wDataSeg,
        WORD cbHeapSize, LPSTR lpszCmdLine)
{
    return TRUE;
}

long FAR PASCAL CInterface(long arg1)
{

}
```

Your goal is simply to return arg1 + 1, which you can do in the following way:

```
#include <Windows.H>

int FAR PASCAL LibMain(HANDLE hModule, WORD wDataSeg,
        WORD cbHeapSize, LPSTR lpszCmdLine)
{
    return TRUE;
}


long FAR PASCAL CInterface(long arg1)
{
    return (arg1+1);
}
```

And you are done with Cuser.C, which appears in listing 12.2; that is all the C code you need for a dynamic link library. (You will see a great deal more C in Chapter 14.) Note that real library functions are supposed to be bulletproof; in a real library function, you would have to check whether adding 1 to arg1 would cause an overflow and, if so, indicate that in some fashion.

 Listing 12.2. Cuser.C

```
#include <Windows.H>

int FAR PASCAL LibMain(HANDLE hModule, WORD wDataSeg,
        WORD cbHeapSize, LPSTR lpszCmdLine)
{
   return TRUE;
}

long FAR PASCAL CInterface(long arg1)
{
    return (arg1+1);
}
```

QuickC for Windows also needs a .def file to create a working dynamic link library (.dll) file. In that file, Cuser.Def, you indicate with the following lines that you want to create a dynamic link library which can be used in Windows, will operate in protected mode, as follows:

```
LIBRARY    CUSER

EXETYPE    WINDOWS

PROTMODE
      :
```

Next, you give Windows the capability to move your code and data around in memory as necessary and to allocate a small amount of memory for free usage by your code in a C-style heap, as follows:

```
LIBRARY    CUSER

EXETYPE    WINDOWS

PROTMODE

CODE       PRELOAD MOVEABLE DISCARDABLE
DATA       PRELOAD SINGLE
SEGMENTS 'WEP_TEXT' FIXED PRELOAD

HEAPSIZE   1024
      :
```

> **How to get more memory in Windows.**
> You can allocate extra memory from the heap for your program by using the LocalAlloc()/GlobalAlloc()set of Windows functions; using the traditional C malloc()/free() functions in Windows is inadvisable.

Finally, indicate that you want to use the default WEP() function and that you want to export (that is, make available to the rest of the Windows system) your function CInterface(), in the following way:

```
LIBRARY    CUSER

EXETYPE    WINDOWS

PROTMODE

CODE       PRELOAD MOVEABLE DISCARDABLE
```

```
DATA        PRELOAD SINGLE
SEGMENTS 'WEP_TEXT' FIXED PRELOAD

HEAPSIZE  1024

EXPORTS
   WEP           @1 RESIDENTNAME
   CInterface  @2
```

And that's it for the .def file, which appears in listing 12.3.

Listing 12.3. Cuser.Def

```
LIBRARY    CUSER

EXETYPE    WINDOWS

PROTMODE

CODE       PRELOAD MOVEABLE DISCARDABLE
DATA       PRELOAD SINGLE
SEGMENTS 'WEP_TEXT' FIXED PRELOAD

HEAPSIZE  1024

EXPORTS
   WEP           @1 RESIDENTNAME
   CInterface  @2
```

> **About libraries that include more than one function.**
> If your library includes more than just one function, list them
> under the CInterface line as @3, @4, and so on.

QuickC for Windows keeps track of which files to use in creating Cuser.Dll
by using a .mak file for the Cuser project, just as you would in Visual Basic.
However, the Cuser.Mak file is pretty complex (it is in listing 12.4). To use
it to create your own .dll, just change the name CUSER wherever it appears

to the name of your project. This file indicates which files QuickC for Windows is to use to create Cuser.Dll, what linker and library options you require, and so on. And that is all there is to it; this is a very small project, as .dll libraries go.

Now that you have the three files—Cuser.C, Cuser.Def, and Cuser.Mak—you can create Cuser.Dll with QuickC for Windows. To do that, simply load the Cuser project into QuickC for Windows, using the QCW Project menu's Open... item to open Cuser.Mak. If you want to edit Cuser.C, open that file with QCW's File menu, as shown in figure 12.4.

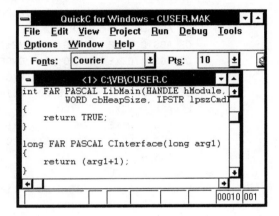

Figure 12.4. Using QuickC for Windows.

 Listing 12.4. Cuser.Mak

```
ORIGIN     = QCWIN
ORIGIN_VER    = 1.00
PROJ      =CUSER
DEBUG     =1
PROGTYPE      =2
CALLER    =c:\vb\vb.exe
ARGS    =
DLLS    =
CVPACK      =1
CC    =cl -qc
```

continues

Listing 12.4. continued

```
RC      =rc
CFLAGS_WEXE     =/AS /G2w /Zp /W3 /D_WINDOWS
CFLAGS_D_WEXE   =/Gi /Od /Zi
CFLAGS_R_WEXE   =/O /Os /DNDEBUG
CFLAGS_WDLL     =/AS /G2w /Zp /Aw /W3 /D_WINDOWS /D_WINDLL
CFLAGS_D_WDLL   =/Gi /Od /Zi
CFLAGS_R_WDLL   =/O /Os /DNDEBUG
CFLAGS_WTTY     =/AS /G2w /W3 /D_WINDOWS
CFLAGS_D_WTTY   =/Gi /Od /Zi
CFLAGS_R_WTTY   =/O /Os /DNDEBUG
CFLAGS_DEXE     =/AS /W2
CFLAGS_D_DEXE   =/Gi /Od /Zi
CFLAGS_R_DEXE   =/O /Ot /DNDEBUG
CFLAGS   =$(CFLAGS_WDLL) $(CFLAGS_D_WDLL)
LFLAGS_WEXE     =/ST:5120 /A:16
LFLAGS_D_WEXE   =/CO
LFLAGS_R_WEXE   =
LFLAGS_WDLL     =/A:16/ST:5120
LFLAGS_D_WDLL   =/CO
LFLAGS_R_WDLL   =
LFLAGS_WTTY     =/ST:5120 /A:16
LFLAGS_D_WTTY   =/CO
LFLAGS_R_WTTY   =
LFLAGS_DEXE     =/NOI /ST:2048
LFLAGS_D_DEXE   =/CO
LFLAGS_R_DEXE   =
LFLAGS   =$(LFLAGS_WDLL) $(LFLAGS_D_WDLL)
RCFLAGS   =
RESFLAGS   =/t
RUNFLAGS   =
DEFFILE =    CUSER.DEF
OBJS_EXT =
LIBS_EXT =

    .rc.res: ; $(RC) $(RCFLAGS) -r $*.rc


all:    $(PROJ).DLL


CUSER.OBJ:   CUSER.C $(H)


$(PROJ).DLL:    CUSER.OBJ $(OBJS_EXT) $(DEFFILE)
    echo >NUL @<<$(PROJ).CRF
```

```
CUSER.OBJ +
$(OBJS_EXT)
$(PROJ).DLL

\qcwin\lib\+
/NOD sdllcew oldnames  libw
$(DEFFILE);
<<
    link $(LFLAGS) @$(PROJ).CRF
    rc $(RESFLAGS)  $(PROJ).DLL

run: $(PROJ).DLL
    $(PROJ) $(RUNFLAGS)
```

To make Cuser.Dll, select the Project... item in QCW's Options menu, indicating that you want to create a .dll file by clicking the correct buttons in the resulting window (see figure 12.5).

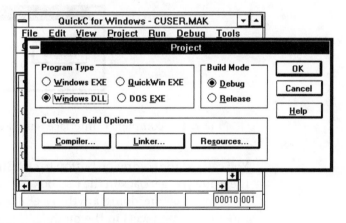

Figure 12.5. Creating a dynamic link library.

Finally, select the Build item in QCW's Project menu, which creates Cuser.Dll. Now you have created your own .dll file, ready to be used. To use it, place it in a directory Windows will search for dynamic link libraries—c:\windows or c:\windows\system, for example.

The Visual Basic Part of the Code

Now start Visual Basic so that you can use your Cuser.Dll library from VB. Call the new VB project, say, Vbcuser.Mak (for Visual Basic C user), giving Form1 the caption C Interface (see figure 12.6) and setting its AutoRedraw property to True.

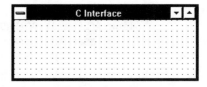

Figure 12.6. Creating the C interface.

Next, add a command button (Command1) and a text box (Text1), as shown in figure 12.7.

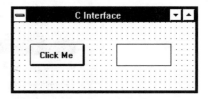

Figure 12.7. The complete C interface template.

You can use the command button to call CInterface() and you can display the value you get back in the text box to make sure that it is incremented each time. Before doing anything else, you can declare the Cuser.Dll function CInterface() in the module, Vbcuser.Bas, as follows:

```
'Module ---------------------------------
```

```
Declare Function CInterface Lib "Cuser.Dll" (ByVal x&) As Long
```

Next, you can declare a form-level variable called TheVal, initialize it to 1 in Form_Load, display it in the text box, and instruct the user to click the button to increment the displayed value:

```
Dim TheVal As Long
```

```
Sub Form_Load ()
```

```
      Print "Click the button to interface to C"
      Print "and increment the displayed value."
      TheVal = 1
      Text1.Text = Str$(TheVal)
End Sub
```

Now, when the user clicks the button Command1, you can call CInterface() to increment TheVal and display its new value, in the following way:

```
Dim TheVal As Long

Sub Form_Load ()
      Print "Click the button to interface to C"
      Print "and increment the displayed value."
      TheVal = 1
      Text1.Text = Str$(TheVal)
End Sub

Sub Command1_Click ()
      TheVal = CInterface(TheVal)
      Text1.Text = Str$(TheVal)
End Sub
```

That's all there is to it. When the user runs the program, it displays a value of 1. When the user clicks the button, you pass that 1 to CInterface(), where it is incremented and passed back. Then you display the resulting 2, and so on; the .dll routine is called each time the user clicks the button, so the displayed value is incremented (see figure 12.8). The final listing of Vbcuser appears in listing 12.5.

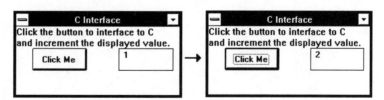

Figure 12.8. Your C interface at work.

Listing 12.5. Vbcuser.txt

```
Form Form1 ------------------------
  Caption      =      "C Interface"

CommandButton Command1
  Caption      =      "Click Me"

TextBox Text1
  TabIndex     =      0

'Module ------------------------------------

Declare Function CInterface Lib "Cuser.Dll" (ByVal x&) As Long

'Form1 Declarations -------------------------------------------

Dim TheVal As Long

'Form1 ---------------------------------------

Sub Form_Load ()
  Print "Click the button to interface to C"
  Print "and increment the displayed value."
  TheVal = 1
  Text1.Text = Str$(TheVal)
End Sub

Sub Command1_Click ()




  TheVal = CInterface(TheVal)
  Text1.Text = Str$(TheVal)
End Sub
```

That's all there is to creating your own .dll files, which let you link C code directly to Visual Basic. You have come far in this chapter: You have seen how to use the wealth of Windows functions in the dynamic link libraries that come with Windows, as well as how to create your own dynamic link libraries. In the next chapter, you will see how to extend Visual Basic even more when you begin adding the custom controls Microsoft provides in Visual Basic Professional Edition.

Summary

You have learned two major new skills here: How to connect your programs to the Windows library functions and to C code you write yourself. In particular, you developed a screen-capture program that used the Windows library calls to do a number of things not usually allowed in Visual Basic: Capture all mouse events whether they occur in your window or not, draw outside your window, and copy graphics from the screen outside your window. By doing this, you created a useful program and saw how to set up the interface to Windows library calls simply by declaring them to Visual Basic. You also saw how to get a handle to the whole screen in Windows by referencing the "Display" object.

The Windows library functions are stored in dynamic link libraries. After you saw how to connect to such libraries, you learned how to write dynamic link libraries yourself. You did that so that you could connect your Visual Basic programs to some C code you have written, and you saw how to pass parameters back and forth between C and Visual Basic. Together, these techniques augment Visual basic tremendously—now you can call any Windows function you want (which means that if you can do it in Windows, you can do it in Visual Basic), and you also can interface to C, the language Windows programs often are written in.

New Windows	Functions
BitBlt GDI library	Copies bitmaps between device contexts. The arguments are these: The destination device context handle for the copied bitmap; the new (x, y) location of the bitmap in the destination; the width and height of the bitmap; the source

continues

579

New Windows	Functions
	device context handle; the location of the bitmap in the source device context; and an argument that indicates what you want done with the bitmap (a value of &HCC0020, for example, indicates that you want the bitmap copied from the source to the destination—this value is also stored as the constant SRCCOPY in Winapi.Txt). Use it like this: BitBlt(ByVal hDestDC As Integer, ByVal X As Integer, ByVal Y As Integer, ByVal nWidth As Integer, ByVal nHeight As Integer, ByVal hSrcDC As Integer, ByVal XSrc As Integer, ByVal YSrc As Integer, ByVal dwROP As Long) As Integer.
ClientToScreen	User library. Converts coordinates pointed to by lpPoint from client area to screen. Use it like this: ClientToScreen (ByVal hWnd As Integer, lpPoint As ApiPoint).
CreateDC	GDI library. Creates a new device context. Use it like this: CreateDC (ByVal lpDriverName As String, ByVal lpDeviceName As Any, ByVal lpOutPut As Any, ByVal lpInitData As Any) As Integer.
DeleteDC	GDI library. Deletes the device context whose handle you pass. Use it like this: DeleteDC (ByVal hDC As Integer) As Integer.
LineTo	GDI library. Draws a line from the current graphics position to (X, Y). Use it like this: LineTo (ByVal hDC As Integer, ByVal X As Integer, ByVal Y As Integer) As Integer.
MoveTo	GDI library. Sets the location of the current graphics position. Use it like this: MoveTo (ByVal hDC As Integer, ByVal X As Integer, ByVal Y As Integer) As Long.

New Windows	Functions
ReleaseCapture	User library. Releases the mouse (see SetCapture). Use it like this: ReleaseCapture ().
SetCapture	User library. Captures all mouse events no matter where they happen. Use it like this: SetCapture (ByVal hWnd As Integer) As Integer.
SetROP2	GDI library. Sets binary raster drawing operation for a device context. Use it like this: SetROP2 (ByVal hDC As Integer, ByVal nDrawMode As Integer) As Integer.

13

Using the Professional Edition's Custom Controls

In this chapter, you will see how to use the custom controls that come with Visual Basic's Professional Edition. The topics covered here include the following:

▼ Key status controls

▼ 3-D buttons

▼ Custom control graphs

▼ Line, bar, and pie charts

▼ Prewritten font, file open, file save, and color dialog boxes

▼ Animated buttons

▼ Pen computing

▼ Windows gauges

In this chapter, you are going to examine the series of professional-level controls that Microsoft provides in the Visual Basic Professional Edition. Customized controls can augment the controls already available in Visual Basic, dramatically extending what is possible. The Professional Edition also includes the Custom Development Kit (CDK), which you will use in the next chapter. Here you will put the custom controls to use, along with 3-D buttons, animated buttons, line charts, bar charts, and pie charts, as well as pen computing, and prewritten dialog boxes (called common dialog boxes) that let you pop font, file open, file save, and color-selection dialog boxes on the screen from a simple control. You will see how to use these new controls as you upgrade some of the programs from the previous chapters. For example, your plotter program will be updated with the new common dialog boxes and you will use of some of the common dialog boxes in your notepad, also.

This chapter shows you how to use the Professional Edition's custom controls. In fact, using them is as simple as using other controls in Visual Basic. You just select the custom control you want, draw it on your program's form, and then add it to the code.

Although there are about 20 new controls in Visual Basic's Professional Edition, this chapter looks at only a few of them. (Examining all of them in detail would merit another book—and not everyone has Visual Basic's Professional Edition.) We will examine many of the properties and methods of the most interesting controls, including key status controls (which display the status of the Caps Lock, Num Lock, Ins, and Scroll Lock keys), gauge controls, animated buttons, graph controls (which graph data in what looks like a picture box), pen controls, and others. One such control—CMDialog—is actually a series of very useful dialog boxes; you will put them to use in this chapter as well.

To see each new control at work, you will use them in programs you have already written. For example, you will see that graph controls work well in your sample plotter and that an animated control button fits in nicely with your animated rocket ship. You will start by adding key status controls to your notepad.

Selecting which .Vbx files to preload yourself.
You can change which .Vbx files are loaded by changing the Autoload.Mak file in the Visual Basic directory.

Updating Your Notepad with Key Status Controls

Table 13.1 lists the .Vbx files that come with Visual Basic's Professional Edition and are in the Vbx directory. These controls are added to the Professional Edition as soon as you start it and are ready for use.

Table 13.1. The Professional Edition's Custom Controls, by File

File	Custom Control
anibuton.vbx	Animated buttons
cmdialog.vbx	Ready-to-use dialog boxes

continues

Table 13.1. continued

File	Custom Control
gauge.vbx	Windows-type gauges
graph.vbx	Controls that graph data
grid.vbx	Matrix of cells
keystat.vbx	Key status controls
mci.vbx	Multimedia
mscomm.vbx	Communications
msmapim.vbx	Mail message MAPI
msmapis.vbx	Mail session MAPI
msmasked.vbx	Masked edit
oleclien.vbx	DDE controls
pencntrl.vbx	Pen controls
penskb.vbx	Windows for Pen keyboard
picclip.vbx	Picture-clipping controls
spin.vbx	Spin buttons
threed.vbx	Three-dimensional appearance controls

The key status controls are the first custom controls you will look at, because their operation is automatic (that is, you do not have to add any code to support them). These controls are in the Keystat.Vbx file. Remember the working notepad you developed in Chapter 2? (For reference, see figure 13.1 and listing 13.1 (Pad.Mak on the Disk).) Load that project back into Visual Basic now. With the key status controls, you can add a few easy-to-read indicators on the side of the pad to show you what the status of the Caps Lock, Num Lock, and Scroll Lock keys is. Figure 13.2 shows the key status tool in the toolbox.

Listing 13.1. The Pad Application (Pad.Mak on the Disk)

```
Form Form1 — — — — — — — — — — — — — — — —
    Caption        =    "Pad"
```

```
TextBox PadText
        MultiLine        =    -1  'True
        ScrollBars       =    2   'Vertical
        TabIndex         =    0

CommandButton CutButton
        Caption          =    "&Cut"
        Enabled          =    0   'False

CommandButton PasteButton
        Caption          =    "&Paste"
        Enabled          =    0   'False

CommandButton ClearButton
        Caption          =    "Clear &All"
        Enabled          =    0   'False


Pad.Bas (Global) — — — — — — — — — — — —


        Global CutText As String


Pad.Frm — — — — — — — — — — — — — — — — — —

Sub ClearButton_Click ()
    PadText.Text = ""
    PadText.SetFocus
End Sub


Sub CutButton_Click ()
    CutText = PadText.SelText
    PadText.SelText = ""
    PasteButton.Enabled = True
    PadText.SetFocus
End Sub


Sub PasteButton_Click ()
    PadText.SelText = CutText
    PadText.SetFocus
End Sub


Sub PadText_Change ()
```

continues

Listing 13.1. continued

```
    CutButton.Enabled = True
    ClearButton.Enabled = True
End Sub
```

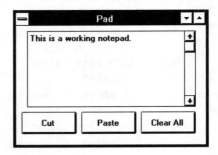

Figure 13.1. The notepad example.

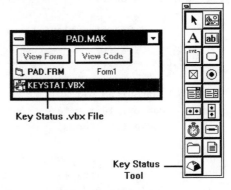

Key Status .vbx File

Key Status
Tool

Figure 13.2. The key status custom control tool.

You can make use of that tool in the toolbox by stretching the notepad form to the right to make room for more controls and double-clicking on the key status tool three times, adding three new controls to the notepad (see figure 13.3).

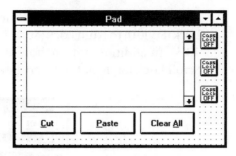

Figure 13.3. The Notepad with the key status template.

By default, each key status control shows the Caps Lock state; if you were to run this program, each key status control would change automatically as you toggle the Caps Lock state, alternately showing "Caps Lock ON" and "Caps Lock OFF." However, three controls doing the same thing is a bit much; these controls also can watch the Num Lock and Scroll Lock keys.

To change the middle key status control to Num Lock, you can use its Style property. As you might expect, each custom control comes with its own set of properties and methods. However, most custom controls support a standard set of properties and methods. You have already seen all the standard properties in this book. They include: Caption, DragIcon, DragMode, Enabled, FontName, Height, hWnd (window handle), Index (for control arrays), Left, MousePointer, Name, TabIndex, TabStop, Tag, Top, Visible, and Width. The standard methods include: Click, DragOver, GotFocus, KeyDown, KeyPress, KeyUp, LostFocus, MouseDown, MouseUp, MouseMove, and Move. Not all custom controls support every one these properties and methods, but most will. To see all the properties available at design time for a new control, you can check the properties window; you can see the Style property for a key status control in figure 13.4. To see all the methods for a custom control, look in the code window.

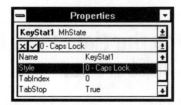

Figure 13.4. The key status control properties.

You can change the setting of the middle key status control from Caps Lock (Style 0) to Num Lock (Style 1) by setting its Style property (see figure 13.5). In addition, set the bottom key status control's Style property to Scroll Lock (Style 3; the Insert Key is Style 2) and run the program.

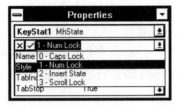

Figure 13.5. Setting the key status Style property.

Now you can see the state of these three keyboard keys as you use your notepad (see figure 13.6). It has not cost you any more code to add this capability. Usually, however, you have to make some small changes to a program's code to use the new custom controls. For example, say that you wanted to update the Cut button in your notepad, giving it a three-dimensional appearance with the 3-D custom controls. We will look into that next.

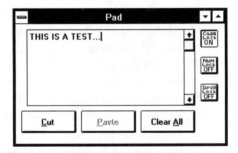

Figure 13.6. The augmented notepad in action.

Updating the Notepad's Buttons to 3-D Appearance

An entire series of 3-D controls in Visual Basic's Professional Edition is packed into the file Threed.Vbx. The 3-D controls—3-D check boxes,

3-D command buttons, 3-D frames, 3-D option buttons, 3-D panels, and 3-D group buttons—appear in the toolbox (see figure 13.7).

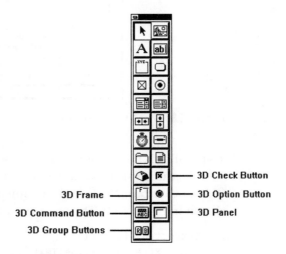

Figure 13.7. The 3-D custom controls.

The 3-D controls primarily are concerned with appearance. By using them, you can create some good three-dimensional effects. For example, the 3-D panel can give the appearance of a panel slightly raised (or lowered) from the surface of your window, and that can set off text or graphics nicely.

In addition, some of these controls can support a font that looks three-dimensional; you will convert the Cut button in your notepad to use them. Double-click on the 3-D command button tool now, creating a 3-D command button in the center of the notepad's form, and give it the caption Cut. Next, set the Font3D property to 2, which makes the caption text appear raised with heavy shading. Other options here include not raised or inset, raised with light shading, and inset with light or heavy shading. In addition, you can raise or lower the bevel_-0 width—the bevel is the slanted surface that seems to slope up from or in toward the screen, on the side of controls—from its default of 2 (which makes 3-D controls look like other VB controls) to, say, 4, by changing the BevelWidth property. You can see the result in figure 13.8.

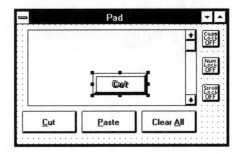

Figure 13.8. The 3-D Cut button.

To install this button, give it the name CutButton3D (note that because Visual Basic insists that Names begin with a character, you cannot name it 3DCutButton). Next, find the notepad's CutButton_Click() event, as shown in figure 13.9. The code looks like the following:

```
Sub CutButton_Click ()
    CutText = PadText.SelText
    PadText.SelText = ""
    PasteButton.Enabled = True
    PadText.SetFocus
End Sub
```

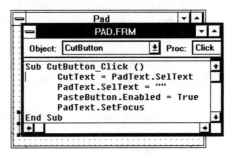

Figure 13.9. The code window.

You have to supplant this with CutButton3D_Click(), which is very easy to do; just change Sub CutButton_Click () to Sub CutButton3D_Click () in the code window, like the following:

```
Sub CutButton3D_Click ()
    CutText = PadText.SelText
```

```
        PadText.SelText = ""
        PasteButton.Enabled = True
        PadText.SetFocus
End Sub
```

Because that control already exists, Visual Basic will automatically associate this code with CutButton3D now. (You can cut the old CutButton now, using Cut in VB's Edit menu.) At this point, you can run the program; the result, complete with new Cut button, appears in figure 13.10. Keep in mind that this is only one of six new 3-D controls; using them in your programs can add some striking effects.

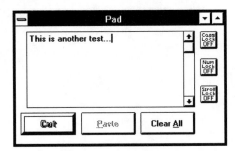

Figure 13.10. Your notepad with 3-D Cut button.

You can put the other types of buttons in Visual Basic's Professional Edition to work also. For example, there is a type of button that displays an animated series of pictures when you click it (in addition to generating a Click event, of course). A perfect place to add that is to your animation example, which sends a small rocket ship up the screen.

Updating Your Animation Example with Animated Buttons

Remember your animation example that drags a rocket ship icon up the screen when you click on a button marked Click Me (see figure 13.11)? Although the Click Me button is acceptable, you can use the Visual Basic Professional Edition's animated button custom control to create an animated button (that is, the displayed image changes when you click on it). That control is in the file Anibuton.Vbx; the animated button tool appears in the toolbox, as shown in figure 13.12.

Figure 13.11. The animated rocket ship example.

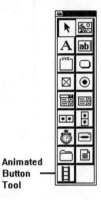

Figure 13.12. The animated button customized tool.

Double-click on that tool now, creating a new animated button. At this point, the animated button—Name AniButton1—is just a blank white rectangle; you need to put something in it. To do that, you have to load images that can be played one after the other when the button is clicked on. For example, you can use the Visual Basic moon icons in icons\misc\moon01.ico - icons\misc\moon08.ico (see figure 13.13). In fact, you can place a full moon in the sky above the rocket; when the user clicks on it, it can change phases and launch the rocket.

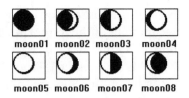

Figure 13.13. Visual Basic's moon icons.

To load the moon images, you can use the animated button's Frame property. Find the Frame property in the properties window and click on it now. The number 1 (indicating frame 1) appears in the settings box, and the drop-down button to the right of the settings box now displays an ellipsis ("..."), which means that if you click on it, a dialog box will appear. Click on it now, opening the Select Frame dialog box. You can use the Load... button to load icons; click on it and load the full moon image (icons\misc\moon05.ico). That image appears as frame 1 (see figure 13.14).

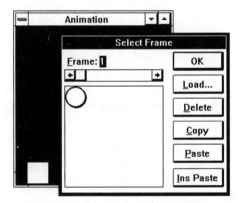

Figure 13.14. The animated button's Select Frame box.

Next, switch to frame 2 by clicking on the scroll bar above the picture box in the Select Frame box. Then load icons\misc\moon06.ico. Keep going, loading moon07.ico as frame 3 and moon08.ico as frame 4. Then click on the OK button to close the Select Frame box. Note that you can use the Ins and Del buttons to insert and delete images.

Animated buttons display their first frame—frame 1—until you click on them. When you click them, they play the first half of the loaded frames

595

while the mouse button is down. When you release the mouse button, the second half of the frames are played. Now you have to use the animated button—AniButton1—to replace the Click Me command button whose Name is Command1. You do that by double-clicking on Click Me, bringing up this Sub procedure:

```
Sub Command1_Click()
    For loop_index% = Picture1.Top To 0 Step -50
        Picture1.Move Picture1.Left, loop_index%
    Next loop_index%
End Sub
```

As before, you have to make only one change—just change Command1 to AniButton1, like this:

```
Sub AniButton1_Click()
    For loop_index% = Picture1.Top To 0 Step -50
        Picture1.Move Picture1.Left, loop_index%
    Next loop_index%
End Sub
```

As before, now that you have changed the name of the Sub procedure, Visual Basic will connect this procedure with AniButton1, not Command1. Cut the Command1 button now, leaving AniButton1 as the only button in the program. Animated buttons also can display captions, so add the caption "Click" to AniButton1 now (the moon icon is too small to hold the string "Click Me"). Now you are ready to run.

In this example, the moon will appear full at first—unfortunately, it will be inside a white box, but you can design your own icons for a black background if you want. When the user clicks on it, the first half of the phases of the moon appear. When the mouse button is released, the second half of the images appear and the rocket is launched. The working program appears in figure 13.15.

> **More about animated buttons.**
> You can change the playing cycle of the images with the animated button's Cycle property. In addition, you can use the DrawMode property to make the animated button any size and automatically stretch images to fit, or use the Speed property to change the speed with which the images are played.

Figure 13.15. The improved animation example, with Moon button.

So far, the new controls you have added have required very little change in code. All you have done is to use new controls that do not need any code support or that replace buttons; you have kept the Click event code intact. However, the Visual Basic's Professional Edition controls have much more to offer here. In fact, some of the new controls offer capabilities that are completely new. For example, one of the Professional Edition controls is Graph, which enables you to graph data automatically inside a control (there is no such control in standard Visual Basic). If you recall, you put together a program named Plotter in Chapter 6 to do exactly that—plot data. The current version of Plotter appears in figure 13.16, but you can improve it with graph controls. That is what you will look into next.

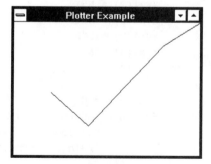

Figure 13.16. Your plotter—standard version.

Improving Your Plotter with Custom Control Graphs

The listing for your Plotter program is in listing 13.2. You want to plot the following set of points (which track phone bills over a set of months):

```
(1, 200)
(2, 95)
(4, 350)
(5, 425)
```

 Listing 13.2. The Plotter Program

```
Form Form1 — — — — — — — — — — — —
    Caption          =    "Plotter Example"

    Dim XVal(4), YVal(4) As Single
    Dim XBiggest, YBiggest As Single

Sub Form_Paint ()
    'Plotting program. Assumes origin is (0, 0)

    Cls

    XVal(1) = 1
    YVal(1) = 200
    XVal(2) = 2
    YVal(2) = 95
    XVal(3) = 4
    YVal(3) = 350
    XVal(4) = 5
    YVal(4) = 425

    XBiggest = 0
    For loop_index% = 1 To UBound(XVal)
        If XVal(loop_index%) > XBiggest Then
            XBiggest = XVal(loop_index%)
        End If
    Next loop_index%
```

```
        YBiggest = 0
        For loop_index% = 1 To UBound(YVal)
              If YVal(loop_index%) > YBiggest Then
                    YBiggest = YVal(loop_index%)
              End If
        Next loop_index%

        Scale (0, YBiggest)-(XBiggest, 0)'Assume (0, 0) origin

        CurrentX = XVal(1)
        CurrentY = YVal(1)
        For loop_index% = 1 To UBound(XVal)
              Line -(XVal(loop_index%), YVal(loop_index%))
        Next loop_index%

End Sub

Sub Form_Resize ()
        Call Form_Paint
End Sub
```

You can do this with a Graph control as well, but for simplicity you will include a point (3, 0) as well:

```
(1, 200)
(2, 95)
(3, 0)
(4, 350)
(5, 425)
```

Now, to put this into action, start a new project named, say, Graph.Mak. The graph tool appears in figure 13.17. Double-click on the graph control and stretch the graph to cover most of the form. The default Name for this graph is Graph1. To load data into the new graph, you use the GraphData property like the following for the first point:

```
Graph1.GraphData = 200
    :
```

Graph
Tool

Figure 13.17. The custom graph tool.

This loads a value of 200 as your first point—and GraphData automatically increments itself to point to the next data point, point 2. For that reason, you can enter that point (2, 95), as follows:

```
Graph1.GraphData = 200
Graph1.GraphData = 95
        :
```

Notice that you did not increment a counter to point to the next x value; that was done automatically (you will see how to customize the x scale later). In addition, the Graph control automatically scales the y axis. You can add all the data for your graph, as follows:

```
Graph1.GraphData = 200
Graph1.GraphData = 95
Graph1.GraphData = 0
Graph1.GraphData = 350
Graph1.GraphData = 425
```

Notice also that you did not include this code in an event procedure (for example, Form_Load()) because most properties of graph controls are available at design time. In other words, you can put together your graph at design time and change it at run time if you wish—including the data you want to graph. To add the data, simply find Graph1's GraphData property in the properties window and type the following:

```
200 <Enter> 95 <Enter> 0 <Enter> 350 <Enter> 425 <Enter>
```

Your graph's data is automatically graphed, as in figure 13.18.

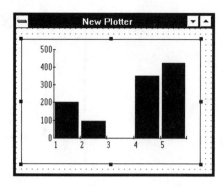

Figure 13.18. A new version of the plotter.

Changing the colors used in a graph control.
You can change the color of the bars in figure 13.18, bar by bar, if you enter values for the ColorData property. These values cycle like GraphData, so if you enter five values, the five bars will use those colors. Here, the colors are not typical VB color values (long integers); instead, they use the 16 colors of QuickBasic, so you can put values 1-15 in ColorData. If you want to print in color, change the PrintStyle property from 0 (the default— monochrome printing) to 1—color printing.

You also can change the PatternData property so that you use hatch shading instead of colors in your bar graph. PatternData takes values from 1-31 (the hatch shadings appear in figure 13.19). This property also cycles through the data points, so you can assign different hatch patterns to all your points, as follows:

```
Graph1.GraphData = 200
Graph1.GraphData = 95
Graph1.GraphData = 0
Graph1.GraphData = 350
Graph1.GraphData = 425
Graph1.PatternData = 1
Graph1.PatternData = 2
Graph1.PatternData = 3
Graph1.PatternData = 4
Graph1.PatternData = 5
```

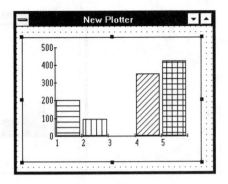

Figure 13.19. Your chart with hatch shading.

Adding hatch patterns to a graph control.
If you graph in DrawStyle 0, monochrome (the default is 1, meaning Color), the graph control will convert automatically from the colors it normally uses for data bars to hatch patterns; so you do not have to set a different PatternData value for each bar.

Other Types of Graphs

The default graph uses vertical bars in a bar graph, as you have been doing so far. However, there are many other types and you can switch quickly between them just by changing the GraphType property, whose values are shown in table 13.2.

Table 13.2. Graph Control's GraphType Values

GraphType	Means
0	None (no graph)
1	2-D Pie
2	3-D Pie
3	2-D Bar
4	3-D Bar
5	Gantt

GraphType	Means
6	Line
7	Log/Lin(ear)

For example, your original Plotter program graphed the data as a connect-the-dots line, and you can do that here as well, simply by switching to GraphType 6 (at either design-time or at run-time). The result is shown in figure 13.20.

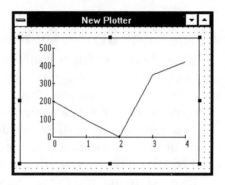

Figure 13.20. The new version of the Plotter, with lines.

There's a great deal more here. For example, you might be a little uncomfortable with the idea of automatically cycling through the points by successively placing values in the GraphData property. What if you just wanted to change one of the data points? You can do that as well, using the ThisPoint property.

Using ThisPoint To Set Graph Data

You might recall that your original data did not have a point 3.

```
(1, 200)
(2, 95)
(4, 350)
(5, 425)
```

It turns out that, using the ThisPoint property, you can enter data without entering anything for point 3. Because ThisPoint determines the point that will receive the data you next place in the GraphData property, you can enter the preceding data, as follows:

```
Graph1.GraphData = 200
Graph1.GraphData = 95
Graph1.ThisPoint = 4     <- 'Skip point 3
Graph1.GraphData = 350
Graph1.GraphData = 425
```

When you want to single out a data point to change its data or work with it in some other way—"explode" it from a pie chart, for example—you can use the ThisPoint property.

Setting Your Own X Coordinates

In addition, you might notice that your graph is actually shifted over along the x axis by one place. To fix that, you can specify the x position of your data by setting its XPosData property. You can do that now, point by point (the XPosData property cycles as well), shifting everything over by one unit. At design-time, you do it by using ThisPoint to make the first point the current point, and then by entering the new x values for the XPosData properties, starting at 0. The result is shown in figure 13.21. Using XPosData, you can set the x coordinates of your points; the graph will adjust automatically.

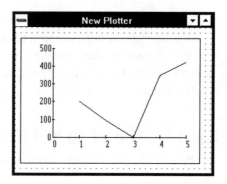

Figure 13.21. The graph, with fixed x axis.

Let's turn to pie charts next.

Pie Charts

As you might expect, switching to pie charts is easy; all you need to do is to check table 13.2 to see that GraphType 1 is a 2-D pie chart and GraphType 2 is a 3-D pie chart. You can switch to a 2-D pie chart just by switching to GraphType 1, or to a 3-D pie chart with GraphType 2 (see figure 13.22).

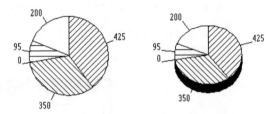

Figure 13.22. Two- and three-dimensional pie charts.

In addition, you can *explode* one or more slice(s) of a pie chart—display it (or them) slightly pulled out of the pie—by using the ExtraData property. This property holds information about how you want each point displayed. (You can use it not only to explode pie sections, but also to indicate the color of the sides of the 3-D bars in 3-D bar charts.) Usually, ExtraData is 0 for all points, but by setting it to 1, you can explode that point. For example, you can start by filling GraphData and drawing a 2-D pie chart, as follows:

```
Graph1.GraphData = 200
Graph1.GraphData = 95
Graph1.GraphData = 350
Graph1.GraphData = 425
GraphType = 1              '2D pie chart
      :
Now select, say, point 2 (the one with a value of 95):
Graph1.GraphData = 200
Graph1.GraphData = 95
Graph1.GraphData = 350
Graph1.GraphData = 425
GraphType = 1              '2D pie chart
Graph1.ThisPoint = 2
      :
```

Next, you can explode it, in the following way:

```
Graph1.GraphData = 200
Graph1.GraphData = 95
Graph1.GraphData = 350
Graph1.GraphData = 425
GraphType = 1              '2D pie chart
Graph1.ThisPoint = 2
Graph1.ExtraData = 1       '"Explode this slice"
```

The result appears in figure 13.23. That is all there is to creating useful pie charts.

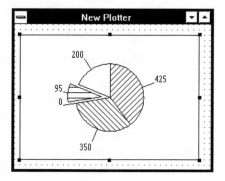

Figure 13.23. The pie chart, with an exploded slice.

Besides exploding pie sections like this, you can do a great deal more with a graph control. In addition to the types you have seen, you can create scatter graphs or Gantt (time-line) graphs. You can graph sets of data, creating stacked graphs. You can add a grid to your graphs simply by changing the GridStyle property (see table 13.3). For example, to add the horizontal and vertical grid shown in figure 13.24, simply set GridStyle to 3.

Table 13.3. Graph Controls' GridStyle Property

GridStyle	Means
0	No grid
1	Horizontal grid
2	Vertical grid
3	Horizontal and vertical grid

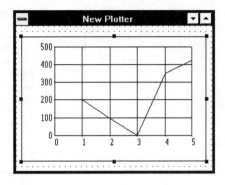

Figure 13.24. Your graph, with grid added.

As you might expect, you also can add titles to your graphs. For instance, you can give your graph the title "The Data," simply by setting the GraphTitle property to "The Data." The result appears in figure 13.25. In fact, you also can label the x and y axes, using the LeftTitle and BottomTitle properties. Because this data is supposed to be telephone bill data, by month, you can label the graph accordingly (see figure 13.26).

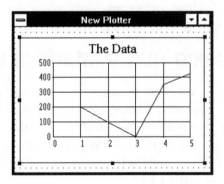

Figure 13.25. Your graph, with a title.

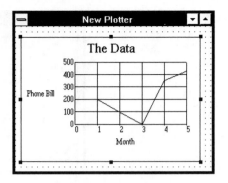

Figure 13.26. Your graph, with left and bottom titles.

Finally, you can reset the data in the graph control as needed, using the DataReset property. You can reset any type of data—graph data, color data, label data, even all data—depending on what value you place in this property. The values, which range from 1-9, are all defined in the settings box of the properties window.

That ends our exploration of graphs, although there is plenty more depth here for the interested programmer. Next, we turn to gauge controls.

Updating Your C Interface with Windows Gauges

You may recall that, in the last chapter, you set up a C interface that started with a 1 in its text box; every time you clicked on the button marked "Click Me," you sent the value in the text box to your C function, got it incremented, and displayed the result. Successive clicks steadily incremented the value. The Visual Basic code for this program appears in listing 13.3.

Listing 13.3. Your C Interface

```
Form Form1 — — — — — — — — — — — —
    Caption      =      "C Interface"


CommandButton Command1
    Caption      =      "Click Me"
```

```
TextBox Text1
     TabIndex     =     0

'Module — — — — — — — — — — — — — —

   Declare Function CInterface Lib "cuser.dll" (ByVal x&) As Long

'Form1 — — — — — — — — — — — — — —

   Dim TheVal As Long

   Sub Command1_Click ()
       TheVal = CInterface(TheVal)
       Text1.Text = Str$(TheVal)
   End Sub
```

You can adapt this code to display the value in the variable TheVal with
a gauge control. Gauges are very popular in Windows. You probably have
seen them when some software package performs an action that takes a
long time (such as installation). The gauge—usually a growing or shrink-
ing horizontal bar—indicates the status of the operation. As time passes,
the bar shrinks or grows to show you how close you are to completion.

Supplanting the text box in your program with a gauge is easy; just use the
gauge tool from Gauge.Vbx, which appears in figure 13.27.

Figure 13.27. The custom gauge tool.

Double-click on it now, creating a gauge named Gauge1. This new control functions much like a scroll bar: The setting of the gauge is kept in the Value property. Value can go from Min (default 0) to Max (default 100). Change Max to, say, 10 now so that you can see the gauge move as you steadily increment Gauge1.Value. The command button's Click event appears as follows now:

```
Sub Command1_Click ()
    TheVal = CInterface(TheVal)
    Text1.Text = Str$(TheVal)
End Sub
```

You can change that to use Gauge1 instead, like this:

```
Sub Command1_Click ()
    TheVal = CInterface(TheVal)
    Gauge1.Value = TheVal
End Sub
```

And that's all there is to it; now when you run the program, you can make the gauge bar grow as you click on the "Click Me" button (see figure 13.28).

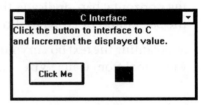

Figure 13.28. Your C interface with a gauge control.

Note that the gauge in figure 13.28 could use a border around it to indicate how big it can grow. In fact, the gauge control comes with a whole series of bitmaps you can use to provide a suitable background for your gauges in the directory bitmaps\gauge. Several types of gauge are possible: Horizontal bar, vertical bar, semicircle (180 degree) needle gauges, and full circle (360 degree) gauges. To put this capability to use, make the Gauge1 control a semicircle gauge by setting its Style property to 2. Next, change the NeedleWidth property from 1 (the default) to 10 (pixels). Finally, load, say, bitmaps\gauge\speedo.bmp into the gauge's Picture property. Now when you run the program, you get the elaborate gauge shown in figure 13.29.

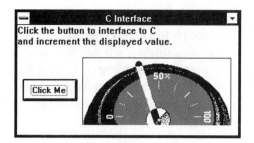

Figure 13.29. Your C interface with a bitmap gauge control.

Gauges make your program look professional and can be very useful. There are still several additional controls in the Professional Edition; next, we will turn to the Professional Edition's prewritten dialog boxes.

Updating Your Notepad with Prewritten Dialog Boxes

Visual Basic's Professional Edition provides five prewritten dialog boxes in the CMDialog—common dialog box—custom control. These dialog boxes are shown in table 13.4.

Table 13.4. CMDialog Dialog Boxes

Dialog Box	CMDialog Action Property
None	0
File Open	1
File Save	2
Color Selection	3
Font Selection	4
Print	5
Windows Help	6

Each CMDialog control can present any of these dialog boxes—File Open, File Save, Color Selection, Font Selection, Print Dialog, or Windows Help.

To distinguish between them, you use the appropriate Action property (see table 13.4). When you set this property in a CMDialog control, the corresponding dialog box is shown (as opposed to using the Show method, which you do with other dialog boxes). Now you are ready to see the common dialog boxes at work. You will start by adding the font selection dialog box—Action 4—to your notepad.

> **Using common dialog boxes to display Windows help.**
> Note in particular that if you set a CMDialog's Action property to 6, it displays Windows help (Winhelp.Exe). This is a useful asset to many Windows programs, especially if you have a Windows help (.Hlp) file ready for your program (see Appendix A).

A Font Selection Dialog Box

You begin by loading your notepad program into Visual Basic and then, using the Menu Design window, adding a File menu (Name: FileMenu) that includes the following six items: Font... (Name: FontItem), Open File... (Name: OpenItem), Save File... (SaveItem), Text Color... (ColorItem), Print... (PrintItem), and Exit (ExitItem) (see figure 13.30).

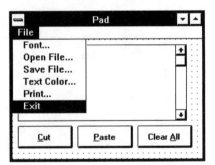

Figure 13.30. Notepad, with File menu.

It is easy to make the Exit item active. Simply add the Visual Basic End statement to ExitItem_Click(), as follows:

```
Sub Exitem_Click ()
    End
End Sub
```

The next step is to work on the Font... item; that is, FontItem_Click(), as follows:

```
Sub FontItem_Click ()
End Sub
```

To add a CMDialog control, use the controls from the file Cmdialog.Vbx, as shown in figure 13.31.

CMDialog Tool

Figure 13.31. The custom CMDialog tool.

Double-click on this tool to add the control CMDialog1. To display this dialog control as a font selection dialog box, you just have to set CMDialog1.Action to 4. Before you do that, however, you should load all the current font properties into CMDialog so that you can display the defaults. CMDialog controls have all the properties they are capable of setting (such as FontSize, FontUnderline, and so on for Font Selection dialog boxes); you can load the properties in the following way:

```
Sub FontItem_Click ()
    CMDialog1.FontName = PadText.FontName
    CMDialog1.FontItalic = PadText.FontItalic
    CMDialog1.FontStrikethru = PadText.FontStrikethru
    CMDialog1.FontSize = PadText.FontSize
    CMDialog1.FontUnderline = PadText.FontUnderline
    CMDialog1.Color = PadText.ForeColor
    :
    :
End Sub
```

Now set the CMDialog control's Flags property to indicate that you are interested in setting the screen fonts only, and that you want to allow the user to select special effects (like underlining or strikethrough), in the following way:

```
Sub FontItem_Click ()
    CMDialog1.FontName = PadText.FontName
    CMDialog1.FontItalic = PadText.FontItalic
    CMDialog1.FontStrikethru = PadText.FontStrikethru
    CMDialog1.FontSize = PadText.FontSize
    CMDialog1.FontUnderline = PadText.FontUnderline
    CMDialog1.Color = PadText.ForeColor
    CMDialog1.Flags = CF_SCREENFONTS Or CF_EFFECTS
        :
        :
End Sub
```

This is the way you will communicate many settings to the CMDialog controls—through the Flags property. The possible settings for this property (when you are selecting fonts) appear in table 13.5; note that you can combine options with the Or operation, in the following way:

```
CF_SCREENFONTS Or CF_EFFECTS
```

This code makes the font selection dialog box limit itself to the available screen fonts and display an effects box as well. These and many other constants that are useful with Visual Basic's Professional Edition can be found in the file proconst.txt, which comes with the Professional Edition.

Table 13.5. Font Selection Flags from PROCONST.TXT

Flag	Means
CF_SCREENFONTS	Allow selection of screen fonts only
CF_PRINTERFONTS	Allow selection of printer fonts only
CF_BOTH	Allow selection of both screen and printer fonts
CF_SHOWHELP	Display Help button in dialog box
CF_EFFECTS	Allow effects selection, including underline and strikethrough
CF_APPLY	Enable Apply Button

614

Flag	Means
CF_ANSIONLY	Allow only fonts that use the Windows character set (not symbols)
CF_NOVECTORFONTS	Disallow vector fonts
CF_NOSIMULATIONS	Disallow GDI font simulations
CF_LIMITSIZE	Limit font size Min < FontSize < Max
CF_FIXEDPITCHONLY	Allow only fixed-pitch fonts
CF_WYSIWYG	Allow only fonts available on printer and screen. (WYSIWIG stands for "what you see is what you get.") If used, also must use CF_BOTH and CF_SCALABLEONLY.
CF_FORCEFONTEXIST	Allow only fonts that exist
CF_SCALABLEONLY	Allow only scalable fonts
CF_TTONLY	Only allow True Type fonts

Next, you display the CMDialog control as a font selection dialog box (also called a ChooseFont dialog box) simply by setting its action property to 4, as follows:

```
Sub FontItem_Click ()
    CMDialog1.Flags = CF_SCREENFONTS Or CF_EFFECTS
    CMDialog1.FontName = PadText.FontName
    CMDialog1.FontItalic = PadText.FontItalic
    CMDialog1.FontStrikethru = PadText.FontStrikethru
    CMDialog1.FontSize = PadText.FontSize
    CMDialog1.FontUnderline = PadText.FontUnderline
    CMDialog1.Color = PadText.ForeColor
    CMDialog1.Action = 4
    :
    :
End Sub
```

At this point, the font selection dialog box is popped on the screen and the user makes font selections and clicks on the OK or Cancel button. Then the dialog box disappears and you can place values from the properties back into the pad's font properties, as follows:

```
Sub FontItem_Click ()
    CMDialog1.FontName = PadText.FontName
    CMDialog1.FontItalic = PadText.FontItalic
    CMDialog1.FontStrikethru = PadText.FontStrikethru
    CMDialog1.FontSize = PadText.FontSize
    CMDialog1.FontUnderline = PadText.FontUnderline
    CMDialog1.Color = PadText.ForeColor
    CMDialog1.Flags = CF_SCREENFONTS Or CF_EFFECTS
    CMDialog1.Action = 4
    PadText.FontName = CMDialog1.FontName
    PadText.FontItalic = CMDialog1.FontItalic
    PadText.FontStrikethru = CMDialog1.FontStrikethru
    PadText.FontSize = CMDialog1.FontSize
    PadText.FontUnderline = CMDialog1.FontUnderline
    PadText.ForeColor = CMDialog1.Color
End Sub
```

This, however, is not ideal. What if the user changes a few properties and then clicks on the Cancel button? In that case, you do not want to transfer property settings from the font dialog box to the pad. The way to determine whether the Cancel button was clicked on in a CMDialog box is a little clumsy—you have to let it generate an error. (This is a little clumsy because you could be watching for other errors in your program, and this would add to the confusion.) You do that by setting the CMDialog property CancelError to True (-1). This means that an error will be generated if the user clicks on the Cancel button. You can test that in the following way (using the Visual Basic On Error statement):

```
Sub FontItem_Click ()
    On Error Resume Next
    CMDialog1.CancelError = -1    'True
    CMDialog1.FontName = PadText.FontName
    CMDialog1.FontItalic = PadText.FontItalic
    CMDialog1.FontStrikethru = PadText.FontStrikethru
    CMDialog1.FontSize = PadText.FontSize
    CMDialog1.FontUnderline = PadText.FontUnderline
    CMDialog1.Color = PadText.ForeColor
    CMDialog1.Flags = CF_SCREENFONTS Or CF_EFFECTS
    CMDialog1.Action = 4
    If Err = 0 Then
        PadText.FontName = CMDialog1.FontName
        PadText.FontItalic = CMDialog1.FontItalic
```

616

```
        PadText.FontStrikethru = CMDialog1.FontStrikethru
        PadText.FontSize = CMDialog1.FontSize
        PadText.FontUnderline = CMDialog1.FontUnderline
        PadText.ForeColor = CMDialog1.Color
    End If
End Sub
```

It turns out that the CMDialog control's properties are not updated if the Cancel button is clicked on, so you are okay. But this demonstrates how to determine whether the Cancel button was clicked on or not—and you will have to know that soon. When you use the font selection dialog box, it looks like the one shown in figure 13.32. You can set fonts with it, as shown in figure 13.33.

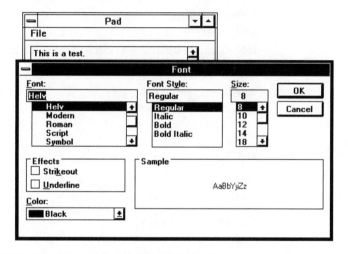

Figure 13.32. The font selection dialog box.

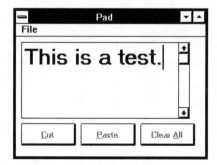

Figure 13.33. A new font in the notepad example.

Next, you will make the File Open... menu item active.

A File Open Dialog Box

If you give a CMDialog control an Action setting of 1, you will get a File Open dialog box (refer to table 13.4). You can put that to use in your notepad program by connecting it to the Open File... menu item. Open the OpenItem_Click () Sub procedure, as follows:

```
Sub OpenItem_Click ()

End Sub
```

In this case, it is very important to know whether the user clicked on the Cancel button; if he or she did, you do not want to execute the code you will use to open the file. For that reason, you will use the error generated if the Cancel button was clicked on. This means that you will have to use error checking, as follows:

```
Sub OpenItem_Click ()
    On Error Resume Next
    CMDialog1.CancelError = -1
        :
End Sub
```

In addition, you can specify a title for your dialog boxes by filling the CMDialog DialogTitle, as follows:

```
Sub OpenItem_Click ()
    On Error Resume Next
    CMDialog1.CancelError = -1
    CMDialog1.DialogTitle = "Open File"
    :
    :
End Sub
```

To specify the extension for the files the File Open dialog box will display initially in its list box, use the Filter property, a string you set in the following way:

```
"Comment1 ¦ Filter1 ¦ Comment2 ¦ Filter2 ..."
```

For example, "Text Files (*.txt) | *.txt | Data Files (*.dat) | *.dat" makes the dialog box display the names of files matching the pattern *.txt. As you will see, the user can switch to the second preset pattern, *.dat, by using a list box that displays the pattern options: "Text Files (*.txt)" and "Data Files (*.dat)" (and users can enter their own pattern). You will see how this works soon.

In addition, you can specify that you only want to read from the file by setting the OFN_READONLY flag in CMDialog1.Flags, as follows:

```
Sub OpenItem_Click ()
    On Error Resume Next
    CMDialog1.CancelError = -1
    CMDialog1.DialogTitle = "Open File"
    CMDialog1.Filter = "Text Files ¦ *.txt"
    CMDialog1.Flags = OFN_READONLY
        :
End Sub
```

The other flag settings (from Proconst.Txt) for CMDialog File Open/Save dialog boxes appear in table 13.6.

Table 13.6. CMDialog File Open/Save Flags

Flag	Means
OFN_READONLY	Check Read-Only box in dialog box
OFN_OVERWRITEPROMPT	Generate a message box if file already exists—users must confirm that they want to overwrite it
OFN_HIDEREADONLY	Hide the Read-Only box
OFN_NOCHANGEDIR	Disallow directory changes
OFN_SHOWHELP	Makes dialog box show a help button
OFN_ALLOWMULTISELECT	Allow multiple files to be selected; they will be separated by spaces in the final string.
OFN_PATHMUSTEXIST	User can enter only valid pathnames
OFN_FILEMUSTEXIST	User can select only names of files that exist
OFN_CREATEPROMPT	Ask whether user wants to create a file, if the file does not already exist

continues

619

Table 13.6. continued

Flag	Means
OFN_SHAREAWARE	Make OF_SHARINGVIOLATION error ignored
OFN_NOREADONLYRETURN	Specify that file selected will not be read-only and will not be in a write-protected directory

How to avoid overwriting preexisting files.
Note that the OFN_OVERWRITEPROMPT flag displays a message box if the file selected exists; if the user wants to overwrite it, he or she has to confirm that fact.

Now display the File Open dialog box by setting CMDialog1.Action to 1, as follows:

```
Sub OpenItem_Click ()
    On Error Resume Next
    CMDialog1.CancelError = -1
    CMDialog1.DialogTitle = "Open File"
    CMDialog1.Filter = "Text Files ¦ *.txt"
    CMDialog1.Flags = OFN_READONLY
    CMDialog1.Action = 1
        :
        :
End Sub
```

Finally, after the user closes the dialog box, you check to make sure that they did not click on Cancel. If you are supposed to read a file into your notepad, you do, taking its name from the CMDialog1.FileName property, as follows:

```
Sub OpenItem_Click ()
    On Error Resume Next
    CMDialog1.CancelError = -1
    CMDialog1.DialogTitle = "Open File"
    CMDialog1.Filter = "Text Files ¦ *.txt"
    CMDialog1.Flags = OFN_READONLY
```

```
        CMDialog1.Action = 1
    If Err = 0 Then
        Open CMDialog1.FileName For Input As #1
        PadText.Text = Input$(LOF(1), #1)
        Close #1
    End If
End Sub
```

Now you can open files and read them into your notepad. For example, now you can read in the file Proconst.Txt. The File Open dialog box appears in figure 13.34; the new version of the notepad, in figure 13.35.

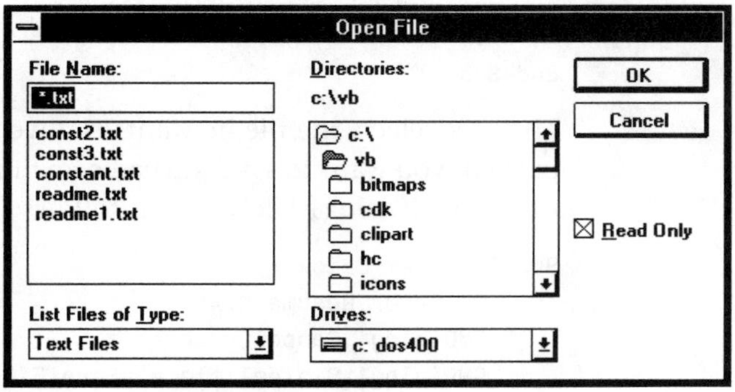

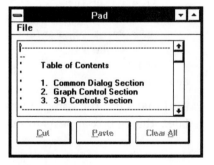

Figure 13.34. The File Open dialog box.

Figure 13.35. Your notepad reading Proconst.Txt.

Next, you will make the File Save... item active.

621

A Save File Dialog Box

To create a Save File... dialog box, you set CMDialog1's Action property to 2. For example, you can use the same properties and then display the Save File box, as follows:

```
Sub SaveItem_Click ()
    On Error Resume Next
    CMDialog1.CancelError = -1
    CMDialog1.DialogTitle = "Save File"
    CMDialog1.Filter = "Text Files ¦ *.txt"
    CMDialog1.Action = 2
        :
        :
End Sub
```

The user selects the file he wants to save. If the Cancel button was not pushed, you want to save the pad's text in the file whose name you will find in CMDialog1.FileName, as follows:

```
Sub SaveItem_Click ()
    On Error Resume Next
    CMDialog1.CancelError = -1
    CMDialog1.DialogTitle = "Save File"
    CMDialog1.Filter = "Text Files ¦ *.txt"
    CMDialog1.Action = 2
    If Err = 0 Then
        Open CMDialog1.FileName For Output As #1
        Print #1, PadText.Text
        Close #1
    End If
End Sub
```

And that's it; now you can save files as well as reading them. The Save File... dialog box appears in figure 13.36.

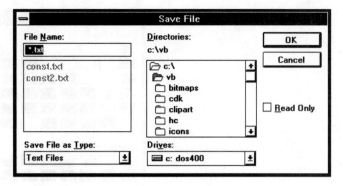

Figure 13.36. The Save File... dialog box.

Next, you can make the Text Color... dialog box active.

A Color Selection Dialog Box

You can use the color-selection dialog box if you set CMDialog1's Action property to 3. To do that, just add the following code to ColorItem_Click() to set PadText's ForeColor property, as follows:

```
Sub ColorItem_Click ()
    CMDialog1.Action = 3
    PadText.ForeColor = CMDialog1.Color
End Sub
```

That is all there is to selecting the new text color. The color-selection dialog box appears in figure 13.37. In addition, table 13.7 lists the flags you can use with color-selection dialog boxes. The last of the CMDialog dialog boxes is the Print dialog box; you can install it in your notepad now.

623

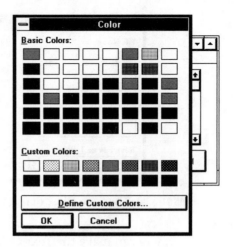

Figure 13.37. The color-selection dialog box.

Table 13.7. CMDialog's Color Properties

Flags	Means
CC_RGBINIT	Set initial color value
CC_FULLOPEN	Make dialog box open fully (including custom color design portion)
CC_PREVENTFULLOPEN	Do not allow dialog box to open fully
CC_SHOWHELP	Show help button

A Print Dialog Box

You can use the Print dialog box if you set CMDialog1's Action property to 5. This dialog box has plenty of options: the user can select a range of pages to print (returned in the dialog box's FromPage and PageTo properties); a Copies box allows the user to select the number of copies printed (returned in the Copies property); and the user can even switch printers. In addition, you can tailor these options by using the Flags settings shown in table 13.8.

More about switching printers.

If the user switches printers, you can no longer use the default Printer object in Visual Basic; instead, the dialog box will return a device context handle in its hDC property (CMDialog1.hDC). You can use this handle with Windows functions to print on the new printer.

Table 13.8. CMDialog's Print Flags

Flags	Means
PD_ALLPAGES	Sets or returns the All Pages button state
PD_SELECTION	Sets or returns the Selection button state
PD_PAGENUMS	Sets or returns the Pages button state
PD_NOSELECTION	Disallows use of the Selection button
PD_NOPAGENUMS	Disallows use of the Pages button state
PD_COLLATE	Sets or returns the Collate button state
PD_PRINTTOFILE	Sets or returns the state of the Print to File box
PD_PRINTSETUP	Makes CMDialog display the Print Setup dialog box instead of the Print dialog box
PD_NOWARNING	Disables warning message when there is no default printer
PD_RETURNDC	Returns an hDC handle (for use if user selects a printer other than the default printer)
PD_RETURNIC	Returns an information context for the printer selected
PD_SHOWHELP	Shows a help button

continues

Table 13.8. continued

Flags	Means
PD_USEDEVMODECOPIES	If a printer does not support multiple copies, does not enable the Copies box
PD_DISABLEPRINTTOFILE	Disallows "Print to File" box
PD_HIDEPRINTTOFILE	Hides "Print to File" box

You will put this to use in your PrintItem_Click() Sub procedure to make the Print... item active in your notepad, as follows:

```
Sub PrintItem_Click ()


End Sub
```

You will check whether the Cancel button was clicked to let you know whether you should execute code to print, so you have to set up error checking here, as follows:

```
Sub PrintItem_Click ()
    On Error Resume Next
    CMDialog1.CancelError = -1
    :
    :
End Sub
```

You can even set up (in the Print dialog box) the boxes that hold the page to start printing from (CMDialog1.FromPage) and the page to print to (CMDialog1.ToPage). In this case, assume that the document has only one page, and fill the From and To boxes accordingly. Now, place the dialog box on the screen, as follows:

```
Sub PrintItem_Click ()
    On Error Resume Next
    CMDialog1.CancelError = -1
    CMDialog1.FromPage = 1
    CMDialog1.ToPage = 1
    CMDialog1.Action = 5
    :
    :
End Sub
```

Peter Norton's Visual Basic for Windows, Third Edition, Covering Release 3.0

Finally, if the user did not click on Cancel, you can print the document (assuming that the user did not select a new printer), as follows:

```
Sub PrintItem_Click ()
    On Error Resume Next
    CMDialog1.CancelError = -1
    CMDialog1.FromPage = 1
    CMDialog1.ToPage = 1
    CMDialog1.Action = 5
    If Err = 0 Then
    Printer.Print PadText.Text
    Printer.EndDoc              'Cause printer to print
    End If
End Sub
```

Figure 13.38 shows the Print dialog box. The Professional Edition listing for your notepad program appears in listing 13.4.

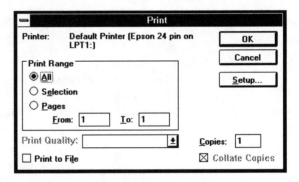

Figure 13.38. The Print dialog box.

Listing 13.4. Your Notepad (Pad.Mak on the Disk)

```
Form Form1 — — — — — — — — — — — — — — — —
    Caption         =    "Pad"

TextBox PadText
        MultiLine       =    -1   'True
        ScrollBars      =    2    'Vertical
        TabIndex        =    0
```

continues

Listing 13.4. continued

```
CommandButton CutButton
        Caption         =    "&Cut"
        Enabled         =    0    'False

CommandButton Pastebutton
        Caption         =    "&Paste"
        Enabled         =    0    'False

CommandButton ClearButton
        Caption         =    "Clear &All"
        Enabled         =    0    'False

Sub ClearButton_Click ()
    PadText.Text = ""
    PadText.SetFocus
End Sub

Sub CutButton_Click ()
        CutText = PadText.SelText
        PadText.SelText = ""
        PasteButton.Enabled = True
        PadText.SetFocus
End Sub

Sub Command1_Click ()
    PadText.SelText = CutText
    PadText.SetFocus
End Sub

Sub Pastebutton_Click ()
    PadText.SelText = CutText
End Sub

Sub PadText_Change ()
    CutButton.Enabled = True
    ClearButton.Enabled = True
End Sub

Sub FontItem_Click ()
```

```
        On Error Resume Next
        CMDialog1.CancelError = -1
        CMDialog1.FontName = PadText.FontName
        CMDialog1.FontItalic = PadText.FontItalic
        CMDialog1.FontStrikethru = PadText.FontStrikethru
        CMDialog1.FontSize = PadText.FontSize
        CMDialog1.FontUnderline = PadText.FontUnderline
        CMDialog1.Color = PadText.ForeColor
        CMDialog1.Flags = CF_SCREENFONTS Or CF_EFFECTS
        CMDialog1.Action = 4
        If Err = 0 Then
            PadText.FontName = CMDialog1.FontName
            PadText.FontItalic = CMDialog1.FontItalic
            PadText.FontStrikethru = CMDialog1.FontStrikethru
            PadText.FontSize = CMDialog1.FontSize
            PadText.FontUnderline = CMDialog1.FontUnderline
            PadText.ForeColor = CMDialog1.Color
        End If
End Sub


Sub ExitItem_Click ()
        End
End Sub


Sub OpenItem_Click ()
        On Error Resume Next
        CMDialog1.CancelError = -1
        CMDialog1.DialogTitle = "Open File"
        CMDialog1.Filter = "Text Files ¦ *.txt"
        CMDialog1.Flags = OFN_READONLY
        CMDialog1.Action = 1
        If Err = 0 Then
            Open CMDialog1.FileName For Input As #1
            PadText.Text = Input$(LOF(1), #1)
            Close #1
        End If
End Sub


Sub SaveItem_Click ()
        On Error Resume Next
        CMDialog1.CancelError = -1
```

continues

Listing 13.4. continued

```
        CMDialog1.DialogTitle = "Save File"
        CMDialog1.Filter = "Text Files ¦ *.txt"
        CMDialog1.Action = 2
        If Err = 0 Then
            Open CMDialog1.FileName For Output As #1
            Print #1, PadText.Text
            Close #1
        End If

End Sub

Sub PrintItem_Click ()
    On Error Resume Next
    CMDialog1.CancelError = -1
    CMDialog1.FromPage = 1
    CMDialog1.ToPage = 1
    CMDialog1.Action = 5
    If Err = 0 Then
        Printer.Print PadText.Text
        Printer.EndDoc
    End If
End Sub

Sub ColorItem_Click ()
    CMDialog1.Color = PadText.ForeColor
    CMDialog1.Action = 3
    PadText.ForeColor = CMDialog1.Color
End Sub
```

Now you will take a look at Pen computing.

Pen Computing

If you have a pen-ready version of Windows (that is, Windows for Pens), you can use the Pen controls that come in the file Pencntrl.Vbx.

> **About installing Windows for Pens.**
> To install Pen computing in your version of Windows, see the Pen ReadMe file in the Windows Software Development Kit (SDK).

The rest of the process is easy; the Pen edit controls that replace the standard text boxes in your program appear as follows:

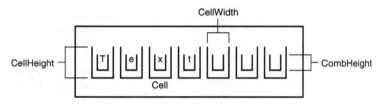

Two important properties of Pen controls are DelayRecog and OnTap. If DelayRecog and OnTap are both False, all writing in the Pen control will be "recognized" immediately after it is written. If DelayRecog is False and OnTap is True, the characters will be recognized only after the user taps the control with the pen. If DelayRecog is True, recognition is delayed until the property becomes False. To read the text, just examine the control's Text property as you would for a text box. That's all there is to it. Visual Basic even makes using Pen controls easy.

As you can see, custom controls can be very useful. Note, however, that this chapter has not covered all the custom controls available—and not even all the properties and methods of those it did cover. Covering everything about these new controls in depth is beyond the scope of this book. Clearly, however, there is a rich set of resources here, ready for use by the Visual Basic programmer. In fact, not only are custom controls useful, but you can even design them yourself. That is exactly what you will do in the next chapter.

Summary

Here you have seen how to use many of the custom controls that come with the Professional Edition of Visual Basic. In particular, you have worked through the following: key status controls, 3-D buttons, graph controls (including line charts, bar charts, and pie charts), prewritten dialog boxes (including font, file open, file save, and color-selection dialog boxes), animated buttons, pen controls, and windows gauges. The common dialog boxes are very useful. As you saw in Chapter 5, it is often difficult to design File Open and File Save dialog boxes just the way you want them; when you use the CMDialog controls, the job is already done for you. The same is certainly true for graph controls, which enable you to plot line, bar, and pie charts simply by selecting a Style property. In all, these controls can save a great deal of time and program development.

New Property	Description
Action	CMDialog property that determines what kind of dialog box appears (see table 13.4 for choices available).
ColorData	Cyclical property determining the color of bars or pie sections in a graph control.
DelayRecog and OnTap	Used in pen controls. If DelayRecog and OnTap are both False, all writing in the Pen control is recognized immediately after being written. If DelayRecog is False and OnTap is True, the characters are recognized only after the user taps the control with the pen. If DelayRecog is True, recognition is delayed until the property becomes False. (To read the text, use the control's Text property as you would for a text box.)
DialogTitle	Holds title to be used in a common dialog box (CMDialog controls).
ExtraData	Holds information, point by point, about how each point is to be displayed in a graph control (for example, allows exploding pie sections or sets the color of the sides of 3-D bars in 3-D bar charts).

New Property	Description
FileName	Holds the filename in file-oriented CMDialog controls.
Filter	Used in file-oriented CMDialog boxes. A string set like this: "Comment1 | Filter1 | Comment2 | Filter2 ...". (for example, "Text Files (*.txt) | *.txt | Data Files (*.dat) | *.dat" makes the dialog box display the names of files matching the pattern *.txt. The user can switch to the second preset pattern, *.dat, by using a list box that displays the pattern options: "Text Files (*.txt)" and "Data Files (*.dat)".)
Flags	Set of flags used to communicate with CMDialog controls (see table 13.5).
Font3D	Holds the 3-D setting for 3-D button controls.
Frame	Holds the current frame of an animated button control; animation occurs when you flip through these frames.
FromPage	Holds the page to start printing from in a Print common dialog box (CMDialog Action = 5).
GraphData	Cyclical property you load with the data to be graphed in a graph control.
GraphTitle	Holds the graph's title in a graph control.
GraphType	Indicates what type of graph you want (for example, a pie chart) in a graph control (see table 13.2 for available choices).
GridStyle	Indicates the type of grid you want in a graph control (see table 13.2 for available choices).

continues

633

New Property	Description
NeedleWidth	Sets the width of the needle in gauge controls (default = 10); measured in pixels.
PageTo	Holds the page to print to in a Print common dialog box (CMDialog Action = 5).
PatternData	Cyclical property, holding the types of patterns you want to use for bars or pie sections in a graph control.
Style	Sets the control wanted in key status and gauge controls.
ThisPoint	Holds the current point in graph controls.
XPosData	Holds the current x coordinate of data in graph controls.

14

Creating Custom Controls

I n this chapter, you will see how to write your own custom controls. The following topics are covered:

▼ Designing a new control for Visual Basic

▼ What it takes to support a control in Visual Basic

▼ Initializing a control

▼ Registering a control with Visual Basic

▼ Creating a Visual Basic property for your custom control

▼ Registering a property with Visual Basic

▼ Handling your control's events

▼ Registering an event with Visual Basic

▼ Designing a control's tool box bitmap

▼ Creating a custom control's procedure

635

Here you are actually going to create and implement a custom control, like a text box or command button, for Visual Basic. You will see how the process of writing and supporting such a new control works in code. Then you will be able to add your new control to the Visual Basic toolbox; Visual Basic programmers will be able to double-click on the tool and draw your control on a form. When they run the program, you will have your own events and properties (and you will see how to support them). In fact, these properties will appear in the properties window and can be set at design time, or in code. The utility of this approach is that you can design your own control—a database control, a control that encrypts files, one that searches entire hard disks for files, another that supports pop-up help, and so on. There is a thriving market for such add-on controls for Visual Basic—and this chapter shows you how to write them. Note also that the code in this chapter is written almost entirely in C, the standard development language in Windows when you want to go past what is possible in Visual Basic.

At this point, you are ready to see how to create custom Visual Basic controls, just like the ones you used in the preceding chapter. That is, you will create your own custom control file—a .Vbx file—which users can add to their programs simply by using Visual Basic's Add File... item. (This is the way to install .Vbx files as custom controls: using Add File....) When they do, your new control will be added as a tool in the tool box.

Note that you will need additional software to work through this chapter. You will be using the Visual Basic Custom Development Kit (CDK), which is included in the Visual Basic Professional Edition. As before, you also will need a package that can create dynamic link libraries. And because the CDK's documentation assumes that you are using Microsoft C Version 6 or 7, you will use those packages in this chapter. (The process is different for each one, so the differences will be pointed out.) You also will use the Windows 3.1 Software Development Kit (SDK). Finally, some readers will be using Visual Basic Version 1.0 and some will be using 2+ (the 2+ means Visual Basic versions later than 2.0, including Version 3.0); the ways to create custom controls in those two packages are slightly incompatible, and the chapter will point out the differences. With all that in mind, then, it is time to start designing your custom control.

The Box Custom Control

Your new control will draw a simple geometrical figure, say a box, and you can call it a Box control. Say, for example, that this is the size of your control in a Visual Basic program:

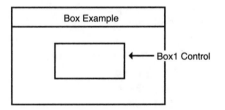

Then you could draw the box inside your control (the name "box control" refers to the box inside the control) like the following, and even color it, say, blue:

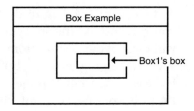

Box Example

Box1's box

In fact, you can define a custom property for this control, say BoxColor, that specifies whether the box in the center of the control will be colored in or left blank (white). That is, if Box1.BoxColor is set True (at design-time or at run-time), the box in the center of the control will be colored blue. Your final program can determine whether the user clicks the control and if so, whether he or she clicked inside the box. This will allow you to create two new custom events: ClickInside (the box) and ClickOutside (the box, but still inside the control), which then can be used as follows in Visual Basic:

```
Sub Box1_ClickOutside ()
     'Visual Basic code
End Sub

Sub Box1_ClickInside ()
     'Visual Basic code
End Sub
```

For example, you could beep once if the user clicks outside the box (but still in the control) and twice if he or she clicks inside the box, as follows:

```
Sub Box1_ClickOutside ()
     Beep
End Sub

Sub Box1_ClickInside ()
     Beep
     Beep
End Sub
```

That is, you will create a program with a custom control you can name Box1. Box1 will have a box in the middle of it and will work in the following way:

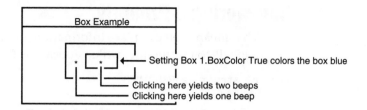

To do this, you have to make Box.Vbx, the custom control file that will let you create box controls. To make Box.Vbx, you use the following six files:

Init.C	Initializes and registers your control with Visual Basic
Box.C	Control's event and message handler
Box.H	Header file: Holds prototypes and variable declarations
Box.Rc	Holds bitmap information for your control's toolbox bitmaps
Box.Def	Specifies that you are creating a Windows type library
Makefile	Used by C 6/7's NMake facility to produce Box.Vbx

You will start with Init.C, which holds the initialization code you will need.

Initializing and Registering a Control

You are going to start by creating Init.C, the initialization file. The first step in setting up a custom control is to register its properties and events with Visual Basic, using VBRegisterModel(), and you will do that in Init.C. This information is passed in a series of structures; that is, you place properties in a PROPINFO structure, events in an EVENTINFO structure, and you place all of them in a MODEL structure that you pass to VBRegisterModel() (here, *model* refers to the class of control you are registering).

Registering a Property

That means you can place information about your BoxColor property in a PROPINFO structure, which appears as follows:

```
typedef struct tagPROPINFO
{
    PSTR    npszName;      /* Property name                       */
    FLONG   fl;            /* PF_ flags                           */
    BYTE    offsetData;    /* Offset into structure               */
    BYTE    infoData;      /* 0 or _INFO value for bitfield       */
    LONG    dataDefault;   /* 0 or _INFO value for bitfield       */
    PSTR    npszEnumList;  /* NULL or a near ptr to a string      */
    /* containing values for prop. listbox */
    BYTE    enumMax;       /* Maximum legal value for enum.       */
}
PROPINFO;
```

The second field, fl, holds the flags that tell Visual Basic how this property acts (those flags appear in table 14.1). By using this field, you will see how you can create properties that are only run-time accessible, or cannot be changed at run time, and so on. Note also in table 14.1 that Visual Basic will communicate with you, as you might expect, with a series of messages (which have the prefix VBM_). That is, you will be processing both normal Windows messages (WM_ messages) and Visual Basic messages (VBM_ messages) in your programs. You will see more about Visual Basic messages later.

Table 14.1. Visual Basic Property Flags

Property Flag	Means
DT_HSZ	Property is a string.
DT_SHORT	Property is a short.
DT_LONG	Property is a long.
DT_BOOL	Property is a bool.
DT_COLOR	Property is a color value.
DT_ENUM	Property is an enumeration.
DT_REAL	Property is a real value.
DT_XPOS	Property is x coordinate in twips.

Property Flag	Means
DT_XSIZE	Property is x size in twips.
DT_YPOS	Property is y coordinate in twips.
DT_YSIZE	Property is y size in twips.
DT_PICTURE	Property is a picture.
PF_fPropArray	Property is an array (must use DATASTRUCT to get or set property values).
PF_fSetData	Set property by setting data in programmer-supplied data structure.
PF_fSetMsg	VBM_SETPROPERTY when attempting to set property.
PF_fNoShow	Do not show property in the property window.
PF_fNoRuntimeW	Property is read-only at run time.
PF_fGetData	Get property value from programmer-supplied data.
PF_fGetMsg	VBM_GETPROPERTY message sent when property value is requested.
PF_fSetCheck	VBM_SETPROPERTY message sent before property is set.
PF_fSaveData	Save property setting along with form when file is saved to disk.
PF_fSaveMsg	VBM_SAVEPROPERTY/VBM_LOADPROPERTY sent when property value saved/loaded to/from file.
PF_fGetHszMsg	VBM_GETPROPERTYHSZ sent when property value is displayed in the properties window.
PF_fUpdateOnEdit	Property is updated as characters are typed in the settings box of the properties window.
PF_fEditable	Enable programmer to edit text in settings box.

continues

Table 14.1. continued

Property Flag	Means
PF_fPreHwnd	Load property before control's window struct is created.
PF_fDefVal	Avoid saving and loading property to and from disk when it is equal to dataDefault in the PROPINFO structure.
PF_fNoInitDef	Do not load property from dataDefault in PROPINFO when loading control.

In this example, you will make the BoxColor property a short value. To keep track of your box control's properties, you set up a BOX structure, in the following way:

```
typedef struct tagBOX
{
    RECT     rectDrawRegion;
    SHORT    BoxColor;
} BOX;
```

Here, you are storing both the dimensions of the box inside the control and the current value of BoxColor. You can place the BOX struct's definition in, say, Box.H. The RECT type in your definition is actually the Windows rectangle type, which will let you store the dimensions of the box, as follows:

```
typedef struct tagRECT
    {
    int    left;
    int    top;
    int    right;
    int    bottom;
    } RECT;
```

In fact, you also can ask Visual Basic to store the settings of your control's properties in a BOX structure. Then, when a property is changed, it will pass us a pointer to its internal BOX structure, which you can use to read values from. That is, Visual Basic enables you to configure the data structure it will use to store your control's properties in a manner that is convenient for you. You do that by setting up the structure you have named BOX. You can specify that Visual Basic should update the control's properties in its internal structure, or you can do it yourself, depending on how you set the property's PF flags, as indicated in table 14.1. You will use the PF_fGetData flag, which indicates to Visual Basic that you will be responsible for updating its internal BOX structure (as opposed to using PF_fSetData, which causes Visual Basic to handle that itself). You also will use PF_fSetMsg, which means that you will get a VBM_SETPROPERTY message when a property changes and, by reading the new value of the property as passed to you, you will be able to decide whether you want to update Visual Basic's internal BOX structure.

To let Visual Basic set up such a structure internally, you have to let it know how big a BOX structure is. After you do, it sets aside that many bytes in its own memory. Next, you have to let it know what is in the structure, and at what locations. To indicate that, you pass the offset of the various properties in the structure to Visual Basic, as follows:

In this way, Visual Basic sets up its own BOX structure the way you want it. When it has to update the data in the structure, Visual Basic will pass us a pointer to that structure, along with the new value of the property that has changed. The next step, then, is to pass the offset of BoxColor in a BOX structure to Visual Basic; you do that with a PROPINFO structure (you must pass one PROPINFO—property information—structure for each of the control's properties), which appears as follows—as you saw earlier:

```
typedef struct tagPROPINFO
{
    PSTR    npszName;      /* Property name                       */
    FLONG   fl;            /* PF_ flags                           */
    BYTE    offsetData;    /* Offset into structure               */
    BYTE    infoData;      /* 0 or _INFO value for bitfield       */
    LONG    dataDefault;   /* 0 or _INFO value for bitfield       */
```

```
      PSTR      npszEnumList;   /* NULL or a near ptr to a string      */
      /* containing values for prop. listbox */
      BYTE      enumMax;        /* Maximum legal value for enum.       */
}
PROPINFO;
```

In this case, you fill the fields of this structure like this for BoxColor (notice that you are passing the offset of BoxColor inside the BOX structure here):

```
#include <windows.h>
#include "vbapi.h"
#include "box.h"

PROPINFO Property_BoxColor =
{
    "BoxColor",
    DT_SHORT ¦ PF_fGetData ¦ PF_fSetMsg ¦ PF_fSaveData,
    (USHORT)&(((BOX *)0)->BoxColor), 0, /* get offset */
    0,
    NULL, 0
};
```

Note also that you included Windows.H here in Init.C, as you might expect, and Box.H, where the BOX structure is declared, and Vbapi.H. This last file, Vbapi.H, holds the prototypes for the functions you will need to interface with Visual Basic. (These functions have the prefix VB—VBRegisterModel()for example. You will see them throughout this chapter.)

Now you can add additional properties. Visual Basic provides a number of pointers to default PROPINFO structures for some standard properties (see table 14.2). You can use some of them to easily include a number of standard Visual Basic properties, including Name, Index, BackColor, Left, Top, Width, Height, Visible, Parent, DragMode, DragIcon, and Tag. In this way, Visual Basic has already done a lot of work for you—you can use the default PROPINFO structures for each of these properties.

Table 14.2. Predefined Properties in the Visual Basic CDK

Property	Constant defined in Vbapi.h
Name	PPROPINFO_STD_NAME
Index	PPROPINFO_STD_INDEX
BackColor	PPROPINFO_STD_BACKCOLOR
ForeColor	PPROPINFO_STD_FORECOLOR
Left	PPROPINFO_STD_LEFT
Top	PPROPINFO_STD_TOP
Width	PPROPINFO_STD_WIDTH
Height	PPROPINFO_STD_HEIGHT
Enabled	PPROPINFO_STD_ENABLED
Visible	PPROPINFO_STD_VISIBLE
MousePointer	PPROPINFO_STD_MOUSEPOINTER
Caption	PPROPINFO_STD_CAPTION
FontName	PPROPINFO_STD_FONTNAME
FontBold	PPROPINFO_STD_FONTBOLD
FontItalic	PPROPINFO_STD_FONTITALIC
FontStrike	PPROPINFO_STD_FONTSTRIKE
FontUnder	PPROPINFO_STD_FONTUNDER
FontSize	PPROPINFO_STD_FONTSIZE
TabIndex	PPROPINFO_STD_TABINDEX
Parent	PPROPINFO_STD_PARENT
DragMode	PPROPINFO_STD_DRAGMODE
DragIcon	PPROPINFO_STD_DRAGICON
BorderStyleOff	PPROPINFO_STD_BORDERSTYLEOFF
TabStop	PPROPINFO_STD_TABSTOP
Tag	PPROPINFO_STD_TAG
Text	PPROPINFO_STD_TEXT
BorderStyleOn	PPROPINFO_STD_BORDERSTYLEON

To create this list of properties in preparation for passing them to Visual Basic in VBRegisterModel(), you have to set up a NULL-terminated array of pointers to PROPINFO structures (one pointer per property). You can call this array of pointers, say, Box_Properties[]. You will include a pointer to the PROPINFO property you declared for BoxColor (you called that PROPINFO structure Property_BoxColor), and the predefined pointers to the other properties you want in your control. Because the predefined pointers are of type PPROPINFO, the array of pointers to PROPINFO structures, which you are calling Box_Properties[], appears as follows:

```
#include <windows.h>
#include "vbapi.h"
#include "box.h"

PROPINFO Property_BoxColor =
{
    "BoxColor",
    DT_SHORT | PF_fGetData | PF_fSetMsg | PF_fSaveData,
    (USHORT)&(((BOX *)0)->BoxColor), 0, /* get offset */
    0,
    NULL, 0
};

PPROPINFO Box_Properties[ ] =      <-
{                                    :
    PPROPINFO_STD_NAME,              :
    PPROPINFO_STD_INDEX,             :
    PPROPINFO_STD_BACKCOLOR,         :
    PPROPINFO_STD_LEFT,              :
    PPROPINFO_STD_TOP,               :
    PPROPINFO_STD_WIDTH,             :
    PPROPINFO_STD_HEIGHT,            :
    PPROPINFO_STD_VISIBLE,           :
    PPROPINFO_STD_PARENT,            :
    PPROPINFO_STD_DRAGMODE,          :
    PPROPINFO_STD_DRAGICON,          :
    PPROPINFO_STD_TAG,               :
    &Property_BoxColor,              :
    PPROPINFO_STD_HWND,              :  //For VB2+—remove for VB1
    NULL                             :
};
```

Note the last property you add, a HWND property, which all Visual Basic controls are expected to have, starting with Version 2.0. However, that property does not exist in Visual Basic 1.0; if you are using that version, omit that line.

Now you are set as far as properties go. The next step is to register the events, including ClickInside and ClickOutside.

Registering an Event

To register events, you have to put together an array of EVENTINFO structures, each of which is defined in Vbapi.H, like this:

```
typedef struct tagEVENTINFO
{
    PSTR      npszName;       /* Event procedure name             */
    USHORT    cParms;         /* Number of parameters to pass to it */
    USHORT    cwParms;        /* Number words words of parameters   */
    PWORD     npParmTypes;    /* List of parameters by type         */
    PSTR      npszParmProf;   /* Event parameter profile string     */
    FLONG     fl;             /* EF_ flags                          */
}
EVENTINFO;
```

To indicate that your ClickOutside event does not need any parameters passed to it, you place 0s or NULLs in its EVENTINFO structure:

```
EVENTINFO Event_ClickOutside =
{
    "ClickOutside",
    0,
    0,
    NULL,
    NULL
};
```

If you want, you can add parameters in the ClickInside event. For example, you might pass the mouse cursor's x and y coordinates in the following way (in Visual Basic):

```
Sub Box1_ClickOutside ()
    Beep
End Sub
```

647

```
Sub Box1_ClickInside (X As Single, Y As Single)
    Beep
    Beep
End Sub
```

To do that, you have to indicate the type of arguments you want passed to your event procedure (you will pass them yourself), their number, and their names, all in the EVENTINFO structure. Visual Basic has defined these constants in Vbapi.H, which will allow you to specify the data types of the arguments you will pass:

ET_I2   16-bit signed integer scalar or array variable

ET_I4   32-bit signed integer scalar or array variable

ET_R4   32-bit real scalar or array variable

ET_R8   64-bit real scalar or array variable

ET_CY   64-bit currency scalar or array variable

ET_SD   String scalar or array variable

ET_FS   Fixed-length string variable

In the ClickInside() event, for example, you will pass two arguments for a total of four words; each will be a 32-bit single, and the argument list will be "X As Single, Y As Single," like this:

```
WORD Paramtypes_ClickInside[ ] = {ET_R4, ET_R4};

EVENTINFO Event_ClickInside =
{
    "ClickInside",           /* Name of event                */
    2,                       /* Pass 2 parameters            */
    4,                       /* Total number of words to pass */
    Paramtypes_ClickInside,  /* Parameter specification      */
    "X As Single,Y As Single" /* Argument names               */
};
```

As you might expect, there are a number of predefined events (just as there are predefined properties). If you use these events, which appear in table 14.3, Visual Basic automatically adds support for them to your control. In this case, you add, say, DragDrop and DragOver.

Table 14.3. Predefined EventInfo Pointers

Event	Predefined EventInfo Pointer
Click	PEVENTINFO_STD_CLICK
DblClick	PEVENTINFO_STD_DBLCLICK
DragDrop	PEVENTINFO_STD_DRAGDROP
DragOver	PEVENTINFO_STD_DRAGOVER
GotFocus	PEVENTINFO_STD_GOTFOCUS
KeyDown	PEVENTINFO_STD_KEYDOWN
KeyPress	PEVENTINFO_STD_KEYPRESS
KeyUp	PEVENTINFO_STD_KEYUP
LostFocus	PEVENTINFO_STD_LOSTFOCUS
MouseDown	PEVENTINFO_STD_MOUSEDOWN
MouseMove	PEVENTINFO_STD_MOUSEMOVE
MouseUp	PEVENTINFO_STD_MOUSEUP

As with properties, you have to set up an array of pointers (here, to EVENTINFO structures) so that you can assemble your events in one place. And, as before, you will use some default pointers (type PEVENTINFO) to include the standard events you have decided on (DragDrop and DragOver). That means that your array of pointers to EVENTINFO structures, which you can call Box_Events[] (the counterpart of Box_Properties[]), will appear as follows in Init.C:

```
#include <windows.h>
#include "vbapi.h"
#include "box.h"

PROPINFO Property_BoxColor =
{
:
:
};

PPROPINFO Box_Properties[ ] =
{
```

```
            PPROPINFO_STD_NAME,
            :
            :
            NULL
    };

    WORD Paramtypes_ClickInside[ ] = {ET_R4, ET_R4};

    EVENTINFO Event_ClickOutside =
    {                                            :
            "ClickOutside",                      :
            0,                                   :
            0,                                   :
            NULL,                                :
            NULL
    };

    EVENTINFO Event_ClickInside =
    {                                            :
            "ClickInside",                       :
            2,                                   :
            4,                                   :
            Paramtypes_ClickInside,              :
            "X As Single,Y As Single"
    };

    PEVENTINFO Box_Events[ ] =
    {                                            :
            &Event_ClickInside,                  :
            &Event_ClickOutside,                 :
            PEVENTINFO_STD_DRAGDROP,             :
            PEVENTINFO_STD_DRAGOVER,             :
            NULL
    };
```

Now you have all your properties in one array, Box_Properties[], and all your events in another array, Box_Events[]. The final step is to place pointers to those arrays in a larger MODEL structure and pass it to VBRegisterModel( ). The MODEL structure appears as follows:

```
typedef struct tagMODEL
{
    USHORT      usVersion;              /* VB version used by control    */
    FLONG       fl;                     /* Bitfield structure            */
```

```
    PCTLPROC     pctlproc;                /* the control proc.              */
    FSHORT       fsClassStyle;            /* window class style             */
    FLONG        flWndStyle;              /* default window style           */
    USHORT       cbCtlExtra;              /* # bytes alloc'd for HCTL structure */
    USHORT       idBmpPalette;            /* BITMAP id for tool palette      */
    PSTR         npszDefName;             /* default control name prefix    */
    PSTR         npszClassName;           /* Visual Basic class name        */
    PSTR         npszParentClassName;     /* Parent window class if subclassed */
    NPPROPLIST   npproplist;              /* Property list                  */
    NPEVENTLIST  npeventlist;             /* Event list                     */
    BYTE         nDefProp;                /* index of default property      */
    BYTE         nDefEvent;               /* index of default event         */
    BYTE         nDefValue;               /* index of default control value */
}
MODEL;
```

Here you will store the current Visual Basic version, a pointer to the routine you will use to handle events for your control. The routine itself—named BoxCtlProc( )—is in Box.C. You will use the default Windows style of your control (each control is itself a window, as you might expect) and the size of the data structure to store data about your control, the name of your control, the name of the control class you are setting up, and pointers to the PROPINFO and EVENTINFO arrays you already set up. You can name this model structure, say, modelBox, because it determines the model (class) of your box control. You can put it to work in the following way:

```
MODEL modelBox =
{
    VB_VERSION,                  /* VB version */
    0,                           /* No additional params */
    (PCTLPROC)BoxCtlProc,        /* Control's event proc */
    CS_VREDRAW | CS_HREDRAW,     /* Window class style */
    WS_BORDER,                   /* Window style */
    sizeof(BOX),                 /* Size of BOX */
    IDBMP_BOX,                   /* Resource number of tool box bitmap */
    "Box",                       /* Control name prefix (—> Box1, Box2...) */
    "BoxClass",                  /* Name of our control class */
    NULL,                        /* No parent class */
    Box_Properties,              /* Point to properties we want */
    Box_Events,                  /* Point to events we want */
    IPROP_BOX_COLOR,             /* index of default property       */
    IEVENT_BOX_CLICKINSIDE,      /* index of default event          */
    IPROP_BOX_COLOR              /* index of default control value  */
};
```

Note that when you pass the size of the control's data structure—
sizeof(BOX)—Visual Basic sets aside that many bytes, in effect duplicating
that structure. As mentioned, you also tell Visual Basic the byte offset of
each property in that data structure (you pass that in the PROPINFO
structures), so that it knows where to store them. Later, you will be able
to get a pointer to that internal Visual Basic structure; and that is where
you can read or write the data Visual Basic will associate with your control.
One of the preceding values, IDBMP_BOX, is a resource number you have
not seen yet but will define soon. This resource number corresponds to
the bitmap you want to use for your Box control tool in VB's toolbox. You
will add IDBMP_BOX later (after designing the corresponding bitmap).

This MODEL structure is the structure you will pass to VBRegisterModel( ).
We will examine that process now. Because Box.Vbx is set up as a dynamic
link library, the first thing that happens when your .Vbx file is loaded is
that you get a call to a function named LibMain( ), where you can perform
initialization, you can put LibMain( ) in Init.C.

In fact, you can set up LibMain( ) now. A number of parameters will be
passed to you that you will not actually use—but you will copy over all
unused parameters to avoid "unused parameter" warning messages from
the compiler. Following that, you will execute UnlockData(0), which
simply makes sure that your data segment is not locked in place when not
used. In addition, you need the instance handle, hMod, when you register
your control; this handle is passed to you in LibMain( ), so you save it in
the variable hmodDLL, as follows:

```
MODEL modelBox =
{
    VB_VERSION,
    0,
    (PCTLPROC)BoxCtlProc,
    CS_VREDRAW | CS_HREDRAW,
    WS_BORDER,
    sizeof(BOX),
    IDBMP_BOX,
```

```
        "Box",
        "BoxClass",
        NULL,
        Box_Properties,
        Box_Events,
        IPROP_BOX_COLOR,
        IEVENT_BOX_CLICKINSIDE,
        IPROP_BOX_COLOR
};


HANDLE hmodDLL;             /* Instance handle  */

int FAR PASCAL LibMain       //C7 version
(
        HANDLE hModule,
        WORD   wDataSeg,
        WORD   cbHeapSize,
        LPSTR  lpszCmdLine
)
{
        wDataSeg     = wDataSeg;
        cbHeapSize   = cbHeapSize;
        lpszCmdLine = lpszCmdLine;

        hmodDLL = hModule;

        return 1;
}
```

This is the MS C 7.0 version of LibMain. You will see the MS C 6.0 and 6.10
version later, in the listing. You use the instance handle hmodDLL when
you register your control using VBRegisterModel( ). In fact, after LibMain( )
returns, you get a call to the function VBINITCC( ). It is here that you call
VBRegisterModel( ). You pass it hmodDLL, your instance handle (you
need an instance handle because you can have multiple instances of your
program running), and a pointer to modelBox, your MODEL structure for
the Box control, like the following:

```
MODEL modelBox =
{
        VB_VERSION,          :
        IPROP_BOX_COLOR
};
```

```
HANDLE hmodDLL;              /* Instance handle  */

int FAR PASCAL LibMain          //C7
{
:
}


BOOL FAR PASCAL _export VBINITCC
(
    USHORT usVersion,
    BOOL   fRuntime
)
{
    fRuntime = fRuntime;
    usVersion = usVersion;


    return VBRegisterModel(hmodDLL, &modelBox);
}
```

Now you have registered your control with Visual Basic. That is all for Init.C. Now Visual Basic is aware of your control, including all its properties and events. To make those events and properties active, Visual Basic will send you messages (letting you know what is going on with your control) to the function BoxCtlProc( ), which you have previously registered. You handle those messages in that function, taking the correct action as needed (turning your control's box blue if BoxColor becomes True, for example, or causing a ClickInside event if the user clicks inside your box). The entire listing for Init.C is in listing 14.1 (Init.C on the Disk). This listing is written for MS C 7.0. If you are using MS C 6.0 or MS C 6.10, uncomment the lines labelled with a C6 in the listing (and comment out the C 7.0 LibMain( ) procedure).

You might have noticed that one of the values you placed in the MODEL structure was a BITMAP id for the Visual Basic toolbox, IDBMP_BOX. Because Visual Basic uses that bitmap in the toolbox, you will see how to create it in the next section.

Listing 14.1. Init.C—Vbx Initialization (Init.C on the Disk)

```c
#include <windows.h>
#include "vbapi.h"
#include "box.h"

PROPINFO Property_BoxColor =
{
    "BoxColor",
    DT_SHORT | PF_fGetData | PF_fSetMsg | PF_fSaveData,
    (USHORT)&(((BOX *)0)->BoxColor), 0, /* get offset to BoxColor */
    0,
    NULL, 0
};

PPROPINFO Box_Properties[ ] =
{
    PPROPINFO_STD_NAME,
    PPROPINFO_STD_INDEX,
    PPROPINFO_STD_BACKCOLOR,
    PPROPINFO_STD_LEFT,
    PPROPINFO_STD_TOP,
    PPROPINFO_STD_WIDTH,
    PPROPINFO_STD_HEIGHT,
    PPROPINFO_STD_VISIBLE,
    PPROPINFO_STD_PARENT,
    PPROPINFO_STD_DRAGMODE,
    PPROPINFO_STD_DRAGICON,
    PPROPINFO_STD_TAG,
    &Property_BoxColor,
    PPROPINFO_STD_HWND,           //VB2+—comment out for VB version 1.0
    NULL
};

WORD Paramtypes_ClickInside[ ] = {ET_R4, ET_R4};

EVENTINFO Event_ClickOutside =
{
    "ClickOutside",
    0,
    0,
```

continues

Listing 14.1. continued

```
        NULL,
        NULL
    };

    EVENTINFO Event_ClickInside =
    {
        "ClickInside",
        2,
        4,
        Paramtypes_ClickInside,
        "X As Single,Y As Single"
    };

    PEVENTINFO Box_Events[ ] =
    {
        &Event_ClickInside,
        &Event_ClickOutside,
        PEVENTINFO_STD_DRAGDROP,
        PEVENTINFO_STD_DRAGOVER,
        NULL
    };

    MODEL modelBox =
    {
        VB_VERSION,
        0,
        (PCTLPROC)BoxCtlProc,
        CS_VREDRAW | CS_HREDRAW,
        WS_BORDER,
        sizeof(BOX),
        IDBMP_BOX,
        "Box",
        "BoxClass",
        NULL,
        Box_Properties,
        Box_Events,
        IPROP_BOX_COLOR,
        IEVENT_BOX_CLICKINSIDE,
        IPROP_BOX_COLOR
    };

    HANDLE hmodDLL;                  /* Instance handle  */
```

```c
int FAR PASCAL LibMain        //MS C 7.0 version of LibMain
(
    HANDLE hModule,
    WORD   wDataSeg,
    WORD   cbHeapSize,
    LPSTR  lpszCmdLine
)
{
    wDataSeg    = wDataSeg;
    cbHeapSize  = cbHeapSize;
    lpszCmdLine = lpszCmdLine;

    hmodDLL = hModule;

    return 1;
}

BOOL FAR PASCAL _export VBINITCC
(
    USHORT usVersion,
    BOOL   fRuntime
)
{
    fRuntime  = fRuntime;
    usVersion = usVersion;

    return VBRegisterModel(hmodDLL, &modelBox);
}

//C6 BOOL FAR PASCAL LibMain(HANDLE hmod, HANDLE segDS, USHORT cbHeapSize)
//C6 {
//C6    cbHeapSize = cbHeapSize;    /* Not used, but necessary for no warn */
//C6    segDS = segDS;
//C6    hmodDLL = hmod;
//C6    UnlockData(0);              /* Leave DS unlocked when not used */
//C6    return TRUE;
//C6 }

//C6 VOID FAR PASCAL _export WEP(BOOL fSystemExit)
//C6 {
//C6    fSystemExit = fSystemExit; /* Not used, but necessary for no warn */
//C6 }
```

Designing the Control's Toolbox Bitmap

Now you can design four bitmaps for the toolbox, corresponding to the following monitors and tool icon positions (up or down—unselected or selected respectively):

VGA up position (unselected)

VGA down position (selected position)

Monochrome up position

EGA up position

Each of these bitmaps needs to be exactly the right size. Fortunately, the CDK comes with several sample bitmaps that you can modify for exactly this purpose. In the directory c:\vb\cdk\pix, for example, you will find Pixcd.Bmp (VGA down position), Pixcu.Bmp (VGA up position), Pixeu.Bmp (EGA up position), Pixmu.Bmp (Monochrome up position). You can copy those files over and rename them for your Box control, like the following:

Boxcu.Bmp   VGA up position (unselected)

Boxcd.Bmp   VGA down position (selected position)

Boxmu.Bmp   Monochrome up position

Boxeu.Bmp   EGA up position

Next, load these files into SDKPaint or the Image Editor in the Windows SDK and change the figures in them to, say, a simple box for the Box control. That is, your toolbox icon will be a simple box, as shown in figure 14.1. After you finish editing these bitmaps with SDKPaint or the Image Editor (put a box figure in the center of each bitmap), you simply write them out to disk. That's it; you have created the icons you will need. (You can even use Windows Paint to modify these bitmaps, although that is a much more difficult task.)

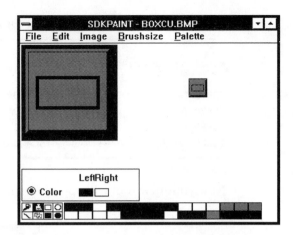

Figure 14.1. Using SDKPaint.

After creating these files, you can assign the corresponding bitmaps arbitrary resource numbers in Box.H, like the following:

```
#define IDBMP_BOX          5000          /* boxcu.bmp */
#define IDBMP_BOXDOWN      5001          /* boxcd.bmp */
#define IDBMP_BOXMONO      5003          /* boxmu.bmp */
#define IDBMP_BOXEGA       5006          /* boxeu.bmp */


typedef struct tagBOX
{
    RECT     rectDrawRegion;
    SHORT    BoxColor;
} BOX;
```

Then you have to associate those resource IDs with the bitmap files themselves, which you do in Box.Rc, as follows:

```
IDBMP_BOX          BITMAP  DISCARDABLE "boxcu.bmp"
IDBMP_BOXDOWN      BITMAP  DISCARDABLE "boxcd.bmp"
IDBMP_BOXMONO      BITMAP  DISCARDABLE "boxmu.bmp"
IDBMP_BOXEGA       BITMAP  DISCARDABLE "boxeu.bmp"
```

In fact, that is all you need in Box.Rc (one of your six files for Box.Vbx), because the bitmaps are the only resources you will use here. The whole thing appears in listing 14.2 (Box.Rc on the Disk).

Listing 14.2. Box.Rc (Box.Rc on the Disk)

```
#include "box.h"

IDBMP_BOX          BITMAP  DISCARDABLE "boxcu.bmp"
IDBMP_BOXDOWN      BITMAP  DISCARDABLE "boxcd.bmp"
IDBMP_BOXMONO      BITMAP  DISCARDABLE "boxmu.bmp"
IDBMP_BOXEGA       BITMAP  DISCARDABLE "boxeu.bmp"
```

Now your new tool will appear in the toolbox, as shown in Figure 14.2.

Our Box
Tool

Figure 14.2. The box tool in Visual Basic's toolbox.

Your Box Control Procedure

The second C procedure you will need, now that your Box control is installed, is Box.C, which handles the operation of Box controls. The function BoxCtlProc( ), which is where Visual Basic will pass messages intended for your control, is in this procedure. You start Box.C by including the include files you will need:

```
#include <windows.h>
#include "vbapi.h"
#include "box.h"
    :
    :
```

Next come the prototypes of the functions you will use in this code in addition to BoxCtlProc( ). You do not put these prototypes in Box.H because these functions are designed to help BoxCtlProc( ) and are entirely internal to Box.C. These functions are as follows: PaintBox( ), which paints box controls; InBox( ), which lets you determine whether a mouse event occurred inside or outside the box in the middle of your control (that is the difference between ClickInside( ) and ClickOutside( )); FireClickInside( ), which lets you fire, or cause, a Visual Basic event—in this case, ClickInside( )—and FireClickOutside( ):

```
#include <windows.h>
#include "vbapi.h"
#include "box.h"

VOID NEAR PaintBox(PBOX pbox, HWND hwnd, HDC hdc);
BOOL NEAR InBox(PBOX pbox, SHORT x, SHORT y);
VOID NEAR FireClickInside(HCTL hctl, SHORT x, SHORT y);
VOID NEAR FireClickOutside(HCTL hctl);
    :
    :
```

In other words, you will divide your C code between Init.C and Box.C, like this:

Init.C

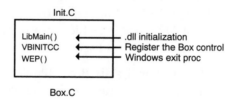

Box.C

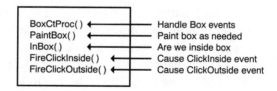

Earlier in this section, you set up a BOX structure to store the properties of your box control, like this:

```
typedef struct tagBOX
{
    RECT     rectDrawRegion;
    SHORT    BoxColor;
} BOX;
```

As you have seen, Visual Basic sets up the same structure internally. When necessary, it passes a pointer to that structure (for you to set values in, or to read the values you set previously), which means that it will be useful to define a type of pointer to BOX called PBOX in Box.H:

```
#define IDBMP_BOX          5000        /* boxcu.bmp */
#define IDBMP_BOXDOWN      5001        /* boxcd.bmp */
#define IDBMP_BOXMONO      5003        /* boxmu.bmp */
#define IDBMP_BOXEGA       5006        /* boxeu.bmp */


typedef struct tagBOX
{
    RECT     rectDrawRegion;
    SHORT    BoxColor;
} BOX;


typedef BOX FAR * PBOX;
```

Note that this is the type of argument you can pass to PaintBox( ) and InBox( )—passing them the BOX pointer you got from Visual Basic. Next in Box.C comes BoxCtlProc( ) itself; this is where you process messages sent to your control. These messages are of two kinds: WM_ messages (like WM_PAINT), that come from Windows, and VBM_messages (like VBM_DRAGDROP, which means that your control was just dropped) that come from Visual Basic.

Now you will start BoxCtlProc( ). Five parameters are passed to that function: hctl, the control handle Visual Basic gives to your control; hwnd, the Windows handle to your control; msg, the message intended for your control (for example, WM_PAINT, WM_SIZE, or messages from Visual Basic, such as VBM_SETPROPERTY); wp, a message parameter (either the customary wparam parameter from Windows for WM_ messages or additional information from Visual Basic for VBM_ messages); and lp (the customary lparam or additional Visual Basic information for VBM_ messages). The code is as follows:

```
#include <windows.h>
#include "vbapi.h"
#include "box.h"


VOID NEAR PaintBox(PBOX pbox, HWND hwnd, HDC hdc);
BOOL NEAR InBox(PBOX pbox, SHORT x, SHORT y);
```

```
VOID NEAR FireClickInside(HCTL hctl, SHORT x, SHORT y);
VOID NEAR FireClickOutside(HCTL hctl);

LONG FAR PASCAL _export BoxCtlProc(HCTL hctl, HWND hwnd, USHORT msg,
    USHORT wp, LONG lp)
    :
```

In general, you pass hctl to Visual Basic API functions and hwnd to
Windows API functions, although they both refer to the same control. In
fact, hctl gives you the pointer you need to VB's internal BOX structure.
To get that pointer, you simply dereference hctl with the VBDerefControl( )
function. That is, you get the pointer to Visual Basic's currently active
BOX structure, as follows:

```
#include <windows.h>
    :
    :
LONG FAR PASCAL _export BoxCtlProc(HCTL hctl, HWND hwnd, USHORT msg,
    USHORT wp, LONG lp)
{
    PBOX pbox;
    LPRECT prect;

    /* Note: Must again dereference hctl whenever we invalidate */
    /* pbox—including after calls to VB API */
    pbox = (PBOX)VBDerefControl(hctl);
    :
```

Note that you should use VBDerefControl( ) again whenever you do
something that might cause Visual Basic to change your BOX structure in
some way—including calls to the Visual Basic API of each function that
begins with the prefix Visual Basic. (Do not, of course, dereference hctl
after calls to VBDerefControl( ).) This API provides the means of connecting to Visual Basic through such functions as VBXPixelsToTwips( ) or
VBFireEvent( ), both of which you will see soon.

Now that you have a pointer (pbox) to the box control's data, you can start
interpreting the message sent to you in msg with a switch statement, as
follows:

```
#include <windows.h>
#include "vbapi.h"
```

```
#include "box.h"
     :
     :
    pbox = (PBOX)VBDerefControl(hctl);

    switch (msg){
     :
     :
```

For example, when your control is first created, you get a WM_CREATE message, as would any normal Windows program. You can perform initialization when you get that message; for example, you might set the BoxColor property to FALSE to start:

```
#include <windows.h>
#include "vbapi.h"
#include "box.h"
     :
     :
    pbox = (PBOX)VBDerefControl(hctl);

    switch (msg){
    case WM_CREATE:                    /* Perform initialization here */
    pbox->BoxColor = FALSE;
    break;
```

This is the way you will interface to the BoxColor property: pbox->BoxColor, which enables you to set or reset Visual Basic's own internal setting of that property.

Next, you will handle the case in which your control was (re)sized—the WM_SIZE case. You want to fill in or update the RECT structure in which you store the size of the box inside your control, which you have called rectDrawRegion in the BOX structure (from Box.H):

```
#define IDBMP_BOX          5000        /* boxcu.bmp */
#define IDBMP_BOXDOWN      5001        /* boxcd.bmp */
#define IDBMP_BOXMONO      5003        /* boxmu.bmp */
#define IDBMP_BOXEGA       5006        /* boxeu.bmp */

typedef struct tagBOX
{
    RECT      rectDrawRegion;
```

```
    SHORT    BoxColor;
} BOX;

typedef BOX FAR * PBOX;
```

You can do that by getting a pointer to rectDrawRegion in VB's BOX structure. That is, this rectangle defines the box inside your control; when you get a resize event, you will have to adjust its coordinates accordingly because you will have to redraw the box in WM_PAINT events, which will read its size from this same RECT structure. Because your control is simply a window, you can find its (new) size with the Windows function GetClientRect( ). After that, all that remains is to recalculate the size of the box in your control (you will just make it occupy the middle region of the control) and store it in VB's BOX data structure, like this:

```
#include <windows.h>
#include "vbapi.h"
#include "box.h"
    :
    :
    switch (msg){
    case WM_CREATE:                    /* Perform initialization here */
    pbox->BoxColor = FALSE;
    break;

    case WM_SIZE:                      /* Our control was (re)sized */
    prect = &pbox->rectDrawRegion;

    GetClientRect(hwnd, prect);        /* Draw box in the control */
    prect->left = prect->right / 4;
    prect->right = 3 * prect->right / 4;
    prect->top = prect->bottom / 4;
    prect->bottom = 3 * prect->bottom / 4;
    break;
        :
```

That also means that when you paint, you will be able to use the coordinates in the box structure. In fact, you will add the WM_PAINT case now. You will set up a separate Paint function called PaintBox( ), because it is usually convenient to call such a function from several places in the program. You will pass the pointer to the box structure—pbox—to PaintBox( ), along with a handle to the device context, hdc, in which it is supposed to paint.

That means you can set up the WM_PAINT case easily. It turns out that if the wp parameter is non-zero, you are being asked to print on the printer and wp holds the correct device context handle. Otherwise, you can simply use BeginPaint( ) and EndPaint( ) as you would normally to get a device context handle, like this:

```
#include <windows.h>
#include "vbapi.h"
#include "box.h"
    :
    :
    pbox = (PBOX)VBDerefControl(hctl);

    switch (msg){
    case WM_CREATE:                    /* Perform initialization here */
        pbox->BoxColor = FALSE;
        break;

    case WM_SIZE:                      /* Our control was (re)sized */
        prect = &pbox->rectDrawRegion;

        GetClientRect(hwnd, prect);        /* Draw box in the control */
        prect->left = prect->right / 4;
        prect->right = 3 * prect->right / 4;
        prect->top = prect->bottom / 4;
        prect->bottom = 3 * prect->bottom / 4;
        break;

    case WM_PAINT:                     /* Repaint our control */
        if (wp)
        PaintBox(pbox, hwnd, (HDC)wp);      /* Printer */
        else{
        PAINTSTRUCT ps;

            BeginPaint(hwnd, &ps);
            PaintBox(pbox, hwnd, ps.hdc);
            EndPaint(hwnd, &ps);
        }
        break;
        :
```

Now you have to set up PaintBox( ), which does the real work. Even so, all you really have to do in PaintBox( ) is to find the coordinates of the box (that you set in WM_SIZE) and draw a rectangle. That looks like this, where you are finding the coordinates of the rectangle in the BOX structure pointed to by pbox and drawing it:

```
VOID NEAR PaintBox (PBOX pbox, HWND hwnd, HDC hdc)
{
    LPRECT   prect = &pbox->rectDrawRegion;

    Rectangle(hdc, prect->left, prect->top, prect->right, prect->bottom);
}
```

You might recall, however, that the box is supposed to be colored blue (RGB(0, 0, 255)) if the BoxColor property is set. That property is stored in the box structure's BoxColor field, like this:

```
typedef struct tagBOX
{
    RECT     rectDrawRegion;
    SHORT    BoxColor;
} BOX;

typedef BOX FAR * PBOX;
```

You can check it in PaintBox( ), using the standard Windows functions CreateSolidBrush( ) and SelectObject( ) as needed to color the box blue, as follows:

```
VOID NEAR PaintBox (PBOX pbox, HWND hwnd, HDC hdc)
{
    HBRUSH   hbr;
    HBRUSH   hbrOld = NULL;
    LPRECT   prect = &pbox->rectDrawRegion;

    f(pbox->BoxColor){
        hbr = CreateSolidBrush(RGB(0, 0, 255)); /* Blue brush */
        hbrOld = SelectObject(hdc, hbr);
    }
    Rectangle(hdc, prect->left, prect->top, prect->right, prect->bottom);
    if(pbox->BoxColor){
        SelectObject(hdc, hbrOld);              /* Restore old brush */
    }
}
```

That takes care of the WM_PAINT case. Next, you will handle the case in which the mouse button goes down in the control. In that case, you will

667

get a WM_MOUSEDOWN message; now you have to determine whether the mouse went down inside the box in your control (you have to "fire" a ClickInside event) or not (ClickOutside). You can use the InBox( ) function for that if you pass it the location of the mouse cursor and a pointer to the box structure, and have it return a BOOL value (TRUE if we are inside the box):

```
BOOL NEAR InBox(PBOX pbox, SHORT x, SHORT y)
{

}
```

All you need to do is get a pointer to rectDrawRegion—as before—and then check whether the mouse coordinates, x and y, indicate that the mouse cursor was inside the box or not:

```
BOOL NEAR InBox(PBOX pbox, SHORT x, SHORT y)
{
    LPRECT  prect = &pbox->rectDrawRegion;

    return ((prect->left < x) & (prect->right > x) & \
        (prect->top < y) & (prect->bottom > y));
}
```

Now you can determine whether the mouse clicked inside or outside the box in your control simply by using InBox( ). In the WM_LBUTTONDOWN case, then, you can find the x and y coordinates of the mouse click from the lp parameter—x = LOWORD(lp) and y = HIWORD(lp). If you are indeed in the box (as determined by InBox( )), you want to fire the ClickInside event with FireClickInside( ), which you will write in a moment. If you are not inside the box, you want to use FireClickOutside( ), which you also will write in a moment. In code, then, the WM_LBUTTONDOWN event looks like this:

```
#include <windows.h>
#include "vbapi.h"
#include "box.h"
    :
    :
    case WM_PAINT:                    /* Repaint our control */
        if (wp)
            PaintBox(pbox, hwnd, (HDC)wp);   /* Printer */
        else{
```

```
        PAINTSTRUCT ps;

        BeginPaint(hwnd, &ps);
        PaintBox(pbox, hwnd, ps.hdc);
        EndPaint(hwnd, &ps);
    }
    break;

case WM_LBUTTONDOWN:              /* Button down in our control */
    if (InBox(pbox, LOWORD(lp), HIWORD(lp))){
        FireClickInside(hctl, LOWORD(lp), HIWORD(lp));
    }
    else
        FireClickOutside(hctl);
    break;
    :
```

Now we will take a look at FireClickOutside( ), followed by
FireClickInside( ). When the user clicks on your control, he or she
generates a ClickInside or ClickOutside event (you decide which one).
You can fire—generate—events with VBFireEvent( ); but how do you tell
Visual Basic which event you are firing? You may recall that you set up the
array of pointers to events structures (in Init.C) like this:

```
PEVENTINFO Box_Events[ ] =
{
    &Event_ClickInside,
    &Event_ClickOutside,
    PEVENTINFO_STD_DRAGDROP,
    PEVENTINFO_STD_DRAGOVER,
    NULL
};
_H
```

Visual Basic will take them in order—ClickInside is considered event 0 for
your control; ClickOutside, event 1; DRAGDROP, event 2; and DRAGOVER,
event 3. In fact, you can define these constants in Box.H for easy reference:

```
#define IDBMP_BOX        5000
#define IDBMP_BOXDOWN    5001
#define IDBMP_BOXMONO    5003
#define IDBMP_BOXEGA     5006
```

```
typedef struct tagBOX
{
    RECT     rectDrawRegion;
    SHORT    BoxColor;
} BOX;

typedef BOX FAR * PBOX;

#define IEVENT_BOX_CLICKINSIDE       0
#define IEVENT_BOX_CLICKOUTSIDE      1
#define IEVENT_BOX_DRAGDROP          2
#define IEVENT_BOX_DRAGOVER          3
```

Similarly, we assembled the array of properties like this (in Init.C):

```
PPROPINFO Box_Properties[ ] =
{
    PPROPINFO_STD_NAME,
    PPROPINFO_STD_INDEX,
    PPROPINFO_STD_BACKCOLOR,
    PPROPINFO_STD_LEFT,
    PPROPINFO_STD_TOP,
    PPROPINFO_STD_WIDTH,
    PPROPINFO_STD_HEIGHT,
    PPROPINFO_STD_VISIBLE,
    PPROPINFO_STD_PARENT,
    PPROPINFO_STD_DRAGMODE,
    PPROPINFO_STD_DRAGICON,
    PPROPINFO_STD_TAG,
    &Property_BoxColor,
    PPROPINFO_STD_HWND,             //For VB2+—remove for VB version 1
    NULL
};
```

So you can add them to Box.H, as well:

```
#define IDBMP_BOX         5000
#define IDBMP_BOXDOWN     5001
#define IDBMP_BOXMONO     5003
#define IDBMP_BOXEGA      5006

typedef struct tagBOX
{
    RECT     rectDrawRegion;
```

```
        SHORT    BoxColor;
} BOX;

typedef BOX FAR * PBOX;

#define IPROP_BOX_NAME                 0
#define IPROP_BOX_INDEX                1        :
#define IPROP_BOX_BACKCOLOR            2        :
#define IPROP_BOX_LEFT                 3        :
#define IPROP_BOX_TOP                  4        :
#define IPROP_BOX_WIDTH                5        :
#define IPROP_BOX_HEIGHT              6        :
#define IPROP_BOX_VISIBLE             7        :
#define IPROP_BOX_PARENT              8        :
#define IPROP_BOX_DRAGMODE            9        :
#define IPROP_BOX_DRAGICON           10        :
#define IPROP_BOX_TAG                11        :
#define IPROP_BOX_COLOR              12        :
#define IPROP_BOX_HWND               13 //VB2+ – remove          for VB1

#define IEVENT_BOX_CLICKINSIDE        0
#define IEVENT_BOX_CLICKOUTSIDE       1
#define IEVENT_BOX_DRAGDROP           2
#define IEVENT_BOX_DRAGOVER           3
```

That completes Box.H, which you can find in listing 14.3 (Box.H on the Disk). Again, remove the definition of IPROP_BOX_HWND if you are using Visual Basic 1.0.

Listing 14.3. Box.H (Box.H on the Disk)

```
#define IDBMP_BOX          5000
#define IDBMP_BOXDOWN      5001
#define IDBMP_BOXMONO      5003
#define IDBMP_BOXEGA       5006

LONG FAR PASCAL _export BoxCtlProc(HCTL, HWND, USHORT, USHORT, LONG);

typedef struct tagBOX
{
    RECT     rectDrawRegion;
```

continues

Listing 14.3. continued

```
    SHORT    BoxColor;
} BOX;

typedef BOX FAR * PBOX;

#ifndef RC_INVOKED

#define IPROP_BOX_NAME              0
#define IPROP_BOX_INDEX             1
#define IPROP_BOX_BACKCOLOR         2
#define IPROP_BOX_LEFT              3
#define IPROP_BOX_TOP               4
#define IPROP_BOX_WIDTH             5
#define IPROP_BOX_HEIGHT            6
#define IPROP_BOX_VISIBLE           7
#define IPROP_BOX_PARENT            8
#define IPROP_BOX_DRAGMODE          9
#define IPROP_BOX_DRAGICON          10
#define IPROP_BOX_TAG               11
#define IPROP_BOX_COLOR             12
#define IPROP_BOX_HWND              13 //VB2+—remove for VB version 1.0

#define IEVENT_BOX_CLICKINSIDE      0
#define IEVENT_BOX_CLICKOUTSIDE     1
#define IEVENT_BOX_DRAGDROP         2
#define IEVENT_BOX_DRAGOVER         3

#endif
```

For a ClickOutside( ) event, then, you only have to fire event number IEVENT_BOX_CLICKOUTSIDE. As you set things up, ClickOutside( ) has no arguments passed to it, so you only need to use VBFireEvent( ) like this in FireClickOutSide( ) (which is called from the WM_LBUTTONDOWN case):

```
VOID NEAR FireClickOutside(HCTL hctl)
{
    VBFireEvent(hctl, IEVENT_BOX_CLICKOUTSIDE, NULL);
}
```

The first argument you pass to VBFireEvent( ) is hctl, the control's handle, the next is the number of the event (IEVENT_BOX_CLICKOUTSIDE), and the last is a pointer to the additional parameters you want to pass to the event procedure. Here, there are no additional parameters, so you are done with FireClickOutside( ).

However, you also have to set up FireClickInside( ) in case the user clicks inside the box. For that, you need the actual mouse coordinates, because you planned to pass them to the ClickInside( ) event:

```
Sub Box1_ClickInside (X As Single, Y As Single)
    Beep
    Beep
End Sub
```

You can get the mouse coordinates from lp (x = LOWORD(lp) and y = HIWORD(lp)) in the WM_LBUTTONDOWN case, like this:

```
    case WM_LBUTTONDOWN:            /* Button down in our control */
        if (InBox(pbox, LOWORD(lp), HIWORD(lp))){
            FireClickInside(hctl, LOWORD(lp), HIWORD(lp));
        }
        else
            FireClickOutside(hctl);
        break;
```

Now you have to design FireClickInside( ) to handle and pass these parameters correctly:

```
VOID NEAR FireClickInside(HCTL hctl, SHORT x, SHORT y)
{
}
```

To pass these parameters to Visual Basic, so that they will be passed to Box1_ClickInside( ), you have to set up a structure and pass a pointer to it when you use VBFireEvent( ). That structure holds the arguments to pass to the event procedure, but in reverse order. You do not have to set up an argument list if no parameters are passed to the event procedure, but ClickInside( ) does take parameters, so you will have to set up an argument list here.

Note that your box control supports the Index property, which means that you can have arrays of box controls and that an Index can be passed. You did not have to take that into account before because you did not pass a parameter structure before. That is, if an event procedure takes no parameters, you do not have to pass a parameter structure—even if you support control arrays. In that case, Visual Basic itself takes care of passing an Index. But now that you are passing a parameter structure to VBFireEvent( ), it turns out that you do have to include space for a (possible) Index property. Because Index is always passed first, it comes last here (and you give it the expected LPVOID type):

```
typedef struct tagCLICKINSIDEPARMS
{
    float    far *Y;
    float    far *X;
    LPVOID   Index;
} CLICKINSIDEPARMS;


VOID NEAR FireClickInside(HCTL hctl, SHORT x, SHORT y)
{

}
```

That's all there is to setting up the parameter structure. Now you just have to fill that parameter structure with the mouse cursor location and pass it to VBFireEvent( ). However, it is very important to note that you have to convert to twips for Visual Basic from the pixel coordinates you extracted from lp like this:

```
    case WM_LBUTTONDOWN:            /* Button down in our control */
        if (InBox(pbox, LOWORD(lp), HIWORD(lp))){
            FireClickInside(hctl, LOWORD(lp), HIWORD(lp));
        }
        else
            FireClickOutside(hctl);
        break;
```

You do that with a common Visual Basic API call, VBXPixelsToTwips( ), like this in FireClickInside( ):

```
typedef struct tagCLICKINSIDEPARMS
{
    float    far *Y;
    float    far *X;
    LPVOID   Index;
} CLICKINSIDEPARMS;
```

```
VOID NEAR FireClickInside(HCTL hctl, SHORT x, SHORT y)
{
    CLICKINSIDEPARMS EventParams;
    float       VisBasX, VisBasY;

    VisBasX = (float)VBXPixelsToTwips(x);
    VisBasY = (float)VBYPixelsToTwips(y);
    EventParams.X = &VisBasX;
    EventParams.Y = &VisBasY;

    VBFireEvent(hctl, IEVENT_BOX_CLICKINSIDE, &EventParams);
}
```

That's it for FireClickInside( ). Now you have made your two events—ClickInside and ClickOutside—active. All that remains is to take care of the property, BoxColor, when someone changes it. To do that, you will handle the VBM_SETPROPERTY message, which indicates that someone has changed a property of the control. The number of the property changed is passed to you in wp, and the new value in lp. Here, you can handle the case in which the BoxColor property—which you have given the number IPROP_BOX_COLOR in Box.H—changes by checking the value in wp. If it is equal to IPROP_BOX_COLOR, you should load the new setting from lp into the BOX structure. You can do that like this in Box.C:

```
#include <windows.h>
#include "vbapi.h"
#include "box.h"

VOID NEAR PaintBox(PBOX pbox, HWND hwnd, HDC hdc);
BOOL NEAR InBox(PBOX pbox, SHORT x, SHORT y);
VOID NEAR FireClickInside(HCTL hctl, SHORT x, SHORT y);
VOID NEAR FireClickOutside(HCTL hctl);

LONG FAR PASCAL _export BoxCtlProc(HCTL hctl, HWND hwnd, USHORT msg,
    USHORT wp, LONG lp)
{
    switch (msg){
    :
    :
    case WM_LBUTTONDOWN:            /* Button down in our control */
            :
            :
        break;
```

```
        case VBM_SETPROPERTY:                    /* BoxColor was set */
            switch (wp){
            case IPROP_BOX_COLOR:
                pbox->BoxColor = (SHORT)lp;
                InvalidateRect(hwnd, NULL, TRUE);
                return 0;
            }
            break;
        }
        return VBDefControlProc(hctl, hwnd, msg, wp, lp);
    }
```

Notice that you repaint the control when the BoxColor property changes (actually, you use InvalidateRect( ) so that a WM_PAINT message will be sent). This enables you to add or remove the blue coloring, as necessary. Note also that at the end of the code you used VBDefControlProc( ), which has the same use as DefWindowProc( ) does in most Windows programs—that is, you pass on to it the messages you do not want to handle. That's it for Box.C, which handles the messages for your control; the full code appears in listing 14.4 (Box.C on the Disk). Now you are almost ready to go.

Listing 14.4. Box.C (Box.C on the Disk)

```
#include <windows.h>
#include "vbapi.h"
#include "box.h"

VOID NEAR PaintBox(PBOX pbox, HWND hwnd, HDC hdc);
BOOL NEAR InBox(PBOX pbox, SHORT x, SHORT y);
VOID NEAR FireClickInside(HCTL hctl, SHORT x, SHORT y);
VOID NEAR FireClickOutside(HCTL hctl);

LONG FAR PASCAL _export BoxCtlProc(HCTL hctl, HWND hwnd, USHORT msg,
    USHORT wp, LONG lp)
{
    PBOX pbox;
    LPRECT prect;

    /* Note: Must again dereference hctl whenever we invalidate */
    /* pbox—including after calls to VB API */
    pbox = (PBOX)VBDerefControl(hctl);
```

```
switch (msg){
case WM_CREATE:                    /* Perform initialization here */
     pbox->BoxColor = FALSE;
     break;

case WM_SIZE:                      /* Our control was (re)sized */
     prect = &pbox->rectDrawRegion;

     GetClientRect(hwnd, prect);         /* Draw box in the control */
     prect->left = prect->right / 4;
     prect->right = 3 * prect->right / 4;
     prect->top = prect->bottom / 4;
     prect->bottom = 3 * prect->bottom / 4;
     break;

case WM_PAINT:                     /* Repaint our control */
     if (wp)
          PaintBox(pbox, hwnd, (HDC)wp);   /* Printer */
     else{
          PAINTSTRUCT ps;

          BeginPaint(hwnd, &ps);
          PaintBox(pbox, hwnd, ps.hdc);
          EndPaint(hwnd, &ps);
     }
     break;

case WM_LBUTTONDOWN:               /* Button down in our control */
     if (InBox(pbox, LOWORD(lp), HIWORD(lp))){
          HDC hdc = GetDC(hwnd);
              /* Do work if desired */
              ReleaseDC(hwnd, hdc);
          FireClickInside(hctl, LOWORD(lp), HIWORD(lp));
     }
     else
     FireClickOutside(hctl);
     break;

case VBM_SETPROPERTY:                      /* BoxColor was set */
     switch (wp){
     case IPROP_BOX_COLOR:
          pbox->BoxColor = (SHORT)lp;
```

continues

677

Listing 14.4. continued

```c
                InvalidateRect(hwnd, NULL, TRUE);
                return 0;
            }
            break;
        }
    return VBDefControlProc(hctl, hwnd, msg, wp, lp);
}


VOID NEAR PaintBox (PBOX pbox, HWND hwnd, HDC hdc)
{
    HBRUSH  hbr;
    HBRUSH  hbrOld = NULL;
    LPRECT  prect = &pbox->rectDrawRegion;

    if(pbox->BoxColor){
        hbr = CreateSolidBrush(RGB(0, 0, 255)); /* Blue brush */
        hbrOld = SelectObject(hdc, hbr);
    }
    Rectangle(hdc, prect->left, prect->top, prect->right, prect->bottom);
    if(pbox->BoxColor){
        SelectObject(hdc, hbrOld);              /* Restore old brush */
    }
}


BOOL NEAR InBox(PBOX pbox, SHORT x, SHORT y)
{
    LPRECT  prect = &pbox->rectDrawRegion;

    return ((prect->left < x) & (prect->right > x) & \
        (prect->top < y) & (prect->bottom > y));
}


VOID NEAR FireClickOutside(HCTL hctl)
{
    VBFireEvent(hctl, IEVENT_BOX_CLICKOUTSIDE, NULL);
}


typedef struct tagCLICKINSIDEPARMS
{
    float   far *Y;
    float   far *X;
```

```
    LPVOID  Index;
} CLICKINSIDEPARMS;

VOID NEAR FireClickInside(HCTL hctl, SHORT x, SHORT y)
{
    CLICKINSIDEPARMS EventParams;
    float      VisBasX, VisBasY;

    VisBasX = (float)VBXPixelsToTwips(x);
    VisBasY = (float)VBYPixelsToTwips(y);
    EventParams.X = &VisBasX;
    EventParams.Y = &VisBasY;

    VBFireEvent(hctl, IEVENT_BOX_CLICKINSIDE, &EventParams);
}
```

In fact, the code is finished, but you still need to complete Box.Def, which indicates to the linker that you want to create a Windows dynamic link library. You can use the same .def file you used in Chapter 12, updated to BOX from the CINTERFACE example. That file appears in listing 14.5 (Box.Def on the Disk).

 Listing 14.5. Box.Def (Box.Def on the Disk)

```
LIBRARY        BOX
EXETYPE        WINDOWS
DESCRIPTION    'Visual Basic Box Custom Control'

CODE           MOVEABLE
DATA           MOVEABLE SINGLE

HEAPSIZE    2048

EXPORTS
    WEP    @1     RESIDENTNAME

SEGMENTS
    WEP_TEXT FIXED
```

The final file you need is the Makefile used by the nmake utility. That file, simply called Makefile, is more or less standard for creating .Vbx files, but it is different for different versions of Microsoft C. The Makefile for MS C 7.0 (Makefile on the Disk) is in listing 14.6; the Makefile for MS C 6.0 and 6.10 (Makefile.C6 on the Disk) is in listing 14.7. They specify all that the various linkers, compilers, and libraries need to know to create Box.Vbx. Now, if you simply type **nmake** at the DOS level with the appropriate files in place, the C nmake utility will create Box.Vbx. At this point, then, Box.Vbx is at last ready to use.

Listing 14.6. Makefile (Makefile on the Disk)

```
.SUFFIXES:  .c .def .VBX .h .lnk .map .obj .rc .res .sym

Default: box.vbx

.c.obj:
    echo >con Compiling $(<F)
    cl /c /W4 /G2cs /Zp /BATCH /Osge /GD -AS $<

box.obj: box.c box.h

init.obj: init.c box.h

box.VBX: init.obj box.obj box.lnk box.res box.def
    echo >con Linking box.VBX...
    link /co @box.lnk
    echo >con RCing box.VBX...
    rc -30 box.res box.VBX
    echo >con mapsyming box.VBX...
    mapsym box
    echo >con Done Linking box.VBX

box.lnk: makefile
    echo >con Making <<box.lnk
    box.obj + init.obj
    box.VBX /co /align:16 /batch /far /li /map /nod /noe /nopackc /w
    box.map
    vbapi.lib libw.lib sdllcew.lib
    box.def
<<KEEP

box.res: box.rc box.h \
    boxcd.bmp \
```

```
boxcu.bmp \
boxmu.bmp \
boxeu.bmp
echo >con Resource compiling box.RC
rc -R $(RCINCS) box.rc
```

Listing 14.7. Makefile.C6 (Makefile.C6 on the Disk)

```
.SUFFIXES:   .asm .c .def .vbx .h .lnk .map .obj .rc .res .sym

Default: box.vbx

.c.obj:
    echo >com **** Now Compiling $(<F)
    if exist $@ del $@
    cl -W3 -c -G2csw -Alnw -Zip $<

.asm.obj:
    echo >com **** Now Assembling $(<F)
    masm -W2 -V -E -P -Zi $<,$@;

init.obj:    init.c box.h

libinit.obj:    libinit.asm

box.obj: box.c box.h

box.vbx: libinit.obj init.obj box.obj box.lnk \
    box.res box.def
    echo >com **** Now Linking box.vbx...
    link /co @box.lnk
    echo >com **** Now CVPACKing box.vbx...
    cvpack -p box.vbx
    echo >com **** Now RCing box.vbx...
    $(RCPATH)rc box.res box.vbx
    echo >com **** Now MAPSYMing box.vbx...
    mapsym box
    echo >com **** Finished linking box.vbx
```

continues

Listing 14.7. continued

```
box.lnk: makefile
    echo >com **** Now Making <<box.lnk
    libinit.obj+
    init.obj+
    box.obj
    box.vbx /co /align:16 /batch /far /li /map /nod /noe /w
    box.map
    vbapi.lib mdllcew.lib libw.lib
    box.def
<<KEEP

box.res: box.rc box.h \
    boxcd.bmp \
    boxcu.bmp \
    boxmu.bmp \
    boxeu.bmp
    echo >com **** Now Resource compiling box.RC
    $(RCPATH)rc -R -i$(TOOLS)\inc $(RCINCS) box.rc

cln:
    -del *.obj
    -del *.res
    -del *.lnk
    -del *.vbx
    -del *.map
    -del *.sym
```

Using Your New Custom Control

All that remains is to put Box.Vbx to work, and you do that in Visual Basic. Start a new project and call it, say, Box.Mak. Now add Box.Vbx with the Visual Basic File menu's Add File... menu item, and you will see that your new control appears in the toolbox (refer to figure 14.2). You can create a new box control as you would any other control—just double-click on the box tool and move the box control that appears into place on the form. Next, you can open the code window, where you will find the following events, among others:

```
Sub Box1_ClickOutside ()
End Sub
Sub Box1_ClickInside (X As Single, Y As Single)

End Sub
```

As was our original plan, we put this code in the event procedures:

```
Sub Box1_ClickOutside ()
    Beep
End Sub
Sub Box1_ClickInside (X As Single, Y As Single)
    Beep
    Beep
End Sub
```

Now, find the BoxColor property in the properties window; when you do, you will see that it has a setting of 0, as in figure 14.3. To set the BoxColor property to True, set it to -1. At that point, and as you might expect, the box inside the control turns blue. Finally, run the program, giving the window shown in figure 14.4. When you click inside the control but outside the central box, you get a beep. When you click inside the box, you get two beeps. Box.Vbx is a success—you have actually designed and implemented your own Visual Basic control, extending the language. Your new control is now viable.

Figure 14.3. The BoxColor property in the Properties window.

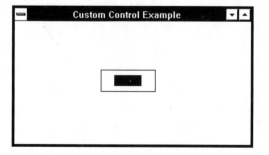

Figure 14.4. The box control at work.

And That's It

And that's it. You have come far in Visual Basic—from the introductory material through the intermediate level, up through truly advanced material. You have seen a great deal—from the basics to extending Visual Basic with Windows calls to using DDE and OLE; from using multiple windows to advanced control handling; from text I/O to creating graphic animation; from sorting, searching, and advanced data handling to connecting Visual Basic to C; from exploring the Professional Edition's custom controls to creating custom controls and .Vbx files. Now all that remains is to put it all to work. Visual Basic is a powerful set of tools and resources: there is hardly a more enjoyable programming platform available. Have fun with it!

Summary

Here you saw how to design and implement a new control in Visual Basic. You saw what it takes to support such a control, and how you can indicate to Visual Basic what properties your control has, as well as what type of events it can support. (Also, you saw how to add a number of standard properties and events automatically.) You saw how to register a control with Visual Basic, how to design its appearance—by painting it on the screen—and how to handle events connected with it. You also saw how to create bitmaps that Visual Basic will use in the toolbox as the control's icon, and how to get them installed. You linked together all your files into a .Vbx file, creating a working custom control, and you put that custom control to work.

New C Function	Description
VBDefControlProc (hctl, hwnd, msg, wp, lp	Visual Basic's default control-handling procedure; the parameters are the same as those passed to a Visual Basic control procedure and should be passed along unchanged.

New C Function	Description
`VBDerefControl(hctl)`	Should be used whenever you do something that causes Visual Basic to change the control's data.
`VBFireEvent` `(hctl, IEVENT_NUMBER, &EventParams)`	Fires a Visual Basic event. The hctl parameter is the control's handle; IEVENT_NUMBER, is the event number as registered with VBRegisterModel( ); and &EventParams is a pointer to an event parameter structure (so Visual Basic knows what values to pass to the Visual Basic event procedure).
`VBXPixelsToTwips(px)`	Converts the point px (a Windows point structure) from screen pixels to Visual Basic's twips.
`VBRegisterModel` `(hmodDLL, &modelStruc)`	Used to register a control with Visual Basic. The hmodDLL parameter is passed to LibMain( ); modelStruc is a Visual Basic Model structure defining this control.

A

Creating Customized Windows Help

You might have noticed that many Windows programs have their own help system. You select an item in the Help menu and a Help window opens. In fact, most applications use the built-in Windows help system, and only provide a .Hlp file which that system can use. To show how that is done, we will develop a file named Editor.Hlp to use with the Editor application you put together earlier. (This help file is intended for demonstration purposes only.)

Creating the Help Text: Editor.Rtf

To create Editor.Hlp for the Windows help system, you must first create Editor.Rtf, a rich text file. *Rich text*—the first step in creating a help file—includes all kinds of embedded items, such as footnotes and hidden text. After you create Editor.Rtf—which specifies how you want your help topics set up and the text in them—you use the Help Compiler (Hc31.Exe, which comes with the Visual Basic Professional Edition) along with a help project file, Editor.Hpj (coming up next), to create Editor.Hlp.

To create Editor.Rtf, you need a word processor capable of creating rich text files. Here, we use Microsoft Word for Windows, Version 2.0 (other word processors also can create rich-text format files). If you have that package, start it in Windows now. Next, you are going to design the help file. The first screen the user sees might present an overview, something like this:

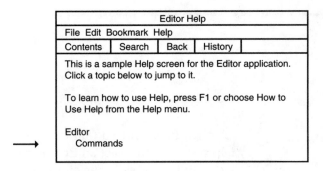

The user can then select help topics.

You will include a section on Commands here. When the user clicks on that word, a new screen might open, showing the available options for help on Editor commands, something like the following:

```
                        Editor Help
 File  Edit  Bookmark  Help
 Contents  |  Search  |  Back  |  History  |
 Click the Editor command you want to know more about.


 Load File...
 Save File...


```

When the user clicks on one of these options, such as Load File..., the appropriate help screen can open (with demonstration text only), as follows:

```
+-----------------------------------------------------+
|                    Editor Help                      |
+-----------------------------------------------------+
| File  Edit  Bookmark  Help                          |
+-----------+----------+--------+----------+-----------+
| Contents  |  Search  |  Back  | History  |           |
+-----------+----------+--------+----------+-----------+
| Load File...                                        |
|                                                     |
|          Loads a file.                              |
|                                                     |
|                                                     |
|                                                     |
+-----------------------------------------------------+
```

Moving from one screen to another is called *jumping* in a help file. There are two kinds of jumps—jumps to another help screen and jumps to pop-up windows. You make a jump to another window by selecting an underlined topic in Windows help; you display a pop-up window by selecting a topic with a dotted underline. Both types of underlined items are green on a color monitor. A *pop-up* window is a window that appears next to or below the item it is connected to. For example, if the word *file* had a dotted underline under it, the user could click it for more information, perhaps opening a pop-up window, as follows:

```
+-----------------------------------------------------+
|                    Editor Help                      |
+-----------------------------------------------------+
| File  Edit  Bookmark  Help                          |
+-----------+----------+--------+----------+-----------+
| Contents  |  Search  |  Back  | History  |           |
+-----------+----------+--------+----------+-----------+
| Load File...                                        |
|                                                     |
|          Loads a file.                              |
|          +------------------------------------+     |
|          | The file should not be larger than 64K |  |
|          +------------------------------------+     |
|                                                     |
+-----------------------------------------------------+
```

All these things are possible, depending on the way in which you set up your Editor.Rtf file. Type the first screenful of information into WinWord now, as shown in figure A.1.

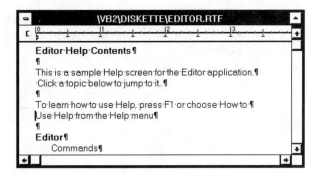

Figure A.1. The first help screen.

Next, you add the *tags* that indicate to the help system what you want to do. In this case, you want to jump to a new screen when the user clicks on the word *Commands*:

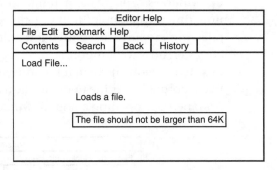

To indicate that, highlight the word *Commands* now and select the Format menu's Character... item. A dialog box labelled Character opens. Select the Double Underline option in the Underline drop-down list box (this will become a single solid underline in the final help file). Next, place the cursor immediately after the word *Commands* and check the Hidden Text box in the Character dialog box. There must be no spaces between the word *Commands* and the hidden text that follows. Now you can add the jump tag, which will indicate what topic you want to jump to. Here you might type **EDITOR_COMMANDS** (note that no spaces are used in a jump tag like this), as shown in figure A.2.

Next, you have to create that new screen (the one with the Load File... and Save File... jump tags). You do that by starting a new page. To insert a page break, select the Break item in WinWord's Insert menu. In the dialog box that opens, click on the item marked Page Break.

690

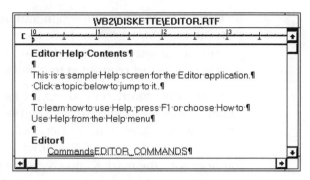

Figure A.2. A completed jump reference.

Now that you have started a new page, you should indicate that this is the target of the jump tag you just created (that is, you have to associate it with the term EDITOR_COMMANDS). You can indicate this with WinWord footnotes. For example, to associate this page of information with the jump to EDITOR_COMMANDS, place the cursor at the very beginning of this new page and select the Footnote... item in the Insert menu. A new dialog box labelled Footnote appears. Click on the option button marked Custom Footnote Mark and type a number sign (#) in the text box next to it, then select OK to close the box. At this point, WinWord will cut the window you are working on in half, displaying a new section at the bottom labelled Footnotes and placing the cursor after the mark you selected (#, which also appears in the text you are working on). Now type **EDITOR_COMMANDS** and return to the text window (the window above the Footnotes window) by clicking on it. The result should be something like that in figure A.3.

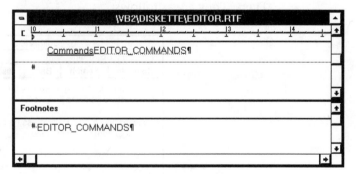

Figure A.3. A jump target.

691

By using a footnote with a # sign and by giving that footnote the text EDITOR_COMMANDS, you have connected the jump on the previous page to the current page. When the user clicks on the word *Commands*, the page you have just connected to it will appear.

There are other footnotes you can use here as well. For example, insert a footnote with the footnote mark $ and give it the text Editor:Commands. This gives the current page a title; it will appear in the list box when you use the Search feature of Windows Help. In addition, add another footnote with the mark K and give it the text Commands; this defines a keyword with which the user can search for a topic. Finally, add the text Editor:Commands, your title, right after the footnotes you inserted into the text window itself. The result should be something like that in figure A.4.

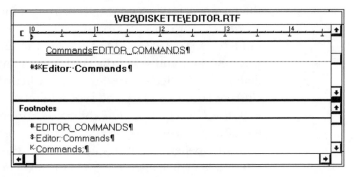

Figure A.4. The tag, title, and keyword marks.

There are two jumps to be made on this new page, Load File... and Save File.... They are as follows:

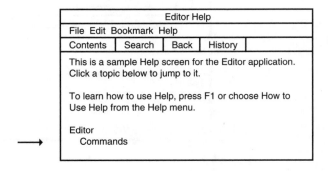

Give these two items the tags LOAD_FILE and SAVE_FILE (as hidden text) and type the rest of the text into the window, as shown in figure A.5.

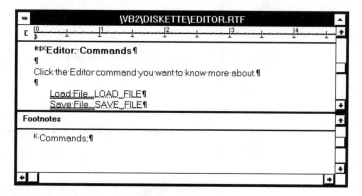

Figure A.5. The Load and Save File help tags.

Now you will create new help screens for each of these items, Load File... and Save File.... Do that by inserting a hard page break with the Break item in the Insert menu and by typing the text of the Load File... demonstration help screen:

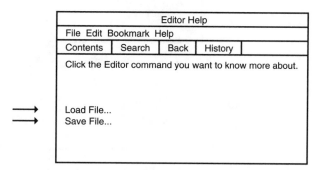

Now connect this screen to the jump LOAD_FILE by inserting a footnote at the very beginning of this page with the footnote mark #, as before. Use the text LOAD_FILE for the footnote itself (see figure A.6).

Now do the same for the Save File... help screen (use the text Save File... and the explanation "Saves a file." as shown earlier. Tie the Save File... help screen to the tag SAVE_FILE with another # footnote, as shown in figure A.7.

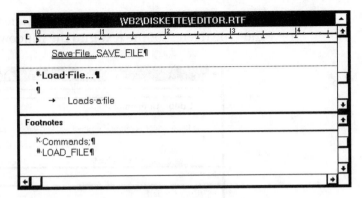

Figure A.6. Tying the Load File jump to its text.

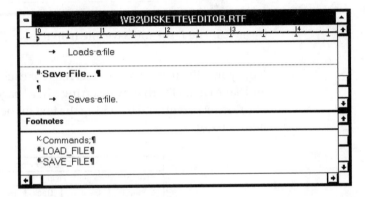

Figure A.7. Tying the Save File jump to its text.

Now you are almost done with Editor.Rtf. The final step is to add a pop-up Help window to the word *file* in the Load File... help screen, like this:

Editor Help				
File Edit Bookmark Help				
Contents	Search	Back	History	

Load File...

Loads a file.

Doing this is as easy as inserting the jumps you already have added. The only difference here is that instead of giving the word *file* a double underline, you give it a single underline (that is, select the Underline option in the Format menu's Character item). Next, as you have done before, you connect it to the text that will appear, using a jump tag—which you might call FILE_POPUP—and connecting that to a new page of text (insert a hard page break) that starts with a # footnote. Give this footnote the text FILE_POPUP. The result of all this appears in figure A.8.

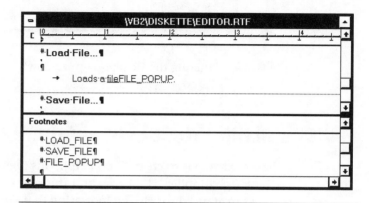

Figure A.8. Creating a Help pop-up window.

Finally, type the text **"The file should not be larger than 64K"** into the FILE_POPUP page (see figure A.9). That's it; your file Editor.Rtf is done. Save this file now in .Rtf format by selecting the Save As... item in WinWord's File menu, and by selecting Rich Text Format (the Rtf option in the Save File As Type box).

All that remains is to convert Editor.Rtf into Editor.Hlp, which the Windows help system will read. That is done with the assistance of a help project file, Editor.Hpj, and we will look into that next.

> **Creating context-sensitive help.**
> It is possible also to create context-sensitive help by using the HelpContextID properties of most forms. Doing this allows you to provide help information on a control-by-control level.

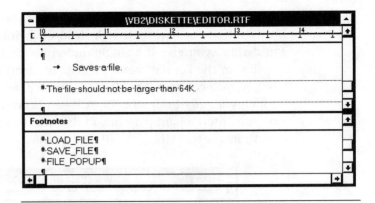

Figure A.9. Entering the Help pop-up window's text.

Creating the Project File: Editor.Hpj

The next step is to create Editor.Hpj. This file is the one you will pass to the Help compiler, Hc31.Exe, and this compiler will create Editor.Hlp. You can start Editor.Hpj by indicating that you want to save a record of errors that occurred during compilation in the file Editor.Err, that the title of the help system should be Editor Help, that you do not want to compress this file (an option that can produce more compact results). You also want to see all warnings. The code for this follows:

```
[OPTIONS]
errorlog = editor.err
title = Editor Help
compress = false
warning = 3
   :
   :
```

Next, you indicate that the rich text format file which holds the help text is called Editor.Rtf, as follows:

```
[OPTIONS]
errorlog = editor.err
title = Editor Help
```

```
compress = false
warning = 3

[FILES]
editor.rtf
    :
    :
```

Finally, you can specify the location, title (Editor Help), and size of the Help window on the screen, as follows:

```
[OPTIONS]
errorlog = editor.err
title = Editor Help
compress = false
warning = 3

[FILES]
editor.rtf

[WINDOWS]
main = "Editor Help", (0,0,1023,1023 ),,, (192,192,192 )
```

That completes Editor.Hpj—it was that quick. Now that you have Editor.Rtf and Editor.Hpj, you are ready to produce the actual help file, Editor.Hlp. You will do that next, with the Help compiler.

Creating the Help File: Editor.Hlp

You will use the Help compiler for Windows 3.1, which is called Hc31.Exe. Simply start that program (it is in the Visual Basic Professional Edition's subdirectory vb2\hc) and pass it the name of your project file Editor.Hpj, as follows:

```
C:\VB2\HC>HC31 EDITOR.HPJ
```

Microsoft ® Help Compiler Version 3.10.445
© Copyright Microsoft Corp 1990 - 1992. All rights reserved.

That's all there is to it; the Help compiler creates Editor.Hlp from your two files. All that remains is to connect it to the Editor itself.

Connecting Editor.Hlp to the Editor Program

Reaching the Editor.Hlp file from your Editor program is not hard. First, add a Help menu to the Editor with a menu item called Commands (Name:CommandsItem), as shown in figure A.10.

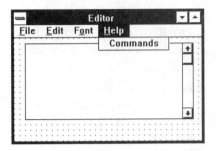

Figure A.10. The Editor program with a Help menu.

Next, click on that menu item to bring up the Sub procedure CommandsItem_Click( ), as follows:

```
Sub CommandsItem_Click ()

End Sub
```

When you makes this selection, you want to call up the help system. You can do this with the Windows function WinHelp( ), declared as follows:

```
Declare Function WinHelp Lib "User" (ByVal hWnd As Integer,
                                      ByVal lpHelpFile As String,
                                      ByVal wCommand As Integer,
                                      dwData As Any) As Integer
```

Adding this function declaration to Editor.Bas is easy; just load the file vb2\hc\Winhelp.Txt into that module, using Visual Basic's Load Text... menu item. Besides the declaration for WinHelp( ), the following global constants are defined there too, as follows:

```
Global Const HELP_CONTEXT = &H1      ' Display topic identified by
dwData
Global Const HELP_QUIT = &H2         ' Terminate help
Global Const HELP_INDEX = &H3        ' Display index
Global Const HELP_HELPONHELP = &H4   ' Display help on using help
Global Const HELP_SETINDEX = &H5     ' Set an alternate Index for
```

```
help file
Global Const HELP_KEY = &H101          ' Display topic for keyword
in dwData
Global Const HELP_MULTIKEY = &H201  ' Lookup keyword in alternate
table
```

You can use these constants as the wCommand parameter—the third parameter you pass to WinHelp( ). For example, passing the HELP_INDEX constant makes WinHelp( ) display the help file's index, and you will do that here. The parameters you pass to WinHelp are as follows: the main window's handle (Form1.hWnd); the location of the help file (which you can assume is, say, c:\vb2\Editor.Hlp); wCommand (you will use HELP_INDEX here); and additional data that might be needed (this is a long integer you set to 0). In this example, that results in the following code in CommandsItem_Click( ).

```
Sub CommandsItem_Click ()
    R = WinHelp(Form1.hWnd, "c:\vb2\Editor.Hlp", HELP_INDEX,
CLng(0))
End Sub
```

Note that although you pass a 0 as the last parameter, you first convert it to a long value. This will bring your help file up on the screen.

Now to see this at work. Run the Editor and select the Commands item in the Help menu to bring up the Help window (see figure A.11). You can click on the Commands item (shown underlined) to switch to another window, just as you can in normal Windows Help. In addition, you can select items with a dotted underline (the word *file*, as you have set it up) to bring up a pop-up Help window (see figure A.12). When you release the mouse button, the pop-up window disappears.

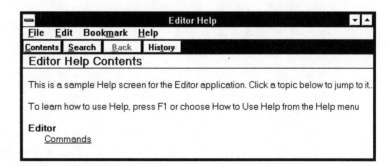

Figure A.11. The completed Help window.

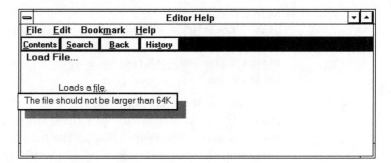

Figure A.12. The completed pop-up Help window.

To close the Help window, select the Exit item in the Help window's File menu. That's it; your demonstration help system is finished.

B

Windows Program Design

This appendix is about the conventions Windows programmers will expect your programs to adhere to. If you are going to develop products that you will sell or distribute on a large scale, this appendix is for you. Windows programs are different from DOS programs in many ways, and one of the primary ones is consistency—that is, supporting a common user interface. We will see more about that in this appendix.

Windows Programming Philosophy

If you are a developer working in Windows, you should certainly be expected to be familiar with most Windows applications. The people who use your program will have a set of standard expectations they expect you to fulfill. This is part of the attraction of Windows: If you know how to use a particular type of application (a word processor, for example), you can often use other ones without additional instruction. In fact, Windows developers should try to make their programs as intuitive as possible so that almost no instruction is required. Ideally, a simple set of Windows skills (such as clicking the mouse, selecting text, using menus) should be enough to let the user use your program, although that is not usually possible with larger, specialized applications.

In addition, you should strive to make your program robust, in the sense that users feel that they have a useful tool that will perform in expected ways. A *robust* program can operate under a wide variety of conditions and inputs and not fail; it is one that the user comes to regard as trustworthy. This is important: If some kind of trappable error occurs, your program should handle it with recovery code of some sort, not simply halt. You should minimize or eliminate any commonly encountered conditions your application cannot handle.

It is important to realize that the user should be the one controlling the program and the program flow in Windows, not the other way around. A Windows developer should try to give the user as much usefullness as possible—and have that utility presented in an easy-to-understand way. Windows customarily uses graphical objects to provide a set of tools for the user, and as many of these should be available as simultaneously as possible. However, do not overwhelm the user; if your window is becoming crowded with buttons, put some options into menus (that is, you should continually display only options that will be in continual use). Also, a Windows program should provide feedback to the user about what is going on when he or she uses the options that are available. For example, do not let your program "freeze" when undertaking a long operation—at least switch the mouse cursor to the hourglass symbol, or use a gauge control to show the status of the operation.

A Windows program operates in an environment where other programs also are operating, so it should not hog resources. For example, even though Timer controls are available in Visual Basic, you should use them only sparingly. Using them too often comes very close to the sequential processing that DOS programs use, as opposed to the event-and-message style of Windows programs.

One other point here is that no matter how minimal your program, it should meet at least one Windows expectation: it should provide the user with a way to quit. That is usually done with the File menu's Exit item (whose shortcut key is Ctrl-X).

Now we will examine the accepted mouse and keyboard Windows standards.

Mouse Actions

The mouse actions that have become standard are probably already familiar to you: clicking, double-clicking, and so on. Clicking is usually done with the left mouse button (left-handed users can use the Windows control panel to switch the buttons if they wish); there is no standard use yet for the right mouse button. In addition to the single click (which makes a selection or activates a control) and double click (which opens applications and selections), you can also use the mouse with the Shift and Ctrl keys. These two operations are used primarily in making selections. Table B.1 shows how they—and the other mouse operations—work.

Table B.1. Windows Mouse Conventions

Action	Means
Click	Control: Activates Selection: Selects Text: Positions insertion point
Ctrl-Click	Selection: Toggles current selection only
DblClick	Control: Activates Selection: Opens
Drag	Control: Moves control, if draggable Selection: Encloses area for selection Navigation: Moves selection
Shift-Click	Selection: Extends selection

Keyboard Actions

There are many standard operations for the keyboard in Windows—mainly because all mouse actions are supposed to be possible with the keyboard alone, a fact you should always keep in mind. If the user types a simple letter or number, he or she is supplying your program with data input. On the other hand, Ctrl-Letter key combinations are usually reserved for (menu) shortcut commands, and Alt-Letter combinations are reserved for (menu and button) access key commands. A number of the function keys, F1 through F12, have predefined meanings (for example, F1 gives Help); they are listed in table B.2. You probably are familiar with many of these—such as using the Tab key to move from control to control in a dialog box (and Shift-Tab to go backwards), but some of them may take you by surprise. For example, Alt-F4 is supposed to close the application, whereas Alt-F6 moves to an MDI window's next open document.

Table B.2. Windows Keyboard Conventions

Key	Means
Alt	Used with letters to create access keys
Alt-Esc	Switches to next application window in Windows
Alt-F4	Closes application
Alt-F6	MDI: Moves to next open window
Alt-Shift-Esc	Switches to previous application window in Windows
Alt-Shift-F6	MDI: Moves backwards to next open window
Alt-Shift-Tab	Reverses order of Alt-Tab
Alt-Tab	Shows application stack, activates top application
	Backspace Selection: deletes entire selection Text: Deletes character to the left
Ctrl	Used with letters to create shortcut keys
Ctrl-B	Text: Bold

Key	Means
Ctrl-D	Text: Double underline
Ctrl-Down	Text: Next paragraph
Ctrl-End	Navigation: Moves to bottom right of document
Ctlr-Esc	Shows all running applications, lets you choose
Ctrl-F4	Closes window
Ctrl-F6	MDI: Moves top document to bottom of stack
Ctrl-Home	Navigation: Moves to top left of document
Ctrl-I	Text: Italic
Ctrl-PgUp	Navigation: Moves to top of window
Ctrl-PgDown	Navigation: Moves to bottom of window
Ctrl-Shift-F6	MDI: Reverses operation of Ctrl-F6
Ctrl-Space	Text: Stops character formatting
Ctrl-U	Text: Underline
Ctrl-Up	Text: Previous paragraph
Ctrl-W	Text: Word-by-word underline
Ctrl-X	Quits an application
Del	Selection: Deletes entire selection Text: Deletes character to the right
Down Arrow	Controls: Next choice Text: Down one line
End	Navigation: Moves to rightmost position of row
Enter	Controls: Presses selected button
Esc	Dialogs: Closes dialog Modes: Exits current mode Selection: Cancels current selection
F1	Help

continues

Table B.2. continued

Key	Means
F6	Moves clockwise to next pane
F8	Mode: Toggles extend mode
F10	Mode: Toggles menu bar
Home	Navigation: Moves to leftmost position of row
Insert	Mode: Toggles between overstrike and insert
Left Arrow	Text: One position to the left Controls: Next choice to left
PgDown	Navigation: Next screenful of data
PgUp	Navigation: Previous screenful of data
Right Arrow	Text: One position to the right Controls: Next choice to right
Scroll Lock	Navigation: Scrolls data, does not move cursor
Shift	Changes function keys and Tab to opposite
Shift-F6	Moves counterclockwise to next MDI pane
Shift-Tab	Reverses operation of Tab
Space	Controls: Clicks buttons with focus
Tab	Dialogs: Next field or control Text: Inserts a tab
Up Arrow	Controls: Previous choice Text: Up one line

There are also some accepted entries in a standard set of menus; we will take a look at the Edit, File, and Help menus here. In general, this is the accepted order of menu names in the menu bar: File, Edit, View, Tools, Window, Help (Help is always last).

The Edit Menu

The Edit menu—if present—usually has these items in it (note that these items are in the order in which they usually appear in an Edit menu), as follows:

Undo	Undoes the last operation
Cut	Cuts selected text
Copy	Copies selected text (usually to clipboard)
Paste	Pastes (usually from clipboard) to selection
Paste Link	Pastes a DDE link
Find...	Finds text (opens Find dialog box)
Replace...	Replaces text (opens Replace dialog box)

NOTE

It is often helpful to the user if you separate menu items into logical groups, using separator bars.

The File Menu

The File menu usually has these standard entries (in the order shown here):

New	Creates a new document
Open...	Opens a document (displays Open dialog box)
Save	Saves a document
Save As...	Saves a document (opens a dialog box allowing the user to set options—commonly, name, path, file type, etc.)

| Print... | Prints a document (displays Print dialog box) |
| Exit | Exits the application (almost always present) |

The Help Menu

The Help menu usually has these standard items (in the order shown):

Contents	Displays list of help topics available
Search	Searches for a help topic
Index	Displays an index of help topics
About xxx	Provides "About" information on application

For the interested developer: There are more Windows standards than are covered here; in fact, there are books on this topic alone. If you are unsure about a Windows standard, you should check on it by doing research before you release your product.

1	2	3	4	5	6				9	10
	11	12	13	14	A	B			D	E

C

Converting Visual Basic for Windows to DOS and Back: A Few Problems

Programs can be converted from Visual Basic for Windows to Visual Basic for DOS—and vice versa—but you must take some considerations into account. For example, because the system of measurement in VBDOS is different from that used in VBWin (VBDOS is run in 80-column character mode but VBWin can work pixel by pixel), all measurements (including form dimensions) have to be redone and code that relies on such measurements (such as code that uses mouse location data) has to be changed. In addition, many controls and mouse icons look quite different in the two versions, and many more keywords are available in VBDOS

709

than in VBWin. Table C.1 lists VBDOS keywords that are not available in VBWin, and table C.2 lists keywords available in VBWin but not in VBDOS.

Table C.1. VBDOS Keywords Not Available in VBWin

ABSOLUTE	INPUT	RESTORE
ALIAS	INSERT	RETRIEVE
ALL	INTERRUPT	ROLLBACK
BEGINTRANS	INTERRUPTX	ROLLBACK ALL
BLOAD	IOCTL	RUN
BOF	IOCTL$	SADD
BSAVE	ISAM	SAVEPOINT
CALLS	KEY	SEEKEQ
CDECL	LINE	SEEKGE
CHAIN	LINE INPUT	SEEKGT
CLEAR	LLIST	SEG
CLS	LOCATE	SELECT CASE
COLOR	LPOS	SETINDES
COM	LPRINT	SETMEM
COMMITRANS	LPRINT USING	SHARED
CREATEINDEX	LSET	SLEEP
CSRLIN	MKC$	SOUND
CVC	MKD$	SSEG
CVD	MKI$	SSEGADD
CVI	MKL$	STACK
CVL	MKS$	$STATIC
CVS	MKDBMF$	STICK
CVDMBF	MKSMBF$	STRIG
CVSMBF	MOVEFIRST	STRINGADDRESS

710

DATA	MOVELAST	STRINGASSIGN
DEF FN	MOVENEXT	STRINGLENGTH
DEF SEG	MOVEPREVIOUS	STRINGRELEASE
DEF USR	OPEN COM	SWAP
DELETE	OUT	SYSTEM
DELETEINDEX	PAINT	TEXTCOMP
DELETETABLE	PALETTE	TROFF
DRAW	PALETTE USING	TRON
$DYNAMIC	PCOPY	UEVENTUPDATE
EQV	PEEK	USING
ERDEV	PEN	VARPTR
ERDEV$	PLAY	VARPTR$
EVENT	PMAP	VARSEG
FIELD	POKE	VIEW
FILES	POS	VIEW PRINT
$FORM	PRESERVE	WAIT
FRE	PRESET	WIDTH
$INCLUDE	PRINT	WINDOW
INKEY$	PRINT USING	
INP	READ	

Table C.2. VBWin Keywords Not Available in VBDOS

GETDATA	LINKPOKE	SENDKEYS
GETFORMAT	LINKREQUEST	SETDATA
GLOBAL	LINKSEND	SHELL
LINKEXECUTE	SCALE	

In addition, VBWin has 256 colors to work with, whereas VBDOS has only 16. Also, VBDOS has more border styles. Note that controls and forms have a different appearance in the DOS and Win versions. To translate projects between VBDOS and VBWin, you can use the Trnslate.Exe program that comes with VBDOS. This program automates the entire translation process.

Translating Visual Basic Projects with Trnslate.Exe

To translate a project, the controls, and their properties, use Trnslate.Exe, which comes with VBDOS. Start it under Windows with the command Win Trnslate. A dialog box labelled Microsoft Visual Basic Project Translator will appear; use the left side of the box to specify the source project (VBDOS or VBWin) and the right side to specify the destination project (VBWin or VBDOS). Make sure that you leave the Adjust Code check box checked so that Trnslate.Exe will convert the code for you as well, and make sure that the destination directory is different from the source directory (or the destination files would overwrite the source files).

After selecting a VBDOS/VBWin project to translate and a destination VBWin/VBDOS project to create, click on the Translate button in the upper right corner. This will create a translated VBDOS or VBWin project that you can load and work on. If you are going from VBWin to VBDOS, Trnslate.Exe will start VBWin (make sure that VBWin is not already running when you run Trnslate.Exe). Save all code as text, use Ft.Exe (which also comes with VBDOS) to convert form files, and load the text into the new VBDOS project. If you are going from VBDOS to VBWin, Trnslate.Exe will start VBDOS and save all the code as text, use Ft.Exe to convert form files, and load the text into the new VBWin project. After the translator runs, you should have a converted project, ready to be loaded into Visual Basic.

Note also that in Visual Basic 2.0 and 3.0, you can save forms and files in ASCII format, which means that for small projects you can often transfer files over from VBWin to VBDOS easily (save them as ASCII and read them in), but you will still have to adjust the form and control's sizes to take into account the different coordinate systems.

Now, however, we still have to take into account several programming differences.

712

Rewriting for Compatibility

Besides the incompatible keywords, there are programming differences that have to be taken into account. For example, VBWin allows dynamic data exchange but VBDOS does not; bit-mapped graphics cannot appear in VBDOS forms; multiple coordinate systems and alternate fonts are available only in VBWin; you cannot set the segment in VBWin, and so on. These differences are made clear by the unsupported keywords in tables C.1 and C.2. A major difference is that VBDOS cannot display graphics while forms are visible; you have to plan around that, toggling between graphics and text, using the SCREEN statement. In addition, Trnslate.Exe will change your properties. An overview of the changes you are likely to see, grouped by property, as follows:

Color Properties	More colors are available in VBWin; colors are mapped to the nearest QB equivalent when going to VBDOS.
Drawing Properties	DrawWidth, DrawStyle, DrawMode, FillColor, FillStyle do not apply in VBDOS.
Font Properties	There is only one VBDOS form font (the MS-DOS font).
Measurement Properties	Measurement properties such as Left, Top, Width, and so on will be adjusted for coordinate systems.
MousePointer Properties	Mouse-pointer properties are brought over from VBWin to VBDOS, but the mouse pointer will look different.
Scale Properties	Scale properties do not work in VBDOS.
Windows Properties	Image, hDC, hWnd do not apply in VBDOS.

In addition, you should know that global memory is handled differently in VBDOS and VBWin. Objects declared with Global in VBWin are declared with COMMON SHARED in VBDOS and, in addition, the

COMMON SHARED declaration must appear in every module in the VBDOS project. Trnslate.Exe handles this automatically. That's it for cross-platform programming.

About the Disk

This appendix lists the projects on the disk that accompanies this book. Run the install.bat program on the disk, or place all the files on the disk into the c:\vb directory on your hard disk (that is, Visual Basic's working directory). Load them into Visual Basic by using the Open Project... menu item, and run them with the Start menu item in the Visual Basic Run menu.

Project	What It Does
alarm.mak	An alarm clock; run it and place a time (for example, 9:30:00) in the Alarm Setting Box. Click on the Alarm On button if you want the alarm to be active.
box.mak	Your custom control. When you run this example, a copy of your custom control will appear in the middle of the window. When you click inside the control but outside the central box, there will be one beep. Click inside the central blue box, and you will get two beeps. This is an example of the custom VB Box control you set up. Using custom controls like this, you can extend Visual Basic, designing your own types of buttons, list boxes, and menus.

NOTE

To make the custom control file box.vbx yourself (there is no need to do this; the file is included on the disk), you should have Microsoft C 7+. Copy these files: init.c, box.c, box.h, box.rc, box.def, and makefile into c:\c700\bin and type **NMAKE** to create box.vbx. Make sure that you have Windows libraries in your LIB path. If you have MS C 6.0 or 6.1, use Makefile.C6 and modify the files as shown in the book.

Project	What It Does
calc.mak	A simple addition calculator; just enter a number in the top text box, another in the second text box, and click the button marked = to see the result of the addition.
capture.mak	A screen-capture program for Windows. Run it and move the mouse cursor to the top left area of the screen you want to capture. Press the left mouse button and move the mouse, stretching a rectangle until you have enclosed the area of the

Project	What It Does
	screen you want. When you release the mouse button, that area will be copied into Capture's window.
cascade.mak	A multiwindow application. When you run it, four windows will appear. Click on the button on window Form1; the four windows will arrange themselves in a cascade, Form1 on top. This example shows how to program multiple window applications.
clipper.mak	A data entry form with cut-and-paste capabilities. Type a name in the top text box, highlight it with the mouse, and select Copy in the File menu. Next, put the insertion point in the second text box and select Paste in the File menu to paste the name in that text box. In this way, you see how to use Copy and Paste, and the code also shows how to determine which control is active (that is, which text box the user is copying from or pasting to) even though you are not in the controls' event procedures.
database.mak	Your database example, capable of holding three fields: Name, Number, and Comment. Put values in these fields and select Add Item in the File menu to add them to the database. To retrieve data, use Find Item... to double-click on items from the sorted list or to type in a name to search for. Also supports file handling.
desktop.mak	An example that lets you drag labels and position them where you want them. This program mimics the Windows Program Manager—you can move program names around the window, organizing them as you like, and start them with a double click. Start the application, which shows some program names in two boxes (labelled

continues

Project	What It Does
	Business and Home). Drag and drop these names as you like; when you double-click on one,the corresponding application starts.
editor.mak	A file editor that lets you examine the contents of files from Windows. You can even modify the files (including cut-and-paste capability) and write it back out to disk. Use the File menu to open and save files, and the Edit menu for cut-and-paste operations. Also included: Editor.Hlp, which loads into Windows Help when you select from the Help menu.
ole.mak	Object Linking and Embedding (OLE) example. Here the program tries to load a section of an Excel for Windows spreadsheet—Sheet1.Xls (supplied on the disk; move it into the c:\excel directory). If successful, you can use the section of worksheet that appears just as you would in Excel.
pad.mak	A notepad, complete with cut and paste. Use the mouse to mark text after you type it; then you can cut the text and paste it in elsewhere. The text in the pad can be up to 64K.
panel.mak	A control panel example. The main application lets you draw freehand with the mouse when you press the left mouse button. To adjust the height, width, and caption of the main window—as well as the drawing color—pop up the control panel from the File menu and use the scroll bars there.
phone.mak	A phonebook program. Run it and type someone's name and phone number in the two text boxes, then choose Add Current Name in the File menu. When you do, that

Project	What It Does
	person is added to the File menu and the text boxes are cleared so that you can add more names. When you select a name from the File menu, that person's name and phone number are retrieved and displayed in the text boxes.
plotter.mak	An example showing how to use a customized scale. Here you simply set the scale of your window to match the range of your data and then plot it. The resulting graph is not much to look at, but it does show how to use the Scale method in code, and how to make plotting data values easier.
prnstrg.mak	A print string example, using word wrap on a form (that is, not automatically, as in a text box). Here, you do the word wrap yourself; this code shows you how to do it (taking into account that Windows uses a variable-width font).
qsort.mak	A Quicksort example. Here you simply sort an array of 10 numbers; what you see here are the before and after contents of the array. The code shows how the Quicksort was done.
spread.mak	A spreadsheet example, using the Grid control. Supplies a number of "expense account" items. As you fill in numbers in all labelled cells (except the Total cell), you will see the running sum in Total be continually updated. WARNING: does not guard against overflow.
sprite2.mak	An animation example. For super speed, you use an icon with a rocketship in it so that Visual Basic can move it around the window for you. Click on the button marked Click Me to see the rocketship fly to the top of the window. (The special

continues

719

Project	What It Does
	file sprite2.ico is also included on the disk and loaded automatically by the program.)
ssort.mak	A shell sort example. Here you simply sort an array of 10 numbers; what you see here are the before and after contents of the array. The code shows how the shell sort was done.
tictac.mak	A rudimentary tic-tac-toe game. All we are trying to demonstrate here are control arrays (that is, how to handle multiple controls); there is no game logic—you will have to be both players. As you click the buttons, their captions alternate between x and o. The game will tell you if x or o won.

This disk also contains three bonus projects that do not appear in the book.

Project	What It Does
bship.mak	A battleship game. Use the New Game item in the File menu to start a new game. The computer will play against you in this game.
colors.mak	A color editor that lets you design the Red, Green, and Blue values of colors. There are three scroll bars here; by adjusting them, you can design your own color in the main box. As you do, you will see what values of Red, Green, and Blue (all of which range from 0 to 255) you are using. When you want to use the final color in Visual Basic, use the RGB() function and pass it the Red, Green, and Blue color values you have designed.

Project	What It Does
hyper.mak	A hypertext example. Run it and press the mouse button when the mouse cursor is over the underlined words. When you do, a temporary box comes up, explaining the meaning of those words. Next, click on the bold underlined words to switch to another window; then click on the bold underlined words there to switch back. This is how hypertext works—by clicking on specially marked words, you can get quick definitions or switch to another context.

More About the Diskette

CSMeter \CRESCENT\

Custom control contained in CSMETER.VBX

Purpose

The CSMeter control gives a visual representation of percentage data. CSMeter operates in two modes set by the PercentMode property. Standard percent mode (0 to 100 percent) or in user mode (–32768 to 32767). In Standard mode, percentages in the 0 to 100 range are passed to CSMeter through the PercentValue property. The percentage value may be displayed in the center of the control when the value of the ShowPercent property is –1. The ShowPercent property default is 0. In UserMode, the MinValue and MaxValue properties set a range that Uservalue is

723

compared to. The percentage of UserValue in relation to the range is then displayed graphically as well as numerically by CSMeter.

When in UserMode, the PercentValue property may be read to get the percent value that is being displayed. The PercentValue property is read only in UserMode.

Properties

BackColor	Height	*PercentValue
*BevelWidth	Index	*ShowPercent
*BorderEffect	Left	Tag
BorderStyle	*MaxValue	Top
*Direction	*MinValue	*UserValue
Enabled	Name	Visible
ForeColor	*PercentMode	Width

* = Custom property or event (see the following paragraphs)

BevelWidth

Purpose
The BevelWidth property sets the width of a CSMeter control's border as specified by BorderEffect.

Syntax
[form.]CSMeter.BevelWidth[= integer%]

Design Time Interface
Edit window

Data Type
Integer

Usage
Read/Write at design and run time

Comments
The BevelWidth property accepts pixel values only.

BorderEffect

Purpose
The BorderEffect property lets you create a sunken or raised effect for an Edit control by drawing an additional frame around the control.

Syntax
```
[form.]CSMeter.BorderEffect[ = integer%]
```

Design Time Interface
List Box:

      0 — None

      1 — Pop (Convex Frame)

      2 — Drop (Concave Frame)

      3 — Drop Shadow

Runtime Data Type
Integer

Usage
Read/Write at runtime and design time

Comments
When this property is set to either 1 or 2, an additional border is drawn around the control (outside any existing border drawn when BorderStyle = 1). When BorderEffect = 1, the top and left sides are drawn in white, and the bottom and left sides are grey. All four sides are drawn 15 Twips wide.

When BorderEffect is set to 3, a drop shadow will be drawn along the bottom and right sides of the control's frame.

PercentMode

Purpose
The PercentMode property determines whether a CSMeter control uses the PercentValue property for input in a range of 0 to 100 or the UserValue property based on the MinValue/MaxValue range.

Syntax

`[form.]CSMeter.PercentMode[ = integer%]`

Design Time Interface

List Box:

> 0 — Standard (0 to 100%)
>
> 1 — User Value (Min/Max)

Data Type

Integer

Usage

Read/Write at design and run time

Comments

If PercentMode is to be changed at runtime, the value properties—PercentValue for standard mode or user value for user mode—must be set afterwards in order for it to take effect.

PercentValue

Purpose

The PercentValue property sets or returns a standard percentage value (0 to 100) in a CSMeter control.

Syntax

`[form.]CSMeter.PercentValue[ = integer%]`

Design Time Interface

Edit window

Data Type

Integer (0 to 100)

Usage

Read/Write at design time

Read/Write at runtime when in Standard percent mode; Read only at runtime when in User percent mode

Comments

Use this property to set or retrieve the current percentage represented by the CSMeter control.

ShowPercent

Purpose

The ShowPercent property enables/disables the numeric percentage display on a CSMeter control.

Syntax

```
[form.]CSMeter.ShowPercent[ = boolean%]
```

Design Time Interface

True/False List Box

Data Type

Boolean Integer

Usage

Read/Write at design and run time

UserValue

Purpose

The UserValue property sets the value on a CSMeter control within the range determined by the MinValue and MaxValue properties.

Syntax

```
[form]CSMeter.UserValue[ = integer%]
```

Design Time Interface

Edit window

Data Type

Integer

Usage

Read/Write at design and run time when in user PercentMode. Not active when in standard PercentMode.

Comments

UserValue sets a value converted into a percentage of the MinValue to MaxValue range. The resulting percentage is displayed and also set into the PercentValue property. If the control is in Standard mode, this property is ignored.

Copyright (c) 1992 Crescent Software Inc.

WARNING

This product is licensed to you pursuant to the terms of the Crescent license agreement included with the original software and is protected by copyright law and international treaties. Unauthorized reproduction or distribution may result in severe civil and criminal penalties and will be prosecuted to the maximum extent possible under the law.

Crescent Software makes many more fine tools for Basic Programmers.

For more information call us at (203) 438-5300.

VBToolsKan

Kansmen Corporation

Due to space requirements, the entire manual for VBToolsKan cannot be printed in this appendix.

The documentation for the individual tools have been placed on the disk with each tool. They are in Word for Windows format.

The VTToolsKan manual is available for $25 plus shipping and handling. (This price is subject to change without notice.) To purchase the manual for VBToolsKan, please contact Kansmen at (408) 988-0634 or write to the following address:

Kansmen Corporation
2080-C1 Walsh Avenue
Santa Clara, CA 95050

Please read the license agreement before using the tools in VBToolsKan.

Each tool from VBToolsKan has been placed in its own directory on the accompanying disk. Each tool and documentation is in a self-extracting archive. To use a particular tool, copy the archive onto your hard disk and execute the name of the tool. The name and directory for each tool will be given with the properties here. For a complete reference, see the Word for Windows document in each archive or contact the Kansmen Corporation for a complete reference manual.

TKCHART   \TOOLSKAN\CHART\CHART.EXE

This TKChart control can serve either as a regular charting tool or as a database front-end for displaying data. More than 30 2-D and 3-D charts (area, line, bar, pie, and column charts) and more than 50 different styles (legend styles, label styles, axes styles, chart title, and so on) are available. This control supports rotation for 3-D charts so that charts can be viewed from different angles. To facilitate 3-D rotations, an automatic self-rotation about the y axis is also implemented in this module. Besides rotation, this TKChart control supports scrolling along the x axis (y axis for bar charts). This is particularly useful when a large set of data points is to be displayed.

If the chart is used as a database front-end, a memory cache of a range of data will be used. The TKChart control will prompt the application for more data only when needed. If the chart is used as a regular plotting device, all data will be kept in memory.

Properties for the TKChart module are listed in the following table.

Table E.1. TKChart Properties Directory

Properties for Chart Configuration			
*AppSendTimer	DragMode	Height	TabIndex
*BorderColor	FontBold	Index	TabStop
*BrushPatternArr	FontItalic	Left	Tag
*cElement	FontName	*LegendAlign	*TitleArr
*ChartStyle	FontSize	*MaxCache	Top

continues

729

Table E.1. continued

Properties for Chart Configuration

---

*ChartType	FontStrike	*Perspective	*TotalData
*DataStart	FontUnder	*PiePosArr	Visible
*DataType	*GridColor	*ProjectStyle	Width
DragIcon			

* = Custom property or event

Custom Properties for Axis Configuration

AxisStyle	dMinVal	iMinVal*	lMinVal
dIncVal	GapStyl	LabelTyp	zLabelArre
Division	iIncVal	lIncVal	

Custom Properties To Be Used with Custom Methods

AxisIndex	dMin	iMin	lMin
ColorArr	iDataArr	lDataArr	xIndex
dDataArr	iMax	lMax	xLabel
dMax			

Custom Properties To Be Used with Custom Events

---

dNeedDataArr	lNeedDataArr
iNeedDataArr	NeedDataxLabel

Custom Properties Used as Methods

AddData	GetAxisConfig	Redraw
AxisConfig	GetCachedDataCount	Rotate
ChartConfig	GetDataCount	SelfRotate
ChTimer	GetElementColorArr	SetElementColorArr

Custom Properties Used as Methods		
CopyChart	GetFirstDataCached	WriteData
DeleteAllData	InsertData	yMinMax
DeleteData	ReadData	

Ribbon/Icon Bar   \TOOLSKAN\RIBBON\RIBBON.EXE

The following are a few of the design options that are available:

▼ Windows 3-D look and feel.

▼ Supports combo boxes and edit controls.

▼ Color customization.

▼ Various item selection styles—multiple selection, single selection, no-state action elements.

▼ Any number of groups and items.

▼ Variable gap widths.

▼ 32-bit private item data.

Table E.2 is a list of properties for the TKRib module.

Table E.2. TKRib Properties Directory

Properties for Ribbon			
*BkColor	FontName	*GroupType	Left
*BtnHeight	FontSize	*GutterSize	*Light3DColor
*BtnWidth	FontStrike	Height	*Style
*cGroup	FontUnder	Index	TabIndex
*cItem	*GroupCurSel	*ItemBitmap	TabStop
*Dark3DColor	*GroupID	*ItemData	Tag
DragIcon	*GroupState	*ItemID	Top

continues

Table E.2. continued

Properties for Ribbon			
DragMode	*GroupStyle	*ItemSel	Visible
FontBold	*GroupText	*ItemState	Width
FontItalic			

* = Custom property or event

Custom Properties Used as Methods	
SetConfig	SetGroup

Custom Properties for Combobox Groups	
ComboAdd	ComboItemID
ComboCount	ComboSelLength
ComboCurIndex	ComboSelStart
ComboDelete	ComboSelText
ComboInsert	ComboText

Custom Properties for Edit Groups	
EditSelLength	EditSelText
EditSelStart	EditText

Status Bar   \TOOLSKAN\STATBAR\STATBAR.EXE

The status bar can be used to display text or information such as time, date, status of caps-lock, num-lock and scroll-lock keys. All text can be continuously scrolled across its designated display area. Progress meters are also available for showing the progress of processes.

The following are a few of the available design options:

▼ Different style for the status bar elements.

▼ Color customization of progress bars.

▼ Variable length of the status bar.

▼ Various text display style.

Table E.3 shows properties for the TKStat control.

Table E.3. TKStat Properties Directory

Properties for Status Bar

*Align	FontBold	*IsScrolling	*Timer
*AppSendTimer	FontItalic	Left	Top
BackColor	FontName	*Percent	Visible
*BarColor	FontSize	*SetEltText	Width
*cElement	FontStrike	*Stretch1	*xMargin
DragIcon	FontUnder	*Style	*xSeparator
DragMode	*GetTextLen	TabIndex	*yMargin
*EltID	Height	TabStop	
*EltWidth	Index	Tag	

* = Custom property or event

Properties Used as Methods

SetConfig	StartMeter
SetElement	StopAutoScroll
SetMeter	StopMeter
StartAutoScroll	

Table   \TOOLSKAN\TABLE\TABLE.EXE

The ToolsKan Table control allows you to display data in a tabular format. The Table control can serve either as a regular table or a database front end. For the regular table, all data is kept in memory. For the database front-end table, a memory cache of a range of data is used. The table will prompt the application for more data only when needed.

This programmer's reference manual documents the ToolsKan Table control for Visual Basic.

The ToolsKan Table control can be used with Visual Basic Version 1.0 or higher. We recommend Visual Basic Version 2.0 because with Version 1.0, the Tab and Return keys cannot be used to move the current selection of the table to adjacent cells.

Table E.4 is a list of properties for the TKTable control.

Table E.4. TKTAB Properties Directory

Properties for Table			
*BkColor	*DataHour	*GetCachedRowCount	*RecSize
*BkColorFlag	*DataInt	*GetCurRowCount	*RedrawFlag
*cCol	*DataLong	*GetFirstRowCached	*RowID
*ColAlign	*DataMin	*GetHScrollPos	*RowOrigin
*ColDataType	*DataMonth	*GetRowSplitOffset	*RowSelCount
*ColID	*DataRadioCheck	*GetVScrollPos	*RowSplitPos
*ColOffset	*DataSec	Height	*ScrollbarID
*ColShow	*DataString	Index	*Style
*ColSelCount	*DataYear	*IsColSplit	TabIndex
*ColSize	DragIcon	*IsCurRowModified	TabStop
*ColSplitPos	DragMode	*IsPastable	Tag
*ColStyle	FontBold	*IsRowSelected	*TextColor
*ColTitle	FontItalic	*IsRowSplit	*TextColorFlag
*ColWidth	FontName	Left	Top

Properties for Table

*CurRow	FontSize	*MaxCache	Visible
*DataBitmap	FontStrike	*MaxRow	Width
*DataDay	FontUnder	*PrivateData	

* = Custom property or event

Custom Properties Used as Methods

AddRow	GetRowSel	SetConfig
ClearAllColSel	GetTableColor	SetCurSel
ClearAllRowSel	InsertRow	SetRowColor
CopyData	InvalidateCell	SetRowHeadingCfg
DeleteAllRow	MoveRow	SetRowSel
DeleteRow	PasteData	SetTableColor
GetColColor	ReadAddRowCell	ShowCol
GetColSel	ReadCell	WriteCell
GetCurSel	ReadModifiedCell	WriteInputCell
GetRowColor	SetColColor	WriteNeedDataCell
SetColSel		

Custom Properties for Columns with TDT_LISTONLY Data Type

ComboAdd	ComboItemID
ComboCount	ComboSelLength
ComboCurIndex	ComboSelStart
ComboDelete	ComboSelText
ComboInsert	ComboText

continues

735

Table E.4. continued

Custom Properties for Columns with TDT_TEXT Data Type	
EditSelLength	EditSelText
EditSelStart	EditText

Custom Properties for Columns with TDT_TEXT Data Type and TDS_VALIDATE Style
FormatString
GetInputTextLen
InputText

TKTBOX   \TOOLSKAN\TOOLBOX\TOOLBOX.EXE

The following are a few of the available design options:

▼ 3-D look and feel.

▼ Color customization.

▼ Item selection style—multiple selection, single selection, no-state action elements.

▼ Any number of groups and items.

▼ Variable gap widths.

▼ Private 32-bit item data.

▼ Displays both bitmap and text.

▼ Optional scroll bar or scroll buttons for a large toolbox.

Table E.5 is a list of properties for the TKTbox module.

Table E.5. TKTbox Properties Directory

Properties for Toolbox		
*BitmapType	*GroupCurSel	*ItemText
*BkColor	*GroupID	*LayoutStyle

Properties for Toolbox

*BtnHeight	*GroupState	Left
*BtnWidth	*GroupType	*Light3DColor
*cCol	*GutterSize	*SelectedTextColor
*cGroup	Height	*Style
*cRow	Index	TabIndex
*Dark3DColor	*ItemBitmap	TabStop
*DisableTextColor	*ItemData	Tag
DragIcon	*ItemID	Top
DragMode	*ItemSel	Visible
*DrawTextStyle	*ItemState	Width
*EnableTextColor		

* = Custom property or event

Custom Properties Used as Methods

SetConfig

SetGroup

737

Appendix E: More About the Diskette

Disk Contents

READ.ME
INSTALL.BAT
ALARM.BAS
ALARM.FRM
ALARM.MAK
BOX.BAS
BOX.C
BOX.DEF
BOX.FRM
BOX.H
BOX.MAK
BOX.RC
BOX.VBX
BOXCD.BMP
BOXCU.BMP
BOXEU.BMP
BOXMU.BMP
BSHELP.FRM
BSHIP.BAS
BSHIP.FRM
BSHIP.ICO
BSHIP.MAK
BSHIP1.FRM
BSHIP2.FRM
BSMOD.BAS
CALC.BAS
CALC.FRM
CALC.MAK
CAPTURE.MAK
CASCADE.BAS
CASCADE.MAK
CASCADE1.FRM
CASCADE2.FRM
CASCADE3.FRM
CASCADE4.FRM
CLIPPER.BAS
CLIPPER.FRM
CLIPPER.MAK

COLORS.BAS
COLORS.FRM
COLORS.MAK
COLPAINT.FRM
DATABASE.BAS
DATABASE.FRM
DATABASE.MAK
DB2.BAS
DB2.FRM
DESKTOP.BAS
DESKTOP.FRM
DESKTOP.MAK
EDITOR.BAS
EDITOR.FRM
EDITOR.FRX
EDITOR.HLP
EDITOR.HPJ
EDITOR.LOG
EDITOR.MAK
EDITOR.RTF
HYPER.BAS
HYPER.FRM
HYPER.MAK
HYPER1.FRM
HYPER2.FRM
INIT.C
L2.FRM
LOADFORM.FRM
LODPAINT.FRM
MAKEFILE
MAKEFILE.C6
OLE.BAS
OLE.FRM
OLE.MAK
PAD.BAS
PAD.FRM
PAD.MAK
PAINT.BAS

PAINT.FRM
PAINT.MAK
PANEL.BAS
PANEL.FRM
PANEL.MAK
PANEL1.FRM
PHONE.BAS
PHONE.FRM
PHONE.MAK
PLOTTER.BAS
PLOTTER.FRM
PLOTTER.MAK
PRNSTRG.BAS
PRNSTRG.FRM
PRNSTRG.MAK
QSORT.BAS
QSORT.FRM
QSORT.MAK
S2.FRM
SAVEFORM.FRM
SAVPAINT.FRM
SHEET1.XLS
SPREAD.FRM
SPREAD.MAK
SPRITE2.BAS
SPRITE2.FRM
SPRITE2.ICO
SPRITE2.MAK
SSORT.BAS
SSORT.FRM
SSORT.MA
TICTAC.BAS
TICTAC.FRM
TICTAC.MAK
WINUSER.BAS
WINUSER.FRM

Index

Symbols

symbol, 53-54
... (ellipsis) in menus, 87
.Bas files, saving as text, 32
.BMP files (Windows Paintbrush), loading, 260-261
.Frm files, saving as text, 32
.Mak files, 31
.WMF (Windows metafiles), LoadPicture( ) function, 259
< operators, 70
> logical operator, comparing strings, 435
> operator, 70
^ operator, 319
0 symbol, 53-54
3-D custom controls, 590-593

A

access keys
   adding to menus, 118-119
   fonts, 118
   notepad program, 65-67
Action property, 498, 500-501, 611-612
activating
   menu items, 105
   shortcut keys, 120
active controls and forms, 530-532
ActiveControl property, 490-491, 530-532
ActiveForm property, 532
Add command, File menu (Database.Mak program), 168-169
Add File... command (File menu), 327
AddAnItem_Click( ) function, 170
adding menu items, 127-134
AddItem method, 170-171, 227-228
AddNameItem_Click( ) Sub procedure, 130

aggregate data types, 44
Alarm Application listing (2.2), 80-83
alarm clock program, 67-68
  Alarm Off/On option button, 73-74
  event handlers, 76-79
  global variables, 73
  menu, 124-126
  selecting fonts, 79-81
  template, 75
  updating display, 74
alarm clock property, displaying time, 71
Alarm.Bas module, 68
Alarm.Frm form, 68
Alarm.Mak project, 68, 80-83, 716
anchor points, 302-303, 556, 557
  Screen Capture program, 546-547
AnchorX/Y global variables, 308-310
And operators, 250
AniButton1_Click( ) Sub procedure, 596
animated button
  custom control, 593-597
  tool, 593-594
animating picture box controls, 280
animation templates, 283-284
ANSI characters, returning, Chr$( ) function, 212
ANSI code, 69
API (external) functions, linking to programs, 543-545

AppActivate statement, 484
Append command (File menu), sequential files, adding to, 220
applications
  adding control panels, 154-156
  exiting, Cancel button, 153
  multitasking, 457
Pad
  3-D controls, 590-593
  Color Selection dialog boxes, 623-624
  File Open dialog boxes, 618-621
  Font Selection dialog boxes, 612-618
  key status controls, 586-590
  Print dialog boxes, 624-627
  Save File dialog boxes, 622-623
Paint
  clipboard, 341-342
  drawing , 316-326, 331-339
  printing graphics, 339-340
  reading files from disk, 328-330
  saving files to disk, 326-328
  scaling graphics, 353-354
Paintbrush for Windows (Microsoft), transferring files with, 330

starting, OK button, 153-154
Windows
  Shell( ) function, 144
  writing, 9
arcs, drawing, 258
arguments
  Button, 299-304
  Index arguments, 89
  KeyCode, 69-70
  Shift, 69-70, 299-302
  type, 140-144
  X/Y, 299-300
arrays, 361-365
  Box_Events[], 649-650
  Box_Properties[], 646
  control, 76-79
  data types, 178-183
  declaring, 178
  general object, 132
  of forms, creating, 529
  passing to Windows calls, 553
  retrieving data from, GetItem( ) Sub procedure, 229
  string
    Names( ), 131
    Numbers( ), 131
    TheData( ), 179
Asc( ) function, 70
aspect argument/ratio, drawing ellipses, 257
assigning indexes to menu items, 111
associating icons, 122
automatic links, 458
automatic word wrap, multiline text box, 211

AutoRedraw property
redrawing forms, 236,
288-289
redrawing graphics, 287
restoring graphics, 261,
266-267
Autosize property, picture
box size changing, 260
average character, finding
width, 271
axes, setting x coordinates,
604

B

BackColor property, 161,
307
command buttons, 245
form background color,
239-240
setting form background,
283-284
text boxes, 17-20
bar graphs, 599-602
.Bas files, saving as text, 32
Basic Beep statement, 70,
73-74
Basic Chr$( ) function, 70
Basic code, replacing with
text boxes, 38-39
battleship game, 720
Beep statement, 140
beta versions of programs,
412
BevelWidth property, 591,
724
binary files,
executable (.Exe), 196
reading data, 213

Binary Input/Output file
mode, 195
binary raster operation,
setting, 555, 556
Binary Tree listing (8.1),
378-379
binary trees, 372-379
BitBlt( ) API function,
562-564
bitmaps
copying, 562-564
designing for toolbox,
658-660
blue setting, Windows
colors, 161-162
.BMP files (bitmap files),
LoadPicture( ) function,
259-261
boldface event names, 27
Boolean integer type
(Visual Basic), 74
BorderEffect property, 725
borders, omitting in
custom controls, 652
BorderStyle (label tool), 71
option 1, 42-43
property, 202-204
Fixed Single, 150-151
NewColor label, 161
BottomTitle property, 607
bounds, values, 412
Box custom control
control procedure,
660-682
creating, 637-639
designing bitmaps for
toolbox, 658-660
initializing and registering, 639-657
using, 682-683

BOX structures, 642-647
Box tool, 316-318
Box.C file listing (14.4),
676-679
Box.Def file listing (14.5),
679
Box.H file listing (14.3),
671-672
Box.Mak project, 716
Box.Rc file listing (14.2),
660
Box_Events[] array of
pointers, 649-650
Box_Properties[] array of
pointers, 646
Box1_ClickInside/Outside( )
Sub procedures 638
BoxColor property, 638,
675-676
BoxCtlProc( ) function,
654, 662-663
drawing, 316-318,
323-326
around tables, 265-266
versus using frames,
509
Break command (Insert
menu), 690-694
Break command (Run
menu), 437
break states, 440
breaking links, 466
Breakpoint tool, 438
breakpoints, 439-444
Bship.Mak project, 720
buffers
circular, 371-372
temporary, 61-65
bugs (logic errors), 411,
433-444
see also debugging

built-in data types, 44
Button argument, 299-304
buttons
  3-D, 590-593
  animated, 593-597
  Cancel, determining if
    clicked, 616-617
  changing colors, 307
  Clear, 308
  command
    creating for drawing
      tools, 307
    cutting/pasting text,
      60-65
  debugging type, 438
  mouse
    testing for being
      pushed/released,
      300-301, 306
    using Ctrl or Shift keys
      with, 301-302
  radio (option), 67-70
  toolbox, hiding, 339
  Windows controls, 38-83

C

C interface
  adding gauges, 608-611
  connecting with Visual
    Basic, 568-579
  listing (13.3), 608-609
Calc.Mak project, 716
calculator programs, 39-43,
  48-52, 55
  investment, debugging,
    445-453
calculator template, 40-42

Call statements, 175-176
CallHello( ) Sub procedure,
  527-528
Calls tool, 438
Cancel button
  activating, 203-204
  determining if clicked,
    616-617
  exiting programs, 153
Cancel options, 151
CancelButton, 156
CancelButton_Click( )
  function, 195
CancelError property, 616
Caps Lock key, 586-590
caption bar (Windows 3+
  version), 4-5
Caption property (proper-
  ties window), 39-44
captions
  menus, 91
  properties, 95
Capture.Mak project,
  565-568, 716-717
capturing screens, 542-568
caret, see insertion point
Cascade program, 524-527
  listing (11.3), 527
Cascade( ) Sub procedure,
  524-527
Cascade.Mak project, 527,
  717
CDK (Control Develop-
  ment Kit), 541
cells
  current, 402
  sending data from
    multiple, (DDE), 471

Change event, 65
  Dir1_, 205
  drop-down list boxes, 204
  moving scroll bar
    thumb, 157-158
change event, 161
Character... command
  (Format menu), 690-691,
  695
characters of data types, 45
charts ,TKChart control,
  729-731
ChDir statement, file list
  box, opening files, 208
ChDrive statement, file list
  box, opening files, 208
check box tool, 465
check boxes, 3-D, 590-593
check marks, menus,
  114-117, 126
Check1_Click( ) Sub
  procedure, 465-471
checked menu items, 87
choosing with single
  mouse click, 5-6
Chr$( ) function, 211-212
CInterface( ) C function,
  569-570
Circle method, 257-295,
  318-326
Circle tool, 318-319
CircleFlag global variable,
  308-310, 318-319
circles, drawing, 318-326
circular buffers, 371-372
Class property, 497-500
Clear All Breakpoints
  command (Run menu),
  441

Clear All button, 105
Clear All command, 59-60
Clear button, 308
ClearButton_Click( ) Sub
  procedure, 105, 308
clearing drawing area, 308
click events, 207-208
ClickInside/Outside( )
  events, 669-675
client area (Windows
  version 3+), 5
client links, 458-459
  design-time, 459-463
  run-time, 465-471
clients, sending data to
  sources from, 480-482
ClientToScreen( ) API
  function, 547-548
clipboard with Paint
  program, 341-342
clipper.mak project, 717
Close statement, 200-201
closing
  links, 488-489
  windows
    End statement, 96
    Menu Design Window,
      93
closing all files, 201
Cls method, clearing
  screen, 248
clusters, 367
CMDialog (common
  dialog box) custom
  control, 611-630
Code menu
  Load/Save Text... com-
    mand, 32

code window, 94
  finding events, 22-23, 30
  procedure box, 24-27
  templates, 22-27
    FFF_Click( ), 112
coded events, 27
codes
  ANSI, 69
  Basic, 38-39
  displaying numericals, 43
coding
  events, 7-8, 27
  programs, 26
color editor, 720
color filling, IconWorks
  program, 282-283
Color Selection dialog
  boxes, 623-624
color values, 241-242
  hexadecimal, 242
  predefined, Constant.Txt
    file, 239-243
ColorData property, 601
ColorItem_Click( ) Sub
  procedure, 623
colors
  buttons, changing, 307
  custom controls, chang-
    ing, 675-676
  drawing, 331-339
  graphs, 601
  lines, 245
  RGB function, 241
  screen position determi-
    nation, (Point method),
    243
  setting, 162-167
Colors.Mak project, 720
Cols property, 401

combo boxes
  database programs,
    185-187
  list and text boxes,
    183-187
  properties, List/Text, 185
  types, 184
command button tool,
  20-23
command buttons
  3-D, 590-593
  control arrays, 89
  cutting text, 60-65
  drawing tools, 307
  enabling, 105
  focus, 95
  menu items, 101
  options, 99
  procedures, 102
  properties, 89
  references, 106
Command1_Click( ) Sub
  procedure, 479, 596
commands
  Add File... (File menu),
    327
  Append (File menu), 220
  Break (Insert menu),
    690-694
  Break (Run menu), 437
  Character... (Format
    menu), 690-691, 695
  Clear All, 59-60
  Clear All Breakpoints
    (Run menu), 441
  Continue (Run menu),
    438
  Copy (Edit menu),
    492-496

Cut, 59-60
Edit menu, 707
End (Run menu), 12, 151
Exit (File menu), 5-6,
   326-327
File menu, 707-708
FileCopy (Visual Basic
   Main menu), 230
Footnote (Insert menu),
   691
Grid Settings...command
   (Edit menu), 12
Help Editor menu,
   688-689
Help menu, 708
Load File... (File menu),
   214, 330
Make Exe File... (File
   menu), 27-28, 62-65
New Drawing Color...
   (File menu), 332-333
New Form (File menu),
   147, 155, 202
New Module... com-
   mand (File menu),
   29-30, 47-48, 61-65,
   139-140
Open (File menu), 30-31,
   195-199
Page Break (Insert
   menu), 690-691
Paste, 59-60
Paste From Clipboard
   (File menu), 341-342
Paste Link (Edit menu),
   459, 489-490
Paste To Clipboard (File
   menu), 341-342
Print (File menu),
   339-340

Remove File (File menu),
   139-140
Save File (File menu),
   31-32, 193-195, 326-328
Save File As... (File
   menu), 31-32
Save Project As... (File
   menu), 30-32, 39-42
Save Text... (Code/File
   menu), 31-32
Search (Help Editor
   menu), 692
sending through DDE
   links, 483-484
Set Startup Form... (Run
   menu), 524
Single Step (Run menu),
   448
Startup Form... (Options
   menu), 148-149
Toggle Breakpoint
   (Debug menu), 439
Undo (File menu), 327
View Code (View menu),
   436
CommentField text box,
   Database.Mak program,
   168-169
Comments( ) global array,
   176
constant RED, 241
Constant.Txt file, 69-70,
   239-243
Continue command (Run
   menu), 438
control arrays, 76-79
Control Development Kit
   (CDK), 541
Control Panel Application
   listing (4.2), 164-167

control panels, 160,
   163-164
   adding to applications,
      154-156
   creating menus, Menu
      Design Window, 159
   drawing colors, custom-
      izing for, 331-339
   hiding, CancelButton,
      156
controls
   3-D, 590-593
   active, 530-532
   animated button,
      593-597
   associating text strings
      with, 517
   CMDialog (common
      dialog box), 611-630
   colors, changing, 675-676
   CSMeter, 723-728
   custom, 585-586
      control procedures,
         660-682
      designing bitmaps for
         toolbox, 658-660
      initializing and
         registering, 639-657
      creating/installing
         .Vbx files as, 637-639
   designing, 90
   gauge, 608-611
   graph, 598-608
   graphic objects, 14
   Grid, 401-406
   key status, 586-590
   labeling on forms, 42-44
   linking to DLLs, 679
   Masked Edit, 70

Name property, 15-20
OleClient, 496-502
passed, 515, 520-523
Pen, 630-631
processing messages sent
   to, 662-664
program I/O, 14
resizing, 664-665
tab order, 532-535
TK, 729-733
TKTable, 734-737
Zorder, 535
coordinate system
   defaults, 236, 287-292
   new, (Scale method), 288
   Paint event, 288-289
   Plotter.Mak project,
      288-290
Copies property, 624
Copy command (Edit
   menu), 492-496
copying bitmaps, 562-564
CopyItem_Click( ) Sub
   procedure, 493-494
CreateDC( ) API function,
   551-554
creating
   menus, 91
      activating options, 96
      adding items, 92
      Clear All button, 105
CSMeter custom control,
   723-728
Ctrl key, 301-302
Ctrl+C (accessing control
   panels), 159
Ctrl+X (exiting control
   panels), 159
currency data type, 44-46

Currency variables, 360
current cell, 402
current directory,
   directory list box,
      205-206
   file list box, 207-210
current pages, titles, 692
CurrentX property, 241,
   263
CurrentY property, 241,
   263
cursor, 299-300, 307-308
Cuser.C listing (12.2), 570
Cuser.Def listing (12.3), 572
Cuser.Mak listing (12.4),
   573-575
custom controls, 585-586
   3-D, 590-593
   animated button,
      593-597
   Box, 637-639, 682-683
   CMDialog (common
      dialog box), 611-630
   colors, 675-676
   control procedures,
      660-682
   CSMeter, 723-728
   designing bitmaps for
      toolbox, 658-660
   gauge, 608-611
   graph, 598-608
   initializing and register-
      ing, 639-657
   installing .Vbx files as,
      637
   key status, 586-590
   linking to DLLs, 679
   omitting borders, 652
   Pen, 630-631

processing messages sent
   to, 662-664
resizing, 664-665
Custom Footnote Mark
   button (Insert menu), 691
customizing
   dialog boxes, 147,
      150-154
   tabs, 265
   windows, 11-14
Cut button (3-D), 591-593
Cut command, 59-60
CutButton/Item_Click( )
   Sub procedure, 103
CutButton3D_Click( ) Sub
   procedure, 592-593
cutting text, 60-65
Cycle property, 596

D

dashed lines, 246-247
data
   editing, 603-604
   organizing, 359-406
   reading, binary files, 213
   searching, 395-401
   sorting
      Quicksorts, 389-395
      shell sorts, 379-389
Data statement, 360
data structures, 366
data types
   aggregate, 44
   built-in, 44
   changing, 45-46
   characters, 45
   currency, 44-46
   default changing, 45-46

Peter Norton's Visual Basic for Windows Third Edition, Covering Release 3.0

integer, 45
Record, 178
single, 45
type declaration, 178
Database program, 168-177
Database Program listing
  (4.3), 176-177
Database.Bas module, 170
Database.Mak project,
  176-177, 717
databases
  AddItem method,
    227-228
  combo boxes, 185-187
  dialog boxes, 172
  error message box,
    186-187
  exiting, 174
  fields, 168
  Load File... dialog box,
    225
  random files, 222
  records, 168, 226-227
DataReset property, 608
DDE (Dynamic Data
  Exchange), 457-458
  Copy command, 492-496
  design-time client/source
    links, 459-465
  establising/terminating
    links, 488-489
  pasting links, 489-492
  picture box links,
    477-480
  sending commands,
    483-484
  sending data, 480-482
  trappable errors, 484-488

Debug menu, Toggle
  Breakpoint command,
  439
Debug window, 440-444
debugging
  breakpoints, 439-444
  Debug window, 440-444
  single-stepping through
    programs, 448-453
  text boxes, 433
  with program running,
    436-438
declarations, 45-46
declaring
  API (external) functions,
    543
  arrays, 178
  dynamic arrays, 364-365
  Static arrays, 363-364
  variables, 89
default button, 51
default data types, 45-46
Default property
  OK button, 153
defaults
  coordinate system,
    287-292
  coordinate system,
    twips, 236
  data types, 45-46
  drive names, 204
  forms, 148, 236-239
  graphics pen tool, 249
  measuring units (twips),
    156
  Min property, 158
  OK button, 153-154
  properties, 194-195
  solid lines, 246-247

tab length, 264
text box names, 22-23, 51
variables, 45
Deftype statement, 45-46
DelayRecog property, 631
DeleteDC( ) API function,
  559-560
deleting
  check marks, 114-116
  device context handles,
    559-560
  menu items, 127-134
  text, 256-259
delimiters, 471
design-time OLE objects,
  499-500
design-time links, 459-465
design-time errors, 411
designing menus, 90-99
Desktop Organizer pro-
  gram, 508-520
Desktop.Mak project,
  717-718
  listing (11.1), 518-519
device context handles
  551-554, 559-560
dialog boxes
  Cancel options, 151
  Color Selection, 623-624
  customizing, 147,
    150-154
  Database.Mak program,
    172
  Editor's Save File..., 198
  file loading, 222-223
  File Open/Save, 618-621
  Font Selection, 612-618
  Hide method, 149,
    152-154, 213-214

Insert Object, 500
Load File..., 202, 213-214
Load Icon, 123
LoadForm, 328-330,
    204-205
modal, 149
Print, 624-627
RunItem_Click( ) event,
    151-154
Save File, 622-623
SaveForm, 194
Select Frame, 595
Shell statement, 151-154
Show method, 149
Visual Basic Professional
    Edition, 193
DialogTitle property, 618
Dim statement, 45
dimensions
    strings on screen,
        267-277
Dir1.Path property,
    205-206
Dir1.Path—> File1.Path
    property, 206
Dir1_Change event,
    205-206
directories
    changing, 209
    directory list box,
        205-206
    ICONS, 122
directory list boxes,
    203-206
disk list boxes, 202-204
Display label, 79-83
DLLs (dynamic link
    libraries), 542-579
Do Until loop, 211

documents, 197
DOS, 6-7
dot (.) operator, 60, 179
dotted lines, 246-247
double-click events, 2,
    185-186, 207-208
doubly linked lists, 372
Drag method, 516
DragDrop event, 509
DragMode property,
    509-513
DrawFlag global variable,
    308-310
drawing
    arcs, 258
    boxes, 316-318, 323-333,
        252, 509, 265-266
    circles, 257-295, 318-326,
    colors, changing, 331-339
    ellipses, 257
    forms, 235-259
    freehand, 306-316
    invisible objects, Xor
        pen (DrawMode
        property), 251
    lines, 244-246, 302-303,
        306-316, 323-326
    multiple rectangles, 253
    picture boxes, 235-259
    pixel-by-pixel,
        IconWorks program,
        282-283
    rectangles, Shape Con-
        trol, 252-254
    single diagonals, Line
        method, 244
    text, 322-326
    tools, 308-310
DrawingItem_Click( ) Sub
    procedure, 332-333

DrawMode property,
    311-313, 596
    Invert pen, 249-250, 254
DrawStyle Property, 247,
    253, 318
DrawWidth property,
    246-248
drive list boxes, 202-204
drive list tool, 202-204
drive names, 204
Drive1.Drive —> Dir1.Path
    property, 206
Drive1.Drive property, 204
Drive1_Change event, 206
Drive1_Change procedure,
    204
drives, 204-209
drop-down list boxes,
    202-204
dynamic arrays, 364, 365
Dynamic Data Exchange,
    see DDE

E

Edit menu, 707
    Copy command, 492-496
    Grid
        Settings...command, 12
    Paste Link command,
        459, 489-490
editing data points,
    603-604
Editor program, 99-109
    Code listing (5.1),
        214-220
    connecting Editor.Hlp
        file, 698-700

icon, 122-124
templates, 101
Version 2 listing (3.2),
108-109
Version 2 listing (3.3),
116-117
Editor.Hlp file, 698-700
editor.mak project, 718
editors, color, 720
Editor's Save File... dialog
box, 198
element-by-element
comparison, 379-389
ellipses, 257
ellipsis (...), 87
embedding in OLE,
496-502
empty strings, 274-275
Enabled property, 64-65,
106
encrypting data, Xor
encryption, 251
End command (Run
menu), 12, 151
End statement, 96
Enter key, default button,
51
EOF( ) function, 211, 212
erasing rectangles around
screens, 557-558
Erl( ) function, 419-420
Err( ) function, 415-418
error handlers
customizing, 421-423
turning off, 415
error message box,
142-144, 186-187
Error$( ) function, 420-421

errors
bugs (logic), 411, 433-444
see also debugging
opening files, file list
box, 210
run-time (trappable),
411-413, 420-421
trappable, 199, 413-415
types, 411
event handlers, 76-79
event names, (coded), 27
event procedures, 24
event-driven program-
ming, I/O handling, 154
event-driven programming
(Windows), 7-8
EVENTINFO structures,
647-654
events
Change, 65, 157-158
ClickInside( ), 669-675
ClickOutside( ), 669-675
coding, 7-8
Dir1_Change, 206
DragDrop, 509
Drive1_Change, 206
Form_Click( ), 238
Form_Load, 148
GotFocus, 62-65
identifying coded, 27
KeyPress, 68-70, 68-74
KeyPress KeyAscii, 69-70
KeyUp, 68-70
LinkClose, 488-489
LinkError, 487-488
LinkOpen, 488-489
LLL_MouseDown( ),
512-513
LostFocus, 62-65

MouseDown, 299-306
MouseUp, 306
of dragging, 511-513
OK_Button_Click, 163
predefined, 648-649
read-only text boxes,
33-35
RunItem_Click( ),
151-154
scroll bar change, 161
text box changes, 33-35
Timer, Interval property,
71-74
Excel (Microsoft) as DDE
client/source, 464-471
executable (.Exe) files, 196
Exist( ) function, 428-430
Exit command, File menu
(Database.Mak program),
168-169
Exit command (File
menu), 5-6, 145-146,
326-327
exiting applications,
Cancel button, 153
exiting Database.Mak
program, 174
ExitItem_Click( ) Sub
procedure, 100, 612
exploding pie chart slices,
605-606
expressionlist, printing
strings, 264
extensions, .Bas (Basic),
30-31
external (API) functions,
543-545
ExtraData property,
605-606

Peter Norton's Visual Basic for Windows Third Edition, Covering Release 3.0

F

F option (All color), 256-257

FFF_Click( ) sub procedure, 113

fields, 168

figures with patterns, 255

file list box, 203-204
  current directory files, 207-210
  errors opening files, 210
  FileName property, 208
  files specification, 207
  Path property, 205-210
  Pattern property, 207-210
  working directory change, 206

file list boxes
  click events, 207-208
  default names, 205
  double-click events, 207-208
  searching files, 202-204

File Manager window, 3

File menu, 707-708
  Add File... command, 327
  Append command, 220
  creating for Paint application
    Exit command, 326-327
    Load File... command, 330
    New Drawing Color... command, 332-333
    Paste From Clipboard command, 341-342

Paste To Clipboard command, 341-342

Print command, 339-340

Save File... command, 326-328

Undo command, 327

Exit command, 5-6, 145-146

Load File... command, 214

Make Exe File... command, 62-65

New Form command, 147, 155, 202

New Module... command (File menu), 47-48, 61-65, 139-140

Open command, 195-199

Open Project... command, 30-31

Remove File command (File menu), 139-140

Run command, 145-146

Save File command, 31-32, 193-195

Save Project As... command, 30-32, 39-42

File menu (Database.Mak program), 168-169

File menu (Visual Basic), Make Eex File...option, 27

File menu (Windows version 3+), 4-5

File Open dialog boxes, 618-621

File Save dialog boxes, 619-620

FileCopy command (Visual Basic Main menu), 230

FileError label, 199

FileName property, 620-621

files
  adding Help windows, 694-695
  Basic (.Bas), 30-31
  binary, 196, 213
  BMP, 259-261
  Box.C, 676-679
  Box.Def, 679
  Box.H, 671-672
  Box.Rc, 660
  closing all, 201
  Constant.Txt, 69-70, 239-243
  copying, 230
  current directory, 207-210
  dialog boxes, 222-223
  errors opening, 210
  Exe, 27
  Help Editor, 698-700
  ICO, 281, 259
  Init.C, 655-657
  length in bytes, LOF( ) function, 212
  loading, 203-204
  .Mak, 31, 32
  Makefile, 680-681
  Makefile.C6, 680-682
  modes, 195
  names, 509, 513-516
  opening, 195-199, 208-209
  Panel.*, 155
  random-access, 196, 222-230
  reading sequential, 210-220

751

rich text files, 688-696
saving
  .Bas and .Frm as text, 32
  current documents, 197
  data, 193-195
searching, 202-204
sequential, 196, 202-220
specification, 207
storing, 202, 223
tying to text, 693-694
Vbrunxxx.Dll, 27
.Vbx, installing as custom controls, 637
.WMF, 259
FillColor property, 256-257
FillStyle Property, 255-256
Filter property, 618-619
Find command, File menu (Database.Mak program), 168-169
FireClickInside/Outside( ) function, 661, 668-675
fixed length strings, 179
flags
  CMDialog dialog boxes, 614-615, 619-620, 624-626
  property, 640-642
  showing usage of drawing tools, 308-310
focus (command buttons), 95
Font menu, 111-116
Font properties, 79-81, 270-271
Font Selection dialog boxes, 612-618
Font3D property, 591

FontItem_Click( ) Sub procedure, 613
FontMenu, 110
FontName text boxes, 17-20
FontName property, 110
fonts
  access keys, 118
  alarm clock project, 79-81
  monospace, 262
  Print method, 110
  selecting, 109-114
  standard, 109-110
  variable-width, 262
  word-wrap problems, 270-271
Footnote command (Insert menu), 691
footnotes (Microsoft Word for Windows, Version 2.0), 691-694
for loop, 95
ForeColor property, 161, 311-313, 331-332, 623
  drawing line color, 245
  graphics pen tool default, 249
  graphics/text color changing, 245-246
Form 1.Height, 156-158
Form 1.Width, 156-158
form level, 47-48
Form_Click( ) event, 238
Form_Click( ) Sub procedure, 473
Form_DragDrop( ) Sub procedure, 514-515
Form_Link( ) Sub procedure, 488

Form_Load event, 148
Form_Load( ) Sub procedure, 237, 283-284, 361-362
Form_Mouse( ) Sub procedure, 299-307, 310-313, 316-318
Form_Paint( ) event, 261
Form_Resize event, 290-291
Form1 properties, 156-158
Form1 window, 11-14
Form1.Control.Property, 156
Format menu
  Character... command, 690-691, 695
Format$( ) function, 53-55
formatting text in restricted space, 271
forms
  active, 532
  Alarm.Frm, 68
  arrays of, 529
  centering text, 271
  control names, 149
  customizing windows, 11-14
  DDE sources, 458-459, 464-465
  default names, 30-31
  defaults, 148, 236-239
  dimensions, 237
  drawing, 235-259
  events, 25
  labeling controls, 42-44
  LoadForm, 202
  modal, 149-150
  naming, 148-149
  Pad.Frm, 55-56

passing to procedures,
523-528
printing, 287
property names, 149
redrawing, 236
resizing, 290-291
Visual Basic, 29
Frame property, 595
frame tool, 75-76
frames, 3-D, 590-593, 509
FreeFile function, 429
freehand drawing, 306-316
.Frm files, saving as text, 32
FromPage property, 624
Function procedures
returning values, 23-27
scope of variables, 46-54
taking arguments, 23-24
functions
AddAnItem_Click( ), 170
API (external)
BitBlt( ), 562-564
ClientToScreen( ),
547-548
CreateDC( ), 551-554
DeleteDC( ), 559-560
GlobalAlloc( ), 571
LineTo( ), 557-558
LocalAlloc( ), 571
MoveTo( ), 556-557
ReleaseCapture( ), 561
SetCapture( ), 543-545
SetROP2( ), 555-556
WEP( ), 568
Asc( ), 70
Basic Chr$( ), 70
BoxCtlProc( ), 654,
662-663,

C
CInterface( ), 569-570
LibMain( ), 569
VBDefControlProc( ),
676
VBDerefControl( ),
663-664
VBFireEvent( ), 669
VBRegisterModel( ),
653-654
VBXPixelsToTwips( ),
674-675
CancelButton_Click( ),
195
Chr$( ), 211-212
EOF( ), 211-212
Erl( ), 419-420
Err( ), 415-418
Error$( ), 420-421
Exist( ), 428-430
FireClickInside( ), 661,
668-675
FireClickOutside( ), 661,
668-675
Format$( ), 53-55
FreeFile, 429
Get #, 226-227
GetItem( ), 175-176, 180
GetWord$( ), 271-275
InBox( ), 661-662, 668
Input$, 212
InputBox$( ), 144-147
InStr( ), 275
Lbound( ), 384
Left$( ), 275
LibMain( ), 652-653
LoadPicture( ), 329-330
loading pictures,
259-261
reading pictures, 280

LOF( ), 212
Ltrim$( ), 180-186
MsgBox( ), 140-144
Name, 77-78
Now, 55
PaintBox( ), 661-667
PrintString( ), 276-281
PSet( ), 235-239
QBColor( ), 242-243
RGB( ),162, 241
Right$( ), 275
Rnd( ), 477-478
Rtrim$( ), 180-186
Shell( ), 144-147
Sqr( ), 319
Str$( ), 50, 53-54
Tab( ), 264-265
Time$, 68
Ubound( ), 384
Val( ), 50, 156-158

G

games, battleship, 720
gamma versions of pro-
grams, 412
gauge custom controls,
608-611
gauge tool, 609
general object
arrays, 132
Get # function, 224-227
GetData method, 341-342
GetItem( ) function,
175-176, 180
GetItem( ) Sub procedure,
229
GetText( ) method, 490

GetWord$( ) function, 271-275
global arrays
  Comments( ), 176
  Names( ), 176
  Numbers( ), 176
global integers, 224
Global keyword, 61-62
global variable declaration, 47-48
global variables
  AlarmOff, 73
  AlarmOn, 73
  AnchorX/Y, 308-310
  BoxFlag, 308-310
  CircleFlag, 308-310, 318-319
  CutText, 61-65
  Database.Bas module, 170
  declaring, 89
  DrawFlag, 308-310
  LineFlag, 308-310
  TextFlag, 308-310
GlobalAlloc( ) API function, 571
GotFocus event, 62-65
graph custom controls, 598-608
graph tool, 599-600
GraphData property, 599-600
graphic objects, 14
graphical text, 262-267, 286
graphical text output (Visual Basic), 235-295
Graphical User Interfaces (GUIs), 2-6

graphics
  drawing, 306-326
  drawing colors, changing, 331-339
  pasting to/from clipboard, 341-342
  printing, 339-340
  reading from disk, 328-330
  saving to disk, 326-328
  scaling, 353-354
graphics (Visual Basic), 235-295
graphics controls, Shape, 252-254
Graphics form, default, 236-239
graphics methods, 294-295
graphics output position, 263
graphics pen, 246
graphics properties, 293-294
Graphics.Mak program, 236-259
graphs
  bar, 599-602
  colors, 601
  editing, 603-604
  grids, 606-607
  hatch shadings, 601-602
  pie charts, 605-606
  resetting data, 608
  titles, 607-608
  types, 602-603
  x axis, 604
GraphTitle property, 607
GraphType property, 602-603

grayed menu items, 87, 107-08
green setting, 161-162
Grid controls, 401-406
Grid Settings...command (Edit menu), 12
Grid tool, 401
grids, 606-607
GridStyle property, 606
group buttons, 3-D, 590-593

H

handles, 543-544, 551-554, 559-560
hatch shadings, 601-602
hBitmap handle, 544
hDC handle, 544
heads, circular buffers, 371
Height property, 237
Help compiler, 696-697
Help compiler (Windows 3.1), 697
Help Editor file, creating, 696-697
Help Editor menu, 688-692
Help Editor rich text file, 688-696
help files, 689
help index, 246
Help menu, 708
Help message box, 142
Help windows, 694-695
HelpContextID property, 695-696
hexadecimal color values, 242

Hide method, 149
hiding
   dialog boxes, 152-154
   Load File dialog box,
      213-214
   options, 126
   toolbox buttons, 339
horizontal scroll bar
   (Windows version 3+), 5
hWnd handle, 543-544
Hyper.Mak project, 721
hypertext, 721
hyphens, 100

I

I/O statements, 224
ICO files, 281
ICO files (icons)
   LoadPicture( ) function,
      259-295
icon bar, VBToolsKan,
   731-732
icon library, 281-282
Icon property, 285
iconic states, 4-5
icons
   associating, 122
   creating ICO files, 281
   customized, adding to
      programs, 285
   designing, 277-281
   Editor application,
      122-124
   libraries, 122
   loading, 122
   loading into picture
      boxes, 259
Program Manager, 123
   Windows version 3+, 4-5
ICONS directory, 122,
   281-282
IconWorks program,
   281-283
Image control, 259
Image controls, 280
Image property, 342
images, 261
Immediate window, see
   Debug window
implicit declarations, 45-46
InBox( ) function, 661-662,
   668
indenting menu items, 93
Index arguments, 89
Index property, 76-79
Indexes, passing, 111
Init.C file listing (14.1),
   655-657
initializing custom con-
   trols, 639-657
Input # statement, 210-220
Input$ function, 212
Input$ statement, 210-220
input/output, handling
   event-driven program-
   ming, 154
InputBox$( ) function,
   144-147
InputBox$( ) statement,
   139
Insert menu
   Break command,
      690-694
   Custom Footnote Mark
      button, 691
   Footnote command, 691
Page Break command,
   690-691
Insert Object dialog box,
   500
insertion point, 26
Inside Line drawing style,
   253
inside lines, DrawStyle
   property 6, 247
installing .Vbx files as
   custom controls, 637
InStr( ) function, 275
integer data type, 45
integer type (Visual Basic),
   74
integers
   global, 224
interfaces, Multiple
   Document Interface
   (MDI), 138-139
Interval property, 72-74
Invert Pen, DrawMode
   property, 249-250, 254
investment calculator
   program, debugging,
   445-453
items, see commands

J

jump tags, 690-691
jumping, 689
jumps, Load/Save File...,
   692

K

key status custom controls, 586-590
key status tool, 588
keyboard shortcuts
  accessing control panel (Ctrl+C), 159
  exiting control panel (Ctrl+X), 159
  Single Step (F8), 448
  table of, 704-706
  Toggle Breakpoint (F9), 439
KeyCode argument, 69-70
KeyPress event, 68-74
KeyPress event KeyAscii, 69-70
KeyUp event, 68-70
keywords
  checking passed controls against, 515
  Global, 61-62
  Me, 528
  Parent, 520
  searching for topics, 692
  Setup, 95
  Step, 241
  TypeOf, 494-495
  Visual Basics for DOS, not in Visual Basic for Win, 710-711
  Visual Basics for Windows, not in Visual Basic for DOS, 711

L

label tool, 42-43, 70-71
labels
  borders, 71
  DDE clients, 458
  Display, 79-83
  double-clicking to start applications, 517
  dragging and dropping, 513-516
  FileError, 199
  form controls, 42-44
  framing, BorderStyle option 1, 42-43
  NewColor, 161
  text boxes, 42-43
  word wrapping, 155
LargeChange property, 157-159
Lbound( ) function, 384
Left and Top property, 17-20
Left$( ) function, 275
LeftTitle property, 607
LibMain( ) function, 569, 652-653
libraries
  icons, 122, 281-282
  Visual Basic Open Database Connectivity (ODBC), 176
license agreement, VBToolsKan, 737-738
Line control tool, 244-251
Line Input # statement, 210-220
Line method, 244, 252-253, 305-306, 316-318

Line tool, 310-311
LineFlag global variable, 308-310
lines
  changing color, 245
  dashed/dotted, 246-247
  drawing, 246, 302-303, 306-316, 323-326
  drawing in code, 244
  drawing with mouse, 303-306
  solid (default), 246-247
  stretching into shape while drawing, 310-313
LineTo( ) API function, 557-558
LinkClose event, 488-489
linked lists, 367-372
LinkError events, 487-488
linking in OLE, 496-502
LinkItem property, 463, 468-469
LinkMode property, 461-462
LinkOpen events, 488-489
LinkPoke method, 481-482
LinkRequest method, 470-471
links
  breaking, 466
  client, 459, 465-471
  DDE types, 458-459
  establising and terminating, 488-489
  pasting in code to unspecified programs, 489-492
  picture box, 477-480
  source, 464-465, 472-476

LinkSend method, 479-480
LinkTimeout property, 463
LinkTopic property, 462
list box properties
    List, 173
    Text, 173
list box tool, 171-172
list boxes, 183-187
    creating, 167-177
    directory, 203-206
    drive, 202-204
    drop-down, 202-204
    file, 203-204
        current directory files,
            207-210
        default names, 205
        working directory
            change, 206
List property, 173, 185
ListCount property, 173,
    185
ListIndex property, 173,
    185
listings
    2.1. Pad Application,
        66-67
    2.2. Alarm Application,
        80-83
    3.1 Tic-Tac-Toe Game,
        97-98
    3.2 Editor Version 1,
        108-109
    3.3 Editor Version 2,
        116-117
    3.4 Phone Book Applica-
        tion, 133-134
    4.1. Windows Shell
        Application, 153-154
    4.2. Control Panel
        Application, 164-167

    4.3 Database Program,
        176-177
    4.4. Revised Database
        Program, 181-183
    5.1. Editor Application's
        Code, 214-220
    6.1. PrintString Sub
        Procedure, 276-277
    6.2. The Rocket Ship
        Sprite—First Try,
        278-279
    6.3. Sprite2, Anima-
        tion—Second Try, 284
    6.4. Plotter.Mak, 291-292
    7.1. Paint Program with
        Drawing and Lines,
        314-316
    7.2. Paint Program:
        Drawing, Lines, Boxes,
        Circles and Text,
        323-326
    7.3. Paint Application
        with File Capability
        and Color Selection,
        333-338
    7.4. Complete Paint
        Application (Paint.Mak
        on the diskette),
        342-352
    8.1. Binary Tree Ex-
        ample, 378-379
    8.2. Shell Sort (Ssort.Mak
        on the diskette),
        387-388
    8.3. A Quicksort
        (Qsort.Mak on the
        diskette), 393-395
    8.4. Ordered Search
        Program, 400-401

    8.5. Spread.Mak
        (Spread.Mak on the
        diskette), 405-406
    11.1. Desktop.Mak
        (Desktop.Mak on the
        diskette), 518-519
    11.2. The PrintString Sub
        Procedure (Prnstrg.Mak
        on the diskette),
        522-523
    11.3. Cascade Program
        (Cascade.Mak on the
        diskette), 527
    12.1. Screen-capture
        Program (Capture.Mak
        on the Disk), 565-568
    12.2. Cuser.C, 570
    12.3. Cuser.Def, 572
    12.4. Cuser.Mak,
        573-575
    12.5. Vbcuser.txt, 578
    13.1. The Pad Applica-
        tion (Pad.Mak on the
        Disk), 586-588
    13.2. The Plotter Pro-
        gram, 598-599
    13.3. Your C Interface,
        608-609
    13.4. Your Notepad
        (Pad.Mak on the Disk),
        627-630
    14.1. Init.C—Vbx
        Initialization (Init.C on
        the Disk), 655-657
    14.2. Box.Rc (Box.Rc on
        the Disk), 660
    14.3. Box.H (Box.H on
        the Disk), 671-672
    14.4. Box.C (Box.C on
        the Disk), 676-679

14.5. Box.Def (Box.Def on the Disk), 679

14.6. Makefile (Makefile on the Disk), 680-681

14.7. Makefile.C6 (Makefile.C6 on the Disk), 681-682

graphics methods, 294-295

graphics properties, 293-294

LLL_DblClick( ) Sub procedure, 517-518

LLL_MouseDown( ) event, 512-513

Load command, File menu (Database.Mak program), 168-169

Load File... command (File menu), 214

Load File... dialog box, 202, 225

Load File... jump, 692

Load File... command (File menu), 330

Load Icon dialog box, 123

Load statement, 127-129, 148

Load Text... command (Code menu), 32

LoadForm dialog box, 202-205, 328-330

loading
.BMP files (Winodws paintbrush), 260-261
icons, 122
pictures, 259-261
screen copies, 281

loading dialog box files, 222-223

LoadPicture function, 280

LoadPicture( ) function, 329-330, 259-261

LoadPicture( ) function
.WMF (Windows metafiles), 259
BMP files, 259-261
ICO files (icons), 259

local variable declarations, 46

local variables, 46-48, 209

LocalAlloc( ) API function, 571

LOF( ) function, 212

logic errors (bugs) *see* debugging

logical > operator, 435

loops
conditions, EOF( ) function, 212
Do Until, 211
for loop, 95

LostFocus event, 62-65

Ltrim$( ) function, 180-186

M

Main menu, 230

main text box, 202

main window, 156-161

Main( ) Sub procedure, 139-140

.Mak files, saving as text, 31-32

Make Exe File... command (File menu), 27-28, 62-65

Makefile file listing (14.7), 680-681

Makefile.C6 file listing (14.7), 681-682

manual links, 458

manual run-time client links, 469-471

marking menu items, 114-117

Masked Edit control, 70

Max scroll bar property, 157-159

Me keyword, 528

member functions (C++), 14

memory
allocating from heap for programs, 571
loading RunDialog form, 151-152

menu bar (Windows version 3+), 4-5, 87

Menu Design Window, 90, 145-146
closing, 93
control panel menus, 159

Menu Design window
adding menus, 110
captions, 91

menu driven program, 88-90

menu items
adding, 127-134
changing at run time, 124-127
check marks, 114-117
command buttons, 101
deleting, 127-134
enabling/disabling, 107
grayed, 107-108
indexes, 111
properties, Enabled, 106

menu separators, 99, 129
menus, 87
... (ellipsis), 87
access keys, 118-119
activating items, 105
adding, 110
alarm clock program,
124-126
captions, 91
checked items, 87
command buttons, 95,
105
creating, 91
activating options, 96
adding items, 92
Clear All button, 105
designing, 90-99
adding items, 92
indenting, 93
grayed items, 87
grouping items, 100
Help Editor commands,
688-689
options, hiding, 126
pop-up, 92
selecting fonts, 109-114
separator bar, 87
shortcut keys, 119-121
message boxes
displaying with
MsgBox( ) function,
140-144
error, 142-144
Help, 142
messages
sent to controls, processing, 662-664
VBM_SETPROPERTY,
675-676
WM_CREATE, 664

WM_MOUSEDOWN, 668
WM_PAINT, 665-667
WM_SIZE, 664-665
methods
AddItem, 170-171
Circle, 318-326
clipboard, 341
Drag, 516
GetData, 341-342
GetText( ), 490
Hide, 149
Line, 305-306, 316-318
LinkPoke, 481-482
LinkRequest, 470-471
LinkSend, 479-480
listing of graphics types,
294-295
Move, 516-517
of dragging, 511-513
Point( ), 318
Print, 442
PrintForm, 339-340
RemoveItem, 171
SetData, 342, 495
SetFocus, 60, 62
SetText, 494
Show, 148-149
methods (Visual Basic), 14
Microsoft Excel
as DDE client, 464-465
as DDE source, 465-471
Microsoft Paintbrush for
Windows, 330
Microsoft Windows 3+
version, 4-5
Microsoft Word for
Windows, Version 2.0
footnotes, 691-694
rich-text files, 688

Min property, 158
Min scroll bar property,
157-159
mini-database programs,
167-177
modal dialog boxes,
149-151
modal forms, 149-150
MODEL structures, 650-654
modes, 195
module level variable
declarations, 47-48
module window, 61
modules
Alarm.Bas, 68
Visual Basic projects,
29-30
monospace fonts, 262
mouse
buttons
testing, 300-301, 306
using Ctrl or Shift keys
with, 301-302
clicking to choose or
select, 5-6
cursor, 561
dragging objects, 6
moving, 303-306
operations, 703
receiving input, 543-545
MouseDown events,
299-303
MouseMove events,
303-306
MousePointer property,
281, 308
MouseUp events, 306
Move method, 280, 284,
516-517

MoveTo( ) API function, 556, 557

MsgBox( ) function, 140-144

MsgBox( ) statement, 139

Multiline properties, 56

multiline text box, 211

multiline text boxes, 39, 55-58

Multiple Document Interface (MDI), 138-139

Multiple Document Interface (MDI) programs, 187-189

multiple-form programs, 147

multitasking, 457

N

Name function, 77-78

Name OKButton, 155-156

Name property, 15-20, 150-154

NameField text box (Database.Mak program), 168-169

Names( ) array, 131

Names( ) global array, 176

naming forms, 148-149

New Drawing Color... command (File menu), 332-333

New Form command (File menu), 147, 155, 202

New Module command (File menu), 61-65

New Module... command (File menu), 29-30

New Module... command (File menu), 47-48, 139-140

NewColor label, 161

NewHeight scroll bar, 158

NewPage method, 286

NewWidth scroll bar, 159

NNN_Click( ) event, 132

notepad project, 55-67
Clear All command, 59-60
Cut command, 59-60
Paste command, 59-60

notepads
3-D controls, 590-593
Color Selection dialog boxes, 623-624
File Open dialog boxes, 618-621
Font Selection dialog boxes, 612-618
key status controls, 586-590
Print dialog boxes, 624-627
Save File dialog boxes, 622-623

Now function, 55

NULL pointers, 552-553

Num Lock key, 586-590

(number) symbol, 53-54

NumberField text box (Database.Mak program), 168-169

NumberNames variable, 130

Numbers( ) array, 131, 176

numerics, 43

O

Object Linking and Embedding (OLE), 496-502

object-oriented programming (Windows), 7-8

objects, 14
filling with patterns, 255
focus, 105
general object arrays, 132
Move method, 280, 284
properties, 12-14

ODBC (Visual Basic Open Database Connectivity), 176

OK button, 153-154

OK_Button_Click event, 163

OKButton_Click( ) Sub procedure, 152-154, 327-332

OLE (Object Linking and Embedding), 496-502

ole.mak project, 718

OLE2 tool, 500

OleClient control, 496-502

OleClient tool, 497

On Error GoTo statements, 198, 413-415

OnTap property, 631

Open command (File menu), 195-199

Open Project... command (File menu), 30-31

Open statement, 197-198, 209

opening links, 488-489

opening files, 195-199, 208-209

OpenItem_Click( ) Sub
   procedure, 618
operating environments,
   2-3
operations, Windows, 5-6
operators
   <, 70
   >, 70
   > logical, 435
   ^, 319
   And, 250
   dot (.), 60, 179
   Xor—Exclusive, 250
option buttons
   3-D, 590-593
options, 99
   menus, 126
   see also commands
Options menu, 148-149
Or property, 250
Ordered Search Program
   listing (8.4), 400-401
output, positioning on
   page, 286

P

Pad application
   3-D controls, 590-593
   Color Selection dialog
      boxes, 623-624
   File Open dialog boxes,
      618-621
   Font Selection dialog
      boxes, 612-618
   key status controls,
      586-590

listings
   2.1, 66-67
   13.1, 586-588
   13.4, 627-630
   Print dialog boxes,
      624-627
   Save File dialog boxes,
      622-623
Pad.Frm (form), 55-56
Pad.Mak project, 55-56,
   586-588, 627-630, 718
PadText.SetFocus state-
   ment, 60
Page Break command
   (Insert menu), 690-691
PageTo property, 624
Paint application
   clipboard, 341-342
   drawing colors, chang-
      ing, 331-339
   drawing lines, 302-303
   listings
      7.1, 314-316
      7.2, 323-326
      7.3, 333-338
      7.4, 342-352
   printing graphics,
      339-340
   reading files from disk,
      328-330
   saving files to disk,
      326-328
   scaling graphics, 353-354
Paint events, 261-262,
   288-289
Paint.Mak project, 342-352
PaintBox( ) function,
   661-662, 665-667
Paintbrush for Windows
   (Microsoft), 330

Paintbrush program,
   472-476
Panel.* file, 155
Panel.Mak program,
   154-156, 164-167
panel.mak project, 718
panels, 3-D, 590-593
Parent keyword, 520
parent windows, 520
passing
   controls to procedures,
      520-523
   forms to procedures,
      523-528
   Indexes, 111
password controls, 49-52
Paste command, 59-60
Paste From Clipboard
   command (File menu),
      341-342
Paste Link command (Edit
   menu), 459, 489-490
Paste To Clipboard com-
   mand (File menu),
      341-342
PasteButton_Click( ) sub
   procedure, 104
PasteItem( ) Sub procedure,
   489-490
PasteItem_Click( ) sub
   procedure, 105
pasting
   DDE links in code to
      unspecified programs,
      489-492
   graphics to/from clip-
      board, 341-342
   text, 63-65, 104
Path property, 205-210

Pattern property, 207-210
PatternData property, 601-602
Pen custom controls, 630-631
PercentMode property, 725-726
PercentValue property, 726-727
phone book application, 132-134
phone.mak project, 718-719
picture box controls, 280
picture box tool, 238
picture boxes
    DDE clients, 458, 472-476
    drawing, 235-259
    loading sprites, 280
    maintaining DDE links, 477-480
    moving, 284
    printing text in, 520-523
    printing to, 266, 275-280
Picture property, 259
pie charts, 605-606
(x!, y!) pixel location, 241
pixel-by-pixel drawing, IconWorks program, 282-283
pixels
    drawing, 236-237
    location, (x!, y!), 241
    setting scale to, 352-353
Plotter program
    custom control graphs, 598-608
    plotting coordinate values, 288-289

Plotter.Mak project, 719
listings
    6.4, 291-292
    13.2, 598-599
Point method, 243
point structures, 547-550
Point( ) method, 318
pointers, 367
    NULL, 552-553
    predefined EventInfo, 648-649
pop-up menus, 92
pop-up windows, 689
predefined constant RED, 241
Print # statement, 200
Print command (File menu), 339-340
Print dialog boxes, 624-627
Print method, 442
    applying fonts, 110
    printing tables, 265
    printing graphical text, 262
printer, positioning output on page, 286
PrintForm method, 339-340, 287
printing
    forms, 287
    graphic text, 262, 286
    Paint application graphics, 339-340
    strings, expressionlist, 264
    tables, 265
    text in picture boxes, 520-523
    to forms, 43, 276-281
    to picture boxes, 266, 275-280

PrintItem_Click( ) Sub procedure, 339-340, 626
PrintString( ) function, 276-281
PrintString( ) Sub procedure, 521-523
    listing (6.1), 276-277
    listing (11.2), 522-523
PrintStyle property, 601
Prnstrg.Mak project, 522-523
prnstrg.mak project, 719
procedure box, 24-27
procedure level, 46-54
Procedure Step tool, 438
procedure templates, 69-70
procedure-level variables, 47-48
procedures
    command buttons, 102
    connecting to buttons, 24
    Drive1_Change, 204
    Function, 23-27
    passing controls to, 520-523
    passing forms to, 523-528
    sharing information, 47-48
    Sub, 23-27
        Main( ), 139-140
        OKButton_Click( ), 152-154
    Sub procedures templates, 89
    Sub Timer1_Timer( ), 73-74
    taking arguments, 23-24
Program Manager
    adding icons, 123
    managing small programs, 187-189

Peter Norton's Visual Basic for Windows Third Edition, Covering Release 3.0

Program Manager window, 3

programming
event-driven, 154
Windows, 9

programs
adding customized icons, 285
beta versions, 412
C interface, 568-579, 608-611
calculator, 39-43, 48-52, 55
Cascade, 524-527
coding, 26
Database.Mak, 168-177
debugging, 433-453
Desktop Organizer, 508-520
directories, 209
drives, 209
Editor, 698-700
gamma versions, 412
Graphics.Mak, 236-259
IconWorks, 281-283
investment calculator, debugging, 445-453
menus, 90-99
Microsoft Excel
as DDE client, 464-465
as DDE source, 465-471
mini-database, 167-177
Multiple Document Interface (MDI), 187-189
multiple-form, 147
Paintbrush, 472-476
Panel.Mak, 154-156, 164-167

Plotter, 598-608
QuickC for Windows, 573-575
renaming, 12-14
robust, 702
saving project files, 32-33
Screen Capture, 542-568
spreadsheet, 401-406
testing, 412-413
Trnslate.Exe, 712-714
Windows, 9
Windows Program Manager, 187-189
Windows shell, 138-190
Word for Windows, 459-461

project window, 30-31

projects
.Mak files, 31
alarm clock, 67-68
Alarm.Mak, 68
Capture.Mak, 565-568
Cascade.Mak, 527
Database.Mak, 168-177
Desktop.Mak, 518-519
Graphics.Mak, 236-259
notepad, 55-67
Pad.Mak, 55-56, 586-588, 627-630
Paint.Mak, 342-352
Plotter.Mak project
plotting coordinate values, 288-289
Prnstrg.Mak, 522-523
Qsort.Mak, 393-395
Spread.Mak, 405-406
Ssort.Mak, 387-388
Visual Basic, 28-30
Windows Shell, 145-147

projects on disk, 715-721

properties
Action, 498-501, 611-612
ActiveControl, 490-491, 530-532
ActiveForm, 532
alarm clock, 71
AutoRedraw
redrawing forms, 236, 288-289
restoring graphics, 261, 266-267
Autosize
picture box size changing, 260
BackColor, 161, 307
command buttons, 245
form background color, 239-240
setting form background, 283-284
BevelWidth, 591, 724
BorderEffect, 725
BorderStyle, 202-204
Fixed Single type, 150-151
NewColor label, 161
BottomTitle, 607
BoxColor, 638, 675-676
CancelError, 616
Caption, 39-44
captions, 95
changing, 18-20
changing Name, 150-154
Class, 497-500
ColorData, 601
Cols, 401
command buttons, 89
Copies, 624

CurrentX
  forms and picture
    boxes, 241
  graphics output
    position, 263
CurrentY
  forms and picture
    boxes, 241
  graphics output
    position, 263
Cycle, 596
DataReset, 608
defaults, 153, 194-195
DelayRecog, 631
DialogTitle, 618
Dir1.Path, 205-206
Dir1.Path—> File1.Path,
  206
DragMode, 509
DragMode property,
  511-513
DrawMode, 311-313, 596
  pen types, 249
  value settings, 249
  Xor Pen (animation),
    250
DrawMode property, 249
DrawStyle, 247, 318
DrawWidth, 246, 248
Drive1.Drive, 204
Drive1.Drive —>
  Dir1.Path, 206
Enabled, 64-65
ExtraData, 605-606
FileName, 208, 620-621
FillColor, 256-257
FillStyle, 255-256
Filter, 618-619
Flags, 614-615

Font3D, 591
FontBold, 79-81, 270-271
FontItalic, 79-81, 270-271
FontName, 79-81,
  270-271
FontSize, 79-81, 270-271
FontStrikeThrough, 79-81
FontStrikethru, 270-271
FontTransparent, 270-271
FontUnderline, 79-81,
  270-271
ForeColor, 161, 311-313,
  331-332, 623
  drawing line color, 245
  graphics pen tool
    default, 249
  graphics/text color
    changing, 245-246
Form1.Control., 156
forms as part of name,
  149
Frame, 595
FromPage, 624
GraphData, 599, 600
GraphTitle, 607
GraphType, 602-603
GridStyle, 606
Height, 237
HelpContextID, 695-696
Icon, 285
Image, 342
Index, 76-79
Interval, 72-74
LeftTitle, 607
LinkItem, 463, 468-469
LinkMode, 461-462
LinkTimeout, 463
LinkTopic, 462
listing of graphics types,
  293-294

menu items, Enabled,
  106
Min, 158
MousePointer, 281, 308
Multiline
  False, 56
  True, 56
of dragging, 511-513
OnTap, 631
Or, 250
PageTo, 624
Path, 205-210
Pattern property, 207-210
PatternData, 601-602
PercentMode, 725-726
PercentValue, 726-727
Picture, 259
predefined in Visual
  Basic CDK, 645
PrintStyle, 601
Protocol, 497-498
registering, 640-647
Rows, 401
ScaleHeight, 237, 353
ScaleMode, 353-355
ScaleWidth, 237, 353
Scrollbars, 56
SelLength, 58-65
SelStart, 58-65
SelText, 58-65
ServerType, 497-498
ServerTypeAllowed, 500
Shape, 252
ShowPercent, 727
Sorted, 168-169, 172
SourceDoc, 497-500
SourceItem, 497-500
Speed, 596
Stretch, 259

TabIndex, 78-79, 533-534
TabStop, 51
Tag, 517
Text, 41, 53, 65, 70
text boxes, 16-20, 49-50,
    110
ThisPoint, 603-604
UserValue, 727-728
Value, 76, 159-160, 610
Visible, 153
Width, 237
Xor Pen (DrawMode),
    251
XPosData, 604
Properties List Box, 21-23
properties of objects, 12-14
properties window, 12-14,
    39-42
PROPINFO structures,
    640-647
Protocol property, 497-498
PSet( ) function, 235-239
PSet( ) method, 277-279
PSet( ) statement, 236-237
Put # statement, I/O
    random files, 224

Q

QBColor( ) function,
    242-243
Qsort.Mak project, 393-395
qsort.mak project, 719
Quick Basic functions,
    QBColor( ), 242-243
QuickC for Windows,
    573-575
Quicksort listing (8.3),
    393-395
Quicksorts, 389-395

R

radio (option) buttons,
    67-68, 75-76
random files, 196
    accessing, 222
    Get # function, 226
    global integers, 224
    I/O statements, 224
    reading, 221-222,
        225-230
    storing, 223
    writing, 222-225
    writing to disk, 225
Random Input/Output file
    mode, 195
random-access files, 223,
    226
read-only text boxes, 33-35
reading Paint files from
    disk, 328-330
reading random-access
    files, 225-230
reading strings, 212
Record type, 178
records
    adding new to database
        AddItem method,
        227-228
    databases, 168
    reading into databases,
        226-227
    specifying reading, 230
rectangles
    drawing around screens,
        551-554
    drawing solid white
        (hiding text), 256-259
    erasing, 557-558
    stretching, 318

recursion, 390
RED constant (predefined),
    241
red setting, 161-162
ReDim statement, 364-365
redrawing images, 261-262
registering
    events, 647-654
    properties, 640-647
ReleaseCapture( ) API
    function, 561
Remove File command
    (File menu), 139-140
RemoveItem method, 171
removing grids, 12
renaming programs, 12-14
repainting images, 261
repainting images, 261
resizing custom controls,
    664-665
Resume Line # statement,
    430-432
Resume Next statement,
    426-432
Resume statement, 199,
    423-426
return values, 141
Revised Database Program
    listing (4.4), 181-183
RGB function, 162, 241
RGB values (Visual Basic),
    242-243
Ribbon, VBToolsKan,
    731-732
rich text files
    Help Editor, 688-696
    saving, 695-696
rich-text files (Microsoft
    Word for Windows,
    Version 2.0), 688

Right$(String$, n) function, 275
Rnd( ) function, 477-478
robust programs, 702
roots, binary trees, 373
Rows property, 401
Rtrim$( ) function, 180-186
Run command (File menu), 145-146
Run menu
  Break command, 437
  Clear All Breakpoints command, 441
  Continue command, 438
  End command, 12, 151
  Set Startup Form... command, 524
  Single Step command, 448
Run menu (Visual Basic), 11-14
run time, 124-127
run-time client links, 465-471
run-time errors, *see* trappable errors
run-time source links, 472-476
Run... dialog box, 150-154
RunDialog form, 151-152
RunItem_Click( ) event, 151-154

S

Save command, File menu (Database.Mak program), 168-169

Save File As... command (File menu), 31-32
Save File command (File menu), 31-32, 193-195, 326-328
Save File dialog boxes, 201, 622-623
Save File... jump, 692
Save Form dialog box default properties, 194-195
Save Project As... command (File menu), 30-32, 39-42
Save Project command (File menu), 31-32
Save Text... command (Code menu), 32
Save Text... command (File menu), 31-32
SaveForm dialog box, 194, 223
SaveItem_Click( ) Sub procedure, 327-328, 622
SavePicture( ) function, 259-267
saving
  Paint application files to disk, 326-328
  project files, 32-33
  rich text files, 695-696
Scale method, 288
Scale properties, 237, 353
scaling graphics, 353-354
scope of variables, 46-54
Screen Capture program, listing (12.1), 542-568
screen copies, 281

screens
  clearing, Cls method, 248
  color of position, Point method, 243
  string length, TextWidth method, 267-277
scroll bar change event, 161
scroll bars
  blue, 161-162
  green, 161-162
  LargeChange, 157-159
  Max, 157-159
  Min, 157-159
  moving thumb, Change event, 157-158
  NewHeight, 158
  NewWidth, 159
  red, 161-162
  setting main window dimensions, 156-161
  SmallChange, 157-159
  Value, 157-159
  Value property, 159-160
  vertical scroll bar tool, 157-158
Scroll Lock key, 586-590
Scrollbars property, 56
Search command, 692
searching
  binary trees, 374-379
  data, 395-401
  topics, keyword, 692
Seek statement, 230
Select Frame dialog box, 595
selecting
  drives, 206
  fonts, 109-114
  with single mouse click, 5-6

Sel properties, 58-65
sending commands
  through DDE, 483-484
  data from DDE clients to
    sources, 480-482
  DDE data to non-
    running programs,
    484-488
  keystrokes to other
    programs, 484
  see also links
SendKeys statement, 484
separator bars, 87, 129
Sequential Append file
  mode, 195
sequential chains of data,
  367-372
sequential files, 196
  Append command (File
    menu), 220
  opening
    Append, 197
    Input, 197
    Output, 197
  reading
    Input # statement,
      210-220
    Input$ statement,
      210-220
    Line Input # state-
      ment, 210-220
  writing to, 200-202
Sequential Input/Output
  file mode, 195
ServerType property,
  497-498
ServerTypeAllowed prop-
  erty, 500
Set Startup Form... com-
  mand (Run menu), 524

SetCapture( ) API function,
  543-545
SetData method, 342, 495
SetFocus method, 60, 62
SetROP2( ) API function,
  555-556
SetText method, 494
setting colors, 162-167
settings box (label tool)
  BorderStyle
    Fixed Single, 71
    None, 71
Setup keyword, 95
Shape Control, 252-254
Shape property, 252
Shell function window
  types, 144
Shell Sort listing (8.2),
  387-388
shell sorts, 379-389
Shell statement, 484
Shell statements, activat-
  ing dialog boxes, 151-154
Shell( ) function, 144-147
Shift argument, 69-70,
  299, 301-302
Shift key, 301-302
shortcut keys, 6
  activating, 120
  adding to menus,
    119-121
shortcut keys (Windows
  version 3+), 6
  see also keyboard short-
    cuts
Show method, 148-152
ShowPercent property, 727
single data type, 45
Single Step command (Run
  menu), 448

single-precision variable
  data storage, 49
sizing handles, 16-20, 244
skipping to next page, 286
SmallChange property,
  157-159
Sorted property, 168-169,
  172
sorting data
  Quicksorts, 389-395
  shell sorts, 379-389
SortQuick( ) subprogram,
  390-393
source applications, DDE,
  492-496
source links, 458-459
  design-time, 464-465
  run-time, 472-476
SourceDoc property,
  497-500
SourceItem property,
  497-500
sources, sending data from
  clients to, 480-482
specifying files, 207
Speed property, 596
Spread.Mak project (listing
  8.5), 405-406, 719
spreadsheet program,
  401-406
Sprite2, Animation—
  Second Try listing (6.3),
  284-292
Sprite2.Mak project,
  719-720
sprites, 280
Sqr( ) function, 319
Ssort.Mak project, 387-388
ssort.mak project, 720

starting Visual Basic, 10
Startup Form... command
  (Options menu), 148-149
statements
  AppActivate, 484
  Basic Beep, 70, 73-74
  Beep, 140
  Call, 175-176
  ChDir, 208
  ChDrive, 208
  Close, 200-201
  Data, 360
  Dim, 45
  End, 96
  End (File menu), 146
  Input #, 210-220
  Input$, 210-220
  InputBox$( ), 139
  Line Input #, 210-220
  Load, 127-129, 148
  MsgBox( ), 139
  On Error GoTo, 198,
    413-415
  Open, 197-198, 209
  PadText.SetFocus, 60
  Print #, 200
  PSet( ), 236-237
  ReDim, 364-365
  Resume, 423-426
  Resume Line #, 430-432
  Resume Next, 426-432
  Seek, 230
  SendKeys, 484
  Shell, 151-154, 484
  Type, 366
  Unload, 127-129, 148
  Write #, 200
Static arrays, 363-364
static local variables, 46-48

status bar, VBToolsKan,
  732-733
Step keyword, 241
Step tool, 438
storing files, 202
Str$( ) function, 50, 53-54
Stretch property, 259
stretching
  circles, 320
  lines, 310
  rectangles, 318
string arrays
  Names( ), 131
  Numbers( ), 131
string height
  TextHeight method,
    267-270
string width
  TextWidth method,
    267-270
strings
  comparing, 435
  converting to numeric,
    49-50
  empty, 274-275
  fixed length dot (.)
    operator, 179
  length on screen,
    267-277
  temporary, 272-273
  text
    associating with
      controls, 517
    passing to Windows
      calls, 551-552
    printing in picture
      boxes, 520-523
  variable length, 45-46

structures
  BOX, 642-647
  EVENTINFO, 647-654
  MODEL, 650-654
  PROPINFO, 640-647
Sub CancelButton( )
  procedure, 156
Sub GetItem( ) procedure,
  186
Sub NewBlue_Change( )
  Sub procedure, 163
Sub NewGreen_Change( )
  Sub procedure, 163
Sub OKButton_Click( )
  procedure, 156
Sub PadText_Change( )
  Sub procedure, 65
Sub procedure Command
  1 (calculator project), 49
Sub procedure templates,
  61-65, 208
Sub procedures, 23-27
  AniButton1_Click( ), 596
  Box1_ClickInside( ), 638
  Box1_ClickOutside( ), 638
  CallHello( ), 527-528
  Cascade( ), 524-527
  Check1_Click( ), 465-471
  ClearButton_Click( ), 308
  ColorItem_Click( ), 623
  Command1_Click( ),
    479, 596
  CopyItem_Click( ),
    493-494
  CutButton3D_Click( ),
    592-593
  DrawingItem_Click( ),
    332-333
  ExitItem_Click( ), 612

FontItem_Click( ), 613
Form_Click( ), 473
Form_DragDrop( ),
514-515
Form_LinkClose( ) Sub
procedure, 488
Form_LinkError( ), 488
Form_LinkOpen( ) Sub
procedure, 488
Form_Load( ), 237,
283-284
Form_Load( ), 361-362
Form_MouseDown( ),
299-303
Form_MouseMove( ),
304-307, 310-313,
316-318
Form_MouseUp( ), 306,
313, 316-318
LLL_DblClick( ), 517-518
OKButton_Click( ),
327-330, 332
OKButton_Click( ),
152-154
OpenItem_Click( ), 618
PasteItem( ), 489-490
PrintItem_Click( ),
339-340, 626
PrintString( ), 521-523
SaveItem_Click( ),
327-328, 622
scope of variables, 46-54
Sub CancelButton( )
hiding control panel,
156
Sub NewRed_Change( ),
162
Sub OKButton_Click( )
setting main window's
caption, 156

Sub PadText_Change( ),
65
taking arguments, 23-24
templates, 89, 205
Text1_LinkError( ),
487-488
TextButton_KeyPress( ),
322
sub procedures
AddNameItem_Click( ),
130
ClearButton_Click( ), 105
FFF_Click( ), 113
PasteButton_Click( ), 104
PasteItem_Click( ), 105
Sub Timer1_Timer( )
procedure, 73-74
subdirectories, icon library,
281-282
subprogams
SortQuick( ), 390-393
symbols,
(number), 53-54
0 (zero), 53-54
System colors (Visual
Basic), 240
system menu box (Win-
dows 3+ version), 4-5
System menus (Windows
version 3+), 6

T

tab length, default, 264
tab order, 78-79
tab order of controls,
532-535
Tab( ) function, 264-265

TabIndex property, 78-79,
533-534
tables, VBToolsKan,
734-736
tabs, 265
TabStop property, 51
Tag property, 517
tags, 690-691
tails, circular buffers, 371
Task List window, 3
templates
alarm clock, 75
animation, 283-284
C interface, 576
calculator, 40-42
Cascade program, 524
Check1_Click( ) Sub
procedure, 465-466
code window, 22-27
FFF_Click( ), 112
Command1_Click( ) Sub
procedure, 479
DrawingItem_Click( )
Sub procedure, 332-333
Editor, 101
Exist( ) function, 428
Form_Click( ) Sub
procedure, 473
Form_LinkOpen( ) Sub
procedure, 488
Form_MouseDown( ) Sub
procedure, 299
Investment Calculator,
446
key status, 589
Paint application, 307
Paint application control
panel, 332
Paste Link application,
489

PrintItem_Click( ) Sub procedure, 339
procedure, 69-70
procedures
   Sub procedures, 61-65, 89
Run-time Client application, 466
Screen Capture program, 546
Source application, 472
spreadsheet, 402-403
Sub procedures, 208, 205
   NewBlue_Change( ), 163
   NewGreen_Change( ), 163
   NewRed_Change( ), 162
   Text1_LinkError( ) Sub procedure, 487
temporary buffers, 61-65
temporary strings, 272-273
testing programs, 412-413
text
  centering on forms, 271
  cutting, 60-65
  deleting rectangles, 256-259
  drawing, 322-326
  formatting restricted space, 271
  graphic, printing, 286
  graphical forms, 262-267
    picture boxes, 262-267
    printers, 262-267
  length, 266-267
  pasting, 63-65, 104
  rich text files, 688-696

translating into numerics, 43
tying files to, 693-694
text box
  focus, 105
  properties, 110
text box change event, 33-35
text box property, 49-50
text box tool, 15-20, 40-42, 56, 68
text boxes, 40-42, 183-187
  Application Caption:, 155
  as DDE clients, 458-463, 465-471
  CommentField
    Database.Mak program, 168-169
  debugging with, 433
  default names, 22-23, 51
  drawing, 15-20
  multiline, 39, 55-58
  NameField
    Database.Mak program, 168-169
  NumberField
    Database.Mak program, 168-169
  numbers as text
    Str$( ) function, 53-54
  password controls, 49-52
  read-only, 33-35
  replacing Basic code, 38-39
  Run... dialog box, 150-154
  SelLength property, 58-65
  SelStart property, 58-65

SelText property, 58-65
setting properties, 16-20
  BackColor, 17-20
  FontName, 17-20
  Left and Top, 17-20
  Width and Height, 17-20
sizing handles, 16-20
switching, 51-52
Windows controls, 38-83
word wrapping, 56-57
Text property, 41, 53, 65, 70, 173
  combo boxes, 185
  Properties List Box, 21-23
Text property (Properties List Box), 21-23
text strings
  associating with controls, 517
  passing to Windows calls, 551-552
  printing in picture boxes, 520-523
Text tool, 322-323
Text1_LinkError( ) Sub procedure, 487-488
TextButton_KeyPress( ) Sub procedure, 322
TextFlag global variable, 308-310
TextHeight method, 267
  string height, 267-270
TextWidth method, 267
  string width, 267-270
  text length, 266-267
The Rocket Ship Sprite—First Try listing (6.2), 278-279

TheData( ) array, 179
ThisPoint property,
603-604
thumb, 157-158
Tic-Tac-Toe Game, 97-98
tictac.mak project, 720
time
checking in alarm clock
project, 73-74
Time$ function, 68, 73-74
Timer event, 71-74
timer tool, 72-74
titles
current page, 692
dialog boxes, 618
graphs, 607-608
TKChart control, 729-731
TKRib control, 731-732
TKStat control, 732-733
TKTable control, 734-736
TKTbox control, 736-737
Toggle Breakpoint com-
mand (Debug menu), 439
toolbar, 438
Toolbox
drive list tool, 202-204
frame tool, 75-76
label tool, 42-43, 70-71
Line control tool,
244-251
list box tool, 171-172
picture box tool, 238
text box tool, 15-20,
40-42, 56, 68
timer tool, 72-74
vertical scroll bar tool,
157-158

toolbox
animated button tool,
593-594
Box tool, 316-318
buttons, 339
check box tool, 465-466
Circle tool, 318-319
Clear button, 308
CMDialog tool, 613
creating for drawing
tools, 307
designing bitmaps for,
658-660
gauge tool, 609
graph tool, 599-600
Grid tool, 401
key status tool, 588
Line tool, 310-311
OLE2 tool, 500
OleClient tool, 497
Text tool, 322-323
VBToolsKan, 736-737
Toolbox (Visual Basic),
14-20
tools, text box, 56
transferring
references, 106
trappable (run-time) errors,
199, 411-432, 484-488
Trnslate.Exe program,
712-714
turning off error handling,
415
twips
changing to pixels,
352-353
coordinate system
(Visual Basic), 236
default measuring unit,
156

Visual Basic units of
measure, 18-20
type argument, 140-144
type arguments
MsgBox( ) Function, 141
Type statements, 366
type-declaraction charac-
ters, 45-46
type-declaration charac-
ters, 44
TypeOf keyword, 494-495

U

Ubound( ) function, 384
Undo command (File
menu), 327
units of measure (Visual
Basic), twips, 18-20
Unload statement, 127-129,
148
updating
Form_MouseUp( ) Sub
procedure, 313
UserValue property,
727-728

V

Val( ) function, 50, 156-158
Value property, 76,
159-160, 610
Value scroll bar property,
157-159
values
bounds, 412
color, 241-242

coordinate system, 290
RGB, 242-243
settings, 249
variable declarations
form level, 47-48
local, 46
module level, 47-48
variable length strings,
45-46
variable-width fonts, 262
word-wrap problems,
270-271
variables
Currency type, 360
default types, 45
global
AnchorX, 308-310
AnchorY, 308-310
BoxFlag, 308-310
CircleFlag, 308-310
CutText, 61-65
declaring, 89
DrawFlag, 308-310
LineFlag, 308-310
TextFlag, 308-310
global declaration, 47-48
local, 209
NumberNames, 130
procedure-level, 47-48
scope, 46-54
Function procedures,
46-54
procedure level, 46-54
Sub procedures, 46-54
single-precision data
storage, 49
types, 359-360
Visual Basic, 43-48
Vbcuser.txt listing (12.5),
578

VBDefControlProc( ) C
function, 676
VBDerefControl( ) C
function, 663-664
VBFireEvent( ) C function,
669
VBM_SETPROPERTY
message, 675-676
VBRegisterModel( ) C
function, 653-654
Vbrunxxx.D11 file
Visual Basic .Exe files, 27
VBToolsKan (Kansmen
Corporation), 728-729
license agreement,
737-738
Ribbon/icon bar,
731-732
status bar, 732-733
tables, 734-736
TKChart control, 729-731
toolbox, 736-737
.Vbx files, installing as
custom controls, 637
VBXPixelsToTwips( ) C
function, 674-675
vertical scroll bars, 161-162
vertical scroll bar tool,
157-158
View Code command
(View menu), 436
View menu, View Code
command, 436
Visible property, 153
Visual Basic
connecting
to C, 568-579
to Windows DLLs
(dynamic link
libraries), 542-568

controls, 14
files loading controls,
203-204
forms, 14, 29
methods, 14
objects, 14
projects, 28-29
Run menu, 11-14
starting, 10
System colors, 240
Toolbox, 14-20
units of measure
twips, 18-20
variables, 43-48
Visual Basic .Exe files
Vbrunxxx.D11 file, 27
Visual Basic File menu
Make Eex File...option, 27
Make Exe
File...command, 27-28
Make Exe File...option,
27-28
New Module...
command, 29-30
Open Project... com-
mand, 30-31
Save Project As... com-
mand, 30-31
Visual Basic Main menu,
FileCopy command, 230
Visual Basic Open Data-
base Connectivity
(ODBC), dynamic link
libraries, 176
Visual Basic Professional
Edition, common dialog
boxes, 193
Visual Basic project
modules, 29-30

Visual Basics for DOS
  keywords not in Visual
  Basic for Windows,
  710-711
  measurement system,
  · 709-710
  translating Visual Basic
  for Windows projects,
  712-714
Visual Basics for Windows
  keywords not in Visual
  Basic for DOS, 711
  measurement system,
  709-710
  translating Visual Basic
  for DOS projects,
  712-714

W

Watch tool, 438
WEP( ) API function, 568
width, finding for average
  character, 271
Width and Height prop-
  erty, 17-20, 237
Windows
  3+ version, 4-5
  applications, 167-177
    Shell( ) function, 144
    without mouse, 6
    writing, 9
  calls, NULL, 552-553
  colors, 161-162
  comparing to DOS, 6-7
  controls
    buttons, 38-83
    text boxes, 38-83
  conventions, 5-6

declaration conventions,
  553-554
DLLs (dynamic link
  libraries), 542-568
Edit menu, 707
event-driven program-
  ming, 7-8
File menu, 707-708
Graphical User Interfaces
  (GUIs), 2-6
Help menu, 708
insertion point focus, 51
keyboard shortcuts
  (table), 704-706
keyboard support, 5-6
managing small applica-
  tions, 187-189
mouse operations, 703
object-oriented program-
  ming, 7-8
operations, 5-6
Program Manager,
  187-189
shell program, 138-190
windows
changing main color, 161
changing names
  Name OKButton,
    155-156
closing
  End statement, 96
  Menu Design Window,
    93
code window, 94
Debug, 440-444
File Manager, 3
iconic states, 4-5
main, setting height/
  width with scroll bars,
  156-161

Menu Design, 90
module, 61
parent of passed con-
  trols, 520
Program Manager, 3
Task List, 3
Windows (Microsoft) 3+
  Form 1 window, 11-14
  insertion point, 26
  properties window, 12-14
  thumb, 5
  vertical scroll bar, 5
Windows character set
  (ANSI), 69
Windows Paintbrush,
  loading .BMP files,
  260-261
Windows Shell Application
  listing (4.1), 153-154
Windows shell program,
  138-190
Windows Shell project,
  145-147
Windows version 3+
  caption bar, 4-5
  client area, 5
  File menu, 4-5
  horizontal scroll bar, 5
  iconic states, 4-5
  icons, 4-5
  menu bar, 4-5
  shortcut keys, 6
  system menu box, 4-5
  System menus, 6
WM_CREATE message, 664
.WMF (Windows
  metafiles), LoadPicture( )
  function, 259
WM_MOUSEDOWN
  message, 668

773

WM_PAINT message,
665-667
WM_SIZE message,
664-665
Word for Windows as DDE
source, 459-461
word wrapping, 56-57,
155, 211, 270-271
working directories, 206
working drive, 206
Write # statement, 200
writing random files,
222-225

X–Y–Z

X argument, 299, 300
x axis, 604
Xor encryption, 251
Xor pen, 311-313
Xor Pen (DrawMode
property), 250-251
XPosData property, 604

Y argument, 299-300

0 (zero) symbol, 53-54
Zorder, 535

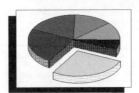